ENCYCLOPEDIA
of Indian Wars
Western Battles and Skirmishes
1850–1890

Gregory F. Michno

2003
MOUNTAIN PRESS PUBLISHING COMPANY
MISSOULA, MONTANA

© 2003 Gregory F. Michno

Second Printing, September 2005

Cover art credits: War bonnet (Quanah Parker, Comanche),
Panhandle-Plains Historical Museum Research Center, Canyon, Texas;
Shield (Crow), Smithsonian Institution/National Museum of the American Indian; Mountain Howitzer and Springfield .45 caliber Model 1873
carbine, Fort Larned National Historic Site

All photographs are by the author unless otherwise indicated.

Library of Congress Cataloging-in-Publications Data
Michno, Gregory, 1948-
  Encyclopedia of Indian wars : western battles and skirmishes,
1850-1890 / Gregory F. Michno.
      p. cm.
Includes bibliographical references and indexes.
  ISBN 0-87842-468-7 (pbk. : alk. paper)
  1. Indians of North America—Wars—1862-1865—Encyclopedias.
  2. Indians of North America—Wars—1866-1895—Encyclopedias.
  I. Title.
  E83.863.M53 2003
  973.8'02'02—dc21

                                        2003008753

PRINTED IN CANADA

Mountain Press Publishing Company
P. O. Box 2399 • Missoula, MT 59806
(406) 728-1900

Contents

Arizona 1850-70

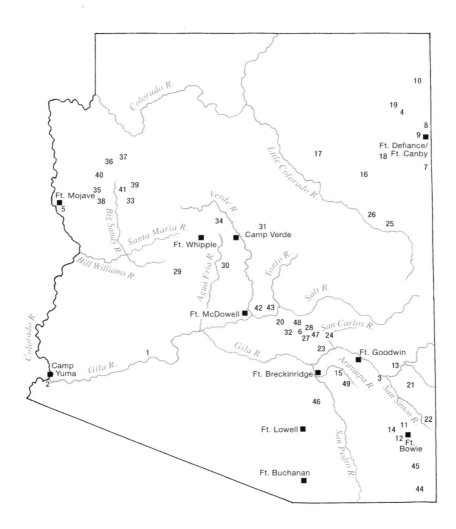

Colorado R.

10

19
4

8

9 ■
Ft. Defiance/
18 Ft. Canby
7

17

16

36 37

40

35
Ft. Mojave
38   33
5

41 39

33

Big Sandy R.

Santa Maria R.

Verde R.

34

31
Camp Verde

26

25

Ft. Whipple ■

30

Bill Williams R.

Agua Fria R.

29

Tonto R.

Salt R.

Ft. McDowell ■

42 43

San Carlos R.

20 48
32 6 28
27 47 24
23

Ft. Goodwin ■

13

Gila R.

Colorado R.

Camp
Yuma ■

Gila R.

1

2

Ft. Breckinridge ■

15

Aravaipa R.

3

San Simon R.

21

49

22

46

14 11
12 Ft.
Bowie

Ft. Lowell ■

San Pedro R.

45

Ft. Buchanan
■

44

Little Colorado R.

Arizona 1871–90

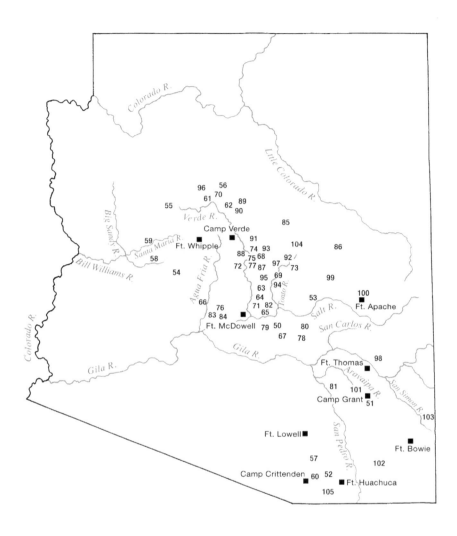

California

Colorado

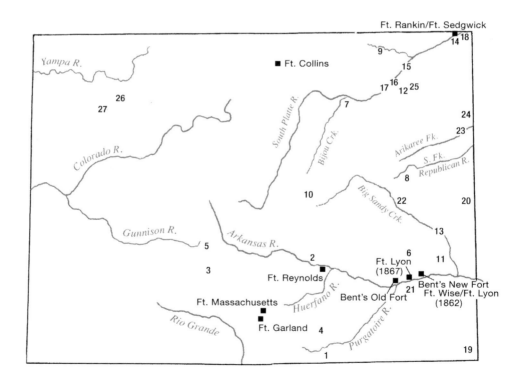

Idaho

1 (Ca. 1 October 1851) Ft. Hall
2 (19 August 1854) Lake Massacre
3 (20 August 1854) Ward Massacre
4 (15 July 1855) Ft. Boise
5 (25 February 1858) Ft. Lemhi
6 (27 July 1859) Cold Springs
7 (31 August 1859) Miltimore Massacre
8 (9–10 September 1860) Utter Fight/
    Castle Creek
9 (9–10 August 1862) Massacre Rocks

10 (12 September 1862) City of Rocks
11 (29 January 1863) Bear River
12 (15 February 1865) Bruneau Valley
13 (17 June 1877) White Bird Canyon
14 (1 July 1877) Clear Creek
15 (3 July 1877) Cottonwood Creek/Craig's Mtn.
16 (4 July 1877) Cottonwood House
17 (5 July 1877) "Brave Seventeen" Fight
18 (11–12 July 1877) Clearwater River
19 (17 July 1877) Weippe Prairie
20 (15 August 1877) Birch Creek
21 (20 August 1877) Camas Meadows
22 (8 June 1878) South Mtn.
23 (21 July 1878) Middle Fork Clearwater River
24 (29 July 1879) Big Creek/Vinegar Hill

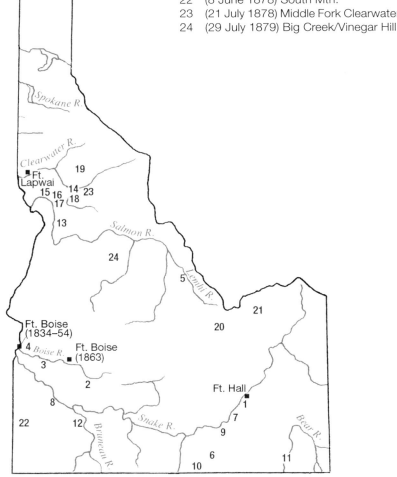

Kansas

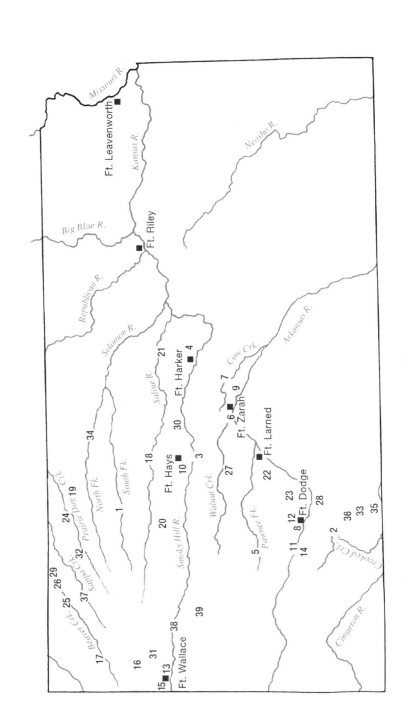

Missouri R.

Ft. Leavenworth

Kansas R.

Neosho R.

Big Blue R.

Ft. Riley

Republican R.

Solomon R.

Arkansas R.

Cow Crk.

Saline R.

7
4
21

9

Ft. Harker

6
Ft. Zaran

North Fk.
South Fk.
1
18
34
30

Prairie Dog Crk.
19
24

Walnut Crk.

Ft. Hays
10
3

Ft. Larned
27
22

Smoky Hill R.
20

Pawnee Fk.
23
12
28
8
Ft. Dodge
11
14

33
36
35

Crooked Crk.
2

Saw Crk.
32

Beaver Crk.
25
26
29

37

16
31

17

39

Ft. Wallace
38

15
13

Minnesota

1 (18 August 1862) Redwood Agency
2 (18 August 1862) Lower Sioux Ferry
3 (19–23 August 1862) New Ulm
4 (20–22 August 1862) Ft. Ridgely
5 (2–3 September 1862) Birch Coulee
6 (3 September 1862) Hutchinson
7 (23 September 1862) Wood Lake
8 (29 June 1863) Dustin Massacre

Northern Iowa

1 (8–26 March 1857)
   Spirit Lake Massacre
2 (16 May 1864) Spirit Lake

Montana

1   (1–8 September 1865) Powder River
2   (1 August 1867) Hayfield Fight
3   (7 April 1869) Sixteenmile Creek
4   (23 January 1870) Marias River
5   (14 August 1872) Pryor's Fork
6   (4 August 1873) Tongue River
7   (11 August 1873) Bighorn
8   (17 March 1876) Powder River/
     Reynold's Fight
9   (17 June 1876) Rosebud Creek
10 (25 June 1876) Little Bighorn
11 (21 October 1876) Cedar Creek
12 (18 December 1876) Ash Creek
13 (8 January 1877) Wolf Mtn.
14 (7 May 1877) Little Muddy Creek/
     Lame Deer Fight

15 (9–10 August 1877) Big Hole
16 (12 August 1877) Horse Prairie
17 (13 September 1877) Canyon Creek
18 (23 September 1877) Cow Island
19 (25 September 1877) Cow Creek
20 (30 September–5 October 1877)
     Bear's Paw/Snake Creek
21 (4 September 1878) Clark's Fork
22 (17 April 1879) Careless Creek
23 (17 July 1879) Milk River
24 (12 February 1880) Pumpkin Creek
25 (2 January 1881) Poplar River
26 (5 November 1887) Crow Agency

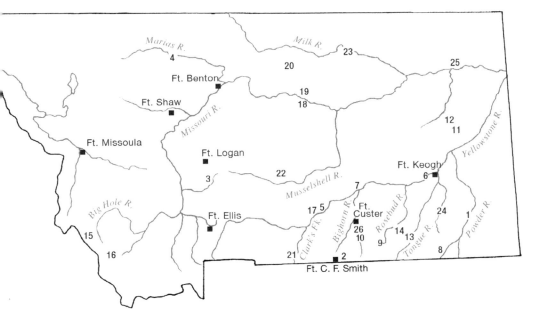

Nebraska

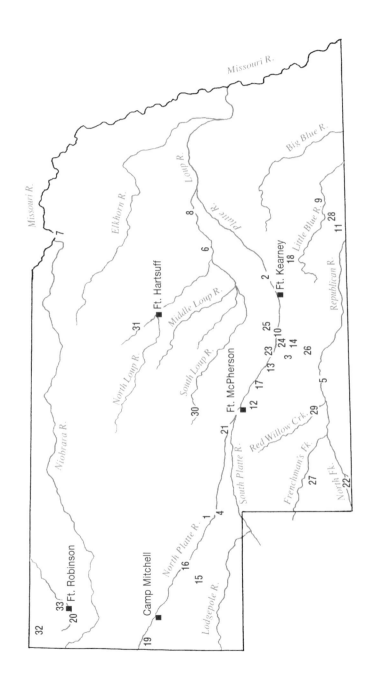

Missouri R.

Missouri R.

Big Blue R.

Elkhorn R.

Loup R.

Platte R.

Little Blue R. 9

7

8

28

6

11

Ft. Kearney

18

2

Republican R.

Middle Loup R.

Ft. Hartsuff

31

25

24 14

North Loup R.

23

10

South Loup R.

13

3

26

17

5

30

Ft. McPherson

12

29

Red Willow Crk.

21

Frenchman's Fk.

South Platte R.

27

North Fk.

22

North Platte R. 1

4

16

Camp Mitchell

15

Ft. Robinson

33

20

Niobrara R.

Lodgepole R.

32

19

Nevada

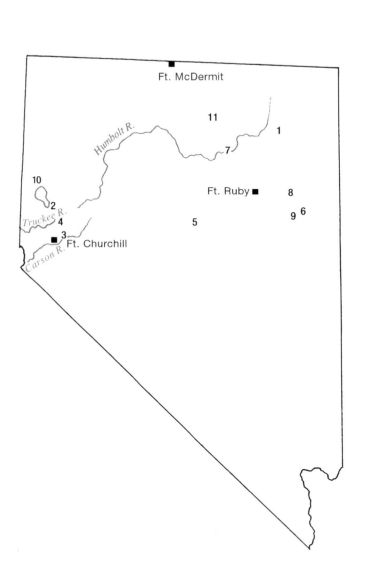

Ft. McDermit

11

Humbolt R.

7

1

10

2

Truckee R.

4

Ft. Ruby

8

9 6

5

3

Ft. Churchill

Carson R.

New Mexico 1850~70

 1 (6 April 1850) Rayado
 2 (May 1850) Wagon Mound
 3 (26 July 1850) Headwaters of the
      Canadian River
 4 (26 August 1851) Gila and Pinto Rivers*
 5 (24–25 January 1852) Laguna*
 6 (6 February 1852) Ft. Webster
 7 (5 March 1854) Congillon River
 8 (30 March 1854) Cieneguilla
 9 (8 April 1854) Ojo Caliente
10 (30 June 1854) Sapello Creek
11 (16 January 1855) Manzano Mtns.
12 (18–19 January 1855) Rio Penasco
13 (23 February 1855) Whiteface Mtn.
14 (13 June 1855) Delaware Creek
15 (20 March 1856) Sierra Almagre
16 (9 March 1857) Mimbres Mtns.
17 (11 March 1857) Ojo del Muerto
18 (24 May 1857) Canyon de los
      Muertos Carneros
19 (10 October 1858) Ojo del Oso
20 (4 December 1860) Ft. Webster
21 (Ca. 28 March 1861) Stein's Peak
22 (21–22 July 1861) Cooke's Spring
23 (2 September 1861) Gallinas Mtns.
24 (9 September 1861) Placitas
25 (13 September 1861) Ft. Fauntleroy
26 (3 March 1862) Comanche Canyon
27 (Ca. 25 October 1862) Graydon Affair
28 (18 January 1863)
      Mangas Coloradas Affair
29 (19 January 1863) Pinos Altos Mines

30 (29 January 1863) Pinos Altos Mines
31 (16 June 1863) Jornada del Muerto
32 (20 June 1863) Warm Springs
33 (4 July 1863) Ft. Craig
34 (10 July 1863) Cooke's Canyon
35 (12 July 1863) Ft. Thorn
36 (18 July 1863) Rio Hondo
37 (19 July 1863) Paraje
38 (22 July 1863) Conchas Springs
39 (24 July 1863) Cooke's Canyon
40 (27 August 1863) Las Animas Creek
41 (27–28 August 1863) Salt Lakes
42 (27 September 1863) Jemez
43 (16 December 1863) Ft. Sumner
44 (4 January 1864) Bosque Redondo
45 (12 January 1864) Datil Mtns.
46 (29 January 1864) San Andres Mtns.
47 (25 February 1864) Pinos Altos
48 (25 August 1864) Sacramento Mtns.
49 (1 December 1864) Red River
50 (9 July 1867) Ft. Sumner
51 (20 November 1867) Dona Ana Mtns.
52 (11 March 1868) Tularosa
53 (17 April 1868) Nesmith's Mills
54 (13 June 1868) Apache Springs
55 (27 August 1868) Hatchet Mtns.
56 (22 April 1869) Sangre Canyon
57 (2 May 1869) San Augustin Pass
58 (7 May 1869) San Augustin Pass
59 (18 November 1869) Guadalupe Mtns.
60 (26–30 December 1869) Sanguinara Canyon

*Site uncertain

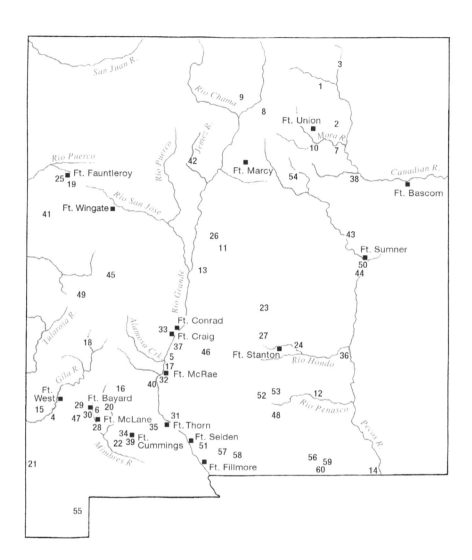

San Juan R.

Rio Chama

3

1

9

8

Ft. Union

2

Mora R.

10

7

Rio Puerco

Rio Puerco

Jemez R.

42

Canadian R.

25 Ft. Fauntleroy

19

Ft. Marcy

54

38

Rio San Jose

Ft. Bascom

41

Ft. Wingate

26

43

11

Ft. Sumner

45

13

Rio Grande

50

44

49

Tularosa R.

Alamosa Crk.

23

18

Ft. Conrad

33

37

Ft. Craig

27

24

Gila R.

5

46

Ft. Stanton

36

17

Rio Hondo

32

Ft. McRae

40

16

Ft.

53

12

West

Ft. Bayard

52

Rio Penasco

15

29

6

20

48

4

47 30

Ft. McLane

31

28

35

Ft. Thorn

34

Ft.

Ft. Selden

22 39

Cummings

51

57

58

56

59

21

60

14

55

Mimbres R.

Pecos R.

New Mexico 1871~90

61 (26 February 1873) Ft. Bascom
62 (13 July 1873) Canada Alamosa
63 (15 September 1876) Florida Mtns.
64 (9 January 1877) Animas Mtns.
65 (24 January 1877) Florida Mtns.
66 (18 December 1877) Animas Mtns.
67 (5 August 1878) Dog Canyon
68 (29 May 1879) Black Range
69 (4 September 1879) Ojo Caliente
70 (18 September 1879) Las Animas Creek
71 (29–30 September 1879)
        Cuchillo Negro Creek
72 (13 October 1879)
        Lloyd's and Slocum's Ranches
73 (12 January 1880) Percha Creek
74 (17 January 1880) San Mateo Mtns.
75 (30 January 1880) Caballo Mtns.
76 (3 February 1880) San Andres Mtns.
77 (9 February 1880) San Andres Mtns.
78 (7–8 April 1880) Hembrillo Canyon/
        San Andres Springs

79 (9 April 1880) Shakehand Springs
80 (16 April 1880) Mescalero Agency
81 (17 April 1880) Dog Canyon
82 (24 May 1880) Palomas River
83 (5 June 1880) Cooke's Canyon
84 (1 September 1880)
        Agua Chiquita Canyon
85 (7 September 1880) Ft. Cummings
86 (25 July 1881) San Andres Mtns.
87 (1 August 1881) Red Canyon
88 (3 August 1881) Monica Springs
89 (12 August 1881) Carrizo Canyon
90 (16 August 1881) Cuchillo Negro Creek
91 (19 August 1881) Gavilan Canyon
92 (23 June 1882) Mescalero Agency
93 (28 March 1883) McComas Massacre
94 (22 May 1885) Devil's Creek
95 (8 November 1885) Florida Mtns.
96 (19 December 1885) Little Dry Creek

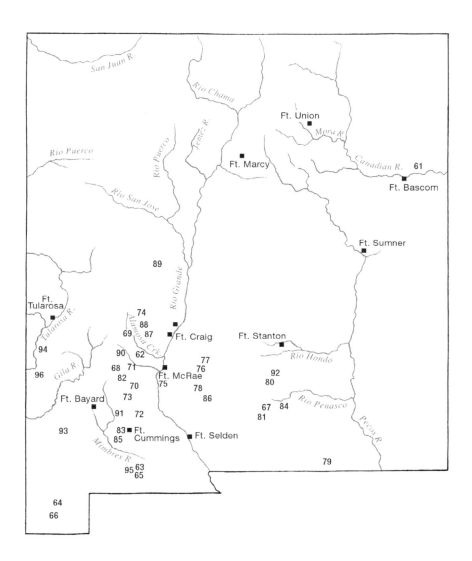

San Juan R.

Rio Chama

Rio Puerco

Rio Puerco

Jemes R.

Ft. Union

Mora R.

Ft. Marcy

Canadian R. 61

Ft. Bascom

Rio San Jose

Ft. Sumner

89

Rio Grande

Ft.
Tularosa

Tularosa R.

74

Alamosa Crk.

88

69   87

Ft. Craig

Ft. Stanton

Rio Hondo

94

90   62

77

76

92

80

96

Gila R.

68   71

82

70

Ft. McRae

75

78

86

Ft. Bayard

73

67   84

Rio Penasco

Pecos R.

91   72

81

93

83 ■ Ft.
85   Cummings

Ft. Selden

Mimbres R.

95 63

65

79

64

66

North Dakota

1 (3–6 September 1862) Ft. Abercrombie
2 (24 July 1863) Big Mound
3 (26 July 1863) Dead Buffalo Lake
4 (28 July 1863) Stony Lake
5 (3 August 1863) Mackinaw Massacre
6 (3 September 1863) Whitestone Hill
7 (16 December 1863) St. Joseph
8 (28 July 1864) Killdeer Mtn.
9 (7–9 August 1864) Badlands
10 (2 September 1864) Red Buttes/Ft. Dilts
11 (21–27 November 1864) Ft. Rice
12 (12–26 April 1865) Ft. Rice
13 (28 July 1865) Ft. Rice

South Dakota

1 (9 September 1876) Slim Buttes
2 (29 December 1890)
  Wounded Knee Creek
3 (30 December 1890) White Clay Creek/
  Drexel Mission

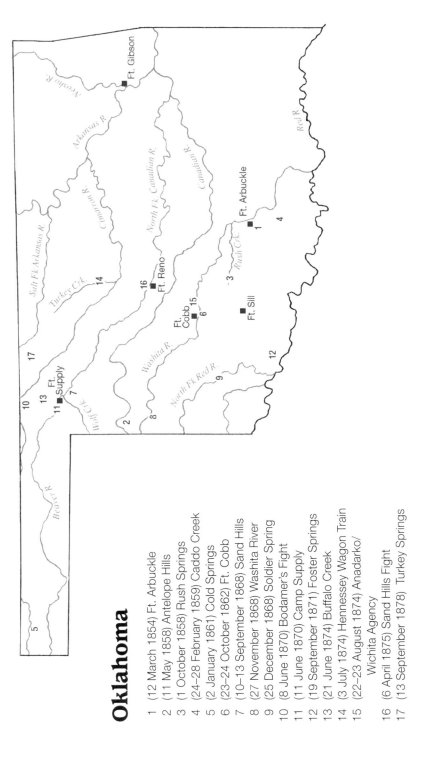

Oklahoma

1 (12 March 1854) Ft. Arbuckle
2 (11 May 1858) Antelope Hills
3 (1 October 1858) Rush Springs
4 (24–28 February 1859) Caddo Creek
5 (2 January 1861) Cold Springs
6 (23–24 October 1862) Ft. Cobb
7 (10–13 September 1868) Sand Hills
8 (27 November 1868) Washita River
9 (25 December 1868) Soldier Spring
10 (8 June 1870) Bodamer's Fight
11 (11 June 1870) Camp Supply
12 (19 September 1871) Foster Springs
13 (21 June 1874) Buffalo Creek
14 (3 July 1874) Hennessey Wagon Train
15 (22–23 August 1874) Anadarko/
      Wichita Agency
16 (6 April 1875) Sand Hills Fight
17 (13 September 1878) Turkey Springs

Oregon

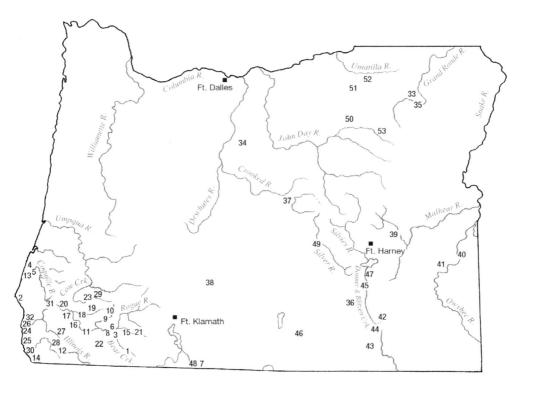

Columbia R.
Ft. Dalles
Williamette R.
Umatilla R.
52
51
33
35
Grand Ronde R.
Snake R.
John Day R.
50
53
34
Crooked R.
Deschutes R.
37
Malheur R.
Umpqua R.
49
39
Silver R.
Ft. Harney
Silver R.
4
5
13
Coquille R.
Cow Crk.
Rogue R.
38
23 29
Donner & Blitzen Crk.
47
45
36
40
41
2
31 20
19 10
Ft. Klamath
42
44
Owyhee R.
32
26
17 18
9
6
43
24
16
11 8 3 15 21
46
25
27
30
28
Illinois R.
22
14
12
Bear Crk.
1
48 7

Texas 1850–70

1   (7 April 1850) Laredo
2   (13 May 1850) Arroyo San Roque
3   (29 May 1850) Agua Dulce Creek
4   (12 June 1850) Laredo
5   (Ca. 15 July 1850) Nueces River
6   (Ca. 23 December 1850) Burleson's Fight
7   (7 February 1852) Stanger's Fight
8   (17 September 1852) San Roque Creek
9   (Fall 1852) Hynes Bay
10 (9 May 1854) Lake Trinidad
11 (11 July 1854) San Diego
12 (3 October 1854) Eagle Pass
13 (11 October 1854) Live Oak Creek
14 (1 November 1854) Ft. Davis
15 (22 July 1855) Eagle Springs
16 (22 February 1856)
       Headwaters Nueces River
17 (8 March 1856) Guadalupe River
18 (13 April 1856) Turkey Branch
19 (1 July 1856) Source of Colorado River
20 (26 November 1856) Concho River
21 (18–21 December 1856) Ft. Clark
22 (22 December 1856)
       Headwaters Concho River
23 (31 January 1857) Howard's Well
24 (12 February 1857)
       North Fork Concho River
25 (13 February 1857) Kickapoo Creek
26 (27 March 1857) Johnston's Station
27 (20 July 1857) Devil's River
28 (3 November 1859)
       Headwaters Llano River
29 (28 June 1860) Paint Creek
30 (26 August 1860) Clear Fork Brazos River
31 (19 December 1860) Pease River
32 (11 August 1861) Mays's Fight
33 (31 August 1862) Dead Man's Hole
34 (9 August 1864) Ellison Springs
35 (13 October 1864) Elm Creek Raid
36 (25 November 1864) Adobe Walls
37 (8 January 1865) Dove Creek
38 (1 June 1866) Wild Rose Pass
39 (October 1866) Cedar Gap
40 (12 March 1867) Pecos River
41 (11 July 1867) School House Massacre
42 (1 October 1867) Howard's Well
43 (26 December 1867) Ft. Lancaster
44 (6 March 1868) Paint Creek
45 (August 1868) Van Horn's Well
46 (14 September 1868) Horsehead Hill
47 (7 May 1869) Paint Creek
48 (7 June 1869) Johnson Draw
49 (12 September 1869) Lookout Point
50 (16 September 1869)
       Salt Fork Brazos River
51 (28–29 October 1869)
       Freshwater Fork Brazos River
52 (24 November 1869) Llano River
53 (20 January 1870) Delaware Creek
54 (19–20 May 1870) Kickapoo Springs
55 (12 July 1870)
       North Fork Little Wichita River
56 (5 October 1870) Cameron Creek

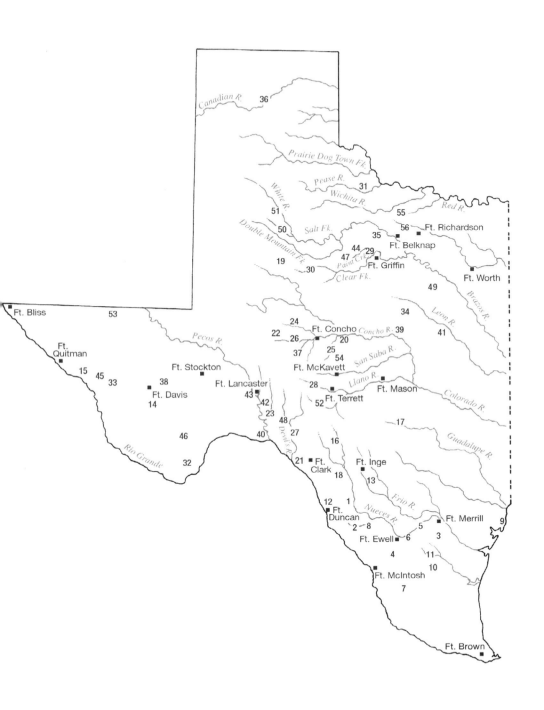

Canadian R.   36

Prairie Dog Town Fk.

Pease R.   31

Wichita R.   55

White R.   Red R.

51

50   Salt Fk.   56   Ft. Richardson

Double Mountain Fk.   35   Ft. Belknap

44   29
47   Paint Cr.   Ft. Griffin
19   30   Clear Fk.   49   Ft. Worth

Ft. Bliss   53   34   Leon R.   Brazos R.

Pecos R.   24   Ft. Concho   Concho R.   39

Ft.   22   26   20   41
Quitman   37   25   54   San Saba R.
15   45   33   Ft. Stockton   Ft. McKavett
38   Ft. Lancaster   28   Llano R.   Ft. Mason
Ft. Davis   43   52   Ft. Terrett   Colorado R.
14   42
23
48   17
46   40   27
Rio Grande   32   16   Guadalupe R.
Devil's R.
21   Ft.   Ft. Inge
Clark   18   13

12   1
Ft.   Nueces R.   Frio R.
Duncan   2   8   5   Ft. Merrill   9
Ft. Ewell   6   3
4   11
Ft. McIntosh   10
7

Ft. Brown

Texas 1871~90

Coahuila

Canadian R.

71

76 74
66 75

79 80

77 Salt Fk Red R.

73 Prairie Dog Town Fk

Pease R.

Wichita R.

Red R.

88 61

87 64 84 Ft. Richardson
62 Salt Fk. 57 60 58

White R. 72
78 70 59

Double Mountain Fk.

Paint Crk.

Ft. Griffin

Clear Fk.

Leon R.

Brazos R.

Ft. Bliss

90

96

91

Pecos R.

89

Ft. Concho 81

Concho R.

Ft.
Quitman

94

85 65 Concho R.

San Saba R.

93 92 Ft. Stockton Ft. McKavett 82

95

Ft. Davis

Ft. Lancaster 68

67

63

Llano R.

Colorado R.

TEXAS

86 83

Guadalupe R.

Devil's R.

69

5 Ft. Inge

Ft. Clark

Rio Grande

4

1

2 3 Ft.
Duncan

Leona R.

Frio R.

COAHUILA,
MEXICO

Nueces R.

Ft. McIntosh

Utah

1   (26 October 1853) Gunnison Massacre
2   (7–11 September 1857)
        Mountain Meadows Massacre
3   (14 August 1859) Devil's Gate Canyon
4   (Mid-June 1860) Willow Creek Station
5   (23 July 1860) Smithfield
6   (23 November 1862) Cache Valley
7   (6 December 1862) Empey's Ferry
8   (12–15 April 1863) Spanish Fork Canyon

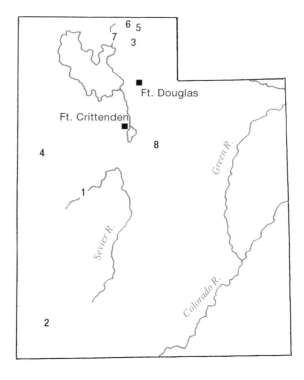

Washington

1   (6–8 October 1855) Toppenish Creek
2   (4–7 November 1855) White River/
     Puyallup River
3   (4 December 1855) Bennan's Prairie
4   (7–10 December 1855) Waiilatpu
5   (1 March 1856) Muckleshoot Prairie
6   (4 March 1856) Connell's Prairie
7   (13 March 1856) Tasawicks
8   (26–28 March 1856) Cascades
9   (10 April 1856) Satus Creek
10 (17 May 1858) Steptoe's Fight/
     Tohotonimme Creek
11 (15 August 1858) Yakima River
12 (1 September 1858) Four Lakes
13 (5 September 1858) Spokane Plain

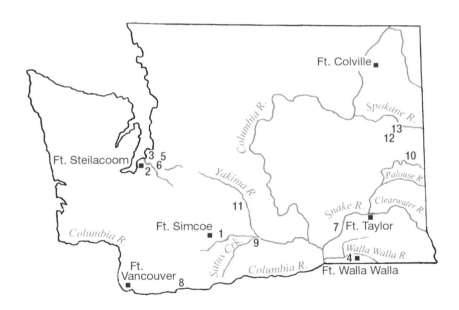

Wyoming

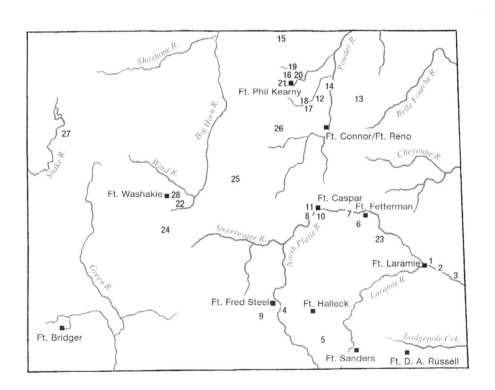

Sonora

1 (8 June 1885) Guadalupe Canyon
2 (23 June 1885) Bavispe Mtns.
3 (22 September 1885) Teres Mtns.
4 (3 May 1886) Pinito Mtns.
5 (15 May 1886) Pinito Mtns.

Chihuahua

1 (27 October 1879) Guzman Mtns.
2 (28 April 1882) Sierra Enmedio
3 (15 May 1883) Rio Bavispe
4 (7 August 1885) Casas Grandes

Introduction

I had several reasons for compiling this survey of battles and skirmishes in the trans-Mississippi West, beginning with the personal. My own library of a few thousand books, scattered among several rooms and covering various subjects, did not contain a fast and easy reference to the hundreds of American Indian versus military fights. There are a few reference books on the subject out there, but none are sufficiently comprehensive, detailed, or accurate for my satisfaction. I realized that if I wanted such a volume, I would have to write it myself. This conclusion was not an unhappy one; I have long had a fascination with the Indian wars and the personalities and places involved. Digging up and cataloguing the whos, whats, wheres, and whys—as well as tabulating statistics to reveal mosts, leasts, bests, and worsts—satisfies my peculiar itch to organize information.

The resulting product, this book, contains entries for 675 fights. In total, I have compiled and studied data from 1,470 fights to formulate my conclusions about warfare during the period; the reader will find these conclusions later in the book. Hundreds more conflicts took place than those cited here, but information about them is so scarce and hard to find that the research hits a point of diminishing returns. Though not complete, this survey offers enough information to be a useful resource and a sampling sufficient to draw conclusions.

I chose to limit my study to the years between 1850 and 1890 because, in the 270-odd years of Indian warfare, these decades recorded the greatest number of conflicts between Indians and the U.S. military. While I would have liked to include battles from the 1830s and 1840s, especially the tough fighting during the Seminole Wars, doing so would have created an impractically massive tome. The steady increase in fighting in the 1850s, as more and more white immigrants moved west, and the drastic drop in hostilities after 1890, the year the Census Bureau declared the frontier closed, seemed natural boundaries for the study.

Geographically, the study includes Indian battles from nineteen western states. After 1850, almost every fight of note took place west of the Mississippi River; therefore I incorporated all those states except Missouri, Arkansas, and Louisiana, in which no significant Indian battles unrelated to the Civil War took place. I have also included some battles fought in Mexico—Sonora, Coahuila, and Chihuahua—that were organized by the U.S. army and involved U.S. soldiers and citizens. Most of the battles were between Indians and the U.S. or state military, but in many cases civilians took part in the fights as well, either on their own or as volunteer auxiliaries to military units.[1] I have also included a number of Indian attacks on settlers, civilian wagon trains, and the like. By and large, the ones I list and describe are the most infamous or most significant incidents.

The battle names listed are the names most commonly used in my main sources. They are usually derived from the name of the place in which the fight occurred, which may or may not match a modern place name. In the text, I have listed the battle's name followed by a location; whenever possible, this is the nearest present-day town to the battle site. I have included entries for some obscure fights, and, so as not to repeat already familiar information, I have limited the descriptions of the best-known ones. Thus, for instance, entries for the Battle of Bone Pile Creek and the Battle of the Little Big Horn are similar in length.

The entries vary in the amount and types of information they include, according to the data I was able to gather. In addition to dates, military units involved, and numbers of casualties, many entries also list other particulars such as numbers engaged, names of leaders and tribes, time of day, specific locations, and so on. In many cases, tribal affiliations were unidentified in my sources or otherwise uncertain. In those instances I have used the generic "Indians" without further explanation.

I used five main sources in collecting my data: Francis B. Heitman's *Historical Register and Dictionary of the United States Army,* 1903, a chronological list of fights that does not include casualties; the Adjutant General's Office's *Chronological List of Actions with the Indians,* printed in the early 1890s; George W. Webb's *Chronological List of Engagements between the Regular Army of the United States and Various Tribes of Hostile Indians,* 1939, a narrative list that combines much information from the above two sources; Joseph P. Peters's *Indian Battles and Skirmishes on the American Frontier,* 1966, which is a composite of some of the above sources and others plus Peters's own addendum; and the 128-volume *War of the Rebellion: A Compilation of the Official Records of the Union and Confederate Armies,* which gives primary reports of battles during the Civil War years. I supplemented these sources with numerous others.

I hope this survey is a handy reference tool for scholars and a source of interest for readers seeking knowledge of western American Indian wars.

---

1 *Many battles during the Indian Wars were fought with state and territorial volunteer forces rather than the United States, or "regular," army. The circumstances surrounding volunteer regiments were often haphazard. Some were officially sanctioned. Others were gathered from within a community at a moment's notice. Yet others started informally but evolved into an official or semiofficial group. The Texas Rangers are an example of this.*

In addition to the entries, a summary of the conclusions I drew from the data appears at the end of this book. In it I attempt to challenge some widely accepted generalizations about the Indian wars and the frontier military, generalizations based on deductions I believe are faulty. Among these generalizations is a revisionist assertion that may surprise the average American: the Wild West was not wild. The frontier was, according to this theory, an unexceptional place in its era, the Wild West image simply a creation of the popular media.

In addition to supposedly debunking the idea that the nineteenth-century American West was violent, these historians question whether we should even continue to study western warfare in any detail. At a roundtable discussion at the 1999 Western History Association conference, some participants went so far as to suggest that historians should deemphasize violence and warfare in history in the hopes that this might curb the violence in our culture. I believe that while we need not glorify violence, we must be careful not to distort the facts to conform to our own political agenda.

The survey of battles and skirmishes presented here certainly shows that all was not serene on the frontier between 1850 and 1890. Fighting was almost a daily occurrence. Still, why study and analyze violent conflicts? In discussing the horror of the 1832 fight between the army and the Sauk at the Battle of Bad Axe, historian Patricia Nelson Limerick asked, "What good can knowledge of this miserable story do? What exactly does knowledge of this event add to American self-understanding and well-being?" Some historians, dreaming of a kinder, gentler world, believe there is little reason to add up war casualties. Limerick answers her own questions, however, pointing out that these stories are part of our national heritage. They shaped our culture, and in order to understand ourselves we need to know our past.[2]

Was the West wild or mild? Perhaps after perusing the survey and reading the conclusions, readers can form their own opinions.

((

I would like to encourage readers who have personal geographical knowledge of the locations of the more obscure battle sites to contact me through the publisher, Mountain Press. The exact sites of a number of these fights are unknown to many except a handful of local citizens. The stated locations of certain battle sites are only best estimates. I would be grateful to any readers who can assist me in pinpointing the sites to insure the greatest accuracy possible.

---

2 Limerick, *Something in the Soil*, 35–36.

4

—1850—

6 APRIL 1850
RAYADO (Rayado, New Mexico)

Near Rayado Creek, about 50 miles south of Raton, a band of Jicarilla Apaches stole horses and seriously wounded two Mexican herders. Captain W. N. Grier of the 1st Dragoons sent out Sgt. William Holbrook and ten men of Company I to protect the Rayado settlement. Riding with Holbrook were Christopher "Kit" Carson and two other frontiersmen, William New and Robert Fisher.

They rode to the scene of the attack, then followed the trail 25 miles to the camp of nine unsuspecting Apaches. At daybreak on 6 April, Holbrook charged in, killed five of the nine, wounded two others, and recaptured the stock. Holbrook returned the next day with five scalps as "vouchers," which he claimed he did not take from the bodies himself; rather, a couple of Mexican herders who came by after the fight did the scalping.[1]

7 APRIL 1850
LAREDO (Laredo, Texas)

On 6 April, during a scout near Laredo, Lt. Walter W. Hudson and Companies G and I of the 1st Infantry, out of Fort McIntosh, attacked a camp of Indians on the Nueces River and recovered 30 stolen horses. Hudson pursued the Indians and the next day caught up with them. In the ensuing fight, four enlisted men were wounded and one was killed. Hudson received a mortal wound and died on 19 April. Four Indians were wounded.[2]

21 APRIL 1850
GLANTON MASSACRE (Winterhaven, California)

John Glanton, a Texan and notorious leader of a band of soldiers of fortune, arrived at the Colorado River near the mouth of the Gila. Glanton and his men had just left Mexico after killing Apaches for the bounties on their heads. They decided that overcharging emigrants for ferrying them across the river would be an easier money-making scheme. Early in April, a party of Americans refused to pay Glanton's prices, built their own boat, crossed the river, and left the boat to the Quechan Indians living nearby. The Indians began their own operation in direct competition with Glanton.

Glanton marched down to the Indians' ferry, destroyed the boat, bound a man named Callahan who worked for the Indians, and threw him in the river. The Quechans would not stand for this. Soon thereafter Glanton and some of his men went to San Diego to transact business. When they returned from the long trip, they lay down near the ferry, got drunk, and fell asleep. Quechans armed with clubs entered their camp and, at a signal, jumped in and began beating the sleeping men. Glanton, hit while asleep, tried to rise and was clubbed to death. Within three minutes, the Indians had killed ten others as well.

Three more of Glanton's gang were downriver and escaped the massacre. They saw the Indians coming for them, jumped into a small boat, and fled farther downriver, where they were taken in at a Mexican settlement. Meanwhile the Quechans carried the white men's bodies to a pile of combustibles and burned them. The *San Francisco Daily Alta California* reported on 8 January 1851, "their bones can be seen there to this day."[3]

MAY 1850
WAGON MOUND (Wagon Mound, New Mexico)

A band of Jicarilla Apaches jumped a train of U.S. mail wagons on its way from Independence, Missouri, to Santa Fe. The Indians attacked in the morning, and the fighting lasted all day. Two whites were wounded and placed in a wagon; the remainder managed to hold their own.

That night, a band of Utes joined the Apaches. The Utes said they did not know how to fight Americans, so the Apaches said they would show them. In the morning the mail wagons were moving closer to the high ground at Wagon Mound when the combined force of raiders attacked again, this time with overwhelming force. The Indians killed ten men and every animal.[4] Soldiers from Santa Fe buried the dead. They found some of the men stripped, but none scalped. Arrows covered the ground and the mail was scattered across the plains.

Wagon Mound (New Mexico)

13 MAY 1850
ARROYO SAN ROQUE (Catarina, Texas)

Capt. John S. "Rip" Ford of the Texas Mounted Volunteers was assigned with his company to Fort McIntosh. They were patrolling along the Nueces River when a band of Comanches attacked them near Arroyo San Roque, a tributary west of the Nueces. One Texan was wounded, while 4 Comanches were killed and 4 were wounded. The Texans captured 11 horses.[5]

14–15 MAY 1850
CLEAR LAKE (Lakeport, California)

In the winter of 1850, Pomo Indians murdered some miners around Clear Lake, about 80 miles north of San Francisco. Commanding the Department of the Pacific, Gen. Persifor Smith sent an expedition under Capt. Nathaniel Lyon to punish the offenders.

Lyon led Company C of the 1st Dragoons, companies A, E, and G of the 2nd Infantry, and a detachment of Company M of the 3rd Artillery to Clear Lake. They brought along boats and a howitzer. Lt. John W. Davidson, Company C, chased 400 Pomos along the western lakeshore until they got in canoes and crossed over to an island at the lake's north end. He killed four Indians and captured one.

On 15 May, Lyon and his men crossed the lake by boat and drove the Pomos off the island, back to the tule-covered shores, where they shot down more than 60 Indians. The surviving Pomos scattered into the woods.[6]

19 MAY 1850
RUSSIAN RIVER (Healdsburg, California)

Heading west after the Clear Lake battle, Capt. Lyon crossed the divide from Clear Lake to the south-flowing Russian River looking for an Indian named Chapo, who was implicated in murdering settlers. Lyon found the Pomo camp deserted and marched downstream 22 miles to find Preesta's band of about 400 Indians. Lyons attacked them in what Lt. Davidson called "a veritable jungle" along the river. Some of the Pomos escaped to an island in the river. There, Lyon closed in and commenced firing. He claimed the place had become "a perfect slaughter pen." The Indian dead were estimated at more than 75; only 2 enlisted men of Company G were wounded.[7]

29 MAY 1850
AGUA DULCE CREEK (Midway, Texas)

Capt. John S. "Rip" Ford led a scout of about 40 Rangers in southern Texas below the Nueces River. After dividing the party into two squads, Ford came across a band under Comanche chief Otto Cuero in present-day Jim Wells County, about 14 miles north of the town of Alice. The Rangers attacked, and the Comanches turned to do battle. Each side had about 16 men. Otto Cuero rode out in front as if daring the Rangers to charge. "Be steady, boys!" Ford said. "He wants to draw your fire and then charge you with the lance!"[8] The chief came on, and Sgt. David M. Level shot him in the arm. When he turned back, the Rangers charged. William Gillespie was shot through the lung with an arrow, and fellow Rangers stopped firing while Gillespie was removed to safety amid long-range sniping. When the Rangers' rear guard arrived, the soldiers flanked the warriors, who tried to pull back to the trees along Agua Dulce Creek. Otto Cuero gave his own horse to a wounded warrior. While the chief was rallying his men, David Steele killed him with a rifle bullet. Then the Comanches took up position along the creek and the Rangers pulled back.

One Ranger was killed and two were wounded. The Comanches suffered four men killed and seven wounded. A slight arrow scratch on Ford's right hand never stopped troubling him. Six years later the hand and arm became paralyzed, and Ford speculated that the arrow was poisoned.[9]

12 JUNE 1850
LAREDO (Laredo, Texas)

Lt. Charles N. Underwood, with detachments of Companies H and K, 1st Infantry, was escorting mail from Fort Merrill to Laredo when Comanches attacked the party. Two soldiers were killed in action; two others were mortally wounded, both succumbing on 16 June. Underwood and three other soldiers were also wounded. One Indian was killed and four were wounded.[10]

CA. 15 JULY 1850
NUECES RIVER (Southern Texas)

In the summer of 1850 Capt. William A. "Bigfoot" Wallace and his 20 men of the Texas Ranging Company were attached to Capt. William J. Hardee's expedition. While Hardee and ten companies of the 2nd Dragoons and 1st Infantry scoured the east bank of the Nueces, Wallace and his Rangers moved down the west bank. After going downriver nearly to Corpus Christi, Wallace turned around and went back up to Fort Merrill, then continued upriver.

At a place called the Black Hills, 20 miles above the old Laredo Road, Wallace's company spotted Indian signs, including a "scalped" mustang, which Wallace interpreted as meaning that if they persisted in following the trail, they would be scalped. But, said Wallace, "the threat did not scare us 'worth a cent.'"[11] Several hundred yards on, they met a Comanche who challenged them to fight. The Texans were game, but soon found themselves facing about 100 warriors. The Indians charged in double file, then when they got within 100 yards, they broke right and left and circled around the Rangers. Wallace was ready, and his men fired intensely, keeping the Indians at bay. Said Wallace, "We pitched the rifle bullets into them so rapidly they couldn't stand the racket, and once more retreated toward their camp."[12]

The Comanches made four charges, the last not dividing but attempting to go right over the Texans. The Rangers shot them to pieces, yet the Indians would not give up the field. After several hours of fighting, Wallace had to make his own charge, hoping to drive the Indians away from their camp and get at the only waterhole in the area. A wild zigzag attack carried the Texans to the camp without casualties, and they drove out the last of the Comanches. Only three Rangers were wounded: Rose, Oget, and Hynyard. Wallace reported 22 Indians killed and 15 wounded.[13]

25 JULY 1850
PIT RIVER (Northern California)

In a planned skirmish with a band of Pit River Indians, detachments from companies A, E, and G, 2nd Infantry; Company M, 3rd Artillery; and Company C, 1st Dragoons, suffered one soldier killed and one mortally wounded.[14]

26 JULY 1850
HEADWATERS OF THE CANADIAN RIVER (Raton, New Mexico)

While patrolling the Santa Fe Trail, Companies C and I of the 1st Dragoons and Company K of the 2nd Dragoons surprised a camp of about 150 Indian lodges, possibly of Jicarilla Apaches, on the upper reaches of the Canadian River. The Indians were able to escape, with unknown casualties. One enlisted man was killed.[15]

CA. 23 DECEMBER 1850
BURLESON'S FIGHT (Loma Alta, Texas)

Lt. Edward Burleson was taking his company of Texas Rangers to Fort McIntosh at Laredo. A few miles from the Nueces River in McMullen County, Burleson spotted some Comanches riding about a mile off the road between San Antonio and Laredo. He took nine men with him to investigate while the rest of the command continued along the road. When they were 50 yards from the mounted Comanches, the Indians wheeled around to expose another 13 of their number, who had been walking unseen in single file in front of the horses. Burleson reined up and called out, "Well, boys, you see what it is, what do you say?" The men were outnumbered two to one, but they told him to make the call. "Well, boys, light in," Burleson ordered.[16]

Both sides dismounted and advanced, firing continuously. Burleson took an arrow through his hat that creased his skull. Jim Carr was hit four times. One arrow pierced his hand and pinned it to the stock of his gun. The fight was hand-to-hand, and almost every man on each side was hit. Interpreter Warren Lyons heard the Comanches calling among themselves. "Lieutenant," Lyons shouted to Burleson, "they are whipped, they are saying to one another they will have to retreat."[17]

The Indians put their most seriously wounded on the horses while the few who remained unhurt covered the retreat. Burleson could not pursue, for every one of his men was dead or wounded. The rest of the command reached the scene as the fight ended, and they packed up the wounded and dead and set out for water. Burleson sent a courier to Laredo for an ambulance and brought his men to the fort, but in rather poor shape for the Christmas festivities.

The fight had lasted barely three minutes, yet about 23 out of 26 combatants were killed or wounded. Two hundred arrows were later retrieved from a half acre of ground. Burleson lost 2 men and 8 were wounded.[18] The Comanches' casualties were 13 killed and wounded.[19]

—1851—

JANUARY 1851
FOUR CREEKS (Bakersfield, California)

About 300 Tulare Indians descended on the small cabin-and-tent settlement at Four Creeks, near present-day Bakersfield, California. Two small civilian parties had joined a few vaqueros herding cattle when the Indians, armed mostly with bows and arrows, quickly wiped them out. Prospectors later found the bodies of 13 whites.

The Tulares then attacked French's Ranch nearby. The 40 or so emigrants there at the time were able to repulse the Tulares, inflicting substantial losses, estimated at 40 killed.[20]

This incident and others led to the establishment of Fort Tejon in 1854, in the Tehachapi Mountains to the south.

CA. 11 JANUARY 1851
SAVAGE'S FIGHT (Madera, California)

James Savage owned trading posts on the Mariposa and Burns Rivers in California's Central Valley. In mid-December 1850, while Savage was at the Burns River post, Indians raided his Mariposa station, killing three employees, kidnapping his two Indian wives, and stealing or destroying $8,000 in goods. Savage went to the Mariposa post, where he raised a company of 43 men, and on 7 January the party marched to the Fresno River. There they built a log fort to hold their supplies and stock, leaving four men as guards.

Savage knew the Indians' stronghold was in the mountains 60 miles east. He and his posse found the camp of perhaps 300 Chowchilla and Yokut Indians in a hollow surrounded by timbered hills, accessible only through one pass. Savage waited until dawn and charged the camp. The Indians fled into the brush, but then rallied and soon forced Savage's company to retreat to the timbers. Some of the Indians knew Savage and called for him to come out and fight. The Indians had few firearms, however, so when they charged, Savage's well-armed men caused great destruction. Before leaving, one Indian called to Savage, saying they would soon meet again.

During the siege, Savage's men had destroyed more than 60 huts and a great amount of mule meat and acorn meal. In all the whites counted 27 Indian dead, and they had certainly wounded a number more. One old woman, severely wounded, had been burned among the huts. Two white civilians were killed, while another had his nose shot off with a rifle ball.[21]

CA. 3 FEBRUARY 1851
FINE GOLD GULCH (Madera, California)

After James Savage returned to the Central Valley following his January fight, he immediately began organizing another paramilitary expedition to avenge the Indian raid on his trading post. This time he started from the Agua Frio River with 210 men. Moving southeast into the foothills, Savage went ahead to reconnoiter with 70 men, leaving the remainder under "Major" James Burney, sheriff of Mariposa County.[22] They were to meet at Fine Gold Gulch.

Savage arrived at the designated spot and waited a day for Burney. When he did not arrive, Savage moved on alone. In the evening of the same day, he surprised a large force of Indians. They skirmished briefly, but nightfall ended the encounter.

Early the next morning, Savage continued on the Indians' trail with 28 men. They found the Indians and attacked, killing 10 and wounding 40. He returned to Fine Gold Gulch without further conflict.[23]

19 MARCH 1851
OATMAN MASSACRE (Gila Bend, Arizona)

In August 1850 Royse and Mary Ann Oatman left Independence, Missouri, for California with their seven children: Lucy, Lorenzo, Olive Ann, Royse Jr., Mary Ann, Charity Ann, and Roland. In a group of about 80 emigrants, they took their wagons along the Santa Fe Trail to the Rio Grande, then continued on the southern route to Tucson.

In February, most of the party elected to remain in Tucson and rest, but the Oatman, Kelly, and Wilder families moved on. By March, they had gotten as far as the Maricopa and Pima villages. There the desert-weakened, short-provisioned party stopped. But Royse Oatman was determined to go on alone. He prodded his family across the desert following the nearly dry Gila River. About 80 miles east of Yuma, Arizona, at the place now known as Oatman Flat, they were waylaid by 19 Yavapais. After demanding to be fed from the Oatmans' pitifully small larder, the Indians attacked them, slaying Royse, his wife, and four of the children. Lorenzo, 16 years old, was badly wounded and left for dead. Olive, 14, and Mary Ann, 7, were taken captive. Lorenzo was eventually rescued and he continued on to California.

The Yavapais took the two girls 100 miles north and sold them to the Mojaves. Mary Ann died the next year. The Mojaves tatooed Olive's face and adopted her into the tribe. She was rescued five years later and eventually reunited with her brother.[24]

29 MAY 1851
SAN TIMOTEO CANYON (Redlands, California)

John Irving, a Texan with an unsavory reputation, and about a dozen soldiers of fortune went to Rancho San Bernardino to engage in some revenge-related robbery and murder.[25] The ranchers had been warned and escaped before the mercenaries arrived. As Irving and his gang plundered the ranches, they were confronted by neighboring Cahuilla Indians. Juan Antonio, a Cahuilla chief, led more than 300 warriors after Irving. He fled southeast for ten miles, then came to a fork in the road. He made a wrong turn up San Timoteo Canyon, just south of present-day Redlands, California. The path narrowed to the width of two horsemen, then ended altogether. The Cahuillas caught up with Irving and his men and shot them down with arrows, then beat them to a pulp with clubs and stones. The entire gang was slaughtered, except George Evans. Evans had warned Irving against taking the canyon, and, riding at the rear, he took the first opportunity to jump off his horse and make his way into the chaparral to hide. Only one Cahuilla was killed.[26]

2 JUNE 1851
BEAR CREEK (Ashland, Oregon)

Thirty-two miners led by Dr. James McBride were returning to Oregon after a stint digging gold in California. On Bear Creek, near present-day Ashland, Oregon, about 150 Rogue River Indians ambushed them. A four-hour battle ensued. The Rogues got the worst of it, with seven men killed and four wounded. Only one miner was injured, but the Rogues got away with horses, packs, and $1,500 in supplies and gold dust.[27]

7 JUNE 1851
SMITH RIVER (Crescent City, California)

Hostile confrontations between Indians and miners in the northern California and southern Oregon gold diggings brought on an escalating series of retaliatory Indian raids and military expeditions. On 7 June, ten armed volunteers under J. B. Long crossed the mountains to the verdant valley of the Smith River, east of present-day Crescent City, California. They walked into a nine-lodge village of Talowa Indians, which included about 30 men, and tried to disarm them. The Indians seized Long, and a fight ensued. Long escaped; the volunteers killed four Indians and wounded four others before pulling out. They recrossed the Siskiyou Mountains boasting of a great victory.[28]

10 JUNE 1851
BATTLE ROCK (Port Orford, Oregon)

Capt. William Tichenor sailed his steamer *Sea Gull* to the southern Oregon coast, hoping to establish a town. He dropped off nine men, supplies, and a cannon to start the fledgling burg, which would later become Port Orford. Tichenor departed promising to bring more men in two weeks. The Quatomah band of Rogue River Indians, however, did not appreciate the intrusion and menaced the new colonists. The newcomers pulled back to a rocky promontory between the ocean and the tidal flats and prepared a defense.

The Indians held a war dance and advanced on the position with about 100 warriors. The colonists' leader, J. M. Kirkpatrick, directed the firing of the cannon, and the defenders fought tenaciously. With only 2 of their own wounded, they killed 17 Rogues, and wounded 10 more. The Indians retreated, but kept the whites under siege for two weeks. When Tichenor did not return on the promised date, the stranded colonists abandoned their rock and fled north, eventually finding safety among the friendly Indians at Coos Bay.[29]

17 JUNE 1851
TABLE ROCK (White City, Oregon)

Maj. Philip Kearny was leading 28 men of the 1st Regiment of Mounted Riflemen from Oregon to California. Desertions to the goldfields had so depleted their ranks that the regiment was being sent back to Jefferson Barracks in St. Louis, Missouri, to recruit. A few miles up the Rogue River from Table Rock, about seven miles north of present-day Medford, Oregon, a band of Rogue River Indians attacked Kearny's army. Army casualties were 2 soldiers wounded and a captain killed. The Rogues lost 11 warriors and 6 were wounded.[30]

26 AUGUST 1851
GILA AND PINTO RIVERS (Southwestern New Mexico)

Indians (probably Apaches) attacked a detachment of Company B, 1st Dragoons, under Lt. Abraham Buford in New Mexico Territory. One soldier was killed; one soldier and one Indian were wounded.[31]

14 SEPTEMBER 1851
COQUILLE MASSACRE (Bandon, Oregon)

The Port Orford settlers, having returned to the area after fleeing to Coos Bay in June, decided to blaze a road from the coast to the Oregon-California Trail. William T'Vault led 23 men on an exploratory expedition, but rough terrain and limited supplies caused 13 of them to give up by mid-August. T'Vault and the other 10 plodded on until 1 September, when they too decided to call it quits.

At the South Fork of the Coquille River, T'Vault's party hired some Coquille Indians to take them downstream in canoes. When they reached the Coquille village on the coast, the Indians pulled ashore, surrounded the explorers, and attempted to disarm them. A fight broke out, and the Indians hacked and bludgeoned the white men. T'Vault, still in his canoe, saw "the most awful state of confusion; it appeared to be the screams of thousands, the sound of blows, the groans and shrieks of the dying."[32]

T'Vault paddled the canoe to the south shore. A few others fought their way through the village and into the woods. Five of T'Vault's men were killed. The Indians suffered no casualties.[33]

CA. 1 OCTOBER 1851
FORT HALL (Fort Hall, Idaho)

A pack train guarded by a small company of men was traveling past Fort Hall when Shoshones, concealed in the brush along the trail, fired upon them. The company disintegrated as eight men were killed and the rest fled. The Indians took $1,000 in cash, $2,000 in property, and 12 horses.[34]

22 NOVEMBER 1851
COQUILLE RIVER (Myrtle Point, Oregon)

In response to the September murder of 5 white men by Coquille Indians, Lt. Col. Silas Casey, 2nd Infantry, led a punitive expedition of 130 men, in companies A, C, and E of the 1st Dragoons, to the mouth of the Coquille River. On 5 November, the Indians fired at them and pulled back upriver. Casey sent to Port Orford for three boats to pursue them.

On 20 November, after rowing upriver for a few days, the soldiers camped at the junction of the north and south forks of the river. Casey sent parties up the branches to locate the Indians. Lt. George Stoneman found the camp on the main stream, eight miles above their camp, near present-day Myrtle Point, Oregon. On the 22nd Casey took the entire force upriver. Half a mile before the camp, they split up to approach the hideout from both sides. A small detachment remained in the boat, which the Coquilles spotted and fired upon. Lt. Thomas Wright immediately attacked them from the shore. As the Indians fled along the river, Casey shouted: "Boys, take good sight, throw no shots away, give them Hell!"[35]

Meanwhile, Lt. Stoneman opened fire from the opposite shore. The Coquilles were caught in the crossfire, and after a short fight they fled into the forest. Casey figured they had learned their lesson and returned to the mouth of the river.

Casey's men killed 15 Indians and wounded several more. On the army side, 2 privates were mortally wounded.[36]

—1852—

LAGUNA (Truth or Consequences, New Mexico)

After several months in the field as part of Maj. Marshall Howe's Apache expedition, detachments of Companies D, E, and H of the 2nd Dragoons, under Lt. Alfred Pleasanton out of Fort Conrad, skirmished with Indians, probably Apaches, in January. Lts. Beverly H. Robertson and Nathan G. Evans distinguished themselves in the fight, which took place near a lagoon on the Jornada del Muerto.

The Indians killed two soldiers of Company E on 24 January, and two of Company K on the 25th. There were no Indian casualties.[37]

6 FEBRUARY 1852
FORT WEBSTER (Hanover, New Mexico)

At the time of this skirmish, Fort Webster was at the Santa Rita copper mines on the southern slopes of the Pinos Altos Range. The post was garrisoned by one company of the 3rd Infantry and one of 2nd Dragoons. On 6 February about 50 Apaches swept down on the post's cattle herd, drawing the soldiers away from the fort. Capt. Israel B. Richardson and Company K, 3rd Infantry, responded. They got the worst of the fight.

Casualties among the soldiers were three dead and one wounded. The Apaches, who did not usually take scalps, did lift the bright red hair of one of the dead soldiers and mutilated his body. On the Indian side, Apache chief Delgadito may have been wounded.[38]

7 FEBRUARY 1852
STANGER'S FIGHT (Zapata, Texas)

In the winter of 1852, Lt. (later Gen.) John Gibbon and a company of the 4th Artillery occupied Camp Drum on the Rio Grande, 50 miles south of Laredo, Texas. Assisting Gibbon were companies of the 2nd Dragoons, split among various Texas posts. On 5 February, Gibbon sent a Cpl. Stanger with 10 men of Company C, 2nd Dragoons, from Camp Drum to chastise a band of Comanche raiders. After a two-day chase, Stanger and his men caught up with and routed about 10 Comanches.

With no casualties of their own, the soldiers killed three Indians, wounded one, and recovered stolen property.[39]

5 MARCH 1852
CAMP YUMA (Yuma, Arizona)

Abandoned for about eight months, Camp Yuma had recently been reoccupied by Capt. Samuel P. Heintzelman, 2nd Infantry, in February 1852. The camp was on the west bank of the Colorado River, below the mouth of the Gila River. On the east bank, Sgt. I. B. Taylor and a detachment of

Col. John Gibbon
—Courtesy Little Bighorn
Battlefield National Monument

Company C, 1st Dragoons, were guarding the post's horses when Yuma Indians attacked. Five soldiers were killed.[40]

22 APRIL 1852
SOUTH FORK OF THE TRINITY RIVER (Forest Glen, California)

On 15 April, a settler named Anderson was murdered near Weaverville, California. Sheriff Dixon got together a band of 36 armed citizens to track the culprits, believed to be the local Indians. The trail led southwest to a valley on the south side of the South Fork of the Trinity River, where about 150 Indians were camped. At midnight on 22 April, Dixon divided his men into three groups, and at dawn they attacked with pistols and knives, devastating the camp.

Some Indian men, women, and children may have escaped into the woods, but Dixon's band killed more than 140 and captured only 3. No white casualties were reported.[41]

17 JULY 1852
TABLE ROCK CONFERENCE (White City, Oregon)

During the summer of 1852, hostilities existed between settlers on the one side and Shasta and Rogue River Indians on the other. In an effort to make peace, Indian agent Alonzo A. Skinner called a meeting near a large gravel bar in the Rogue River below Table Rock. He persuaded some of the Indians to stack their arms and attend the conference, and with difficulty he talked the Oregon Volunteers under John K. Lamerick into doing the same.

When Elisha Steele marched up with his California Volunteers, events took a turn for the worse. Steele refused to stack his arms, and when Skinner crossed the river to talk to some more Indians, the California Volunteers attacked the Indians at the conference. One volunteer shot the son of Shasta chief Sullix in the head, and a melee broke out. The white men killed most of the Indians there.

After the episode, Skinner was unable to negotiate a settlement between the antagonists and gave up. Reports of Indian deaths in the incident ranged between 4 and 20.[42]

SEPTEMBER 1852
BLOODY POINT (Tulelake, California)

When an emigrant wagon train on the Applegate Cutoff to Oregon passed near the shore of Tule Lake, at the foot of a steep bluff, a Modoc war party, hidden in the rocks above, descended on the train. The Modocs killed 62 emigrants. Only one man escaped. Two girls, ages 12 and 14, were taken captive.[43]

17 SEPTEMBER 1852
SAN ROQUE CREEK (Cotulla, Texas)

Citizens of Laredo, Texas, were alarmed when Indians, probably Lipans, crossed the Rio Grande and began raiding up and down the river. A Texas Ranger company under Capt. Owen Shaw intercepted the trail and tracked the Indians north to the Nueces River, then upstream. About 30 miles northwest of Fort Ewell on San Roque Creek, about 12 miles west of present-day Cotulla, the Rangers found the Indians' camp.

The Indians approached the Texans from an arroyo and opened fire with rifles, arrows, and one six-shooter. From 75 yards away, Shaw and his men returned fire with their larger number of rifles. When Shaw charged, the Indians abandoned the arroyo, and the mounted Rangers cut them down on the prairie.

The Rangers killed 9 Indians and wounded 11; only 1 escaped. They also captured 23 horses and mules, plus saddles, bridles, and weapons. Shaw had no casualties.[44]

CA. 15 NOVEMBER 1852
BEN WRIGHT AFFAIR/BLACK BLUFF (Merrill, Oregon)

Wanting to avenge the emigrant killings at Tule Lake (see Bloody Point, September) Ben Wright of Yreka, California, gathered a company of miners and settlers to hunt down the Modoc perpetrators. The vigilantes camped south of the Indian village, near Bloody Point, on a peninsula that jutted out into Tule Lake. For two months they tried to induce the Modocs to return the items they had stolen from the emigrants, without success. Finally, Wright switched to a different tactic. When some of his men returned from Yreka with a supply of food, Wright invited the Modocs to his camp for a feast and a peace talk. But the Indians suspected he had put strychnine in their food and would not eat it.

Tiring of his own game, Wright moved to the north end of the lake by Lost River Bridge, just inside the Oregon border, and camped next to a Modoc village. In the morning, while the Indians were drying meat for the winter, Wright walked calmly into the village, threw open his coat, and began firing. This signaled his men, concealed around the village and on a nearby bluff, to open fire too. The Modocs panicked. Some jumped into the lake and drowned. Others ran into the woods but Wright's men hunted them down.

Only 5 of the 46 Modocs in the village escaped; the rest were killed. The public later censured Wright for not having fought the Indians in an open contest.[45]

FALL 1852
HYNES BAY (Austwell, Texas)

After conflicts with Texans, many of the Karankawa tribe—despised for their cannibalism—moved to Mexico. But sometime in the fall of 1852, one Karankawa band returned to its old campgrounds along Hynes Bay, near present-day Austwell. When they were discovered by local settlers, about 30 militia, led by John Hynes, surrounded the camp and launched a surprise attack.

The militia destroyed the Karankawa village of about 50 people, sparing only a handful of women and children; about 45 Karankawas died. The militia had no losses. This may have been the last fight of the Karankawas on Texas soil. Within a decade, disease and warfare made the Karankawas virtually extinct.[46]

—1853—

31 JANUARY 1853
CHOWCHILLA RIVER (Chowchilla, California)

In the winter of 1852–53, ranchers along the lower Mariposa and Chowchilla Rivers in Merced County, California, lost a considerable number of livestock to Indian raiders of an unidentified tribe. One well-shod stolen horse left deep prints in the dirt, enabling half a dozen ranchers to track down a rancheria of about 100 Indians near the Chowchilla River. The settlers confronted some of the men of the band, but a parley in Spanish produced only "No sabe, no sabe."

During the talk, one of the ranchers, named Starkie, saw some suspicious movement and without warning fired his rifle, killing the Indian he believed was chief. Immediately, several arrows pierced him in return, and the fight was on. A Dr. Westfall was severely wounded in the hand. When it looked as if the Indians were going to cut them off from their horses, the ranchers retreated, leaving Starkie's body behind. A few days later they returned with more men, but the Indians were gone. The settlers burned the rancheria.[47]

CA. 3 FEBRUARY 1853
DRY CREEK (Galt, California)

About ten miles northwest of present-day Lodi, California, on the Mokelumne River near its junction with Dry Creek, the trading post of Bragg and Drew was robbed. The owners suspected nearby Indians and went to their rancheria, a short way up Dry Creek. When the traders saw some of their goods lying about, they confronted the chief. The chief held a pistol to Drew's head and threatened to kill him if the two didn't leave.

After the incident Drew gathered 16 settlers to help him retrieve his property. At the rancheria, Drew told the chief he had come not to fight but to take back what was his. While they talked, an Indian raised his rifle and fired but missed. Gunfire erupted from both sides. Drew's men killed four Indians, and they kept firing until they ran low on ammunition and pulled back. Then more settlers arrived, and the fight was renewed.

The Indians took refuge on a small island in Dry Creek. Without boats, Drew could not get at the Indians, and he could see they were fortifying their position. In a verbal exchange, Drew learned that the chief had committed the robbery, but the Indians would not give him up. They told the settlers that if they wanted him, they would have to come and get him.

Gunfire continued throughout the day, with Drew unable to cross to the island and the Indians unwilling to leave. Darkness brought an end to the fight, and Drew retreated, leaving the Indians and his property behind. The four Indians killed were the only casualties of the fight.[48]

1 MARCH 1853
OAK GROVE (Oroville, California)

When $3,000 in livestock was stolen from a Mr. Carter in Butte County, California, suspicion fell on nearby Tehama Indians. A dozen civilians searched near Deer and Pine Creeks but returned empty-handed. On the way home they seized a half-Indian named Battedou and forced him to reveal the thieves' hideout. Fearing for his life, he agreed to show them the cave in which the Indians were hiding, east of Oak Grove in the Sierra Nevada foothills.

On the last day in February, more settlers assembled in Oak Grove and, at midnight, marched for the cave. They began rolling large rocks into the cave mouth, forcing the frightened Tehamas to flee into the gunfire of the waiting posse.

Thirteen Indians were killed, including three chiefs of different rancherias and three women. At least three women and five children were spared. Two of the children were adopted by the settlers. The *Daily Alta California* (6 March 1853) reported that the other survivors "were disposed of in the same charitable manner among the party."[49]

15 JUNE 1853
FORT LARAMIE (Fort Laramie, Wyoming)

During a gathering of Lakotas and Cheyennes near Fort Laramie to receive their annual treaty goods, an argument occurred in which a Minneconjou fired a shot at a soldier operating a ferry on the Platte River. Lt. Richard B. Garnett, in command at the fort, sent out 23 men of the 6th Infantry under Lt. Hugh Fleming to arrest the offender.

In spite of the approximately 600 Lakota and Cheyenne lodges with over 1,000 warriors nearby, Fleming boldly demanded his prisoner in the Minneconjou camp of 40 lodges. The discussion grew heated and the soldiers fired, killing three Indians, wounding three others, and taking two prisoner. Fleming was extremely lucky to retreat with no losses. Only great exertion on the part of the chiefs prevented a massive retaliation, as they correctly proclaimed that the soldiers had been "the first to make the ground bloody."[50]

11 AUGUST 1853
WILLOW SPRINGS (Medford, Oregon)

In the wake of angry retaliations for numerous raids on settlements in the Jacksonville, Oregon, area, Rogue River Indians attacked a party of five travelers at Willow Springs, near present-day Medford, Oregon. William T'Vault, who had survived a previous attack (see Coquille Massacre, 14 September 1851), escaped, but two others in the party were killed, and the Indians burned several cabins.[51]

17 AUGUST 1853
EVANS CREEK MEADOWS (Shady Cove, Oregon)

After roving bands of Shasta and Rogue River Indians had been raiding settlements in the Jacksonville, Oregon, area, settlers kept retaliating against local, non-nomadic Rogues and other Indians, who were generally innocent. Growing tired of the unfair attacks, the local Indians joined together against the settlements, and the settlers sent to Fort Jones, in northern California, for help.

In response to the threat, and to the attack at Willow Springs (see previous entry), Capt. Bradford R. Alden marched north from Fort Jones with a detachment of ten men of the 4th Infantry. On the way, in Yreka, California, he picked up a company of volunteers. In Jacksonville Alden added three more companies of Oregon volunteers under Joseph Lane, the territorial congressional delegate. The combined force went to Camp Stuart, near present-day Medford, Oregon, to prepare to hunt down the Indians.

Volunteer companies under John Lamerick and John S. Miller were the first to move out. They hoped to trap the Rogue River Indians responsible for the deaths at Willow Springs. A 22-man detachment under Simeon Ely found the band of Rogues under Chief Sam (Toquahear) on Evans Creek, a dozen miles north of Table Rock. Ely sent a messenger to Camp Stuart for help and retired to an open meadow between two willow-lined streams that flowed into Evans Creek.

Chief Sam had seen Ely's volunteers and maneuvered his warriors into the willows for an attack. The Rogues killed two of Ely's men in the first volley. Ely retreated 500 yards to a pine-covered ridge, where the fight went on for three hours. Finally, James P. Goodall's volunteer company arrived and Sam broke off the fight, but not before capturing 18 horses and mules, along with blankets, guns, and ammunition.

The Rogues had only a few wounded, while the volunteers lost six men. Four more were wounded, including Ely.[52]

24 AUGUST 1853
EVANS CREEK (Shady Cove, Oregon)

After Simeon Ely's fight at Evans Creek Meadows (see previous entry), John E. Ross took John S. Miller's and John Lamerick's volunteer companies, and Joseph Lane took Jacob Rhodes's and James P. Goodall's volunteer companies, accompanied by Capt. Bradford R. Alden and ten of his 4th Infantrymen, from Camp Stuart to look for Chief Sam's retreating Rogue River band. Ross went down the Rogue River to the mouth of Evans Creek, then upstream, while Lane went cross-country north of Table Rock. Lane found the Indians' trail and continued north up Evans Creek. The Indians had felled trees as they went to delay the volunteers' passage.

Lane and Alden reached the Indians first, at the headwaters of Evans Creek. There were about 200 of them from the bands of Chiefs Sam, Joe (Apserkahar), and Jim (Anachaharah), defending a log-and-thicket fortification. Alden led a frontal attack and Rhodes circled from the flank. They got no closer than 30 yards to the entrenchments before gunfire halted them. Several volunteers went down, including Capt. Alden, whose wound would cause him to resign the following month. Lane came to the front to renew the assault. He too was wounded, but he directed the fight for another three hours before going to the rear.

The battle sputtered out toward evening, and the Indians signaled for a conference. Concealing his wounded arm under his coat, Lane went out to talk with them. The Rogues agreed to come to Table Rock in seven days for treaty talks. The resultant Treaty of Table Rock would keep the area relatively quiet for a few years. Ross arrived too late for the battle, and Lane had to convince him not to renew the fight.

In addition to Alden's and Lane's injuries, the battle cost the lives of 3 volunteers. Another was mortally wounded, and 3 others were also wounded. Rogue losses were 15 killed or mortally wounded and 13 wounded.[53]

28 AUGUST 1853
LONG'S FERRY (Grants Pass, Oregon)

Although peace plans had been made after the Evans Creek fight (see previous entry), Elias A. Owens's company of Oregon Volunteers continued its search for hostile Indians farther down the Rogue River. They lured several of the Grave Creek band to a council, then murdered five or six of them. The enraged Indians gathered up more tribesmen and burned cabins along Jump Off Joe Creek.

Owens's company continued south on the Rogue River to Long's Ferry, near present-day Grants Pass, Oregon. There, the Indians jumped them and killed three volunteers.[54]

24 OCTOBER 1853
ILLINOIS RIVER (Cave Junction, Oregon)

Miners along the Illinois River in Oregon complained that coastal Indians of an unidentified tribe were stealing cattle in the region and sent a call for help to Fort Lane, built only a month before at Table Rock. Lt. Richard C. W. Radford took detachments of Companies A, C, and E of the 1st Dragoons over the mountains to assist the miners. Upon arriving, Radford realized he did not have enough men to round up the Indians and sent for reinforcements. Lt. Thomas F. Castor came with another detachment.

The company traveled up the Illinois River into the Siskiyou Mountains until they came across a camp of Indians—possibly Talowas who had fled the Smith River area after miners attacked them (see Smith River, 7 June 1851). Radford attacked the camp. The soldiers killed 15 Indians, captured 16 horses, and burned all the property they could gather up. Two soldiers were killed and four were wounded.[55]

26 OCTOBER 1853
GUNNISON MASSACRE (Delta, Utah)

Capt. John W. Gunnison of the U.S. Corps of Topographical Engineers led a 37-man expedition to explore the 38th parallel. Among the members were a topographer, Richard Kern, and a German botanist, Frederick Creuzefeldt. The military escort included a detachment of Company A, Mounted Rifles. The party left Fort Leavenworth, Kansas, on 23 June, surveyed Cochetopa Pass and the San Luis Valley; crossed the San Juan Mountains, the Green River, and the Wasatch Range; and reached the valley of the Sevier River in October.

On 26 October, Gunnison and an advance party of ten men were washing in the river southwest of present-day Delta, Utah, while the others prepared breakfast in camp. A band of Paiutes, or possibly Pahvants (Utes), under the leader Kanosh, struck Gunnison's party from all sides. Gunnison went down, riddled with arrows, as did Creuzefeldt. The soldiers scattered, and the Indians picked them off easily.

In all, seven died, and four escaped. When the main survey party came upon the scene two days later, wild animals had picked clean what the Indians had left behind. Lt. Edward G. Beckwith, 3rd Artillery, took command of the expedition and made winter camp at Salt Lake City.[56]

—1854—

26 JANUARY 1854
KLAMATH CAVE (Yreka, California)

Rogue River and Shasta Indians had been raiding stock in the area of Yreka, California, while renegade white "squaw hunters" raided the Indian camps, kidnapping the tribes' women. A band of 50 Shastas under Chief Bill (Konechequot) killed a group of four squaw hunters and fled the scene, holing up in a cave near the Klamath River, about 20 miles upriver from Yreka. Volunteers cornered them there and requested help from the troops at Fort Jones in northern California.

Capt. Henry M. Judah, 4th Infantry, and a small force of 26 men, including Lts. John C. Bonnycastle and George Crook, marched out. Along the way, 24 volunteers under a "Capt." Geiger joined them. The cave turned out to be on a 45-degree slope with little or no cover for an attacking force; Crook and Bonnycastle persuaded Judah it would be folly to attack it headlong. Judah proposed that Geiger lead his volunteers in, but Geiger declined and instead had the volunteers climb to the bluff above. While peering over the edge, Geiger was shot in the head and killed.

Judah wisely postponed the attack. He sent Crook to Fort Lane to get a howitzer. Capt. Andrew J. Smith accompanied Crook back to the cave with 15 men of the 1st Dragoons. On 26 January, the soldiers shot several shells at the cave mouth, and the Shastas called a truce. They explained that they sought only to defend themselves and did not want to fight. Insisting that they had killed the four white squaw hunters in self-defense, they surrendered.

Geiger's was the only death among the soldiers and volunteers. The shells wounded a few Shastas.[57]

28 JANUARY 1854
COQUILLE VILLAGE (Bandon, Oregon)

Although conflicts in Oregon had lessened during the winter of 1853–54, the settlers and miners in Randolph and at the Whiskey Run Mines thought the Nasomah band of lower Coquille Indians were up to something—if only some mischief—and they decided to do something about it. George H. Abbott, A. F. Soap, and William H. Packwood led 40 volunteers to the sleeping Coquille village, a mile and a half from the coast. They attacked with a fury that the Indians—with only three guns and some bows and arrows among them—could not counter.

With no injuries to themselves, the volunteers killed 15 men and 1 woman, wounded 4 others, and captured 20. The jubilant volunteers believed they had forestalled a planned Indian uprising. In reality, they had only begun another series of reprisals.[58]

15 FEBRUARY 1854
CHETCO RIVER (Brookings, Oregon)

The Chetco River Indians were living peacefully on the river, operating a ferry for miners and packers traveling along the coast. In the fall of 1853, white settler A. F. Miller built a house a quarter of a mile from the river mouth and decided to take over the ferry business. Miller promised the Indians peace and a good trade relationship if they gave up their weapons. They acquiesced.

On 15 February, after calling in friends from the Smith River settlements in California, Miller attacked the unsuspecting Indians. He and his men shot at them and burned the lodges. Two Indians trapped inside a plank house burned to death, and another was shot down as he ran.

The attackers allowed most of the women and children to escape, but they killed 12 men.[59]

5 MARCH 1854
CONGILLON RIVER (Conchas, New Mexico)

When a band of Jicarilla Apaches ran off cattle from the Fort Union herd, Lt. Col. Philip St. George Cooke sent Lt. David Bell in pursuit. Leading 30 men of Company H of the 2nd Dragoons, Bell caught up to Lobo Blanco (White Wolf), the third chief of the Jicarillas, on Congillon Creek, about 70 miles southeast of the fort. Lobo Blanco had massacred members of the White wagon train on the Santa Fe Trail near Point of Rocks, New Mexico, in October 1849.

The adversaries were closely matched in number, but Bell's command was mounted while Lobo and his 22 warriors were on foot. Bell and Lobo had a long, tense parley. Then Lobo defiantly raised his rifle to shoot, and a sharp action ensued. The dragoons charged through the Apaches, who scattered, some escaping into a nearby arroyo. Bell and his men put several balls into Lobo, who refused to die until someone "got a great rock and mashed his head."[60] More Jicarillas appeared, and Bell vacated the area with his wounded, sending a rider back to Fort Union for assistance.

Bell's losses were 2 killed and 4 wounded, while his men killed or wounded about 16 Indians and took 30 horses.[61]

12 MARCH 1854
FORT ARBUCKLE (Hennepin, Oklahoma)

Lt. Arthur D. Tree, Company B, 2nd Dragoons, with 20 enlisted men, captured and killed a Kickapoo named Thunder, who had that day killed a Col. Stein and an enlisted man from the fort.[62]

30 MARCH 1854
CIENEGUILLA (Pilar, New Mexico)

Jicarilla Apaches had been raiding on the road between Taos and Santa Fe in March 1854, and Maj. George A. H. Blake at Cantonment Burgwin, ten miles south of Taos, sent men out to investigate. Lt. John W. "Black Jack" Davidson led 60 men from Company I and a detachment of Company F of the 1st Dragoons into the Embudo Mountains, near present-day Pilar, New Mexico.

Expecting the dragoons, Chacon, first chief of the Jicarillas, set up an ambush with over 200 warriors. From a rocky defile, the Indians fired down into the startled soldiers. Davidson had the men dismount, take cover, and shoot back. After a furious three-hour fight with many dragoon casualties, the Apaches threatened to capture the soldiers' horses, and the dragoons cut their way out in retreat, saber and pistol against arrow and lance.

Davidson managed to get back to Cantonment Burgwin with 38 men, 36 of them wounded, himself included. He left 22 dead soldiers on the field; later, a detail of soldiers that included Kit Carson buried them. The dragoons must have killed a significant number of Apaches, for Chacon also fled the area, leading his band west across the Rio Grande.[63]

Cieneguilla was called "one of the most desperate fights in our Indian record."[64]

8 APRIL 1854
OJO CALIENTE (Ojo Caliente, New Mexico)

After the battles at the Congillon River and Cieneguilla (see 5 March 1854 and previous entry), Lt. Col. Philip St. George Cooke took the field from Fort Union with all the force he could muster against the Jicarilla Apaches. Lt. Samuel D. Sturgis led Company H and a detachment of Company G of the 2nd Dragoons, and Lt. Bell led Company H of the 1st

Dragoons. Lt. George Sykes of the 3rd Infantry followed behind, leading Company D of the 2nd Artillery.

The command marched across the Sangre de Cristo Mountains in a snowstorm, reaching Cantonment Burgwin on 3 April. There they picked up more 1st Dragoons under Maj. George A. H. Blake, plus guide Kit Carson, some Pueblo Indians—longtime foes of the Apaches—and 32 Mexicans under "Capt." James H. Quinn. In all they had, Cooke said, "100 sabres and 89 rifles and irregulars."[65]

The column tracked Jicarilla chief Chacon for 150 miles, across the Rio Grande, through deep snow, and over mountains, thanks to the skill of the Pueblo guides. Unable to shake his pursuers, Chacon set up an ambush with his 150 warriors. The Jicarillas hid behind the huge tumbled boulders that lined the icy waters of the Rio Caliente, but Quinn's Pueblos uncovered the trap and rushed against their foes.

The Jicarillas had a strong position behind their rocky ramparts, and Cooke figured he could take them only with some rough maneuvering over several hours. But the Pueblos had already brought on the battle, so Cooke decided to pitch in. Sykes, leading some riflemen, followed behind the Pueblos. Bell led Company H to the right; they dismounted and clambered onto the rocks to the Apaches' left. Cooke, Blake, and Sturgis pushed the rest of the command into the Apache center. Lt. Jospeh E. Maxwell of the 3rd Infantry cut off the Indians' pony herd far to the left.

The suddenness and enthusiasm of Cooke's response shook the Apaches, and in a short time they broke up and scattered into the mountains. When Bell's men reached the top of the boulders, the Indians were gone. Cooke destroyed their camp and pursued them for three days, finding remnants of their flight along the way: "The tracks of bare and diminutive feet left a feeble memorial of their suffering," he wrote.[66]

Cooke lost one man and another was wounded. The Jicarillas suffered five killed and six wounded. Cooke believed the experience humbled them: they now knew they could be trailed in the worst weather and into the deepest recesses of their lands.[67]

9 MAY 1854
LAKE TRINIDAD (Ben Bolt, Texas)

Lt. George B. Cosby and 11 men of Companies F and I, Mounted Rifles, were riding south out of Fort Merrill, at the end of a long scout, when a Mexican rider informed Cosby that Indians were camped on the shore of Lake Trinidad, near present-day Ben Bolt, Texas. Though the men were armed only with revolvers and were short of ammunition, Cosby spurred ahead.

The band of 40 Lipan Apaches withstood Cosby's charge and fell back to encircle the soldiers. Cosby and his men had no choice but to break out of the tightening ring. The troopers charged ahead, firing their pistols until their bullets were gone, then bluffing with their empty guns. Cosby took an arrow in the chest; it would have killed him if it had not hit his coin-filled pocketbook. When another arrow hit him in the arm, he drew his saber. A warrior charged in for the kill, but Sgt. John Byrne interceded, swinging his sword. The warrior shot an arrow into Byrne's forehead. Byrne's horse ran into a thicket, knocking Byrne off into the arms of the Indians.

The remainder of the squad rode about 200 yards before Cosby fainted. The men dismounted and circled around their fallen lieutenant. Taking over, Cpl. William Wright told the troopers to fight where they stood, distributing the bullets from Cosby's revolver. At the soldiers' bold stand, the Lipans judged it easier to chase after two men who had become sepa-rated. While the Indians were occupied, one trooper rode off to the riflemen's camp at Santa Gertrudes for ammunition and help. Reinforcements ar-rived in less than two hours, but the Lipans had gone.

In addition to Cosby and two other soldiers wounded, Byrne and two enlisted men were killed. Three Lipans were believed killed and two wounded.[68]

24 MAY 1854
KLAMATH FERRY (Yreka, California)

After the signing of the Treaty of Table Rock (see Evans Creek, 24 August 1853) a band of Rogue River Indians living along Bear Creek in Oregon, under their leader Tipsu Tyee, continued minor depredations in the area, and the chief was implicated in a plot to kill another Indian leader. Tipsu Tyee went south to California to encourage the Shastas to join him. Fearing that Tipsu Tyee brought trouble, Shasta chief Bill had him killed about 18 May. The Shastas then waited for the soldiers to come, as they inevitably did.

Lt. John Bonnycastle, 4th Infantry, from Fort Jones investigated the incident. He praised Bill for his timely action and departed. At the same time, however, settlers in the region decided the Shastas ought to be cleared out and moved to Fort Jones. With about 30 DesChutes Indian scouts, volunteers drove 60 miserable Shastas downriver. At Klamath Ferry the party stopped, and the Indians decided to bathe. While five of them were in the river, the volunteers opened fire.

They beat, shot, and scalped Bill, then threw him into the rapids. Two other Shastas were killed and two were badly wounded. The rest of the band ran into the woods, but not before the DesChutes kidnapped four Shasta children. One white man, named McKaney, was killed.[69]

4 JUNE 1854
FISHER'S PEAK (Trinidad, Colorado)

By the spring of 1854, the army had not yet subdued all the Jicarilla Apaches. Capt. James H. Carleton of the 1st Dragoons led 100 of his own men and James Quinn's battalion of irregulars on a sweep to the north. They went to Fort Massachusetts, a post 85 miles north of Taos, midway up the San Luis Valley on the slopes of Sierra Blanca Peak. There, the force found a trail heading southeast, past the Spanish Peaks and up into the Raton Mountains. With Kit Carson guiding, they found the Apache camp in a basin on the east side of treeless Fisher's Peak, about six miles south of present-day Trinidad, Colorado.

Carleton held his troops back in the brush and off the trail until they slowly worked into position. At 2 P.M. on 4 June, they fanned down the mountainside in a surprise attack. The startled Apaches scattered immediately. The soldiers destroyed 22 lodges and captured 38 ponies, but the Apaches fled so fast, Carleton's men killed only 3 of them. The soldiers suffered no casualties.[70]

30 JUNE 1854
SAPELLO CREEK (Watrous, New Mexico)

By the summer of 1854, the Jicarilla Apaches had lost their enthusiasm for large engagements with dragoons, but there were still occasional conflicts. An Apache raiding party north of Las Vegas, New Mexico, was heading back into the Sangre de Cristo Mountains and had reached Sapello Creek, near the Mora River, not far from Fort Union, when they ran into Lt. Sykes, 3rd Infantry, with Company D and a detachment of Company H of the 2nd Dragoons.

Lt. Joseph E. Maxwell, 3rd Infantry, led a charge. A deadly hand-to-hand fight ensued. Maxwell had emptied his revolver and was in the act of sabering an Apache when he went down, bristling with arrows. A Pvt. Allen killed the Indian who shot the last arrow into Maxwell. Two men of Company H were wounded. The rest of the Apaches got away.[71]

11 JULY 1854
SAN DIEGO (San Diego, Texas)

Sixteen enlisted men of companies A and H, Mounted Rifles, under Capt. Michael E. Van Buren were patrolling in the vicinity of San Diego, Texas, about 50 miles west of Corpus Christi, when they met a band of Comanches. In the ensuing skirmish, Van Buren was mortally wounded, two soldiers were wounded, and five Indians were killed.[72]

19 AUGUST 1854
GRATTAN'S FIGHT (Torrington, Wyoming)

While the Lakotas and Cheyennes waited at their camps in the Fort Laramie area for their yearly annuities, emigrants were traveling close by along the Oregon Trail. When a Minneconjou (Lakota) named High Forehead shot an old, lame cow belonging to a Mormon emigrant, the angry owner reported it at the post.

In charge at Laramie, Lt. Hugh Fleming advised caution, perhaps wiser from his experience with the Indians the year before (see Fort Laramie, 15 June 1853). However, young Lt. John L. Grattan, eager to show his Indian-fighting prowess, insisted that he be allowed to make an arrest. The next morning, Grattan led 30 men of Company G, 6th Infantry, plus two artillery pieces to the Indian camp, about eight miles east of the fort.

High Forehead was visiting in the Brule (Lakota) village of Brave (or Conquering) Bear when Grattan marched up to them and demanded the culprit who had shot the cow. Brave Bear could not order the Minneconjou to submit, and a tense 45-minute talk only hardened High Forehead's resolve to die right there. The interpreter, Auguste Lucien, hated the Indians and may have made matters worse by twisting each party's words.

Finally Grattan lost his patience, and his men leveled their muskets. No one knows who fired first, but the killing started in a flash. Brave Bear was wounded in the crossfire. The cannons roared, blowing off tipi tops, then fell silent. Grattan went down, and several hundred warriors engulfed the soldiers. About 18 fought their way out of the camp but were killed as they fled to the fort. One soldier made it to the trading post of James Bordeaux, then to Fort Laramie, where he soon died from his wounds.

Bordeaux spent a harried night giving away his stock to appease the Indians and trying to convince them not to attack the fort. Eventually, he and the older chiefs calmed the excited warriors, but not before they had pillaged another company's warehouse.

Grattan and his 30 men were killed. Brave Bear's brother and a few more Indians were wounded. Brave Bear lingered, but died in November.[73]

19 AUGUST 1854
LAKE MASSACRE (Boise, Idaho)

A large emigrant train heading to Oregon had split up into three sections, and the last four wagons had fallen several miles behind. About 70 miles southeast of the old Hudson's Bay Company post of Fort Boise, 11 Shoshone Indians approached the group of 4 families and 2 unattached young men. Ostensibly, the Indians sought to trade for whiskey. The emigrants said they had none. The Indians shook hands, appearing friendly, then opened fire, killing George Lake and fatally wounding two others in the party, Empson Cantrell and Walter G. Perry. The emigrants returned fire and wounded two Indians. The Shoshones stole five horses and rode off.[74]

20 AUGUST 1854
WARD MASSACRE (Caldwell, Idaho)

The day after the Lake Massacre (see previous entry), the vanguard of the same large but dispersed wagon train to Oregon was about 25 miles southeast of Fort Boise on the Snake River Plain, just east of present-day

Caldwell, Idaho, when a party of 30 Shoshones approached Alexander Ward's five-wagon train of 20 emigrants. One Indian tried to take a horse by force, threatening an emigrant with his weapon. The white man shot the Indian down, starting a slaughter.

The Shoshones killed Ward and raped and tortured several women, killing some. They hung children by the hair over a blazing fire. One boy, 13-year-old Newton Ward, was shot with an arrow and left for dead. His 15-year-old brother, William, took an arrow through the lung but lived. He hid in the brush until the Indians left, then wandered for five days until he reached Fort Boise.

While the massacre was taking place, a group of seven emigrants under Alex Yantis, backtracking in search of stray cows, saw the commotion. They rushed in and rescued Newton Ward, but the Shoshones killed one of them, a young man named Amens, in the process. Outnumbered, Yantis's party had to leave the few survivors to their fate while they raced to Fort Boise. When the Indians left, they took 46 cows and horses and more than $2,000 in money and property. A rescue party of 18 men arrived two days later, only to bury the mutilated bodies.

In addition to Amens, the Shoshones killed 18 of Ward's party. Some Indians may have been wounded, but it is not known for sure.[75]

3 OCTOBER 1854
EAGLE PASS (Eagle Pass, Texas)

When Lipan Apaches stole stock and attacked travelers east of the Rio Grande, Capt. John G. Walker took companies D and K, Mounted Rifles, from Fort Inge to find the culprits. On a trail heading west, Walker and his 40 soldiers rode fast to catch the Indians before they crossed the Rio Grande. The party lost the trail that night, but guide "Polly" Rodriguez picked it up again in the morning.

At about 10 A.M. on the third day, near Eagle Springs, the soldiers came upon about 300 Lipans. Walker drew his saber and ordered the charge. Leading Company K was Lt. Eugene A. Carr. In his enthusiasm, he outpaced his command and suddenly found himself alone. Three Indians turned on him. An arrow whizzed past his cheek and another struck him in the side. A trooper named Booth saw Carr and cried out to the others, "Oh Lord! There's the lieutenant, stuck full of arrows!"[76] Walker and the rest of the command joined the fray. After they had secured Carr, the soldiers broke off the fight.

The Lipans killed one soldier and wounded Carr and Rodriguez during the fight. The soldiers killed about seven Indians. Although Carr brushed off his wound as trifling, Walker thought it serious enough to suspend the expedition and take Carr back to Fort Inge.[77]

11 OCTOBER 1854
LIVE OAK CREEK (Batesville, Texas)

Capt. Benjamin H. Arthur with Company F, 1st Infantry, skirmished with Lipan Apaches along Live Oak Creek near present-day Batesville, Texas, and killed two Indians.[78]

1 NOVEMBER 1854
FORT DAVIS (Fort Davis, Texas)

Near Fort Davis, Lt. Theodore Fink and some men of Company G, 8th Infantry, fought with a party of Apaches. Three soldiers were killed.[79]

13 NOVEMBER 1854
HORSE CREEK (Torrington, Wyoming)

After the Brule chief Brave Bear died from injuries received in the fight with Lt. John L. Grattan (see Grattan's Fight, 19 August), many young warriors wanted to retaliate. Brave Bear's oldest surviving brother, Red Leaf, his half-brother Long Chin, Spotted Tail, and two younger braves headed for the Overland Trail.

About 12 miles west of Horse Creek, near present-day Torrington, Wyoming, they waylaid a mail stage headed for Salt Lake City, killed three men, and robbed the coach of a metal box containing $20,000 in gold, which was never recovered.[80]

25 DECEMBER 1854
PUEBLO (Pueblo, Colorado)

In the fall of 1854, Ute Indian agent Kit Carson had distributed some coats to the tribe to smooth over a feud between the Utes and some Mexicans. The clothing may have carried smallpox, for two tribal leaders who wore the coats caught the disease and died. Their deaths incited a retaliation against settlers in the San Luis Valley.

On Christmas Day, a Ute and Jicarilla Apache war party of 100 attacked the small settlement of Pueblo, on the Arkansas River. They killed 15 men and wounded 2, carried off a woman and 2 children, and stole 200 horses.[81]

—1855—

16 JANUARY 1855
MANZANO MOUNTAINS (Albuquerque, New Mexico)

On 13 January, a small raiding party of Mescalero Apaches attacked the Eaton ranch in the Galisteo Basin near Santa Fe. They raped the women, killed two herders, and drove off 75 horses and mules.

That night, Lt. Samuel D. Sturgis led 16 men of the 1st Dragoons and 8 civilians out of Santa Fe, hot on the trail of the culprits. They tracked the raiders south for three days, coming upon them on 16 January in the eastern foothills of the Manzano Mountains. A dozen Mescaleros met them, apparently professing peace. "Well, men," said Sturgis, "I do not understand one word they are saying; haul off and let them have it, and look out for yourselves."[82]

The dragoons opened fire at 100 yards and closed in. The Apaches ran for cover in the timber. The bitter cold made it difficult for the soldiers to reload their weapons, so Sturgis tried to drive the Apaches out with a saber charge. A Cpl. Katon dueled with an Indian and "took off nearly one side of his head."[83]

The soldiers killed three Apaches and wounded four. The Apaches wounded three dragoons, one fatally, and the rancher Eaton. Eaton recovered all his stock.[84]

18–19 JANUARY 1855
RIO PENASCO (Mayhill, New Mexico)

In December 1854, Mescalero Apaches stole 2,500 sheep from a ranch on the Pecos River. Brig. Gen. John Garland ordered two forces in pursuit. Capt. Richard S. Ewell, later a Confederate general, led 81 men of the 1st Dragoons out of the town of Los Lunas and marched up the Pecos River, then to the Bonito River, joining Capt. Henry W. Stanton with 29 dragoons and 50 infantry out of Fort Fillmore on 7 January.

The combined force marched south to the Rio Hondo near its mouth and followed it up toward the mountains, into country their guides had never seen before. On 9 January they cut south to the Rio Penasco and moved upriver. On the night of the 18th, Mescaleros attacked the soldiers' camp, showering them with arrows and trying to burn them out.

The next morning, the dragoons chased the Indians upstream into the Sacramento Mountains. Progress was slow however, for a persistent rear guard of Mescaleros harassed the soldiers at every step. The Indians' delaying tactic cost them 15 casualties. In the late afternoon, Ewell found an abandoned camp. Stanton had meanwhile taken 12 men to investigate another camp in an adjoining valley about 500 yards distant. He rode into a trap. As his soldiers fell back, Stanton covered the retreat with his Sharps carbine. The Mescaleros cut off and lanced one dragoon, a Pvt. Dugan of Company B, and shot another, and Stanton took a bullet in the head. All three died.

The Apaches had been able to hold off the dragoons long enough for their families to escape, and Ewell lost the trail. After heading south toward the Guadalupe Mountains, he finally gave up the chase. Returning to the Rio Penasco camp, where they had buried the three bodies, the soldiers found the graves open and the remains strewn about. They burned the bodies and carried the bones with them as they returned to the Rio Grande.

Ewell's men had killed about 15 Apaches, including the war chief Santa Anna.[85]

23 FEBRUARY 1855
WHITEFACE MOUNTAIN (Becker, New Mexico)

A few days after Capt. Richard S. Ewell's bone-weary dragoons returned from their trip to the Rio Penasco (see previous entry), a band of die-hard Mescaleros who had followed them back attacked a horse-grazing camp 25 miles from the post at Los Lunas. Four soldiers of Company G, 1st Dragoons, in Ewell's command, were guarding the horses when the Indians struck, late on 23 February. After a bloody fight in which every soldier was hit at least four times, the dragoons drove off the Mescaleros. Two of the soldiers succumbed to their wounds on 21 March.[86]

19 MARCH 1855
SAGUACHE CREEK/COCHETOPA PASS (Saguache, Colorado)

The Utes and Jicarillas, now under the Ute chief Blanco, continued to harass residents of the San Luis Valley (see Pueblo, 25 December 1854). Brig. Gen. John Garland, in charge of the Department of New Mexico, became fed up with the Indian depredations and called for five companies of territorial volunteers to assist the regulars in clearing out the Indians.

Col. Thomas T. Fauntleroy organized the invasion. The forces gathered at Taos and Cantonment Burgwin in late winter: 500 men of Companies B, D, and F of the 1st Dragoons, two companies of the 2nd Artillery serving as infantry, and five companies of New Mexico Volunteers under Ceran St. Vrain, commissioned as a lieutenant colonel for the expedition. Lucien Stewart commanded a company of Pueblo and Mexican scouts, and Kit Carson acted as chief guide.

The columns marched north to Fort Massachusetts, then trekked across the San Luis Valley in snow and freezing temperatures. They found the Ute and Jicarilla camp at the headwaters of Saguache Creek, on the trail to Cochetopa Pass. The Indians swarmed from their lodges and formed a line to oppose the scouts and volunteers, who had arrived before the regulars. But the Indians' brave front could not stand up to the determined volunteers.

Conspicuous in a red shirt, Chief Blanco rallied his men. One Apache charged to and fro, encouraging his warriors to attack. When he charged up to volunteer Don Manuel Chaves, Chaves shot him, and another volunteer, Antonio Tapia, immediately dragged him down and scalped him. The scouts also fought well. When the regulars arrived, with bugles sounding the charge, the Indians fled into the mountains. The columns returned to Fort Massachusetts.

Two soldiers were wounded and eight Indians were killed.[87]

25 APRIL 1855
CHICOSA ARROYO (Trinidad, Colorado)

After the Saguache Creek/Cochetopa Pass engagement (see previous entry), Col. Thomas T. Fauntleroy's expedition rested and provisioned at Fort Massachusetts, then moved out again. Kit Carson guided Ceran St. Vrain and three of his volunteer companies east of the Sangre de Cristo Mountains, trailing the Apaches and Utes to the edge of the plains. At one point along Chicosa Arroyo, north of present-day Trinidad, Colorado, the Pueblo irregulars were out hunting game when the volunteers mistook them for Apaches and nearly attacked them. From that point on, the Pueblos wore distinctive white headbands.

Continuing down Chicosa Arroyo to the headwaters of the Purgatoire River, the column ran into a camp of about 60 Jicarillas. St. Vrain attacked, killed 6 Indians, captured 7, and rounded up 31 horses. The volunteers suffered no casualties.[88]

29 APRIL 1855
PONCHA PASS (Poncha Springs, Colorado)

As Kit Carson guided part of Col. Thomas T. Fauntleroy's expedition east of the Sangre de Cristo Mountains (see previous entry), Fauntleroy led the rest—two companies of regulars and two companies of volunteers—out of Fort Masssachusetts and picked up an Indian trail to the north. It led up to Poncha Pass, the 9,000-foot-high gap between the Sangre de Cristo and San Juan Mountains.

Ute chief Blanco had let down his guard. He and his 150 warriors were holding a war dance by a bonfire. The soldiers crept up on two sides of the camp and were within 150 yards before the Indians' dogs began to bark. Fauntleroy ordered his men to open fire. A semicircle of gun flashes illuminated the night and "swept the enemy like chaff."[89] The startled Indians fled into the darkness, abandoning their camp, provisions, and winter clothing. The soldiers burned everything.

Fauntleroy lost one man and two were wounded, while the soldiers killed 50 Indians. After the defeat, the Utes finally began to lose their defiance.[90]

13 JUNE 1855
DELAWARE CREEK (Rock House, New Mexico)

Capt. Carter L. Stevenson, later a Confederate general, was on an Indian scout east of the Guadalupe Mountains with a detachment of Company I, 5th Infantry, when a band of Apaches surprised them near the junction of the Delaware and Pecos Rivers. The Indians killed four enlisted men.[91]

15 JULY 1855
FORT BOISE (Parma, Idaho)

Still seeking to punish the Shoshones responsible for the Ward Massacre the year before (see 20 August 1854), Capt. Granville O. Haller took 150 men, mostly of the 4th Infantry, from Forts Dalles and Vancouver east along the Oregon Trail. The Indian agent for the Shoshones, Nathan Olney, accompanied the command. Haller traveled from Fort Hall to Camas Prairie to Shoshone Falls, all the while sending word that he wanted a council with the tribes. On 15 July at Fort Boise, 200 Indians gathered to hear Haller's words, but nothing came of it.

Meanwhile, Lt. Edward H. Day had captured 6 of the 30 murderers of the Ward party, although how he knew they were guilty is unknown. Three of the captives tried to escape and were shot down. A military commission tried and convicted the other three. They were taken 25 miles southeast of the fort to the site of the Ward killings and, on 18 July, were hanged over the graves of their purported victims. After the hangings, T. J. Dryer, editor of the *Portland Weekly Oregonian,* said, "Our only regret is that they did not shoot the whole tribe."[92]

22 JULY 1855
EAGLE SPRINGS (Sierra Blanca, Texas)

Operating out of Fort Davis, a detachment of Company I, Mounted Rifles, under Capt. Charles F. Ruff, fought with Mescalero Apaches near Eagle Springs. Of 15 Indians, 13 were reported killed, with no army casualties.[93]

3 SEPTEMBER 1855
BLUEWATER CREEK (Lewellen, Nebraska)

In a retaliatory expedition stemming from Indian depredations of the previous winter, as well as from Lt. Grattan's routing in August of the year before (see Grattan's Fight, 19 August 1854), Col. William S. Harney led more than 600 men of Companies E and K of the 2nd Dragoons; Companies A, E, H, I, and K of the 6th Infantry; Company E of the 10th Infantry; and Company G of the 4th Artillery out of Fort Leavenworth. Lt. Col. Philip St. George Cooke took charge of the dragoons, and Maj. Albemarle Cady led the foot soldiers. The command left in August.

At Fort Laramie, Thomas S. Twiss, the Indian agent for the Lakotas and Cheyennes, had passed the word for all Indians in the area to beware. The "good" bands—those who wanted peace—were to seek refuge south of the Platte River. The "bad" bands, who wanted war, were told to remain north of the river and prepare to be deluged. Many Lakota bands moved out of harm's way, but Little Thunder, successor to Brave Bear, and his 41 lodges of 250 Brules did not. They remained camped on Bluewater Creek, about six miles north of the Ash Hollow Crossing on the Platte.

Site of Bluewater Creek fight (Nebraska)

In a night march, Cooke moved his troopers north of the Brule village, while Cady brought the infantry up from the south. In the morning, meeting under a white flag, Harney told Little Thunder he must either give up the warriors responsible for past raids and the deaths of Grattan and his men or prepare for trouble. The chief, still defiant, hurried back to the village, and Harney ordered the advance. The Indians tried to flee, but they were caught in a deadly trap. As many of them sought refuge in a ravine, mounted troopers cut some of them down and chased the rest for over five miles. Midmorning, Harney ordered a recall. Searching the Brule camp, the soldiers found papers from mail robberies and army clothing presumed to have belonged to Grattan's men.

The soldiers killed 86 Brules, wounded 5, and captured about 70 women and children. Harney lost 7 enlisted men, and 5 others were wounded. Little Thunder escaped.[94]

6–8 OCTOBER 1855
TOPPENISH CREEK (White Swan, Washington)

In September 1855, Yakimas cut the throat of Indian agent Andrew J. Bolon, and Yakima chief Kamiakin announced that he would kill all whites who entered his country. The tribes of the Columbia River basin had united to stop the increasing incursions into the area. In response, district commander

Maj. Gabriel J. Rains ordered an expedition to awe the Indians, and Capt. Granville O. Haller was to lead it. Haller's 4th Infantry Companies I and K and a detachment of H left Fort Dalles in early October with a howitzer.

A three-day march brought Haller to Toppenish Creek, east of present-day Fort Simcoe State Park, Washington, where he ran into Kamiakin, Palouse chief Owhi, and possibly up to 1,500 Yakima and Palouse Indians. Haller's was not a large enough force to intimidate the combined tribes arrayed against him. Nevertheless, the infantry took position on a ridge top and fought for nearly three days before retreating. Haller then struggled for three more days to get his men back in one piece to Fort Dalles. They lost the howitzer and the pack train, and Haller was lucky to escape with most of his command.

Five men were killed and 17 wounded in the expedition. Approximately 20 warriors were wounded or killed. The defeat emboldened the rest of the northwestern tribes to take action.[95]

8 OCTOBER 1855
LITTLE BUTTE CREEK (Eagle Point, Oregon)

Even after their chief, Tipsu Tyee, was killed in the spring of 1854 (see Klamath Ferry, 24 May 1854), Rogue River warriors continued to raid settlements along Bear Creek and the Rogue River. The settlers, needing little prodding to pick up their weapons, joined a crusade led by "Maj." James Lupton, a packer who had come to Oregon with the Mounted Rifles in 1849. Along with volunteers from Yreka, California, Lupton marched to Jacksonville, Oregon, and with about 115 settlers planned an attack.

Lupton led his 36-man company to an Indian village on Little Butte Creek, a short distance from the Table Rock Reservation. They found Chief Jake's Rogue River band asleep in their summer brush huts. It was still dark when the volunteers opened fire, killing everyone they could find.

Though some of the Indians took refuge at Fort Lane, 23 men, women, and children in Jake's band died. Another group of volunteers killed 3 Indians in Sambo's band. The contest was not one-sided, however. Lupton paid for his blood lust, taking a fatal arrow through the lungs, and 11 other volunteers were wounded. Lupton's attack started another spate of revenge killings.[96]

9 OCTOBER 1855
ROGUE RIVER MASSACRE (Grants Pass, Oregon)

The day after the settlers' attack on Chief Jake's village (see previous entry), the rest of the Rogue River Indians, enraged, bolted from the Table Rock Reservation and went on a rampage downstream. They killed one settler before they left the reservation and attacked others along the Rogue River between Evans Ferry and Grave Creek. At George Harris's ranch, Harris and two others were killed and his daughter was wounded, but

Mrs. Harris managed to bolt the door and defend her home. Four people were killed at the Haines ranch, and four teamsters hauling apple trees were killed at the river. The Indians also slaughtered 7 others, 19 people in all—at least 4 of them women or children.[97]

17 OCTOBER 1855
SKULL BAR (Galice, Oregon)

A few days after their 9 October rampage (see previous entry), Rogue River Indians, under Chiefs George (Cholcultah) and Limpy, attacked a miner's camp on the Rogue River near Skull Bar, just below the mouth of Galice Creek. About 40 miners and packers defended their cabins with the aid of earth-and-flour-sack breastworks.

The miners had cut away much of the brush, so the Indians had little cover, but they used the sparse foliage that remained. J. W. Pickett led six men to try to dislodge them. The Rogues killed Pickett and forced his men back. Another squad of miners sortied ahead and fought for four hours before retreating. The Rogues could not close in, but the miners could not break out. The Indians shot flaming arrows into the camp, but the miners doused the flames before they could do much damage. While George and Limpy kept the whites pinned down, other Rogues burned the nearby settlement of Galice to the ground.

At nightfall, the Indians left, dragging all their casualties—about a dozen killed and wounded—from the field. Of the miners and packers, 4 were killed and 11 were wounded.[98]

25 OCTOBER 1855
GRAVE CREEK (Leland, Oregon)

In a continuation of their raids against area settlers (see previous entries), Rogue River Indians ambushed a party of soldiers near the Oregon-California Road. Lt. August V. Kautz, 4th Infantry, and a 12-man detachment from Company H, 3rd Artillery, finishing a 13-day road survey from the coast at Port Orford to the Oregon-California Road, were within three miles of the road when the Indians attacked.

At the first shots, Kautz fell to the ground, clutching his chest. Thinking he was dead, his men started to run, but the ball had hit his pocket diary and only stunned him. The Rogues went after the fleeing soldiers, killing two privates, named Gill and Adams. The rest of Kautz's men ran to Fort Lane, the lieutenant eventually following, and inadvertently discovered the Rogues' hideout near the post.[99]

31 OCTOBER–1 NOVEMBER 1855
HUNGRY HILL (Wolf Creek, Oregon)

The intelligence Lt. August V. Kautz brought to Fort Lane (see previous entry) energized the soldiers and volunteers there. Capt. Andrew J. Smith led 105 soldiers from Companies C and E of the 1st Dragoons and Companies D and E of the 4th Infantry to the hideout of the warring Rogue River Indians. Another "Capt." Smith—a volunteer—led "Col." John E. Ross's 145 volunteers. Together they hurried down the Rogue River, crossing at Vannoy's Ferry, and marched north to the valley of Grave Creek.

On 31 October, near where Kautz's men were ambushed, the party saw a large gathering of Indians on a high ridge to the north. There were about 500 Umpquas, Rogues, Shastas, and Klamaths under Chiefs Old John (Tecumtum), George (Cholcultah), Limpy, and others. The soldiers and volunteers ran to attack. When they reached the summit of a bald peak known as Hungry Hill, they met about 150 warriors in a good defensive position. They gamely charged, but the Indians raked them with bullets and arrows, and soon the company was scrambling back down the mountain. By dark, they had found a safe place to get water and care for their wounded.

At dawn on 1 November, the Indians attacked the white men's camp, which they stoutly defended. After a four-hour fight, with their ammunition, food, and water nearly exhausted, the two Capt. Smiths decided to withdraw. The volunteers went down to Wolf Creek, and government troops made temporary camp on Grave Creek to bury their dead.

Over the two days, 4 regulars were killed and 7 were wounded; volunteer losses were 7 killed and 20 wounded. The Indians lost 20 warriors. The battle was a draw, but it left the recalcitrant bands in possession of a section of their homeland.[100]

4–7 NOVEMBER 1855
WHITE RIVER/PUYALLUP RIVER (Puyallup, Washington)

To cooperate with columns approaching the Yakima Indians from west of the Cascades, Capt. Maurice Maloney organized a force in the Puget Sound area. With a volunteer company of 100 men of Companies A and C of the 4th Infantry, he marched east up the White River, but he found his route over the Cascades blocked with snow. After the soldiers left, several bands of Puyallup, Nisqually, and Squaxon warriors drove white settlers into the main towns and forts around Puget Sound and sent 150 warriors up the White River to find and confront Maloney's troops.

The ensuing battle was sharp. After a daylong fight, the Indians pulled back, but the soldiers pursued them to the Puyallup River. The action continued for another day or two, until the Indians finally broke off and scattered.

In the various confrontations, the Indians had 30 casualties. Of Maloney's regulars, 3 were killed and 2 were wounded; 19 civilian volunteers were killed.[101]

26 NOVEMBER 1855
LITTLE MEADOWS (Mariel, Oregon)

After the battle at Hungry Hill (see 31 October–1 November), soldiers and volunteers again tried to corner the Rogue River Indians and their allies. A battalion of 286 volunteers under Maj. James Bruce joined Capt. Henry M. Judah, 4th Infantry, and his 146 regulars. Bruce went directly down the Rogue River, while Judah took the road to Grave Creek before going downstream.

Judah and his men camped at the mouth of Whiskey Creek, then hiked a dozen miles west into the most isolated part of Rogue country, where they were to meet Bruce and his men. At Little Meadows, an open table-land in the forested mountains, Judah spotted campfires several miles away on the riverbank and thought it was Bruce. Later, however, Bruce showed up at the meadows. Scouts investigated the campfires and found about 150 Indian men with their families fortified on a river bar in a narrow portion of the canyon below.

Judah took his men down the mountain, while Bruce and his volunteers circled back to cross the river and approach from the south. Unwisely, the volunteers chopped down trees to build rafts; the Rogues heard the commotion and hastened to attack. The adversaries exchanged shots throughout the day, and the Indians pulled away before Judah could reach the scene. Just as at Hungry Hill, the expedition had been thwarted.

Four volunteers were wounded and one, William Lewis, was killed. The Rogues had three casualties.[102]

4 DECEMBER 1855
BENNAN'S PRAIRIE (Auburn, Washington)

Since the fight at White River/Puyallup River (see 4–7 November), Lt. William A. Slaughter and his company had been camped at Bennan's Prairie, just east of present-day Auburn, Washington, where the Green and White Rivers flow a mile apart. Slaughter's men, Companies A and C of the 4th Infantry, and a detachment of Company M of the 3rd Artillery had bedded down for the evening of 4 December in heavy fog. That night, Chief Kanaskat and his Klickitat warriors surrounded the camp. They closed in, fired a volley, and withdrew into the darkness.

It was no pitched battle, but three enlisted men were wounded and one was killed. The only officer hit with a fatal bullet was Lt. Slaughter.[103]

7–10 DECEMBER 1855
WAIILATPU (Walla Walla, Washington)

Lt. Col. James K. Kelly left Fort Dalles, Oregon, on 2 December with 350 men of Companies A, B, F, H, I, and K of the 1st Oregon Volunteers, heading up the Columbia River for Fort Walla Walla. Two days later, near the confluence of the Touchet and Walla Walla Rivers, Kelly met with Chief Peopeo Moxmox of the Walla Walla Indians, who had allied with the Cayuses, Umatillas, and Palouses. The conference did not go well, and Kelly, suspecting the chief of trickery, held him and several others hostage.

The next morning, Kelly moved up the Touchet River about 15 miles to find the rest of the Indians, but they had fled. Returning to the confluence, Kelly induced Peopeo Moxmox to send a messenger to tell his band to surrender, but the courier did not return. On 7 December, as Kelly marched up the Walla Walla River, Indians appeared on the hills. Soon, they outnumbered the volunteers three to one, and a ten-mile moving battle ensued.

Kelly advanced to within two miles of Waiilatpu, Washington, the site of the old Whitman Mission. There, the Indians had formed a battle line on the north side of the river, blocking further advance. They fired a sharp volley, causing the volunteers to fall back. With his men, Lt. J. M. Burrows tried to flank the Indians in the hills, but he was killed.

Company A, under Capt. A. V. Wilson, tried to push the warriors back with a bayonet charge, and Capt. Charles Bennett's Company F joined them. Together they drove the Indians about a mile up the river. The warriors took a stand in some abandoned cabins and killed Bennett as he tried to storm the place. During the day's fighting, Peopeo Moxmox allegedly tried to seize a gun from a guard and was clubbed to death. Some of the other hostages bolted and five were shot. When the battle ended for the night, the volunteers set up a field hospital in a settler's house.

The next morning, Kelly faced more than 1,000 warriors. He rallied his men and jockeyed for better position. By the day's end, he had worked his companies into a good defensive position behind improvised breastworks. The worn-out troops remained there all day the following day, repulsing several Indian attacks. Finally, the next day, 10 December, Kelly's men sortied out and drove the warriors from a few key positions. With their flanks threatened, the Indians finally fled the field.

The fight cost the Walla Wallas and Cayuses 100 casualties. Of the Oregon Volunteers, 8 were killed and 18 were wounded. After the battle, the volunteers built a new post two miles up the Walla Walla River from Waiilatpu and named it Fort Bennett in memory of Capt. Bennett.[104]

24 DECEMBER 1855
LITTLE BUTTE CREEK (Lakecreek, Oregon)

As winter set in, 18 inches of snow lay on the ground and the Rogue River froze over at Vannoy's Ferry. Two 30-man companies of volunteers under "Capt." Miles T. Alcorn and "Capt." E. A. Rice fortified themselves with alcohol and marched to Little Butte Creek, where James Lupton's volunteers had massacred Chief Jake's band of Rogue River Indians in October (see Little Butte Creek, 8 October).

On the north fork of the creek, Alcorn and his men viciously attacked a Rogue village. They murdered eight men, burned dwellings and supplies, and left the women and children to starve or die of exposure. At the same time, at the mouth of the creek, Rice's men hit a second village and killed 11 men. They sent the women and children they captured to Fort Lane. Many of the captives died or suffered frostbite. Later, Brig. Gen. John E. Wool, Department of the Pacific commander, equated the volunteers' operations with organized murder.[105]

—1856—

5 JANUARY 1856
APPLEGATE RIVER CAMP (Applegate, Oregon)

On the first of the new year, Maj. James Bruce of the 2nd Oregon Mounted Volunteers continued the winter war with the Rogue River Indians. At Fort Lane, he got 25 regulars to join his and E. A. Rice's companies and convinced Capt. Andrew J. Smith to lend him a howitzer. The column marched west over the mountains to the valley of the Applegate River, where Rogue chief Joe (Apserkahar) and his band were reported to have taken refuge in some abandoned settlers' cabins.

During the column's trek over the mountains, Rogue warriors harassed the men, and on 2 January, they killed Martin Angel, one of the most virulent of the white "exterminators." Before reaching the Applegate River, Bruce lost the howitzer ammunition when the mule carrying it tumbled off a cliff. On the 5th, more ammunition arrived and the fight commenced.

The cannon blasted the houses in which the Indians were sheltered. The Rogues had dug pits into the dirt floors so they could shoot from underneath the bottom logs, and the shooting lasted throughout the day. About 11 P.M., the Indians broke out of the cabins and in the darkness rushed the enemy's lines and escaped into the woods, leaving many women and children behind.

One volunteer, Dr. W. Myers, was killed and three were wounded. Three Rogues were killed, and one man and two children were wounded.[106]

23 JANUARY 1856
COW CREEK (Glendale, Oregon)

While Maj. James Bruce and "Capt." E. A. Rice continued to search for Indians along the Applegate River (see previous entry), Joseph Bailey's volunteers were searching along the tributaries of the Umpqua River. They found no Indians, but a band of Umpquas found them. The volunteers, camped on a prairie in the mountains near where the Oregon-California Road crossed Cow Creek, had posted no sentries. As the men lounged about the fire, the Umpquas fired into the camp, killing two.[107]

22 FEBRUARY 1856
HEADWATERS OF THE NUECES RIVER (Rocksprings, Texas)

On 14 February, Capt. James Oakes with Company C, 2nd Cavalry, left Fort Mason to pursue a band of Waco Indians who had been raiding settlements. The soldiers trailed the Wacos for three days until they cut the Indians' path, then they chased them for six days. When the soldiers found them, the band proved to have only six to eight warriors.

In the ensuing fight, a trooper wounded a Waco and, having used up all his ammunition, killed him with a rock. Two other Indians may have been wounded. Two soldiers were wounded, as were six army horses. Oakes and his men captured all the Indian horses and property, then made the long trip back to Fort Mason. Along the way, as they ran out of food, the men killed and ate several lame horses. Oakes was later recognized for being the first 2nd Cavalryman to have killed an enemy Indian.[108]

23 FEBRUARY 1856
GOLD BEACH (Gold Beach, Oregon)

In November 1855, miners at Gold Beach, at the mouth of the Rogue River, raised a company of volunteers to patrol the area, with John Poland as captain. After three months, thinking the Indians had quieted down, the volunteers pulled back to the coast. The Tututni band of Rogue River Indians, though aware of fighting upriver (see Little Butte Creek, 24 December 1855 ff.), had been living nearby in tentative peace, but a fiery mixed-blood man named Enos roused them to fight. The Gold Beach miners were planning to celebrate George Washington's birthday with an all-night dance, and the Indians decided to strike then.

On the night of the party, Poland left a minimal 14-man guard at the volunteers' camp. As the fiddlers played and the revelers made merry, the Tututnis got ready, and at daybreak they swept in. Overwhelming the sleepy guards, the Indians killed nine volunteers in the first onslaught; five volunteers escaped into the woods. Nearby settlers heard the noise and rushed to alert the volunteers and miners still at the dance hall. The Tututni Rogues attacked other homes along the river, burning buildings and killing 23 settlers.

Poland, unaware of the events, had stopped to see Benjamin Wright on his way home from the dance hall. Wright had perpetrated a notorious attack on the Modoc Indians several years earlier (see Ben Wright Affair, ca. 15 November 1852). Nevertheless, Poland did not suspect treachery when some Tututnis came to Wright's cabin to report that Enos was causing trouble. Heading for the camp, Wright and Poland were jumped, murdered, and mutilated. The Indians cut out Wright's heart and ate it.

The people of Gold Beach and the surrounding area forted up in a makeshift post called Fort Miner while Enos rode about on a white stallion, haranguing his warriors to storm the position. The Indians contented themselves with stealing livestock, burning, and looting. There were no known Indian casualties. In all, 40 settlers and volunteers were killed that day.[109]

1 MARCH 1856
MUCKLESHOOT PRAIRIE (Enumclaw, Washington)

In late February, Capt. Erasmus D. Keyes of the 3rd Artillery captured Kanaskat, the Klikitat chief who had instigated the attack on Lt. Slaughter at Bennan's Prairie (see 4 December 1855). While apprehending him, soldiers shot the chief in the back, but he still struggled furiously. Unable to silence him, a Cpl. O'Shaughnessy placed his musket to Kanaskat's temple and killed him.

With Kanaskat gone, the Puget Sound tribes lost another advocate of war, but they still had fight in them. On 1 March, about 200 warriors of various Puget Sound tribes struck the camp of Lt. August V. Kautz, 4th Infantry, on the White River, not far from the site of Slaughter's fight. Kautz, who was leading Companies D and H of the 9th Infantry, sent for help, and Capt. Keyes arrived with his company of 3rd Artillery. Together the two forces stormed the Indians, who had taken a defensive position on a hilltop. The warriors scattered.

Two soldiers were killed in the fight and eight were wounded, including Lt. Kautz.[110] The Indians suffered no casualties.

4 MARCH 1856
CONNELL'S PRAIRIE (Buckley, Washington)

Two small companies of Washington Volunteers went to the White River crossing at Connell's Prairie, just east of present-day Bonney Lake, Washington, to establish a ferry and build a blockhouse. Before they could accomplish the task, about 150 Klickitats attacked them. The volunteers countercharged the Indians and inflicted about 30 casualties, while only 4 volunteers were wounded. The results discouraged the Puget Sound bands, and this was the last comparatively large-scale battle west of the Cascades.[111]

8 MARCH 1856
GUADALUPE RIVER (Kerrville, Texas)

A detachment of Company I, 2nd Cavalry, under Capt. Albert G. Brackett, scouting to the south out of Fort Mason, discovered a Lipan Apache camp near the Guadalupe River in present-day Kerr County, Texas. The Indians had recently killed settlers, looted cabins, and stolen livestock in the San Antonio area. A small detachment under Sgt. Henry Gordon found the raiders' trail in a dense cedar brake. The terrain was too rough for a mounted charge, so Gordon and his men attacked the camp on foot. The first carbine volley surprised the Lipans and they fled with little resistance.

The soldiers killed three of the Indians, and recovered stolen horses, mules, and a bank draft for 1,000 British pounds.[112]

13 MARCH 1856
TASAWICKS (Kahlotus, Washington)

After spending a miserable winter in the Walla Walla Valley, more than 300 men of the 1st Oregon Volunteers, with their new commander, Thomas Cornelius, went after the Walla Walla and Palouse Indians. Though ill-supplied, Cornelius moved north on 9 March "to win a noble triumph over our common enemy."[113]

On the 13th, Cornelius reached the Snake River at the Palouse village of Tasawicks, about 25 miles upstream from its junction with the Columbia River. Most of the Palouses fled as the volunteers crossed the river in boats. An advance guard killed four older Palouse men who could not keep up with the rest. The volunteers also captured two women and a small boy, whom they named Thomas after their commander. It would be Cornelius's only "victory" of the campaign.[114]

18 MARCH 1856
PISTOL RIVER (Pistol River, Oregon)

In the aftermath of the siege of settlers at Fort Miner (see Gold Beach, 23 February), George H. Abbot gathered up 34 volunteers at Crescent City, California, and marched up the coast to punish the Indians responsible and prevent further trouble. Though his force was small, Abbot hurried north, not waiting for the regulars under Maj. Robert C. Buchanan, 4th Infantry, who followed behind.

At the Pistol River, about ten miles south of Gold Beach, Abbot saw some Rogue River Indians driving a herd of horses in the foothills and went after them. Suddenly many more warriors appeared. Abbot was in trouble. He fell back to the seashore, prepared a barricade from driftwood, and sent a messenger back to Buchanan. Soon the Rogues surrounded the volunteers and peppered them with bullets.

At nightfall, the Indians did not halt the attack but moved in closer. Abbot countered with a charge to drive them back. When it was too dark to see, the volunteers blasted into the night with their shotguns. By dawn, most of the Indians had gone, but they had captured 10 horses and 20 mules from the volunteers. Sporadic fire continued until Maj. Buchanan's force arrived later that day.

Surprisingly, only 1 of Abbot's men was killed and 1 was wounded. The Rogues lost 12 warriors with perhaps 10 wounded.[115]

20−26 MARCH 1856
MOUTH OF THE ROGUE RIVER (Gold Beach, Oregon)

Three columns of soldiers planned to converge at the mouth of the Rogue River and, under Maj. Robert C. Buchanan, trap the last recalcitrant bands of Rogue River Indians, particularly that of Old John. Old John had decided that, since the whites had resolved to kill his people, he might as well die fighting. Two of the columns had little contact with the Rogues, but on the way to the meeting point, Capt. Edward O. C. Ord's Company B, 3rd Artillery, saw plenty of action. On 20 March, Ord fought near the river mouth, killing eight Indians and wounding eight more at a cost of two wounded enlisted men.

Meanwhile, Buchanan had sent one of the three columns, 112 men of the 4th Infantry, upriver to the principal Mikonotunne Rogue village at Skookum House Prairie. On 26 March the soldiers reached the abandoned village and began burning the plank houses, but lingering Rogues fired on them. The Indians wounded one soldier. Five Indians were killed and three more drowned while trying to flee in their canoes.[116]

20 MARCH 1856
SIERRA ALMAGRE (Red Rock, New Mexico)

Detachments from Companies G and I of the 1st Dragoons and D, F, and I of the 3rd Infantry were sent on a retaliatory expedition against some livestock-raiding Mogollon Apaches in west-central New Mexico. Two columns left Forts Craig and Thorn on the Rio Grande for the Mogollon Mountains, to the west. One column of about 100 men under Lt. Col. Daniel T. Chandler of the 3rd Infantry swept into the mountains from the north. Another 100 men, under Lt. Early Steen, came in from the south.

The two columns united on the upper Gila River around present-day Buckhorn. Blas Lucero's scouts indicated that the Apaches' trail went southwest into the Sierra Almagre. On 20 March the soldiers fell upon a Bedonkohe Apache rancheria under the warlike leader El Cautivo. They killed or wounded five Indians and recovered 250 stolen sheep. One enlisted man was wounded.

On the way back to Fort Craig, one mile from the Mimbres River, Chandler mistakenly attacked a friendly Mimbres Apache camp under Delgadito and shot several women and children. Saying he thought they were Mogollon Apaches, he offered his apologies, paid indemnities, and hurried away.[117]

23 MARCH 1856
DEER CREEK (Selma, Oregon)

On Deer Creek, a tributary of the Illinois River, Rogue River warriors ambushed a pack train on the trail between Crescent City and the Illinois River valley settlements. The Rogues killed 4 freighters and ran off 40 horses and 28 mules loaded with supplies and ammunition.

Hurrying to the scene from a nearby farm, Maj. James Bruce and his volunteers caught up with the raiders, but the Indians fired first, killing two men of "Capt." Abel George's company and wounding two from "Capt."

Thomas O'Neal's unit. Three Indians were killed. The fight lasted only a short time before the outnumbered volunteers broke off the action and retreated.[118]

M. C. Barkwell, a volunteer surgeon, lost his horse and all his instruments and medicines. "The volunteers have had so little success," he said, "I am getting tired of it. [I] would like to see the regulars take the field."[119]

24 MARCH 1856
ILLINOIS RIVER (Cave Junction, Oregon)

Capt. Andrew J. Smith led Company C, 1st Dragoons, and a detachment of Company E, 4th Infantry, to the Illinois River country to scout for Rogue River Indians. They found some Indians, and in an ensuing fight, two soldiers were killed and four were wounded.[120]

24 MARCH 1856
COW CREEK (Glendale, Oregon)

While patroling the Oregon-California Road along Cow Creek in the Umpqua Mountains, John M. Wallen's volunteer company, along with 20 men from the company of a Lt. Capron, skirmished with a band of Umpqua Indians. One volunteer was killed and one wounded. The volunteers pursued the Umpquas for six days, but killed only one warrior in the exhausting chase.[121]

26–28 MARCH 1856
CASCADES OF THE COLUMBIA (Stevenson, Washington)

The 9th Infantry moved out from Fort Vancouver, traveling west by boat up the Columbia River to The Dalles, to join an Indian expedition on the upper Columbia River. With the troops heading in their direction, various bands of Yakimas, Chinooks, and Klickitats moved east and attacked settlements downriver, particularly at the Columbia Cascades. On 26 March, at the Middle Cascades, Indians besieged a sergeant and eight men of the 8th Infantry in an old blockhouse built specifically for shelter against Indians.

When word of the attacks reached Fort Vancouver, Lt. Philip H. Sheridan of the 4th Infantry immediately took 40 soldiers upriver on a steamboat. Early on 27 March, the troops landed at the Lower Cascades and started up the narrow trail on the north side of the river, but Indians blocked their way. After a fight in which a soldier standing next to Sheridan was killed, the lieutenant ferried his men over to Bradford's Island. From there, the party continued upriver, towing their boat through the rapids. At the blockhouse, Sheridan's men went ashore to relieve the besieged soldiers.

Meanwhile, at Fort Dalles, Maj. Edward J. Steptoe, having heard about the attacks, took 200 men from the 1st Dragoons, four companies of the 9th Infantry, and Company L of the 3rd Artillery and steamed downriver to the Upper Cascades. Steptoe's men debarked and continued on foot, fighting off the Indians in their path. Steptoe's advance guard reached the blockhouse about the same time as Sheridan's men.

Most of the Indians scattered at this turn of events, the Chinooks escaping to Bradford's Island. Steptoe detached Lt. Alexander Piper, Piper's 3rd Artillery company, and a howitzer and sent them with Sheridan after the Chinooks. Piper's men cornered the Chinooks at the lower end of the island and the Indians surrendered, claiming they had not partaken in killing settlers nor in the blockhouse siege. To test their claim, Sheridan inserted his finger into several of the Chinook's muzzles and found the unmistakable evidence of burnt powder. He arrested 13 warriors.

On 28 March Col. George Wright of the 9th Infantry had marched back to the Upper Cascades, and Sheridan turned the prisoners over to him. A quick trial by military commission judged them guilty, and eight, including Chief Chenowith, were hanged.

The fighting cost the lives of three soldiers, and four others were wounded. About six civilians were killed in the raids preceding the battle. In addition to the eight hanged Indians, three died in battle.[122]

10 APRIL 1856
SATUS CREEK (Granger, Washington)

After their minor skirmish at the Tasawicks village (see 13 March), Thomas Cornelius and his 1st Oregon Volunteers continued across eastern Washington in a vain attempt to find Walla Walla and Palouse Indians. Seeing no Indians as he trekked the Palouse country, Cornelius considered giving up, but instead he sent part of his force south to rest and reconnoiter at The Dalles while he continued on to the Columbia River, downriver to old Fort Walla Walla, and up the Yakima River. There, at last, Cornelius found his Indians.

About 300 Yakimas led by Kamiakin attacked Cornelius and his men near the confluence of Satus Creek and the Yakima River. The five-hour skirmish yielded meager results for both sides. One of Cornelius's volunteer officers was killed, and a few Indians were killed or wounded. The Indians withdrew and Cornelius went on to The Dalles.[123]

13 APRIL 1856
TURKEY BRANCH (Cline, Texas)

After Indians, probably Comanche or Lipan Apache, raided around Laredo, Capt. Thomas Claiborne Jr., in command of companies B and D, Mounted Rifles, and Company F, 1st Artillery, out of Forts McIntosh and Duncan, pursued the raiders for 300 miles. With the soldiers were Laredo mayor Santos Benavides and 25 Laredo citizens. The force surprised a small band of Indians on the Turkey Branch of the Nueces River, west of Uvalde, Texas, and killed one Indian, wounded one, and captured four.[124]

A twelve-pound mountain howitzer, used in the Mexican War, the Civil War, and the Plains Indian wars —Courtesy Fort Larned National Historic Site

29 APRIL 1856
CHETCO RIVER (Brookings, Oregon)

Capt. Edward O. C. Ord, with a detachment of Company B, 3rd Artillery, acting as infantry, was escorting some packers down the Oregon coast from the Rogue River to Crescent City to pick up supplies. As the mules and men forded the Chetco River near present-day Brookings, Oregon, Chetco Indians attacked them.

Ord pursued about 70 of the Chetcos upriver, but they hid in the alders and willows along the banks, firing at the men as they forded the river. One sergeant was mortally wounded in a hand-to-hand fight with an Indian he had driven into the water. One enlisted man was wounded. Two Indians were killed, three were wounded, and several were captured.[125]

27–28 MAY 1856
BIG MEADOWS/BIG BEND (Illahe, Oregon)

Three columns of soldiers under Maj. Robert C. Buchanan had been chasing the southern Oregon tribes for months with only one significant skirmish (see Mouth of the Rogue River, 20–26 March). Finally, they had a major encounter. Before a planned peace conference between soldiers and Rogue River Indians at the Big Bend of the Rogue River, Rogue chief Old John talked Chiefs Limpy and George out of surrendering and instead arranged a surprise for the soldiers.

Capt. Andrew J. Smith and 50 men of his Company C of the 1st Dragoons, with 30 men under Lt. Nelson B. Sweitzer, Company G, 4th Infantry, and a howitzer, reached Big Meadows, near Big Bend, on 25 May, the day before the conference. No warriors appeared the next day, but two Rogue women came to the camp and warned the soldiers of Old John's plan. Smith moved the men from the meadow to a small hill between two creeks and set up a defense. A courier rode out to get help from Buchanan.

At 10 A.M. on 27 May, Old John's braves attacked, but the blazing howitzer kept them at a distance, and the long range of the infantry muskets kept the snipers down. When night fell, the soldiers dug in and built breastworks. The battle continued the next morning, and soon nearly a third of the soldiers had been hit, the water was gone, and the ammunition was getting low.

A first-rate disaster was in the offing for the soldiers when Capt. Christopher C. Auger and his 4th Infantry companies appeared, advancing at double time. Smith's men jumped up and charged the Rogues, who had been about to launch their own last charge. Meanwhile, Auger hit the Indians' rear. Within 15 minutes, the surviving Indians had fled the field. Two days later, George and Limpy surrendered their bands, and late in June Old John bowed to the inevitable. The Rogue River War was over.

Smith and Auger lost 11 men and 20 were wounded. The Indians probably suffered a similar number of casualties. About 1,200 eventually surrendered, and the government removed them to reservations. Perhaps the only positive outcome of this defeat for the Indians was that it saved them from probable slaughter by vengeful citizens and volunteers.[126]

CA. 6 JUNE 1856
PAINTED ROCK (Gold Beach, Oregon)

After the fight at Big Meadows (see previous entry), Capts. Smith and Auger's soldiers traveled down the Rogue River to the coast with many prisoners. Renegade Indian bands still roamed the coast, however, and a number of them attacked the miners at Gold Beach. Capt. Auger's 4th Infantry joined up with the Gold Beach volunteers to corner a band at Painted Rock on the Rogue River. The combined force killed 14 Indians and captured a dozen Indian women and children. More drowned when the canoes in which they were attempting to escape capsized in the rapids.[127]

1 JULY 1856
SOURCE OF THE COLORADO RIVER (Gail, Texas)

In the summer of 1856, Lt. Col. Robert E. Lee led an expedition to the upper Brazos River to look for Indians. Capt. Earl Van Dorn, with Company A of the 2nd Cavalry, was part of the command. Between the headwaters of the Colorado and the Double Mountain Fork of the Brazos, Van Dorn ran into Comanches. With no casualties of their own, his men killed two, wounded and captured one, and took 12 horses.[128]

18 JULY 1856
GRANDE RONDE (LaGrande, Oregon)

Gov. Issac I. Stevens of Washington Territory, frustrated at the military's feeble campaigning to remove Indians from settled areas, planned a summer expedition into Walla Walla and Yakima Indian country. In early July, Lt. Col. Benjamin F. Shaw took a force of 400 volunteers and marched into Oregon Territory.

In the Grande Ronde Valley—nestled between the Blue and Wallowa Mountains—the expedition came upon 300 Walla Walla, Cayuse, DesChutes, Palouse, and Umatilla Indians. Shaw sent a Nez Perce scout to talk to them, but the scout came galloping back, saying he heard one Cayuse order others to shoot him. Without hesitation, Shaw ordered his men to charge.

The volunteers attacked, and the Indians ran for their lives. Some went into the brush and trees on the slopes of the mountains. Others headed for the Grande Ronde River, but the volunteers killed them en masse on the banks. Shaw proudly declared, "We may safely conclude that at least forty of the enemy were slain, and many went off wounded."[129]

Of the volunteers, three were killed and four were wounded. Shaw's men destroyed the village and a large supply of food, tipis, and ammunition, and captured 200 horses. Gov. Stevens declared victory, and the stage was set for Indian surrender, which would take place at a grand council of tribes in the Walla Walla Valley in September.[130]

26 AUGUST 1856
GRAND ISLAND (Wood River, Nebraska)

Cheyenne warriors frequently traveled to the Loup River area, in Pawnee territory, looking for a fight with their inveterate enemies. In August near Grand Island, some Cheyennes flagged down a Salt Lake mail coach to beg tobacco. The driver drew his pistol and bolted, reaching Fort Kearny, on the Platte River, with an arrow in his arm.

Capt. George H. Steuart, with 41 men from detachments of Companies E, G, and K, 1st Cavalry, went in pursuit of the Cheyennes who had stopped the mail coach. Downriver from the fort, the cavalry ran into a camp of about 80 Cheyennes and charged in. The Indians, believing they had done no wrong, did not realize they were being attacked and waited too long to respond. Soon they had no option but to flee.

Steuart's men killed six Indians and wounded ten more. The affair set off another series of raids on emigrants and stages.[131]

26 NOVEMBER 1856
CONCHO RIVER (West-central Texas)

Scouting out of Fort Mason, a detachment of Company G, 2nd Cavalry, under Capt. William R. Bradfute ran into a band of Comanches and skirmished. One soldier was wounded, while four Comanches were killed, two were wounded, and one was captured.[132]

18 AND 21 DECEMBER 1856
FORT CLARK (Del Rio, Texas)

Operating out of Fort Clark, at the site of present-day Brackettville, Texas, Lt. James B. Witherell, with a detachment of Company C, 2nd Cavalry, and two officers of the 8th Infantry had a brush with Lipan Apaches west of the post near the Rio Grande. Witherell killed two Apaches with no loss of his own men. Three days later, Witherell caught another band of Lipans near the Rio Grande. This time his men killed two, wounded two, and captured their horses and weapons.[133]

22 DECEMBER 1856
HEADWATERS OF THE CONCHO RIVER (West-central Texas)

Lt. Richard W. Johnson, in command of a detachment of Company F, 2nd Cavalry, from Camp Cooper, found a band of Comanches near the source of the Concho River. Johnson separated the Indians from their horses and drove the animals into the chaparral. Dismounting his men, Johnson divided them into two squads, surrounded the Indians, and closed in.

In a sharp action amid dense brush, Johnson's men killed three Indians and wounded three. The Comanches killed two soldiers, bugler Ryan Campion and Pvt. Timothy Lamb—the first 2nd Cavalrymen to die in battle—and wounded two. Johnson collared 34 horses and recovered a Mexican captive.[134]

—1857—

31 JANUARY 1857
HOWARD'S WELL (Pandale, Texas)

At Howard's Well, about 20 miles southeast of Fort Lancaster, detachments of companies A, C, F, G, and H, 8th Infantry, fought with Comanches while on escort duty. Four soldiers were killed.[135]

12 FEBRUARY 1857
NORTH FORK OF THE CONCHO RIVER (Sterling City, Texas)

Lt. Robert C. Wood, with Company B, 2nd Cavalry, was scouting out of Fort Mason along the North Fork of the Concho River. After tracking a Comanche trail for three days, the soldiers found and attacked the Indians. Three Comanches were killed and two were taken prisoner. Lt. Wood was wounded.[136]

13 FEBRUARY 1857
KICKAPOO CREEK (Vick, Texas)

When Comanches stole horses near Center Point, Texas, Sgt. Walter McDonald and a detachment of Company D, 2nd Cavalry, rode out of Camp

Verde to catch them. Led by guide "Polly" Rodriguez and two civilians, the cavalry tracked the Comanches west along the Concho River to Kickapoo Creek, southeast of present-day San Angelo, Texas. Upon attacking the Indian camp, McDonald found himself in a sharp contest. His men killed two Comanches and wounded four, but two of his troopers were killed in action and a third was mortally wounded.[137]

8 AND 26 MARCH 1857
SPIRIT LAKE MASSACRE
(Spirit Lake, Iowa, and Springfield, Minnesota)

The Wahpekute Santee called Inkpaduta had been plagued by troubles most of his life. White whiskey-sellers and horse thieves murdered his blood brother's family, and whites had taken his lands and his guns. Homeless in the winter of 1856–57, he saw his son freeze to death. Afterward, a vengeful Inkpaduta and ten renegade Santees raided settlers' homes in northwest Iowa, stealing, injuring, and terrorizing, but not killing.

In March 1857, when the raiders arrived at their sacred lakes around Spirit Lake and found that whites had built cabins, sown seeds, cut down trees, and fished in the waters, Inkpaduta went berserk. Soon his band had killed 26 settlers and abducted 4 women. Inkpaduta then went north to Springfield, Minnesota, where a band of Sissetons under Sleepy Eye joined him. On 26 March, they besieged 21 settlers in a barricaded house, killing 1 boy and wounding 2 men and a woman. Before leaving the village, they murdered 7 more settlers.

Having slain 42 white civilians in all, Inkpaduta escaped to Dakota Territory. When the Santees at the agencies in Minnesota learned that they would not receive their annuities until the murderers had been caught and punished, they organized a manhunt. They killed Roaring Cloud, who was responsible for the death of a white woman, and three other renegades, but Inkpaduta got away.[138]

9 MARCH 1857
MIMBRES MOUNTAINS (Hillsboro, New Mexico)

On 8 March, in the vicinity of the Robledo Mountains, eight Mimbres Apache raiders stole horses from a territorial surveyor, and Lt. Alfred Gibbs with 16 men of Company G, Mounted Rifles, rode after them from Fort Fillmore. The Indians' trail crossed the Rio Grande ten miles north of Dona Ana and headed northwest.

Tracking the raiders doggedly, Gibbs caught them the next day near the northern slopes of the Mimbres Mountains. The Apaches ran for high ground, with Gibbs and his men right behind them. The lieutenant and one of the warriors squared off in a duel. Gibbs wounded the Apache, and the warrior lanced Gibbs, but Gibbs was able to partially parry the thrust with his pistol. Close to fainting, Gibbs dismounted while his men continued the chase to the edge of the mountains. They killed six Apaches and wounded one. Gibbs, the only casualty in the fight, survived his wound.[139]

11 MARCH 1857
OJO DEL MUERTO (Truth or Consequences, New Mexico)

A 35-man detachment of Company B, Mounted Rifles, under Lt. Laurence S. Baker ran into Apaches at Ojo del Muerto (Spring of the Dead), a few miles east of the Rio Grande, at the future site of Fort McRae. In a sharp fight, two soldiers were killed and four were wounded, while the Apaches' losses were seven killed and four wounded.[140]

27 MARCH 1857
JOHNSTON'S STATION (Mertzon, Texas)

Johnston's Station was a small mail station on the Middle Concho River, 28 miles west of present-day San Angelo, Texas, on what would become the Butterfield Overland Stage route. Five single men and a couple, Mr. and Mrs. Evaness, ran the station. On 27 March, a large number of Comanches rode in, hoping to make a quick theft of the horses. The three employees outside with the stock ran into the station. The Indians found the horses side-hobbled with locks and chains. Unable to break the chains, the Indians cut off the horses' legs and let them die.

Approaching the station, the Comanches saw a number of rifle barrels pointing at them through the firing slots and fell back, then sent flaming arrows into the structure. Speaking in Spanish, which some of the Indians understood, the station workers said they would not fire if the Indians let them go. Figuring there would be much to plunder once they put out the flames, the Indians agreed.

As the whites emerged, fingers on the triggers of their weapons, one Indian said in English that the white woman was beautiful and he wanted her for his own. Mr. Evaness heard the comment and shot the Indian, killing him on the spot. The employees ran for cover in a grove of trees. The Comanches fired, wounding both Mr. and Mrs. Evaness. They might have killed all the workers if a stagecoach had not appeared on the road. Believing the coach signaled the approach of a troop of dragoons, the Indians hastily left the station.[141]

24 MAY 1857
CANYON DE LOS MUERTOS CARNEROS (Southwestern New Mexico)

While Brig. Gen. John Garland was on leave from the Department of New Mexico, Col. Benjamin L. E. Bonneville of the 3rd Infantry took his place. Apache raids in the area had not ceased, and Navajo agent Henry I. Dodge was missing and presumed murdered by Mogollon Apaches. The old colonel, determined to lead the next Indian expedition, rounded up troops from across the territory to gather in Albuquerque and at Fort Fillmore.

Col. William W. Loring of the Mounted Rifles led the northern column into the Mogollon Mountains. His command inluded Companies C, D, and I, Mounted Rifles; Companies B and E, 3rd Infantry; and some Pueblo Indian scouts. Loring found no Mogollon Apaches, but he did come across the trail of a band of Mimbres who were in the wrong place at the wrong time. Chief Cuchillo Negro, a progressive leader who had encouraged his people to learn farming, had inopportunely entered the war zone with a herd of 2,000 stolen sheep.

Loring followed the Mimbres' trail northeast into the Black Range, and, on 24 May, surprised the band in a rocky valley. The Mimbres fled into the mountains, leaving behind seven dead, nine captured, and all the stolen sheep. Cuchillo Negro was among the slain.[142]

10 JUNE 1857
PIT RIVER CANYON (Big Bend, California)

After hearing reports of massacres of white settlers in the Pit River Valley during the winter of 1856–57, the military organized an expedition to punish the perpetrators, who they believed were Shasta Indians. On 18 May, Capt. Henry M. Judah led 65 men of Companies D and E of the 4th

Gen. George Crook
—Courtesy Southwest Studies,
Maricopa Community Colleges

Infantry from Fort Jones to the scene of the massacres. At Lockheart's Ferry, they met Sam Lockheart, whose brother Harry had been one of those killed. Lockheart gave the soldiers directions, but Judah could find no Indians.

The captain returned to Fort Jones, leaving Lt. (later Gen.) George Crook with 16 men of Company D to guard the trail and the ferry. Crook scouted southeast of the ferry and, after two days, found a small Indian rancheria. By the time he returned with his men to attack, however, the camp had moved. Crook found a trail and in his excitement went too far ahead. He came upon a warrior, probably a Shasta, and killed him, but when several other Indians appeared, Crook hightailed it back.

Crook then led his little group into a canyon on the Pit River several miles upriver from the ferry. They came upon an Indian camp at the water's edge and attacked. Crook caught an arrow in his right hip after shooting a warrior trying to swim the river. The Indians soon fled, and the short fight was over.

Two Indians were killed in the skirmish. Crook with his wound was the only army casualty. The soldiers thought the arrow was poisoned, for Crook became very sick. A surgeon from Fort Jones hurried to the scene and decided it would be better to leave the arrowhead embedded. It was never removed, but Crook lived for many more years.[143]

27 JUNE 1857
GILA RIVER (Safford, Arizona)

The southern column of Col. Benjamin L. E. Bonneville's expedition (see Canyon de los Muertos Carneros, 24 May) left Fort Fillmore in May and headed west. Lt. Col. Dixon S. Miles of the 3rd Infantry led the column, which consisted of about 600 men in Companies B and G of the 1st Dragoons; B, G, and K of the Mounted Rifles; C, F, and K of the 3rd Infantry; and B, H, and I of the 8th Infantry.

Bonneville accompanied the column, which made a number of officers unhappy. Capt. Richard S. Ewell swore he would rather raise cabbages than chase Indians in a command run by Bonneville and Miles, "who don't know what to do or how to do it if they knew what they wanted."[144] Lt. Henry M. Lazelle described the campaign as "folly," "stupidity," and "asinine." After moving to the headwaters of the Gila River and establishing a supply base, Bonneville moved his men downstream in two wings, each so large that Ewell described them as "solemns"—a solid mass of men. Moving in such large, obvious groups, some grumbled that they would have little chance of catching any Indians.

The soldiers found no Mogollon Apaches, but like Loring's column in May, they ran into other foes. East of Mt. Graham on the Gila River, near present-day Safford, Arizona, they surprised a camp of Coyotero Apaches.

It was discovered later that the Coyoteros had been raiding along the California Trail. Ewell's right wing was in the camp before the Indians knew what hit them, and the fight was over before Bonneville and Miles arrived.

About 40 warriors were killed or wounded, and the soldiers captured 45 Apache women and children. One of the slain was a Mogollon Apache who turned out to be the presumed murderer of agent Henry I. Dodge. Bonneville lost two officers, and seven of his men were wounded. No one called the expedition "Bonneville's Folly" anymore.[145]

2 JULY 1857
FALL RIVER LAVA BEDS (Northern California)

Lt. George Crook, having recovered from his arrow wound (see Pit River Canyon, 10 June), persisted in searching for the Indians who had been raiding cattle along the Pit River. With 32 men of Company D, 4th Infantry, he found a small rancheria in the rough lava beds north of the Pit River and divided his men into three squads, to attack the camp from all sides.

An Indian sentinel, facing the soldiers' guns, gave himself up, but in the attack, a soldier shot him. Crook's entire company charged into the fray. Crook described the pandemonium: "We met them face to face, so close that we could see the whites of each other's eyes. The yelling and screeching and all taken together made my hair fairly stand on end."[146]

The soldiers drove the Indians from their camp, shooting down individual warriors as they broke from cover. Crook reported killing "a great many." Finding many slaughtered beeves in the camp, he assumed he had caught the raiders.

The soldiers captured many women and children but released them. One Indian woman was killed, and about a dozen men. One enlisted man was wounded.[147]

20 JULY 1857
DEVIL'S RIVER (Del Rio, Texas)

Lt. John B. Hood, a future Confederate general, left Fort Mason on 5 July to lead 25 men of Company G, 2nd Cavalry, on a scout. Near the Concho River, the soldiers found an Indian trail heading south toward Mexico. Though the country was rough and dry, Hood figured his men "could live for a short time wherever Indians could subsist," and pushed his command into the wasteland.[148]

After more than 150 miles with only a few water holes, Hood and his men began to think that not only would they find no Indians, but their own survival might be in jeopardy. Many of the soldiers began to drop from exhaustion and were left behind. Approaching the Devil's River near the Rio Grande on 20 July with only 17 men, Hood saw about 50 Comanche warriors materialize just ahead. One waved a white flag. Hood went forward to parley, but within 30 paces, the Comanches threw down the white flag and started firing, joined by others concealed in the surrounding brush.

Warriors rushed up and grabbed the reins of the soldiers' horses before the men could even react. Hood fired his shotgun, and his men blazed away with revolvers. An arrow pinned Hood's hand to his horse's bridle. The soldiers fell back 50 yards and dismounted, firing as they retreated. Years later Hood wrote, "We were nigh meeting a similar fate to that of the gallant Custer and his noble band."[149]

Though the situation was formidable for Hood's men, they held their own, and with what Hood described as "one continuous mourning howl," the Indians quit.[150] The soldiers took the lives of nine Comanches and wounded ten others. Hood suffered wounds to himself and four other soldiers; one soldier was killed and another was missing, probably killed.[151]

27 JULY 1857
PIT RIVER VALLEY (Northern California)

Upon refitting his men after the battle at the Fall River Lava Beds (see 2 July), Lt. George Crook and his Company D, 4th Infantry, set out in search of more Indian raiders. They covered the lava beds again, then moved about eight miles northeast to a glen where some Indians had established a camp under a bluff. Crook estimated that the camp had 500 Indians, quite outnumbering his company, yet he proceeded to attack.

Before Crook could get his men down the rocky bluff, the Indians saw them and scattered. At the bottom, each soldier picked an Indian and chased him down. Crook shot one, then rode after another who was drawing a bead on one of his men. The warrior saw Crook coming and the two faced each other at 60 yards. The Indian dodged from one side to another while singing his death song. Crook kneeled down and fired, breaking the Indian's back. The lieutenant claimed he killed another warrior as he tried to escape into the hills.

After the chase, the soldiers rallied in the village and destroyed everything they could find, including a large supply of grasshoppers drying for the winter food supply. Crook had no casualties. His men killed or wounded about ten Indians.[152]

29 JULY 1857
SOLOMON'S FORK (Penokee, Kansas)

In an attempt to punish Cheyenne Indians for depredations along the Overland Trail, Col. Edwin V. Sumner led Companies A, B, D, E, G, and H, 1st Cavalry, and Companies C, D, and G, 6th Infantry, on an expedition across the central plains from Fort Leavenworth. The force, after combing the plains for months with no luck, combined with Maj. John Sedgwick's men near the junction of the South Platte and Cache la Poudre Rivers to return east.

On 29 July, Sumner, moving south along Rock Creek, reached its junction with the South Fork of the Solomon River, near present-day Penokee, Kansas. There he came upon a large band of Cheyennes prepared to fight. They had recently performed ceremonies that included washing their hands in a magic lake for immunity to soldiers' firearms. About 300 warriors lined up on their ponies, their left flank along the Solomon, their right near the bluffs. Sumner met them with his cavalry in three columns. Instead of firing, the colonel ordered his men to draw their sabers and charge.

The Cheyennes, believing their charm ineffective against sabers, quickly broke up and splashed across the river. The casualties came during the ensuing seven-mile chase. The cavalry followed the Indians south, destroying their camp, 15 miles from the battle site, along the way. The soldiers rode all the way to the site of old Fort Atkinson on the Arkansas River without bringing the Cheyennes to battle again.

Sumner reported that nine Cheyennes had been killed and perhaps ten wounded; the Cheyennes reported only four killed. Two soldiers were killed and eight were wounded.[153]

2–3 AUGUST 1857
PLUM CREEK (Lexington, Nebraska)

In the summer of 1857, the freight company of Russell, Majors & Waddell contracted to carry supplies and drive 2,000 beef cattle for Col. Albert S. Johnston's army, who were heading to Utah to stem trouble with the Mormons. Employees James Rupe, Charles R. Morehead, and 14 herders were to drive a wagon train with the first 800 cattle ahead of the troops. On the Little Blue River, Rupe and Morehead stopped to help a wagonmaster quell a mutiny among his teamsters. The herders went ahead with the rest of the train.

When Rupe and Morehead got to Fort Kearny, eastbound travelers reported seeing many Indians in the vicinity, and the two hurried on. Soon, during a nighttime thunderstorm west of the fort, they met their herders, who informed them they'd suffered an Indian attack. The herders had been camped at the mouth of Plum Creek when about 20 Cheyennes rode in, professing friendship. The herders offered the Indians some food, and while they ate, another band charged in on horseback and stampeded the cattle. One herder, William Sanborn, was killed and another, named Robb, was wounded.

Rupe and Morehead returned to Fort Kearny with their men. The next day, Lt. Elisha G. Marshall of the 6th Infantry sent ten soldiers—all he could spare—out with Rupe, Morehead, and ten of the herders. At Plum Creek they found Sanborn's body, stripped, scalped, pierced by arrows and a lance, and mutilated. The party followed the Cheyennes' trail as best they could, but the rain had obliterated most of it. They were able to round up 65 stray cattle before meeting 150 mounted Cheyennes. Rushing into a small canyon, the herders and soldiers tied their mules to their wagon and prepared a hasty defense line. The first volley checked the Indians, and the second drove them from the field. Morehead estimated they hit six or eight Indians.

In addition to the death of one herder and the wounding of another, the two attacks cost about 735 head of cattle to Russell, Majors & Waddell.[154]

13 AUGUST 1857
HUMBOLDT WELLS (Wells, Nevada)

The Holloway wagon train, a party of only ten emigrants, probably should not have attempted the journey to California on their own. Indians, possibly Paiutes, attacked them at dawn on 13 August near the wells at the head of the Humboldt River. The Indians killed six of the party and wounded three. Mrs. Holloway, one of the wounded, was also scalped. Among those killed was Mrs. Holloway's two-year-old daughter, whom one of the Indians swung by the heels and smashed her head against a wagon wheel.

Three of the emigrant men, two of them wounded, escaped to another wagon train that was coming up behind. At the appearance of the second train, the Indians left. Mrs. Holloway was rescued and her scalp retrieved. She recovered from her physical wounds and fashioned a wig from her own hair, but she ultimately lost her mind as a result of the tragedy.[155]

7, 8, AND 11 SEPTEMBER 1857
MOUNTAIN MEADOWS MASSACRE (Enterprise, Utah)

A large wagon train under Robert and Alexander Fancher, a party of about 140 emigrants, mostly from Arkansas, passed through southwest Utah on its way to California. The emigrants had publicly made flagrant anti-Mormon remarks and damaged Mormon property during their trek, and in Cedar City, some Mormons refused to sell them food. The emigrants threatened to return with the military to punish them.

The Mormons encouraged the Paiutes to attack Fancher's train, and on the morning of 7 September, as the emigrants camped on a creek in Mountain Meadows, just north of present-day Central, Utah, about 200 Paiutes hit them. The Indians, under Chiefs Moquetas and Big Bill, killed 7 emigrants and wounded 16 in the initial assault. Fancher and others hastily corralled the wagons to hold the Paiutes off. The next day, two men broke out of the circle to ride for help. They met a party of Mormons, but instead of helping them, the Mormons shot and killed one man and wounded the other, who then ran back to the wagons.

After a few days, Mormons John D. Lee and William Bateman rode out to Mountain Meadows and offered the emigrants help if they surrendered to the Mormons. The emigrants agreed, and on 11 September they laid down their weapons. Armed Mormons led them back to Cedar City. On the way there, Paiute warriors swept out from behind a ridge and began the slaughter, then the Mormons joined in. Men, women, and children were killed without compunction until all the adults and most of the children were dead.

The Indians and Mormons killed 121 emigrants; only 17 of the youngest children were spared. The Mormons confiscated property amounting to $70,000. It took officials 20 years to catch and convict John D. Lee of the murders, the only perpetrator ever charged in the incident. He was executed on 23 March 1877.[156]

10 SEPTEMBER 1857
ASH HOLLOW (Lewellen, Nebraska)

As in the Plum Creek incident (2–3 August 1857), Cheyennes attacked a Russell, Majors & Waddell beef train, this time near Ash Hollow. William H. Russell's son John hurried to Fort Kearny for help, but with only one company of the 6th Infantry, Lt. Elisha G. Marshall did not have the manpower to take on the 150 or so Indians.

The Cheyennes killed three teamsters and stole 50 head of cattle; they also rifled through one of the wagons, helping themselves to government arms and ammunition.[157]

17 NOVEMBER 1857
TERWAW FLATS (Klamath Glen, California)

Lt. George Crook, with about 90 soldiers of his Company D and other detachments of the 4th Infantry, canoed six miles up the Klamath River from the Pacific Ocean to establish a post at Terwaw Flats, a 100-acre grassy prairie on the Klamath Indian Reservation. The reservation housed two bands of Klamath Indians, the Tolowas and another that Crook called the Alagnas. The two bands were as hostile toward each other as they were toward whites in the area, and Crook expected trouble.

Crook heard from a friendly Indian that the Tolowas intended to kill him, so he made a plan to ambush the Indians first. The plot never went further, however, for before Crook could take action, on 17 November the Tolowas lured Indian agent H. P. Heintzelman to their homes, saying a tribesman was sick. As Heintzelman and another civilian hurried over, the Tolowas ambushed them. Surprisingly, the two men managed to hold off their attackers until Crook came to their rescue.

"We made short work of the disaffected Indians," Crook wrote.[158] The soldiers killed ten and wounded about five. Soon after the incident, the Tolowas captured three white travelers, but they released them at the reservation the next day, then fled north to the Smith River.[159]

—1858—

25 FEBRUARY 1858
FORT LEMHI (Baker, Idaho)

The Mormon mission called Fort Lemhi had become perhaps too successful. Though the Mormons had established good relations among the Shoshones and Bannocks in the Lemhi Valley and had converted many of them, the Indians were becoming unhappy about the growth of Mormon settlements in the area, and they began to rebel. Likewise, Thomas S. Smith, presiding elder at the mission, was becoming unhappy with the Indians, complaining to Brigham Young about how impudent and unmanageable they had become. The old Bannock chief Le Grand Coquin became particularly angry when the Mormons would not give him some white wives, and when Coquin made an impromptu inspection of the mission's horse corral, the Mormons were suspicious.

Suddenly, about 250 Bannock and Shoshone warriors descended on Fort Lemhi. They killed 2 herders, wounded 5 other men, and drove off 255 cattle and horses. After the attack, some Shoshones returned, offering 30 cattle as a peace gesture. They had quarreled with the Bannocks, who, they said, had instigated the raid and who refused to return the rest of the stock. The disheartened Saints abandoned the fort and left the valley on 1 April.[160]

Texas Ranger John S. "Rip" Ford
—From the collection of John N. McWilliams

11 MAY 1858
ANTELOPE HILLS (Durham, Oklahoma)

The Texas Rangers had been fighting Kiowas and Comanches for years, but always within the confines of their own territory. The new governor of Texas, Hardin R. Runnels, was determined to take the war to the Indians' home. Capt. John S. "Rip" Ford organized Runnels's new Ranger command, and in March 1858 he went to the Brazos Indian Reserve—home of Shawnees, Tonkawas, Caddos, Anadarkos, and Wacos—to enlist the Indians' help. The agent, Shapley P. Ross, made a speech to his charges, saying now was the time to avenge themselves on their Comanche enemies.

The talk was effective. Indian spies went north to locate Comanche villages while the expedition prepared for action. In April, Ford led 102 Rangers north with wagons, an ambulance, and pack mules, accompanied by 113 Indians under Ross. On May 11, in the Antelope Hills, on a loop of the Canadian River, the expedition spotted a Comanche camp. The plan was to attack early the next morning, but some impatient Tonkawas jumped in and attacked five lodges. A few Comanches got away to warn the main village.

Ford had to attack quickly. The Comanche camp was still three miles distant, but Ford charged ahead. The Comanches, under Chief Iron Jacket—whose name and supposed invulnerability came from an old Spanish coat of armor he wore—were ready. A resplendent Iron Jacket led his 300 warriors into battle, but his armor proved no match for the five or six lead balls that riddled him at the outset.

The fight spread over six miles of ground, with individual fights the order of the day. When the Comanches between the camp and the river were driven from the field, Ross's Indians let out wild cheers of victory. But soon, Comanches from another camp up the river, alerted by the din of battle, appeared. The reservation Indians and the Comanches faced each other in lines, strutting and shouting insults, firing at long range without doing much damage. Then Rangers entered the contest, and the fighting again became general until about 2 P.M., when the Comanches quit the field.

Ford's men took all the spoils they could and destroyed the rest. They captured more than 300 horses and took 18 prisoners, mostly women and children. The Texans and Ross's Indians killed 76 Comanches, while their own losses were 2 Rangers killed and 2 wounded. The expedition showed the Comanches that they were no longer safe north of the Red River.[161]

17 MAY 1858
STEPTOE'S FIGHT/TOHOTONIMME CREEK (Rosalia, Washington)

In the spring of 1858, after Palouse Indians had run off stock and killed some miners traveling to the diggings in the Colville area of northeastern

Washington Territory, Lt. Col. Edward J. Steptoe decided to look in on the Palouse and Spokane Indians. On 6 May, he led 164 men of Companies C, E, and H of the 1st Dragoons and a detachment of Company E of the 9th Infantry with two howitzers out of Fort Walla Walla. They must not have expected much trouble, for each man was issued only 40 rounds of ammunition.

On 16 May the soldiers crossed the Palouse River heading north and marched across Tohotonimme Creek. Suddenly, nearly 1,000 Spokanes, Coeur d'Alenes, and Palouses confronted them, blocking their way. Steptoe parleyed with the Indians, assuring them he came in peace, but the talk was futile. Steptoe, realizing he was dangerously outnumbered, called for a withdrawal.

The next morning the soldiers went on their way, moving south along Pine Creek, but the Indians stayed menacingly on their flanks. At 8 A.M. they attacked. The dragoon companies shielded the soldiers' ranks as they struggled southward with the pack train and howitzers. The fighting waxed and waned. Two officers commanding flank companies, Lt. William Gaston and Capt. Oliver H. P. Taylor, took mortal wounds. Steptoe rushed to deploy the howitzers on a hilltop just south of present-day Rosalia, Washington. The Indians kept him under fire all day and made one major assault, which he beat back.

That night, Steptoe could see campfires almost ringing his position on the butte. His men were down to three rounds each. Steptoe wanted to fight to the death on the hill, but his lieutenants talked him into a retreat under cover of darkness. They scouted an area that was clear of campfires, and after they buried their dead, they abandoned the howitzers and stole off into the night. Almost miraculously, the exhausted column escaped further attack and made it to Fort Walla Walla on 22 May.

Steptoe lost 5 men in addition to the 2 officers, and 12 others were wounded—a surprisingly light casualty total under the circumstances. The Indians, attacking a defensive position, had greater losses—9 killed and 50 wounded. Nevertheless, they were now fully up in arms.[162]

15 AUGUST 1858
YAKIMA RIVER (Ellensburg, Washington)

After Lt. Col. Edward J. Steptoe's ordeal in May (see previous entry), the military organized more columns to put an end to the Indian troubles. Maj. Robert S. Garnett, with Companies C, G, and I of the 9th Infantry, and Lt. George Crook's Company D, 4th Infantry, marched north from Fort Simcoe. Garnett's orders were to attack and punish all hostile Indians and to capture the Palouses who had participated in killing the miners in April.

It was Garnett's understanding that about 25 Palouse warriors were guilty of the murders and that they had scattered among the Yakima Indians west of the Columbia River. In the gloom of an early morning along the Yakima River, an advance party of 15 men found and attacked a camp suspected of harboring the culprits. In the poor light, Lt. Jesse K. Allen was accidentally killed by his own men. When Garnett's main body of soldiers arrived, 70 Indians surrendered. Garnett executed 5 Palouses believed to have participated in the murders.[163]

1 SEPTEMBER 1858
FOUR LAKES (Four Lakes, Washington)

After their battle with Lt. Col. Edward J. Steptoe (see Steptoe's Fight/ Tohotonimme Creek, 17 May), the Spokane, Coeur d'Alene, and Palouse Indians who had defeated him were exultant and confident. A priest from the Coeur d'Alene Mission sent word to Col. George Wright that the tribes were ready for war and had congregated in the Four Lakes region southwest of present-day Spokane, Washington. Wright prepared to meet the challenge. His command of 600 men consisted of Companies C, E, H, I, and a detachment of D of the 1st Dragoons under Bvt. Maj. William N. Grier; Companies A, B, G, K, and M of the 3rd Artillery under Capt. Erasmus D. Keyes; Companies B and E of the 9th Infantry under Capt. Frederick T. Dent; and 30 Nez Perce scouts under Lt. John Mullan. They left their stone fortification on the Snake River on 27 August.

Marching onto the Spokane Plain, Wright observed Indians lingering just out of range. On the last day of August, the Indians tried to set fire to the prairie but were unsuccessful. The next day at dawn, Wright saw a great number of Indians—Spokanes, Coeur d'Alenes, Pend d'Oreilles, and Palouses—arrayed on a treeless hill in his path, ready to fight.

Wright left the howitzers behind with the pack train and pushed Grier's dragoons and Dent's and Keyes's infantry to seize the hill. They took the hill easily enough but found there were another 500 mounted warriors in the rocky ravines amid the four lakes below them, and still more in the pine trees at the base of the hill. Wright sent some of Keyes's men cautiously down the hill, hoping to entice the Indians out into the open.

Keyes's skirmishers drew out the Indians as planned, and the soldiers held them off with steady fire. With new 1855 rifles, the infantry was able to shoot some warriors off their horses from over 500 yards. Artillery men then brought up the howitzers and blasted the woods, then Dent's infantry closed in on the right. When all his adversaries were out in the open, Grier shouted to his dragoons, "Charge the rascals!"[164] The horsemen raced in and belabored the Indians with sabers and pistols. The Indians broke, and Grier's men chased them for a mile before the soldiers' horses gave out.

The Indians lost about 50 men and as many were wounded. Unbelievably, Wright fought the Battle of Four Lakes with no casualties. He gave most of the credit to his long-range rifles.[165]

5 SEPTEMBER 1858
SPOKANE PLAIN (Spokane, Washington)

Col. George Wright and his men took a three-day rest after their victory at Four Lakes (see previous entry), then they moved north. A short march brought them to the edge of the Spokane Plain, where, on a rocky, tree-covered ridge to the east, 600 or more warriors contested their advance.

Wright formed up his troops, throwing Keyes's artillery men forward as skirmishers, and angled toward the timber. The Indians set fire to the grass and curled around the soldiers' flanks while hidden in the billowing smoke. The soldiers' long-range rifles came to their rescue as they had in the previous battle, allowing the infantry to dash through the flames and drive the Indians back into the trees. Then the artillery men opened up into the timber. One round knocked a limb onto Yakima chief Kamiakin, severely wounding him.

When the howitzers had done their job, the infantry ran into the woods and chased the Indians for over four miles. Once the foot soldiers had driven the Indians out onto the open plain, Grier's dragoons took over, charging them with pistol and saber. The warriors scattered and returned to the trees.

Wright led his men to the Spokane River. At that point, all that the Indians could muster was sporadic harassing fire against the column's flanks. That night, the soldiers camped on the riverbank below Spokane Falls, and within two days the Indians had surrendered as Wright's men rounded up fugitives.

Amazingly, only one soldier was wounded in the battle. The Indians' losses are not known, but they probably suffered at least 30 casualties. Wright slaughtered 900 horses from one captured chief and hanged 15 men he considered major troublemakers. The Yakima called Qualchin was hanged, and when his father, Owhi, tried to escape, four pistol balls brought him down. Wright's victories brought major fighting in the Pacific Northwest to an end.[166]

9–15 SEPTEMBER 1858
CANYON DE CHELLY (Chinle, Arizona)

In July 1858, a Navajo rode into Fort Defiance, Arizona, and murdered the black servant of Capt. William T. H. Brooks, 3rd Infantry. After the tribe ignored demands for the culprit's surrender, the military launched a punitive expedition. Lt. Col. Dixon S. Miles gathered 307 men of Companies A, F, H, and I of the Mounted Rifles and Companies B and C of the 3rd Infantry. A squad of Mexican scouts under Blas Lucero accompanied them.

On their second day out, 10 September, Miles's men captured a Navajo warrior, questioned him, then shot him as a spy. Three days later they entered Canyon de Chelly, a Navajo sanctuary twisting 30 miles into the Defiance Plateau, with cliffs 600 to 1,000 feet high. As Miles's column followed the river down Monument Canyon, Navajos fired at them and rolled boulders down from the cliffs, but these long-range efforts produced few casualties. The troops emerged from the canyon's western mouth and moved south along the west face of the plateau, fending off quick thrusts by the angry Indians.

Miles was back at Fort Defiance on 15 September. Two of his men had been killed and three wounded, while the Navajos lost about ten men.[167]

1 OCTOBER 1858
RUSH SPRINGS (Rush Springs, Oklahoma)

Hoping to keep the Comanches out of Texas, the military organized a punitive expedition in September 1858, the second that year (see Antelope Hills, 11 May). Capt. Earl Van Dorn, later a Confederate general, left Fort Belknap with 225 men of Companies A, F, H, and K of the 2nd Cavalry, a detachment of 1st Infantry, and 135 reservation Indian auxiliaries. On Otter Creek, west of the Wichita Mountains, they built a stockade they called Camp Radziminski and scouted the country for Comanches.

Two Wichita scouts traveled east to their own people's village near Rush Springs in present-day Grady County, Oklahoma, and were surprised to find a Comanche village under Chief Buffalo Hump camped nearby. They returned to Van Dorn with the news, not knowing that the Comanches had just finished preliminary peace talks with soldiers at Fort Arbuckle. Van Dorn marched through the night to attack.

In the fog at daybreak on 1 October, Van Dorn sent Capt. Nathan G. Evans (also destined to be a Confederate general) with one of the cavalry companies and the Indian allies to cut off the horse herd, while the other three cavalry companies hit the village. The Comanches were up at once. They gathered in a ravine that ran across the front of their camp and stretched several hundred yards along the river. With showers of arrows, they covered the withdrawal of their families. The fog in the creek bottom made the adversaries almost invisible to each other and kept the combat at close range.

Leading the Indian allies was Lawrence S. "Sul" Ross (a third future Confederate general), son of Indian agent Shapley Ross. Seeing a group of Comanches escaping, Ross took off after them, calling out for help. Only Lt. Cornelius Van Camp, a soldier named Alexander, and a Caddo scout followed him. Ross found a captive white girl and told the scout to take her back to Van Dorn. Continuing on, he and his two companions ran into 25

Comanches trying to rescue their families. Alexander, hit by arrows, went down. Van Camp blasted his double-barreled shotgun once before being killed, while Ross's Sharps rifle misfired. A Comanche called Mohee grabbed Alexander's rifle and shot Ross in the side. He was about to scalp Ross when Lt. James Majors galloped by and killed him.

Meanwhile, Van Dorn's mounted attack could not dislodge the Indians from the ravine. The cavalry dismounted and began a concentrated sniping that eventually decided the issue. The Comanches broke and fled. Mounted troopers cut them down as they ran. The warriors' determined resistance had allowed most of their families to escape.

During the fight, Van Dorn had been hit with an arrow in his stomach and another in his wrist, and his soldiers thought the wounds would be fatal. Now in charge, Capt. Charles J. Whiting ordered the 120 Comanche lodges burned. After the battle, the soldiers remained on the field waiting for medical help from Fort Arbuckle for the wounded. A doctor cut the arrowhead from the shaft in Van Dorn's gut and pulled the shaft out. Within five days, Van Dorn was well enough to be moved to Camp Radziminski.

The soldiers' losses were 4 killed and 11 wounded; 2 civilians, Sul Ross, and J. J. Ward, were also wounded. The fight cost the lives of 56 Comanche men and 2 Comanche women, and 25 others escaped from the field with wounds that proved fatal. The expedition captured 300 horses. Chief Buffalo Hump escaped, vowing to take revenge on the Texas settlements.[168]

10 OCTOBER 1858
OJO DEL OSO (Fort Wingate, New Mexico)

After Lt. Col. Dixon S. Miles's September expedition to punish the Navajos (see Canyon de Chelly, 9–15 September) had fallen short of its goal, Capt. William T. H. Brooks led a second column from Fort Defiance. It consisted of Company G of the 3rd Infantry and a detachment of Company K of the 8th Infantry, along with Company A of the Mounted Rifles under Capt. Washington L. Elliott. At Ojo del Oso, on the road to Albuquerque north of the Zuni Mountains and near the head of the Rio Puerco, the soldiers clashed with about 150 Navajos. Two enlisted men were wounded, and about 25 Navajos were killed.[169]

—1859—

9 JANUARY 1859
MOJAVE (Mojave, Arizona)

In the late 1850s, Mojave Indian attacks on emigrants and gold seekers heading to California were increasing. The Department of California ordered construction of a fort at Beale's Crossing on the Colorado River to protect travelers and keep the road to California open. Lt. Col. William

Hoffman, 6th Infantry, led 52 men of Companies B and K, 1st Dragoons, across the Mojave Desert from Los Angeles to inspect the fort site, which was across the Colorado River from present-day Needles, California, and construct the fort. Mojaves harassed them as they traveled.

On 9 January, after Hoffman and his men arrived, about 300 Mojaves provoked a fight; however, with few firearms, the Indians were no match for Hoffman's dragoons, who killed 18 warriors. In March, faced with a new force of 700 men under Hoffman, the Mojaves met with Hoffman and conceded the country to him. Hoffman proceeded to build Fort Mojave.[170]

24, 27, AND 28 FEBRUARY 1859
CADDO CREEK (Ardmore, Oklahoma)

After their defeat at Rush Springs (see Rush Springs, 1 October 1858), many Comanches left the area. Some wintered in Chihuahua, Mexico, while others went north of the Arkansas River. Those who remained continued raiding settlers. In February two patrols out of Fort Arbuckle ran into some of the raiders.

On 24 February on Caddo Creek, south of the Arbuckle Mountains, Comanche raiders jumped Lt. James E. Powell, 1st Infantry, and 31 men of Companies D and E, 1st Cavalry, killing one trooper and wounding two. Three days later, again on Caddo Creek, Capt. James M. McIntosh led a detachment of Company D, 1st Cavalry, against a Comanche band. The fight continued into the next day. Seven Indians were reported killed.[171]

13 MAY 1859
CROOKED CREEK (Fowler, Kansas)

Capt. Earl Van Dorn led nearly 500 soldiers of Companies A, B, C, F, G, and H, 2nd Cavalry, and 58 Indians from the Brazos Reservation north out of Camp Radziminski in search of Comanche raiders. A captured Comanche boy confirmed that the raiders were near the Arkansas River.

Van Dorn's men came upon the Comanche camp in a sharp bend of Crooked Creek, south of the Arkansas, about ten miles north of present-day Fowler, Kansas. The troops spotted two Comanches running away, and Lt. William B. Royall and 30 men pursued. After three miles, they overtook about 100 fleeing Comanches. At the sight of the soldiers, the Comanches ran for cover in a steep, brushy ravine and prepared to fight. Royall stopped, rounded up the Indians' horses, and sent to Van Dorn for help.

The rest of the troopers arrived, but the Comanches were positioned so that a mounted charge was impossible. Van Dorn placed some soldiers around the perimeter of the area to prevent the Indians' escape, while the majority of them skirmished in the rain-soaked brush, feeling their way through thickets and often coming face-to-face with the enemy in mutual surprise.

A Comanche hiding behind a log put a pistol ball in the thigh of Capt. Edmund Kirby Smith, the future Confederate general. Another Rebel general-to-be, Lt. Fitzhugh Lee, took an arrow through the chest as he simultaneously blasted his assailant. The Comanches were trapped, and, wrote Van Dorn, "they fought without giving or asking quarter until there was not one left to bend a bow."[172]

The soldiers killed 49 Comanche warriors, wounded 5, and captured 5 men and 32 women. The Comanches killed 2 soldiers and wounded 15, and killed or mortally wounded 4 of the troops' Indian allies.[173]

27 JULY 1859
COLD SPRINGS (Malta, Idaho)

Frequent fighting had occurred between emigrants and Indians along the Hudspeth Cutoff northwest of Salt Lake City, and one act of retribution fell on an innocent party. A wagon train led by Ferguson Shepherd was traversing a canyon near Cold Springs, on the west side of the Sublett Range. When the emigrants stopped to doctor a sick horse, Shoshone bullets rang out of the bushes on both sides of the trail. The bullets killed four emigrants and wounded several others. Four of the emigrant men rode off. The Shoshones grabbed a young child and threw her against some rocks,

Crooked Creek (Kansas)

breaking her leg. The mother managed to mount a mule and escape with her injured daughter. Another woman fled on foot and became so exhausted she left her eight-month-old infant hidden behind some bushes. In all, four were killed and four were wounded, one of them mortally.[174] The Shoshones burned most of the wagons and stole 35 horses.

The next morning another wagon train found some of the survivors huddled under a wagon, being tended by a five-year-old boy. The abandoned infant was found blistered from the sun but otherwise unharmed. The rescuers took the survivors to California.[175]

14 AUGUST 1859
DEVIL'S GATE CANYON (Brigham City, Utah)

After the Shoshone attack on emigrants at Cold Springs (see previous entry), Col. Albert S. Johnston, 2nd Dragoons, sent a force under Maj. Isaac Lynde from Camp Floyd to Bear River Crossing to search for the perpetrators. Once there, Lt. Ebenezer Gay's detachment of men from Company G found a Shoshone encampment in Devil's Gate Canyon between Brigham City and Cache Valley. Before dawn on 14 August, Gay charged the camp. Its inhabitants scattered and took up positions on the steep hillsides of the canyon. Estimates of the number of warriors involved in the ensuing fight vary from 17 to 200.

Gay claimed to have killed 20 Shoshones; 6 of his own men were wounded. However, local Mormons reported that the soldiers killed just one Shoshone man and one boy, and wounded a Shoshone woman.[176]

31 AUGUST 1859
MILTIMORE MASSACRE (American Falls, Idaho)

About 25 miles southwest of Fort Hall on the Oregon Trail, between the Portneuf Bridge and the Snake River, 30 Shoshones, led by Pageah and Sowwich, attacked 19 emigrants in the wagon train of Edwin A. Miltimore. The Indians jumped the rear wagons first, allowing men in the lead wagons to take cover in the brush and begin firing at their assailants with the company's two rifles.

The Indians killed and mutilated five men, one woman, and two children. As the Shoshones worked their way up toward the lead wagons, one of the armed emigrants killed one of the Indians' leaders, effectively dampening the warriors' ardor for a fight, and they left. Three days later, the emigrant survivors met a squad of 2nd Dragoons under Lt. Henry B. Livingston, who escorted them to Camp Floyd.[177]

3 NOVEMBER 1859
HEADWATERS OF THE LLANO RIVER (South-central Texas)

Lt. William B. Hazen, with a mounted detachment of Company F, 8th Infantry, and 30 civilian volunteers, rode out of Fort Inge looking for

Comanches who had stolen horses and killed two settlers near Sabinal, Texas. Northwest of the fort, near the source of the Llano River, Hazen and his men found and attacked the perpetrators. A sharp fight ensued.

The Comanches wounded Hazen and 3 volunteers. Hazen's men killed 7 Comanches, wounded 1, and recovered 30 horses and some guns.[178]

24 DECEMBER 1859
PINAL MOUNTAINS (Globe, Arizona)

In the fall of 1859, Col. Benjamin L. E. Bonneville, commanding the Department of New Mexico in Santa Fe, decided to punish the Pinal Apaches for raids in both Mexico and the U.S. He charged Bvt. Lt. Col. Issac V. D. Reeve of the 8th Infantry with organizing an expedition from Fort Buchanan, near the Mexican border. With only 176 men of Companies D and G, 1st Dragoons, and Company A and detachments of C and F, Mounted Rifles, the scheme seemed to be shaping up as another of "Bonneville's follies."

Reeve established a supply depot on the San Pedro River, then proceeded to sweep the country. Between 12 and 26 November, he rounded up 22 Apaches, all women and children except for 1 warrior. The next month, another sweep in the Pinal Mountains resulted in a battle on Christmas Eve. Dragoons under Capt. Richard S. Ewell attacked a Pinal camp, killing 8, wounding 1, and capturing 23. Only Ewell himself was slightly wounded.

Despite Col. Thomas T. Fauntleroy's later denouncement of Bonneville's campaign as a failure, the Pinals did come to Fort Buchanan early in 1860 to seek peace.[179]

—1860—

13 JANUARY 1860
ROUND VALLEY (Covelo, California)

A party of volunteers calling themselves the Eel River Rangers, led by "Capt." W. S. Jarboe, made it their goal to hunt for Nomlacki escapees from the Mendocino Reservation. If, upon being caught, the refugees refused to return, the Rangers killed them, occasionally excepting women and children. In a severe fight on 13 January near Round Valley in Mendocino County, Jarboe's men killed about 30 Indian men of unidentified tribes and captured 28 prisoners.[180]

17 JANUARY 1860
CIENEGA AMARILLA (Window Rock, Arizona)

The Navajos were determined to force the abandonment of Fort Defiance. At sunrise on 17 January, Chief Huero and about 250 warriors attacked a wagon train and the post's beef herd at the Cienega Amarilla (Yellow Swamp) near Black Creek, about eight miles south of the fort. Then the Indians surprised four soldiers on a wood-cutting detail about 400 yards outside the corral; they immediately cut down three, but the fourth escaped.

The Navajos made for the cattle, but the herd guard of 35 enlisted men from detachments of Companies B, C, E, and G, 3rd Infantry, held them off, shooting two raiders off their horses. Sgt. Gable of Company C tied a message around his dog's neck and sent it off to the fort.

About noon, a friendly Indian approached Fort Defiance with news of the fighting. Officers were skeptical until Gable's dog remarkably trotted in just then with the message. Meanwhile, more Navajos attacked a lumber detail in the mountains near the fort, and word of its predicament also came in. Capt. Oliver L. Shepherd, 3rd Infantry, took 50 men and headed out for the lumber camp, while Lt. Alexander N. Shipley and Lt. Silas Kendrick took 25 men south to Cienega Amarilla.

While the relief parties marched out, Huero's warriors attacked a mule train heading for the fort, severely wounding a teamster and killing one of the soldier escorts. By the time the rescuers arrived, the Navajos were gone. Lt. Kendrick counted 130 arrows protruding from the bodies of the three soldiers outside the corral.[181]

8 FEBRUARY 1860
BONITO CANYON (Fort Defiance, Arizona)

After his failed attempt to drive the soldiers away from Fort Defiance in January 1860, Navajo Chief Huero (see previous entry) led nearly 500 warriors against the fort's beef-herd guard, about seven miles northwest of the post. A Sgt. Werner of Company C, 3rd Infantry, was in charge. His 44 enlisted men—detachments of Companies B, C, E, and G—had a strong position in a partially forested mountain glade outside Bonita Canyon. They had seen Indians in the area for the past few days and they were ready. When Huero attacked, just after sunrise, the cattle were already drawn into the corral and the men were in position. The two-hour fight ended with the arrival of 12 soldiers and a mountain howitzer.

Only one soldier was slightly wounded. Capt. Oliver L. Shepherd reported that 10 Navajos "were shot helpless" and carried off the field, and about 20 were wounded.[182]

25–26 FEBRUARY 1860
HUMBOLDT BAY MASSACRE (Eureka, California)

Settlers in Humboldt County, California, believed the Indians who lived along the coast near the Eel River and Humboldt Bay, south of present-day Eureka, were in league with nearby mountain tribes to kill or steal their cattle. The settlers estimated that Indians had killed or stolen about 1,000 head, one-eighth of the cattle in the county. When one of the settlers, James

Ellison, went after a band that was running off his stock, the Indians killed him and a few other settlers as well.

In response, Humboldt County sheriff B. Van Ness and about 40 volunteers descended on a village near the Eel River and the shore of Humboldt Bay, killing 9 men and 47 women and children. On Indian Island, they killed 60 Indians, and at Eagle Prairie, 35 more.

Van Ness said later that he had killed about 80 Indians, but Maj. Gabriel J. Rains, 4th Infantry, commander at Fort Humboldt, placed the figure at 188. According to Rains, the Indians had been "inoffensive," had "killed nobody, troubled nobody, and nobody's cattle," and had been killed "for no crime whatever."[183]

30 APRIL 1860
FORT DEFIANCE (Fort Defiance, Arizona)

In a continuing attempt to drive soldiers out of Fort Defiance, on Navajo homeland, Navajos returned in force to the post with upward of 1,000 warriors. Stationed at the fort were Bvt. Maj. Oliver L. Shepherd and his Companies B, C, and E, 3rd Infantry. Before dawn on 30 April, three columns of warriors charged in. They penetrated some of the outbuildings, but Shepherd could do little about it until first light. At daybreak, he cleared the Indians out with a series of infantry charges, driving them back into the foothills.

One soldier was killed and two were wounded. About 12 Navajos were killed or wounded. This was one of the few times Indians in the West actually assaulted a fort.[184]

12 MAY 1860
PYRAMID LAKE (Nixon, Nevada)

In April, after many conflicts between whites and Indians along the California Trail, several hundred Paiutes held a council at Pyramid Lake to discuss going to war. The young Paiute leader Winnemucca tried his best to prevent war, but a mixed-race Bannock named Mogoannoga made the decision for the Paiutes when he stole away from the council and, with a small band of warriors, killed five whites at the Williams Station trading post near present-day Silver Springs, Nevada. When Mogoannoga returned and announced his deed, the council broke up and prepared for war.

"Maj." William O. Ormsby was the nominal commander of 105 armed citizens from Virginia City, Carson City, Genoa, and Gold Hill who volunteered to go after the Paiutes. After burying the dead at Williams Station, the volunteers marched down the Truckee River toward Pyramid Lake. Two miles from the southern end of the lake, 25 warriors met them with a shower of arrows. The volunteers fell back to a grove of cottonwoods, only to find it filled with Paiutes. Panicked, Ormsby's force fled back upriver.

Truckee River (Nevada); area of Hays's fight

Ormsby himself, hit in both arms and with a poisoned arrow piercing his mouth, fell from his horse. When the Paiutes approached, he offered his revolver as a token of surrender, but they simply killed him with it. The volunteers' retreat along the narrow bench by the river turned into a rout, the Paiutes chasing the volunteers out of the bottomlands near Black Mountain.

The volunteers may have killed or wounded 10 Paiutes. The Paiutes killed 76 volunteers. Almost all of the 29 volunteers who survived were wounded.[185]

29 MAY 1860
WILLIAMS STATION (Silver Springs, Nevada)

After the Pyramid Lake fight (see previous entry), settlers and volunteers put out calls for help. Former Texas Ranger John C. Hays organized more than 500 men from Carson City into the "Washoe Regiment" and brought them to Virginia City. More volunteers joined Hays from California: 165 men from Downieville and a few hundred more from Placerville, Sacramento, La Porte, and Nevada City. Capt. Joseph Stewart, commanding at Fort Alcatraz, also headed into Nevada with 144 men from detachments of Companies A and F, 1st Dragoons; H, I, and M, 3rd Artillery; and A and H, 6th Infantry.

On 20 May Stewart's troops reached Carson City, where he was ordered to await developments. Hays's Washoe Regiment marched on, however, to Williams Station. Hays and his men found 150 Paiutes waiting there, confident after their victory at Pyramid Lake. In a sharp skirmish, two white men and six Paiutes were killed before the Indians pulled back, heading north toward Pyramid Lake.[186]

3–4 JUNE 1860
TRUCKEE RIVER (Wadsworth, Nevada)

After their fight at Williams Station (see previous entry), John C. Hays and the Washoe Regiment marched north. Capt. Joseph Stewart and his regulars joined them at a campsite on the Truckee River. The next day the combined force moved eight miles down the river and built an earthwork defense. Downriver, in the valley near Pyramid Lake, an advance party found the remains of volunteers from the 12 May rout there. They also spotted 300 Paiute warriors rapidly approaching.

With the Paiutes in pursuit, the vanguard hurried back to the main force. The men formed a skirmish line about a mile long and held the Paiutes back, but they could not drive them from the field. After three hours, at sunset, the Paiutes pulled back north toward the lake. Stewart, Hays, and their men followed for a while, then built a fortification in which to spend the night.

The next morning, the force continued its pursuit, leaving one company in camp to care for the wounded. In a canyon, Paiutes ambushed the five advance riders, killing volunteer William Allen, the expedition's last fatality. After that, the Paiutes vanished; the command reached the south end of Pyramid Lake to find the village gone. After several days, Hays returned to Carson City and disbanded his regiment. Stewart stayed in the area for another month, but the Paiutes did not return.

In all, the regulars and volunteers killed 25 Paiutes and wounded about 20. The Paiutes killed 3 men and wounded 5.[187]

CA. 16 JUNE 1860
DRY CREEK STATION (Austin, Nevada)

Si McCandless ran a small trading post at the Dry Creek Pony Express station near the Simpson Park Mountains, in present-day Lander County, Nevada. McCandless lived with a Paiute woman, and when her tribe asked him to bring her back, he refused. Soon he noticed several of the woman's relatives hanging around the trading post, and he warned the Pony Express workers of impending trouble.

One morning, when stationkeeper Ralph M. Lozier opened his door to fetch water, a Paiute shot him down. Another Pony Express employee, John Applegate, ran to the door and was shot in the hip and groin. A third worker, Lafayette "Bolly" Bolwinkle, who had been asleep inside, bolted out of bed, grabbed his gun, ran to the door, and started firing. McCandless dashed across the road from the trading post and forted up with Bolly. They piled grain bags across the door and exchanged shots with the angry Paiutes. Applegate, in excruciating pain, asked for a revolver to shoot at the Indians, but instead shot himself in the head.

After a short time, the firing stopped. McCandless and Bolwinkle made a run for the next station. A few Indians chased them but soon gave up, content with looting the station and post. When McCandless and Bolwinkle reached the next station, the ten-mile run had left Bolly's bare feet badly cut up.[188]

MID-JUNE 1860
WILLOW CREEK STATION (Callao, Utah)

As Indian hostility continued to heat up in the area, attacks on Pony Express stations and riders increased. Upon reaching Deep Creek Station, eastbound rider Elijah N. Wilson found out that his relief rider had been killed. Wilson kept on riding to Willow Creek Station, at the southwest edge of the Salt Lake desert near the Deep Creek Range. While Wilson was resting there, seven Gosiutes walked in and demanded food from stationkeeper Peter Neece. Neece offered them a 24-pound sack of flour, but they demanded a sack apiece, and Neece threw them out. As they passed the corral, the Gosiutes shot a cow, whereupon Neece drew his revolver and killed two of the Indians.

Aware that about 30 Indians were camped nearby, Neece, Wilson, and the two other men who worked at the station loaded their weapons and hid in the sagebrush outside. Near dark, the angry Gosiutes surrounded the building and were surprised when bullets began flying from the brush. The Indians fired toward the gun flashes, but the workers were able to avoid being hit. Finally, after three more warriors were killed, the Gosiutes left in disgust.[189]

28 JUNE 1860
PAINT CREEK (Throckmorton, Texas)

After Comanche Indians killed settler Josephus Browning and wounded his brother Frank near Hubbard Creek, other settlers in the area wanted revenge. Visiting at the time was rancher and future Civil War officer John R. Baylor with four other men. Upon hearing of the incident, the five visitors joined several local men at the Browning ranch to form a posse, which Baylor led.[190]

The party tracked the Comanches for five days, finally overtaking them on Paint Creek at the Clear Fork of the Brazos River. The posse killed 13 of the Indians, destroyed their camp, and returned to town with 9 Comanche scalps, numerous trophies, and a white woman's scalp they had found in the camp.[191]

Ruins of Dry Creek Pony Express Station (Nevada)

29 JUNE 1860
DESCHUTES RIVER (Northern Oregon)

Capt. Andrew J. Smith and a force including Company C, 1st Dragoons, left Fort Dalles with orders to construct a road from Harney Lake to the Oregon-California Trail near the Raft River. Just east of the Deschutes River, Indians—probably Shoshones or Paiutes—attacked Smith and his men. The soldiers killed one of the Indians and wounded several, with no loss to themselves. Upon hearing of the incident, Maj. Enoch Steen ordered Smith to abandon road-building and go after the attackers. Smith did so, but he was unable to catch the Indians.[192]

11 JULY 1860
BLACKWATER SPRING (Eads, Colorado)

In March 1860, Forts Riley, Cobb, and Union each sent out a column of soldiers to hunt down Kiowa and Comanche Indians. Maj. John Sedgwick led the Fort Riley column—almost 500 men in Companies F, G, H, and K, 1st Cavalry; Companies C and K, 2nd Dragoons; and Delaware Indian scouts under their leader, Fall Leaf.

After several months, the column reached Bent's New Fort without having fought a single Indian. Then Sedgwick received word of a Kiowa war party to the north. On 9 July, Capt. William Steele and Lt. Francis C. Armstrong of the 2nd Dragoons and Lts. George D. Bayard and Joseph H. Taylor of the 1st Cavalry led 86 men on the chase. They went north 56 miles to Big Sandy Creek without finding the warriors and turned back. Meanwhile, Kiowas in the vicinity of Bent's New Fort were spotted fleeing north, and Lt. J. E. B. Stuart and 20 1st Cavalrymen went after them. On 11 July, after a 26-mile, 2½-hour run, the Kiowas found themselves between Steele's men and Stuart's.

In a running fight along Kiowa Creek, the Kiowas wounded two enlisted men, John Smith and Ferdinand Schwartz, and Lt. Bayard received a severe arrow wound below the eye. The soldiers killed 2 Kiowa men and captured 16 women and children, most of them from the lodges of the Kiowa warrior Litarki, along with 40 ponies and mules. The army turned the captives over to Indian agent William Bent.[193]

23 JULY 1860
SMITHFIELD (Smithfield, Utah)

Chief Pagunap and a small band of about ten other Shoshones were arrested at Smithfield, Utah, for stealing a horse from a Mormon settler in Cache Valley. The Indians tried to escape, but Pagunap was shot and killed in the attempt. In revenge, the escaped Shoshones killed three settlers and wounded two others as they fled.[194] A group of Smithfield citizens pursued the Shoshones but succeeded only in wounding one of them before night fell and the Indians escaped.

Two weeks later, local citizens gave Chief Bear Hunter four beeves to bring in the fugitives, but he never returned with them.[195]

3, 4, AND 6 AUGUST 1860
REPUBLICAN FORK (Cambridge, Nebraska)

Capt. Samuel D. Sturgis led an Indian expedition of 419 men of Companies A, B, C, D, E, and I, 1st Cavalry, out of Forts Cobb, Washita, and Arbuckle in early June. Sturgis moved north for several weeks, heading across the Arkansas River to a spot on the Solomon River where Kaw Indian scouts said he would find a camp of 100 "hostile Kioways & Camanches." He found the camp on 2 August, but its inhabitants had fled north. He pursued them.

The next day, five of Sturgis's scouts had a scrape with the warriors. Three scouts were killed and two were wounded; they killed and wounded a like number of Kiowas and Comanches. That night, about 20 warriors raided Sturgis's camp, but they caused little damage. At first light, the column continued north. Capt. James M. McIntosh and 16 men of Company D got into a running fight with 50 warriors. Lt. Oliver H. Fish joined in with 36 men of Company B, and ultimately the whole column followed, chasing the Indians over hill and gully for 18 miles. The soldiers killed 2 more Indians.

After camping on Beaver Creek, the soldiers saw more warriors on a ridge to the north. Lts. Fish and Ingraham chased them eight miles farther to the Republican River valley, south of present-day Cambridge, Nebraska. As the command moved downstream and forded the river, more and more Indians came into sight.

On a mile-wide plain north of the Republican and south of some hills, the soldiers met more than 600 Kiowas and Comanches. Capt. McIntosh took a squadron into the hills, around their opponents' left flank; Capt. William N. R. Beall led the advance squadron on the right; and Capt. Eugene A. Carr of Company I led his squadron through the center. Hardly had they begun the charge when the Indians broke and fled. Scattered parties of 1st Cavalrymen pursued them 15 miles north of the Republican before calling it quits. Sturgis and his men continued on to Fort Kearny, where the expedition ended.

Sturgis claimed that 29 Kiowas and Comanches were killed in the battle and preceding skirmishes. His losses included 3 friendly Indians killed and 2 wounded, and 3 enlisted men wounded and 1 missing, presumed killed.[196]

11 AUGUST 1860
EGAN CANYON (Schellbourne, Nevada)

At the Egan Canyon Pony Express station, in a pass between the Egan and Cherry Creek Mountains, about 80 Paiutes approached, looking for food. A rider named Wilson and stationkeeper Mike Holt (or Holton), the only ones there, grabbed their guns and fired from the building. Though the Paiutes had the numbers, they had few firearms, and the workers kept them at bay for a while. But soon their ammunition was gone. The Paiutes broke through the door and asked for bread. Hoping to escape death, Wilson and Holt gathered up all the food they could find for the warriors. The chiefs were not satisfied. Pointing to the flour sacks, they ordered the white men to bake more. Wilson and Holt prepared food throughout the day.

When the food was gone, the Indians took the two men outside, tied them to a wagon tongue driven into the ground, piled sagebrush at their feet, and set it on fire. The warriors danced while the flames grew. At this point a rider, William Dennis, rode up, saw the trouble, and raced five miles back to a contingent of soldiers he had just passed. Lt. Stephen H. Weed was heading to Salt Lake City with 27 men of Company B, 4th Artillery. When Dennis alerted him, Weed sped to the station, ran off the Indians, and rescued Holt and Wilson before they were badly burned.

Paiutes killed one of Weed's men and wounded two. Paiute losses were three, with about a dozen wounded.[197]

26 AUGUST 1860
CLEAR FORK OF THE BRAZOS RIVER (Snyder, Texas)

Maj. George H. Thomas, later a Union general, led the smallest contingent of the army's summer expeditions of 1860. Company B and a

Site of Utter Fight/Castle Creek (Idaho)

detachment of D, 2nd Cavalry, left Camp Cooper, on the Clear Fork of the Brazos River, on 23 July. For a month Thomas trekked around the headwaters of the Concho and Colorado Rivers, searching for hostile bands.

On 26 August, by the head of the Clear Fork near present-day Snyder, Texas, Thomas encountered 11 Comanches. The soldiers killed 1 of them and wounded 2, but not before the Comanches had killed 1 soldier and wounded 5 others, including Thomas. The column quickly returned to Camp Cooper.[198]

9–10 SEPTEMBER 1860
UTTER FIGHT/CASTLE CREEK (Grand View, Idaho)

Elijah P. Utter's wagon train consisted of the Utter family, three other families, six single men, and six ex-soldiers recently discharged from Fort Hall.[199] Though a relatively small train, the 8 wagons, 100 oxen, and 44 travelers, 16 of whom were adult men, appeared to be strong enough to make it to Oregon. Traveling along the Snake River, the party reached the mouth of Castle Creek, about 12 miles downriver from present-day Grand View, Idaho, early on 9 September. There, a cloud of dust ahead warned of approaching Indians.

Utter corralled the wagons on high ground overlooking the river. A band of Bannocks circled around, shooting, for an hour, then they approached waving a white flag. The Indians indicated that they were hungry, and Utter let some of them inside the corral and fed them. The Bannocks thanked the emigrants and made signs that they could proceed, but when Utter strung the wagons out along the road, the warriors attacked again.

Three men, including the driver of the lead wagon, quickly lost their lives as Utter circled the wagons again. Throughout the day and into the night, the Bannocks besieged the emigrants, and they were still there the next morning. In need of water, Utter tried to move the wagons to the river, but the Indians hit them again, killing another man.

At that point, four of the ex-soldiers and two other men, the Reith brothers, mounted horses and galloped away, leaving the rest of the train to their fate. The party broke up and ran for the thickets along the river. Elijah and Abagel Utter, four of their children, and another man were killed. The Bannocks, busy looting the wagons, left the remaining 27 emigrants alone in their hiding places along the river.

In all, 11 emigrants died in the attack.[200] The survivors took various tragic treks down the Snake. A few wandered away; Indians killed or captured others; and some died of starvation and were eaten by their companions. There were no known Bannock casualties.[201]

13–28 OCTOBER 1860
CHUSKA MOUNTAINS (Chinle, Arizona)

After the audacious Navajo attack on Fort Defiance (see 30 April), Secretary of War John B. Floyd ordered a massive punitive operation. Floyd sent significant reinforcements to Fort Defiance from Utah: the entire 5th and 7th Infantry regiments, three companies of the 10th Infantry, and two companies of the 2nd Dragoons. In September, Maj. Edward R. S. Canby, 10th Infantry, organized the 600-man command, which included nine of the infantry companies from Utah and six companies of Dragoons and Mounted Rifles, accompanied by Ute auxiliaries and Blas Lucero's scouts. Canby divided the command into three columns, one of which he led himself, and the other two directed by Bvt. Maj. Henry H. Sibley and Capt. Lafayette McLaws.

For almost two months, the soldiers scoured the Chuska Mountains and the Defiance Plateau. The Ute auxiliaries raided Navajo stock and burned their fields, but the Navajos themselves managed to stay at the periphery of the columns, which, composed mainly of infantry, could not force the Indians into a major battle. The two main engagements were at Black Pinnacle (13 October) and San Jose (24 October), near the Black Mesa. One officer, Capt. George McLane, was killed on 13 October.

Troops under Capt. Thomas Claiborne, including Companies B and I of the Mounted Rifles, participated in much of the action, accounting for 22 Navajo casualties. Other casualties occurred in numerous isolated skirmishes.

The difficult campaign—conducted in mountain and desert terrain and plagued by drought—took a toll on the men and horses. In November, the soldiers marched back to Fort Defiance. They had killed about 36 warriors, but the main damage was to Navajo homes, crops, and herds.[202]

4 DECEMBER 1860
FORT WEBSTER (Mimbres, New Mexico)

Most of the nearly 400 miners in the Pinos Altos region were not taking enough gold out of the ground to support themselves, and they were looking for scapegoats for their bad luck. The occasional thefts in the mining camp were conveniently blamed on the Mimbres Apaches who were camped on the Mimbres River near abandoned Fort Webster.

Instigator James H. Tevis gathered 28 miners and headed to the peaceful camp on 4 December. They tried to surprise the Mimbres at dawn, but the Indians were alert. At first, the two sides fought at long range, then warriors from another rancheria joined those under attack. Tevis saw Chief Elias, an old acquaintance, on a horse about 200 yards away.

The Apaches later said Elias tried to stop the fighting and moved forward to talk to Tevis. Tevis, however, said Elias only "cussed us in English—and in good English, too." Tevis asked if any of his men could "lift [Elias] out of his saddle."[203] A miner named Davis aimed his rifle and shot the chief off his horse. The Mimbres retreated. Tevis tried to follow, but after several of his men and horses were wounded, he withdrew.

The miners killed 4 Apaches, wounded several, and captured 15 women and children, whom they took to Fort McLane. The incident convinced many peaceful Mimbres Apaches that they could no longer trust the whites.[204]

19 DECEMBER 1860
PEASE RIVER (Margaret, Texas)

In the fall of 1860, Capt. Lawrence "Sul" Ross took his company of Texas Rangers to the northwest Texas frontier, where Comanches had been stealing horses and murdering settlers. Requesting help, Ross received a 21-man detachment of Company H, 2nd Cavalry, from Camp Cooper, led by Sgt. J. W. Spangler. Seventy volunteers under Jack Cureton augmented the force, giving Ross about 150 men.

The troops marched up the Pease River. From the top of a divide, they spotted fresh pony tracks, and on the next hill they found themselves within 200 yards of a small camp of Comanches, at the junction of Mule

Creek and the Pease River. About 25 warriors were packing up and preparing to move. Ross had outmarched Cureton's volunteers, but he decided he did not have time to wait and must attack with his Rangers and the cavalry alone.

Under the cover of a strong wind that stirred up dust, Ross brought his command up to the camp unnoticed. He sent Spangler around some sand hills to cut the Comanches off, then charged with his Rangers. The Indians fled—right into Spangler's waiting troopers—then scattered. The Comanche leader, Peta Nacona, rode off with someone mounted behind him. Ross and Lt. Tom Kelliher chased them down. Within 20 yards of Nacona, Ross fired, hitting both the chief and his passenger, and both fell from the horse.

Nacona got up and shot arrows at Ross; Ross shot back, hitting Nacona three times. The chief crawled away and sang his death song. Lt. Kelliher caught the passenger, who turned out to be a woman, Nacona's wife. When Ross saw her, he noticed she had blue eyes. She was Cynthia Ann Parker, whom the Comanches had captured from her parents 24 years earlier. She had borne Nacona several children. One of them, who escaped during this incident, was Quanah Parker, later the leader of the Quahadi Comanches.

The Pease River fight cost the Comanches 14 lives, and 3 others were captured. There were no white casualties. After her recapture, Cynthia Ann Parker could not readjust to white society and died of self-starvation and influenza in 1870.[205]

—1861—

2 JANUARY 1861
COLD SPRINGS (Boise City, Oklahoma)

Head of the Department of New Mexico, Col. Thomas T. Fauntleroy, commanding at Fort Union, ordered Lt. Col. George B. Crittenden to chastise the raiding Kiowas and Comanches at any opportunity. When news of depredations in the mountains along the Santa Fe Trail came in, Crittenden led out 88 men and four officers of Companies D, H, and K and a detachment of Company E, Mounted Rifles.

In the meantime, the raiders had moved east of the Raton Mountains and were harassing travelers along the Cimarron River. Crittenden ordered forced marches to catch up with them. Near the Cimarron, about ten miles north of Cold Springs, the soldiers found a camp of 175 sleeping Kiowa and Comanche lodges. They surprised the Indians, killing 10 and wounding about 10 more. Three Mounted Riflemen were wounded. Crittenden's men destroyed the camp and took 40 horses back to Fort Union with them.[206]

4–10 AND 19 FEBRUARY 1861
BASCOM AFFAIR (Fort Bowie, Arizona)

In October 1860, Coyotero Apaches raided the ranch of John Ward in the Sonoita Valley, ran off his livestock, and captured his 12-year-old stepson, who would grow up to be known as Mickey Free. Ward asked for help at Fort Buchanan, mistakenly blaming the Chiricahua Apaches. Not until January 1861 could the fort spare troops to hunt for the boy and the stolen stock.

Lt. George N. Bascom took 54 men of Company C, 7th Infantry, and headed for Apache Pass, the home of Chief Cochise's Chiricahuas. Cochise, accompanied by six family members, met with Bascom on 4 February. Inside Bascom's tent, the lieutenant accused Cochise of abducting Ward's stepson. The chief said the Coyoteros had the boy, and if Bascom would wait ten days, he would try to get him back. When Bascom insisted on keeping Cochise's family hostage until then, the chief slit open the tent with his knife and escaped up the mountainside, leaving his relatives behind.

The next day, under a flag of truce, Cochise met with Bascom at a nearby Butterfield mail station. The meeting quickly degenerated. Cochise's warriors took station attendant James F. Wallace hostage and shot two other Butterfield employees, one fatally, before fleeing. That evening, the Indians seized a freight-wagon train entering the pass. They bound eight Mexican freighters to the wagon wheels and burned them to death, and took several other freighters hostage.

On 6 February, Cochise tried negotiating again, offering to exchange Wallace and 16 stolen mules for his 6 relatives. Bascom would not deal without getting Ward's stepson in the bargain, but Cochise did not have the boy. The succeeding days brought more Apache raids, and a few raiders were shot. Bascom called for reinforcements.

On 10 February, help arrived from Fort Buchanan, and the soldiers captured three Coyotero warriors to add to Bascom's captives. On the 14th, dragoons under Lt. Isaiah N. Moore arrived from Fort Breckenridge. They searched the area and found the bodies from the wagon-train massacre. Following circling vultures to the north of the pass, they also found Wallace's body, riddled with lance wounds and horribly mutilated, identifiable only by the fillings in his teeth.

On 19 February, Bascom headed back to Fort Buchanan. At the site of the wagon-train massacre, he hanged three of the Chiricahuas and the three Coyotero prisoners from tree limbs, leaving the bodies dangling as a defiant gesture to Cochise. The other hostages, women and children, were released.

The affair cost the lives of nine Apaches, eight Mexican civilians, and two Butterfield employees, and the wounding of another employee and two soldiers. It was the beginning of 25 years of fighting with the Chiricahuas.[207]

CA. 28 MARCH 1861
STEIN'S PEAK (Lordsburg, New Mexico)

The Bascom affair (see previous entry) brought quick retribution from the Chiricahua Apaches. In late March, a Butterfield stage left Mesilla, New Mexico, for Tucson. The conductor, Anthony Elder, and the driver, a man named Briggs, rode on the outside of the coach; inside were company employee Sam Nealy and two passengers, Michael Neiss and John J. Giddings.

At dawn the stage approached the Stein's Peak station, at the head of Doubtful Canyon, on today's New Mexico–Arizona border. From behind a stone parapet, Cochise and his warriors opened fire on the coach, killing Elder and Briggs. The driverless mules ran for over a mile to the edge of the mountain before the coach capsized. Neiss, who knew Cochise and considered him a great friend, persuaded the Chiricahuas to parley.

Either Cochise had forgotten his friendship with Neiss or the Bascom affair had changed the chief's thinking. Neiss and Giddings, Cochise reported later, "died like poor sick women."[208] Only Nealy put up a good fight, killing three Apaches before succumbing.[209]

14–15 APRIL 1861
VAN DUZEN'S CREEK (Dinsmore, California)

On upper Van Duzen's Creek, near the Mad River, soldiers attacked Indians in reprisal for raids on the soldiers' and settlers' stock. Lt. Joseph B. Collins, 4th Infantry, led a detachment of Company B, 6th Infantry, in a two-day fight against the Indians.

On 14 April, Collins attacked and killed 15 Indians. One soldier was wounded. On 15 April, near Neil's Ranch, Collins attacked again, killing 5 Indians and wounding 3.[210]

23, 26, AND 30 MAY, 2, 8, 16, AND 17 JUNE 1861
EEL AND MAD RIVERS EXPEDITION (Northwestern California)

Lt. Joseph B. Collins, 4th Infantry, led a detachment of 6th Infantry and California Volunteers on a sweep for Indians up the Eel and Mad Rivers and their tributaries. On 23 May, Collins attacked an Indian camp between the head of Larabee Creek and the Eel, killing ten Indians. On the 26th he hit another camp 12 miles farther up Larabee Creek and his men killed four Indians. On 30 May at Keatuck Creek—possibly today's Kekawaka Creek—Collins had a harder fight, but still killed 25 Indians, with only 1 man, packer John Steward, wounded among his own men.

Downriver, near Larabee's Ranch, Collins's men killed 20 Indians on 2 June. Six days later, three miles south of Larabee's Ranch, the soldiers killed four more Indians and wounded one. From there, Collins marched east to the tributaries of the Mad River. At noon on 16 June in the Hettenshaw Valley, he and his men attacked the large rancheria of Chief Lassic's band, whom he described as "probably the most desperate and troublesome Indians in the mountains."[211] The soldiers killed only four Indians; the rest escaped into the nearly impenetrable brush. Volunteer "Cpl." Larabee was wounded.

On 17 June, the soldiers hit another rancheria on the road leading south from Hettenshaw Valley to Round Valley; six Indians were killed and only one escaped. After that fight, Collins called a halt to his operations. He reported having killed 73 Indians, his own force suffering only 2 wounded.[212] Collins wrote, "The number of Indians reported killed and wounded in the several engagements were, of course, all males, competent to bear arms. In no instance have Indians been punished who were supposed to be innocent."[213]

28 MAY, 4, 14, 15, AND 16 JUNE 1861
SOUTH FORK OF THE EEL RIVER (Northwestern California)

Operating out of a camp near Spruce Grove, Lt. James P. Martin, 6th Infantry, with seven enlisted men and six California volunteers, attacked an Indian camp on the South Fork of the Eel River a mile above its mouth. The attack, on 28 May at 11 A.M., resulted in eight Indian men killed and one woman accidentally wounded.

On 4 June, Martin and his men attacked another Indian camp, at Bell Spring on the Eel, killing 16 and wounding a few others. In his report, Martin apologized that, due to darkness, his men accidentally killed 3 women. After returning to his camp at Spruce Grove, Martin left on another scout on 10 June, this time with 11 enlisted men of the 6th Infantry, 6 volunteers, 5 hunters, and 1 interpreter. On the night of 14 June, the party saw two campfires, one on either side of them, and split up to attack both camps.

Half of Martin's party found a rancheria on the South Fork of the Eel, about 15 miles above its junction with the main river, and attacked it, killing seven Indians and wounding one. The other half, which included Martin, found no campfire that night, but the next morning they found a small camp and killed two Indians and wounded one.

Other squads from Martin's camp scoured the surrounding area. On 16 June 11 soldiers and volunteers hit another camp, killing 2 Indians and wounding 3. After Martin's scouting party returned to their own camp on the 16th, the soldiers saw four Indians lurking about. They caught them and killed them as spies.

In all, Martin and his men killed 39 Indians and wounded 8.[214] Martin was not as certain as Collins (see previous entry) that these Indians were hostile. "I do not know positively what depredations, if any, have been committed by the Indians killed by this command," he wrote. "I have no means of finding out whether those that we may come upon are guilty or innocent."[215]

21 JULY 1861
SOUTH FORK OF THE EEL RIVER (Redway, California)

A month after his Indian expedition (see previous entry), Lt. James P. Martin led a small detachment of 6th Infantry, two guides, and one interpreter on an expedition to determine a route from the South Fork of the Eel River to Shelter Cove on the Pacific Coast. Martin's command left their camp on the Mattole River on 20 July. The next day, on the South Fork of the Eel, near present-day Redway, California, they found and attacked a rancheria of about 40 Indians.[216]

"Twelve of the number were killed," reported Martin, "among whom, unfortunately, were two women; the latter were killed through mistake. I do not know positively that these Indians belong to the tribe at Shelter Cove, but I am satisfied that they had committed depredations on the property of white people, because evidence to that effect was discovered before they were fired upon."[217]

21–22 JULY 1861
COOKE'S SPRING (Deming, New Mexico)

After the Civil War began, a group of Unionists abandoned Franklin, Texas (present-day El Paso) and headed for California. The seven well-armed men, under either Freeman Thomas or Emmett Mills—brother of future Union general Anson Mills—were at Cooke's Spring, north of present-day Deming, New Mexico, on the morning of 21 July, when nearly 200 Apache warriors, led by Mangas Coloradas and Cochise, attacked them.[218] At the top of a small hill, the Unionists constructed a stone breastwork and put up a great fight. It was not until the next day that the last two white men fell.

Freighters Alejandro Daguerre and J. J. Thibault found the seven bodies a few days after the fight, along with a penciled note from one of them that described the incident. Indians later said that 40 warriors were slain in the fight. Cochise and his son Taza may have been wounded.

This fight is most likely the same one that other sources say occurred at Doubtful Canyon in April.[219]

11 AUGUST 1861
MAYS'S FIGHT (Marathon, Texas)

Mescalero Apache chief Nicolas and his band frequented the Fort Davis area, occasionally receiving rations but at other times raiding the post's beef herd. On 5 August, Nicolas's band attacked the ranch of Manuel

Musquiz, six miles southeast of the fort. They killed three herders and stole horses and cattle.

A detachment of Capt. James Walker's Company D of Lt. Col. John R. Baylor's 2nd Regiment, Texas Mounted Rifles, was stationed at Fort Davis. Lt. Reuben Mays of Company D took 14 soldiers and civilians to track down the Apache raiders. The Indians' trail led south from the Davis Mountains to the Big Bend country.

On the night of 10 August, camped in a mountain valley, Mays's men heard horses nearby. Quietly, they herded up their own horses, then went to investigate. They found an Indian camp about three miles away, and at sunrise they attacked. Soon Mays and his men discovered they had bitten off more than they could chew. More than 80 Mescalero Apaches put them to flight. The Texans holed up behind a large rock, Mays fighting with a broken arm. His Mexican guide Juan Fernandez, realizing they were trapped, found a way out and brought word back to Fort Davis, but it was too late for a rescue.

Fernandez was the only survivor; 14 soldiers and volunteers were killed. Apache casualties are unknown.[220]

19 AUGUST 1861
SOUTH FORK OF THE PIT RIVER (Likely, California)

On 15 August Lt. John Feilner, Company F, 1st Cavalry, went northeast out of Fort Crook with 27 men of his company to search for stolen cattle. They came to a large valley watered by two creeks. The description in Feilner's report places him in present-day Jess Valley, at the headwaters of the South Fork of the Pit River.

On the evening of 19 August, the cavalrymen came upon a rancheria on a high bluff. According to Feilner, the inhabitants were Goose Lake Indians. The two groups exchanged fire at a distance of over 800 yards. The cavalry attempted to scale the bluffs, but the Indians got away easily. Feilner took about 42 head of cattle and called it quits. He reported one Indian killed and three wounded.[221]

2 SEPTEMBER 1861
GALLINAS MOUNTAINS (Corona, New Mexico)

When Union troops abandoned Fort Stanton to consolidate their forces in the face of the Confederate invasion, Confederate Lt. Col. John R. Baylor sent a detachment of Company D, 2nd Texas Mounted Rifles, to occupy the place, with Lt. John R. Pulliam in command. Pulliam sent a squad of four men—T. G. Pemberton, Joseph V. Mosse, Joseph Emmahacker, and Floyd A. Sanders—to the Gallinas Mountains, 75 miles northwest of the fort, to watch for Union forces.

Pulliam had instructed the four soldiers to reach a certain spring on the morning of the second day, water the horses, fill up their canteens, and move on, because the spring was a popular watering hole for Indians. Convinced they were in no danger, however, the squad made a camp about 100 yards from the spring, in a pine grove easily visible from the trail.

While the soldiers cooked breakfast, they saw three Indians running over an adjoining hill. They immediately saddled up their horses, but a shower of arrows stopped their departure. Soon they were surrounded by an overwhelming force of Mescalero Apaches. Each soldier took up a position behind a tree and fired his revolver. Within two hours, three of the four—Emmahacker, Pemberton, and Mosse—were dead. The survivor, Sanders, jumped on his horse and galloped down an almost vertical mountain amid flying arrows. His attackers followed him for ten miles before he finally eluded them, and he safely reached Fort Stanton.[222]

9 SEPTEMBER 1861
PLACITAS (Lincoln, New Mexico)

When Floyd A. Sanders reached Fort Stanton after the Gallinas Mountains attack (see previous entry), Lt. John R. Pulliam ordered 14 men to head to the scene of the fight. In the meantime, perhaps emboldened by their easy victory, Mescalero Apaches attacked the small village of Placitas (present-day Lincoln, New Mexico), about ten miles southeast of Fort Stanton. Pulliam and 15 men of Company D, 2nd Texas Mounted Rifles, rode to the rescue and, with no casualties of their own, managed to kill five raiders in a running fight.

After these incidents, Lt. Col. John R. Baylor decided he could not send enough troops to Fort Stanton to cope with the Indians in the area, and he ordered his men to abandon the post.[223]

13 SEPTEMBER 1861
FORT FAUNTLEROY (Fort Wingate, New Mexico)

Occasionally, Navajos gathered at Fort Fauntleroy, a Union post established in August 1860 at Ojo del Oso, at the north end of the Zuni Mountains, to wager money and goods on horse races.[224] On 13 September 1861, a race degenerated into a fight when the soldiers' horse won and the Indians cried foul. A warrior scuffled with a sentry, and soldiers fired their muskets. Lt. Col. Manuel Chavez of the 2nd New Mexico Volunteers, believing the place was being attacked, brought out his howitzers. Five shell bursts killed about a dozen Navajos, causing the enraged Indians to withdraw.

In December, the Union army abandoned the fort. The Navajos retaliated for the September fight with raids on settlers, mainly along the Rio Grande.[225]

—1862—

3 MARCH 1862
COMANCHE CANYON (Albuquerque, New Mexico)

Detachments of Companies C and K, 3rd Cavalry, were en route from Fort Craig to Fort Union when, on the road between Peralta and Antelope Springs, in Comanche Canyon, Indians surprised them. The warriors killed one soldier from Company C and wounded the officer in charge, Sgt. (Acting Lt.) Richard Wall, as well as two men from Company C and two from Company K. There were no Indian casualties.[226]

6 APRIL 1862
FORT ANDERSON (Blue Lake, California)

Capt. Charles D. Douglas was commander at Fort Anderson, on the Redwood River about 15 miles east of present-day Arcata, California. With a detachment of Company F, 2nd California Infantry, Douglas engaged a band of Hoopa Indians in the hills a mile east of the post.

With Lt. Parish B. Johnson and five soldiers standing by, Douglas took seven soldiers directly up the mountain, where he found six to eight Hoopas burning a supply train they had attacked. Douglas's men killed one of the Indians and wounded two. The wounded warriors escaped with the others. The dead Hoopa had a U.S. government rifle, ammunition, and tobacco.[227]

9 APRIL 1862
BISHOP'S CREEK (Bishop, California)

Lt. Col. George S. Evans, 2nd California Cavalry, and 33 men of Company D marched north from Los Angeles to the Owens Lake Valley to investigate recent Indian depredations. The Owens Valley Indians had killed a man named Taylor and another known as Yank and had burned every house in the lower Owens Lake Valley. On 6 April the soldiers found and buried two more murdered settlers, a Mr. Talman and a Mr. Hanson.

According to the locals, more than 400 Indians lived in the valley, prompting Evans to ask for assistance. A "Col." Mayfield and 40 civilians volunteered. Near present-day Bishop, California, Evans and Mayfield met up with Lt. H. Noble of Company A, 2nd California Cavalry, and 50 men from Fort Churchill. Evans's force now numbered about 120 men.

On 9 April, the party left Bishop's Creek at sunup and traveled three miles to a canyon. When Evans's scouts entered the canyon, Indians attacked them, killing one, a Pvt. Gillespie of Company A, and wounding another, a Cpl. Harris. Dismounting his men, Evans ordered Lts. Noble and Oliver to ascend a point on the left with 40 men while he took Lt. French and 40 men to the right, leaving the others to guard the stock at the canyon's mouth.

To Evans's surprise, the Indians—comprising Owens Rivers, Tulares, Monos, and Paiutes—numbered more than 600. Armed with good guns, the warriors were positioned among the rocks up to the cliff tops. Evans and his men toiled for two hours to reach their foe, but the Indians simply fired down on them while climbing higher. "I saw that it would be madness and no less than murder to attempt to go any farther," Evans wrote later.[228] He was forced to fall back.

Evans camped for the night at Bishop's Creek. Then, almost out of provisions, he marched his men back to Los Angeles. Most of the settlers in the area left at the same time.

In addition to Gillespie, Mayfield was killed in the canyon; Harris was the only soldier reported wounded. No Indian casualties were reported.[229]

26 APRIL 1862
FORT BAKER (Bridgeville, California)

From Fort Baker, about 25 miles upstream from Hydesville, California, on Van Duzen's Fork, Capt. Thomas E. Ketcham and soldiers from Company A, 3rd California Infantry, attacked a rancheria south of the post. The soldiers killed four Indians, including one woman who was shot accidentally. Ketcham returned to the fort with 24 prisoners—2 men and the rest women and children.

On the same day, Lt. John F. Staples and a detachment of the same company surprised another large band of Indians, killing 15 and taking 40 prisoners, 3 of whom, unable to travel, they left behind.[230]

14 MAY 1862
ANGEL'S RANCH (Northwestern California)

At daybreak on 14 May, on a scout on the North Fork of the Mad River, Lt. Henry Flynn and 15 men of Company E, 2nd California Infantry, found a rancheria at Angel's Ranch. The Indians had spotted Flynn first, however, and crossed the river on their fish dam, cutting it away behind them so the soldiers could not follow. The two sides fought at long range for about an hour. Finally the Indians retreated, and Flynn did not pursue them, as he had counted about 150 of them.

Flynn reported six Indians killed in the fight with no losses of his own. He destroyed all the Indians' provisions, beds, and clothing, and found papers linking the Indians to the murder of a settler named Bates.[231]

31 MAY 1862
EEL RIVER (Northwestern California)

Lt. John F. Staples left Fort Baker on 29 May with a detachment of 20 men of Company A, 3rd California Infantry, on a scout for Indians. On 31 May, the soldiers headed southwest to the Eel River. One mile upriver, they discovered about 30 Indians also traveling up the river. Rushing across a small prairie, Staples attacked them, killing one man and capturing 12 women and children. He took his prisoners back to Fort Baker.[232]

6 JUNE 1862
DALEY'S FERRY (Arcata, California)

At about 4 P.M. on 6 June, approximately 50 Indians attacked the lodging house at Daley's Ferry on the Mad River, five miles from Arcata, California. Only two soldiers guarded the inn, since it was so near town and on a public highway. Both soldiers were outside with owner Daley and his family when the Indians began to fire. One of them, Pvt. Joseph N. Bacon, Company I, was wounded in the first volley, but he and his comrade, Pvt. Henry H. Wyatt, Company H, 2nd California Infantry, rushed into the house and returned fire from the windows.

Daley also ran to the house, leaving his family behind, then, seizing his rifle, fled to his boat on the river. The soldiers directed the women and children to the boat, staying behind to keep the Indians at bay. When the family reached the boat, the soldiers, both wounded, made a run for it. Wyatt got to the boat while Bacon concealed himself behind a log in the brush. Bacon counted 27 Indians entering the house, which unfortuately was still occupied by a hired man and Mrs. Daley's five-year-old nephew. The Indians pillaged the house and set it on fire, killed the hired man, and captured the boy.

Meanwhile about 20 more Indians, on the opposite bank, fired on the party in the boat. Three balls struck and killed Mrs. Daley's mother. Mrs. Daley was wounded in the arm, and Pvt. Wyatt was wounded again. Forced ashore, the whites ran into the brush. Mrs. Daley and two of the children fell down exhausted; her husband threw their infant into the bushes and made for Arcata.

When the Indians caught up, they took Mrs. Daley's rings and purse, but they did not kill the "white squaw." She continued on with her children until rescued by Arcata residents. The wounded soldiers, also rescued and taken to Fort Humboldt, were later cited for admirable coolness and bravery under fire.[233]

7 JUNE 1862
MATTOLE VALLEY (Petrolia, California)

Lt. Charles G. Hubbard, Company K, 2nd California Infantry, took 12 soldiers and 7 volunteers on a scout in the Mattole Valley, about 50 miles south of Fort Humboldt. On the evening of 7 June, he and his men attacked a camp of 20 Indians on a small branch of the Mattole River. They killed or mortally wounded six of the camp's inhabitants and took six prisoners; the rest escaped in the darkness. Two of the dead were reputed to be some of the most dangerous Indians in that country.

The soldiers also recognized one of the prisoners, a 12-year-old boy, as having stolen arms and ammunition from them before. Hubbard spared the boy's life, but he had great difficulty keeping the other Indians from killing him, since the boy had a $100 reward on his scalp.[234]

Hubbard disapproved of slaughtering Indians: "If the Indians are hostile they will always be so until some stringent measures are taken to protect them, and to wipe out the perpetrators of these most horrible crimes against humanity."[235]

24 JUNE 1862
OWENS LAKE (Lone Pine, California)

Lt. Col. George S. Evans returned to Owens Valley after his failed April expedition (see Bishop's Creek, 9 April). A forced march of 35 miles on 23 June brought Evans and more than 120 men of Companies D, G, and I, 2nd California Cavalry, to the southern shore of Owens Lake, where they attacked a party of Indians, killing two men and capturing two men, seven women, and two children.[236]

15–16 JULY 1862
APACHE PASS (Fort Bowie, Arizona)

After the Confederate invasion of New Mexico, Union Brig. Gen. James H. Carleton marched his brigade of 1,800 California soldiers east to catch the Rebels on the Rio Grande. As the advance guard—126 men of the 1st California Infantry, a detachment of cavalry under Capt. Thomas Roberts, 2 howitzers, and 22 wagons—labored up the western approach to the springs at Apache Pass, between the Chiricahua and Dos Cabezas Mountains, several hundred Apache warriors waited.

Near the springs, the warriors opened fire on the troops from the rocks above. Unable to reach their assailants, the soldiers had no choice but to blast the Indians out of the rocks. Roberts opened up with his two howitzers. Faced with exploding shells and flying rock fragments, the Indians fell back, and Roberts secured the springs.

Roberts sent six horsemen back to Capt. John C. Cremony, who waited at Dragoon Springs with the rest of the cavalry and the supply wagons. On the way, the horsemen ran into more Apaches. One of the soldiers, Pvt. John Teal, lagged behind, and the Indians cut him off from the others and shot his horse. Laying down beside his dying animal, Teal resolved to take at least one Apache with him. With a breech-loader and a pistol, he kept up a steady fusillade, preventing the Indians from rushing him. Teal shot one tall Apache in the chest, and it caused much commotion—the Indians took the warrior away and soon disappeared completely. Teal did not know it, but he had desperately wounded the great Apache leader Mangas Coloradas. The soldier picked up his saddle, bridle, and blanket and walked

Apache Pass (Arizona), from the Apache positions;
the howitzers were fired from the center of the valley.

eight miles to Dragoon Springs, meeting Cremony just before he set out
for Apache Pass.

When they arrived at the pass the next morning, Cremony and his men
found the Apaches had reoccupied the cliffs. Once again, the artillery blasted
them, clearing the path to the springs. The soldiers filled their canteens
and departed on 17 July.

The two-day battle cost Roberts and Cremony two men; two others
were wounded. Some of the men reported more than 60 Indians killed,
but, more realistically, Roberts estimated 9 slain and perhaps 12 wounded.[237]

28 JULY 1862
WHITNEY'S RANCH (Northwestern California)

When a large band of Indians attacked Whitney's Ranch, on Redwood
Creek four miles downriver from Fort Anderson, on 28 July, Whitney was
with two hired men, an Indian boy, and three soldiers from Company F,
2nd California Infantry. The Indians killed one hired man, named Mitchell,
and one soldier, Pvt. Campbell, and they mortally wounded Whitney,
taking all their guns. The surviving soldiers, a Cpl. Kennedy and a Pvt. Lee,

Massacre Rocks (Idaho)

and the Indian boy bravely held the house (50 bullet holes were later counted), returning fire until the Indians departed at the approach of Capt. Charles D. Douglas with 20 men of the 2nd California Infantry. The Indian losses were not known.[238]

9–AUGUST 1862
MASSACRE ROCKS (Neeley, Idaho)

Approximately 150 Shoshones and Bannocks fell upon several wagon trains on the Oregon Trail, along the Snake River between American Falls and Massacre Rocks. In the first attack, about half a mile east of the rocks, the Indians swept through the wagons of the Smart train and killed two emigrants. Continuing east two miles, the warriors hit the Adams train, killing three more men and badly wounding a woman, Elizabeth Adams.

That night, the Indians pulled away as the Kennedy train joined the survivors of the two attacks. With 86 wagons, the emigrants formed a corral. In the morning, John K. Kennedy led out 40 well-armed, mounted men to recover the stolen stock. The emigrants found the Indian camp, with nearly 300 Indians, five miles south. In the recovery attempt, Kennedy lost three men and a few more were wounded, Kennedy himself mortally. The Indians chased Kennedy and his men back to the river, but by then another train, the Wilson party, had come up, adding 46 wagons to the defense. The Indians chose not to attack, and the combined trains moved on.

Including the subsequent deaths of Kennedy and Elizabeth Adams, emigrant fatalities totaled ten, with nine wounded.[239]

14 AUGUST 1862
GRANDE RONDE PRAIRIE (LaGrande, Oregon)

Capt. George B. Curry took 30 men of Company E, 1st Oregon Cavalry, from Fort Walla Walla to the Grande Ronde Prairie to investigate Cayuse depredations on settlers, hoping to arrest the leaders of the attacks. He ordered ten men to remain at the Umatilla Reservation and continued on. In the Grande Ronde, the settlers described several instances in which Cayuse chiefs Tenounis and Wainicut-hi-hi threatened to kill them if they didn't leave.

Making a night ride, Curry and his soldiers surrounded Tenounis's lodge and held the chief hostage in his tent. The next morning, intending to take Tenounis to Fort Walla Walla for questioning, Curry sent a boy out for horses. But instead of horses, 15 or more Cayuses showed up at the tent. After arguing with the Indians, Curry ordered his men to tie up Tenounis and Wainicut-hi-hi. Just then the two chiefs sprang up, seizing the arms they had concealed in their blankets. Tenounis leveled his gun, but Curry fired first and struck him in the breast. Wainicut-hi-hi was also killed in the tent. Outside, the warriors fired on the soldiers, who were drawn up in a line in front of the lodge. The soldiers returned fire, killing two Cayuses. The remaining Indians fled into the brush.[240]

17 AUGUST–23 SEPTEMBER 1862
MINNESOTA SIOUX UPRISING (Southwestern Minnesota)

The Minnesota Sioux Uprising of 1862 was the result, generally, of unpaid annuities, unscrupulous traders, and poor diplomacy. It began after an incident on 17 August, when four Sioux hunters attacked a group of white settlers near Acton, Minnesota, killing several of them. That night, the four told other Sioux at the Redwood Indian Agency what they had done, and some hot-tempered Mdewakanton Sioux convinced the rest that, now that blood had been spilled, war was the only answer. Soon after the uprising began, wavering Sioux bands, including the Wahpeton and Sisseton Sioux, were drawn into the bloodletting.

The killings, which had mostly subsided by the end of August, provoked months of white reprisals. The exact number of whites massacred is unknown, but according to Minnesota state records, 644 persons were killed and 23 Minnesota counties were virtually depopulated. The uprising was one catalyst for the 1863–64 Dakota (Sioux) Indian campaigns.

The major incidents of the uprising are described individually in succeeding entries.

18 AUGUST 1862
REDWOOD AGENCY (Morton, Minnesota)

As soon as the Sioux decided to wage a major rebellion against the whites (see previous entry), the attacks began. Early the next morning at the Redwood Agency, Sioux warriors slew two dozen people, mostly traders and government employees. Among them was trader Andrew J. Myrick, who, upon hearing of the Indians starving, once sneered, "If they're hungry, let them eat grass for all I care."[241] The Sioux killed Myrick in front of his store and stuffed his mouth with grass.

From there, Sioux attacked settlers on farms and in villages up and down the Minnesota River, slaughtering men and taking women and children captive. On the first day alone, they killed about 200 settlers, especially in Renville County and the Lake Shetek area.[242]

18 AUGUST 1862
LOWER SIOUX FERRY (Morton, Minnesota)

Immediately after the attack at the Redwood Agency (see previous entry), survivors began to pour into Fort Ridgely, 13 miles away. Capt. John Marsh, stationed there with the 5th Minnesota Infantry, sent a messenger to Fort Snelling to get help. He then took 46 men and interpreter Peter Quinn and marched to Lower Sioux Ferry, on the north bank of the Minnesota River, across the river from the agency.

At the ferry, White Dog, a Santee Sioux whom Marsh had seen before at the fort, motioned to Marsh for a parley. While they talked, other Santees crept up around the soldiers. At a signal from White Dog, 100 muskets opened fire, killing half a dozen soldiers and Quinn. More gunfire came from across the river. Marsh ordered a volley, then a retreat into some timber.

For over an hour, Marsh and his men held off the warriors as they slowly retreated downriver toward Fort Ridgely. Then, in an attempt to lead his men to swim across the river, the captain drowned in the swift current. The 14 leaderless soldiers, two of them wounded, made their way back to the fort, staggering in late that night. Of the 48 soldiers who had gone out that day, 34 were killed. The Indians lost perhaps 10 men.[243]

19 AND 23 AUGUST 1862
NEW ULM (New Ulm, Minnesota)

After the Minnesota Sioux Uprising began (see previous entries), Chief Little Crow of the Mdewakanton Santee band wanted to attack Fort Ridgely, but a number of his council members thought the town of New Ulm, having more supplies, food, and women, made a better target. The bands split; Little Crow led one party to the fort, while the other headed to New Ulm.

Hearing that a force of Sioux warriors was headed for their town, New Ulm residents Charles Roos and Jacob Nix organized a militia of 44 men with firearms, and a reserve unit armed with pistols, axes, and pitchforks. Another 15 men stayed at their homes to defend their families. The militia made barricades in the town center.

At 3 P.M. the Sioux warriors charged New Ulm from the south, then from the northwest. But the attackers, few in number, essentially leaderless, and hampered by a severe thunderstorm, fell back after an hour and a half. In the fight, 5 white defenders and a 13-year-old girl were killed and 5 were wounded; Indian losses were approximately the same. Later, a party of 16 whites were out searching for survivors when Mdewakantons jumped them and killed 11 of them.

That evening about 100 volunteers arrived in New Ulm under Judge Charles E. Flandreau, an honorary colonel. Over the next two days, another 300 volunteers and 1,000 refugees arrived from settlements to the east. On 23 August, after being repulsed at Fort Ridgely (see next entry), Little Crow and his followers appeared at New Ulm and surrounded the town.

Hoping to keep the attackers away from the town's outer buildings, Flandreau went out to meet the advancing warriors on the prairie. But when the Indians charged, the judge's raw volunteers ran back to the barricades in the center of town. The Indians, however, fearing a trap, did not rush straight after them. Instead, Little Crow decided to set fires, hoping to blind the defenders with smoke so his warriors could close in. The plan failed and the defenders held.

Late in the afternoon, Little Crow began to fear he would not gain the town by nightfall. In a last effort, he assembled 60 warriors by the river for one swift charge up Main Street. Flandreau, seeing them gathering, charged first with 60 volunteers. This time the Sioux broke and ran. Now beyond town, however, Flandreau and his men were in an exposed position. To prevent the Indians from occupying the unprotected houses on the outer edges of town, Flandreau ordered 40 of them burned. By sunset, Little Crow knew the fight was over and pulled back.

The Sioux had killed 32 white defenders and wounded over 60. About 100 of their warriors were killed or wounded. About 190 buildings burned.[244]

20 AND 22 AUGUST 1862
FORT RIDGELY (Fort Ridgely, Minnesota)

When Capt. John Marsh left Fort Ridgely on 18 August to respond to the Sioux attack on the Redwood Agency that morning (see Lower Sioux Ferry), he left behind Lt. Thomas P. Gere and about 30 men to guard the

Fort Ridgely (Minnesota)

fort. As reports of further attacks poured in, Gere wondered nervously how he could defend the post with so few soldiers. On 19 August, Lt. Timothy J. Sheehan brought reinforcements, then another detachment arrived. Now with 180 soldiers, as well as about 250 civilian refugees, the fort stood a chance of survival.

On 20 August, Chief Little Crow rode up to the fort alone and demanded a talk. It was only a ruse, however; at the appointed moment about 400 Santees burst from the trees opposite the fort. They soon broke through the first line of defense on the northern perimeter of the fort, a row of log houses.

Sheehan rallied his men on the parade ground, but as the Indians prepared for another charge, the volunteers quailed. Meanwhile, Sgt. John Jones was feverishly teaching some infantrymen how to fire artillery. They wheeled six old howitzers into place and loaded them. Just as Sheehan's line began to melt, Jones ordered his men to fire as rapidly as possible into the center of the Indians. The old guns belched out canister and solid shot. The Sioux wavered and, at the third salvo, broke—they could face the musketry but feared the "wagon guns." Jones had saved the day.

Birch Coulee (Minnesota), near soldiers' position

On 22 August, Little Crow was back at the fort with almost 800 warriors. Meanwhile the soldiers had repaired damage, built up defenses, and covered every angle of approach with their six trump howitzers. Indeed, the Indians attacked from all sides. In the southwest corner of the fort, Chief Mankato's warriors got into the buildings and set fire to haystacks and woodpiles. Cannon fire blasted the buildings, scattering the Indians back onto the prairie. The soldiers kept up their repeated artillery blasts. Little Crow, realizing he could not take the fort, called off the attack.

For all the ferocity of the attacks at Fort Ridgely, only 5 soldiers were killed and 22 were wounded. Soldiers found about 100 Indian graves in the woods and estimated they had wounded about the same number.[245]

It was not yet apparent, but with their defeats at Fort Ridgely and New Ulm, the Sioux had lost their war.

31 AUGUST 1862
DEAD MAN'S HOLE (Valentine, Texas)

After Lt. Edmond D. Shirland and a detachment of 20 Union troops from Company B, 1st California Cavalry, followed some retreating Confederates to San Antonio, they marched to abandoned Fort Davis, flew the Union flag over it for a day, then set out to return to Fort Bliss. The detachment stopped for the night at Dead Man's Hole, near present-day Valentine, Texas.

The next morning the soldiers had ridden about ten miles when a Mescalero Apache appeared with a white flag. Five others followed, all mounted. Shirland tried to talk with them, but they did not respond. About 30 more mounted Mescaleros arrived, and Shirland's men could see another party of warriors approaching on foot. Perceiving that the mounted Mescaleros were simply waiting for the footmen to arrive before surrounding the soldiers, Shirland and his men rode away from them. The mounted Indians pursued for a time in a running fight, then broke off the chase.

The soldiers killed 4 Mescaleros and wounded perhaps 20 more. Two troopers were wounded.[246]

2–3 SEPTEMBER 1862
BIRCH COULEE (Morton, Minnesota)

Minnesota's first governor, Henry H. Sibley, was commissioned colonel of the state militia and given the task of quashing the Minnesota Sioux Uprising. Sibley gathered 1,500 men, including the newly organized 6th Minnesota Infantry, and moved slowly up the Minnesota River, relieving the defenders of New Ulm and Fort Ridgely (see New Ulm, 19 and 23 August, and Fort Ridgely, 20 and 22 August).

Sibley drilled his volunteers at Fort Ridgely, then sent Maj. Joseph R. Brown, Capt. Hiram P. Grant, and 160 men upriver toward the Redwood Agency to bury early victims of the uprising and pick up any survivors. The party of teamsters, civilians, and a military escort had buried 50 bodies by the time they reached Lower Sioux Ferry. There they found 33 more dead from Capt. Marsh's command (see Lower Sioux Ferry, 18 August); beyond that, they buried about 50 more. Preparing to turn back, they camped on the night of 1 September at Birch Coulee, not far from the agency.

During the night, about 200 warriors under Santee Sioux chiefs Mankato, Big Eagle, and Gray Bird followed the river downstream to see what Grant's command was up to. They surrounded the soldiers' camp, bursting in at 4 A.M. on 2 September and killing nearly all the pickets before the others were roused. As the groggy men rolled out of their bedding, Grant bellowed, "Lay on your bellies and shoot, goddamn you!"[247]

The soldiers formed a perimeter as quickly as possible and, remarkably, held off the assault. The army supply wagons were damaged in the crossfire, and ultimately all 87 horses tied to them were killed. Justina Krieger, a recently rescued refugee curled up in one of the wagons, somehow survived the blasts. As the day wore on and Grant's men ran low on ammunition, they opened the reserve to find only .62-caliber bullets for their .58-caliber rifles. They had to whittle the bullets down to fit into their gun barrels. In addition, they had only one bucket of water and one head of cabbage to share among more than 100 people.

Back at Fort Ridgely, Sibley heard the faint sounds of gunfire. He sent out a relief party under Col. Samuel McPhail with 240 men and 2 howitzers. Three miles from Birch Coulee, McPhail ran into a large group of Sioux, including warriors from Big Eagle's band. Deciding there were too many Indians to fight, McPhail had the men fire the howitzers, then pulled back. Big Eagle's men then returned to the fight with Grant, laughingly reporting that they had scared the white soldiers away. Sibley sent out another 1,000 men to reinforce Grant.

At sunrise on 3 September, a Sioux invited the whites to surrender and the mixed-bloods among them to join the Indians. Trader Joe Coursolle and the other mixed-bloods spat at the suggestion. The fight resumed. The Santees were closing in, and Grant's command was down to five rounds per man when Sibley's relief force finally appeared in the east, a sight the Indians described as "three miles of white men."[248]

The remnants of Grant's command were saved, but the Santees had gained some revenge for their defeats at Fort Ridgely and New Ulm. Only 2 warriors were killed and 4 were wounded in the fight, while 24 whites were killed and 67 were wounded. The Indians also embarrassed Sibley in their resistence to his attempt at subjugation and angered the people of Minnesota against him. Sibley tendered his resignation but the army did not accept it. He would receive more men and supplies, and continue on.[249]

3 SEPTEMBER 1862
HUTCHINSON (Hutchinson, Minnesota)

While Chiefs Mankato, Big Eagle, and Gray Bird were fighting Capt. Hiram P. Grant at Birch Coulee (see previous entry), Little Crow, his half-brother White Spider, and Walker Among Sacred Stones led 110 warriors northeast to attack more settlements. The Santees camped near Acton, Minnesota, and prepared to attack the towns of Forest City and Hutchinson the next day.

Camped nearby were 55 green recruits of the 10th Minnesota Infantry under Capt. Richard Strout, en route to defend Forest City. At 3 A.M. on 3 September, a messenger from Forest City found Strout and reported an Indian sighting in the area. Strout alerted the troops. Like Grant's men, Strout's soldiers had been issued the wrong size of bullets and had to whittle them down to fit their gun barrels.

Later that morning, marching north for Forest City, the soldiers ran into a line of Indians led by White Spider. The recruits did well at first, advancing in a skirmish line, until Walker Among Sacred Stones arrived and attacked from the rear. The soldiers fixed their bayonets and charged back through the lines, leaving casualties and supplies behind as they hurried south to Hutchinson. Some Santees pursued them for the eight miles to town then backed off.

The Sioux suffered few casualties and killed 6 whites and wounded 23. The next day, splitting their force, they attacked Forest City and Hutchinson, but both towns, well prepared, rebuffed the smaller groups with ease.[250]

3 AND 6 SEPTEMBER 1862
FORT ABERCROMBIE (Abercrombie, North Dakota)

After the failed attacks at Fort Ridgely (see 20 and 22 August) and elsewhere, many Sioux vacated the Minnesota River area, and the uprising spread outward. On 3 September, they attacked Fort Abercrombie, on the west bank of the Red River of the North, 25 miles south of present-day Fargo, North Dakota. During the six-hour fight, Company D of the 5th Minnesota Infantry held the post without casualties. On 6 September the Indians struck again, gaining possession of some outbuildings until three artillery pieces drove them away.

Two soldiers were killed and two were wounded in the second fight. The Sioux lost about 20 warriors in total.[251]

8 SEPTEMBER 1862
REDWOOD CREEK (Northwest California)

On 7 September Lt. William H. Noyes, Company F, 2nd California Infantry, left Fort Anderson on a scout with 19 men of his company, a guide, and a packer. The next morning, the men were struggling up a long, steep slope when Indians opened up from above with heavy musket fire, killing several mules and wounding a sergeant named Connell in the foot.

A barricade of rocks protected the Indians all along the ridge. Judging the Indians to have three times more men than he did, Noyes fell back. The Indians followed, capturing two pack mules loaded with rations. After wounding one Indian, the soldiers retreated 35 miles back to the fort.[252]

12 SEPTEMBER 1862
CITY OF ROCKS (Almo, Idaho)

A wagon train of 15 men under Charles McBride and John Andrews, returning from California to the States, camped near City of Rocks on the Raft River, near today's Utah-Idaho border. On the morning of 12 September, they rode into a camp just ahead of them, thinking it was that of another emigrant train. Instead it was a village of Shoshones and Bannocks. At first, the Indians appeared friendly, and the whites began negotiating for cattle. But when the tribesmen told the whites they could buy all the beef they wanted if they would bring all their men into the village, the travelers suspected treachery and moved on.

Soon, about 40 warriors ambushed them. McBride and Andrews kept the train rolling, and the fight stretched for 20 miles. Finally the white men took refuge behind rocks along Cassia Creek near the Raft River. They drove the warriors off, but lost six men in the process, with two wounded. In the moonlight that night, the nine survivors crept away, to endure five days without food before making it to the Mormon settlement at Box Elder.[253]

23 SEPTEMBER 1862
WOOD LAKE (Wood Lake, Minnesota)
Col. Henry H. Sibley waited two weeks before retaliating for the Sioux ambush at Birch Coulee (see 2–3 September), and the delay had Minnesota settlers calling for his head. On 19 September he moved out of Fort Ridgely with a large force: 9 companies of the 6th Minnesota Infantry, 5 companies of the 7th, 1 company of the 9th, and 270 men of the veteran 3rd, as well as 38 mounted men of the Renville Rangers, 28 other mounted civilians, and 16 artillerymen, for a total of 1,619 fighters.

Sibley advanced toward Wood Lake, up the Minnesota River from the Yellow Medicine Agency. Meanwhile, several Santee Sioux bands, camped nearby, heatedly debated whether to fight, surrender, or flee. Due to the dissension, Chief Little Crow could gather only 740 warriors to stay and fight. Since the Indians' previous all-out assaults had failed, he organized an ambush along the road he knew Sibley would follow.

Early on 23 September, Company G of the 3rd Minnesota Infantry foraged in the Santees' fields, setting off the trap prematurely. Suddenly 200 Indians popped up and began firing. Company G held on while the rest of the 3rd rushed forward. But the Indians had surprised the soldiers and their leaders, and soon, rattled by confusing bugle calls, they began to retreat. Just then, the Renville Rangers galloped up and stabilized the line, giving the rest of Sibley's men time to deploy. The various companies repelled Sioux charges on the left and right while pushing effectively from the center.

Col. William R. Marshall brought up five companies of the 6th Minnesota just in time to repel an Indian charge from the ravine on the right. With two companies of the 6th, Maj. R. N. McLaren parried another thrust on the left. In the center, the 3rd made a push, while the 6th and 7th joined in on the flanks. It was all over in about two hours.

Many of Little Crow's warriors were posted farther up the road, waiting for the ambush, so only perhaps half of the chief's force were in the fight. The Indians lost 25 warriors; 40 were wounded. A cannonball killed Chief Mankato. Sibley lost 7 of his men and 34 were wounded. Vengeful soldiers scalped some of the Santee dead.

This was the final battle of the Minnesota Sioux Uprising. Little Crow turned his captives over to the faction of Santees who wanted peace, then fled northwest with 200 warriors. Sibley received 269 captives from the peaceful Santees at a site he christened Camp Release. Over the next two weeks, about 2,000 Sioux surrendered.[254]

9–15 OCTOBER 1862
HUMBOLDT EXPEDITION (Northeastern Nevada)

At the end of September, after undocumented reports that Indians had murdered up to 23 emigrants at Gravelly Ford on the Humboldt River earlier that month, two companies of 2nd California Cavalry left Fort Ruby in northeastern Nevada on a sweep to the north, looking for hostile Indians. Company H, under Maj. Edward McGarry, joined Company K, led by Capt. Samuel P. Smith, and searched down the South Fork of the Humboldt River. McGarry had orders from Col. Patrick E. Connor, commander at Fort Ruby, to "destroy every male Indian whom you may encounter."[255] They arrived on 5 October at Gravelly Ford on the Humboldt, near present-day Beowawe, Nevada, then turned back upstream.

On 9 October soldiers captured three Indians, probably Paiutes. McGarry took their weapons and arrested them. Later they broke free, but the soldiers fired after them and wounded all three. Fearing they would escape again, McGarry ordered the guard to kill them. On 11 October, about ten miles upstream of McGarry, Smith caught 14 more Indians. They, too, broke free, jumping into the Humboldt River. Smith and his men fired after them, killing nine. Three succeeded in escaping and two women were caught and brought back to camp. By the end of the next day, soldiers had captured eight more Indians, including a woman and a child.

On 13 October, McGarry let two of the captive warriors go with the understanding that they would return with the Indians who had murdered the emigrants. If they did not come back that night, he told them, he would kill the other prisoners. The two did not return. McGarry shot the four remaining Indian men and released the captive women and child to spread the word that if the Indians did not stop killing emigrants, he would be back the following summer and destroy them all. Two days later, McGarry's soldiers captured eight more Indians, whom they shot in escape attempts.

The troops continued east, arriving at Camp Douglas, outside Salt Lake City, on 28 October. They had killed a total of 24 Indians on the expedition.[256]

23–24 OCTOBER 1862
FORT COBB (Fort Cobb, Oklahoma)

The Confederates took over Fort Cobb on the Washita River during the Civil War, and the Indian agents appointed by the Confederates did not make friends of the tribes in the area. The Indians developed a particular dislike for agent Mathew Leeper, and the Shawnees, Delawares, Osages, and

Christopher "Kit" Carson
—Courtesy Denver Public Library,
Western History Department

other tribes sympathized with the Union. In addition, none of these Indians liked the Tonkawas, who practiced cannibalism.

After two Tonkawas murdered and ate a Caddo boy, the other tribes, led by Ben Simon, took action against all of their enemies in one night. First, raiders swooped down on the agency at Fort Cobb, shooting about ten of the white employees and throwing them into burning buildings. The agent Leeper managed to climb out a window and escape on a horse. Interpreter Horace Jones also jumped out a window and fled.

Downstream from the agency, the Tonkawas heard the uproar and ran to the nearby town of Anadarko, where they thought they would be safe. The other tribes pursued them, however, surrounded their camp, and massacred almost all of them.[257]

CA. 25 OCTOBER 1862
GRAYDON AFFAIR (Fort Stanton, New Mexico)

In 1861, at the start of the Civil War, Union troops abandoned Fort Stanton and other southwestern forts, and Mescalero Apaches in the vicinity stepped up their raiding activities. To get the Indians back in line, in the fall of 1862 Brig. Gen. James H. Carleton directed Kit Carson, now commissioned by the army as colonel of the New Mexico volunteers, to take five companies of the 1st New Mexico Cavalry and reoccupy the fort. One company of Carson's command was to garrison Fort Stanton while the others were to hunt the Mescaleros down. Carleton's orders of 12 October were: "All Indian men of that tribe are to be killed whenever and wherever you can find them."[258] He added, however, that if the Mescaleros begged for peace, their chiefs and 20 principal men must come to Santa Fe to talk.

Carson and his men arrived at the fort on 26 October, but before they had even unfurled the flag Carson learned that Capt. James Graydon and his advance company had run into a band of Mescaleros heading for Santa Fe. The Indians had signed for peace and a parley, but Graydon ordered his troops to fire, killing Chiefs Manuelito and Jose Largo, four other warriors, and a woman. Then, in a running pursuit, the cavalry killed 5 more warriors, wounded 20, and took 17 horses and mules. As soon as Carson arrived, other Mescalero bands began to surrender at the fort.

Word spread that Graydon had lured Manuelito's band into a trap with the help of civilian Charles Beach, who received some of the horses as booty. Carleton wrote to Carson, saying that if the fight had not been "fair and open," Carson should return the stock to the Mescaleros and remove Beach from the country. The incident grew increasingly controversial. Graydon was accused of plying the Indians with liquor then shooting them down, a scenario the captain denied.

J. W. Whitlock, a former surgeon, published the accusations against Graydon in the *Santa Fe Gazette*. At Fort Stanton, Graydon challenged Whitlock to a duel, in which both men were wounded. Afterward, as Whitlock was leaving the fort, Graydon's men shot him from his horse and pumped 130 bullets into him. Carson wanted Graydon to resign after this incident; Carleton wanted him to stand trial. It all became moot when Graydon died on 9 November from the wound he suffered in the duel.[259]

23 NOVEMBER 1862
CACHE VALLEY (Northern Utah)

Maj. Edward McGarry, with a detachment of 2nd California Cavalry from Camp Douglas, headed for the settlements of the Cache Valley along the Bear River to meet with Zacheus Van Ornum, the uncle of a boy captured in an attack on a wagon train in 1860 (see Utter Fight/Castle Creek, 9–10 September 1860). Van Ornum had learned that Chief Bear Hunter and his band of Shoshones had the boy. The troops rode through the night to surround Bear Hunter's camp. When the men arrived, however, the camp was deserted. They found one Shoshone, whom they captured.

Later that morning, more than 30 armed Shoshone warriors approached the soldiers, making defiant gestures. McGarry divided his command into three squads and pursued the Shoshones up a canyon. When the Indians opened fire on Lt. George D. Conrad's party, McGarry hesitated to advance his other men, fearing an ambush. After two hours of fighting, Bear Hunter signaled with the white flag of truce, and McGarry allowed him to come talk.

Had Bear Hunter known McGarry's previous record with hostages (see Humboldt Expedition, 9–15 October), he probably would not have talked with him. Indeed McGarry ordered the chief and four others captured, demanding that the other warriors return with the captive boy. The Shoshones returned with a child the next day, and McGarry released his prisoners. While the rescued child was white, not even Van Ornum was certain it was his nephew.

The soldiers killed three Indians and wounded one in the battle, with no army casualties.[260]

6 DECEMBER 1862
EMPEY'S FERRY (Brigham City, Utah)

After emigrants accused the Shoshones of stealing and holding many of their cattle near the Bear River ferry west of Brigham City, Col. Patrick E. Connor ordered Maj. Edward McGarry to investigate with 100 2nd California Cavalrymen from Camp Douglas. McGarry left on the evening of 4 December, arriving at Empey's Ferry at dawn on 6 December, ready to give the Indians "a little taste of the fighting qualities of the Volunteers."[261]

The Indians, McGarry found, had cut the ferry rope. Leaving their horses behind, the command crossed the river on a scow. They managed to catch only four Shoshones, but McGarry sent word to their kin: deliver the stolen stock by noon the next day or the captives would be killed. But the Shoshones packed up their camp and went north. McGarry promptly ordered the hostages shot.[262]

—1863—

18 JANUARY 1863
MANGAS COLORADAS AFFAIR (Hurley, New Mexico)

Mineral strikes in the Pinos Altos Mountains of southwest New Mexico brought more whites into the area, increasing conflicts between whites and Indians. Indian raids became common, and Brig. Gen. James H. Carleton was determined to stop them. He sent Brig. Gen. Joseph R. West to establish Fort West near the Pinos Altos Mines, on the east bank of the Gila River, with elements of the 1st California Cavalry and 5th California Infantry.

Meanwhile, a detachment of California Cavalry under Capt. Edmond D. Shirland joined a party of 40 mountain men under Joseph R. Walker, who were hunting for gold in the area. Together they lured the notorious Mimbres Apache leader Mangas Coloradas under a flag of truce into a trap, captured him, and took him to Fort McLane, south of present-day Hurley, New Mexico, where Brig. Gen. West was making preparations.

West informed the 70-year-old Mangas, who was still recovering from a chest wound (see Apache Pass, 15–16 July 1862), that he would be a prisoner for the rest of his life, and if he tried to escape he would be killed. Daniel E. Connor, a prospector with the Walker party, reported that he heard West say to the guards, "Men, that old murderer has got away from every soldier command and has left a trail of blood for five hundred miles on the old stage line. . . . I want him dead."[263]

According to Connor, the sentries built a fire and heated their bayonets in it, then touched the hot metal to the chief's feet. Mangas protested, and two of the guards fired their muskets into him, followed by two shots each with their revolvers. Afterward, West reported that Mangas had attempted to escape three times, and the third time he was shot.

The next morning the soldiers buried the chief in a ditch. The death of Mangas Coloradas did not stop Apache hostilities, but it made them wary of trusting the whites.[264]

19 JANUARY 1863
PINOS ALTOS MINES (Pinos Altos, New Mexico)

After the killing of Apache chief Mangas Coloradas (see previous entry), Capt. William McCleave and some men from his 1st California Cavalry were ordered from Fort McLane to the Pinos Altos Mines to protect the miners from retribution. Soon after the cavalry arrived, a party of Mimbres Apaches appeared. McCleave's men attacked, swiftly killing 11 Apaches and wounding a woman who turned out to be Mangas Coloradas's wife.[265]

29 JANUARY 1863
PINOS ALTOS MINES (Pinos Altos, New Mexico)

Shortly after arriving in the area, Brig. Gen. Joseph R. West sent Capt. William McCleave of the 1st California Cavalry to establish Fort West near the mines in the Pinos Altos Mountains. A few companies of the 5th California Infantry garrisoned the post. They had just moved in when Apaches attacked two Company A hunting parties at the mines, killing one soldier, Pvt. William Hussey, and wounding another, Sgt. T. B. Sitton. The other soldiers rallied and drove off the Apaches, killing 20 and wounding 15.[266]

Vicinity of Bear River fight (Idaho)

29 JANUARY 1863
BEAR RIVER (Preston, Idaho)

Col. Patrick E. Connor led troops from Camp Douglas against the Shoshone bands of Bear Hunter and Sagwitch, who were camped in a bend of the Bear River near present-day Preston, Idaho. The 75-lodge village comprised about 450 Indians, about 200 of them warriors. With Company K, 3rd California Infantry; Companies A, H, K, and M, 2nd California Cavalry; 2 howitzers; and a train of 15 wagons, Connor had about 260 men in all.

When Connor and his force splashed across the icy Bear River on the morning of 29 January, the Shoshones were ready for them, positioned defensively along the cutbanks of Beaver (now called Battle) Creek. Maj. Edward McGarry dismounted his soaked and shivering men and launched a frontal attack. About 10 troopers were killed and 20 wounded in the first half hour of this exchange.

Connor then assumed control. He sent out companies to flank the Indians' rear and seal off avenues of retreat. Lt. John Quinn went downstream and Capt. Samuel W. Hoyt went upstream, placing the village in a vise. Many Shoshones began to flee, some by swimming the frigid river, in which they became easy targets. A handful of warriors stayed and defended the village from within a stand of willows along the creek bed.

The four-hour battle was hard fought, not at all the massacre that some have contended. When it was over, the troops counted 224 Indian bodies on the field, including those of Bear Hunter and subchief Lehi. Sagwitch escaped. The soldiers captured 160 women and children and 175 horses and destroyed the village. Connor lost 21 killed or mortally wounded and 46 wounded; 75 sustained frostbitten limbs.

The battle broke the power of the Shoshones in the Cache Valley and Bear River area. One by one, bands began to surrender. Connor was promoted to brigadier general.[267]

20 FEBRUARY 1863
PASS CREEK (Walcott, Wyoming)

Ute Indians attacked the Pass Creek stage station, near the junction of Pass Creek and the North Platte River, driving off stock and destroying equipment. In response, Lt. Henry Brandley and a 20-man detachment of Company B, 9th Kansas Cavalry, rode out from Fort Halleck. They overtook and killed a few of the raiders, but Brandley was badly wounded by a ball through the left arm.[268]

21–24 MARCH 1863
NORTH FORK OF THE EEL RIVER (Northwestern California)

Capt. Henry Flynn and 32 men of Company A, 2nd California Infantry, left Camp Baker on 10 March on a 25-day scout. They went up the Middle Fork of the Eel River, then turned east. When scouts returned with news they had seen Indians on the North Fork of the Eel, Flynn sent Lt. T. C. Winchill and 15 men to attack. On 21 March, Winchill requested that Flynn and his men meet him at Kettenpom Valley (Winchill called it Kitten Valley).

That same day, a captured Indian divulged the location of a camp on the North Fork of the Eel. Winchill went there and surprised the inhabitants, who were spread out for a mile along the river gathering seeds and clover, with two flanking squads. The fight was short but sharp. Two soldiers were hit—one, a Pvt. Lynch, was fatally shot in the heart; the other, a Sgt. Thomas, came to Lynch's assistance and was wounded by an arrow. Ten Indian men and one woman were found dead on the field. Winchill took his prisoners to Kettenpom Valley, where he met up with Flynn.

The command resumed their march the next day and attacked another Indian camp, killing ten men and capturing two women. The prisoners told their captors that there were more Indians near the mouth of the North Fork, so Flynn continued downriver and, on the morning of 24 March, assaulted another camp. Flynn sent Winchill to the left while he and his men hid in a canyon. When Winchill attacked, the fleeing Indians ran straight into Flynn's waiting guns.

The soldiers killed 18 Indians, among them, "unavoidably," 2 women. In a subsequent engagement the same day, the soldiers killed 8 more Indians in another canyon. The four fights produced 46 Indian dead and 37 captured. Soldier casualties were 1 dead, 1 wounded. Flynn returned to Camp Baker on 1 April.[269]

27 MARCH 1863
RIO BONITO (Safford, Arizona)

On the afternoon of 22 March, Gila Apaches ran off 60 horses from a white-owned herd near Fort West. Capt. William McCleave, 1st California Cavalry, started in pursuit with a command consisting of Lts. French and Latimer, 40 men of Company A, 25 men of Company B, and 14 men of Company C. McCleave followed the raiders' trail west about 70 miles, then down the Gila River for 5 miles and across a divide to the Rio Bonito.

Moving upstream, the command saw evidence of Apaches camped close by on 26 March. They made camp two miles farther upstream, then prepared to strike the rancheria. With the only serviceable horses left, Lt. Latimer led 30 mounted soldiers, and Capt. McCleave took 30 on foot. The rest of the men stayed with Lt. French. Leaving camp at 8 P.M., the soldiers ascended a mountain west of the Rio Bonito and traveled about 12 miles, then rested in a light rain until dawn.

Lt. Latimer and his command charged the rancheria first. While the dismounted men gathered the Indians' horses, other soldiers skirmished on the bluffs. In 20 minutes, the soldiers had routed the Apaches, killing 25 of them, and recaptured the stolen horses. One trooper, Pvt. James Hall of Company B, was wounded and later died.

After destroying the rancheria, the command returned to camp by a different trail. Some Apaches followed them and attacked, wounding Lt. French and killing two horses, but the soldiers prevailed, killing three more warriors.

On 30 March, during their return march, the provisions gave out and the soldiers subsisted on horseflesh. They reached the fort on 4 April.[270]

9 APRIL 1863
WILLIAMS VALLEY (Covelo, California)

After Nome Cult Indians of Round Valley were implicated in the murder of Williams Valley settler George Bowers, Capt. Charles D. Douglas, commanding Fort Wright in Round Valley, took 15 men of Company F, 2nd California Infantry, and an Indian guide in pursuit of the perpetrators. On the morning of 9 April, the soldiers found a small Nome Cult camp of Indians who had not been able to keep up with the main band. Douglas tried to take them prisoner, but they would not surrender, so he ordered his men to fire. They killed the six men of the party, and the two old women remaining gave themselves up. When he ran out of rations, Douglas gave up the pursuit.[271]

12–15 APRIL 1863
SPANISH FORK CANYON (Provo, Utah)

In Utah, the Shoshones and Bannocks had been subdued, but Utes and Gosiutes were still attacking the overland mail between Salt Lake and Fort Ruby. Leading about 170 men of Companies A, H, and M, 2nd California Cavalry, Col. George S. Evans left Camp Douglas for the Utah Lake area. Lt. Francis Honeyman and a five-man gun crew moved ahead with a howitzer.

On 12 April Honeyman camped in the town of Pleasant Grove. Later, about 100 Utes attacked his camp. Taking shelter in an adobe house, Honeyman and his crew blasted the attackers with the howitzer. The Indians peppered the building with bullets, but no soldier was hit. The Mormons in the town watched the fight but offered no assistance. Finally the Utes gave up and left.

When the main command arrived in town, Evans, misinformed by the Mormons, searched in Dry and Provo Canyons for the Utes who had attacked Honeyman. On 14 April he realized the Indians must have gone up the nearly impregnable Spanish Fork Canyon, southeast of present-day Provo, Utah. Before sunrise on 15 April, he moved his men up the canyon along Spanish Fork and dismounted two companies, sending Capt. George F. Price and Company M to the south side of the river and Lt. C. D. Clark and Company H to the north side. With Lt. Anthony Ethier and Company A, and Lt. Honeyman and his howitzer, Evans moved up the center.

About 200 Ute warriors, many under Little Soldier, had gathered to fight the soldiers, but they were not expecting the attack so early. In addition, rain had masked the sight and sound of the approaching troops. Honeyman moved ahead and dropped shells into the highest concentration of Indians, while the flanking companies got in close enough to use revolvers. When the Utes began to flee. Evans and his men mounted up and chased them for 14 miles up the canyon; they captured 22 horses and mules.

Only one soldier, Lt. F. A. Peel, the regimental quartermaster, was killed, and two, Sgts. Brown and Booth of Company M, were wounded. Thirty Utes were killed and a dozen or more were wounded. The Spanish Fork fight convinced most of the Utes to sue for peace.[272]

25 APRIL 1863
APACHE PASS (Fort Bowie, Arizona)

Capt. Benjamin F. Harrover and the 5th California Infantry, traveling through Apache Pass, spotted and attacked a band of about 200 Apache Indians, 30 of them mounted but only a few with guns. The Indians fell back at first fire, but they kept up the fight for nearly two hours. One soldier, Pvt. M. B. Wilcox of Company E, was wounded; three Apaches were killed.[273]

7 MAY 1863
ARAVAIPA CANYON (Klondyke, Arizona)

Capt. Thomas T. Tidball of the 5th California Infantry was ordered to clear out an Apache rancheria deep in Aravaipa Canyon, about 20 miles east of the site of old Fort Breckinridge at the junction of Aravaipa Creek and the San Pedro River. His orders stated, "All grown males are fair game."[274] Tidball took 25 men of Companies I and K of the 5th, 10 civilians, 32 Mexicans under Jesus Maria Elias, 20 Papago Indians, and 9 Apache scouts and left Tucson late on 2 May. The command traveled only after sunset for five nights, lighting no fires and sleeping by day. For the final 16 hours of the trip the soldiers traversed treacherous canyon trails. Tidball mounted his offensive on the 7th.

The attack, deep in their canyon haven, shattered the unprepared Apaches. Tidball's troops killed 50 Indians, wounded a like number, and took 10 prisoners and 66 head of stock. One soldier, Thomas C. McClelland, was killed.[275]

9 MAY 1863
SHELTER COVE (Shelter Cove, California)

Capt. William E. Hull, 2nd California Infantry, proceeded from Fort Bragg with a 20-man detachment of Company D to the Shelter Cove area "to chastise a band of hostile Indians who have killed several head of cattle and two valuable horses belonging to Mr. Beall, in that neighborhood." Early on 9 May, Hull and 8 soldiers surprised about 35 of the Indians, killing 4 and wounding 3. Shelter Cove citizens recognized one of the dead Indians as having participated in the murder of two area settlers, named Oliver and Lewis, in 1861. Hull returned to Fort Bragg with six Indian captives, one boy and five women.[276]

16 JUNE 1863
JORNADA DEL MUERTO (Rincon, New Mexico)

Lt. L. A. Bargie of the 1st New Mexico Cavalry, on his way back to Fort McRae from Franklin (now El Paso, Texas) after testifying at a court-martial, was traveling along the Jornada del Muerto, north of the Robledo Mountains, with a detachment of Company H when about 70 Mimbres Apaches attacked. Bargie and some others were killed immediately, but the remainder of the party defended a hastily thrown-up breastwork for three hours. After dark the Apaches renewed their attack but the soldiers repulsed them. Finally the Indians crossed to the west side of the Rio Grande and disappeared.

Three soldiers were killed and four were wounded; no Indian casualties were reported. The Apaches took Bargie's head with them as a trophy. Sgts. Pina and Urliberra were cited for heroic conduct in the fight.[277]

20 JUNE 1863
GOVERNMENT SPRINGS (Cherry Creek, Nevada)

Capt. Samuel P. Smith, operating out of Fort Ruby with a detachment of 2nd California Cavalry, jumped a small party of Gosiutes at Government Springs, killing ten of them. Among the dead were Chief Peahnamp's wife and child.[278]

20 JUNE 1863
WARM SPRINGS (Truth or Consequences, New Mexico)

At a hot springs on the Rio Grande near Fort McRae, 15 to 20 Apaches attacked Capt. Albert H. Pfeiffer of the 1st New Mexico Cavalry, his wife, two servant girls, and an escort of six soldiers. Two soldiers, Pvts. Quintana and Mestas, were killed. Pfeiffer, a Pvt. Dolores, and a civilian named Betts were wounded.

The uninjured men of the party fled back to the fort and reported the incident to the commander, Maj. Arthur Morrison. Morrison took 20 mounted men and went in pursuit, but they could not overtake the Apaches. They found Mrs. Pfeiffer and the servant girls on the trail, badly wounded; Mrs. Pfeiffer and one of the girls later died.

In total, two privates were killed, two women were mortally wounded, and four others—an officer, a private, and two civilians—were wounded. The Indians probably suffered no losses. After his wife's death, Capt. Pfeiffer dedicated his life to killing Apaches.[279]

23 JUNE 1863
EGAN CANYON STATION (Schellbourne, Nevada)

To avenge the killing of his wife and child at Government Springs (see Government Springs, 20 June), Chief Peahnamp and about 17 Gosiute warriors attacked Egan Canyon stage station. William Riley was in charge of the station; a guard of four men of Company E, 3rd California Infantry, was also posted there—a Cpl. Hervey and Pvts. Abbott, Burgher, and Elliott.

On the morning of 23 June, the Gosiutes attacked the station while Hervey and Abbott were out filling the water cart and Burgher and Elliott were hunting. The Indians shot stationkeeper Riley and set his body on fire with the woodpile. When Hervey and Abbott came back, Gosiutes hidden in the sagebrush about 500 yards from the station fired on them. Hervey was killed; Abbott, wounded in the neck, fired back at their attackers as he and the cart driver raced for the station. Cavalry from Deep Creek Station later rescued Abbott and the cart driver.

Upon their return from hunting, Burgher and Elliott were chased south into the mountains. Their bodies were recovered later. Burgher had been shot 4 times; Elliott had 35 wounds and, because he was nearly bald, had his whiskers taken rather than his scalp.[280]

23 JUNE 1863
PAWNEE AGENCY (Cushing, Nebraska)

On 23 June about 50 Brule Lakotas attacked the Pawnee Agency on the Loup River, killing several Pawnees and wounding Capt. Henry L. Edwards, 2nd Nebraska Cavalry. Edwards ordered Lt. Henry Gray to pursue the Brules with 35 men of Company D. Gathering up about 300 Pawnees anxious for revenge, Gray took up the chase. After about 15 miles, Gray came upon more than 400 Lakota warriors drawn up in line, ready to fight.

The Pawnees assured Gray they would fight with him, so he threw out some skirmishers. However, when the Lakotas began firing, killing one soldier, Sgt. Joseph Dyson, and mortally wounding another, Pvt. George Osborn, the Pawnees ran, leaving Gray and his troops to fight alone. The battle lasted an hour. After losing four or five warriors, the Lakotas retreated.

Meanwhile Edwards took 20 men and went to Gray's assistance. However, by the time he reached him, the Lakotas were about six miles away and night was falling, so the men all returned to the agency.[281]

Fort Craig (New Mexico)

29 JUNE 1863
DUSTIN MASSACRE (Howard Lake, Minnesota)

After the Wood Lake battle (see 23 September 1862), Santee chief Little Crow fled to Canada to ask the British for help. Turned down, he returned with a small band of 17 people, including his 16-year-old son Wowinape, to the Big Woods section of central Minnesota, where he had grown up.

Little Crow's once great coalition of Sioux, which had caused such terror and destruction in southwestern Minnesota, had degenerated into little more than a horse-stealing expedition. Nevertheless, some of Little Crow's warriors split off to take more serious vengeance on the whites. Near Howard Lake, west of St. Paul, these Santees jumped the Dustin family as they rode in an oxcart. Four of the six Dustins were killed; two children escaped into the woods and were rescued a week later.

On 3 July, while picking berries at Scattered Lake, six miles north of Hutchinson, Little Crow and his son ran into settler Nathan Lamson and his son out hunting. The two parties exchanged gunfire, and Little Crow was killed. Wowinape fled, but he was captured three weeks later near Devil's Lake.[282]

4 JULY 1863
FORT CRAIG (San Marcial, New Mexico)

Capt. Nathaniel J. Pishon, with 27 men of his D Company, 1st California Cavalry, pursued a party of 8 Indians—perhaps Navajos or Apaches—who had driven off 104 government mules from Fort Craig. Pishon overtook the raiders a few miles from the post, killed four of them, and recovered the mules. Three soldiers—Capt. Julius L. Barbey and Pvts. Jackson and Bancroft—were wounded in the action.[283]

7 JULY 1863
GRAND PASS (Ryan Park, Wyoming)

Since February 1863, Grand River and Uinta Utes had been raiding the mail line west of Fort Halleck and had stolen 173 horses and 34 mules from Ben Holladay's company. To stop this, about 70 men from a detachment of 1st Colorado Cavalry and from Company B, 9th Kansas Cavalry, left Fort Halleck in July in search of the Utes.

At sunrise on 7 July, in a pass in the Medicine Bow Mountains about 25 miles south of the fort, Lts. Henry Brandley and Hugh W. Williams and their men overtook the Indians. When the troopers rode up, 250 Utes opened fire from the timber and underbrush. Undaunted, Brandley and Williams dismounted the men and charged up the slope.

The Utes, well-armed with Hawkins rifles, would likely have killed a great many more soldiers, but, according to Capt. Asaph Allen, commander at Fort Halleck, "in firing down the steep hill-side they invariably fired too

high. It was a perfect hail-storm of lead over the heads of the troops."[284]
The fight lasted two hours. When the soldiers achieved the crest of the
pass, the Utes broke and fled.

One soldier, Sgt. S. N. Waugh of Company B, was killed in the charge,
and 6 were wounded. The Utes left 20 dead on the field; they carried off
another 40 dead and wounded. The fight left the Fort Halleck region in
comparative peace.[285]

9 JULY 1863
REDWOOD CREEK (Northwestern California)

Returning from a trip to deliver government supplies to Fort Gaston,
on the Trinity River, from the Eureka area, a supply train owned by Manheim
& Company, escorted by 18 men from Weaverville, California—recruits
for Company C, 1st Battalion California Mountaineers—camped for the
night at Redwood Creek. The next morning, 9 July, the men were securing
their saddles and packs for an early start when gunfire erupted from the
timber and brush on three sides of them. Three or four soldiers were hit
in the first volley from more than 80 Indians. The recruits conducted
themselves well, holding their ground in a fight that lasted eight hours, at
which point the attackers faded into the woods.

The Indians wounded ten train members, two of them mortally. Several
Indians were reported hit.[286]

10 JULY 1863
COOKE'S CANYON (Deming, New Mexico)

Sgt. E. W. Hoyt of Company D, 1st California Infantry, three men of
Company B, and three men of Company D were taking four supply wagons to Las Cruces through the pass in Cooke's Canyon when Apaches
attacked. Hoyt drove his wagons for a mile before one broke down in the
narrowest part of the pass, forcing him to abandon three wagons and 19
mules. He and his men killed four warriors and wounded several others.
The Apaches wounded four soldiers.[287]

12 JULY 1863
FORT THORN (Hatch, New Mexico)

On a patrol near abandoned Fort Thorn, on the Rio Grande, Capt.
Albert H. French and 27 men of his company of 1st California Cavalry
attacked and routed a band of about 60 Apache warriors. They killed ten
Apaches and captured four horses. Two soldiers, a Sgt. Walsh and Farrier
Burns, were wounded.[288]

18 JULY 1863
RIO HONDO (Roswell, New Mexico)

Attempting to steal horses, about 50 Indians, probably Mescalero
Apaches, attacked Lt. Juan Marques, 1st New Mexico Cavalry, and 15 men

of Company A camped at the Rio Hondo on their way back from an expedition. The Apaches gained possession of the camp, but the soldiers dislodged them and drove them across the river. Soon the Indians recrossed and charged the herd again, but the soldiers drove them back again, this time with a loss—Pvt. Jose Chaves was killed.

The fight continued for several hours. More Indians arrived and joined in until they numbered about 200. Finally the soldiers' ammunition gave out. Marques ordered his men to escape, which they managed to do without further casualties.

Chaves was the only army casualty in the affair, but all the government's animals, including ten mules, were lost. Marques estimated that he and his men had killed six Apaches.[289]

19 JULY 1863
PARAJE (San Marcial, New Mexico)

Near Paraje, on the Rio Grande about seven miles south of Fort Craig, Indians attacked Lt. Col. William McMullen's ambulance and its 1st California Infantry escort. Two men, Asst. Surg. E. L. Watson and Pvt. Robert Johnson, Company G, were killed. The soldiers believed they had killed two Indians and wounded some others.[290]

22 JULY 1863
CONCHAS SPRINGS (Conchas, New Mexico)

Navajo warriors attacked a three-man detachment of Company I, 1st New Mexico Cavalry, guarding a herd of beef cattle at Conchas Springs, near the junction of the Conchas and Canadian Rivers. Though badly outnumbered, the soldiers—Sgt. Jose Lucero and Pvts. Juan F. Ortiz and Jose Banneras—fought the Navajos from 11 A.M. until after sundown, killing and wounding several.

The soldiers fought gallantly, but Lucero and Ortiz were killed and Banneras was severely wounded with eight arrows. Banneras managed to gather the guns of his dead comrades and throw them in the springs. After pounding Banneras's skull with rocks, the Navajos drove the cattle off to the west, leaving him for dead.

Amazingly, the soldier recovered toward morning and made his way to Chaperito, on the Gallinas River. From Camp Easton, Capt. Edward H. Bergmann mounted 30 men and went to intercept the Navajos. At the Pecos River, a squad under a Cpl. Martinez hit the Navajos' rear, killing two, wounding a number of others, and recapturing three beeves.[291]

24 JULY 1863
COOKE'S CANYON (Deming, New Mexico)

At 5 A.M. on 24 July, a band of Apaches attacked Lt. John Lambert, 5th California Infantry, and his men as they were camped with three wagons on the Mesilla-Tucson road in Cooke's Canyon. Lambert succeeded in flushing the Indians from their cover, but two soldiers—a Sgt. Hance of Company H and a Pvt. Queen of Company F—were wounded in the process, Queen mortally.

Lambert fell back east of the canyon, circled the wagons, and maintained a desultory fire. At 10 A.M. he noticed the Indians preparing a triple attack—in front, flank, and rear—and he retreated, abandoning two of the wagons. The Indians captured the wagons and 12 mules but did not pursue the soldiers.[292]

Because of the danger of such attacks at this pass (see also 10 July), the army established Fort Cummings just east of Cooke's Range in October 1863.

24 JULY 1863
BIG MOUND (Tappen, North Dakota)

Promoted to brigadier general after his final quelling of the Minnesota Sioux Uprising (see Wood Lake, 23 September 1862), Henry Sibley was assigned a column of soldiers with which to sweep the Indians (mainly Sioux) out of Minnesota and far into Dakota Territory. Sibley's huge force consisted mostly of Minnesota Infantry units—the 6th, the 7th (9 companies), the 9th (100 engineers), and the 10th (8 companies)—as well as the 1st Minnesota Mounted Rangers (9 companies), the 3rd Battery of Light Artillery, and 70 Indian and mixed-blood scouts. The 3,320 men and 325 wagons formed the largest single force to take the field in the western Indian wars. On 16 June the command pulled out of Camp Pope, on the Minnesota River, in a column five miles long.

By mid-July, Sibley had established a base camp about 40 miles south of Devil's Lake. On 17 July buffalo hunters informed Sibley of a large encampment of approximately 600 Indian lodges about 75 miles southwest. Leaving behind two companies of each regiment, Sibley marched out with 2,056 men. On the 24th the soldiers reached the Indian camp, which consisted mostly of Standing Buffalo's Sisseton and Wahpeton Sioux, but also included Wahpekutes under Inkpaduta, the leader of the Spirit Lake Massacre of 1857 (see 8 and 26 March 1857). Sibley invited the chiefs to talk, and they accepted.

For the talk, Sibley circled his wagons near a small alkali lake, and approximately 1,500 warriors gathered east of the soldiers on a high hill called Big Mound, about seven miles north of present-day Tappen, North Dakota. Approximately equal in number to the soldiers, the Indians lacked comparable firepower—fewer than half of them had guns. Negotiators from each side met in the middle, but with both parties expecting treachery, it wasn't long before violence erupted. When Dr. Josiah S. Weiser of the Mounted Rangers moved in to exchange pleasantries with some

Sissetons he thought he knew, the Santee Tall Crown shot him down. A fight commenced.

Under a sky ominous with thunder and lightning, Sibley's soldiers moved across the prairie toward Big Mound. The howitzers lobbed shells onto the hill, killing a few warriors. A bolt of lightning killed a soldier named John Miller and burned two others. Lt. Col. William R. Marshall with his 7th Minnesota and Col. Sam McPhail with his Mounted Rangers drove the Sioux off the hill and south two miles. McPhail pursued the Indians as they fled west toward the Missouri River. Meanwhile knots of warriors held the soldiers off to allow women and children to escape. The Rangers trailed the Indians as far as Dead Buffalo Lake before darkness ended the chase.

About 40 Sioux were killed and 40 were wounded. Four of Sibley's men were wounded and three, including Weiser, Miller, and Lt. Ambrose Freeman of the Mounted Rangers, were killed.[293]

26 JULY 1863
DEAD BUFFALO LAKE (Dawson, North Dakota)

Two days after the fight at Big Mound (see previous entry), after resting his forces, Gen. Henry Sibley took up his pursuit of the Sioux. He would not find Standing Buffalo's and Sweet Corn's Sisseton and Wahpeton Sioux bands; they had fled northwest toward the Mouse River. But Inkpaduta's Wahpekute warriors, who did not go with the others, joined about 650 Hunkpapas and Blackfeet who were hunting east of the Missouri. This put about 1,600 warriors in the vicinity of Dead Buffalo Lake.

After noon on 26 July, swarms of Indians appeared around Sibley's vanguard, which consisted of Col. William Crooks's 6th Minnesota Infantry and some Mounted Rangers under Capt. Edward B. Taylor. The soldiers repulsed attacks on the left and right. In midafternoon, the Sioux made a rush on the hay-cutters and teamsters at Sibley's bivouac on the south shore of Dead Buffalo Lake. Again the Rangers came to the rescue, along with six companies of the 6th. The fighting lasted half an hour, though with the blinding dust and smoke there was more noise than destruction. At the death of their chief Grey Eagle, the Indians withdrew. Sibley threw up earthworks that night, but the fight was over.

Fifteen Indians lost their lives in the fight, as did one trooper, John Platt—surprisingly few casualties considering the high number of fighters on both sides.[294]

28 JULY 1863
STONY LAKE (Driscoll, North Dakota)

The day after the fight at Dead Buffalo Lake (see previous entry), Gen. Henry Sibley and his troops continued 24 miles southwest to Stony Lake and set up camp. After a predawn reveille, the troops were in motion again.

Two hours later, approximately 2,200 Sioux attacked. Sibley, in the vanguard with Col. James H. Baker's 10th Minnesota Infantry, deployed soldiers to the right and left of the trail to meet the warriors, who kept coming, circling around the soldiers' flanks.

Baker sent two companies back as skirmishers to protect the wagons at the rear and sent the rest of his men, with bayonets fixed, to face the main body of Indians. Just when the soldiers feared they would be overrun, a section of artillery came up and peppered the Indian line. The artillery and long-range infantry fire made the warriors balk at launching an all-out assault. Soon the other regiments were deployed and formed a tough moving cordon the Indians could not penetrate. The warriors fired some parting volleys and withdrew.

Sibley claimed his soldiers recovered 11 Indian bodies. The soldiers had no casualties.[295]

3 AUGUST 1863
MACKINAW MASSACRE (Bismarck, North Dakota)

The Sioux driven west by Sibley's troops (see previous entries), now at the Missouri River, took revenge on the next party of whites they encountered. Traveling down the Missouri from the mines near Boise, a large mackinaw carrying 32 civilians and $100,000 in gold reached Fort Berthold, where the passengers heard of the trouble with Indians farther down the river. Ten passengers left the boat, but 22 stayed, including 2 mixed-blood Sioux men, a white woman, and 2 children.

At a narrow place in the Missouri—near the mouth of the Apple River—Sioux warriors ambushed the mackinaw. Ten miners went down in the first volley. The survivors on the boat fought valiantly, aided by a small cannon, but when their leader fell and the ammunition ran out, it was over. Reaching the boat by canoe and on horseback, the Sioux finished off the last of the passengers.

Indian losses were estimated at between 36 and 90—certainly an exaggeration. More likely, no more than a dozen Sioux were killed or wounded.[296]

5–19 AUGUST 1863
PUEBLO COLORADO EXPEDITION (Northeastern Arizona)

On 5 August, Col. Christopher "Kit" Carson, 1st New Mexico Cavalry, left his camp south of Bonito Canyon, near recently reoccupied Fort Defiance, on a 30-day scout for Navajos. With him were 337 men from Companies B, D, G, H, K, and M, 1st New Mexico Cavalry, and some other units, as well as a group of Ute scouts. On the first day out, the troops found and destroyed 135 acres of Navajo corn and wheat. Some soldiers chased two Navajos but were able only to capture one of their horses.

On 6 August soldiers led by Capt. Albert Pfeiffer and Lt. Charles H. Fitch captured 11 Navajo women and children. They also killed a woman who tried to escape and a child accidentally. Hearing of a Navajo camp near Moqui, Carson and his troops turned west toward the Pueblo Colorado Wash and found the camp on 9 August. There Pfeiffer and 30 cavalrymen rounded up 1,000 sheep and goats, and he also mortally wounded a Navajo; Capt. Joseph Berney's troops rounded up 25 horses; and the Ute scouts captured 5 Navajos, killed 1, and took 20 horses and mules. Afterward the Utes took their captured stock and went home.

A few days later Carson took a 100-man detail and pursued another band of Navajos about 12 miles farther west, but could not catch them. The party made camp nearby. At 2 A.M. the next day, 15 August, Navajos attacked the soldiers' camp to run off horses, but without success. Carson moved his men back to the Pueblo Colorado Wash, and on the 16th, they destroyed about 50 acres of corn and captured a Navajo woman.

Two days later, a concealed Navajo shot Maj. Joseph Cummings through the abdomen, killing him instantly. This was Carson's only casualty of the expedition, which Carson then terminated. The soldiers had killed 4 Navajos and captured 17.[297]

27 AUGUST 1863
LAS ANIMAS CREEK (Caballo, New Mexico)

After Indians attacked a mail stage on the Jornada del Muerto near Point of Rocks, about 20 miles southeast of Fort McRae, Capt. Henry A. Greene, 1st California Infantry, sent 15 mounted men from the fort in pursuit and detailed 9 more to escort the stage. The pursuers spotted three Indians on the bank of the Rio Grande opposite the mouth of Las Animas Creek, about seven miles south of the fort. The rest of the band was hidden in the brush across the river.

The infantrymen, under Lt. A. J. Fountain, fired on the three Indians. One fell, but his fellows helped him up and they crossed the river. Fountain and his men splashed across in pursuit. Skirmishing through the brush, Pvt. George S. Dickey saw an Indian jump into the water and shot at him. The Indian turned and shot back, hitting Dickey. It was the only shot fired by the Indians.

In all, one Indian was killed and three were wounded. Dickey later died of his wound.[298]

27–28 AUGUST 1863
SALT LAKES (Quemado, New Mexico)

Capt. Rafael Chacon, 1st New Mexico Cavalry, left Fort Wingate in August with 40 enlisted men on a scout for Navajo Indians. On the 27th, near the Salt Lakes, the party chased a band of Navajos, killing two and

Whitestone Hill (North Dakota)

capturing eight. Later that day, a soldier killed one of the Navajo captives when he tried to escape.

The next day, Chacon attacked a camp of 150 Navajos, who fled in all directions. His men killed 3 adults, captured 7 children, recovered a captive Mexican boy named Agapito Apodaca, and confiscated about 1,500 head of stock, mostly sheep and goats.[299]

3 SEPTEMBER 1863
WHITESTONE HILL (Merricourt, North Dakota)

Launching his Missouri River column in the 1863–64 Sioux Campaign, Brig. Gen. Alfred Sully left Fort Ridgely with about 1,200 men of the 6th Iowa Cavalry, 8 companies of the 2nd Nebraska Cavalry, 2 companies of the Dakota Cavalry, 1 company of the 7th Iowa Cavalry, 3 companies of the 45th Iowa Infantry, and an 8-gun mountain-howitzer battery.

After waiting at Fort Randall for supplies, Sully took rations for 23 days and set out to look for hostile Sioux and possibly meet up with Gen. Henry Sibley and his column, who were still in the field. After finding nothing for many days, Sully met a friendly Indian who told him that Sibley had moved on and the Indians he sought were back on the east side of the Missouri River, traveling toward the James River to gather food. Sully turned southeast.

On 3 September, near the James River, Sully sent a 300-man battalion of 6th Iowa Cavalry under Maj. A. E. House to look for the Sioux encampment. That afternoon House discovered some 500 lodges about ten miles south, in ravines near Whitestone Hill, in present-day Dickey County.

Ordered to report back about any contact immediately, House sent couriers back to Sully, but he also moved most of his command—Companies C, E, F, and H—forward to contain the village. Yet with 300 soldiers against perhaps 1,200 Santee, Yanktonai, Blackfoot, and Hunkpapa warriors, it was impossible.

The couriers made it back to Sully, who immediately spurred his men to a gallop. Back at the Indian camp, House tried to negotiate a surrender with the Indian leaders, Inkpaduta among them. Looking at the small number of soldiers before them, the Sioux parleyed unworried. Inkpaduta was about to launch an attack when Sully's column appeared.

The 2nd Nebraska Cavalry, under Col. Robert W. Furnas, moved around to the southeast while soldiers from the 6th Iowa Cavalry moved to the other side and advanced. Dismounting 400 yards from the camp, the 2nd Nebraska sent a volley into the lodges. The Sioux went after them, allowing House and Col. David S. Wilson of the 6th Iowa to slip behind and envelop them from the flank and rear. Furnas moved his men in and the battle became general. The troops repulsed flank attacks, then Wilson led a failed mounted charge into the fray. House also advanced but later had to fall back. In the center of the camp, Sully rounded up the friendly bands of Little Soldier and Big Head—about 30 men and 90 women and children in all.

Near dusk, the Sioux pulled back. Sully began to pursue them, but darkness called a halt to the fight. Sully wrote that had he had an hour or two more daylight, "I feel sure that . . . I could have annihilated the enemy. As it was I believe I can safely say I gave them one of the most severe punishments that the Indians have ever received."[300]

Indeed, there may have been more Indian casualties at Whitestone Hill than in any other fight in the West. According to best estimates, over 100 Sioux and Sioux allies died in the battle, another 100 were wounded, and approximately 156 were captured. In addition, the troops burned 300 lodges and over 400,000 pounds of dried buffalo meat. Sully lost 20 soldiers and 38 were wounded.[301]

27 SEPTEMBER 1863
JEMEZ (Jemez Pueblo, New Mexico)

After Pueblo Indians near Fort Marcy complained that a band of Navajos had stolen stock from them, Lt. P. A. J. Russell, 1st California Infantry, and four mounted infantrymen joined a party of Pueblos to pursue the raiders. At Valle Grande, west of present-day Los Alamos, they picked up the trail and followed it down the Jemez River into Jemez Pueblo, where they attacked. They killed 8 Navajos, captured 20 women and children, and recaptured 125 sheep.[302]

THOMAS'S RANCH (Burnt Ranch, California)

From Fort Gaston, Capt. Abraham Miller took a 15-man detachment of Companies B and C, 1st Battalion California Mountaineers, on a scout up the Trinity River. On 13 November, near Thomas's Ranch, they came upon two Indian men and three women, probably Hoopas, dressing a beef they had killed. As soon as they saw the soldiers, the Indians jumped into the river and began swimming away. The soldiers shot at them, killing the two men. The women escaped. The dead men were identified as Handsome Billy and Frank, reputedly "two of the worst" Indians in the area.

The next morning, as the detachment headed back to the fort, a small band of Hoopas fired on them as they crossed the South Fork of the Trinity. Two of Miller's men, named Heckmann and McCracken, were severely wounded, and the pack mules stampeded, though the men recovered all but three. They made it across the river and returned to the post.[303]

ORAIBI EXPEDITION (Northeastern Arizona)

With Companies C, D, G, H, and L, 1st New Mexico Cavalry, and some 5th New Mexico Infantry, Col. Christopher "Kit" Carson left Fort Canby on 15 November to chastise the Navajos west of the Oraibi villages. The next day, 30 men under Sgt. Andreas Herrera overtook a small party of Navajos, killing 2, wounding 2, and capturing 50 sheep.

After passing by a Moqui village without incident, on 25 November the troopers found and destroyed two Navajo encampments in a steep canyon of the Little Colorado River. They took a woman and 2 children prisoner, and captured more than 500 sheep and goats and about 70 horses, then followed the trail of the fleeing Navajos. By the 27th, northeast of the San Francisco Mountains, the troopers were within 25 miles of the Indians, but lack of water and exhausted mounts forced them to turn back.

On 3 December, the soldiers surprised another encampment and captured a horse and four oxen, but the Navajos escaped. The next day the expedition straggled back to Fort Canby. The expedition's results were disappointing, with only two Navajos killed, two wounded, and three captured.[304]

WILLOW CREEK (Weaverville, California)

Immediately after Hoopas fired on Capt. Abraham Miller and his men on 14 November (see Thomas's Ranch), Capt. George W. Ousley left Fort Gaston with a 16-man detachment of Companies B and C, 1st Battalion California Mountaineers, to find the attackers. Traveling up the Trinity River to the mouth of Willow Creek, they found two of Miller's mules early in the morning on 17 November. Meanwhile, a few soldiers out hunting had come upon 30 Hoopas preparing a surprise attack. The soldiers ran back to camp and warned Ousley, undoubtedly preventing many Mountaineer casualties in the fight that ensued.

The battle lasted from 7:30 A.M. to 3 P.M., during which time Ousley figured his command dodged about a thousand bullets. Three soldiers were wounded, Ousley among them. Five Hoopas were killed and several were wounded.[305]

4 DECEMBER 1863
NIOBRARA (Niobrara, Nebraska)

On 1 December a detachment of 7th Iowa Cavalry came across 20 Ponca Indians off their reservation, camped near the mouth of the Niobrara River. When the sergeant in command asked to see the Indians' passes, they could not produce any and were angered by the request. The sergeant decided to let it go.

Three days later, some of the same Poncas harassed some whites outside Niobrara, Nebraska. The settlers complained, and the 7th Iowa cavalrymen went out again. This time, when they found the Poncas, the soldiers fired on them. The Indians returned fire as they retreated. The Iowans killed seven Poncas in the chase.

Ponca agent J. B. Hoffman complained about the Iowans' conduct in the incident, so the army stationed a lieutenant there, thinking an officer "would be likely to act with a greater degree of caution and a deeper sense of responsibility than an enlisted man seems likely to do."[306]

11 DECEMBER 1863
RICONDE MASCARES (Northeastern Arizona)

Shortly after returning from the Oraibi Expedition (see 15 November– 4 December), Col. Christopher "Kit" Carson sent Lt. Donaciano Montoya and Company F, 1st New Mexico Cavalry, out after a party of Navajo warriors. On their third day out, the soldiers came upon a Navajo encampment and attacked, killing 1 man, capturing 13 women and children, and confiscating many supplies.

Later that day, in a skirmish near the Pueblo Colorado Wash, Montoya's troopers wounded a Navajo man and captured another woman. Three members of Company C—Lt. C. M. Hubbell, Sgt. Antonio Nava, and Cpl. Marquez—were wounded.[307]

16 DECEMBER 1863
ST. JOSEPH (Walhalla, North Dakota)

During the fall and frigid winter of 1863–64, with an independent battalion of cavalry, former Blackfoot agent Maj. Edwin A. C. Hatch patrolled the U.S.–Canadian border to keep the Sioux from crossing for British weapons and to accept any Sioux surrenders. He built a post at what would become the town of Pembina, North Dakota, near the junction of the Pembina River and the Red River of the North.

Settlers and Indians wishing to keep the peace told authorities the location of a hostile band of Sioux, near the old British trading post at St. Joseph, about 40 miles west of the Pembina post. Hatch sent out a dismounted detachment of 20 men under a Lt. Cross. At 3 A.M. on 16 December, the troopers attacked the sleeping camp and killed six Sioux; the rest of the Indians fled. Two soldiers were wounded. As a result of Hatch's action, about 90 Sioux surrendered to him early in 1884.[308]

16 DECEMBER 1863
FORT SUMNER (Fort Sumner, New Mexico)

After the Mescalero Apaches began living on the Bosque Redondo Reservation near Fort Sumner, they were constantly raided by Navajos. After Navajos swept through the area in December, running off thousands of sheep, Bosque Redondo agent Lorenzo Labadie and a chaplain named Joseph Fialon requested help from Maj. Henry D. Wallen, 7th Infantry, in command at Fort Sumner. Detachments of infantry companies C and D and eight men of Company B, 2nd California Cavalry, prepared to go out after the raiders, but Labadie and Fialon could not wait.

At 5:30 A.M. on 16 December, Labadie and Fialon left the post with 30 Mescaleros, soon joined by the mounted Californians. They picked up the Navajos' trail and overtook them about 30 miles northwest of the fort. There were about 130 warriors, but only about 20 had rifles. In the ensuing fight, which was severe, the whites and Mescaleros finally routed the Navajos. Lt. Charles Newbold, 5th Infantry, and three others pursued the fleeing Navajos for three miles before giving up.

The soldiers and Mescaleros killed 12 Navajos and wounded several others. They also took 1 Navajo prisoner and recovered 13 burros and 5,259 sheep. The Mescalero Alazan was fatally wounded.[309]

—1864—

4 JANUARY 1864
BOSQUE REDONDO (Fort Sumner, New Mexico)

Less than a month after their last raid (see previous entry), Navajo stock thieves were back at the Bosque Redondo Reservation and Fort Sumner. In the frigid predawn of 4 January, they drove off a number of horses from Fort Sumner as well as 60 Mescalero Apache horses. As before, agent Lorenzo Labadie requested assistance from Fort Sumner, then took off after the raiders with Chief Cadete and about 60 Mescaleros, without waiting for the soldiers. Lt. Charles Newbold, 5th Infantry, joined them later with 15 mounted men, composed of a detachment of Company B, 2nd California Cavalry, and several soldiers of the 5th Infantry.

The Navajos' trail led south along the Pecos River. The temperature was about ten below zero. In a small valley not more than ten miles from the reservation, the Bosque Redondo party encountered about 100 Navajos formed up, waiting for their pursuers. The Navajos fired first, at 80 yards. An answering volley from the Mescaleros and soldiers killed about nine Navajos. Newbold gave the order to draw pistols and charge, and his men "went down among the Navajos like a small tornado."[310]

The battle lasted from 11 A.M. to sundown. Each trooper carried two Colt six-shooters. Their fingers numb with frostbite, the soldiers could hardly load their weapons. Their Apache allies soon abandoned their guns for their quicker and more reliable bows and arrows. At last, splitting their number, the Navajos attempted to flee in two different directions, but only about 25 succeeded.

The soldiers reported 40 Indians dead on the field and at least 25 wounded. In the Bosque Redondo party, no soldier or Apache was hit. Fifty of the Apaches' horses and mules were recovered.[311]

12 JANUARY 1864
DATIL MOUNTAINS (Datil, New Mexico)

Out of Fort Wingate, Lt. Jose M. Sanches and a detachment of Company F, 1st New Mexico Cavalry, attacked a party of Navajos near the Datil

The Pecos River at Bosque Redondo, Fort Sumner (New Mexico)

Mountains. The troopers killed 3 men, captured 2 women and a boy, and took 80 head of stock. A chief variously reported as Sordo or Gordo was killed in the fight.[312]

12–14 JANUARY 1864
CANYON DE CHELLY (Chinle, Arizona)

Having been successfully fighting Navajos since the summer of 1863, Col. Christoper "Kit" Carson received orders from Gen. James H. Carleton to end the campaign with a winter sweep through the Navajo stronghold of Canyon de Chelly. On 6 January, Carson led 375 enlisted men and 14 officers, most from the 1st New Mexico Cavalry, out of Fort Canby. Capt. Albert H. Pfeiffer was to enter the east end of the canyon with about 100 men while Carson marched up from the west end. It was the first time troops had been in Canyon de Chelly since Col. Dixon S. Miles had marched through it in 1858. He had recommended that no command enter it again.

A scouting party under Sgt. Andreas Herrera rode ahead. At the canyon's western end, the scouts killed 11 Navajo warriors and captured 2 women, 2 children, and 130 sheep and goats. The command then headed east, Capt. Joseph Berney leading a company along the north rim and Carson and Capt. Asa B. Carey leading another along the south rim. When Carson came within sight of the canyon's eastern end, he did not see Pfeiffer and hurried back west.

Pfeiffer had missed his entry point in a snowstorm, so he led his men through the Canyon del Muerto, a northern branch, instead, snaking his way along the icy creek at the bottom. There his men killed 3 Navajos, found some who had frozen to death, and captured 90, while others fled. All the while, from the cliff walls, Navajo warriors harassed Pfeiffer's soldiers, shooting and hurling rocks down at them as they made their way through the canyon.

When Pfeiffer and his troops appeared at the west end, Carson instructed Carey to sweep back up the canyon with 75 men, destroying any crops, orchards, and hogans he found. On the way, Carey met 150 starving, freezing Indians who wished to surrender and told them to go to Fort Canby. Upon Carey's return, the entire command headed back to the fort.

When the Navajos realized the soldiers would not slaughter them if they came to the fort, more turned themselves in. The results of the campaign were great. The soldiers killed 23 Navajos and wounded 5, and 234 were either captured or surrendered. In the next several days, 344 more Navajos came in with the supply train under Maj. Jose D. Sena. By mid-February, there were 1,000 Navajos at the fort. Ten days later there were 1,500. All of them would make the long walk to the reservation at Bosque Redondo in eastern New Mexico.[313]

24 JANUARY 1864
FISH CREEK CANYON (Tortilla Flat, Arizona)

In the months after the Walker prospecting party discovered gold in the Lynx and Granite Creeks area of central Arizona (soon to become the town of Prescott), more whites came in, which inevitably led to confrontations between them and Indians. King S. Woolsey—rancher, miner, frontiersman, merchant, legislator, and Indian-hater—lived in the area, and Apaches constantly raided his ranch on the Agua Fria River. Fed up, Woolsey organized a retaliatory expedition of settlers.

With about 40 men, Woolsey rode all the way down to the Salt River, then east up the Salt. At a Pima Indian village, expedition member Abe Peeples went for supplies and returned with 14 Maricopa Indian scouts under Juan Chivaria, a white man named Cyrus Lennan, and some Pimas. The party then continued east.

On the bright sunny morning of 24 January, marching single-file along a narrow path in Fish Creek Canyon, they ran smack into about 250 Pinal and Coyotero Apaches. Woolsey called out, *"Buenos dias."* The Apaches spoke some Spanish, as did Woolsey's Yuma employee Tonto Jack, who parleyed with them. Soon six chiefs stepped up to meet the whites. Chief Paramucka said he would not sit on the bare ground to talk, so Woolsey had a blood-red blanket spread for him and offered pinole (corn flour) and tobacco as gifts.

Woolsey had arranged a signal for his colleagues to start shooting, and knowing the Apaches did not understand English, he laughingly pointed out an Apache target for each man. At Woolsey's good humor, the Apache leaders dropped their guard, and some even joined in the laughter. Then Woolsey raised his hat, the signal, and his men began blasting away. Five of the six chiefs were killed immediately. The sixth, despite having been shot twice, drove his lance into Cyrus Lennan's heart before another white, Joe Dye, killed him. Stunned, the other Apaches took to their heels. Woolsey's men chased them for half a mile up the wash before desisting.

Strapping Lennan's body to a horse, the party started back. They buried Lennan under a cottonwood tree by the Salt River.

Woolsey's party killed an estimated 19 Apaches and wounded several others. Several of Woolsey's men were also wounded, including Tonto Jack; Lennan's was their only death.[314]

29 JANUARY 1864
SAN ANDRES MOUNTAINS (South-central New Mexico)

On 26 January, after Indians (probably Apaches) ran off some of the stock at Fort Craig, Lt. Thomas A. Young, 5th California Infantry; a sergeant and 11 privates of Company B, 5th California Infantry; and Company D,

1st California Cavalry, left the fort on their trail. Three days later, the soldiers overtook the Indians in the San Andres Mountains. At 9 P.M. that evening, before Young could attack the Indians, 60 warriors assaulted them first. Five soldiers, including Young, were wounded.[315] Too diminished to continue the fight, Young and his troops returned to Fort Craig the next day. The lieutenant estimated that they had killed seven Indians.[316]

25 FEBRUARY 1864
PINOS ALTOS (Southwestern New Mexico)

While camped on the Mimbres River, Capt. James H. Whitlock, 5th California Infantry, received word of Apache depredations at the mining town of Pinos Altos. The Apaches, of the Mimbres and Chiricahua bands, had even announced that they would be back on 25 February. With 21 men of Company F, Whitlock went to catch them, taking an old, indirect route. The men hid in a canyon about three miles from town, and Whitlock sent out a spy, who returned saying there were no Indians. The soldiers waited.

At noon the next day, 26 February, Apaches appeared in town. Whitlock and his men went in stealthily and, at dusk, struck before the Indians could form a defense. The troopers killed most of the Apaches right away and chased the survivors eight miles before giving up. They returned to their camp on the 29th.

Whitlock reported killing 13 of the 19 Apaches, including Chief Luis, the alleged successor to Mangas Coloradas, and he believed he'd wounded the other 6. The soldiers also rescued 22-year-old Marijenia Figueira, captured 15 years before and made a slave of Chief Luis.[317]

29 FEBRUARY 1864
REDWOOD CREEK (Northwestern California)

Lt. Knyphausen Geer of Company A, 1st Battalion California Mountaineers, took 30 men on a scout out of Fort Gaston. On Redwood Creek, near the Weaverville-Arcata trail, Geer sent out patrols. One returned reporting an Indian camp eight miles away. That night, the soldiers marched to the camp, and they attacked at 5:30 A.M. They killed three Indians, wounded several, and captured five. One soldier was wounded.[318]

19, 22, 27, AND 28 MARCH 1864
EAST BRANCH, SOUTH FORK OF THE EEL RIVER
(Northwestern California)

Lt. William E. Hull and his Company D, 2nd California Infantry, went on a scout to the headwaters of the east branch of the South Fork of the Eel River. On Red Mountain, about five miles northeast of present-day Legget, California, Hull's scouts discovered a band of Indians (perhaps Eel River) on 17 March and a chase began, but the Indians got away.

On the evening of 19 March, Hull and his soldiers caught up to the Indians on the east branch. They killed two men and captured two women, but most of the band escaped. On the 22nd, Hull's troops found the fleeing band and pursued them into Bell Springs Canyon, killing two more. The soldiers stayed hot on their trail for five more days, and on 27 March a Sgt. McGuire and four men audaciously burst into a large Indian camp on the east branch, guns blazing. They killed 5 men and captured 11 women and children. The next day, in stormy weather, Hull's troops hit another Indian camp on the east branch, this time killing 16 warriors and capturing 2 women.

In all, the soldiers killed 25 Indians and captured 15 on the expedition. Hull sent his prisoners to district headquarters and congratulated himself on having cleared the area of nonreservation Indians.[319]

7 APRIL 1864
SIERRA BONITA (Duncan, Arizona)

On 15 March, Apaches ran off a government herd at Cow Springs, near Camp Mimbres, a supply depot for the California Volunteers. On the 27th, Capt. James H. Whitlock, 5th California Infantry, left the camp with 26 men of Company F, 20 men of Company I under Lt. George A. Burkett, and 10 troopers of Company C, 1st California Cavalry, as well as guides, to find the raiders. At Stein's Peak, the Apaches' trail indicated that they had turned north down the San Simon Valley. Whitlock and his troops also went north, but on a parallel route east of the Peloncillo Mountains.

Cutting west after several days, the soldiers found fresh tracks near Mount Gray in the Sierra Bonita Mountains, and, at 4 A.M. on 7 April, they spotted campfires in the foothills. Whitlock rushed his command forward, and by sunup they were in position to attack the camp of about 250 Chiricahua Apaches. The Apaches fought for an hour, then fled into the mountains.

As they destroyed the camp, the soldiers set fire to a quantity of dried mescal, an important Apache food source, and about 30 warriors reappeared in an attempt to save it. The soldiers ran them off with a rain of fire. With no casualties of their own, Whitlock's men killed 21 Apaches and recovered about 45 horses and mules.[320]

7 APRIL 1864
HARNEY LAKE VALLEY (Burns, Oregon)

On a hunt for 40 stolen mules and horses, Lt. James A. Waymire headed southeast from Camp Lincoln, on the South Fork of the John Day River, with 15 men of Company D, 1st Oregon Cavalry. The stock's owner, a Mr. Davis, had tracked the thieves, believed to be Paiutes, to Harney Lake. Some of his employees went along with Waymire's expedition, and about 50 more armed volunteers under "Capt." C. H. Miller joined the party at Harney Valley. From there, the party found a trail that led about 20 miles south.

Early on 7 April, Waymire moved out with his own troopers, 30 volunteers led by Miller, and one day's rations. Along the way, they saw a large cloud of smoke about three miles off the trail. Waymire sent a Sgt. Casteel with three other men to investigate, then took the rest of the men over a divide, where they found perhaps 150 Paiutes in a large dry lakebed. For hours, the two sides vied for position. Eventually Miller's volunteers became scattered in ineffectual groups of two and three. Growing bolder, the Paiutes intensified their long-range firing, but only one volunteer was slightly wounded.

After four hours moving across the plain, the soldiers' horses grew tired while the Paiutes appeared to be gaining reinforcements. After noon, Waymire wanted to try a saber charge, but Miller convinced him to fall back instead. Waymire called the retreat, and the soldiers barely got out of the valley intact. Yet in a brisk race that followed, Waymire thought he saw five warriors knocked off their mounts.

Sgt. Casteel's party never returned. Waymire's men searched for them without success, and the four were presumed dead. Back at Camp Lincoln, the lieutenant complained in his report, "It is with pain that I am obliged to state, in justice to myself and command, that our defeat on the 7th instant is due to the want of organization under an efficient commander on the part of the citizen volunteers."[321]

12 APRIL 1864
FREMONT'S ORCHARD (Orchard, Colorado)

On 11 April, rancher W. D. Ripley came into Camp Sanborn, on the South Platte River, to report that Cheyennes were stealing cattle and horses along Bijou Creek. Lt. Clark Dunn and 40 men of Companies C and H, 1st Colorado Cavalry, went with Ripley to recover the stock. Dunn split his men into two scouting parties. Neither group, one scouting along Bijou Creek and the other on the South Platte River, found any Indians. Reuniting near the South Platte, the soldiers saw smoke. Again Dunn split them, sending half toward the smoke and accompanying the others to the river.

About three miles from Fremont's Orchard, Dunn spotted 15 to 20 Cheyennes crossing the river a mile upstream with horses. When Ripley confirmed that the horses were his, the men crossed the river and rode over to the party. Dunn and 15 troopers confronted the warriors while Ripley and 4 troopers went after the stock. As Dunn spoke to the Indians they moved closer, trying to shake hands and show that they were friendly. Dunn was wary, however, and sought to disarm them. The Indians bolted, firing at the soldiers as they fled.

Dunn pursued the Cheyennes for 15 miles, but his horses could not catch up. Four of his men were wounded, two of them fatally, and the Cheyennes also had about four casualties.[322]

These and other cattle thefts by Cheyennes in Colorado sparked the Plains War of 1864.

15 APRIL 1864
EAYRE'S FIGHT (Flagler, Colorado)

In early April, Cheyennes reportedly stole 175 cattle belonging to government contractors Irwin & Jackman. On the 8th, Lt. George S. Eayre set out from Denver after the raiders with 54 men of McLane's Battery of Colorado Volunteer Artillery and 26 men of Company D, 1st Colorado Cavalry, under Lt. Charles E. Phillips.

The party headed southeast, where they picked up a man named Routh, who had been herding the cattle before they were stolen. They went downstream on the Big Sandy River, then found a cattle trail and followed it north to the headwaters of the South Fork of the Republican River. On 15 April, near present-day Flagler, Colorado, they found a Cheyenne camp, and Lt. Phillips went ahead with two men to reconnoiter. Within minutes they were galloping back: the Cheyenne noncombatants were fleeing and warriors were coming their way.

As Eayre and his men headed for the river bottom, a Cheyenne approached within 50 yards of the command and shot and wounded a soldier. Eayre ordered a Lt. Beach to pull the artillery out of the draw and organized ten-man squads to fan out. The attacking warriors retreated. Then Eayre rode to the five-lodge camp, which was deserted. Eayre burned it.

The expedition continued northwest the next day. The men burned another deserted village and recovered 19 cattle, but the party's mules were breaking down from the strain of heavy freight wagons. Eayre returned to Denver on 23 April for lighter wagons.[323]

28 APRIL 1864
BIG BEND OF THE EEL RIVER (Northwestern California)

In a scout led by Capt. William E. Hull, Company D, 2nd California Infantry, through the upper Eel River country, a detachment under a Sgt. Wheeler surprised a band of Indians at the Big Bend of the Eel, northwest of Round Valley. To escape, most of the Indians jumped in the river; some may have drowned. The soldiers killed 8, wounded several, and captured 12 women and children.[324]

2 MAY 1864
KNEELAND'S PRAIRIE (Eureka, California)

With ten men of Company E, 6th California Infantry, Lt. John B. Taylor found an Indian trail near Kneeland's Prairie, a treeless hilltop about ten miles southeast of Eureka, California. The next morning, 1 May, Taylor directed Pvts. Mills and Berry to take the mules and packs and wait for the supply train from Fort Humboldt to Camp Iaqua. Instead of waiting, however, the two men went ahead on the road. At Booth's Run they were about a mile in advance of the train when Indians ambushed them, killing Mills. Berry was shot through the hand but escaped.

Traveling along the same road, Lt. Knyphausen Geer, with four men of Company A, 1st Battalion California Mountaineers, encountered the Indians who had jumped Mills and Berry. Later that day, Taylor and his men joined Geer's party, and they found the Indians' camp on a ridge between two deep ravines. At dawn the next morning, 2 May, Taylor and Geer divided their soldiers, Taylor going south of the camp while Geer went north. When Taylor opened fire, the Indians ran north into Geer's rifles.

The soldiers killed four Indian men and three women, wounded one man, and took four women and children prisoner. On their way to Camp Iaqua, the men found and brought in Mills's body. Berry was found alive on 3 May and taken to Fort Humboldt.[325]

3 MAY 1864
CEDAR CANYON (Sterling, Colorado)

After Lt. Dunn's fight near Fremont's Orchard (see 12 April), Maj. Jacob Downing of the 1st Colorado Cavalry took over at Camp Sanborn. On 18 April Downing received word that Cheyennes had attacked a ranch on the South Platte River. He took 60 men downstream but found no Indians. He scouted up and down the river for over a week, with the same result. Finally on 1 May, at Kelley's Station (American Ranch), Downing captured a half-Sioux man named Spotted Horse and induced him to lead the soldiers to a Cheyenne camp in Cedar Canyon.

The next day Downing set out with 40 men of Companies C and H of the 1st Colorado Cavalry. On the morning of 3 May the command found the 14-lodge camp. The inhabitants were on their way north, led by the aged chief Bull Rib, and in fact knew nothing about the ranch siege. Downing's attack caught them totally by surprise, but they fought back well. With his bow and arrows, Bull Rib's son Lame Shawnee killed a Pvt. Isner of C Company, took his rifle, and wounded another, a Pvt. Wilcox, also of C Company. When the Indians took shelter in the rocks of the canyon, Downing could not get at them. After three hours, with his ammunition running low, Downing pulled out, taking about 100 ponies with him.

One soldier was killed and one wounded in the fight. Two Cheyenne women and two children were killed.

Downing hoped to return with some howitzers and finish the job, but he settled for bringing back 80 men a week later. By then the Cheyennes, of course, were gone. Downing burned the lodges.[326]

4 MAY 1864
DOUBTFUL CANYON (San Simon, Arizona)

Lt. Henry H. Stevens, 5th California Infantry, and 54 men of Company I were on a march from Fort Cummings to Fort Bowie. As they passed through Doubtful Canyon near Stein's Peak, about 100 Apaches attacked them. The fight lasted for nearly two hours and resulted in 10 Apaches dead and about 20 wounded, and 1 soldier missing, presumed killed, and 6 wounded, 1 mortally.[327]

16 MAY 1864
BIG BUSHES (Schoenchen, Kansas)

His April expedition against raiding Cheyennes having been hampered by heavy wagons (see Eayre's Fight, 15 April), Lt. George S. Eayre set out on another expedition from Denver with 15 lighter wagons and 84 men, including McLane's Battery (Colorado Volunteer Artillery) and Company D of the 1st Colorado Cavalry. On 1 May the troops were at the headwaters of the Smoky Hill River, on the Colorado-Kansas border, about 160 miles southeast of Denver. Continuing east along the river, Eayre missed the Cheyenne camps of Coon and Crow Chief as well as a village of Brules. At Big Bushes, on the Smoky Hill River south of present-day Hays, Kansas, the soldiers found a Cheyenne camp.

On the morning of 16 May, Cheyenne hunters brought the camp news that soldiers were approaching from the west. Two men in the camp, Black Kettle and Lean Bear, had gone to Washington the year before and considered themselves friends of the whites. President Lincoln had even given Lean Bear a medal, which he wore when he rode out to meet Eayre. But at the Indians' approach, Eayre deployed his men into line and without further ado began firing. Lean Bear and two other Cheyennes went down in the first fusillade.

The Indians shot a few soldiers off their horses, but then the howitzers came up and began blasting the village. At this, more than 500 enraged warriors responded, ready to sweep over the now disorganized soldiers. But Black Kettle rode frenziedly among the warriors, urging them to stop the fighting. If not for him, Eayre's command would probably have been slaughtered. As it was, the soldiers were able to pull away, though warriors followed them and sniped at them most of the way to Fort Larned.

A total of three Cheyennes died in the fight and a dozen were wounded. The Cheyennes killed four soldiers and wounded three. The incident convinced many Cheyennes that war was the only way to deal with the whites.[328]

16 MAY 1864
SPIRIT LAKE (Spirit Lake, Iowa)

On 16 May, ten Sisseton Sioux, possibly from White Lodge's or Sleepy Eye's band, attacked a two-man post at Spirit Lake. The two men of the 7th Iowa Cavalry made a spirited defense, beating off the attack and reportedly wounding or killing three Indians. One of the soldiers, a Sgt. Whitlock, was seriously wounded.[329]

18 MAY 1864
CROOKED RIVER (Paulina, Oregon)

Capt. John M. Drake of the 1st Oregon Cavalry led an expedition southeast from Fort Dalles to look for Indians who had been raiding west of Canyon City. A march of about 170 miles brought them near the junction of the north and south forks of the Crooked River. There Warm Springs Indian scouts brought word of a nine-lodge Shoshone camp a dozen miles to the northeast. Drake sent Lt. J. M. McCall, 26 men of Company D, 13 men of Company B under Lt. Stephen Watson, and 10 of the Warm Springs scouts to strike the camp "without preliminaries."

The party left early on 17 May, proceeding over high, rocky country. At 2 A.M. they reached the camp, which sat in a juniper-shaded basin, and planned their assault. Two hours later, the scouts attacked from the north, McCall and his men from the south, and Watson's command from the west. McCall quickly found himself mired in swampy ground they had not seen in the darkness. Meanwhile about 50 well-armed Shoshones under Chief Po-li-ni retreated 300 yards east to good defensive positions on a boulder-strewn hillside.[330] Watson charged after them. At the edge of a cliff the Indians fired into Watson's squad, killing the lieutenant and two others and wounding five. A civilian, Richard Barker, and the Warm Springs chief Stock Whitley were also wounded.

The battle lasted only 15 minutes. Realizing the Indians' position was impregnable, McCall retreated and sent for help. The messenger reached Drake the next morning, and the captain hurried to the camp with 40 men of Company G. He found McCall's party on a small rise nearly a mile from the battle site. The Indians had fled only an hour before. The soldiers went to retrieve their dead from the field and found the bodies had been stripped and mutilated.

The expedition had killed 3 Shoshones and captured 50 horses, but Drake's losses were 3 soldiers and 1 Warm Springs scout killed, and 5 soldiers, scout Whitley, and civilian Barker wounded.[331]

27 MAY 1864
THOMAS'S RANCH (Burnt Ranch, California)

A Sgt. Wilson took nine men of Company C, 1st Battalion California Mountaineers, up the Trinity River to search for Indians. On the afternoon of 27 May at Thomas's Ranch, the soldiers spotted a camp of a dozen Indians. Wilson and his soldiers charged the camp, killing three men and a woman, and wounding two others. Then, from across the river, about 20 Indians under Chief Frank loosed a volley of bullets. The Mountaineers dove into the timber for cover and returned fire, wounding two more Indians.

The shooting continued until dark, when Sgt. Wilson realized that he could not safely drive the remaining Indians off the ranch. He broke off the fight, having suffered no casualties, and marched his command to their camp at Burnt Ranch, eight miles up the Trinity.[332]

28 MAY 1864
BIG FLAT (Shelter Cove, California)

Detachments of Company E, 1st Battalion California Mountaineers, under Lt. William W. Frazier, searching the coastal mountains from Cape Mendocino to Shelter Cove for Indians, found signs of Indians at the mouth of the Mattole River and began tracking them. At Bull Run Gulch, they came close to an Indian camp, but they frightened a bear into the camp, alerting the Indians, who fled.

The Mountaineers found the band's tracks again on the South Fork of the Mattole River and followed them toward the coast, but at one point the Indians had set fire to the grass to hide their trail. A Sgt. Byrnes and several men cut directly to the coast, then headed north. They discovered about ten of the Indians camped on Big Flat, about eight miles north of Shelter Cove, on 27 May. Byrnes decided to stay hidden and wait. About 5 A.M. the next day, the Indians started down the beach, walking straight into Byrnes's rifles.

Frazier reported that the Mountaineers killed all the Indians, but actually they killed only two, while eight got away.[333]

29 MAY 1864
MESCAL CREEK (Coolidge Dam, Arizona)

In the spring of 1864, Gen. James H. Carleton planned a relentless campaign against the Apaches, much like the one Kit Carson had recently led to defeat the Navajos. Several columns of the 1st and 5th California Infantry, 1st California Cavalry, and 1st New Mexico Infantry left Las Cruces, Tucson, and Forts Whipple, Bowie, Canby, Wingate, McRae, and Craig to punish the Apaches. In addition, the soldiers were to scout along the middle Gila River for a site to build Fort Goodwin. Carleton's inspector general, Lt. Col. Nelson H. Davis, would make the final selection.

Escorted by Capt. Thomas T. Tidball and 86 men of Companies C, I, and K, 5th California Infantry, and 16 men of Companies C and L, 1st California Cavalry, Davis left Fort Bowie on 9 May and headed north. When the party reached the Gila River they headed downstream, examining potential sites along the tributaries and skirmishing with the Apaches they ran into. At the mouth of the San Carlos River they found evidence of Indians and headed upriver for five miles. Coming upon a small rancheria, they killed one Apache. One trooper was wounded.

The soldiers returned to the Gila and followed it into its great canyon, where they captured two Apache children and five women. The women said their husbands were in the Mescal Mountains. With one woman as a guide, Tidball's men found two rancherias in Mescal Creek Canyon. The next day, 29 May, Tidball split his command and surrounded the rancherias, himself charging one of the camps and Lt. George A. Burkett hitting the other. With a two-to-one advantage, the soldiers all but obliterated the camps. They followed a trail of blood down the canyon after Chief Ska-ish-nah for half a mile and killed him.

Tidball and his men killed or captured 42 of the 49 occupants of the two rancherias and destroyed the lodges and supplies. In all, Tidball's excursion killed 51 Apaches, wounded 17, and captured 16 in addition to destroying large quantities of crops, food, and camp equipment. One trooper was wounded.[334]

7–8 JUNE 1864
SAN CARLOS RIVER (San Carlos, Arizona)

With Apaches raiding on both sides of the U.S.–Mexico border, on 25 May Capt. Julius C. Shaw, 1st New Mexico Cavalry, left Fort Wingate on an expedition to the Gila River to stop them. With him were Lt. Jose M. Sanches, 40 men of Company F, 20 men of Company B, 1 civilian guide, and rations for 60 days. On 6 June, Shaw and his men reached the head-waters of the San Carlos River and traveled downstream to the vicinity of an Apache rancheria he hoped to surprise the next morning. Daybreak revealed the rancheria to be deserted.

Continuing down the west bank of the river, Shaw heard a dog barking and sent skirmishers into the dense timber. With rifles blazing, they charged a cluster of wickiups, killing an old woman and a boy and capturing two other women and two boys. One of the captives told Shaw about another rancheria downriver. He went there, but found this camp, too, deserted. Shaw called a halt in the early afternoon, and late in the day several Apaches appeared, bearing a white flag. They thought Shaw and his men were some Mexican traders they had been expecting. Not disabusing them of that notion, Shaw told them to return at sunup.

The next morning, 8 June, Shaw's men stood ready for action. About 76 warriors, plus some women, showed up. Shaw told them to stay on the other side of the river. They asked to parley, so Shaw and Sanches met Chief Soldado, his Mexican interpreter Francisco, and a dozen warriors. When the Apaches asked the two men what they had to sell, Shaw said he was not selling anything, he was there to fight, unless the Indians complied with certain conditions. The Apaches said they already knew it. They said they had a good-conduct pass but could not produce it. They also claimed they had never harmed anyone north of the border. Finally they promised to give Shaw 30 hostages as a token of peace.

Shaw wrote, "I was flattering myself on the successful termination of my negotiation, when the Indians requested permission to retire to their people for the purpose of . . . selecting those that were to go with me."[335] After an hour, no Apaches had returned, and those who had stayed behind began to leave. When Shaw ordered them not to, they ran. Shaw gave the order to fire. About 14 Apaches fell in the first volley; the rest scattered. The soldiers gave chase, shooting down several more Apaches before breaking off the pursuit.

With no losses of their own, Shaw and his men killed about 20 Apaches and confiscated a horse and some weapons and blankets.[336]

11 JUNE 1864
HUNGATE MASSACRE (Parker, Colorado)

After Indians ran off some cattle at the Van Wormer ranch, about 30 miles southeast of Denver on Running Creek, ranch manager Nathan W. Hungate rode out to look for strays. Seeing smoke rising from the direction

Site of Hungate Massacre (Colorado); the house stood between the poles.

of the ranch, he rode back to find the house on fire and his family dead, then he was captured and killed. The perpetrators were believed to be a small band of Arapahos.

The four badly mutilated bodies were brought to Denver and put on display. Outraged Denverites, along with the city's newspaper, the *Rocky Mountain News*, screamed for revenge.[337]

CA. 15 JUNE 1864
LITTLE COLORADO RIVER (Eastern Arizona)

On a scout out of Fort Canby, Capt. Albert H. Pfeiffer, 1st New Mexico Cavalry, 1 lieutenant, and 64 enlisted men attacked a band of Coyotero Apaches near the Little Colorado River. In an eight-mile-long running fight, the soldiers killed five Apaches and wounded seven. Later two Indians came into the troopers' camp. They made signs of peace but soon began shooting, severely wounding Pfeiffer and a private named Pedro Rael. The other soldiers killed the two warriors instantly. The sound of the gunshots brought a large party of Apaches running toward the camp, but the soldiers fired at them, wounding several and scattering the rest. The men returned to Fort Canby with their wounded captain.[338]

24 JUNE 1864
JOHN DAY'S ROAD (Silver Lake, Oregon)

Southwest of present-day Silver Lake, Oregon, on the California–John Day's Road, a band of Klamath and Modoc Indians attacked a wagon train escorted by a detachment of the 1st Oregon Cavalry. The Indians wounded 2 soldiers, stole 7 cattle, and destroyed 3,000 pounds of flour. The train retreated south to the Sprague River to await further escort.[339]

24 JUNE 1864
LOOKING GLASS CREEK (Genoa, Nebraska)

After a hard day's work on 24 June, about half a dozen hay cutters working for Nebraska farmer Patrick Murray, who was contracted to cut hay for the military garrison at the Pawnee Agency near present-day Genoa, Nebraska, were finishing supper in their camp beside Looking Glass Creek. They saw some Indians riding over a hill to the northwest and assumed they were Pawnees from the agency.

Soon the Indians showed up at the workers' camp. They were Lakotas. They demanded to be fed and became increasingly belligerent. When they began untying the hay cutters' horses and mules, one of Murray's men pulled a gun. The camp erupted in chaos. The Lakotas shot, stabbed, and clubbed the hay cutters. The outfit's cook, Bridget Murray, tried to defend herself with a pitchfork before arrows hit her. The fight was over quickly. The Lakotas took the stock and departed.

A boy hidden under a haystack ran to the Pawnee Agency. Capt. James B. David of Company E, 7th Iowa Cavalry, arrived the next morning with troopers and found six civilians wounded, three mortally. Bridget Murray, discovered wandering the prairie, survived.[340]

9–21 JULY 1864
LITTLE COLORADO RIVER EXPEDITION (Eastern Arizona)
Capt. Saturnino Baca, Company E, 1st New Mexico Cavalry, left Fort Canby on 9 July with 53 enlisted men on a scout for Indians. They marched southwest to the Little Colorado River where, over the next two weeks, in a series of skirmishes, they killed six Indians (probably Navajo), took six prisoner, captured livestock, and destroyed large supplies of food.[341]

12 JULY 1864
KELLY WAGON TRAIN (LaPrele, Wyoming)
When a wagon train from Kansas consisting of ten emigrants, including the Josiah S. Kelly family, the Larimer family, and others, reached Fort Laramie, people at the fort assured them that the road ahead was safe and that the Indians were friendly. A few more wagons joined them when they left the fort.

As the train was crossing Little Box Elder Creek, about four miles west of LaPrele Station, more than 200 Oglala Sioux swept in. Professing friendship, the Indians asked for food and supplies, and the emigrants fed them. After the meal, the warriors attacked with guns and arrows. Kelly, Larimer, and a servant were wounded but escaped. The four other men—Gardner Wakefield, a Mr. Taylor, a Mr. Sharp, and a servant named Franklin, were killed. The Indians tore through the wagons, looting and destroying, and captured Kelly's and Larimer's wives and the two children.

It was dark when they rode away, and Mrs. Kelly let her little daughter slide off the horse, hoping she would be rescued. Instead, the girl's father found her body later, filled with arrows and scalped. The next night, Mrs. Larimer and her son managed to steal away and made it to safety. The Sioux returned Mrs. Kelly to Fort Sully in December.[342]

28 JULY–4 AUGUST 1864
PINAL MOUNTAINS EXPEDITION (Globe, Arizona)
On an Indian scout out of Fort Goodwin on 18 July, Maj. Thomas J. Blakeney, 1st California Cavalry, led Company E, 5th California Infantry under Capt. Benjamin F. Harrover; Company I, 1st New Mexico Infantry, under Capt. Smith H. Simpson; and a detachment of Company E, 1st California Cavalry, under Capt. Chauncey R. Wellman. On 24 July the troops reached Camp Rigg, where detachments from each of the companies were detailed to remain with Wellman. On the 26th the remaining command

marched eight miles west to Jaycox's Spring and camped. They hoped to surprise an Apache rancheria believed to be on Pinal Creek.

They marched all the next evening, but became lost. At midnight they chanced upon a camp of Indians in a deep ravine on the divide between Pinal and Mineral Creeks. Blakeney determined to keep going and try to reach the main village before any of the Indians could warn them. The troops came upon the Apache village around noon, but when Lt. Amos J. Stockwell and his men charged in, the wickiups were empty.

Blakeney advanced his command to another rancheria about 30 miles from Jaycox's Spring. There three Apaches appeared with a white flag wanting to talk. One of them told Blakeney she would get the Apaches to surrender, for they did not want to fight the white men. For the next three days the two sides parleyed, Blakeney never allowing more than 20 Apaches at a time into his camp. Chief Crooked Foot said he would advise his people to give themselves up.

Meanwhile one Apache woman recognized a boy who was traveling with the troops as her son, and the Indians took him. In response Blakeney seized two Apache men, two boys, and two women as hostages for the boy's return. That night, one of the women and one boy tried to escape, and the soldiers shot and killed them.

With relations breaking down, on 1 August Blakeney gave his men orders to kill any Apaches big enough to bear arms and to capture women and children. He split up his force, sending Harrover with Company E over the mountain west of Pinal Creek and Simpson over the mountains to the south, with Stockwell scouring the valley. Blakeney himself took 26 men from Company E, 5th California Infantry, into the mountains east of Pinal Creek. Blakeney's party killed only one Apache, who turned out to be a woman, and captured one woman. The other units found no Indians.

In a last attempt to get the stolen boy back, Blakeney let one of the original hostages go. If she did not return with the boy in two days, he told her, he would kill the remaining prisoners. She did not return, and Blakeney hung the two Apache men at sundown on 3 August. The next day Blakeney received orders to return to Camp Rigg, where he brought the two remaining captives.

In total, Blakeney's troops had killed 10 Apaches and destroyed 20 acres of corn.[343]

28 JULY 1864
KILLDEER MOUNTAIN (Killdeer, North Dakota)

On 19 July Brig. Gen. Alfred Sully continued his campaign against the Sioux that had begun the previous fall (see Whitestone Hill, 3 September 1863). He left the newly built Fort Rice and went up the Missouri River with about 3,000 soldiers, along with some emigrants who wanted protection. On 23 July, Sully left the emigrants near the Heart River and proceeded on with 2,200 men. The First Brigade consisted of 11 companies of Lt. Col. Samuel M. Pollock's 6th Iowa Cavalry, 3 companies of Lt. Col. John Pattee's 7th Iowa Cavalry, 2 companies of Capt. Nelson Minor's Dakota Cavalry, 4 companies of Maj. Alfred B. Brackett's Minnesota Battalion, 70 scouts, and 4 mountain howitzers. The Second Brigade, under Col. Minor T. Thomas, had 8 mounted companies of Lt. Col. Henry C. Rogers's 8th Minnesota Infantry, 6 companies of Col. Robert N. McLaren's 2nd Minnesota Cavalry, and 4 howitzers.

The Sioux were waiting for Sully and his soldiers on the wooded slopes of Killdeer Mountain. They had a huge camp there: over 1,600 lodges, an estimated 8,000 Hunkpapas, Santees, Blackfeet, Yanktonais, Sans Arcs, and Minneconjous, probably over 3,000 of them warriors. (Sully estimated that there were over 5,000 warriors, though the Indians claimed it was 1,600.) Sully formed his force into a hollow square over one mile long per side, then advanced to about five miles south of the village. Cautious, he let his artillery predominate instead of charging into hand-to-hand combat.

On the Indian side, many Lakotas under Sitting Bull and Gall formed up on the right while Yanktonais and Dakotas under Inkpaduta took the left. Around noon a young Hunkpapa, Lone Dog, rode up near the soldiers, brandishing his war club and taunting them. Finally Sully tired of his

Killdeer Mountain (North Dakota);
photo taken from position of artillery firing on Indian camp

antics and sent a message to Pattee: "The general sends his compliments and wishes you to kill that Indian for God's sake."[344]

Sharpshooters fired and Lone Dog tumbled down, but bounced back up and rode off. Sully advanced his square slowly north. The Indians made scores of sorties against the flanks. With a few well-placed shots, Sgt. John Jones's battery foiled an assault on Brackett's battalion and another on the supply train.

By late afternoon, Sully had advanced to the camp. Now the Indian women tore down the lodges and prepared to escape over the mountain. To protect them, Inkpaduta led a serious charge against Sully's right. Brackett's men countered it with a mounted charge, and the hand-to-hand fight that Sully had wished to avoid came about. Brackett came out ahead in the fight, and the Indians broke away.

Meanwhile, on the left, the Dakota Cavalry swung out with two howitzers and sent round after round into the village. The artillery fire caused most of the battle's Indian casualties. With darkness gathering, Sully called his men back and let the howitzers finish the job. By sunset no living warrior remained at the Killdeer Mountain camp. Most had fled.

The next day Sully's men burned hundreds of tipis, 40 tons of pemmican, and other supplies, and killed 3,000 dogs. Sully estimated 150 Indians had been killed, almost all of them warriors. Due to his tight, controlled square and judicious use of howitzers, only 5 of his men were killed and 10 were wounded.[345]

5 AUGUST 1864
PINAL CREEK (Burch, Arizona)

When Maj. Thomas J. Blakeney pulled out of the Pinal Creek valley (see Pinal Mountains Expedition, 28 July–4 August), he left Sgt. B. F. Fergusson in charge of 12 men of Company E, 5th California Infantry; 12 of Company I, 1st New Mexico Infantry; and 3 of "Col." King Woolsey's citizen volunteers. Secreted about camp, the men had instructions to remain hidden until evening and to kill any Indians who came in. About three hours after Blakeney left, 15 Apaches approached. Fergusson's men opened fire, and the Indians fled. The dense brush impeded the soldiers' pursuit, but ultimately they killed or mortally wounded five warriors.[346]

7–9 AUGUST 1864
BADLANDS (Medora, North Dakota)

After the battle at Killdeer Mountain (see 28 July), Brig. Gen. Alfred Sully picked up the emigrants he had left at the Heart River and continued west with his large force. A torturous march brought the party on 5 August to the rim of the arid Badlands—40 miles of 600-foot-deep canyons and insurmountable buttes. "Truly hell with the fires burned out," Sully called it.[347] However, knowing that supply boats were waiting on the Yellowstone River on other side, Sully went forward.

On Sunday, 7 August, while the company was camped near the Little Missouri River, a band of Sioux struck. One group of warriors rained down arrows from the top of a 500-foot butte while another ran off some horses. The Sioux said they had 10,000 warriors as well as a white woman captive (Fanny Kelly—see Kelly Wagon Train, 12 July), and they dared the soldiers to attack.

The next day, Sully led his troops across the river and up a plateau, where a large force of Indians was waiting. The warriors surrounded Sully's men on three sides, but the artillerymen heaved their cannons up the slope and saved the day. As the artillery pushed the Indians back, the Dakota and 7th Iowa Cavalries foiled two assaults. Six of Sully's force were wounded, including the troops' Blackfoot guide. Finally, the head of the column reached the far side of Flat Top Butte, where they were able to rest.

The next morning, 9 August, another 1,000 Sioux appeared before the column. With Lt. Col. Samuel M. Pollock's 6th Iowa Cavalry on the right and Lt. Col. John Pattee's 7th Iowa Cavalry on the left, the soldiers pushed forward and cleared the way. With long-range rifles, cannons, and some trickery, the troopers drained the Indians' spirit. By evening, the Sioux had virtually abandoned the fight.

The next day Sully's expedition broke into open country, and they reached the Yellowstone River, another 25 miles, on 12 August. Sully estimated his troopers killed 100 Indians on their three-day journey through the Badlands. Army casualties were placed at 9 killed and 100 wounded.[348]

7–9 AUGUST 1864
LITTLE BLUE RIVER RAID (Oak, Nebraska)

Trouble brewing earlier in 1864 broke out in a fury at the end of the summer as hundreds of Cheyennes and some Sioux rampaged along the Overland Trail. Particularly hard-hit were ranches along a 60-mile stretch of the Little Blue River between present-day Fairbury and Hastings, Nebraska. On 7 August, 23 civilians were killed or mortally wounded. On the 9th, nine people were killed or mortally wounded, most of them at the Gilman ranch; three others were wounded. When the raids were over, Indians had killed 38 settlers, wounded 9, and captured 5.[349]

8 AUGUST 1864
PLUM CREEK MASSACRE (Lexington, Nebraska)

In addition to raiding along the Little Blue River (see previous entry), Cheyennes attacked along the Overland Trail west of Fort Kearny. Two miles west of the Plum Creek stage station, on the south side of the Platte River southeast of present-day Lexington, Nebraska, Mart Bowler's corralled bull

Oak Grove Ranch on the Little Blue River (Nebraska)

train was breaking camp when Cheyennes attacked. With an arrow piercing his buckskin vest, 14-year-old bullwhacker William Gay fired a shot to alert his comrades, who blasted away. The Cheyennes rode right into the circle of wagons, but the teamsters managed to drive them out. After circling a few times, the Cheyennes disappeared, leaving behind two of their own dead and three wounded teamsters.

The same morning, about five miles east of the first attack, a wagon train heading west—consisting of three wagons of Thomas F. Morton, three of William Marble, and six of Michael Kelly—was charged by 100 Cheyennes from bluffs to the south. Some believed there was no cause for alarm at first, but James Smith and his wife urged their team into a run and peeled away from the rest of the wagons. Mrs. Smith jumped from the wagon and hid in the cattails as her husband rushed on.

The warriors swept in and the teams scattered. Nancy Morton, age 19, began to run. She saw her cousin and brother firing at the Indians, but she saw both die before she was captured. Thrust up behind a Cheyenne rider, she noticed she had arrows in her thigh and left side. The Indians also captured young Danny Marble.

At Plum Creek Station, Bowler's bull train had arrived, but they had only one rifle and some short-range weapons. Lt. Joseph Bone, Company

Site of emigrant massacre at Plum Creek (Nebraska)

G, 7th Iowa Cavalry, was unable to do more than telegraph a message to Fort Kearny. But it was too late. The Cheyennes disappeared with their 2 captives, 13 emigrants dead in their wake.[350]

9 AUGUST 1864
ELLISON SPRINGS (Gorman, Texas)

A party of about 35 Kiowas or Comanches on a horse raid several miles northwest of present-day Gorman, Texas, ran into a scout of about 15 Texas militiamen under Lt. Singleton Gilbert. The militia attacked, but the Indians prevailed, escaping with most of the horses. They killed Gilbert and two other militiamen and wounded three, suffering no casualties.[351]

11 AUGUST 1864
SAND CREEK (Lamar, Colorado)

Numerous reports of Indian depredations kept detachments of the 1st Colorado Cavalry in the field. When some Indians chased a soldier near Fort Lyon, Maj. Edward W. Wynkoop sent Lt. Joseph A. Cramer, Company G, and 15 men from Companies D and L in pursuit. Riding down the Arkansas River four miles, then cutting north for three miles, Cramer and his men saw a band of Indians about six miles ahead.

The Indians, 14 Arapahos led by Neva, were traveling to Fort Lyon to inquire about a peace proposal from Colorado governor John Evans. Neva said later that he tried to show a soldier a letter he had from Evans, but the soldier ran away.

Cramer chased the band for more than 15 miles. When the Arapahos finally turned to fight, Cramer's command, with failing horses, was straggling. By the time Cramer pulled his command together, the Arapahos once again fled. The chase continued until exhausted horses and a heavy rainstorm convinced Cramer to return to the fort. Cramer had captured one pony and thought he had wounded four Indians, but the Arapahos said they had no damage.

In the meantime, Neva had received reinforcements and gained a vantage point from which he could have killed all the soldiers, but because he was on a peace mission, he said, he restrained his warriors from attacking.[352]

16 AUGUST 1864
ELK CREEK (Nelson, Nebraska)

Capt. Edward P. Murphy left Fort Kearny on 12 August with about 125 men, including his Company A, 7th Iowa Cavalry, to help the settlers the Cheyennes had attacked along the Little Blue River (see Little Blue River Raid, 7–9 August). Only 50 of the soldiers were mounted. At Hook's Ranch, Murphy "borrowed" some horses belonging to Ben Holladay's stage company.

Continuing along the Little Blue, the troops picked up some civilian volunteers. Two of them were George Constable, who had lost an ox team in the raids, and Joe Roper, whose daughter, Laura, was missing and presumed captured. At Little Blue Station Murphy sent a detail led by Capt. Henry Kuhl, 1st Nebraska Veteran Cavalry, downriver to inter any unburied bodies.

On 16 August, as Murphy and his troops and volunteers scouted the area along Elk Creek, some of the civilians rode ahead of the soldiers, and the Cheyennes saw an opportunity to attack. One quick strike sent the civilians wheeling back. George Constable fell dead, an arrow in his side. Topping a rise, Capt. Murphy sent a howitzer shell into the Indians and drove them back, but the shot cracked the cannon's limber, rendering it useless.

Estimating that there were 500 Indians, Murphy decided to retreat. The Cheyennes followed the soldiers for ten miles, slashing in and out. It was nearly dark when the disorganized companies reached the Little Blue again and forded it to the relative safety of the station.

The Cheyennes killed one soldier, Pvt. John Creek, of the 1st Nebraska Veteran Cavalry, as well as the civilian Constable. Murphy reported killing ten Indians, no doubt an exaggeration.[353]

16 AUGUST 1864
SMOKY HILL CROSSING (Carneiro, Kansas)

A six-man detachment of Company H, 7th Iowa Cavalry, left Salina, Kansas, carrying orders for the commanding officer at Fort Larned to intercept Cheyennes who had been raiding along the Overland Trail near Fort Kearny and were now moving south. However, at about 4 P.M. on Alum Creek, east of the Smoky Hill crossing of the Santa Fe Road, about 200 Cheyennes waylaid the messengers, killing four of them. The two surviving soldiers hightailed it back to Salina.[354]

25 AUGUST 1864
SACRAMENTO MOUNTAINS (Alamogordo, New Mexico)

Capt. Francis McCabe, 1st New Mexico Cavalry, left Fort Sumner with 43 men of Company L and 6 Navajo guides to scout for Apache raiders. At Fort Stanton he met up with Lt. Henry W. Gilbert and 8 men of the same regiment. Gilbert had tracked the raiders to the Sierra Oscura and led McCabe and the men west through the Malpais Lava Beds to find the Apaches' rancheria. But it was not there.

The party moved south to the San Andres Mountains and east across the White Sands to the Sacramento Mountains, where they picked up the trail of about 14 Apaches. McCabe took his broken-down horses and barefoot men north to a camp near Tularosa while Gilbert and 20 men took the best mounts and followed the trail. It led east through the mountains to the Sacramento River, southeast of present-day Alamogordo.

On 25 August, near Almagre Springs, Gilbert dismounted his cavalry to lead the horses up a steep slope. Nearly at the top, the soldiers discovered they had walked into an ambush. One of the first bullets killed Gilbert, and five other troopers were wounded in the volley of arrows and musketry. The soldiers fell back, abandoning most of their horses. [355]

In addition to Gilbert, two of the five wounded men, Pvt. Sandoval and the guide Sanchez, died before they reached camp. One Apache was killed.

2 SEPTEMBER 1864
RED BUTTES/FORT DILTS (Marmarth, North Dakota)

Capt. James L. Fisk was leading 200 emigrants and gold-seekers in 88 wagons to the mines of Montana. At Fort Rice, on the Missouri River, Fisk begged for an escort, and 47 soldiers, led by a Lt. Smith of Company A, Dakota Cavalry, headed out with the train on 23 August. Brig. Gen. Alfred Sully was not happy to be responsible for yet another group of emigrants and feared trouble.

On 2 September, about 130 miles west of Fort Rice, Sully's fear was realized. In the gully of Deep Creek, about 12 miles east of present-day

Site of Fort Dilts (North Dakota)

Marmarth, North Dakota, a wagon turned over, and two other wagons stopped to assist. Leaving nine soldiers behind as guards while repairs were made, the rest of the train moved on. Soon Sitting Bull and 100 Hunkpapa Sioux attacked the isolated wagons, cutting down most of the defenders in the first few minutes. One soldier did manage to put a bullet into Sitting Bull's hip, and White Bull and Jumping Bull pulled their chief to safety.

A mile ahead on the trail, Fisk and the others heard the gunfire. After corralling the train, Fisk hurried back with 50 soldiers and civilian volunteers. A scout, Jefferson Dilts, met one of the survivors running toward the wagon train. By the time Dilts reached the scene, the Hunkpapas were looting the wagons. Recklessly, Dilts charged. Blasting away with a carbine and a six-gun, he shot six Hunkpapas before reining his horse around. He did not retreat fast enough, however, and took three arrows in the back.

Fisk and the rest of the rescuers, running square into the Hunkpapas, quickly forted up and fought until sunset. After dark they crept back to the corralled wagons. The Indians did not show up.

Ten soldiers and two civilians, including Dilts, were killed. Six Hunkpapas were killed, most or all by Dilts, and Sitting Bull was wounded. From the wagons, the Hunkpapas looted rifles and 4,000 bullets, plus liquor and cigars.

The wagon train continued a few miles the next morning, but the Indians attacked again. Fisk corralled the wagons again and the soldiers and emigrants built sod walls for cover, naming their fortification Fort Dilts after the brave scout. They stayed holed up for several days, suffering no casualties. On 5 September, over 400 Indians probed the earthworks, but the defenders held out. That night, Lt. Smith and 13 men crept out and rode to Fort Rice for help. The train members waited at Fort Dilts for two more weeks before an angry Sully dispatched 900 men to rescue them. On 20 September, the Fisk party was escorted back to Fort Rice.[356]

20 SEPTEMBER 1864
COTTONWOOD CANYON (Maxwell, Nebraska)

With a scurvy outbreak at Fort Cottonwood, a small party was sent out to gather some fruit. A Capt. Mitchell, a Cpl. Anderson, and an orderly, 7th Iowa Cavalry, took seven patients in an ambulance wagon to pick plums in Cottonwood Canyon, a few miles south. There they met up with two more troopers, rounding up stray horses.

As the soldiers sat eating some of the fruit, Cheyenne warriors burst from the bushes. Mitchell's party clambered into the ambulance and bounced down the winding trail, while the two troopers mounted up and beat a hasty retreat. The warriors knocked one of the two from his saddle and killed him. The speeding wagon ran into more warriors coming up the canyon. Mitchell ordered the driver to veer off the trail and up the hillside.

With the party's only arms, Mitchell and Anderson tried to shoot, but the lurching ambulance tossed both men out. The Indians found Anderson, who spit out a rapid fire with his Spencer repeater and hit nine warriors before they wounded him, captured him, and exacted a terrible vengeance. Mitchell lay hidden close by and later ran back to the fort.

There were about 60 Indians engaged in the fight, and Anderson killed or wounded 9 of them. He and 3 other soldiers were killed and their bodies were mutilated.[357]

25 SEPTEMBER 1864
PAWNEE FORK (Ravanna, Kansas)

Hoping to "do a little killing," Maj. Gen. James G. Blunt, commander of the Upper Arkansas district, marched out of Fort Larned on 22 September with 400 2nd Colorado Cavalrymen, Companies L and M of the 1st Colorado Cavalry, 2 mountain howitzers, some Delaware Indian scouts, and 10 days' rations. They followed the Arkansas River south to the Cimarron Crossing, where Blunt learned of a large force of Indians (probably Cheyenne) on the Smoky Hill River, many miles to the north. Cutting cross-country, Blunt and his men reached the Pawnee Fork of the Arkansas the next day, 25 September, at dawn.

Blunt sent a scouting party upstream to hunt for a crossing. The scouts ran into a lodge and soon after, Cheyenne warriors. Blunt heard the firing and dispatched Maj. Scott J. Anthony, commander of Fort Larned, and 59 men of the 1st Colorado Cavalry to the scene. Six miles upstream, near present-day Ravanna, Kansas, Anthony and his soldiers collided with a much larger force of Indians.

Anthony sent messengers to alert Blunt but the Indians cut them off. Anthony fell back, firing, for five miles. After 11 soldiers had been hit, he finally formed his men up in a defensive perimeter while the Indians circled around. The soldiers managed to hit one warrior close to the perimeter, and Fall Leaf, a Delaware scout, went out with a war whoop and scalped him. In Anthony's perception, the scalping "seemed to strike more terror into those Indians than anything else we had done that day."[358]

Having heard nothing from Anthony for an hour, Blunt headed upriver with the rest of the command, arriving just in time to drive the Indians away. The soldiers chased the Indians west for two days, until their horses gave out. The Indians then headed north toward the Smoky Hill River.

In total, the Indians killed two troopers and wounded nine. Blunt counted nine Indian bodies.[359]

10 OCTOBER 1864
WHITE BUTTE CREEK (Sterling, Colorado)

Cheyennes were appearing more and more boldly along the Denver Road in the fall of 1864. On 9 October, people at Wisconsin Ranch, a few miles south of present-day Sterling, Colorado, saw a warrior in full war regalia. By sundown, word of the sighting reached Capt. David H. Nichols, Company D, 3rd Colorado Cavalry, at Valley Station on the South Platte River, about five miles downstream from Wisconsin Ranch. A local man, Sam Ashcraft, told Nichols of a spring in the sand hills, about 12 miles southeast, where the Cheyennes might be camped. Nichols decided to "have a little surprise party."

Leaving at 2 A.M., Nichols, accompanied by 2nd Lt. Lewis H. Dickson and 40 men, with 2 civilians as guides, arrived at the spring about sunup on 10 October. They found two lodges containing at least six warriors, three women, and a teenage boy. Nichols dashed in and opened fire, and the Cheyennes, led by Big Wolf, returned the fire. By the time the Indians raised a white flag, it was too late. Nichols had his men wipe out the band.

The soldiers scalped most of the dead. By a pool of water, they found a dead woman bent over a child, who looked up at the soldiers. "Boys, don't kill it," Morse Coffin, a Colorado Volunteer, said.[360] The soldiers didn't, but one of the civilian guides did.

Nichols's men took ten horses and a mule. They also recovered the scalp and clothes of a white woman and documents attesting to Big Wolf's good character and friendship for whites.[361]

12 OCTOBER 1864
MULLAHLA'S STATION (Cozad, Nebraska)

On 12 October, 8 miles west of Plum Creek, 25 Indians attacked a Butterfield Overland Mail coach. Taking shelter in a deserted ranch house, the guards and passengers fired on their assailants. After two hours, two Indians were killed and the rest left. A passenger and a guard were wounded, the latter severely.

In response, a detachment of 40 men under Capt. W. W. Ivory, 1st Nebraska Cavalry, marched out from Plum Creek Station. Capt. H. H. Ribble, commanding at Mullahla's Station to the west, also sent out 15 men. Ribble's men ran into 60 warriors, who instantly killed 2 soldiers, named Jackson and Kelley. While 7 of the soldiers succeeded in reaching Plum Creek, the other 6, cut off by the Indians, dismounted and fought their way back to Mullahla's Station, using their horses as shields.

Ribble's men estimated that they killed three Indians, including a chief. In addition to the two soldiers killed, two were wounded.[362]

13 OCTOBER 1864
ELM CREEK RAID (Newcastle, Texas)

On 13 October 1864 around 500 Comanche and Kiowa raiders struck Young County, Texas, particularly ranches along Elm Creek, a tributary of the Brazos River northwest of Fort Belknap. At the Carter ranch, raiders broke down the door, tomahawked and scalped 21-year-old Milly Durkin, killed a boy named Jim Johnson and an infant, and took seven captives, including Milly Durkin's two daughters. Six were released about a year later; Durkin's two-year-old girl died in captivity.[363]

At the George Bragg ranch, neighbors Thomas Hamby and Thomas Wilson and their families gathered in the house and held off attackers while Hamby's son, Thornton, a Confederate soldier, rode for help. The ranchers killed a number of Indians, including Comanche chief Little Buffalo. Bragg and Thomas Hamby were wounded and Wilson was killed.

As about 300 raiders drove the stolen stock north, Lt. N. Carson, Company D, of Col. James Bourland's Confederate Border Regiment pursued with only 15 men. But the soldiers rode into an ambush and were forced to retreat. As civilian John Wooten tried to escape, his horse was shot out from under him. Pursued by two warriors, he fled on foot, occasionally stopping to shoot. As he did so, one of the Indians called out to him by name and told him to keep running. After running for three miles, Wooten escaped. He later figured his pursuers were Comanches from the Throckmorton County Reservation, where he had worked as a butcher, and they spared his life because he had fed them in the past.

In all, the Indians lost about 20 warriors in the fights at Bragg's ranch and with Carson's soldiers. They killed five soldiers and seven settlers, wounded about five soldiers and two settlers, and took seven captives. They also made off with hundreds of horses and cattle.[364]

20 NOVEMBER 1864
FORT ZARAH (Great Bend, Kansas)

Capt. Henry Booth, Company L, 11th Kansas Cavalry, acting inspector for the District of Upper Arkansas, and Lt. A. Helliwell, 9th Wisconsin Battery, acting Assistant Adjutant General, having just finished their duties at Fort Zarah, were returning to Fort Larned. They told their escort to proceed ahead of them, saying they would catch up. A few miles west of Fort Zarah, about 25 Indians ambushed the officers, and the two ran for the fort.

During the two-mile chase, both men sustained gunshots in the back and arm, and Helliwell was hit twice in the head, though not fatally. Back at the fort, the officers reported that they thought they had killed some of the Indians, but were not certain.[365]

21 AND 27 NOVEMBER 1864
FORT RICE (Fort Rice, North Dakota)

Outside Fort Rice on 21 November, a band of heretofore peaceful Yanktonai Sioux shot and wounded a private, Edwin Durham, of the 1st U.S. Volunteers. On the 27th, another band of Indians, thought to be Santee Sioux, attacked a hunting party under Lt. S. B. Noyes as they returned to the fort from the Cannonball River. The men fought off their assailants, but Noyes and his quartermaster sergeant, C. D. Thompson, were wounded, and Pvt. George Townsend was missing and presumed killed.

After these incidents, Col. Charles A. R. Dimon, 1st U.S. Volunteers, in command of Fort Rice, issued orders that all armed Indians on the west side of the Missouri, except those in soldier uniforms, be regarded as enemies and immediately fired upon.[366]

25 NOVEMBER 1864
ADOBE WALLS (Borger, Texas)

To search for Kiowas and Comanches who had been raiding along the Santa Fe Trail, Col. Christopher "Kit" Carson left Fort Bascom on 12 November with about 335 men from the 1st New Mexico Cavalry, the 1st California Cavalry, and the 1st California Infantry, as well as 75 Ute and Jicarilla Apache scouts. The force surprised Little Mountain's Kiowa village of 150 lodges on the Canadian River in present-day Hutchinson County, Texas, not far from William Bent's abandoned trading post. The Kiowas fled downstream.

Pursuing, Carson found himself in the midst of about 1,000 warriors, from a larger camp of about 350 lodges of Comanches under Stumbling Bear. For several hours, Little Mountain and others led assaults against the cavalrymen. Only Carson's two howitzers under Lt. George H. Pettis held them back.

Carson and his troops fell back to the Kiowa village only to find it reoccupied. The soldiers tried to blast the inhabitants out, but the Kiowas renewed their attacks. Again the howitzers triumphed. Before they left, the troopers torched the lodges and supplies—a severe blow to the Indians at the onset of winter.

Three soldiers and a scout were killed, and 25 soldiers and 4 scouts were wounded. Kiowa and Comanche losses were estimated at 60 killed. The Indians had been holding five white women and two children captive in the village, but Indian women hid them during the battle.[367]

26 NOVEMBER 1864
PLUM CREEK (Lexington, Nebraska)

On 19 November, about 100 Indians (probably Cheyenne) attacked an ox train four miles west of Plum Creek, killing or taking 20 head of cattle. Plum Creek commander Capt. T. J. Majors, Capt. Thomas Weatherwax, and 39 men of the 1st Nebraska Cavalry chased the Indians ten miles southwest, to no avail. Three days later, Indians attacked a stagecoach east of the post, wounding three passengers.

On 26 November Majors learned that 75 Indians had attacked another coach, five miles east of the post, killing two and wounding six aboard. Rushing out with 30 men, Majors found the warriors fleeing south. He chased them for 16 miles to Spring Creek before realizing that some of his men had dropped back, having exhausted their horses. The Indians took a stand in some ravines. Both sides dismounted and a sharp fight ensued, but neither side could pull off a victory. Majors returned to Plum Creek.

One soldier, a Pvt. McGinnis of Company E, 1st Nebraska Cavalry, was wounded. Majors claimed three Indians were killed.[368]

29 NOVEMBER 1864
SAND CREEK/CHIVINGTON MASSACRE (Chivington, Colorado)

Leaving Denver, Col. John M. Chivington and 450 men of the 3rd Colorado Cavalry, under Col. George L. Shoup, and about 100 men in 3 companies of the 1st Colorado Cavalry, under Lt. Luther Wilson, rode southeast to Fort Lyon, where on 28 November they picked up another 125 men of the 1st Colorado Cavalry, under Maj. Scott Anthony. The 3rd Colorado was formed after the Hungate Massacre (see 11 June), and revenge was no doubt on the minds of many of the men. The column headed northeast about 40 miles to a Cheyenne encampment at Sand Creek.

Sand Creek (Colorado), upstream from the Cheyenne village, where the inhabitants fled

About 115 lodges of Cheyennes under Black Kettle and White Antelope, and 8 lodges of Arapahos under Left Hand were camped on the north side of the creek, where Maj. Anthony had ordered them to go after driving them away from Fort Lyon. Many there thought they were safe, though Anthony had not promised them a place of refuge. A number of them had participated in the summer raids along the Little Blue River and Plum Creek (see 7–9 August and 8 August).

Chivington planned to attack the Cheyennes, peaceful or hostile, and indeed the Indians seemed to prepared to fight: the first casualty occurred when the horse of George Pierce, Company F, 1st Colorado, bolted near the edge of the village, and the Indians shot and killed the rider. The fight broke out in earnest. Wilson and his battalion cut off the Indians' access to their horses, while Shoup and Anthony rode into battle. Some of the men, however, including Capt. Silas S. Soule of Company D, 1st Colorado Cavalry, refused to fire at the Indians, which suggests that there were questions about the integrity of the action.

The battle lasted from dawn until 3 P.M. and stretched a few miles along the creek, the Cheyennes taking positions along the cutbanks. With the soldiers surrounding the camp, many women, unable to escape, stayed with their husbands and were hit in the crossfire. Though most of the Indians fled, Chivington's men devastated the village and destroyed the lodges.

Cheyenne and Arapaho chiefs, left to right:
top row, Bosse, Notanee, Heap of Buffalo;
bottom, Bull Bear, Black Kettle, Neva, White Antelope
—Courtesy Denver Public Library, Western History Department

Col. John M. Chivington —Courtesy Denver Public
Library, Western History Department

About 130 Indians were killed at Sand Creek, many of them noncombatants. Among the dead were chiefs White Antelope, Left Hand, Yellow Wolf, One-Eye, Notanee, and Little Robe. No Indians were left wounded, and the soldiers took no prisoners.

The Coloradans were later condemned for the attack and for mutilating the Indian bodies. Historically the fight has been labeled a massacre, but the number of cavalry casualties shows that Sand Creek was a tough fight for the soldiers: Chivington lost 15 soldiers killed and more than 50 wounded—among the highest losses of soldiers during the Indian wars.[369]

1 DECEMBER 1864
RED RIVER (Mangas, New Mexico)

After citizens of Lemitar, on the Rio Grande, reported that raiders with Manuelito's Navajo band had stolen stock, Maj. E. W. Eaton, 1st New Mexico Cavalry, left Fort Wingate on 23 November with some of his cavalrymen and rode southeast to the Datil and Mangas Mountains. On Mangas Creek, between the two ranges, the men picked up the trail of about 55 Apaches and Navajos.

On 1 December at about 3:30 P.M., Eaton found the band camped in a narrow, timbered canyon near the Red River. The Indians scattered, but the cavalrymen killed one warrior, captured a woman and a boy, rounded up about 160 sheep, and destroyed the camp.[370]

4 DECEMBER 1864
COW CREEK (Lyons, Kansas)

The driver and four-man escort of a wagon loaded with ammunition for Fort Zarah were camped on Cow Creek, 15 miles east of the post, when Indians attacked. Just after dark, while the men ate supper, the Indians approached from along the high creek bed and began firing arrows. The teamster was killed, but all four troopers, one of them wounded, escaped. Three of them went to Fort Ellsworth, about 30 miles north, arriving about 3 A.M. The fourth was later picked up by a stagecoach and taken to Fort Zarah.

Capt. Theodore Conkey, 3rd Wisconsin Cavalry, in command at Fort Zarah, sent out two parties to recover the wagon and ammunition, half of which had been stolen. Conkey complained to headquarters that the wagon's escort had been inadequate given that the route used was known to be "swarming" with hostile Indians.[371]

15 DECEMBER 1864
HASSAYAMPA RIVER (Wickenburg, Arizona)

Capt. Allen L. Anderson, 5th Infantry, rode out of Fort Whipple on 10 December with five civilians, a Ute guide named Dick, and 22 men of Company K, 1st New Mexico Cavalry, led by Capt. J. Thompson to look for Apaches. The party traveled southwest through the Bradshaw Mountains to the Hassayampa River, near Walnut Grove, where miners working in the Weaver Mountains faced constant Indian harassment.

From the soldiers' camp on the Hassayampa, scouts found two Tonto Apache rancherias. Thompson and Anderson split the men to attack both simultaneously. Removing their boots for a quiet approach, Thompson's group hit their target first, killing 11 of the 15 Apaches in the camp and wounding the other 4. A Pvt. Brandon of Company K was wounded. The rancheria Anderson and his men hit contained just seven Indians. The soldiers killed three and captured three, and a wounded man escaped. None of the Apaches had firearms.[372]

—1865—

1 JANUARY 1865
SYCAMORE SPRINGS (Cordes Junction, Arizona)

In late December, Lt. Samuel L. Barr, 5th Infantry, took Company F, 5th Infantry; a detachment of 1st New Mexico Cavalry; and guides named Cooler and Rice from Fort Whipple on a scout for Apaches. They followed a trail down the Agua Fria to near present-day Cordes Junction, Arizona. From there they went east into the high country north of Turret Peak, up Ash Creek and over to Sycamore Creek.

At noon on 1 January, in a canyon about six miles south of the head-waters of Sycamore Creek, the men found a small Indian camp. But when a guide thought he saw a smoke signal from the top of a hill, Barr believed they had been discovered. He hurriedly led his men into the camp without setting up a proper attack. The Apaches, who were busy butchering a steer, were no more ready for a melee than were the soldiers.

The soldiers killed four Indians; at least one warrior escaped in a canyon to the east. The army suffered no casualties. In his report, Barr suggested that the pack covers be painted dark brown rather than white to make them harder to see.[373]

7 JANUARY 1865
JULESBURG (Julesburg, Colorado)

A great force of Cheyennes and Lakotas were up in arms after the Sand Creek fight of the previous November (see Sand Creek/Chivington Massacre, 29 November 1864). About 1,000 warriors planned to hit Julesburg's stage station, store, and warehouse in northeastern Colorado, one mile east of Fort Rankin.

Fort Rankin was guarded by only one company of the 7th Iowa Cavalry, under Capt. Nicholas J. O'Brien. Before the attack, an Indian decoy party under Big Crow lured O'Brien and 38 soldiers and civilians toward the sand bluffs south of the Platte River, but undisciplined warriors sprung the trap too soon. O'Brien saw the other Indians half a mile away and spun his command around back to the fort. They made it back with the aid of a howitzer blasting away from the fort's gates, but not without casualties. The Indians killed 14 soldiers and 4 civilians, and wounded 2 soldiers. No Indians were killed or wounded.

In the meantime, the inhabitants of Julesburg and an arriving stage escaped safely to the fort. The Indians sacked the abandoned burg, stealing $40,000 in goods from the store and destroying thousands of dollars in paper money before returning to their camp south of the Platte.[374]

7 JANUARY 1865
VALLEY STATION (Sterling, Colorado)

While a large force of Lakotas and Cheyennes attacked Julesburg (see previous entry), more than 70 warriors raided along the road to Denver on both sides of Valley Station. Wagon driver W. G. Cross was heading east from American Ranch with seven passengers when, halfway to Valley Station, Indians jumped the party. The warriors were led by a white man, probably Charles Bent. A man named Andrews was killed and Cross was shot in the elbow. The wagon then careened down the road until it crashed, killing the mules. The passengers scrambled out and fought their way down the river to Valley Station. All were injured, one with a fractured skull. Cross had to have his arm amputated. Two Indians were killed.

Meanwhile, five miles downriver from the station, at Dennison's Ranch, the Indians hit a large wagon train that was encamped for the winter. They burned all the wagons and killed 12 men. The raiders also fired on a stage from the east, but it got through safely.

At Valley Station, the Indians plundered the buildings outside the telegraph office, stealing $2,000 in goods and burning 20 tons of hay. The station operator, John Hines, tapped out a final message before fleeing: "I am going to take all my things and go down the road until things get more quiet."[375]

8 JANUARY 1865
DOVE CREEK (Knickerbocker, Texas)

In December 1864, Texas scouts found an abandoned Indian camp that they assumed to be that of hostile Kiowas or Comanches. Actually it was the camp of a band of about 500 Kickapoos who were migrating to Mexico from the Pottawatomie Agency in Kansas to escape the strife of the Civil War. The Texans quickly gathered 325 militiamen, under the command of Capt. S. S. Totten. Meanwhile, 161 troops of the Confederate Frontier Battalion, under Capt. Henry Fossett, waited for the militia at Fort Chadbourne. Impatient, Fossett left on his own, and the two forces trailed the Indians independently, finally joining up about one mile north of the Kickapoo camp on Dove Creek, in present-day Irion County, about 20 miles southwest of San Angelo.

At 9 A.M. on 8 January, Totten and the militia circled east and struck the camp of about 160 lodges while Fossett and his mounted troops circled west and captured 1,000 Indian horses. Lt. Brooks with 75 troopers attacked the camp from the southwest. The uncoordinated assault quickly fell apart, for the Kickapoos had a good defensive position, protected by thick brush and timber, with the dry branches along the creek making fine rifle pits.

The militia were met by hundreds of warriors with Enfield rifles, and a score of men went down in the first few minutes. The militia were driven away in full rout, the Kickapoos in pursuit. Brooks's detachment rejoined the other Confederates and took cover in the timber in scattered groups. By noon, the Kickapoos had almost overrun the Confederates' right flank. One Indian, with two children beside him, held up his hands, possibly to show that the village was friendly, but the soldiers shot him down. After that, the Kickapoos kept up their fire until nightfall. The soldiers pulled back across Dove Creek but met more fire. The retreat turned into a rout and the captured horses were lost. The Confederates eventually joined up with the militia three miles away on Spring Creek. They had to kill many of their remaining horses for food.

The Kickapoos' casualties were 23 killed and perhaps 20 wounded. The Confederates lost 8 men, including a Lt. Giddens, and the militia lost 18, including a Capt. Gillentine. About 60 Texans were wounded.

The Kickapoos made it to Mexico, but they continued to raid into Texas for years because of the Texans' ill-advised attack.[376]

14 JANUARY 1865
AMERICAN RANCH (Merino, Colorado)

During their January raids in the Valley Station area (see Valley Station, 7 January), Lakotas and Cheyennes hit American Ranch, about 13 miles upriver from present-day Sterling, Colorado. On the morning of 14 January, ranch hands Gus Hall and a man known as Big Steve were crossing the South Platte River to cut wood when 100 Indians appeared. Big Steve was killed and Hall was shot in the ankle.[377] Hall holed up in the sandy bluffs by the river and held his ground.

At the ranch were the current owners, Bill and Sarah Morris, their two little boys, and several hired hands. The warriors rode in shooting and set the stables and hay on fire. When the main house caught fire, the occupants ran out to the corral, where they were surrounded and the men were cut down. A Minneconjou named White White stopped the other warriors from killing Sarah Morris, offering them a horse for her, and took her for his own. The two boys were also taken prisoner, but the younger was later killed.

As Hall watched the events helplessly from the riverbank, a warrior came upon him and shot an arrow, which cut Hall across the chest but landed on the ice behind him, and Hall shot the Indian. When the Indians left, Hall stumbled 12 miles down the frozen South Platte River to Wisconsin Ranch, also recently raided. There he found a store of grain and flour and buried himself in it for warmth until soldiers rescued him.

At the ruins of American Ranch, soldiers counted seven white bodies and three Indian. Near the dead Indians were open whiskey decanters, making Hall later speculate that Bill Morris had laced the liquor with strychnine, as he once said he intended to do.[378]

14–15 JANUARY 1865
GODFREY'S RANCH (Merino, Colorado)

Due to frequent Lakota and Cheyenne attacks in the area, rancher Holon Godfrey made his home, about two miles upriver from American Ranch, into a fortress, surrounded by a six-foot-high adobe wall with fire ports. Next to his house was a tower, also with fire ports. Inside was abundant food, water, and ammunition. Godfrey was on his early-morning watch when Indians appeared on 14 January. Standing by that day were several travelers and employees.[379]

When 130 Lakotas and Cheyennes arrived that morning, the rancher was ready. The Indians circled around the fortress to draw fire, but the fire never slackened, and several Indians were hit as they closed in. The defenders moved from portal to portal, firing away, while the women and children kept the weapons loaded.

When the Indians broke into the corral to steal the stock, Godfrey said, "Let 'em go! We ain't gettin' outside these walls."[380]

The Indians set a fire to burn the settlers out, but they formed a bucket brigade and soaked the ground. When Godfrey ran out to throw a last bucket of water, a warrior jumped in front of him, but Godfrey pumped a bullet through his shield and into his chest. Later, the Indians shot flaming arrows onto the roof; the defenders carried water up a ladder to douse the fire.

The siege lasted through the next day. On the second night, one of the settlers rode out to get help at Valley Station. Though only four soldiers would accompany him back to Godfrey's the next morning, by the time they got there, the Indians were gone.

Outside Godfrey's adobe walls were 17 Indian bodies. No one on the inside was hurt. The Lakotas and Cheyennes gave Godfrey a nickname: Old Wicked. He then christened his ranch Fort Wicked. It was one of the few ranches in the area to survive the January attacks.[381]

20 JANUARY 1865
POINT OF ROCKS (Dodge City, Kansas)

Sutler supply trains destined for Fort Lyon left Fort Larned on 17 January, escorted by 25 men of the 1st Veteran Colorado Cavalry and 6 men of the 2nd Colorado Cavalry. They proceeded unmolested for three days, until they reached Point of Rocks, or Nine Mile Ridge, 65 miles west of Fort Larned and about 2 miles west of present-day Dodge City, Kansas. There, about 45 Cheyennes and Arapahos attacked.

In the skirmish, three Indians were killed and three were wounded. One private was killed and two were wounded. The trains were so harassed that they returned to Fort Larned.[382]

2 FEBRUARY 1865
JULESBURG (Julesburg, Colorado)

A month after the January attack on Julesburg (see 7 January), the Cheyenne and Lakota raiders hit the town again before leaving the area and heading for the Powder River country. The day of the attack, Capt. Nicholas J. O'Brien, in charge of Fort Rankin near Julesburg, was on his way back from an aborted expedition with Lt. Eugene Ware, ten soldiers, and a howitzer. From a hill about three miles east of the fort, the soldiers saw smoke rising from Julesburg. While about 1,000 warriors plundered the town, O'Brien decided to cut through to the fort, blasting a path through the startled Indians with the howitzer. About a mile from the fort, warriors blocked the troopers' way, but they charged ahead, opening the path. Said Lt. Ware: "We made a royal bluff, and it won."[383]

The 100 soldiers and 50 civilians staying at Fort Rankin expected an attack. The mixed-blood George Bent, who lived among the Cheyennes, later told about the incident, saying that warriors rode around the fort and taunted the soldiers, but to no avail. The Indians, left alone, finished sacking the town. Before leaving, they scattered shelled corn taken from the warehouse over the ice on the South Platte River to make it easier for their ponies to cross, then disappeared over the bluffs.[384]

4–6 FEBRUARY 1865
MUD SPRINGS (Dalton, Nebraska)

After their second attack on Julesburg (see previous entry), the Cheyennes and Lakotas who had raided along the Platte in January moved their village to Lodgepole Creek, south of Mud Springs. Mud Springs, in a small, boggy, bowl-shaped valley, was the only water source between Lodgepole Creek and the North Platte River.

On 4 February, an advance party of warriors ran off a horse herd that was grazing near the Mud Springs telegraph station. Defending the station

Mud Springs Station (Nebraska)

was a small force of nine 11th Ohio Cavalrymen and five civilians. The operator tapped out messages to Forts Laramie and Mitchell for help. Col. William O. Collins started immediately from Fort Laramie with 120 men from various companies of the 11th Ohio Cavalry and part of Company D of the 7th Iowa Cavalry. From Fort Mitchell, Lt. William Ellsworth took 36 men of Company H, 11th Ohio Cavalry.

After a tough march, Ellsworth reached Mud Springs Station on the morning of the 5th. The 1,000 warriors who arrived to attack that day were surprised by the increase in soldiers, but they surrounded the place and peppered it with bullets. The buildings were almost impregnable to small arms fire, however, and the soldiers fired through loopholes cut in the walls. Some warriors crept closer to shoot, but neither side would come out in the open to fight. The soldiers then tried a ploy. They turned loose the stock in the corrals, and the Indians, finding the bait more attractive than desultory firing at buildings, scattered after the animals. The fighting died out for the day.

The next morning, Collins, after a grueling march that gave many of his men frostbitten limbs, made it to the springs. The Indians, planning to renew their assault, again found more soldiers opposing them. Collins placed his men outside to keep the Indians out of the valley, but the character of the ground allowed for only hide-and-seek action, with men popping up to shoot and ducking down to dodge. About 200 Indians got within 75 yards of the corral and angled a mass of arrows into it, hitting horses and men alike. Collins organized two charges to clear the ground, then dug a rifle pit to squelch trouble from that direction.

After four hours of fighting, the soldiers expanded the perimeter and drove the Indians out of the valley. According to Cheyenne observer George Bent, the Indians just got tired of fighting and left. Collins estimated that they hit 30 Indians; Bent said no Indians were killed. Collins reported 3 soldiers killed and 4 wounded.[385]

8–9 FEBRUARY 1865
RUSH CREEK (Broadwater, Nebraska)

While many of their warriors were fighting at Mud Springs (see previous entry), the rest of the Lakota-Cheyenne village moved down Rush Creek, crossed the North Platte River, and camped east of present-day Broadwater, Nebraska. At the Mud Springs telegraph station, before the Indians cut the lines, Col. William O. Collins had requested aid from Fort Laramie. Lt. William H. Brown of the 11th Ohio Cavalry arrived with a howitzer on the morning of 8 February, two days after the raiders left, and Collins decided to go on the offensive. The troops left immediately to follow the Indians' trail.

On Rush Creek at about noon, a mile from the North Platte, Collins spied the great pony herd across the river. Then through his field glasses he saw 2,000 warriors. But while he was looking for a place to ford, the Indians, alerted, swarmed back over the frozen river, coming in two miles above and below Collins's position. Collins was barely able to corral his train before he was surrounded. The troopers hastily dug rifle pits in the small sand hills around the train. The Indians' first mounted charge aimed at the north side of the perimeter, but the soldiers' gunfire split the charge around to the east and west sides. Then the Indians began a tactic of skulking and sharpshooting.

Several persistent warriors had crawled down the bank of the creek to a hillock 400 yards behind the soldiers. Sixteen men of Company D, 7th Iowa Cavalry, and the 1st Battalion, 11th Ohio Cavalry, led by Lt. Robert Patton of the 11th Ohio, made a charge with revolvers in hand to clear them out. About 200 Indians who saw the charge rode to the rescue, and a hand-to-hand fight ensued.

Yellow Nose and another warrior were wounded. Two privates were killed—one after his unruly horse carried him into Indian lines.[386]

The fighting simmered down to sharpshooting again until evening, when the Indians pulled back and moved toward the river for water. At the river the warriors discovered an Indian body on the ice and galloped back to the fight. After Collins recalled the troops, the warriors left, taking the body. The next morning about 400 Indians returned and the combatants exchanged a few shots, then the warriors rode off to the north. Collins abandoned further pursuit and headed back to Fort Laramie.

In the battle, the army's casualties were 2 killed and 9 wounded, plus 7 disabled from frostbite. Collins thought he had hit perhaps 100 Indians, but realistically the totals were probably about 3 killed and 6 wounded.[387]

15 FEBRUARY 1865
BRUNEAU VALLEY (Bruneau, Idaho)

After eight head of cattle were stolen near Fort Boise, four settlers and six soldiers from Company I, 1st Washington Territory Infantry, under Sgt. John Storan, tracked the thieves. The trail went up the Snake River to Bruneau Valley, near the junction of the Bruneau and Snake Rivers, about 20 miles southwest of present-day Mountain Home, Idaho.

Sgt. Storan's small group found the culprit Indians, probably Bannocks, in a little canyon eight miles from Bruneau Valley, dressing the carcasses of the eight steers. Though outnumbered about eight to one, Storan attacked, and in a tough, hour-and-a-half fight that ended with rain and darkness, he succeeded in driving off the Indians.

Fort Churchill (Nevada)

Storan reported killing 30 Indians, with no casualties to his own party, and having fired only 83 shots. Storan's superior officer, a Capt. O'Regan, added that Storan's men wounded an additional 30 Indians. These casualties are certainly an embellishment.[388]

14 MARCH 1865

MUD LAKE (Northwestern Nevada)

After several cattle thefts in the area, Capt. Almond B. Wells took 50 men of Company D, 1st Battalion Nevada Cavalry, from Fort Churchill and Camp Nye to Pyramid Lake. There Chief Winnemucca told Wells that a band of Smoke Creek Paiutes, camped about 11 miles north of their position near Mud Lake, were probably the thieves. Wells detached 21 men to stay with the Indians at Pyramid Lake and left on 14 March at 3 A.M. for the Mud Lake camp.

With 29 troopers and two civilian guides, Wells reached the camp at sunup.[389] He divided his command into three squads, one each under Sgts. Wadleigh and Besat, and the other he led himself. The soldiers approached the sleeping Paiutes, intending to arrest the thieves. They were not yet 150 yards from the camp when the Indians began firing. The first shot hit a corporal in the shoulder, and another passed through Wells's overcoat. The captain ordered a saber charge.

"The Indians fought like veterans," Wells later reported, yet his men beat them back into the bushes on both sides of the slough. Wadleigh and Besat had them nearly surrounded. Wells recounted, "I killed twenty-nine in all; but one escaped. . . . I destroyed several guns, a quantity of powder, and fresh beef. I pursued and fought them for about ten miles up into the mountains. Some of my men had hand-to-hand conflicts with them. Several were beaten on the arms with the Indians' guns."

After the battle, Winnemucca reportedly called on Wells. Through an interpreter, Winnemucca said he was pleased by Wells's victory. He said he had been admonishing the Indians all winter, "telling them not to steal the white men's cattle, and he thought that the punishment they had received would teach them a lesson."[390]

12 AND 26 APRIL 1865
FORT RICE (Fort Rice, North Dakota)

It was a hard winter for Col. Charles A. R. Dimon and his 1st U.S. Volunteers, the "Galvanized Yankees," Confederate prisoners who had joined the Union Army rather than languish in prison. Many had died of scurvy and hundreds were sick. When the weather got better, Indians showed up. Lt. Jeremiah Cronan of Company H captured two Santees on 30 March.

On 12 April, 200 Santees and Yanktonais suddenly swept down from the bluffs west of the fort and attacked the herders outside the stockade. Killing 2 soldiers, the Indians got away with 68 cattle, mules, and horses.[391] In reprisal, Dimon ordered the two captured Santees shot.

Two weeks later, on 26 April, about 300 more warriors attacked a horse herd a mile from the post. Only 7 guards were on duty, but they managed to stave off the Indians and saved all but 2 horses and 2 mules.

One man, Pvt. Hiram Watson, Company E, suffered a severe arrow wound in the chest but later recovered. Eight Indians were wounded.[392]

12 MAY 1865
SMITH'S RANCH (Gothenburg, Nebraska)

Dan Smith's Ranch, about three miles southwest of present-day Gothenburg, Nebraska, was guarded by a detachment of four soldiers of Company A, 1st Battalion Nebraska Veteran Cavalry. About 30 Lakotas attacked the ranch, killed Sgt. Hiram Creighton, wounded another soldier, and took about 30 head of cattle.

Another detachment of the 1st Nebraska, this one from Midway Station, ten miles east, were out gathering wood when they came upon the fight in progress and chased the Indians across the North Platte River. The soldiers wounded one Indian. In a stand that allowed the other soldiers to return safely to Smith's Ranch, Pvt. Francis W. Lohnes, Company H, was wounded. Lohnes received the Medal of Honor for his action. Though the

Nebraskans rallied and chased the Lakotas for 25 miles, they called off the pursuit after Indian reinforcements appeared.[393]

18 MAY 1865
ELM CREEK STATION (Ayr, Nebraska)

Fifteen convalescents of various companies of the 3rd U.S. Volunteers (the "Galvanized Yankees") and the 1st Nebraska Veteran Cavalry were marching from Leavenworth to Fort Kearny with a six-mule wagon and a civilian teamster. The highest-ranking soldier among them was Sgt. Jefferson Fields of C Company. Through some administrative foul-up, no arms had been issued to them.

At 2 P.M. on 18 May, the party was two miles from Elm Creek Station, about six miles south of present-day Hastings, Nebraska, where at least 20 Indians found them. The Indians, carrying U.S. cavalry sabers, rode up, killed two men, wounded six, and plundered the wagon. The soldiers could offer no resistance. Pvt. John W. Twyman was struck down and scalped while still alive, but he lived to tell about it. Sgt. Fields was helpless to do anything except order his men to walk down the road. The Indians followed them a short distance then let them go.

The Indians were strange: one spoke English, some had their hair roached on top in the Pawnee fashion, and another made a point of announcing that he was a Cheyenne chief and presented Lakota and Cheyenne arrows to prove it. The teamster, Washington Fulton, heard them say that they were friendly Sioux.[394] Had they been Lakotas or Cheyennes, they probably would have killed everyone, so they were most likely Pawnees.

20 MAY 1865
DEER CREEK STATION (Glenrock, Wyoming)

In May 1865 Companies D and L of the 11th Kansas Cavalry were garrisoned at Deer Creek Station, about 28 miles east of Platte Bridge Station and just east of present-day Glenrock, Wyoming. Several Indian battles occurred near the post on the same day.

Three miles above their camp on Deer Creek, 25 Indians assaulted Lt. W. B. Godfrey of Company D and 3 soldiers. After a brisk two-hour fight the men succeeded in repulsing their attackers without suffering casualties. Godfrey estimated they killed 2 Indians and wounded 4.

At the same time, 50 Indians besieged the camp of a Sgt. Smythe and 6 men of Company L, 11th Kansas. After two and a half hours the Indians withdrew but ran off with 26 cavalry horses. The Indians lost 3 warriors and 5 were wounded. One soldier was killed.

After the attacks, at Camp Plumb on Mud Creek, about ten miles west of Deer Creek Station, Lt. Col. Preston B. Plumb of the 11th Kansas Cavalry directed Lt. Jacob Van Antwerp of Company L to take 24 men in pursuit of the Indian raiders. Antwerp tracked them southeast to Deer Creek, then to Box Elder Creek, and down to the North Platte River. About seven miles east of Deer Creek Station, he found 100 warriors, but they were on the opposite bank and the river was running too high to ford. Antwerp returned to Camp Plumb empty-handed on 22 May.[395]

20 MAY 1865
TUSCARORA (Tuscarora, Nevada)

Trouble with Paiutes in Nevada's northern Humboldt country and Paradise Valley sent hundreds of miners and ranchers scurrying to the area's few towns for safety. Lt. Col. Charles McDermit, 1st Nevada Cavalry, was told by his commander, "If the Indians have not come to terms, take the force yourself and give them a lesson which they will not forget."[396]

McDermit sent Capt. Almond B. Wells from Fort Churchill with 50 men to find the Paiutes. Ten miles southwest of present-day Tuscarora, Nevada, Wells met up with several hundred Paiutes under Zeluawick. The Indians were well-armed and forted up in the rocky hills, almost inaccessible to cavalry. Wells tried to drive them out, but succeeded only in getting two soldiers killed and four others badly wounded. Seeing the futility of further attack, Wells retreated.[397]

3 JUNE 1865
DRY CREEK (Casper, Wyoming)

Lt. Col. Preston B. Plumb, in command of the 11th Kansas Cavalry, made his headquarters at Camp Dodge, about seven miles southeast of Platte Bridge Station, which was guarded by soldiers from Company G of the 11th Ohio Cavalry. At about 3 P.M. on 3 June, a band of ten Indians fired on Platte Bridge Station from across the North Platte River. When a messenger brought Plumb the news, he took ten men of Company B and rode to the station. There he gathered ten more men from the 11th Ohio Cavalry and a few more from Companies A and F, 11th Kansas Cavalry, and headed west after the raiders.

A chase of five miles had half the cavalry's horses dropping back in exhaustion, but Plumb's men were close enough to fire on and hit two Indians. The warriors abruptly turned and charged at Plumb, who did not turn away. The Indians then broke off, at a considerably faster speed than they had been going before. These Indians, Plumb discovered, were a decoy. "This purpose was quite apparent immediately after," Plumb later said, "as a party of about sixty Indians came charging down the bottom of Dry Creek half a mile to our left, with the apparent purpose of getting between us and the station and cutting off the stragglers."[398]

At this time another 20 men from Companies A and F of the 11th Kansas Cavalry showed up, and the Indians turned around. The soldiers chased the warriors for two miles. Six men of A and F Companies and one of Company G, 11th Ohio, pursuing a party considerably in advance, were ambushed by about 30 Indians, front and rear. Before assistance arrived two privates were killed.[399] One was scalped after his horse fell on him and pinned him to the ground; the other's body was saved from mutilation when a Pvt. Martin of Company A, taking cover in a ravine, drove the Indians off with his carbine.

Plumb reported one Indian killed and about five wounded. The two soldiers killed were the only army casualties.[400]

8 JUNE 1865
SAGE CREEK STATION (Saratoga, Wyoming)

Just a few days after Lt. James A. Brown detached five men of Company K, 11th Ohio Cavalry, to guard the Sage Creek Station on the Overland Road west of Fort Halleck, they were attacked by about 100 Lakotas and Cheyennes. After one hour's fighting and with dwindling ammunition, they were compelled to evacuate with two civilians.

Though well mounted, the fleeing men faced a desperate eight-mile run west to reach Pine Grove Station, with the Indians in pursuit. During the chase, Pvts. George Bodine and Perry Stewart were killed, Cpl. W. H. Caldwell and Pvt. William Wilson were wounded, and Pvt. Orlando Ducket was wounded and captured. The two civilians were presumed killed. Caldwell and Wilson made it to Pine Grove Station, where they joined a detachment of ten men of their own company, commanded by a Sgt. McFaddin, as they retreated to Sulphur Springs.

The next morning, the soldiers found the bodies of Stewart and Bodine lying in the road horribly mutilated, the latter scalped. They also found the body of one of the civilians, but the other civilian and Pvt. Ducket were not found. It was thought that the Indians burned their bodies at Sage Creek Station.[401]

11 JUNE 1865
COW CREEK (Alden, Kansas)

Lt. Richard W. Jenkins, Company I, 2nd Colorado Cavalry, along with three men of his company and three men of Company G, 7th Iowa Cavalry, left Cow Creek Station on 11 June to accompany the mail coach to Fort Zarah. Three miles from the station, the soldiers passed a slow-moving wagon train, and one mile beyond that, they were stormed by 100 Indians, probably Kiowas. As the mail coach spun around, with Jenkins and his men blasting away, the raiders rode up to the windows, stabbing at the guards inside with their lances.

One Indian was killed and four Indian ponies were shot. Two soldiers, Pvts. Cutting and Platt, Company G, took lance wounds to the head.

Watching the scene from the roof of Cow Creek Station, Capt. Elisha Hammer, Company G, 7th Iowa Cavalry, quickly readied 29 men of his own company and 26 men of Company I, 2nd Colorado Cavalry, and rushed to Jenkins's relief. At Hammer's approach, the Indians pulled back. Jenkins took command of the Company I contingent and joined with Hammer to chase the Indians. They rode about six miles southwest to the Arkansas River, where they caught the warriors fording to the south bank. The Indians were, Hammer said, "close enough to empty eight saddles."[402]

As some of the Indians floated down the river, the soldiers killed or wounded at least 15 of them. They also killed or wounded 3 on the south bank with carbines from the north side.

Jenkins crossed over with his men to pursue the Indians, then Hammer crossed with his. They continued the chase three miles farther south, but the Indians had gotten too far ahead, and Hammer called it off.[403]

14 JUNE 1865
SPRING CANYON (Campo, Colorado)

A 70-ox train owned by Semon Baca of Las Vegas, New Mexico, was traveling the Santa Fe Trail to the States. At the recently established Camp Nichols, about four miles east of the present-day panhandle border of Oklahoma, the train picked up an army escort of 49 men from Company F, 1st California Cavalry, under Capt. Thomas A. Stombs. After one day's

Cow Creek battle site (Kansas)

march east, at the Willow Bar Crossing of the Cimarron River, they came upon another train. Stombs searched the party for deserters from the California and New Mexican cavalry, but he came up empty-handed.

The Baca train continued east the next day, but at about 2 P.M., near Spring Canyon on the Cimarron, in the extreme southeast corner of Colorado, more than 40 Kiowa and Comanche warriors charged into the train's cattle herd. The Indians lanced one Mexican herder, killing him instantly, and wounded another with an arrow. Stombs's troopers immediately fired and drove the raiders back before they could cut out any cattle from the herd. The Indians ran off with only one mule and three ponies. While the remainder of the company corralled the stock, 30 soldiers pursued the Indians for about six miles before giving up.

Baca requested that Stombs escort his train all the way to Fort Larned, but the captain's orders would not permit it, so they all turned around and went back to Camp Nichols, where Baca hoped to pick up another escort.

Stombs estimated hitting five Indians in the skirmish, with no army casualties and one civilian killed and one wounded.[404]

14 JUNE 1865
HORSE CREEK/FOUTS'S FIGHT (Morrill, Nebraska)

On 11 June, the government moved the "friendly" Indians who generally camped near Fort Laramie to Fort Kearny so they would be out of the way during the upcoming campaigns. About 185 lodges of Lakota, probably over 1,500 Indians, started eastward under guard of 135 men of Companies A, B, and D of the 7th Iowa Cavalry, with Capt. William D. Fouts in command. About 30 white civilians also rode along, as did Charles Elliston and his uniformed Indian police. The Indians were allowed to keep their weapons.

On the 13th the party camped at the mouth of Horse Creek, the soldiers on the east bank and the Indians on the west. At 5 A.M. the next morning, Capt. John Wilcox of Company B was ordered to proceed two miles ahead and wait for the Indians and the wagons. When Fouts set out, expecting the Lakotas to follow, they did not move—they were having a great argument about whether to continue to Fort Kearny. Some had cut saplings and placed them across a ford on the North Platte River for the women and children to cross. When Fouts saw that the Indians were not behind him, he rode back to hurry them up. As he approached, some of the Indians went after him, while others fought among themselves. The captain and three privates were shot to death, and a few others were wounded.

The rear guard, Company D under Lt. Haywood, hurried ahead to Wilcox to report the fight. Wilcox demanded to know why Haywood had not stayed to help, and the lieutenant replied that they had no ammunition because Fouts had told them they would not need it. Lts. Triggs and Smith and 65 men stayed to corral the wagons and dig a defensive position, while Wilcox, Haywood, and 70 men rode back to Horse Creek.

The soldiers crossed to the west bank of the creek and saw Fouts's body, then they rode to the North Platte, where the Indians were wading their families across. About 500 warriors turned back on Wilcox and his men and drove them back to their corral. After replenishing his ammunition, Wilcox took Lt. Smith and 50 men, all he could mount on the only serviceable horses, and went out again. Once more he was repulsed.

At 9 A.M., Capt. Shuman, 11th Ohio Cavalry, arrived with reinforcements from Fort Mitchell, and Wilcox tried again. When the troopers reached the North Platte, the Indians had all crossed and taunted them from the north shore. Wilcox rightly decided not to cross.

Eight Lakota prisoners had been riding with Fouts, and the Indians managed to rescue seven of them, with balls and chains still on their legs. Only one called Osape, who had been riding in a wagon because his legs were swollen from the manacles, was left behind. When the soldiers returned, they took Osape out and shot him. Mrs. Fouts, hysterical over the death of her husband, wanted to kill all the Indians who remained. One, Green Plum, who was taking care of four orphans, went to Mrs. Fouts and offered himself to quench her vengeance; the distraught woman relented.

The army casualties were four dead and four wounded.[405] The Lakotas killed four of their own chiefs while arguing, the old men Little Thunder and Bad Wound among them. The captive Osape was the only known Indian killed by the whites, and perhaps half a dozen were wounded.[406]

17 JUNE 1865
DEAD MAN'S FORK (Crawford, Nebraska)

When Col. Thomas Moonlight, in command at Fort Laramie, heard by telegraph of Fouts's Fight (see previous entry), he quickly organized an expedition to catch the renegade Lakotas. Leaving at 8 A.M. on 15 June, Moonlight took 234 men of Companies L and M of the 2nd California Cavalry, Company L of the 11th Kansas Cavalry, Company L of the 11th Ohio Cavalry, and a detachment of the 16th Kansas Cavalry in a rapid march to Horse Creek. From there the men followed the Indian trail north to Dead Man's Fork, a small creek flowing into the White River, about four miles southwest of present-day Crawford, Nebraska.

Moonlight had marched hard—120 miles in two days—and 100 of his men had to turn back when their mounts gave out. On the 17th, the command had gone 20 miles before breakfast, when they stopped for a rest by the stream's steep banks. Few of the California Cavalry had picket ropes or

Dead Man's Fork (Nebraska)

pins, so their horses were herded. The Lakotas, camped on Soldier Creek on the other side of the White River, saw the soldiers' camp and recognized an opportunity.

At 10 A.M., about 200 warriors charged in and stampeded the horses. The troopers tried to corral the animals, but the shooting and war whoops made them frantic. Moonlight and Capt. Joel Huntoon placed themselves in front of the stampede but failed to stanch it. The horses ran to the mouth of Dead Man's Fork, where waiting warriors gathered them up and headed over the mountains. As Capts. James A. Brown, George D. Conrad, and Henry Booth and about 25 troopers pursued the raiders, nearly 400 warriors confronted them, some taunting the troops in English. The soldiers prudently gave up the chase.

Moonlight later wrote, "After losing the horses there was nothing left for me to do but to return, after destroying the saddles and other property which we had no means of transporting." The colonel ascribed no blame for the loss of his horses, but he did complain that he was provided with no hobbles, which he thought was the only way to secure the animals properly in hostile territory. "Nor will I ever attempt again to march a command, large or small, unless provided in this way."[407] Moonlight never had to worry about it again, however, for when his "foot soldiers" returned to Fort Laramie, the colonel was relieved of command.

Two soldiers were wounded and 74 horses were captured. Moonlight claimed to have seen 4 Indians shot dead off their horses, and several more wounded.[408]

9 JULY 1865
MALHEUR RIVER (Drewsey, Oregon)

Cattle thefts and depredations near the Burnt River in the summer of 1865 led to a punitive expedition by the Oregon Volunteers. Lt. Charles Hobart took 40 men of Companies A, B, and D, 1st Oregon Cavalry, out of Camp Lyon on 2 July. The circuitous trail of stolen stock led to the Malheur River, where Hobart spotted several Indians on various trails and split up his command to follow them. The soldiers camped on a flat near the Malheur on the 8th.

Before daylight the next morning, Indians, probably Paiutes, were seen lurking near the camp. Hobart ordered the stock driven in and called the men to arms. The warriors, about 70 mounted and maybe 70 more on foot, opened fire from all sides, heaviest from a bench on the mountain behind the camp. The troopers threw a canister charge at them and they fell back. A party under a Sgt. Wallace and a Cpl. Walker, Company B, charged the hill, while fire from the front wounded a private from Company D. Blasts from the troopers' howitzer dissuaded subsequent attacks.

Hobart pursued the marauders in a running fight of five miles. He later speculated that they had white men among them, "for they told us in good English to 'come on, you sons of bitches, we can whip you anywhere.'"[409] The Indians escaped down a steep canyon, carrying off the bodies of three of their dead and a number of wounded but leaving behind one body and nine horses.

During the pursuit, Cpl. Walker and a Pvt. Phillips of Company B were cut off from the main body and had to fight their way back. Phillips was seriously wounded, and Walker killed the Indian who was about to knock Phillips off his horse.

Hobart had two men wounded. Indians losses were placed at five killed and perhaps five wounded.[410]

17 JULY 1865
OWYHEE RIVER (Southeastern Oregon)

Having recently returned from the Malheur River expedition (see previous entry), a detachment of Company B, 1st Oregon Cavalry, under Sgt. Wallace, was out again searching for stolen stock. About 45 miles south of Camp Lyon, in an 800-foot canyon of the Owyhee River, Wallace found the raiders. Dismounting, he split his command into two squads and approached the Indians' camp from two sides. There were about a dozen warriors.

The squad under a Sgt. Phillips reached the Indians first, and two Indians washing in the river spotted them. Phillips had to open fire before Wallace's squad was in place. Nevertheless, the surprised Indians offered little resistance. Several were wounded but managed to splash across the river and get away. Four were killed on the field. Wallace gathered up several head of livestock, along with weapons, furs, blankets, and hundreds of pounds of dried meat, then burned the camp.[411]

26 JULY 1865
PLATTE BRIDGE (Casper, Wyoming)

After their winter raids (see Julesburg, 7 January ff.), the Cheyennes and Lakotas who had left Colorado and Kansas for the Powder River country in February joined with the Lakotas who had escaped from the army during a relocation march (see Horse Creek/Fouts's Fight, 14 June) to form a great force. Together they planned a major attack of about 2,500 warriors against Platte Bridge Station, commanded by Maj. Martin Anderson of the 11th Kansas Cavalry. The garrison consisted of about 120 men of Companies C, I, and K of the 11th Kansas Cavalry, detachments of Company G, 11th Ohio Cavalry, and some 3rd U.S. Volunteers under Capt. A. Smith Lybe.

Among the officers at the Platte Bridge post was Lt. Caspar Collins, son of the retired colonel of the 11th Ohio Cavalry. On 26 July, soldiers saw

Reconstruction of Platte Bridge (Wyoming), near site of Caspar Collins's death

numerous Indians north of the North Platte River; this posed a threat to a wagon train expected soon from the west. When Collins was ordered to take some men out to help guard the train, he fully expected to die. Turning to his friend, he said, "Jim, I know I shall never get back alive. Here is my cap that you have admired so much. Keep it to remember me by."[412] With that, he led out 25 men from Companies I and K.

Collins and his men crossed the long wooden bridge across the river and turned west. Riding along the banks near the bluffs, they were jumped by about 1,000 warriors. The soldiers spun around and tried to cut their way back to the bridge. There were so many Indians on both sides that they shot and hit more of their own warriors than cavalrymen.

Meanwhile, Lt. Henry C. Bretney of the 11th Ohio was crossing the bridge with 40 men to help Collins in case there was trouble. Concealed near the bridge were about 200 Arapahos, but when they jumped out, some well-placed volleys drove them back. The path was open for Collins if he could break through.

Collins's fight was so close that the troopers could almost touch the warriors riding alongside them. Collins was wounded in the hip, but he continued riding until he saw a trooper go down and stopped to help him. As he tried to get the man up on his horse, they were both overwhelmed. Bretney held off the Indians until the retreating troopers galloped back across the bridge.

Four other men died with Collins, and eight more were wounded.[413]

Later that day, Lt. George M. Walker, 11th Kansas Cavalry, led 15 men out to repair a telegraph line the Indians had cut in their raid. Capt. Lybe posted a small force to their rear for support. Walker had barely reached the broken line when Lybe signaled that Indians were coming. The men fell back pell-mell as the Indians closed in. The warriors caught four troopers and speared two of them, killing Pvt. James A. Porter and seriously wounding farrier Joseph Hilty, whose horse carried him to safety. Sgt. Duncan McDougal placed his revolver against the ribs of an Indian riding next to him and fired his last cartridge into him. The howitzer at the station held the Indians long enough for the soldiers to retreat behind its walls.

Six soldiers were killed and nine wounded in the second fight. Indian casualties are difficult to separate from the additional losses they took later in the day (see next entry). It seems probable that five were killed and ten wounded.[414]

26 JULY 1865
RED BUTTES/CUSTARD'S WAGON TRAIN (Casper, Wyoming)

After the Cheyennes and Lakotas chased the soldiers at Platte Bridge Station back into the post (see previous entry), they were distracted from

Site of Custard's fight, Red Buttes (Wyoming)

pursuing the fight by word of a wagon train approaching from the west. Sgt. Amos J. Custard of Company H, 11th Kansas Cavalry, was in charge of the 14 teams, 5 wagons, and about 25 men of Companies H and D. Custard left Sweetwater Station on 25 July and camped for the night at Willow Springs, halfway to Platte Bridge. That evening Lt. Henry C. Bretney and Capt. A. Smith Lybe with their detachments, also on their way to Platte Bridge, stopped at Custard's camp and suggested he join them, but the sergeant thought the mules were too tired.

The next morning Custard took his train down the telegraph road near the North Platte River. Past Red Buttes, he met a 30-man patrol of the 11th Ohio Cavalry, who warned him that thousands of Indians were besieging the station just ahead and urged him to turn back. "No sir," said Custard, "we don't stop here. We are going to Platte Bridge in spite of all the redskins this side of hell."[415]

Farther on, Custard heard the gunfire and sent five men to scout ahead. The scouts were soon attacked and dashed to the river for safety. Two of them were shot at the river, but three others eventually made it to the station.[416] On the way they killed the Cheyenne Left Hand, brother of the famous war leader Roman Nose.

Shortly after the scouts left, the Indians swarmed on Custard. He hurriedly corralled his wagons, and the remaining 20 men fired from

Sitting Bull, Hunkpapa chief
—Courtesy Little Bighorn
Battlefield National Monument

beneath or inside the wagons. The warriors got in close, some rolling logs and rocks in for cover as they tightened the circle. Though hopelessly outnumbered, Custard and his men held out for four hours. When Roman Nose finally directed the warriors to rush in for the final combat, there were only a handful of soldiers still alive. The few they captured were subjected to horrible tortures, for the soldiers had shot a substantial number of Indians. The Cheyennes threw away the scalps they took, for too many warriors had died to celebrate the battle.

Killed were Custard, 19 soldiers at the wagons, and the 2 shot at the river. The Cheyennes lost 6 warriors, with another 6 wounded.[417] The Lakotas lost about 6 killed and 12 wounded.[418]

28 JULY 1865
FORT RICE (Fort Rice, North Dakota)

The U.S. government made hostile tribes a number of peace offers in 1865, but fiery leaders such as Sitting Bull refused the gestures. At Fort Berthold, Sitting Bull slashed himself with a knife to show the wavering warriors how the soldiers at Fort Rice had cut him while trying to kill Indians who came near the fort. He then recruited nearly 400 warriors to attack Fort Rice.

As soon as the Lakotas gathered on the hills, Lt. Col. John Pattee of the 6th Iowa Cavalry, in charge at the post, led his men out. Four companies of the 1st U.S. Volunteers, two companies of the 4th U.S. Volunteers, and one company of the 6th Iowa Cavalry made a long line that curled around the stockade walls. Sitting Bull's warriors charged in, shooting arrows at long range. Pattee's men responded with musketry. When the howitzers were put into action, the Lakotas lost their enthusiasm. The three-hour, long-distance fight favored the soldiers' weapons, assuring victory as long as they kept their lines and did not rush out in response to Indian taunts. The discouraged Lakotas finally melted away. After Sitting Bull's terrible performance, some angry warriors flailed him with horsehide whips.

Probably a dozen warriors died in the battle. Two soldiers were killed and three wounded.[419]

13 AUGUST 1865
CRAZY WOMAN'S FORK (Buffalo, Wyoming)

The Powder River campaign against the Cheyenne and Lakota had been in the planning stages all spring and early summer, and after interminable supply delays, it finally got under way. Brig. Gen. Patrick E. Connor led the "Left Column" out of Fort Laramie on 30 July. It consisted of 90 men each of the 7th Iowa and 11th Ohio Cavalries, 116 of the 2nd California Cavalry, 95 Pawnee scouts under Capt. Frank North, and 84 Omaha scouts. Accompanying them were 200 men of Col. James H. Kidd's 6th Michigan Cavalry, who were to build and garrison a new fort on the Powder River.

While the troops looked for a place to build a post, North led a scout of Pawnees down the Powder River, north of the main command. On 13 August, near Crazy Woman's Fork, North chased a war party until he became separated from his support. The warriors shot North's horse, and things looked grim for him when one of his scouts, Bob White, rode up. North ordered White to go for help. The scout stated, according to teamster Finn Burnett, "Me heap brave, me no run, you and me killem plenty Sioux, that better."[420]

After possibly wounding a few warriors, other Pawnee scouts arrived to end the action.[421]

13–15 AUGUST 1865
BONE PILE CREEK (Gillette, Wyoming)

Hoping to pioneer and publicize a shorter route to Montana, prominent Iowa merchant James Sawyers organized an expedition to build a road along the proposed route. He left the mouth of the Niobrara River, in northern Nebraska, on 13 June with 53 men and 15 wagons pulled by 45 yoke of oxen. His escort was a rather unwilling Capt. George Williford leading 143 men of the 5th U.S. Volunteers and a detachment of Dakota

Cavalry. Joining them was an emigrant train of 5 wagons and 36 freight wagons owned by C. E. Hedges & Company of Sioux City, Iowa.

The party traveled slowly up the Niobrara, at times struggling through sand hills with temperatures climbing over 100 degrees. By the time they reached the badlands of the upper White River, Williford was running out of provisions. On 21 July he sent 15 men to Fort Laramie, about 75 miles southwest, for the needed supplies.

By 9 August, the expedition had reached the Belle Fourche River and decided to strike northwest to the Powder River. A nearly waterless 32-mile trek over the next two days convinced Sawyers that it was not the place for a wagon road, and he retraced his steps. On 13 August the party camped on Bone Pile Creek, about ten miles southwest of present-day Gillette, Wyoming. About a mile and a half from camp, a band of Cheyennes jumped Nathaniel D. Hedges, a 19-year-old partner in the freighting firm. They killed him and ran off eight horses.

The distressed expedition moved a few miles down Bone Pile Creek, corralled, and placed a strict guard. They burried Hedges in the center of the corral and concealed his grave. On the 14th, the Indians appeared in force and made a dash at the camp's herd, but the group drove them off. The next day over 500 warriors appeared on the bluffs. They swept onto the plain and circled around shooting, but the camp repelled them again. At noon the Indians asked for a parley. Sawyers gave them a wagonload of sugar, bacon, coffee, flour, and tobacco to buy his way out.

Williford objected to the gift, doubting it would work, and he proved correct. No sooner had the expedition started to get under way again than a melee erupted. Some Lakota had come in after the gifts were distributed. Two Dakota cavalrymen of Company B, John Rawze and Anthony Nelson, were shot down. Finally the Indians left, and Nelson's body was recovered and buried in the corral as Hedges had been. Rawze's body could not be found. The expedition turned south to Fort Connor.

The two soldiers and one civilian killed were the whites' total casualties. Five Lakotas were wounded, two of them mortally.[422]

16 AUGUST 1865
POWDER RIVER (Northeastern Wyoming)
While construction began on Fort Connor, near present-day Sussex, Wyoming, Frank North's Pawnee scouts kept up a vigilant search for Cheyennes and Sioux. They trailed a band of Cheyennes who had been raiding along the Platte River and were heading north. The signs showed about 40 horses and mules and 1 travois. North, with 48 Pawnees and a number of white soldiers and civilians, caught up with the raiders on the Powder River about 50 miles north of Fort Connor.

The Cheyennes assumed the approaching Indians were Cheyennes or Lakotas, for they made a friendly sign. Suddenly the Pawnees charged in, shouting. The fight was one-sided, the exuberant Pawnees killing 27 Cheyennes, including Yellow Woman, stepmother of George Bent. A wounded Cheyenne in the travois rolled himself over a steep cutbank, but a Pawnee saw him, climbed down, and killed him with a saber.

North's scouts lost 4 horses but captured 18 horses and 17 mules, many with government brands showing they had been taken in the Platte Bridge fight. Back at Fort Connor, the Pawnees held a great scalp dance long into the night. North was praised after the battle, which earned him the name "Pawnee Chief" from his scouts.[423]

29 AUGUST 1865
TONGUE RIVER (Ranchester, Wyoming)

Launching the Powder River campaign (see Crazy Woman's Fork, 13 August), Brig. Gen. Patrick E. Connor led his Left Column north from Fort Laramie on 30 July. They moved up the Bozeman Trail to the Powder River, where the 6th Michigan Cavalry, who had accompanied the column to build a new post at the river, began constructing Fort Connor.

Connor continued north with his column on 22 August, trailing along the east edge of the Bighorn Mountains to the Tongue River and moving downstream toward the planned meeting place with other columns under Col. Nelson Cole and Col. Samuel Walker. On the 28th, scouts brought

Site of Tongue River fight (Wyoming)

word of an Indian village 40 miles upstream at the head of the Tongue. Connor prepared to backtrack and attack.

Leaving part of the command with the 184-wagon train, Connor led 125 cavalrymen and 90 scouts in a night march to Black Bear and David's Arapaho village, a mile south of present-day Ranchester, Wyoming. There were nearly 300 lodges with about 700 Indians. Though it was early in the morning, the Indians were dismantling the camp. Connor lined up his men, who fired a volley then barreled into them. The soldiers fought with the warriors while the women and children fled. A battery of howitzers under Maj. Nicholas O'Brien of the 7th Iowa Cavalry blasted the village.

Capt. Henry E. Palmer of the 11th Kansas Cavalry said of the fight: "I was in the village in the midst of a hand to hand fight with warriors and their squaws, for many of the female portion of this band did as brave fighting as their savage lords. Unfortunately for the women and children, our men had no time to direct their aim . . . squaws and children, as well as warriors, fell among the dead and wounded."[424]

Connor led a pursuit up the valley for ten miles. At about 11 A.M., at the edge of a canyon, he turned around and found he had outdistanced most of his support and now had only about 13 men with him. He retreated to the Indians' village site and spent the rest of the day destroying the lodges and burning tons of buffalo robes, blankets, furs, and meat. The number of horses Connor captured was estimated between 500 and 1,100. In the late afternoon, Connor marched his men the 40 miles back to the wagon train. The soldiers had been in the saddle for 100 miles and without rest for 40 hours.

Connor lost 2 soldiers and 3 scouts, and 7 soldiers were wounded. He captured 7 women and 11 children, but later freed them. Connor estimated that 35 Indians were killed, while Palmer said 63 were slain.[425]

1, 4, 5, AND 8 SEPTEMBER 1865
POWDER RIVER (Powderville, Montana)

As Brig. Gen. Patrick E. Connor led the Left Column of the Powder River campaign (see previous entry), the other two columns were having a tough time of it, troubled by troops near the end of their enlistments who were threatening mutiny. Col. Nelson Cole's Right Column left Omaha on 1 July with 1,400 men who made up eight companies of his own 2nd Missouri Light Artillery, equipped as cavalry, and eight companies of the 12th Missouri Cavalry. Col. Samuel Walker led the Center Column out of Fort Laramie on 5 August with 600 men of his own 16th Kansas Cavalry and a detachment of the 15th Kansas Cavalry.

The two columns met northwest of the Black Hills and continued north along the Little Missouri River, then crossed west through badlands to the

Vicinity of battle at Powder River (Montana)

Powder River, where they ran into serious trouble. On 1 September, as the men camped near the junction of Alkali Creek and the Powder River, about 300 Lakotas of the Hunkpapa, Sans Arc, and Minneconjou bands attacked the soldiers' horse herd a mile from camp. Capt. E. S. Rowland and six men responded and were cut to pieces. Only Rowland escaped.

Cole and Walker marched the men downstream to the mouth of the Mizpah River, plagued by poor grass and cold, rainy weather. About 200 horses and mules perished. On 4 September, the column marched back upriver. A detachment of the 12th Missouri Cavalry, sent back to destroy some of the column's own abandoned property, were jumped by Indians but beat them off.

The next morning, warriors tried to cut off the column's herders, starting a three-hour fight that engaged over 1,000 Lakotas and Cheyennes. The Indians made several attacks, hoping to draw the troops out in pursuit. The Cheyenne Roman Nose made several brave runs in front of the soldiers' blazing guns and remained untouched. The howitzers kept the Indians at bay but killed only an old man named Black Whetstone. Several soldiers were killed in the battle.

The Cheyennes left the scene and moved east to the Black Hills, leaving the Lakotas behind to harass the soldiers as they moved upriver. The Lakotas attacked the column on 8 September, but artillery held them back. That night a great hail- and snowstorm struck and continued through the 9th, forcing the soldiers to hole up in the vicinity of present-day Powderville,

Montana. About 400 horses perished, and the famished soldiers pounced on the carcasses.

When the weather abated Cole and Walker's men limped farther up the Powder, constantly dogged by warriors, but there were no more serious engagements. On 13 September, Connor's scouts found them and directed them to continue 80 miles upriver to the newly built Fort Connor, which they reached on the 20th.

Cole reported 12 men killed, with 2 missing, presumed killed. He reported only 1 man wounded, but Lt. Charles H. Springer of Company B, 12th Missouri Cavalry, reported at least 4 wounded in the engagement on 5 September alone. Cole estimated they might have killed 200 warriors, an extremely high number. Springer estimated a more likely figure of 20. Walker, although he saw a number of Indians shot off their horses, said in frustration and anger, "I cannot say as we killed one."[426]

Although the Powder River Expedition kept the Indians away from the Overland Road for some months, it was not a great success. About 700 government and civilian horses and mules died, along with much property abandoned and destroyed.[427]

—1866—

13 FEBRUARY 1866
GALLEGOS'S FIGHT (Pine, Arizona)

After the Civil War ended and the California Volunteers were mustered out, the citizens of Arizona Territory needed to take their defense into their own hands and organized the Arizona Volunteers. Most of the corps were Pima and Maricopa Indians and Mexicans, recruited at Tucson and elsewhere south of the Gila River.

Capt. Hiram H. Washburn, with the assistance of Lt. Manuel Gallegos, once a captain in the Sonoran army, organized Company E, posted at Camp Lincoln, later called Camp Verde, near the junction of Beaver Creek and the Verde River. After getting word of the location of an Apache rancheria, Gallegos led 45 men of Company E east out of Camp Lincoln on 11 February.

Traveling by night and resting by day, Gallegos scoured the Mogollon Rim. On the second night he discovered Indian campfires around some caves and positioned his small force nearby. At about 2 A.M. the troopers went in shooting. They took the lower caves with sharp fighting; the upper caves could not be taken without sacrifice, and Gallegos decided to withdraw.

Thirty Apaches were killed and 12 women and children were captured and taken back to Camp Lincoln. Seven volunteers were wounded. They brought back 13 scalps.[428]

WALKER'S FIGHT (Globe, Arizona)

Company C of the Arizona Volunteers, Pima Indians under the half-Wyandotte Indian Lt. John D. Walker, and Company B, Maricopa Indians under Lt. Thomas Ewing, went after a band of Apaches in March 1866. Leaving from a Pima village on the 27th, the volunteers trailed the Apaches for four days before finding them in the Pinal Mountains. They surprised the Apache camp near the edge of a perpendicular bluff with many deep crevasses.

The surprise overwhelmed the Apaches, and Walker, dressed in breech-clout like his Pimas, showed them no mercy. Those not shot were driven off the cliffs. The Pimas even shocked some of the local miners with their exuberant smashing of Apache skulls.

About 25 Apaches were slain, though estimates went as high as 75. Walker lost 1 man and 2 were wounded. It was said that for years later one could still see the skeletons of the Apaches in the crevices.[429]

WILD ROSE PASS (Fort Davis, Texas)

Supply freighter William Edgar, with his brothers John and James, were returning to San Antonio after taking two wagon trains to El Paso. On 31 July William Edgar, with 28 men and part of the train, stopped at Fort Davis to wait for a load of corn from Presidio. The next day, they traveled ten miles down Limpia Canyon and nooned.

While the others rested, Edgar, his cook, and a man named Forbes went ahead to Wild Rose Pass to look for a place to camp for the night, but they were attacked by Mescaleros and driven back. At the same time, about 60 Lipans and Mescaleros were charging the wagons, but the freighters held them off, and the 3 made it safely back to the train.

The next day, Navajos from Bosque Redondo under Chief Gordo joined the siege. After an impasse of several days, the Indians said they were starving and would leave if given some corn. Edgar reluctantly agreed to the deal and the Indians withdrew.

Edgar claimed that several Indians were killed in the fight; the freighters had no casualties.[430]

CAZEAU WAGON TRAIN (Banner, Wyoming)

Traders Peter Cazeau and Henry Arrison were traveling along the Bozeman Trail in two wagons with three employees, Cazeau's Oglala wife Mary, and their four children. On 16 July they were camped on Peno Creek, six miles north of Fort Phil Kearny, when a group of Northern Cheyennes joined them. Later, some angry Oglalas appeared, demanding that the Cheyennes join them in a war against the soldiers at the fort. When the Cheyennes refused, the Oglalas called them cowards, whipped them, and drove them from the camp.

Early the next morning, the Oglalas returned and killed Cazeau, Arrison, and the three hired men. Mary and the children escaped into the brush and safely reached the fort.[431]

20 JULY 1866
CRAZY WOMAN CREEK (Buffalo, Wyoming)

A small 18th U.S. Infantry detachment of 29 soldiers under Lt. George Templeton was heading north to Fort Phil Kearny as escort for the wives of Lt. Alexander Wands and Sgt. F. M. Fessenden, a servant, and several children. After passing Fort Reno (formerly Fort Connor), the party went down Dry Creek to its junction with Crazy Woman Creek. Scouting ahead, Templeton and Lt. Napoleon H. Daniels were jumped by over 50 warriors, probably Lakotas, perhaps with some Cheyennes. Daniels was killed. The Indians chased Templeton back to the train with an arrow in his back and a wound on his face. He ordered the train corralled and organized the defense. Several men were wounded and a few mules were shot down.

At sunset, two men volunteered to ride back to Fort Reno for help. Just then, another train of 34 wagons and 47 men, under Capt. Thomas B. Burrowes, approached from the northwest. Burrowes was unaware that anything was wrong until he saw Templeton's corralled train, then came across the body of Pvt. Terrence Callery, one of his own men who had gone out to hunt. Burrowes's train forted up with Templeton's.

Crazy Woman Creek (Wyoming)

The next morning the soldiers found the body of Lt. Daniels stripped, scalped, and pierced with 22 arrows. Responding to the call for help, Lt. Thaddeus S. Kirtland and 13 men rode in on 21 July, but the Indians had gone by then. The entire party went back to Fort Reno the next day.

Two men were killed in the siege and six were wounded. Indian casualties are unknown.[432]

24 JULY 1866
CLEAR CREEK (Buffalo, Wyoming)

At Fort Reno, after the siege at Crazy Woman Creek (see previous entry), the soldiers buried Lt. Daniels, then Capt. Burrowes and his train joined the Templeton party to Fort Phil Kearny. On 23 July the train caught up with two large civilian wagon trains that had left the fort the day before, led by Hugh Kirkendall and William Dillon. The conglomeration consisted of about 200 wagons and stretched 6 miles across the plains.

The first wagons reached Clear Creek, at present-day Buffalo, Wyoming, on the afternoon of the 24th and corralled. Kirkendall's train, 6 miles south, had to corral on their own when 25 Indians tried to run off their mules. In the meantime, William Dillon and five other men had left camp to see what was holding Kirkendall up, when they were attacked. The six men shot their horses and made a small circle to hold off the Indians. After four hours of fighting, they tried to make a run for Kirkendall's corral. Dillon was critically wounded, and one of the men carried him while three others walked backward, shooting at their pursuers. Kirkendall recognized what was happening and sent a party out to rescue them.

At the first corral, at Clear Creek, Burrowes heard of the attack and sent couriers to Fort Phil Kearny for help. He also dispatched 16 men to assist Kirkendall and Dillon, and Kirkendall was able to move his wagons to Clear Creek. Dillon died that night. The next morning, 60 men and a howitzer arrived from Fort Phil Kearny, and they all proceeded to that post.

Dillon was the only casualty from the wagon trains. Two Lakotas were killed in the fight.[433]

OCTOBER 1866
CEDAR GAP (Brownwood, Texas)

About 16 miles southwest along the road from Comanche to San Saba, Texas, ranchers Larkin Stone, Frank Brown, John Roach, and another man were attacked by about 30 Comanches. Firing hotly, they knocked several Indians from their ponies, then made their escape. Brown got away with a facial wound, but Roach was hit thrice. Nevertheless, he rode far enough away to escape before dropping from his mule. The three others made it to a settlement and spread the alarm.

James Cunningham and his son David raised a number of settlers to take up the chase. Near the attack site they found Roach, still alive. The trail led them northwest into Brown County, and soon they discovered a fresh grave, which held the body of a recently shot Comanche. The posse, which included about 40 men with a few bloodhounds, rode through the night into the hills near Gap Creek. There they discovered a sleeping Comanche camp and surrounded it.

At first light they charged the Indians with a Texas yell. Five warriors died in the first fire, and their scalps were soon hanging from the Texans' belts. Eighteen-year-old Freeman Clark's revolver misfired and a Comanche shot him in the ribs. A bullet shattered Larkin Stone's pistol grip in his hand. When the Indians mounted up and fled, the Texans chased them for several miles before losing them.

All told, the Texans lost one man and one was wounded. They killed and scalped seven Comanches and wounded four.[434]

23 OCTOBER 1866
NORTH PLATTE RIVER (Western Nebraska)

Lt. George A. Armes arrived at Fort Sedgwick with Company M, 2nd Cavalry, on 1 October 1866. On the 22nd, Lakotas attacked a wagon train a few miles from the post and drove off all the stock. The next day, Armes and Lt. Randolph Norwood took 25 men in pursuit.

The soldiers followed the Indian trail east through the day and part of the night. At 11 P.M., after riding 98 miles, they crossed the forks of the Platte River. Finding the Indians camped on the banks of the North Platte, Armes disregarded Norwood's orders and, with 17 men, barreled into the camp in the darkness. Even though they had superior manpower, the surprised Lakotas put up little resistance.

Armes and his men killed 4 warriors and wounded 7, at the cost of 2 enlisted men wounded. He captured 22 Indian ponies, took back nearly all the stolen stock, and burned the camp.[435] The praise of Brig. Gen. Philip St. George Cooke made Armes feel "as if I were a man of great importance in this part of the country."[436]

6 DECEMBER 1866
PENO CREEK (Banner, Wyoming)

After Indians (probably Lakotas) attacked a wood-cutting detail about four miles from Fort Phil Kearny, post commander Col. Henry B. Carrington, 18th Infantry, led 25 mounted infantrymen under Lt. George W. Grummond north of Lodge Trail Ridge, and sent Capt. William J. Fetterman and Lt. Horatio S. Bingham with a squad of mounted infantry and about 30 troopers of Company C, 2nd Cavalry, northwest toward the wood wagons. The idea was for Fetterman to drive the Indians from the west side of Lodge Trail Ridge to the east side, where Carrington would be waiting for them.

The plan quickly came unraveled either through miscommunication or from deliberately disobeyed orders. Bingham rode ahead of Fetterman, far in advance of the command. Likewise, Grummond rode out ahead of Carrington. On his way to Lodge Trail Ridge, Carrington had a skirmish with 100 warriors, delaying him. Fetterman arrived in time only to check Bingham's fleeing troopers, who had gone chasing after a few Indians along Peno Creek and were nearly annihilated by a large force of warriors—the first Indians had been decoys. The green soldiers stopped their flight only after Lt. Alexander Wands threatened to have them shot by their own comrades. Bingham, however, did not stop. He continued on with a handful of troopers toward Carrington, whom he saw on the ridge. He never made it. Carrington and Fetterman pulled back to the fort.

Carrington killed one Indian himself and estimated that ten warriors were killed. Bingham and Sgt. G. R. Bowers were killed, and another sergeant and four privates were wounded. Bingham's body was found lying over a stump with more than 50 arrows in it.[437]

21 DECEMBER 1866
FORT PHIL KEARNY/FETTERMAN FIGHT (Buffalo, Wyoming)

In a near repeat of the 6 December incident (see previous entry), a train of wood wagons came under attack outside Fort Phil Kearny, and Col. Henry B. Carrington sent Capt. William J. Fetterman out with 80 men, including 27 horsemen of Company C, 2nd Cavalry; detachments of Companies A, C, E, and H of the 18th Infantry; and 2 civilians, James S. Wheatley and Isaac Fisher.

"Under no circumstances," ordered Carrington, "pursue over . . . Lodge Trail Ridge."[438] Fetterman, however, was pulled into a chase by a decoy party that included the Lakotas Crazy Horse, Black Shield, and White Bull. Fetterman and his command followed the Indians over the ridge. As soon as the soldiers were out of sight of the fort, the concealed warriors struck.

On a north-south ridge that would become known as Massacre Hill, perhaps 1,000 warriors, perfectly following the plan of the Minneconjou chief High Back Bone, rose up from the valley of Peno Creek and charged up the hill. The cavalrymen under Lt. George W. Grummond, who were farthest north, fell back toward the infantry along the trail as they all tried desperately to find a place to make a stand. The two civilians, behind a pile of rocks at the north end of the ridge, put up one of the best fights with their Henry rifles.

The battle lasted only about half an hour. All 81 soldiers and civilians were killed; Fetterman and Capt. Frederick H. Brown reportedly shot each

Site of Fort Phil Kearny (Wyoming)

other in the head simultaneously at the end of the battle. The Cheyennes lost 2 men, the Arapahos 1, and the Lakotas about 60. Perhaps 100 were wounded.[439]

26 DECEMBER 1866
OWYHEE RIVER (Southeastern Oregon)

Lt. Col. George Crook, 23rd Infantry, arrived in Boise City, Idaho, to join his regiment in December 1866. Within a week, word came of depredations, probably by Paiutes, near the mouth of the Boise River. On 18 December, Crook took 45 men of Capt. David Perry's Company F, 1st Cavalry, on a punitive expedition. In freezing weather the men trailed the Indians up the Owyhee River. Crook's chief scout, Cayuse George, was unreliable, and the troops were opposed to continuing the march, but Crook forced them on.

On the morning of the 26th, Crook's men caught the raiders sleeping. At the cost of 1 enlisted man wounded and Sgt. O'Toole mortally wounded, Crook killed 30 Indians and captured 7, plus all their stock. "That ended any more depredations from that band," wrote Crook.[440]

—1867—

CA. 15 JANUARY 1867
AQUARIUS MOUNTAINS (Wikieup, Arizona)

Believing the army was not providing sufficient protection, the miners and settlers of Prescott, Arizona, met in November 1866 to take matters into their own hands. Forming a company they called the Yavapai Rangers, they set off in pursuit of the "red rascals." On one expedition they found signs of Indians northwest of Prescott at the Willows oasis. The trail led south into a rugged canyon in the southern Aquarius Mountains, where the Rangers found an unsuspecting rancheria of Apache and Mojaves. Surrounding the camp on two sides, they attacked, unleashing their fury on many noncombatants.

Only 1 Indian woman was known to have escaped, while 23 men, women, and children were slaughtered. One Ranger was killed and 3 were wounded.[441]

29 JANUARY 1867
STEEN'S MOUNTAIN (Burns Junction, Oregon)

Continuing his winter expedition (see Owyhee River, 26 December 1866), Lt. Col. George Crook, after scouting up the Malheur River, headed southeast to Camp Lyon, on the Jordan River near Silver City, Idaho. There he released Capt. David Perry to return to Boise and took Capt. James C. Hunt's Company M, 1st Cavalry, and 12 Indian and 4 white scouts to continue the search for Indians.

At the eastern foot of Steen's Mountain, the soldiers found a rancheria of Paiutes under Paunina. Crook drew up his company on a low sagebrush plain only 200 yards from the village and sent scouts around the flanks to cover escape routes. When he ordered the charge, his horse bolted and he found himself leading the command, bullets whistling all around him. Crook's unmanageable steed carried him right through the village, but his men followed him. When Crook and a civilian from Silver City approached a wickiup, an Indian popped out of the entrance and shot the civilian through the heart. The warrior was then blasted with a volley from the sagebrush.

The troopers of Company M were deadly efficient. They killed 60 Indians and captured 27. Only 2 Paiute men and 2 women escaped. Crook lost 1 scout and another was wounded, and 3 soldiers were wounded.[442]

26 FEBRUARY 1867
PUEBLO MOUNTAIN (Fields, Oregon)

After his success at Steen's Mountain (see previous entry), Lt. Col. Crook and his men rested at Camp C. F. Smith on Whitehorse Creek, east of the Pueblo Mountains. Crook marched out with Companies H and M, 1st

Cavalry, during a February blizzard. Scouting around Pueblo Mountain, the soldiers ran into a small camp of Paiutes. They killed two warriors and captured five women and children. Afterward, Crook halted operations because of the bad weather and returned to Camp Smith.[443]

12 MARCH 1867
PECOS RIVER (Langtry, Texas)

While camped on Live Oak Creek near the abandoned Fort Lancaster, Capt. John A. Wilcox and a detachment of Company C, 4th Cavalry, picked up the fresh trail of what appeared to be about 200 Indians. They followed it for four days, twisting through the hills west of the lower Pecos River. On 12 March, Wilcox overtook the Indians, burned their camp, and recovered one Mexican captive. The soldiers then had to make a fighting withdrawal as the Indians pursued them for 15 miles.

Four of Wilcox's men were missing, presumed killed; guide Severino Patino was killed and five soldiers were wounded. Wilcox claimed to have killed between 25 and 40 Indians, but 10 is a more likely number.[444]

10, 16, 17, AND 18 APRIL 1867
BLACK MOUNTAIN (Cottonwood, Arizona)

In early April, word reached Fort Whipple, near Prescott, Arizona, that a large party of Indians was in Hell Canyon, which joined the Verde River northeast of the fort. Capt. James M. Williams took Companies B and I of the 8th Cavalry out to investigate. On 10 April, a detachment under Lt. William Owens of the 32nd Infantry jumped a band of Yavapais, killing three and wounding several others while incurring no losses of their own.

Williams continued hunting through the Black Mountains between Fort Whipple and the Verde River, and on 16 April he found and destroyed a rancheria of 30 lodges. The inhabitants fled. The next day Williams left the horses with Sgts. Golden and Terran and 18 troopers, and took the main body up the mountainside after the Indians. Seeing about 35 of the Yavapais circling back to the horse herd, Golden and Terran mounted up with their men and fought the Indians, killing 20 and routing the rest, without loss to themselves.

On the 18th Williams discovered a rancheria near the Verde River, attacked, and killed another 30 Indians. In this fight, George W. Drummond, a saddler in B Company, was killed and another soldier was wounded. In all, Williams reported killing 53 Yavapais, but the figure was more likely half that number.[445]

15 APRIL 1867
LOOKOUT STATION (Antonino, Kansas)

On 14 April, 250 lodges of Lakotas and Cheyennes fled their Pawnee Fork camp to escape Maj. Gen. Winfield Scott Hancock and his command, which included Lt. Col. George A. Custer and the 7th Cavalry. The Indians moved quickly north, crossing the Smoky Hill Trail and attacking stage stations along the way.

On the evening of the 15th, employees at Big Creek Station saw smoke rising from the direction of Lookout Station, about eight miles west, near present-day Antonino, Kansas. A freighter called "Capt." Barron and a trader, John H. Betts, went to Lookout and found that the station had been burned, the bodies of the stock tender and cook had been nailed to the barn, which was also burned, and the stock had been driven off. Another man had also been killed and burned.[446]

19 APRIL 1867
CIMARRON CROSSING (Cimarron, Kansas)

When Gen. Winfield Scott Hancock and his command approached a large Cheyenne and Lakota village on the Pawnee Fork (see previous entry), a party of six Cheyennes from Black Kettle's village, south of the Arkansas River, had the misfortune to be visiting at the time. The six fled south on foot. One Bear suggested they steal some horses at Anthony's Stage Ranch, near the Cimarron crossing of the Arkansas.

Meanwhile, Lt. Matthew Berry with Company C, 7th Cavalry, from Fort Lyon, and Maj. Wycliffe Cooper with Company B, from Fort Dodge, had been scouting along the Arkansas. As the Cheyennes approached Anthony's Stage Ranch, they ran into Cooper and Berry's companies. They ran for the river, the soldiers on both sides of them. Reaching the cottonwoods on the bank, the Indians split up. Two slipped away along the cutbanks, and the other four crossed to an island and tried to hold off the soldiers, who had dismounted and were peppering them with gunfire. Finally the Indians splashed across to the south bank, but the soldiers followed close behind.

One Bear was shot and killed as he climbed the bank, and Plenty of Horses was wounded. Eagle Nest ran off in another direction but was pursued into the sand hills and killed. One enlisted man was wounded. Lt. Berry took One Bear's beaded belt, pistol, and quiver as souvenirs.[447]

30 MAY 1867
BEALE'S SPRINGS (Kingman, Arizona)

Cpl. J. Brown and three privates of a detachment of Company E, 14th Infantry, were posted at Beale's Springs Station, near present Kingman, Arizona, along with six civilians. Suddenly confronted by more than 200 Hualapai Indians, the men defended the station admirably, causing a number of casualties. One civilian was killed.

The Hualapais pulled away at the approach of 20 troopers of Company K, 8th Cavalry, under Lt. Jonathan D. Stevenson. The troopers chased them east toward Peacock Springs and brought them to bay, but Stevenson, realizing he had bit off more than he could chew, retreated to Beale's Springs. The Hualapais lost 15 men in the encounters.[448]

11 JUNE 1867
BIG TIMBER (Arapahoe, Colorado)

Lt. James M. Bell, Company I, 7th Cavalry, stationed at Fort Wallace, constantly juggled his few troopers among the western stage stations, trying to protect the passengers that traveled to Denver and back. On one return trip from Denver, the fear of Indians was so bad that the stage had no passengers. With only one driver and one mail guard, Bell started east.

In eastern Colorado the stage picked up three men of Company I, and at the next station the men took aboard a sick private from Company E, 3rd Infantry. When they reached Cheyenne Wells, the station keeper's wife insisted upon going east with them.

At a dry fork of the Smoky Hill River, four miles from Big Timber Station, just east of today's Kansas-Colorado border, about 25 warriors, probably Cheyennes, opened fire on the stage, riddling it with bullets. Bell and his three troopers grabbed their Spencers and returned fire. Across the creek bed, they got out to shoot, and Bell told the woman to lie on the floor. The sick infantryman tried to clamber down from the top, but he was hit in the open doorway. He tried to give Bell his dying message to his mother, but the hot fire kept Bell otherwise occupied.

The quick-shooting Spencers drove the Indians off for a time. Bell saw them place the bodies of two warriors on horseback. As the stage continued on to Big Timber, the warriors returned for another try. The soldiers shot one more Indian from his mount. After two more hours, the attackers gave up. Bell's stage, with the horses badly wounded, pulled into Big Timber Station.

One soldier and three Indians were killed.[449]

12 JUNE 1867
FORT DODGE (Fort Dodge, Kansas)

Company B of the 7th Cavalry, under Capt. William Thompson, was stationed at Fort Dodge when the troop's horses, grazing about two miles from the post, were stampeded by a band of Kiowas. The Indians succeeded in running off 71 head. While trying to prevent the theft, Pvt. James Spillman was hit by several arrows and died the next day.[450]

14 JUNE 1867
YAMPAI VALLEY (Truxton, Arizona)

In the Yampai Valley (Truxton Wash), north of the Peacock Mountains, Capt. James M. Williams, scouting with Company I, 8th Cavalry, struck a party of Hualapais. The veteran desert troopers scattered the band, killing 20 and capturing 9.[451]

19 JUNE 1867
STEEN'S MOUNTAIN (Burns Junction, Oregon)

While Lt. Col. George Crook operated out of Camp Smith and Camp McIntosh on the Quinn River, just across the present-day Oregon-Nevada line, his chief of scouts scored a victory. Archie McIntosh, a half-blood Shoshone, with a detachment of Shoshone and Warm Springs Indians, surprised a camp of Paiutes near Steen's Mountain, Oregon. The scouts killed 12 Paiutes, wounded 1, and captured 2 more.[452]

21–22 JUNE 1867
FORT WALLACE (Wallace, Kansas)

Fort Wallace was virtually under siege in June 1867. On the 21st, Cheyenne Dog Soldiers under Roman Nose struck nearby Pond Creek Station, ran off stock, killed one soldier, and wounded another. The next morning they came back with reinforcements, led by Charles Bent, the half-Indian son of trader William Bent. After a making a feint at Pond Creek Station, they directed their full attention to the fort.

While some Indians drew the attention of the soldiers at Fort Wallace, 50 others threatened a railroad-surveying party working in the area under a Col. Greenwood. In response, a Sgt. Dummell rode from the fort with ten men. He ordered a charge, but only three soldiers obeyed. Although they fired their Spencers furiously, the little party was nearly trampled by the warriors. They were all unhorsed and shot or lanced. Two were killed and two were wounded. Greenwood's men rushed forward to assist the others.

Meanwhile, at a rock quarry about three miles from the post, the Cheyennes attacked two teams hauling stone to the fort in wagons. The drivers sped back to the quarry. One made it, but the other, Pat McCarty, was killed and his horses were stolen. The soldiers at the quarry grabbed their rifles and headed back for the fort. Mounted soldiers met them and escorted them back safely. The Indians burned the tents and equipment at the quarry.

White casualties totaled five dead and five wounded over the two days.[453]

22 JUNE 1867
BACA'S WAGON TRAIN (Cimarron, Kansas)

A train of 80 wagons heading for Santa Fe, led by Capt. Francisco Baca, were camped at the Cimarron crossing of the Arkansas River on 22 June. Among those traveling with Baca were the first Catholic bishop of Santa Fe, Jean Baptiste Lamy, ten other priests, and six nuns. The Cheyenne Lame Bear and 75 warriors, including George Bent, another half-Indian son of William Bent, coming from their camp on the Washita River, encountered Baca's party. After successfully stealing 50 mules, the Indians were repelled by the fast shooting of Baca's men.

Though eastern papers reported that all the priests were killed and the nuns abducted, the only casualties were ten people, including one nun, who died of the cholera that was sweeping Kansas in the summer of 1867.[454]

24 JUNE 1867
NORTH FORK OF THE REPUBLICAN RIVER (Benkelman, Nebraska)

Lt. Col. George A. Custer and Companies A, D, E, H, K, and M of the 7th Cavalry, about 357 troopers, left from Fort McPherson on the Platte River and traveled southwest to the forks of the Republican, looking for Indians. Camping for a few days just south of present-day Benkelman, Nebraska, Custer dispatched Companies D and K with 12 wagons to Fort Wallace for supplies.

On the morning of 24 June, Custer's camp was surprised by Sioux trying to run off the horses. The raiders badly wounded one of the guards, but other soldiers drove them off before they could lift his scalp. The warriors stopped one mile away, and Custer signaled them for a parley. He learned the band was under the Oglala Pawnee Killer. Both sides suspected treachery, and after some tense moments, the parties drew apart.

Several hours later the Indians returned, snooping around the camp, and Capt. Louis M. Hamilton took his Company A and pursued them. The Indians drew Hamilton on for some distance, and he split his command. Suddenly 43 more warriors appeared and turned on his squad of 25. One of the men with Hamilton, Dr. Isaac T. Coates, had fallen behind, and upon seeing the attack he raced back to camp, just ahead of the pursuing warriors. His alarm sent more troopers to the rescue. But en route the relief men ran into Hamilton returning at an easy pace. He had beaten off the attackers, killing two warriors and wounding four more.[455]

26 JUNE 1867
POND CREEK STATION (Wallace, Kansas)

About 6 A.M. on 26 June, a band of Cheyennes tried to run off the stock from Pond Creek Station, three miles west of Fort Wallace. Capt. Albert Barnitz of Company G, 7th Cavalry, left the fort with 50 men of his company and a few from Companies E and I to run after them. The soldiers galloped north, then swung west to cut off what appeared to be 75 mounted Indians. Barnitz stopped to form a line on open ground about three miles northwest of present-day Wallace, Kansas.

As Barnitz began the move against the Indians, more warriors appeared from over the crest of a slight ridge to the northwest, and others came up from the southwest out of the Pond Creek valley. The 200 Cheyennes and Lakotas did not follow their usual custom of circling, but charged right in for a hand-to-hand struggle. Barnitz termed it "quite a desperate little fight."[456]

The fight was most savage on the south side, where the Dog Soldier Bear With Feathers lanced a trooper off his horse and another Cheyenne, Big Moccasin, scooped up bugler Charles Clark and carried him off. Sgt. Frederick Wyllyams was cut off and overwhelmed. Barnitz himself was shot at several times but came out unscathed. The line held its own briefly, but a portion fell back at the order of Sgt. William Hamlin of Company I, who was later tried for cowardice. Barnitz managed to extricate his command and make it back to the fort.

The next day Barnitz returned for the bodies. Clark and Wyllyams were horribly mutilated. Six troopers had been killed and six wounded. Barnitz surmised that the Indians lost an equal number.[457]

26 JUNE 1867
BLACK BUTTE CREEK/COOKE'S FIGHT (Wallace, Kansas)

The wagon train Custer sent south to Fort Wallace (see North Fork of the Republican River, 24 June) consisted of about 50 men, led by Lt. William W. Cooke, and included Lt. Samuel M. Robbins and his D Company escort. Capt. Robert M. West of Company K traveled with them as far as Beaver Creek, then left on a scout. The wagons safely made it to Fort Wallace, loaded up with supplies, and headed back Custer's camp.

After Indians attacked his camp on 24 June, Custer feared the wagon train might be in danger. He sent a squad of Company E, under Capt. Edward Meyers, to find Capt. West and give him orders to meet Cooke's train and escort it back.

Meanwhile the train, halfway back to Beaver Creek, was indeed attacked. More than 600 Cheyenne and Lakota warriors, some fresh from the morning's fight at Pond Creek Station (see previous entry), surrounded the wagons. Cooke and Robbins deployed the train into two parallel columns, with the horses in between. The unmounted troopers formed a circle around the perimeter while the wagons kept moving. The first attack came from the flank. The troopers, kneeling, used their seven-shot Spencers to good effect, and several Indians and ponies went down. The Indians fell back while scout William Comstock taunted them in their own language.

In the next assault, the warriors circled around the train, constricting ever closer until the soldiers opened fire, again driving them back. The Indians kept up the pressure for three hours, drawing fire to use up the soldiers' ammunition. All the while the wagons kept going.

The standoff ended when Capts. West and Meyers finally appeared on the northern horizon. The Indians pulled away, and Cooke's men and their rescuers returned to Custer's camp.

The Indians suffered five killed and half a dozen wounded in the fight. Two troopers were wounded.[458]

2 JULY 1867

KIDDER'S FIGHT (Goodland, Kansas)

While Lt. Col. George Custer was scouting the forks of the Republican River, Lt. Lyman S. Kidder of Company M, 2nd Cavalry, was sent to find him and deliver messages from Gen. William T. Sherman. Kidder left Fort Sedgwick, on the South Platte River, on 29 June, heading south with ten men of Company M and the Lakota scout Red Bead.

It was after dark when Kidder reached Custer's campsite at the forks. He found it abandoned. Unbeknownst to Fort Sedgwick, Custer had left the area and marched to the Platte River. In the moonlight, Kidder mistook the trail of the train Custer had sent to Fort Wallace for Custer's own trail. Kidder left, on the wrong road.

About midday on 2 July, a group of Lakotas discovered Kidder's party north of Beaver Creek. The warriors alerted 12 nearby Cheyennes, including the Dog Soldier Tobacco. At the Indians' approach, Kidder and his men veered off to the southeast, making for the valley of Beaver Creek, 12 miles north of present-day Edson, Kansas. Some of Kidder's men were shot down on a ridge above the creek, but the rest of them made it to a small gully 50 yards north of the creek. The Lakotas dismounted and crept up on foot while the Cheyennes circled around, shooting. Kidder's men fired from the gully, shooting Tobacco's and Good Bear's horses out from beneath them.

Author at site of Kidder's Fight (Kansas)

Hopelessly outnumbered, Kidder and his ten men were killed and mutilated, some of them tortured and burned. Red Bead was cut down with the soldiers. Two Lakotas were killed, among them the young chief Yellow Horse.[459]

5 JULY 1867
DONNER AND BLITZEN CREEK (Burns, Oregon)

While operating in eastern Oregon, chasing small bands of hostile Paiutes, Lt. Col. George Crook, 23rd Infantry, left Camp Warner, 20 miles east of Warner Lake, and headed northeast toward Malheur Lake with Companies F and M, 1st Cavalry, and a detachment of Indian scouts. South of Malheur Lake on Donner and Blitzen Creek, Paiutes surprised Crook's camp, stampeding and running off most of his horses. The troopers managed to kill five raiders, but the loss of the horses forced Crook to end the expedition and return to Camp Warner with the remaining mules.[460]

9 JULY 1867
MUSIC MOUNTAIN (Truxton, Arizona)

Col. John Irvin Gregg, commanding the District of Prescott and the Upper Colorado, joined Capt. James M. Williams and Companies B and I, 8th Cavalry, in a search for raiding Indians around the Yampai Valley. They bivouacked at the foot of the Music Mountains on 5 July and scouted the area.

On the 9th, Gregg, Williams, and eight men began a climb up a peak, but they never reached the summit. A band of Hualapais were already there. In the ensuing fight, the Indians lost three warriors but wounded an enlisted man and put two arrows into Williams's back, one piercing his kidney. With some difficulty, Gregg got the wounded men back down to Truxton Springs. The Hualapais did not pursue them. The wounds effectively ended Williams's Indian-fighting career.[461]

9 JULY 1867
FORT SUMNER (Fort Sumner, New Mexico)

On 8 July, Theodore H. Dodd, agent at Bosque Redondo, learned that Navajo outlaws had hidden a herd of stolen horses in a canyon 25 miles south of Fort Sumner. Temporary commander Capt. Elisha W. Tarlton, 3rd Cavalry, sent out Lt. Henry M. Bragg, 3rd Cavalry, with 18 troopers to recapture the horses.

Bragg found the canyon in the morning and talked to the Navajos through a Mexican interpreter. The interpreter was not certain these were stolen horses, but Bragg had his orders and began driving about 100 head back to the fort. The Navajos, believing the soldiers were stealing their herd, stampeded the horses. The persistent Bragg tried again, collecting 50 horses and heading back to Fort Sumner. Five miles from his destination, the

Indians caught him again and took the horses back. Bragg sent three men after the horses but the Navajos fired at them, and Bragg wisely returned to the post.

At the fort, Tarlton had been drinking with Lt. Charles Porter, 5th Infantry. Perturbed at Bragg's failure, Tarlton ordered Porter to take 20 men from Companies G and I, 3rd Cavalry, to round up the horses. On the way, Porter found 200 Navajos, some under Chief Narbono, blocking his path. This time without an interpreter, both sides ended up gesticulating and shouting without communicating. When an old Navajo rode up and apparently demanded to know why the army was taking his horses, a soldier fired at him. The Indians returned the fire and drove Porter away.

The Navajos chased the soldiers all the way to the hill overlooking the fort, killing five soldiers and wounding four, including Porter. The affair was patched up over the next few days, preventing a major conflict.[462]

11 JULY 1867
SCHOOL HOUSE MASSACRE (Hamilton, Texas)

A score of farms and ranches scattered along the Leon River and in the hills around Hamilton, Texas, sent their children to a one-room school on the south bank of the river, under the guidance of Ann Whitney. On 11 July, through the school's only door, which opened to the south, a little girl saw people who looked like Indians approaching. She told Miss Whitney, but the teacher said they were probably ranchers.

The girl looked again and exclaimed that they *were* Indians. She grabbed her brother by the hand and crawled out through the north-facing window. Then Whitney looked for herself and saw the Indians taking her horse and the other animals in the yard. She slammed the door and told the children to escape through the window. All of them got out except Mary Jane Manning, three Kuykendall children, and Whitney.

One Indian peered through the chinks of the poorly constructed cabin and said in rough English, "Damn you, we have got you now." Though Whitney implored the warrior not to harm the children, the Indians began to shoot arrows through the openings. Whitney was hit, but she succeeded in pushing Mary Jane out the window. The little Kuykendall girl was hit in the back.

The Indians burst through the door. Whitney was dead. The English-speaking warrior asked the two Kuykendall boys if they wanted to go with them, whereupon one uttered "no" and the other said "yes." Strangely enough, the Indians left behind the one who said no and carried off the other, John Kuykendall. Outside, a girl, Olivia Barbee, was almost taken, but she struggled free. The other children were hiding under the schoolhouse floor.

Just then two riders, Amanda and Sarah Howard, approached. The Indians went after them. Sarah leapt over a rail fence and made it to a neighbor's house. Amanda, riding in the other direction, broke through to spread the warning. The Indians hurriedly finished their plundering and rode west. On the way out they killed a Mr. Strangeline and wounded Mrs. Strangeline, a girl, and a baby.

John Kuykendall was later purchased from his captors and brought home.[463]

27 JULY 1867
CAMP WARNER (South-central Oregon)

Based in southeastern Oregon in summer 1867, Lt. Col. George Crook increased his force to 100 men of Companies F, H, and M, 1st Cavalry, and about 100 Wasco, Warm Springs, and Shoshone scouts in three companies under Lt. W. C. McKay, Capt. John Darragh, and chief scout Archie McIntosh. On 20 July, Crook and his men rode out of Camp Smith to seek Indians, first traveling to the Pueblo Mountains, then turning west toward Camp Warner. The three scout companies competed with one another to see which one could find the most trails and kill the most Indians, and the scouts did find several small bands during the march. But on the night of 26 July, in spite of all the scouts, the party became lost in the barren country of south-central Oregon and made a dry camp.

Daylight found the men only a few miles off the Camp Smith–Camp Warner trail, not far from the latter post, and they continued on. At noon, surprisingly close to the fort, they ran right into a Paiute rancheria. McKay's and Darragh's scouts barreled into the camp, followed closely by Joe Wasson, a newspaper reporter who'd been traveling with the command and who now kicked in with his quick-firing Henry rifle. The fight rolled across half a mile of sagebrush and rocks before the Paiutes, armed with only bows and arrows, holed up in a boulder field. They fought there for another half hour. Wasson wrote that three hostile Indians were literally burned out of the rocks, one Indian being "cooked white." The scouts ransacked the camp for spoils.

The Paiutes lost 11 warriors, and 11 women and children were captured. During the weeklong march Crook had killed or captured 46 Indians.[464]

1 AUGUST 1867
HAYFIELD FIGHT (Yellowtail, Montana)

After the annual Sun Dance in 1867, many bands of Lakotas and Cheyennes decided to attack the posts on the hated Bozeman Trail. About two and a half miles northeast of Fort C. F. Smith, on the Bighorn River, a willow-and-log stockade protected the employees of A. C. Leighton, contracted to cut hay for the fort.

On the morning of 1 August, 20 enlisted men of various companies of the 27th Infantry, under Lt. Sigismund Sternberg, guarded 6 civilians cutting hay. At about 11 A.M., more than 800 warriors descended upon the stockade. After a failed decoy, the Indians charged in and were surprised by the amount of fire the soldiers could muster with their new Springfield-Allin breech-loaders. Falling back, the warriors set fire to the hay upwind. The flames were within 20 feet of the stockade when a providential change in wind direction moved the blaze away.

The Indians attacked again. Lt. Sternberg admonished his command, "Stand up, men, and fight like soldiers!"[465] They were his last words, for just then he caught a bullet in the head. Sgt. James Norton took command, but he too was hit. Then Pvt. Thomas Navin of F Company was killed. By default, civilian Al Colvin took over. Colvin was a whirlwind, firing his 16-shot Henry rifle incessantly from all around the perimeter.

Pvt. Charles Bradley of Company E volunteered to ride to Fort Smith for help. Though knocked off his horse by a blow from a pursuing warrior, Bradley reached the post. Lt. Col. Luther P. Bradley was slow in responding; it was 4 P.M. before he sent out Capt. Thomas B. Burrowes with Company G and a howitzer, and shortly afterward, Lt. Reuben N. Fenton with Company H. The relief force got to the hay stockade at sundown. By then the Indians had given up the attack. Perhaps 450 Indians still hovered on the bluffs, and Burrowes drove them off. In the gathering night, the exhausted defenders rode back to Fort Smith.

Sternberg and Navin were killed, and 3 other soldiers were wounded, as was 1 civilian. About 8 warriors were killed and 30 wounded.[466]

1–2 AUGUST 1867
SALINE RIVER (Hays, Kansas)

In the midafternoon of 1 August, 30 warriors, probably Cheyennes and Lakotas, attacked a party of railroad workers near the North Fork of Big Creek, west of present-day Victoria, Kansas. The workers had left their firearms behind that day. Six men were killed, including the foreman, P. S. Ashley. Afterward, Capt. George A. Armes of the 10th Cavalry, one of two black "buffalo soldier" regiments, arrived at the site from Fort Hays, ten miles west, and carried the last wounded man back to the post hospital, where he soon died.

Armes and F Company then followed the Indians' trail north. On 2 August, about 20 miles north of the fort, near the Saline River, Armes and his 35 troopers ran into more than 300 warriors. The Indians charged in, and Armes dismounted his troopers, placed them around the horses, and slowly walked back toward the fort. Although the warriors circled around for six hours, nearly all the way to Fort Hays, they did not break Armes's perimeter.

The Indians fired about 2,000 rounds but killed only one soldier, Sgt. William Christy—the first fatality in the 10th Cavalry—and wounded four, including Armes, hit in the hip. Armes reported six Indians killed. In addition, six soldiers contracted cholera during the scout and had to be strapped to their horses to get back to the fort.[467]

2 AUGUST 1867
WAGON BOX FIGHT (Story, Wyoming)

A crew of civilian woodcutters were camped on Little Piney Creek, about five miles northwest of Fort Phil Kearny, with their military escort, Capt. James W. Powell and Lt. John C. Jenness, 27th Infantry, and 51 men of Company C, who had just relieved Company A. Early in the morning of 2 August, nearly 1,000 Sioux warriors, mainly Oglalas, Minneconjous, and Sans Arcs, under Red Cloud and High Back Bone, struck the camp.

Some soldiers and civilians were caught outside camp or in transit between the camp and the fort, and they had their own fights or escaped. All Powell could muster to his wagon corral were Jenness, 24 enlisted men, and 6 civilians. Perhaps 800 warriors concentrated on the wagons. A mounted charge from the southwest was beaten back by judicious fire from the soldiers' new Springfield-Allin breech-loading rifles. When the initial charge failed, the warriors dismounted and crept close to the north and east side of the corral, where the terrain provided cover.

In the second attack, Lt. Jenness remained standing, ignoring the entreaties of his men. "I know how to fight Indians," he said.[468] Just then a

Left: Site of the Wagon Box fight, Bighorn
Mountains (Wyoming)

Right: Chief Red Cloud
—Courtesy Denver Public Library,
Western History Department

bullet hit him square in the forehead. Also killed were Pvts. Henry Haggerty
and Tommy Doyle. A Minneconjou named Jipala brazenly advanced with
a spear and a buffalo hide, challenging the soldiers to shoot him. He remained unscathed for a long time, but Pvt. Max Littman finally brought
him down. The defenders repulsed eight charges between 7 A.M. and 1:30 P.M.

Eventually survivors outside the corral brought word to Fort Phil
Kearny. Maj. Benjamin Smith took 100 men and a mountain howitzer to
their relief. The howitzer's boom announced the rescue, and the Sioux, tired
and frustrated at their inability to overrun the corral, pulled back. About
4 woodcutters and 14 soldiers hiding in the woods came back when the
fight was over.

Three men in the corral were killed and two were wounded; four more
defenders were killed outside the enclosure. Historian George Hyde wrote
that six Indians were killed and six were wounded. Some estimates of Sioux
casualties were as high as an absurd 1,500. Powell estimated 60 Indians
killed and 120 wounded; the real figure was likely half that.[469]

6 AUGUST 1867
TURKEY LEG'S RAID (Lexington, Nebraska)

When Cheyennes under Turkey Leg and Spotted Wolf sabotaged the
train track three and a half miles west of Plum Creek Station, six Union
Pacific workers took a handcar out to repair the damage. When they found
the break in the track, the Indians jumped up from behind some tall
grass and attacked, killing five of them. An Englishman named William

Thompson was clubbed down and feigned death while a warrior sawed off his scalp. "I just thought then that I could have screamed my life out," he later reported. "It just felt as if the whole head was taken right off."[470]

Thompson's attacker mounted and rode off, but he dropped the scalp. Thompson retrieved it and lay in the grass until dark. He watched as a train came chugging along from the east, hit the torn-up tracks, and derailed in a crash of steam and twisted metal. The engineer and a fireman were killed, but in the caboose, another fireman, two brakemen, and the conductor got out. They ran down the track until they saw the lights of another oncoming train and managed to flag it down. They scrambled aboard while the engineer threw it in reverse and backed away.

Thompson saw the Indians throwing the dead bodies from the train into a roaring bonfire and dragged himself away, clutching his scalp. He made it to Plum Creek Station and got aboard a train, carrying his scalp in a bucket of water, hoping in vain that a doctor could sew it on. Thompson eventually returned to England, but his scalp, tanned and preserved in alcohol, was kept in the Omaha Public Library Museum.

Seven civilians were killed in the raid.[471]

17 AUGUST 1867
PLUM CREEK (Lexington, Nebraska)

After the bold attacks on the Union Pacific trains near Plum Creek Station (see previous entry), Col. Richard I. Dodge ordered Maj. Frank North and his Pawnee Battalion to the scene, 220 miles west. North and his men took a train there and arrived in 24 hours, but the Indians had gone. North decided to wait.

Ten days later, Lt. Isaac Davis and 20 scouts were repairing cut telegraph wire around old Plum Creek Station, on the south side of the Platte River, when about 100 of Turkey Leg's warriors attacked from the south. They pushed Davis back to the river. Upon learning of the assault, North was about to charge into the fray, but Capt. James Murie implored him to give him the command. North agreed, and Murie took the remaining 30 Pawnee scouts and approached the Cheyennes on their right flank. The Cheyennes spotted the blue uniforms, however, and prepared to attack. The scouts left their horses along the riverbank and walked into full view, slapping their breasts and shouting, "Pawnees!"

The surprised Cheyennes saw the shaved heads and scalp locks of their old enemies and hesitated. The Pawnees, armed with seven-shot Spencers, fired into them. Turkey Leg had never faced Spencers before, and seven of his braves went down in the first volley, while the rest lost their desire to fight. Murie recorded, "I ordered a charge and it had the desired effect, which was a stampede of the enemy."[472]

The scouts pursued the Cheyennes 12 miles before giving up the chase. The Pawnees were jubilant. They had garnered 15 scalps and captured 31 horses and mules. They had also taken a Cheyenne woman, a boy, and a girl—the children were Turkey Leg's own nephew and niece.[473]

21–22 AUGUST 1867
PRAIRIE DOG CREEK (Prairie View, Kansas)

Only 19 days after being wounded in the Saline River fight, Capt. George A. Armes was back in the saddle, leading a scout north out of Fort Hays. The command consisted of 40 men of Company F of the 10th Cavalry and 90 men of Companies B and C of the 18th Kansas Volunteer Cavalry under Capts. Edgar A. Barker and George B. Jenness.

After crossing the Solomon River, the soldiers set out for Beaver Creek, a small tributary of the North Fork of the Solomon in present-day Phillips County, Kansas. On the night of 20 August, Jenness saw a light to the east and went to investigate. It was an abandoned Indian camp with the remains of a campfire. Jenness decided not to try to find his way back that night, but the next morning, when he went back to Armes's camp, he found that Armes had already moved out. Jenness joined up with the supply wagons following the command.

Near the head of Beaver Creek, not far from Prairie Dog Creek, several hundred Cheyenne and Lakota warriors attacked the wagons. Jenness formed them up in a hollow square and kept the circling warriors away with his seven-shot Spencers. Even so, the Indians gave the wagoneers a hot time, shaking their lances and flapping blankets to frighten the horses. A warrior on a white pony, possibly Roman Nose, charged right through the square and out the other side, emerging unscathed.

Meanwhile Armes, in the Prairie Dog valley, was beset by a like number of Indians. Both commands held off their attackers until dark. That night, Jenness went back to the North Fork of the Solomon, where he took refuge in a canyon.

The battle resumed at daybreak. Armes fought his way south and eventually linked up with Jenness, but the Indians still had them surrounded. Many came close enough to taunt them—one of them, possibly Charley Bent, in English: "Come out of that hole you sons of bitches and give us a fair fight."[474]

Armes made a charge that drove his tormentors away for awhile. About 4 P.M., the Indians and soldiers tried a parley, but neither side trusted the other. Concealed weapons came out and firing began once more. The fight continued until dark, when the Indians pulled away, and Armes took his battered command back to Fort Hays.

The army suffered 8 killed and 35 wounded. Armes claimed 150 Indian casualties, but 10 killed and 20 wounded are more likely numbers.[475]

SURPRISE VALLEY (Cedarville, California)

While Lt. Col. George Crook prepared for a new campaign at Camp Warner, his chief scout, Archie McIntosh, took 18 of his Shoshones to explore the territory south and east of Goose Creek. In Surprise Valley, McIntosh ran into a large band of Paiutes and Pit River Indians under Cheeoh. The encounter cost the hostiles two killed and seven wounded; McIntosh had several wounded. Realizing he could not defeat the warriors in a protracted battle, McIntosh tried a parley. There would be no peace, the hostiles declared. If anyone came into their country they would be killed. "Archy," wrote reporter Joe Wasson, was "whipped back." He reported the affair to Crook.[476]

15 SEPTEMBER 1867
DAVIS'S FIGHT (WaKeeney, Kansas)

Sgt. Ed Davis and nine men of Company G, 10th Cavalry—"buffalo soldiers"—were guarding a railroad crew near the Saline River about 45 miles west of Fort Hays. Pvt. John Randall and 2 civilians left camp on a hunt and were attacked by 70 Cheyennes. The civilians were killed and the wounded Randall reached dubious sanctuary in a hole under a railroad cut. Amused warriors poked lances into the hole, hitting Randall 11 more times before they tired of the sport. Then they turned to attack the camp.

In the meantime, Davis, having seen the Indians, took his soldiers on foot to help Randall. The Cheyennes went after two passing railroad workers with an ox team. Davis blocked the move, allowing the men to reach camp. The Cheyennes backed off, and Davis searched for Randall. The soldiers found Randall by his cries for help and dragged him from his crumbling shelter to safety.

The Indians came back to finish off the buffalo soldiers but found them very handy with their carbines—13 warriors went down, dead or wounded. Other than Randall, there were no additional soldier casualties.[477]

26–28 SEPTEMBER 1867
INFERNAL CAVERNS (Northeastern California)

Lt. Col. Crook began a new expedition on 30 August, leaving Camp Warner with about 280 men of Companies F and H, 1st Cavalry; the mounted Company D, 23rd Infantry; and 100 Warm Springs and Shoshone scouts. They found many Indian trails but could not bring the elusive bands to battle. South of Goose Lake, they moved down the Pit River to within 20 miles of Fort Crook, then cut back east toward the South Fork of the Pit River.

On the morning of 26 September, Lt. W. C. McKay reported that he had found a group of Indians holed up in some lava beds. Crook placed the cavalry under Lt. William R. Parnell to the south of the Indians' position and the infantry under Lt. John Madigan to the north of it. About 75 Paiutes, 30 Pit River Indians, and a few Modocs, all under Cheeoh and Sieta, were waiting for them.

The Indians had made a fort out of the jumble of sharp lava rocks amid the cliffs, ravines, and boulders. When Crook attacked, his men were blasted all day without capturing the position. The next day, Parnell and Madigan fought against a fortification to the east while the scouts went after a western one. In the first charge of the morning, Lt. Madigan was killed and seven others were wounded. Nevertheless, they kept up the assault, scrambling up the rocks. Sgt. Michael Meara of Company H reached the top of the fortification and shouted, "Come on, boys, we've got 'em!" only to be shot dead, falling at reporter Joe Wasson's feet.[478]

The soldiers eventually captured the position, but the Indians were still hidden in the labyrinth below. Said Crook: "I never wanted dynamite so bad as I did when we first took the fort and heard the diabolical and defiant yells from down in the rocks."[479] Fighting continued through the day and into the night, but by the next morning, the Indians had crawled out of the caves and made their escape.

It was a dear victory for Crook, who suffered 8 killed and 11 wounded. The Indian casualties were 20 killed, 12 wounded, and 2 captured.[480]

1 OCTOBER 1867
HOWARD'S WELL (Pandale, Texas)

A party of Kickapoos who had crossed over from Mexico ambushed and killed Cpl. Emanuel Wright and Pvt. E. T. Wright of Company D, 9th Cavalry, as they escorted the mail from Fort Clark to Fort Stockton. The coach driver and passengers were wounded. In his frantic escape, the driver dropped all the mail four miles from Howard's Well.[481]

6 OCTOBER 1867
HUALAPAI MOUNTAIN (Kingman, Arizona)

Lt. Almond B. Wells, 8th Cavalry, led one column of 50 men of Company L out of Fort Mohave in search of Chief Scherum's Hualapais. He traveled east through Beale's (Sitgreaves) Pass in the Black Mountains, scouting for 12 days between there and the Hualapai Mountains. A severe drought had dried up the known water holes, and the Indians were hard to locate. Finally, on 6 October, Wells attacked a small party in the northern Hualapai Mountains, killing seven Indians with no loss to his own command.[482]

THE WILLOWS (Kingman, Arizona)

Lt. Patrick Hasson, 14th Infantry, was ordered to take 50 men of Company E, 1st Cavalry, and a detachment of the 8th Cavalry to "meet conditions"—find and fight the enemy. Hasson and his men left Fort Whipple and headed northwest. They stopped to camp near the Willows oasis at the base of the Cottonwood Cliffs, about 30 miles east of present-day Kingman, Arizona.

Indian signs were plentiful, and scout Dan O'Leary soon found a Hualapai rancheria in the hills above the oasis. At dawn on 7 November, the soldiers were in position to attack, but some overeager men got too far ahead and gave away the surprise. Hoping to get them back, someone sounded recall on the bugle, to the extreme chagrin of the poised soldiers. Nevertheless, the uncoordinated charge began, and it turned out to be a hot battle.

Although many Hualapais escaped, Hasson reported 19 killed and 17 women and children captured. Hasson and 5 enlisted men were wounded.[483]

DONA ANA MOUNTAINS (Dona Ana, New Mexico)

About 50 Apaches raided Fort Selden on the Rio Grande, stealing the quartermaster herd of 13 horses and 30 mules. A handful of black soldiers and a detachment of Company K, 3rd Cavalry, under Lt. Oscar Elting, quickly mounted up and pursued them. They chased the raiders six miles east into the Dona Ana Mountains and in a running battle killed three Indians and captured about eight Indian ponies. They recaptured all the stock except for six head that were killed during the fight. The soldiers also shot down one Hispanic hay cutter whom they mistook for an Indian.[484]

FORT LANCASTER (Sheffield, Texas)

Capt. William Frohock and Company K of the black 9th Cavalry were guarding a herd of horses for the military at Fort Lancaster, on Live Oak Creek near its junction with the Pecos River, when they were attacked by a huge force of Lipans, Kickapoos, Mexicans, and white renegades, estimated at nearly 900 men. About 200 mounted raiders came out of the north and surprised some troopers who were moving the herd to water, overwhelming them and running off the horses. Another 400 mounted men came from the west and assaulted the main Company K camp. The troopers formed a defensive semicircle and tried to corral the remaining horses, but they were swamped and the horses were run off.

The soldiers took refuge in the ruins of a settler's store near the fort. Frohock thought the renegades were too busy with the horses to annihilate his command at first charge, so he would try to make them pay for their mistake. He advanced some of his men on foot and drove the renegades back, but fire halted the advance. As the defenders repelled a second charge from the north, the foot soldiers returned to the store.

Frohock assumed the raiders would charge from all sides and probably overwhelm them, but they were apparently satisfied with the horses and pulled back at nightfall. The plucky Frohock mounted several troopers on his last available horses and pursued. After a four-mile chase, the soldiers returned empty-handed.

Surprisingly, Frohock's only casualties were three herd guards who were caught in the initial attack—they were roped, dragged away, and killed. Twenty attackers were killed; one Confederate uniform was retrieved from the battlefield.[485]

—1868—

14 JANUARY 1868
DIFFICULT CANYON (Chloride, Arizona)

Capt. Samuel B. M. Young, convinced that the scouting missions sent through the Hualapai country would not be decisive, left Fort Mojave on 11 January with Company K of the 8th Cavalry and a party of scouts under Dan O'Leary. The men marched through a furious storm, protesting, but Young reasoned that if he wanted to pay Chief Scherum a visit, the chief was more likely to be at home during a storm.

The trail wound over the Black and Cerbat Ranges and into the Hualapai Valley. Thinking Scherum must have seen the column, Young ordered Lt. Jonathan D. Stevenson with a platoon to head southeast as a deception, then took his men northwest into a canyon below Cherum Peak. In the false dawn of the parting clouds, Young, O'Leary, and 13 dismounted troopers went around a bend and found themselves 30 yards from Scherum's camp. Both sides were equally startled. About 100 Indians took to the rocks of the canyon walls and fired away, but the soldiers' Spencers took a toll and seven Indians fell in the opening round. O'Leary wounded Scherum, but the chief dragged himself to cover behind a boulder. After an hour and twenty minutes of fighting, Young's ammunition was low and he pulled back.

Meanwhile, Lt. Stevenson had gone several miles across the valley and then doubled back. Seeing smoke from the canyon, he headed for the fight. Young, however, had already left the scene when Stevenson and his platoon arrived, and they ran into the large force of warriors. With the first shots, Stevenson took six bullets and went down. His men carried him away, but the Hualapais followed them three miles down the canyon, firing at them until darkness brought an end to the fight.

During the night Young sent a courier to Beale's Springs for an ambulance. In the morning, the wounded were taken to Fort Mojave and Young made another feint to the southeast. That night he reversed course to approach Scherum's camp, but at dawn he found that the Indians were gone.

Both Stevenson and Scherum survived their wounds. Two enlisted men were wounded; 21 Indians were killed and 6 wounded.[486]

6 MARCH 1868
PAINT CREEK (Haskell, Texas)

On the morning of 5 March, Capt. Adna R. Chaffee, 6th Cavalry, with detachments of Companies F and I, left Fort Griffin to scout for Indians. The next morning they crossed the Clear Fork of the Brazos River about 12 miles below old Fort Phantom Hill and soon found an Indian trail. They followed it northwest through cold, stormy weather. About 10 A.M., on the banks of Paint Creek in the southeast corner of present-day Haskell County, Texas, he came upon a Comanche camp.

Chaffee charged right in, scattering the Indians and killing five Comanches, plus one Mexican and one mulatto, whom he reported were the leaders of the band. The soldiers took five ponies and destroyed a large number of shields, weapons, and camp equipment. Three privates were wounded in the offensive.[487]

11 MARCH 1868
TULAROSA (Tularosa, New Mexico)

In a raid on settlements around Tularosa at the foot of the Sacramento Mountains, Mescalero Apaches killed and mutilated 11 men and 2 women, captured a child, and drove off about 2,200 sheep. Lt. Peter D. Vroom, 3rd Cavalry, with a detachment of Company H, chased the raiders. With a three-day head start, the Apaches disappeared into the Guadalupe Mountains. Vroom could only round up some abandoned sheep.[488]

14 MARCH 1868
DONNER AND BLITZEN CREEK (Burns, Oregon)

While hunting down the last of the recalcitrant Paiute bands, Lt. Col. George Crook led several scouts out of Camp Warner during the winter of 1867–68. It was bitterly cold, below zero, on 14 March, when Crook discovered a small rancheria of Indians on Donner and Blitzen Creek in the lowlands south of Malheur Lake. The usually marshy sloughs were frozen over, and Crook, with Company H, 1st Cavalry; Company C, 8th Cavalry; and Company D, 23rd Infantry, had no trouble crossing over to attack.

The soldiers entered an area of brush and willows, which blended in with the Indians' wickiups. Crook and a guide mistakenly rode right into the door of a wickiup. The dogs began howling and gave the alarm. The troopers dismounted, chasing the Indians through the brush. Most of the Indians escaped over a muddy creek that had not frozen over. One officer and two enlisted men were wounded. Twelve Paiutes were killed and two were captured.

Crook assumed the Indians had fled to a camp several miles down the valley, where he had earlier seen smoke. They marched there in the darkness, spending the night without fires, stomping their feet and pounding their bodies with their arms to keep from freezing. "Our beards were one mass of ice," said Crook.[489]

At daylight they found another partly frozen slough barring their path, and by the time they sloshed across, most of the Indians had run away. In the afternoon, a warm Chinook blew in out of the southwest, rapidly melting the snow. Marching over ice with up to two feet of meltwater running over it, Crook had to retreat "for fear of being waterbound."[490]

21 MARCH 1868
CAMP WILLOW GROVE (Kingman, Arizona)

At 9:00 A.M. on 21 March, mail carrier Charles Spencer and escorts Cpl. D. Troy and Pvt. Flood of the 14th Infantry left Camp Willow Grove with mail for Hardyville. Four miles from the post they were ambushed by 75 Hualapais. In the first volley, Troy and Flood were killed and Spencer's mule went down. Spencer grabbed his seven-shot rifle and ran behind the nearest greasewood bush.

When the warriors came up to strip and mutilate the two dead soldiers, Spencer fired, killing two of them. The others ran for cover, and Spencer did the same, running behind some boulders. The combatants sniped at each other for several hours. The Indians hit Spencer in the thigh and thought they had him, but when they approached, Spencer fired again. Later the Hualapais tried to talk the white man out of his hole, assuring him they wouldn't kill him. To test their word, Spencer raised his hat on a stick, and it was peppered with bullets.

Finally the gunfire drew the attention of the soldiers at Camp Willow Grove. They rode in and drove away the Indians, then brought up a wagon to carry out the bodies. Spencer, too weak to crawl out of his hole, fired a few times to let the soldiers know where he was. They found him and carried him back to camp.

The wounded Spencer and the two soldiers killed comprised the army's casualties. On the Hualapais' side, two were killed and several were wounded.[491]

17 APRIL 1868
NESMITH'S MILLS (Tularosa, New Mexico)

In the foothills of the Sacramento Mountains near Tularosa, New Mexico, a detachment of Company H, 3rd Cavalry, commanded by Sgt. E. Glass and aided by a party of armed citizens, fought with the Mescalero Apaches. One trooper and 5 civilians were wounded. The party reported killing 10 Indians and wounding 25, very likely an exaggerated count.[492]

29 APRIL 1868
TOBIN MASSACRE (Overton, Nebraska)

As the Union Pacific built west, Indians were inexorably pushed away from the main travel routes, but not without resistance. At the Overton siding in central Nebraska, about ten miles east of the Plum Creek train station, were the homes of rail workers Timothy Tobin and Richard Costin. While Tobin, the section foreman, and several workers were repairing rails two miles away, Mrs. Tobin saw a dust cloud approaching and thought it was buffalo. She was soon disabused of that notion—it was Indians. She ran with her children to the Costin home.

The Indians, about 40 of them, approached Tobin and 3 other men.[493] Caught too far from the handcar where the workers' weapons lay, Tobin walked up to the nearest warrior and tried to talk. "Tobak!" exclaimed the Indian, asking for tobacco and indicating that he was a friendly Pawnee. Then,

Sugarloaf Mountain (Arizona)

seeing that the white men were unarmed, the Indian suddenly proclaimed himself a Lakota and opened fire.

Tobin fell; the others broke and ran, to be picked off in turn. One of the men, Williams, made it to the handcar and began furiously pumping for his life. He took an arrow in the back but made it to the Overton siding. There Mrs. Costin got aboard, and the two headed for Plum Creek Station. Meanwhile, Mrs. Tobin and her children watched the Indians disappear into the hills.

At Plum Creek, rescuers commandeered a waiting train and rushed to Overton, only to find the three scalped, mutilated bodies of the unfortunate work crew.[494]

13 JUNE 1868
APACHE SPRINGS (Apache Springs, New Mexico)

On 6 June, just as the government was finalizing a treaty to move the Navajos back to their homeland, four white men were discovered face down in the water on Twelve Mile Creek, in New Mexico Territory. Navajo arrows pierced the bodies, and three of the victims appeared to have been tortured. Navajo leaders Barboncito, Delgadito, and Manuelito, not wanting the incident to ruin the treaty, cooperated fully in finding the criminals.

The guilty men fled the reservation, but the chiefs reported them to the soldiers at Fort Sumner. Lt. Deane Monahan, with detachments of Companies G and I, 3rd Cavalry, caught up with the culprits before dawn at Apache Springs, less than 20 miles south of Las Vegas, New Mexico. While the soldiers surrounded the sleeping Navajos, the band's leader, Juh Sanchez, awoke and roused his warriors. A fight erupted, but the Navajos, outgunned, were forced into a ravine, where two Indians were killed and Sanchez was mortally wounded. The 11 remaining renegades surrendered soon after daylight.[495]

16 JUNE 1868
SUGARLOAF MOUNTAIN (Fort McDowell, Arizona)

Sgt. J. Lemon and four privates of Company E, 1st Cavalry, were assigned to carry mail from Camp Reno, in the Tonto Basin, to Camp McDowell, about 25 miles away.[496] When they reached Sugarloaf Mountain, 12 miles east of their destination, one of the men, Pvt. Theeley, noticed Indians ahead and shouted out a warning. Lemon, in front, tried to spur his horse on, but a volley from nearly 100 Apache warriors crashed into them from three sides. All five men and all the horses were hit. Lemon managed to kill one warrior before being overwhelmed. One of the privates ran to a hill and held on for a time before being hacked in two. Only Theely got away, making it back to an outpost of Camp Reno with 20 Apaches in pursuit.

The total losses were four soldiers killed and one wounded, and one Apache killed.[497]

8 JULY 1868
BIG RUMP CANYON (Roosevelt, Arizona)

Inveterate enemies of the Apaches, the Pimas spent much time tracking them for the white soldiers or for their own edification. In early July some Pima warriors jumped a band of Apaches, killed two, and chased six more into a cave in Big Rump Canyon, in the Four Peaks area between the Salt and Verde Rivers. Unable to get at them, the Pimas hurried north to Camp Reno and alerted the soldiers. Lt. Camillo C. C. Carr, 1st Cavalry, took detachments of Companies E, 1st Cavalry, and I, 8th Cavalry, to the scene.

The troops halted on the rim of the canyon, unable to descend the cliffs. They shot one Apache off the ledge, the body falling more than 100 feet to the rocks below. While the soldiers paused on the rim, Apache reinforcements arrived, and as Carr's columns moved up the mountain, about 200 warriors laid in wait. The Apaches let Carr's main force ride by unmolested, then opened fire on the trailing supply train. Fourteen soldiers and a number of packers fought a seesaw battle with the Apaches, losing the mules, recapturing them, and losing them again. By the time Carr rode to the rescue, the Indians had retreated, and after a 60-mile chase the lieutenant gave up the pursuit.

Three Indians were reported killed and eight wounded. A few packers were wounded.[498]

AUGUST 1868
VAN HORN'S WELL (Van Horn, Texas)

Former Texas Ranger "Bigfoot" Wallace and eight companions were driving the mail stage between El Paso and Fort Davis when they saw dust rising in the distance. They hurried to a defensive position at Van Horn's Well as the Indians (probably Apache) became visible. The Indians charged then withdrew a short distance. Wallace killed a few horses for breastworks and waited behind them. The night passed without incident, but in the morning the Indians, thirsty, tried to get to the well. They hid among their horses as they turned the animals loose to go to the water. The ruse failed, costing them several mounts as Wallace and his men blasted away. The Indians then rode in circles around the barricade, showering the defenders with arrows and bullets, wounding three of them. That afternoon, a great thunderstorm struck, blunting the Indians' ardor for attack. They soon departed.

Three of Wallace's men were wounded; they estimated they hit 11 Indians.[499]

13 AUGUST 1868
ELKHORN CREEK (Lincoln, Kansas)

More than 200 Cheyennes, Arapahos, and Lakotas, under prominent warriors such as Man-Who-Breaks-the-Marrow-Bones, Tall Wolf, Porcupine Bear, and Bear-That-Goes-Ahead, moved north from their villages in central Kansas and descended on the settlements along the Saline and Solomon Rivers. Some may have been carrying arms and ammunition recently issued to them by Indian agent Edward W. Wynkoop at Fort Larned. On 10 August, they raided the farms along Spillman Creek in Grant County, raping three women.[500]

Capt. Frederick W. Benteen, with Company H, 7th Cavalry, and Lt. Owen Hale, with Company M of the same regiment, were sent from Fort Larned to the scene of the attacks, about 80 miles away. Benteen took a detachment of H and moved rapidly, reaching Fort Harker in two days. From there, he took 40 men from his company and several he rounded up at the fort and moved north.

Benteen's party arrived at the farmhouse of a family called Schermerhorn on Elkhorn Creek, about five miles southeast of Lincoln, Kansas, where 50 Indians were threatening a family. After dropping off ten men with the pack mules, Benteen and his men "were into that gang of astounded reds before they were aware of it."[501]

The 30 soldiers chased what turned out to be nearly 200 warriors down the Elkhorn and up the Saline toward Spillman Creek. The troopers got so close, said Benteen, they were "almost trampling on their 'gee-strings.'"[502] During the 20-mile romp the Indians abandoned two captured girls, Maggie and Esther Bell, who were rescued the next day.

The cavalrymen put their repeating Spencers to work, killing three Indians and wounding ten; Benteen lost not a man.[503]

18–21 AUGUST 1868
PAWNEE FORK (West-central Kansas)

On 18 August Indians attacked a wagon train carrying supplies for Fort Dodge and the upcoming expedition under Brig. Gen. Alfred Sully as it was leaving the Pawnee Fork. The drivers corralled the wagons and fought the Indians to a standoff, but the siege did not break. On the 20th, Lt. David W. Wallingford and 38 men of Company B, 7th Cavalry, rode out of Fort Dodge and dispersed the Indians. During the night, the Indians returned to attack again, but the soldiers repulsed them. Wallingford brought the wagons safely to the fort on 23 August.

Five citizens were wounded in the attack; Wallingford estimated that five Indians were killed and ten wounded.[504]

27 AUGUST 1868
HATCHET MOUNTAINS (Hachita, New Mexico)

Convinced that Apaches from south of the border were crossing to steal stock, Capt. Alexander Moore, 38th Infantry, set out to halt the practice. He left Fort Cummings on 23 August with 85 soldiers, mostly from Company F, 38th Infantry, and scouted the international boundary.

On 27 August, in the Hatchet Mountains near Ojo Alamo, Moore surprised a rancheria and killed three Apaches. The soldiers captured three Indian children and seized many pounds of powder, one ton of mescal, skins, blankets, rifles, and livestock. After many more days of scouting, Moore returned to Fort Cummings on 14 September.[505]

2 SEPTEMBER 1868
LITTLE COON CREEK (Spearville, Kansas)

On Little Coon Creek, east of Fort Dodge, about 40 Kiowas attacked supply wagons heading from Fort Larned to Fort Dodge. The train's escorts included a detachment of 3rd Infantry under Sgt. Dittoe, Company A, and four 7th Cavalrymen under Cpl. J. Goodwin, Company B. The wagons corralled and put up a good defense while one of the men rode to Fort Dodge for help.

Three enlisted men were wounded, and three Indians were killed and one wounded before help arrived from Lt. Wallace and the 3rd Infantry.[506]

10 SEPTEMBER 1868
RULE CREEK (Toonerville, Colorado)

Company L, 7th Cavalry, recently restationed at Fort Lyon, were temporarily under the command of Capt. William H. Penrose, 3rd Infantry. When stock was stolen in the vicinity, Penrose led a hard-riding scout up Rule Creek, about six miles from the fort. Five horses died of exhaustion in the chase before the soldiers engaged a band of Cheyennes in a sharp fight, killing 4 Cheyennes and recovering 12 head of stock. Two troopers were killed in the encounter and one was wounded.[507]

10–13 SEPTEMBER 1868
SAND HILLS (Woodward, Oklahoma)

Due to constant Indian raiding in Kansas during the summer of 1868, the army sent an expedition to punish the tribes south of the Arkansas River. Brig. Gen. Alfred Sully led 500 men in 9 companies of the 7th Cavalry under Maj. Joel H. Elliot, and Company F of the 3rd Infantry, out of Fort Dodge on 7 September.

On 10 September, near the confluence of Crooked Creek and the Cimarron River, the expedition's scouts were attacked by Indians (probably Cheyennes) but escaped. Shortly afterward, Elliot's vanguard repulsed another attack, killing two Indians. Early the next morning, a war party burst into the soldiers' camp, tried to run off the horses, and bodily carried off two men of Company F. Capt. Louis Hamilton of Company A, in command of the rear guard, took up the chase. He pressed the raiders so closely that they were forced to drop one of the soldiers, but not before severely wounding him. The other, James Curran, was killed after Sully ordered Hamilton to return to the column.

Sully forged across the divide toward the North Fork of the Canadian River, harassed all the way by Cheyenne Dog Soldiers, one of whom blew bugle calls. Elliot's troopers killed eight of the Indians. Six miles from the river, the expedition came upon a deserted village, where they were confronted by more warriors, whom they drove off after inflicting several more casualties. Heading down the North Fork, the soldiers were harassed by Indians in the sandy bluffs. Sully ordered his men to dismount, and for two hours they chased the Indians back into the hills, causing 12 more casualties. They then continued another 15 miles downriver.

At about 11 A.M. on the 12th, the soldiers crossed the divide from the North Fork to Wolf Creek and marched southeast for two miles. There they met a large force of Kiowas, Comanches, and Cheyennes. The Indians had made false trails in the sand to set a trap. With difficulty Sully extricated

Brig. Gen. Alfred Sully
—Courtesy Denver Public Library,
Western History Department

his wagons from the surround, and while the 3rd Infantry guarded the train, the 7th Cavalry troops fanned out into the sand hills to drive away the tenacious warriors.

The next day Sully continued about 20 more miles down the North Fork and encountered more conflicts with Indians in the sand hills south of the river. Fed up, he turned the troops around and headed upriver, assuming the Indians had fled that area. Two days later, harassed the entire way by Indians whom Sully thought had gone, the soldiers made camp at Bluff Creek, 45 miles southeast of Fort Dodge.

Three enlisted men had been killed and 5 wounded. Sully reported 22 Indians killed and 12 wounded.[508]

14 SEPTEMBER 1868
HORSEHEAD HILL (Marathon, Texas)

Late in August, west of Fort Stockton, 200 Apaches attacked a wagon train owned by a man named Morales and stole 100 mules. Morales recruited 45 armed Mexicans to get them back, but he knew it was not enough. He requested help from the army, and Lt. Patrick Cusack responded with 60 men of Companies C, F, and K, 9th Cavalry. The combined parties left Fort Davis on 8 September.

In the Santiago Mountains, Cusack found the Indians—Alsate's Mescaleros and Sabier's Lipans—and chased them in a running fight for five miles. The warriors retreated up Horsehead Hill, which was too steep for the horses to climb, so Cusack's men dismounted and fought them amid the rocks. The soldiers thoroughly defeated the Apaches. Some of Cusack's troops rode back to Fort Davis painted like Indians and carrying lances with Apache scalps attached.

At a cost of one enlisted man wounded, Cusack claimed his men killed 25 Indians and wounded 25 more. They also captured two Mexican boys and an Indian girl and took 450 skins and 198 horses and mules. Morales's mules were returned to him. Cusack was brevetted a captain for "conspicuous gallantry."[509]

15 SEPTEMBER 1868
BIG SANDY CREEK (Aroya, Colorado)

Scouting along the road from the Arkansas River to Denver, Capt. George W. Graham of Company I, 10th Cavalry, a black unit, saw an Indian trail heading west. With his 36 troopers, Graham followed the path into present-day eastern Colorado. At Big Sandy Creek they ran into about 100 Cheyenne Dog Soldiers.

The warriors attacked and engaged the soldiers in a bitter fight at close quarters. It was Company I's first battle, and they handled themselves handsomely, fighting like "cornered wildcats."[510]

By the time nightfall ended the fighting, 7 soldiers had been wounded and 18 horses had been killed or were missing; they had killed 11 Cheyennes and wounded 14.[511]

17–21 SEPTEMBER 1868
BEECHER'S ISLAND (Wray, Colorado)

To assist Kansas settlers with their Indian problem, Gen. Philip Sheridan directed Maj. George A. Forsyth to enlist a company of 50 frontiersmen to patrol the state's northwest frontier. The men moved out of Fort Hays on 29 August and traveled west to Fort Wallace, east to the railhead at Sheridan, then northwest toward the Republican River.

After two weeks in the saddle, the patrol picked up an Indian trail and followed an ever-increasing number of tracks up the Arikaree Fork of the Republican. At dawn on 17 September, several Cheyennes drove off some of Forsyth's horses. The major was saddling up to chase them down when he saw the few warriors turn into more than 500. His only hope was to take his command to a small nearby island in the river and try to hold the Indians off. They splashed across to what would come to be called Beecher's Island, and the Cheyennes quickly surrounded them. Some men wanted to make a run for it. "Stay where you are men," shouted Forsyth. "It's our only chance. I'll shoot down any man who attempts to leave the island."[512]

Beecher's Island (Colorado)

There the company stayed, fighting off numerous mounted Cheyenne and Lakota charges and dodging snipers hidden in the tall grasses along the banks. Three times they held off massed frontal charges under Pawnee Killer, Tall Bull, Bull Bear, and White Bull, splintering their forces at the last moment. The defenders' repeating Spencers saved the day.

Forsyth was hit twice. As Dr. John Mooers crawled over to help him, he took a bullet in the forehead and slumped to the sand. Later Forsyth suffered a third hit, a bullet that grazed the top of his head and knocked him senseless. The second-in-command, Lt. Frederick Beecher, was mortally wounded. "My poor mother," he mumbled before he died.[513]

The prominent Cheyenne warrior Roman Nose, though he believed his spiritual medicine was not working, had entered the fray. True to his presentiment, Roman Nose, leading a charge, was cut down by a Spencer bullet.

The battle faded with the setting sun. That night, two scouts slipped out to try to reach Fort Wallace for help. At dawn the fighting picked up again with a halfhearted Indian charge, then settled down to desultory sniping at the trapped defenders. The second night, two more scouts broke out to get help.

The fight continued for five days. By 21 September, it appeared that almost all the Indians had disappeared. Now the company faced a fight with starvation. All the horses were dead, and there were too many wounded men to travel on foot. The meals were now of rancid horse meat. One of the scouts, Chauncey Whitney, scrawled in his diary, "My God! Have you deserted us?"[514]

On 25 September, Company H of the black 10th Cavalry, the "buffalo soldiers," under Capt. Louis Carpenter, came to the rescue.

In the final count, 6 of Forsyth's men had been killed and 18 were wounded. The Indians suffered casualties of about 30 killed and 60 wounded.[515]

14 OCTOBER 1868
PRAIRIE DOG CREEK (Norton, Kansas)

To increase protection of settlers, the 5th Cavalry assembled in Kansas in the fall of 1868. Companies A, B, F, H, I, L, and M were stationed at Fort Harker and placed under the temporary command of Maj. William B. Royall. On 1 October, Royall led the seven companies on a reconnaissance north of the Kansas Pacific Railroad toward Beaver Creek. After searching a wide area, on 12 October the troops bivouacked on Prairie Dog Creek. Royall sent out a battalion of Companies B, F, and M under Capt. William H. Brown to scout Beaver Creek, and another of Companies A, H, and I under Capt. Gustavus Urban to scout the Republican River. Royall waited in camp with Company L.

On the 14th a party of Cheyennes, led by Tall Bull, struck the camp, killing one trooper, wounding another, and driving off 26 horses. The frustrated Royall recalled his battalions and headed back to Buffalo Tank rail station, arriving on 22 October, where Carr met them a few days later.[516]

18 OCTOBER 1868
BEAVER CREEK (Atwood, Kansas)

Maj. Eugene A. Carr of the 5th Cavalry arrived at Fort Wallace on 12 October, looking for Maj. William B. Royall and his regiment, who had been out on reconnaissance since the 1st (see previous entry). Two days later, with an escort of about 100 men of Companies H and I of the 10th Cavalry under Capts. Carpenter and Graham, Carr headed north to Beaver Creek. The party reached the creek the next day and followed it downstream.

After traveling nearly 50 miles without a sign of the regiment, Lt. Myron Amick took ten men and scout Sharp Grover and headed south, cross-country, to look for a trail, while Carr continued downriver. At sunset on 17 October, Amick returned, having gone as far as Prairie Dog Creek (also called Short Nose Creek) but finding no trace of the 5th Cavalry. Camping near the present-day town of Traer, Kansas, Carr decided to search downstream one more day before turning back. Early the next morning, they had not gone far before Indians appeared. Said Carr: "As we had not found Royall but had found the Indians, or rather they had found us, it was no use to go farther down the Beaver, and I determined to move toward home."[517]

It was not that easy, however. For several hours the soldiers moved upstream under mild resistance from Cheyenne and Lakota warriors. Then, around noon, 600 Indians forced the men onto a knoll. Capt. Carpenter formed the troops into an oval-shaped stockade, with the horses and mules inside and the soldiers around the perimeter. The Indians circled around, shooting, seemingly under the command of one warrior with a bugle. According to Carr, they were outnumbered about seven to one. "I really did not expect to get out of that fix," he said.[518]

Carr stood by Grover, firing at the warriors; they killed three within 50 feet of the wagons. Grover had one wounded Indian, named Little Crow, brought to him for questioning. When the Indians ceased firing, Little Crow motioned to indicate his "heart is bad," meaning the warriors wanted to give up and wanted the soldiers to go away so they could gather up their dead and wounded. Carr ordered his column to pack up and move out. The Indians followed for a few miles, but did not attack. The tired command reached Fort Wallace on 21 October.

After eight hours of fighting, the army had only 3 men wounded. The Indians lost 10 men and about 20 were wounded.[519]

25–26 OCTOBER 1868
BEAVER CREEK (Herndon, Kansas)

When Maj. Eugene A. Carr returned to Fort Wallace after the fruitless search for his regiment, the 5th Cavalry (see previous entry), he learned they were at Buffalo Tank Station and boarded a train to join them. Hoping to find a village that the wounded Indian captive Little Crow had told them about. Carr headed north on 23 October with 480 men of Companies A, B, F, H, I, L, and M and a company of scouts under Lt. Lewis Pepoon of the 10th Cavalry.

Two days later, at about 2:30 P.M. along Beaver Creek, Company M skirmished with Lakota and Cheyenne warriors. Carr moved the rest of the command forward, and a six-mile running fight commenced. About 200 warriors, keeping just out of range, set fire to the dry grass to impede the soldiers' progress. As Carr's advance slowed, nearly 300 more warriors appeared.

The next day, Carr advanced with his troops around the wagons in a protective ring. After ten miles, the Indians gathered in front of them. A battalion of cavalry under Capt. John H. Kane, Lt. William C. Forbush, and Lt. Jules Schenofsky charged out to disperse the warriors, pursuing them for three miles. The Indians then countercharged, and Lt. Pepoon's scouts rode out to help resist them. The Indians, it turned out, were distracting the soldiers while their village fled. Carr pushed on and found hundreds of cedar lodgepoles, 400 dried buffalo hides, and other abandoned property.

About 4 troopers were wounded over the two days; the Indians lost about 10 warriors and 70 ponies.

For the next four days, Carr relentlessly pursued the fleeing Indians, tracking them north nearly to the Republican River, then looping back south to Beaver Creek. By 31 October the trails had dissipated into a few scattered pony tracks. "The enemy," said Carr, "suddenly disappeared like a mist before the morning sun."[520] Carr marched back to Fort Wallace.[521]

19 NOVEMBER 1868
WILSON'S FIGHT (Rush Center, Kansas)

A detachment of ten troopers from Capt. Nicholas Nolan's Company A of the 10th Cavalry, on a scout from Fort Larned led by Sgt. Augustus Wilson, came upon a small party of Indians. In a chase of nearly 20 miles, the soldiers killed two of them.[522]

27 NOVEMBER 1868
WASHITA RIVER (Cheyenne, Oklahoma)

On 12 November, 11 companies of the 7th Cavalry under Lt. Col. George A. Custer, 3 companies of the 3rd Infantry, 1 of the 5th Infantry, 1 of the

38th Infantry, and about 450 wagons set out from Fort Dodge for Indian territory to seek out hostile Indians. Across a snow-covered landscape Custer followed Indian trails to a 50-lodge Cheyenne village on the banks of the Washita River. Early on the frigid morning of 27 November, nearly 700 men of the 7th Cavalry prepared to attack.

To the tune of "Garryowen," Custer charged into the village with his four battalions: Maj. Joel Elliot with Companies G, H, and M came in from the northeast; Capt. William Thompson with Companies B and F, from the south; Lt. John M. Johnson with E and I attacked from the southwest; and Custer with A, C, D, and K, from the west. The troops burst into the village, cutting down the Indians as they fled their lodges. The soldiers were also hit: one captain was killed by a bullet in the chest, and another was severely wounded in the abdomen. Maj. Elliot cut loose with 18 men of various companies to chase some Indians who had escaped to the east, reportedly calling out, "Here goes for a brevet or a coffin."[523] Elliot was cut off and his party killed.

During the battle, the Cheyennes killed two of four white captives. It is uncertain whether Custer was able to rescue the other two. After soldiers killed Chiefs Black Kettle and Little Rock, Custer captured the camp, burned tipis and supplies, and shot 875 Indian ponies. As more Indians gathered from other camps downriver, Custer made a feint downstream, sending them back to protect their villages. Doubling back in the gathering darkness, Custer returned to his supply train and headed home, reaching Camp Supply on 1 December.

Custer captured 53 women and children during the mission and reported 103 Indians killed, though the Cheyennes claimed it was half that number. The army lost 21, with 16 wounded.[524]

25 DECEMBER 1868
SOLDIER SPRING (Lugert, Oklahoma)

Leading one of three columns that Gen. Sheridan sent in a campaign against Indian winter camps, Maj. Andrew W. Evans left Fort Bascom, New Mexico, on 17 November with 536 men of Companies A, C, D, F, G, and I of the 3rd Cavalry; Companies F and I of the 37th Infantry; and four mountain howitzers. Evans took his men down along the Canadian River to the Antelope Hills, where he struck a broad trail. It was the trail of the Cheyennes who had moved south after the Washita battle with Custer just days earlier (see previous entry). Through sleet and snow, Evans and his men followed the tracks for weeks, the horses dying of exhaustion and lack of forage. At the North Fork of the Red River, the troops continued downstream.

After a dry camp on 24 December, Evans headed northeast toward some small mountains on the opposite side of the Red, about six miles northeast of present-day Blair, Oklahoma. He saw two Indians shadowing him and sent Capt. Elisha W. Tarlton with one company of the 3rd to chase them down. After crossing to the north bank, Tarlton headed southeast and nearly ran into 60 Noconee Comanche lodges, probably under Chiefs Arrow Point and Howea.

The Indians had seen the soldiers coming and rode out to delay them long enough for the village to flee. The Comanches charged Tarlton with rifles, pistols, and lances. Tarlton was hard-pressed, but soon Capts. Monahan and Hawley brought up their companies. During the confrontation Chief Arrow Point suffered a gunshot wound to the mouth, from which he later died. The howitzers then arrived and shot into the Indian camp, causing the inhabitants to abandon much of their property as they fled.

Tarlton had almost reached the village when more Indians arrived from downstream—Kiowas under Chief Woman's Heart. They hit Tarlton's flank but were chased off when Evans arrived with the rest of the command. They pushed the Indians out of the village, but their mounts were in poor condition and they could not give chase. After sending Capt. James H. Gageby's infantry to flush out the remaining Indians, Evans spent the rest of the day destroying the village, a task not completed until midnight.

After watching hungrily as Evans destroyed hundreds of pounds of dried buffalo meat, a number of Indians went to Fort Cobb to surrender. The remainder went west to join the Quahadi Comanches on the Staked Plains. Evans declined to pursue them, claiming he was out of supplies, though he had destroyed enough to have kept his column going for several more weeks.

Only 1 soldier was killed in the battle and 3 were wounded. Evans reported 25 Comanches killed, but there were more likely only half a dozen casualties.[525]

—1869—

29 JANUARY 1869
MULBERRY CREEK (Ford, Kansas)

In January a band of raiders, thought to be Pawnees from their reservation in Nebraska, ran off with horses from frontier settlements in central Kansas. Capt. Edward Byrne, with 25 troopers from Company C, 10th Cavalry, rode out of Fort Dodge in pursuit. He caught the thieves on Mulberry Creek and recovered the horses.[526]

Two troopers were wounded in the pursuit; seven Pawnees were killed and one was wounded.[527]

7 APRIL 1869
SIXTEENMILE CREEK (Ringling, Montana)

In the Gallatin Valley northwest of Fort Ellis, just west of Bozeman, Montana, about ten Blackfeet drove off the cattle and horses from a ranch on Dry Creek sometime in the spring. The neighboring ranchers started after them but then decided to go to Fort Ellis for help. Capt. Emory W. Clift took 40 mounted soldiers from Companies D, F, and G, 13th Infantry, and, with 15 ranchers, started in pursuit.

At noon on 7 April, Clift caught up with the Blackfeet on the North Fork of Sixteenmile Creek, in present-day Meagher County. The Indians went up a rough mountain to a nearly impregnable position and waved their blankets in derision. Clift divided his command, sending a Lt. Thompson around from the east and having his own squad scale the west side. Suddenly the Indians found themselves surrounded atop the craggy peak.

Clift closed in, firing at any head that popped up over the rocks. Soon the trapped Blackfeet began singing their death songs. Clift kept up the fire for about two hours. At dusk he called for volunteers to charge. One dozen men responded and went in with revolvers in hand. The Blackfeet were still game, however; they killed a private named Conry and wounded two other soldiers.

In the morning Clift counted nine Indian bodies amid the rocks.[528]

22 APRIL 1869
SANGRE CANYON (Southeastern New Mexico)

On 9 April an expedition composed of Companies A, F, and H, 3rd Cavalry, and Company I, 37th Infantry, left Fort Stanton to search for renegade Apaches. The party scouted through the Sacramento Mountains and down the Rio Penasco toward the Pecos. After establishing a supply camp at Rio Azul, the expedition turned south into the Guadalupe Mountains.

In Sangre Canyon the expedition attacked a rancheria and wounded five Apaches, suffering no casualties themselves. The soldiers recovered 19 stolen horses and a $500 check.[529]

2 MAY 1869
SAN AUGUSTIN PASS (Organ, New Mexico)

The pass between the San Augustin and Organ Mountains, east of Fort Selden, was considered the most dangerous place in the area. On 2 May, Apaches ambushed a wagon train guarded by soldiers of the 38th Infantry, killing two and wounding four in a failed attempt to capture the wagons. The soldiers claimed to have killed five Indians and wounded ten, but the numbers were probably exaggerated.[530]

7 MAY 1869
SAN AUGUSTIN PASS (Organ, New Mexico)

Cpl. C. Younge and a two privates of Company K, 3rd Cavalry, were escorting a civilian through San Augustin Pass when approximately 40

Apaches attacked them. Younge was killed, and one private and the civilian were wounded.[531]

7 MAY 1869
PAINT CREEK (Stamford, Texas)

Capt. George W. Smith took a detachment of mounted 35th Infantry and a company of Tonkawa scouts to search for some Comanches who had been raiding in Texas and discovered about 25 of them camping at the headwaters of Paint Creek in present-day southwest Haskell County. With no loss to his party, Smith routed the Indians, killing 14 and wounding 3. Smith gave the 14 captured horses to the Tonkawa scouts.[532]

13 MAY 1869
ELEPHANT ROCK (Traer, Kansas)

After leading an unsuccessful mission as the third prong of Gen. Sheridan's winter campaign into Indian territory, Maj. Eugene Carr and his 5th Cavalry marched back to Fort Wallace in Kansas. With Companies A, B, F, H, I, and L, he left the fort on 10 May, heading north to Fort McPherson on the Platte River. They reached Beaver Creek and headed downstream to Elephant Rock, near present-day Cedar Bluffs, Kansas. There they found an Indian trail going downriver.

Carr sent Lt. Edward W. Ward and ten men with scout William F. "Buffalo Bill" Cody to investigate. They followed the trail 12 miles until they topped a rise and found a Lakota village of perhaps 400 lodges. "This

Elephant Rock (Kansas)

is no place for us, Lieutenant," Cody said to Ward. "I think we have important business at the camp to attend to as soon as possible."[533]

Ward agreed, and they hightailed it back to Carr, but not before being seen by several Indian hunting parties. Cody, on the fastest horse, took off alone to deliver the news while Ward followed behind. At Cody's announcement Carr left one-third of each regiment with Capt. William H. Brown to pack up the camp and took the rest of his men downstream after the Indians. Ward, in the meantime, had skirmished with a hunting party, killing one warrior before Carr reached him.

Five miles farther, Carr ran into about 500 warriors, now fully aware that there were soldiers pursuing them. The warriors formed a line across Carr's path, but he went around the flank. Lt. Jules Schenofsky with Company B angled to the left and chased some warriors out of sight into the bluffs.

Carr reached the village as it was getting dark, so he turned around and went back toward Maj. Brown and the wagons. Carr's retreat emboldened the Indians, and they threatened him enough to make him march his men in a square. The company joined the wagons about 9 P.M. One other soldier had been killed and three wounded during the fighting.

The next morning Carr returned to the village, abandoned during the night, and destroyed what had been left behind. Schenofsky finally returned. He had chased Indians for seven miles, lost three men, and spent the night in the hills.

The encounter had cost Carr a total of 4 men killed and 3 wounded. He reported 25 Indians killed and 20 wounded.[534]

16 MAY 1869
SPRING CREEK (Oxford, Nebraska)

On 14 May, the morning after the battle at Elephant Rock (see previous entry), Maj. Carr's men found the Lakotas' trail, which led out of the Beaver Valley and headed northeast toward the Republican River. With "Buffalo Bill" Cody's dogged tracking, the 5th Cavalry followed in the Indians' wake. When they reached the Republican, the trail turned east, downstream. At this point Carr ordered Lt. William C. Forbush to take the expedition's wagons on to Fort McPherson, while he kept two ambulances and all the provisions his men could pack on the horses, and the company pushed on.

The soldiers marched for two more days. During that time, they came upon two buffalo robes laid in the trail, with the heads pointing in the direction the Indians were traveling. The Indians probably believed they had shaken their pursuers and had left the sign for their tribesmen. Carr continued on.

At noon on 16 May, the tired command reached Spring Creek, northeast of present-day Oxford, Nebraska. Here they saw the Indians in the hills. Carr had sent Cody, Lt. William J. Volkmar, and ten men ahead to scout, and, suspecting trouble, he ordered Lt. John B. Babcock and his company to assist them. When Babcock caught up with Volkmar, they were ambushed by 200 warriors. Babcock led his command to high ground and formed a circle. While the bullets flew fast and furious around them, Babcock remained mounted to inspire the men. His action earned him a Congressional Medal of Honor. The soldiers held their position for half an hour, until a relief company under Lt. Bradley came into view, whereupon the Indians rapidly dispersed.

Three soldiers were killed, and three enlisted men and one civilian were wounded. No Indian casualties were reported.

The Indians fled south, back toward the Republican River, dropping much property in their haste to escape. Carr followed with his troops to the banks of the river. Here the trail split up in a dozen directions, and Carr, with horses and supplies exhausted, gave up the chase. He sent Cody to Fort Kearny, about 50 miles northeast, with dispatches, and the tired cavalry rode behind, reaching the post on 18 May.[535]

28 MAY 1869
FOSSIL CREEK STATION (Russell, Kansas)

About 30 Cheyennes attacked 7 railroad hands who were cutting weeds two miles west of Fossil Creek Station, in present-day Russell, Kansas. The workers jumped on a handcar and pumped furiously toward the station. Four of them had rifles, but succeeded only in killing an Indian pony. Shot and unable to hang on to the car, two of the workers fell to the ground. Their bodies were later found mutilated and scalped. The other five, four of them wounded, escaped. The injured were taken to Fort Harker's hospital, where they recovered.

That evening the Indians tore up two rails and sabotaged a third, derailing the westbound train around midnight.[536]

7 JUNE 1869
JOHNSON DRAW (Juno, Texas)

In the spring of 1869, Fort McKavett was headquarters of the 41st Infantry, a black regiment under Col. Ranald S. Mackenzie. On 19 May, Mackenzie rode out with a scout of two lieutenants and 42 men from detachments of Companies G, L, and M, 9th Cavalry, along with a few civilians and two guides. About 50 miles from the mouth of the Pecos River, the company fell upon a party of Indians and scattered them in the first charge. The Indians fled south toward the Rio Grande; the soldiers' weary horses could not keep up a pursuit.

One enlisted man and two Indians were killed in the skirmish.[537]

19 JUNE 1869
SHERIDAN (Wallace, Kansas)

Near the end of the railroad tracks at Sheridan, Cheyenne Dog Soldiers attacked a surveying party escorted by a detachment of Company E, 7th Cavalry. One Indian rode up so close to surveyor Howard Schuyler that Schuyler touched him with the muzzle of his gun as he fired. Schuyler's horse was shot four times and collapsed as Schuyler reached the surveyors' camp.

Two surveyors, including Schuyler, were wounded. Two soldiers were also wounded, while reportedly 4 Indians were killed and 12 wounded.[538]

6 JULY 1869
FRENCHMAN'S FORK (Champion, Nebraska)

After his 16 May battle at Spring Creek, Maj. Carr had little time to rest before the next expedition was planned and ready. He was to take eight depleted companies of the 5th Cavalry, only about 300 men, supplemented with three 50-man companies of Frank and Luther North's Pawnee scouts, on another sweep through the Republican River country. Leaving Fort McPherson on 9 June, they traveled south down Medicine Creek to its junction with the Republican, then headed east to scout the mouths of Short Nose (Prairie Dog), Sappa, and Beaver Creeks, after which they would continue up the Republican.

On the 15th, about eight miles above the mouth of Sappa Creek, Cheyennes jumped the expedition, trying to steal their horses. One herder was hit with an arrow as the soldiers chased them off. Luther North and his Pawnees charged off in pursuit, and Maj. William Royall followed after them with some soldiers. North and Royall's men killed two of the marauders.

The expedition followed the Cheyennes' trail south toward the Solomon River, but soon the tracks scattered in all directions. By 19 June, the Cheyennes having apparently disappeared, the men were back following the Republican. On 3 July, Carr found a trail leading up the North Fork of the Republican. Carr sent Royall ahead with three companies of the 5th and one company of scouts. The orders were the same as they had been for the past month: "Try to surprise them," Carr said, "kill as many warriors as possible and capture their families and animals."[539]

While Carr waited in camp, near the junction of the North and Arikaree Forks of the Republican, Royall's party followed the trail north to Frenchman's Fork (Frenchman Creek). There, on 6 July, they ran into a small band of Dog Soldiers returning to their village. Two of the warriors, Shave Head and Little Man, were dragging their wounded cousin, Howling Magpie, on a travois. The rest of the Indians fled when the soldiers appeared, but the two cousins would not leave their injured relative. They put up a good fight but were overwhelmed; Howling Magpie was killed on his litter.

Royall decided the other Cheyennes were too far ahead and returned to Carr's camp. Entering camp on the 7th, the Pawnee scouts, brandishing the three scalps, whooped and hollered so much that for a moment Carr's men thought they were being attacked.[540]

8 JULY 1869
DOG CREEK (Laird, Colorado)

When Maj. Royall returned to camp from his pursuit of Cheyennes on Frenchman Creek during Maj. Carr's June–July expedition on the Republican River (see previous entry), he reported that in his estimation, the Cheyennes were too far ahead of them to be caught, and, furthermore, that the country was too dry and barren to make a pursuit practical. Carr nevertheless decided to keep up the chase, backtracking downstream to where the North and Arikaree Forks of the Republican converged, then forcing a march over the divide to Frenchman Creek. Spying Indians saw his retrograde move and assumed he was leaving.

As Carr left, he sent Cpl. John Kyle with three men of Company M back up the North Fork to bring in a few horses they had left behind at their previous camp. After several miles Kyle spotted 13 Indians watering their horses. He tried to elude them but they saw him and gave chase. Kyle directed his men to some sheltering rocks, where they killed a horse and defended their position, killing three warriors and compelling them to retreat. After the fight, Kyle's squad rejoined Carr's command, who were camped near the mouth of the Arikaree Fork about 12 miles away.

That night, the camp was attacked by Cheyennes trying to steal the Pawnees' horses. The Pawnee Angry Bear was wounded, and the Ute-Cheyenne Yellow Nose was thrown from his horse and broke his arm. He crawled into a slight gully and hid in the darkness while Pawnees jumped right over him. He got back to his camp two days later.[541]

11 JULY 1869
SUMMIT SPRINGS (Sterling, Colorado)

Maj. Eugene Carr, continuing to lead his tired Companies A, C, D, E, G, H, and M of the 5th Cavalry and three companies of Pawnee scouts after the elusive Cheyennes (see previous entry), resumed the march on 9 July. Carr requested that Royall take the lead since he had been over the territory a few days earlier. When Royall declined, Carr put Capt. George F. Price in the vanguard and stubbornly pushed the column north through the sand hills along the present-day Nebraska-Colorado border. "March[ed] 30 miles without water," wrote Frank North, "and oh how hot and dry."[542]

Tall Bull Ravine, Summit Springs (Colorado)

The next day the expedition reached Frenchman Creek and slogged another 32 miles upstream. They were rewarded when they found an abandoned Indian camp with the prints of a white woman's shoe. Farther upriver they found another abandoned camp, and then another, indicating the Cheyennes had slowed down and the soldiers were gaining. The Indians, believing Carr was leaving the country, may have relaxed their vigilance.

The Cheyennes were mostly Dog Soldiers under Tall Bull and other Cheyennes under Black Shin, about 84 lodges with 400 people, including 100 fighting men. Lakotas under Two Strikes and Whistler were with them. They were traveling west toward the South Platte. Tall Bull stopped to rest his tired people at Summit Springs, a watering place about 15 miles south of present-day Sterling, Colorado.

Early on 11 July, his men and horses bedraggled, Carr scraped together 244 cavalrymen and 50 Pawnees, all that could be mounted on the last serviceable horses, and forged on. In the early afternoon the party reached the South Platte and were about to ford the river when some sharp-eyed scouts saw Tall Bull's horses to the south. Between the camp and the river, Carr formed three battalions and headed in. At about 3 P.M. he struck the village from the west, north, and east, and the surprised Cheyennes had no avenue of escape except to the south. Many of the warriors were determined to die fighting while their families escaped. They took vengeance on two white captives they had taken in Kansas, killing one, Susanna Alderdice, and severely wounding the other, Maria Weichell. Tall Bull and some Dog Soldiers holed up in a ravine east of the camp, but the troopers picked them off.

With only one soldier wounded, Carr's troops killed 52 Cheyennes and captured 17 women and children and more than 300 horses and mules. Maria Weichell recovered from her wounds. Some warriors and their families managed to escape and joined up with the Southern Cheyennes, but the Dog Soldiers never again regained their power and influence.[543]

12 SEPTEMBER 1869
LOOKOUT POINT (Bluff Dale, Texas)

A small band of Indians, possibly Kiowas or Comanches, raiding through Hood County, Texas, stole horses as they made their way down Squaw Creek almost to the Brazos River, then cut west toward the Paluxy River. When citizens discovered them driving nearly 200 head, they hastily gathered up posses from the Squaw Creek and Thorp settlements to converge at Lookout Point, 12 miles west.

After riding hard all night, ten men from Squaw Creek surprised the Indians, only seven in number, and the Indians took refuge in a small ravine beneath the tangled roots of some large trees. The ten-man posse from Thorp soon arrived, and around 8 A.M. on 12 September, they rushed the ravine. The fight was over quickly. The white men killed and scalped all seven Indians; one was a woman. Two of the posse were wounded, one of them mortally.[544]

14 SEPTEMBER 1869
POPO AGIE (Lander, Wyoming)

On the Shoshone reservation near the Little Wind River, civilian James Camp and Pvt. John Holt, Company K, 7th Infantry, were killed, possibly by Shoshones or Bannocks, who shared the reservation, but more likely by wandering Lakotas in the vicinity. The same day, at Camp Augur, to the southeast on the Popo Agie River, soldiers spotted hostile Lakotas within three miles of the post. Lt. Charles B. Stambaugh, with a 28-man detachment of Company D, 2nd Cavalry, rode out to investigate.

After following a trail for 14 miles, Stambaugh ran into 200 Lakotas and engaged them in battle. In a three-hour fight, two soldiers were wounded, two Indians were killed, and ten Indians were wounded. Stambaugh also had eight horses killed and four injured, so he could not pursue the retreating Lakotas.[545]

16 SEPTEMBER 1869
SALT FORK OF THE BRAZOS RIVER (North-central Texas)

After raiding in the Fort McKavett vicinity, a group of Kiowas and Comanches returned north to Indian territory. Following them were Capts.

Henry Carroll and Edward M. Heyl with 95 men of Companies B, E, F, and M, 9th Cavalry. The soldiers left the fort on 2 September. After losing the trail and running out of supplies, they reprovisioned at Fort Concho, then picked up the trail at the edge of the Staked Plains, heading north.

At the headwaters of the Salt Fork of the Brazos River, Carroll found a camp of nearly 200 lodges. His hungry troopers only had time to gnaw off a chunk of tobacco before Carroll gave the order to charge. The thunder of the hooves was enough to send the Indians running. Carroll chased them for eight miles, until his mounts wore out.

About 20 Indians were killed or wounded, and all their camp equipment was destroyed. Three soldiers were wounded.[546]

26 SEPTEMBER 1869
PRAIRIE DOG CREEK (Dresden, Kansas)

Although Maj. Eugene Carr had beaten the Dog Soldiers at Summit Springs in July (see Summit Springs, 11 July), there were still Indians raiding the Kansas and Nebraska frontiers. An expedition of 449 men left Fort McPherson on 15 September under Lt. Col. Thomas Duncan, 5th Cavalry. The party consisted of Companies B, E, F, L, and M of the 5th, Companies B, C, and M of the 2nd Cavalry, the Pawnee scouts, and "Buffalo Bill" Cody as guide. They marched southeast to the Republican River and followed it downstream to Prairie Dog Creek, which they reached on 22 September.

For the next four days the expedition scouted Prairie Dog Creek, marching upstream about 80 miles to a point near present-day Dresden, Kansas. Two miles in advance of the column, Lt. William J. Volkmar, acting engineering officer, and Lt. George F. Price were leading about 30 soldiers toward the river. A mile in front of them, Cody, Frank North, and several Pawnees were hunting buffalo. Six Lakotas spotted the hunting party and attacked, not knowing other whites were close by.

The Lakotas soon found themselves facing Volkmar's men, charging in from 200 yards away. The six warriors spun around and headed west, up the creek. As Volkmar and North pursued, more and more Lakotas began to appear on their flanks. The chase continued until dusk. One Lakota was killed and several were wounded. Just as Volkmar was calling off the pursuit, Lt. Price climbed a rise above the creek and saw a village farther upstream, which he reported to Lt. Col. Duncan upon returning to camp.

The next morning, Duncan moved his men upstream and found Pawnee Killer's and Whistler's abandoned village of 56 lodges, which he destroyed, along with 9,000 pounds of dried buffalo meat and other items. The men found two tripods stolen in an attack on some railroad surveyors the previous August.

Duncan continued on to the headwaters of the Republican, where he searched fruitlessly for more Indians until late October, then returned to Fort McPherson.[547]

8 OCTOBER 1869
CHIRICAHUA PASS/PEDREGOSA MOUNTAINS (Douglas, Arizona)

On 5 October Apache chief Cochise and his warriors waylaid a stage near Dragoon Springs, killing the six white passengers.[548] The next day, the same Apaches ran off a herd of cattle in the area, then shot up a government train. The 21st Infantry men escorting the train had just discovered the remains of the stage party. A messenger rushed to Fort Bowie to alert the troops.

Lt. William H. Winters mounted all the available men at the post—25 troopers of Company G, 1st Cavalry—and rode to the scene. Cochise was herding the cattle southeast across the Sulphur Springs Valley, and Scout Merejildo Grijalva found the trail. Winters and his men followed Cochise's trail for 22 hours without sleep. At 8 A.M. on the 8th, they caught up with the Indians on the east slope of the Pedregosa Mountains. The fatigued soldiers charged the Apache rear guard, killing three of five warriors, then barreled on to the main body.

Winters tried to stop the Apaches who were on foot from reaching the mountains, but Cochise and other mounted Apaches held him back. The battle flowed back and forth. The soldiers made a special target of Cochise, but no one could knock him off his gray horse. The 90 minutes of fighting allowed the unmounted Indians to escape into the southern Chiricahua Mountains. Cochise also escaped.

Two troopers were wounded in the skirmish, and Winters reported killing 12 Indians. The soldiers recovered the entire cattle herd and most of the mail stolen from the stage. The *Prescott Arizona Miner* reported, "Cochise, for the first time since 1861, has been badly whipped."[549]

19 OCTOBER 1869
CHIRICAHUA MOUNTAINS/TEX CANYON (Southeastern Arizona)

When Capt. Reuben F. Bernard, 1st Cavalry, arrived at Fort Bowie after a scout, he learned of Lt. Winters's encounter with Cochise (see previous entry). Hoping to cut Cochise off, Bernard took detachments of Company G, 1st Cavalry, and Company G, 8th Cavalry, and rode along the east side of the Chiricahua Mountains. On 18 October, he arrived at the scene of Winters's fight, where the scout Grijalva picked up Cochise's trail. The trail did not lead into Cochise's home territory in Mexico but went north into the Chiricahua Mountains.

Later the soldiers found a deserted rancheria and moved up Tex Canyon. Within ten miles they found fresh tracks and another abandoned campsite.

A little farther up the canyon, the men were suddenly attacked by perhaps 150 Apaches, firing, Bernard said, "from all parts of the rocks above us."[550] Three soldiers were hit in the initial onslaught.

Bernard tried to flank the Apaches to drive them from their position, but Cochise had warriors covering all angles. Bernard could get no closer than 100 yards to them. The fighting continued through the afternoon. Lt. John Lafferty was badly wounded in the jaw as he tried to recover the bodies of some of his men. Near sunset, Bernard, deciding he would need twice as many soldiers to dislodge the Indians, gave up the assault.

Army casualties were 2 men killed and 3 wounded. Bernard reported killing 18 warriors, probably an exaggeration.[551]

28–29 OCTOBER 1869
FRESHWATER FORK OF THE BRAZOS RIVER (Crosbyton, Texas)

In October, disappointed with the lack of success in quelling Indian raids, Col. Edward Hatch, 9th Cavalry, called for an all-out campaign to drive the Kiowas and Comanches out of the region. Companies B, C, G, and L, 9th Cavalry, under Capt. John M. Bacon, left Fort Concho to meet Lt. Frederic W. Smith's Company F, 9th Cavalry; Lt. Byron Dawson's Company M, 9th Cavalry; detachments of Companies D and M, 4th Cavalry; a detachment of the 24th Infantry; and 20 Tonkawa scouts. On 5 October, Bacon took his 200 men and headed west.

The soldiers scouted the headwaters of the Colorado and Brazos Rivers for three weeks with no results. At sunrise on 28 October, camped on the Freshwater Fork of the Brazos (the White River), Bacon was about to send out another round of scouting parties when 500 Comanche and Kiowa warriors attacked. The Indians found they had stirred up a hornet's nest. In a bitter, sometimes hand-to-hand fight, they were thrashed and forced to flee.

The next morning Bacon pursued the Indians. He found their camp in the midafternoon and charged, scattering the demoralized Indians in all directions.

The two days of fighting cost Bacon 8 men wounded; the Indians suffered 40 men killed and 7 women captured. Bacon and Dawson received brevets for their meritorious service.[552]

18 NOVEMBER 1869
GUADALUPE MOUNTAINS (Southeastern New Mexico)

Lt. Howard B. Cushing, transferred to the 3rd Cavalry in May 1867, was operating out of Fort Stanton when about 150 head of stock were stolen from a ranch on the Rio Hondo. Cushing took his Company F on a 200-mile chase that led into the Guadalupe Mountains in New Mexico, just north of the Texas border. There he found the Mescalero Apache raiders and recovered most of the stock, along with 30 Apache ponies.

Cushing's men killed one Indian; one corporal and one private were severely wounded. The soldiers returned to Fort Stanton on 30 November.[553]

24 NOVEMBER 1869
LLANO RIVER (Sonora, Texas)

Capt. Edward M. Heyl took 20 men from Companies F and M, 9th Cavalry, from Fort McKavett to scout the headwaters of the South Fork of the Llano River, west of old Fort Terrett. There the soldiers ran into a small party of Apaches and engaged them in battle. The troopers killed one Indian and took seven horses and mules. Heyl received a serious wound.[554]

1 DECEMBER 1869
HORSESHOE CREEK (Glendo, Wyoming)

At Horseshoe Creek near present-day Glendo, Wyoming, about 150 Lakotas attacked the mail stage heading from Fort Fetterman to Fort Laramie. Riding escort were ten soldiers of the 4th Infantry under Sgt. Conrad Bahr, Company E. The Indians sought to overwhelm the escort, but the men fought back, hitting several attackers. Three soldiers were wounded. The mail got through.[555]

26 AND 30 DECEMBER 1869
SANGUINARA CANYON (Southeastern New Mexico)

As part of a punitive operative against Mescalero Apaches, Lt. Howard B. Cushing left Fort Stanton on 10 December with a detachment of Company F, 3rd Cavalry, and 28 civilian volunteers, moving into the Guadalupe Mountains in New Mexico. Near the old stage stop at Pine Spring, just inside the Texas border, the men attacked an Apache rancheria. After a quick exchange of shots, the troopers burned the huts, destroyed the winter provisions, and captured a large number of ponies. Several Mescaleros were hit in the fight, and Lt. Franklin Yeaton, fresh out of West Point, was wounded in the wrist and hand.

Yeaton's wound was severe but did not appear life-threatening. The soldiers fashioned a travois to carry the injured man out, through heavy snow, to a sheltered camp on the Rio Penasco. Though he lived for two and a half more years, Yeaton's wound ultimately proved fatal. On 30 December Cushing took his strongest men and horses back to the scene. At the mouth of McKittrick Canyon, about five miles northeast of his first assault, Cushing found the Apaches mourning their dead. He attacked, scattering them.

Casualties were not recorded.[556]

—1870—

DELAWARE CREEK (Pine Springs, Texas)

Capt. Francis S. Dodge continued Col. Edward Hatch's campaign (see Freshwater Fork, 28–29 October 1869) despite frigid weather, leading 200 men of Companies A, C, D, H, I, and K, 9th Cavalry, north from Fort Davis, following a Mescalero Apache trail up Delaware Creek into the Guadalupe Mountains. In a nearly inaccessible spot, the soldiers found the rancheria. But the Mescaleros had seen Dodge's men coming, so they climbed into the rocks above the gorge and began firing. Dismounting, the troopers began an ascent, though rain made footing precarious. By dusk they had reached the top, but the Indians were gone.

In the exchange, the Apaches wounded two troopers. Dodge counted ten dead warriors. The soldiers captured 25 ponies and destroyed the Indians' weapons and supplies.[557]

23 JANUARY 1870
MARIAS RIVER (Shelby, Montana)

The previous fall, Blackfeet had raided stock and killed several settlers near Helena, Montana. At the beginning of 1870, Maj. Eugene M. Baker took Companies F, G, H, and L, 2nd Cavalry, and 55 mounted men of the 13th Infantry from Fort Shaw on a punitive expedition. Baker headed for the camp of the Pikuni Blackfoot (Piegan) leader Mountain Chief, on a bend of the Marias River about 12 miles southeast of present-day Shelby, Montana. Mountain Chief had gotten wind of Baker's plans, however, and left. Heavy Runner, Black Eagle, Big Horn, and Bear Chief moved into his camp with their people, thinking Baker was interested only in Mountain Chief's band.

When a scout informed Baker that the camp was not Mountain Chief's, he replied, "One band or another of them; they are all Piegans and we will attack them."[558] Baker's command killed 173 Blackfeet, wounded 20, captured 140, rounded up about 300 horses, and burned the encampment. One enlisted man was killed. Weather cut short any further pursuit of Mountain Chief.[559]

4 MAY 1870
MINER'S DELIGHT (South Pass City, Wyoming)

When the Shoshone Reservation was placed beside mines in the Sweetwater District, near South Pass in the Wind River Range, miners demanded protection from the army. Responding to a report of alleged depredations, Capt. David S. Gordon and Lt. Charles B. Stambaugh, Company D, 2nd Cavalry, moved out of Camp Auger, in the Popo Agie Valley near present-day Lander, Wyoming.

Early in the morning the troopers charged some Arapahos driving stolen stock, killing two of the Indians and wounding one. Later, near Twin Creek, Stambaugh and 10 soldiers fought sharply with more than 60 Arapahos. The soldiers killed five warriors and wounded one. The Arapahos wounded a Sgt. Brown and killed Stambaugh.[560]

17 MAY 1870
SPRING CREEK (Ruskin, Nebraska)

A five-man detachment of Company C, 2nd Cavalry, left Camp Bingham on the Little Blue River to search for lost horses. On Spring Creek, a few miles west of present-day Ruskin, Nebraska, 50 Indians jumped the soldiers, wounding one, Pvt. Thomas Hubbard. Sgt. Patrick A. Leonard killed some of the detachment's horses and used their bodies for breastworks. For two hours, the troopers held off the Indians, killing one and wounding seven. Then, at the approach of a survey party, the raiders left, probably mistaking it for a column of cavalry.

A family of frightened settlers returned to Camp Bingham with the soldiers. The fight marked the last Indian foray into southern Nebraska.[561]

19–20 MAY 1870
KICKAPOO SPRINGS (Eden, Texas)

Sgt. Emanuel Stance took ten men from Capt. Henry Carroll's Company F, 9th Cavalry, on a scout to Kickapoo Springs, about 20 miles north of Fort McKavett. Halfway there Stance saw some Indians, probably Comanches, driving a herd of horses. He and his men charged, and the surprised Indians fled. The soldiers captured nine horses.

After spending the night at Kickapoo Springs, Stance's men were heading back to Fort McKavett the next morning when they saw warriors preparing to attack a wagon train. The soldiers charged in and "set the Spencers to talking and whistling about their ears so lively that they broke in confusion and fled to the hills."[562] The soldiers captured five more horses in the confrontation. As they moved on, the Indians reappeared, taking long-range shots at them. Stance and his men charged them again, and after a few volleys they left the troopers in peace.

Four Indians were wounded in the two exchanges. For his actions, Stance was given the Medal of Honor.[563]

26 MAY 1870
ISRAEL-KENNEDY WAGON TRAIN (Oracle, Arizona)

Merchants Newton Israel and Hugh Kennedy pulled out of Tucson with a well-stocked supply train for Camp Grant, 55 miles northeast. With them were 2 women, some children, and 21 men. Only four of the party had weapons. Halfway to their destination, near present-day Oracle, Arizona, more than 50 Pinal Apaches attacked them.

A rescue party from Camp Grant found Kennedy with an arrow in his lung, but still alive, and Israel's partly burned body with its heart cut out. Similar fates had befallen most of the party, though the Apaches may have kidnapped the women and children. Kennedy died the next day at Camp Grant. At least 20 of the party had been killed.[564]

31 MAY 1870
BEAR CREEK STATION (Ashland, Kansas)

On 31 May a band of more than 40 Kiowas who had been following an escorted wagon train turned their attention instead to the mail station on Bear Creek, near present-day Ashland, Kansas, about 45 miles south of Fort Dodge. Sgt. James Murray and four privates from Companies B and F, 3rd Infantry, were guarding the station. Calling themselves Arapahos, the Kiowas approached in a friendly manner and asked for food. Cautious, Murray returned their greetings and fed them what he could. Most drifted away, but a few remained in the station house and around the stable.

Ordering two soldiers to guard the weapons in the station, Murray went with the other two to check the stable. A moment later, shots rang out; Murray rushed back to find the two guards dead, and the Kiowas attacked him with bows and arrows. Murray fought back with his only weapon, an ax, but he was hit seven times. At the stable, the two remaining soldiers fought the Indians with pitchforks.

The fight would have ended quickly but for the appearance of Maj. Milo H. Kidd and 50 men from Companies A and K, 10th Cavalry. They killed five of the Kiowas and drove the rest off. Murray recovered at Fort Dodge.[565]

1 JUNE 1870
NORTH FORK OF THE SOLOMON RIVER (North-central Kansas)

Shortly after Lt. Charles C. DeRudio and Company K, 7th Cavalry, had escorted a train of settlers to the plains along the North Solomon River, about 75 Indians, probably Cheyenne, stole the emigrants' cattle. DeRudio and his men, camped downstream, rode after the raiders, wounding four Indians and recovering much of the stock. Later, at Ellsworth, Kansas, the thankful citizens presented DeRudio with a gold-mounted saber. Six years later, DeRudio would carry the saber into battle at the Little Bighorn.[566]

5 JUNE 1870
SIGNAL PEAK (Globe, Arizona)

Lt. Howard B. Cushing received orders to track down the Pinal Apaches responsible for the Israel-Kennedy wagon train massacre (see 26 May). Cushing left Camp Grant with a detachment of Company F, 3rd Cavalry; 14 men of Company B, 3rd Cavalry, under Lt. A. Sidney Smith; and a 30-man detachment of Company K, 1st Cavalry. Cushing's scouts Joe Felmer

Pinal and Signal Peaks (Arizona)

and skilled tracker Manuel Duran followed a complex trail the Apaches had made into the Pinal Range. The trail led north to the San Carlos River, doubled back to the San Pedro, and turned north again into the mountains. At last Duran spotted smoke in a valley northeast of Signal Peak, southwest of present-day Globe, Arizona.

The soldiers found the camp and, in the darkness, surrounded it. An Apache discovered them and called out an alarm. Cushing ordered his men to shoot, and pandemonium erupted. The soldiers were everywhere; escape for the camp was impossible. With no casualties of their own, the soldiers killed about 30 Apaches and captured several women and children.[567]

8 JUNE 1870
RED WILLOW CREEK (McCook, Nebraska)

With a detachment of Company I, 5th Cavalry, Lt. Earl D. Thomas set out from Fort McPherson on 7 June in pursuit of Indians who had stolen stock from area settlers. Knowing his quarry was moving fast, Thomas, his troops, and guide "Buffalo Bill" Cody left in a hurry and traveled until dark. Early the next morning, the soldiers surprised the raiders in their camp on Red Willow Creek, northeast of present-day McCook, Nebraska, killing two. The rest of the Indians fled. The soldiers destroyed the camp and recovered the stock.[568]

BODAMER'S FIGHT (Buffalo, Oklahoma)

Lt. John A. Bodamer and 25 men of Company F, 10th Cavalry, were escorting a large ox train from Fort Dodge to Camp Supply, about 80 miles south. Near the edge of Indian territory, about 100 Cheyennes attacked. Bodamer corralled the wagons and fought off the Indians until nightfall, then dispatched Pvt. William Edmonson to Camp Supply for reinforcements. Narrowly escaping capture, Edmonson reached the post at 11 P.M. When Capt. Nicholas Nolan arrived the next morning, the Cheyennes were gone.

During the fight Bodamer and his men killed three Cheyennes and wounded ten. Two soldiers, a Cpl. Freeman and a Pvt. Winchester, were wounded.[569]

CAMP SUPPLY (Fort Supply, Oklahoma)

Camp Supply, under the command of Lt. Col. Anderson D. Nelson, 3rd Infantry, was a focal point for Indian raids in 1869 and 1870. In June 1870, elements of Companies A, F, H, I, and K, 10th Cavalry, and B, E, and F, 3rd Infantry, were stationed at the post. On 11 June, at 3:30 P.M., Indians dashed into the 10th Cavalry camp and stole three horses. Capt. Nicholas Nolan led a counterattack, and the action headed up the Beaver, or North Canadian, River.

On a hill, watching through a spyglass, Nelson saw about 200 Comanches and Kiowas along the river ahead of Nolan and sent Lt. Mason M. Maxon with 18 men to assist him. After half a mile, some Indians stopped Maxon and his troopers. Nelson dispatched Lt. J. P. Davis and a 3rd Infantry howitzer crew to help him, but in the meantime Lt. Myron J. Amick and Company I joined Maxon, and together they chased off the Indians.

The soldiers killed six Comanches and Kiowas and wounded ten. The Indians wounded three soldiers.[570]

NORTH FORK OF THE LITTLE WICHITA RIVER (Archer City, Texas)

Accused of being cowardly and too cooperative with the whites, Kiowa Chief Kicking Bird left the reservation in north Texas with about 250 warriors and attacked a mail stage near Rock Station. At Fort Richardson, Capt. Curwen B. McClellan took 56 men from detachments of Companies A, C, D, H, K, and L, 6th Cavalry, in pursuit. On 12 July, in a severe rainstorm, McClellan and his men headed up the North Fork of the Little Wichita River.

After five miles the soldiers ran into a small force of Kiowas. When more Kiowas joined the fight, McClellan found himself outnumbered and outgunned, since several Indians had seven-shot Spencer rifles. The warriors surrounded the troopers, but McClellan led his men in a fighting withdrawal to the south that lasted four hours. During the chase, Kicking Bird restored his status as a great warrior when he lanced a trooper off his horse.

In the afternoon, after the troops forded the Middle Fork of the Little Wichita, then the South Fork, the Kiowas gave up the chase. The Indians had killed 2 of the 6th Cavalrymen and wounded 11. McClellan reported 15 Kiowas killed.[571]

1 AUGUST 1870
SKIRMISH CANYON (Miami, Arizona)

After his victory in June (see Signal Peak, 5 June), Lt. Howard B. Cushing led Company F, 3rd Cavalry, and Company K, 1st Cavalry, on a summer-long chase of Pinal Apaches. In Skirmish Canyon, on the north slope of the Pinal Mountains, the men located a rancheria. Indian lookouts discovered their approach and the two sides exchanged fire. One soldier, blacksmith Joseph Graff of Company K, was killed. Cushing's men killed six Apache men and captured two women.

The captured women led the soldiers to a second campsite. The inhabitants were waiting for them in the hills. The troopers exchanged long-range shots with them, without casualties, then destroyed 13 lodges before returning to Camp Grant.[572]

5 OCTOBER 1870
CAMERON CREEK (Jermyn, Texas)

In pursuit of Indian raiders, Capt. William A. Rafferty led Company M, 6th Cavalry, and a detachment of Tonkawa scouts out of Fort Richardson. On Cameron Creek near Spy Knob, the soldiers skirmished with about a dozen Wichitas, killing two and wounding another. After the survivors fled, troopers found clothing and other items that indicated the Indians had been raiding settlements. One of the dead Wichitas had a pass signed by an Indian agent saying that the man, Keesh-Kosh, should be treated well.[573]

6 OCTOBER 1870
DEER CREEK (Fort Grant, Arizona)

On 30 September Lt. Howard B. Cushing and his Company F, 3rd Cavalry, now based at Camp Lowell in Tucson, left to pursue Apaches who had robbed an army paymaster. Five days' searching brought them to Deer Creek between the Pinaleno and Galiuro Mountains, close to an Apache rancheria. When the soldiers stopped to water their horses, mounted Apaches attacked, wounding two privates, Andrew Smith and Lewis Shire.

Cushing's men fought the Apaches off, killing two and capturing some stolen livestock. The warriors counterattacked, recaptured the stock, and fled into the mountains. Deciding not to chase them, Cushing returned to the fort to get medical help for his wounded men.[574]

—1871—

24 JANUARY 1871
FLAT TOP MOUNTAIN/TURTLE HOLE (Graham, Texas)

At least 25 Kiowas under Chiefs Mamanti and Quitan came down from Flat Top Mountain to attack three black settlers hauling supplies across the prairie to their homes near Fort Griffin. One of the men was Brit Johnson, who had earned a reputation as an Indian fighter during the Elm Creek Raid (see Elm Creek, 13 October 1864). Spotting the Kiowas, Johnson moved his companions, Dennis Cureton and Paint Crawford, into a hollow between Flint Creek and Briar Creek known as Turtle Hole, where they killed their horses to use as barricades.

The Kiowas hit one of the men early on, but Johnson and his remaining mate fought back tenaciously (more than 170 empty cartridges were found by the bodies). It was hopeless, however. The Kiowas overran and slaughtered them, scalping and mutilating their bodies.[575] Whether Johnson and his companions wounded or killed any Kiowas is unknown.[576]

Turtle Hole battle site (Texas)

7 FEBRUARY 1871
COBB'S FIGHT (Chico, Texas)

About 50 miles east of Flat Top Mountain, in northeast present-day Wise County, Texas, Sgt. E. H. Cobb and 9 Texas Rangers ran into 40 Kiowas and Comanches who were well-armed with Henry rifles, six-shooters, and bows and arrows. The Indians moved back over a hill and into a stand of tall grass, and when Cobb's men topped the rise, the warriors tried to surround them. Cobb pulled his men back to a better position and fought them off.

The Rangers killed two Indians and wounded a few others. One Ranger, "Little Billy" Sorrells, was wounded.[577]

4, 11, AND 12 APRIL 1871
APACHE MOUNTAINS (Miami, Arizona)

In March, Lt. Howard B. Cushing took his Company F, 3rd Cavalry, north from Tucson to Camp McDowell, then east to the Sierra Ancha. On 4 April they destroyed a rancheria and killed one Apache. Dropping south into the Apache Mountains, on 11 April Cushing and his men laid waste to another camp, killing four Apaches, capturing two, and destroying supplies. The next day, the relentless lieutenant found yet another camp on the southern slope of the same mountains. The soldiers killed 24 Apaches and wounded many. Cushing was back in Tucson on 17 April.[578]

16 APRIL 1871
ROCK CREEK (Graham, Texas)

In the spring of 1871, 12 ranchers were engaged in their annual cattle roundup near Rock Creek when more than 40 Comanches and Kiowas attacked them. The only protection the ranchers could find in the flat prairie was a shallow ravine, and their pistols put them at a disadvantage to the Indians' rifles.

By late afternoon, eight of the ranchers were either dead or wounded. Had the Indians known only four of the men were still capable of firing, they would have rushed the ravine and killed them all. Knowing this, rancher I. E. Graves had all the men who could stand rise and gesture their defiance. The stratagem worked; the Indians took the stock and left.

Three ranchers died in the fight; five were wounded.[579]

30 APRIL 1871
CAMP GRANT MASSACRE (Dudleyville, Arizona)

In accordance with President Ulysses S. Grant's peace policy with western Indians, Brig. Gen. George Stoneman attempted to collect peaceful Apaches on reservations, where they could receive supplies and education in agriculture. But some of the Apaches continued to slip out to raid settlers. Enraged Arizonans labeled the reserves nothing more than "feeding stations."

Approximately 500 Apaches lived at Camp Grant, on the lower San Pedro River. Lt. Royal E. Whitman, 3rd Cavalry, in command there, had gained the trust of resident Aravaipa and Pinal Apaches under Chief Eskiminzin. When a number of settlers and mail riders were murdered around Tucson, about 50 miles southwest of Camp Grant, reports traced the culprits back to "Whitman's Indians."

The murders put the people of Tucson into a frenzy. On 28 April two citizens, William S. Oury and Jesus Maria Elias, took a force of 92 Papago Indians, 42 Mexicans, and 6 white Americans to Camp Grant. It took them two days to reach the reservation. According to Oury, as soon as they arrived, the Papagos "bounded forward like deer," and there was "no time for anything but a haphazard dash, and kill all we could."[580]

The slaughter was over in half an hour. Whitman was not at the camp when the mob arrived. When he got there, the camp was burning and dead littered the ground. With no troops at his disposal, Whitman could do nothing.

The mob killed 144 Apaches, all but 8 of them women and children. They also captured 27 children, who were sold into slavery in Mexico. Chief Eskiminzin lost four wives and five children. The surviving Apaches retained a surprisingly unshaken faith in Whitman and believed he was genuinely repulsed by the affair.

Those responsible for the massacre were brought to trial, but a Tucson jury exonerated them.[581]

Aravaipa Creek (Arizona); the Camp Grant Massacre
took place near the entrance to Aravaipa Canyon.

5 MAY 1871
WHETSTONE MOUNTAINS (Huachuca City, Arizona)

Lt. Howard B. Cushing and others, convinced that Cochise was insti-gating Indian troubles in Arizona, appealed to territorial governor Anson P. K. Safford, who urged the army to find the Apache leader and end the depredations. On 27 April Cushing left Camp Lowell in Tucson with a detachment of Company F, 3rd Cavalry, that was surprisingly small for such an ambitious undertaking: 1 sergeant, 1 packer, and 16 privates. The party marched south, dipping into Mexico, then circled back north to the Babocomari River.

On 5 May, they followed a slight trail north into the Whetstone Moun-tains. Cushing stayed on the main trail and sent Sgt. John Mott and three men to follow a side trail. In an arroyo south of Granite Peak, the sight of Apaches—probably Juh and his band—confirmed Mott's suspicion that they were entering a trap. He sent one man for Cushing and made a stand with the other two. In a fighting withdrawal, both soldiers with Mott, Pvts. Green and Pierce, were wounded, Green mortally.

At last Cushing and his men rode up, but with only 11 soldiers alto-gether in his fighting line. Nevertheless, Cushing pushed his men forward, killing five Apaches, and sent three men back to the pack train. Judging the

Whetstone Mountains (Arizona)

soldiers to be outnumbered 15 to 1, Mott questioned the prudence of advancing further, but Cushing kept on, with only 8 men left. In the next volley from the rocks, however, he was hit.

Mott and a private grabbed Cushing and fell back. The lieutenant was wounded in the chest, then he was shot again in the head as he was being carried out. Mounting up and fighting their way out, the remaining soldiers had to leave three bodies behind, including Cushing's. They reached Camp Crittenden at 1 A.M. the next morning.

The army casualties were 3 dead, 1 wounded. Mott estimated that the soldiers had killed 13 Apaches.[582]

18 MAY 1871
SALT CREEK PRAIRIE/WARREN WAGON TRAIN (Loving, Texas)

From their reservation at Fort Sill, the Kiowas and Comanches continued to raid into Texas. Kiowa prophet Mamanti foretold that the next raid would be a major success. In May 1871 about 150 Kiowas and Comanches joined him, crossing the Red River into Texas and waiting by the road between Forts Griffin and Richardson.[583]

On 18 May Gen. William T. Sherman passed along the road with Inspector Randolph B. Marcy and a small escort. The warriors wanted to attack, but Mamanti held them back—in his vision, they had attacked the

Site of Salt Creek Prairie/Warren Wagon Train fight (Texas); Cox Mountain in distance

second group they saw, not the first. Later that afternoon, a ten-wagon train belonging to freight company Warren & DuBose was traveling under wagonmaster Nathan Long with supplies for Fort Griffin. A warrior blew his bugle and the Indians charged out from behind a ridge.

Long did not have time to completely corral his wagons. Three teamsters were killed instantly. The others fought hard, killing Comanche warrior Ord-lee and wounding the Kiowa Red Warbonnet and the Kiowa-Apache Light-Haired Young Man. Another teamster was killed in the fight. Seven teamsters ran for the timber on Cox Mountain to the east. Two were killed; the other five were all wounded but escaped.

The Indians turned their concentration to the wagons. A teamster, Sam Elliot, was hiding in one of them. When a Kiowa, Hau-tau, ran up to it, Elliot sat up and shot him in the face, mortally wounding him. The Indians apprehended Elliot, chained him to a wagon tongue, and roasted him over a fire. Then they plundered the wagons, burned what they could not carry, and rode away.

That night two of the teamsters stumbled into Fort Richardson, where Gen. Sherman dispatched a patrol to the scene. The soldiers buried seven dead teamsters. Indian casualties in the raid were one warrior killed and three wounded, Hau-tau dying, his face infected with screw worms, back on the reservation.[584]

20 MAY 1871
LITTLE WICHITA RIVER (Henrietta, Texas)

After the Warren wagon train raid (see previous entry), some of the Kiowas remained south of the Little Wichita River to hunt buffalo. Also coming to the Little Wichita that day was Lt. Peter M. Boehm and 25 men of Company A, 4th Cavalry, returning to Fort Richardson after a 30-day scout. Near present-day Henrietta, Texas, the soldiers jumped the hunters, killing and scalping one named Tomasi; the others escaped. One trooper was wounded in the skirmish.[585]

CA. 1 JULY 1871
SALT RIVER (East-central Arizona)

Capt. Guy V. Henry took three companies of the 3rd Cavalry out of Camp Apache, on the White River, and headed west on a scout toward Camp McDowell. Near the Salt River, Henry surprised an Apache band, killing 7 men and capturing 11 women.[586]

19 SEPTEMBER 1871
FOSTER SPRINGS (Southwestern Oklahoma)

Capt. John B. Vande Wiele of Company B, 10th Cavalry, and a patrol from Otter Creek Camp in Oklahoma were scouting southeast toward the Red River. On 19 September, Kiowas and Comanches ambushed three troopers who were riding ahead of the rest. Kiowa warrior An-pay-kau-te killed bugler Larkin Foster, while the soldiers killed two warriors and wounded three.

Col. Benjamin Grierson was so angry at the death of one of his 10th Cavalrymen that he wanted to strike the Kiowas at Fort Sill, but Indian agent Lawrie Tatum talked him out of it.[587]

10 AND 19 OCTOBER 1871
BLANCO CANYON (Crosbyton, Texas)

Guided by Tonkawa scouts, Col. Ranald S. Mackenzie and eight companies of the 4th Cavalry, about 600 men, led an expedition against the Kotsoteka and Quahadi Comanches. The troops moved up the Freshwater Fork of the Brazos River, or White River, to the foot of the Staked Plains. On 9 October they camped at the mouth of Blanco Canyon. After midnight, a party of Comanches led by Parra-o-coom, also known as Bull Bear, drove off 70 of the cavalry's horses.

At sunrise, Lt. Robert G. Carter, Capt. Edward M. Heyl, and a dozen soldiers left in pursuit. When they rode into a few hundred warriors, Heyl retreated, leaving Carter and five troopers to fight. As they fell back, the Comanches killed one of them, a Pvt. Gregg, and wounded another, a Pvt. Melville, before Lt. Peter M. Boehm's scouts came to the rescue. Carter later received a Medal of Honor for gallantry.

After this episode, Mackenzie continued up Blanco Canyon, which was a terra incognita to the scouts as well as the soldiers. Quanah Parker and his Quahadis hovered at the column's flanks, though without provoking battle. On the Staked Plains, a blizzard turned Mackenzie back. Back in Blanco Canyon, on 19 October, soldiers caught and killed two Comanches, while Mackenzie and a farrier named Stiegel were wounded.

The expedition disturbed the Comanches—especially the presence of the once-cannibalistic Tonkawa scouts. The army casualties were one soldier killed and two wounded, plus Mackenzie's wound. The soldiers killed two Quahadi Comanches. Dr. Rufus Choate took the two Indians' heads for scientific study.[588]

5 NOVEMBER 1871
WICKENBURG MASSACRE (Wickenburg, Arizona)

About 1,000 Apache-Yumas and Apache-Mojaves lived on the Date Creek Reservation, about 25 miles northwest of Wickenburg. Some reservation Indians sought to live under the white man's terms, but others saw the reservations as temporary sanctuary between raids. On 5 November, a band of Indians from the Date Creek Reservation attacked a stagecoach eight miles west of Wickenburg, killing six men. A woman named Shephard and a man named Kruger, both badly wounded, managed to crawl back to town.[589]

—1872—

HOWARD'S WELL (Pandale, Texas)

Wagonmaster Anastacio Gonzales was leading a ten-wagon train loaded with supplies, lumber, and kerosene, along with some travelers and livestock, up the Devil's River to Fort Stockton. At midday the train had stopped at Howard's Well, about 20 miles southeast of Fort Lancaster, when more than 100 Kiowas and Comanches under White Horse and Big Bow tore into camp and began shooting. They killed most of the men, lashing several herders to wagon wheels, soaking them with kerosene, and burning them. The Indians killed Marcela Sera's baby and captured Sera and her mother.

Col. Wesley Merritt, traveling from Fort Stockton to Fort Clark with Companies A and H, 9th Cavalry, soon came across the scene. Two badly burned survivors told Merritt the story. He sent a detachment from both companies in pursuit under Capt. Michael Cooney and Lt. Frederick R. Vincent.

When the soldiers caught up, the Indians hid Sera in a thicket with some Indian women, having killed her mother when she could not keep up. Then, on the brow of a hill, they turned to fight, hitting the troops with sharp fire as they came up the incline. Nine of the soldiers' horses went down. Cooney's leg caught in the stirrup and he was dragged. Vincent was shot in both legs.

Near dusk the troopers dislodged the Indians from the hill and recovered Marcela Sera. With night coming on and ammunition low, they pulled back to Howard's Well. Big Bow and White Horse watched the soldiers' camp that night, but the cavalry's strong guard discouraged the Indians from attacking.

That evening Merritt and his men buried 11 civilians from the wagon train. Vincent, the only army casualty, died of his wounds before reaching camp. Two warriors, White Horse and Tau-ankia, the son of Lone Wolf, were wounded; none were killed. Sera incorrectly believed that ten Indians had been killed.[590]

SOUTH FORK OF THE LOUP RIVER (Stapleton, Nebraska)

When Minneconjou Lakotas stole horses from a Union Pacific Railroad station near Fort McPherson, Capt. Charles Meinhold and elements of Company B, 3rd Cavalry, went in pursuit, guided by "Buffalo Bill" Cody. The trail led north toward the South Fork of the Loup River, west of present-day Stapleton, Nebraska. At the river, Cody, Sgt. John H. Foley, and ten men stayed on the south bank to scout while the main command crossed to the north bank.

The squad on the south bank found the Minneconjou camp and charged in. In the short fight, Cody killed one Indian and Foley's troopers killed two others. Six other warriors escaped.[591]

19 may 1872
ROUND TIMBERS (Westover, Texas)

A band of Comanches and Kiowas including Kom-pai-te, the young brother of Kiowa chief White Horse, attacked a survey party, led by L. H. Luckett, seven miles east of Round Timbers, about 25 miles northwest of Fort Belknap near present-day Megargel, Texas. One of the surveyors was killed; Kom-pai-te and another Kiowa boy were also killed, and Pohocsucut, brother of Comanche chief Tabananica, was wounded.[592]

19 may 1872
CAMP HUALPAI SCOUT (Central Arizona)

When Apaches ran off stock from Williamson Valley ranchers, a small expedition left Camp Hualpai, 40 miles northwest of Prescott, in pursuit. Sgt. Rudolph Stauffer, guides Ed Clark and Dan O'Leary, and a detachment of Company K, 5th Cavalry, went on a winding 110-mile chase into the Tonto Basin. Four Apaches were killed and two soldiers were wounded, but only a single head of stock was recovered.[593]

22 may 1872
CIMARRON CROSSING (Ashland, Kansas)

Cheyenne warriors jumped two couriers of Company E, 6th Cavalry, on the Camp Supply to Fort Dodge road about eight miles north of the Cimarron River. The Cheyennes took the soldiers' mail, horses, and equipment, killing one of the men, Pvt. Alexander Christopher. Pvt. Henry Weusserman, mortally wounded, died at Camp Supply on 1 June.[594]

10 june 1872
BILL WILLIAMS MOUNTAIN (Williams, Arizona)

Lt. Thomas Garvey left Fort Whipple with a detachment of Company A, 1st Cavalry, and guides Archie McIntosh and Bill McCloud, in pursuit of Apaches who had stolen mules near Prescott. The Indians' trail went north across the Chino Valley, over the Verde River, and up a plateau to Bill Williams Mountain. In a canyon southeast of the peak, the party caught the raiders, but they had killed and skinned the mules. Garvey attacked; in the ensuing fight, one Apache was killed and one wounded; there were no army casualties.[595]

15 june 1872
JOHNSTON'S STATION (Mertzon, Texas)

A band of Indians, perhaps Comanches, attacked Johnston's Station, a small mail station 20 miles west of Fort Concho. A detachment of

Company H, 11th Infantry, under a Cpl. Hickey, defended the station without casualties, killing two Indians.[596]

14 AUGUST 1872
PRYOR'S FORK (Billings, Montana)

Out of Fort Ellis, Maj. Eugene M. Baker led a 370-man column consisting of Companies F, G, H, and L, 2nd Cavalry, and Companies C, E, G, and I, 7th Infantry, east along the Yellowstone River to meet Col. David S. Stanley's escort of a party of Northern Pacific Railroad surveyors. On 13 August Baker and his men camped near the junction of Pryor's Fork and the Yellowstone River, east of present-day Billings, Montana. At 3 A.M. Lakotas and Cheyennes tried to run off some of the army's horses. Pickets fired in the darkness. In the sharp fight that ensued, several soldiers were hit. The Indians managed to run off 4 mules and 15 cattle.

By 7 A.M., more than 400 Lakotas and Cheyennes were in position on benchlands half a mile away; however, they did not engage when Baker moved his men out, and the two sides sniped at each other from long range. Some warriors made "bravery runs," riding out and daring the soldiers to shoot them. When one of them was indeed knocked from his pony, the Indians broke off the action, crossed the river, and by 2 P.M., were gone.

Baker estimated that the soldiers killed two warriors and wounded ten. The Cheyennes and Lakotas killed one enlisted man and one civilian and wounded five soldiers.[597]

27 AUGUST 1872
DAVIDSON CANYON (Sonoita, Arizona)

Despite warnings about daytime ambushes in Davidson Canyon, Lt. Reid T. Stewart, new to Camp Crittenden, left the post to travel to Tucson via the canyon. With him were four enlisted men of Company F, 5th Cavalry, under Cpl. James Brown, two invalid soldiers, and a civilian named Albert Banta. Soon Stewart and Cpl. Joseph P. G. Black, riding together in a buckboard, were an hour ahead of their escort.

When the buckboard entered Davidson Canyon, between the Empire and the Santa Rita Mountains, Chiricahua Apaches did indeed jump the two soldiers, killing Stewart and wounding Black, who ran but was captured. When Brown and the escort arrived, they saw Black tied to a burning dead tree and being tortured. Brown ran to him, but 15 Apaches bore in on one side and 3 on the other, forcing the soldiers to abandon the attempt. Later, Banta commented that they could have beaten the Indians easily "if those dough boys had been any good."

Brown received the Medal of Honor for attempting to rescue Black, securing Stewart's body, and driving the mail through to Tucson.[598]

8 SEPTEMBER 1872
DATE CREEK (Date Creek, Arizona)

Friendly Hualapais told Lt. Col. George Crook that the perpetrators of the Wickenburg Massacre (see 5 November 1871) were living among the Apache-Yumas and Apache-Mojaves on the Date Creek Reservation. They also warned Crook that when he went there, Indians planned to come to his quarters under the pretext of talking, and during the customary smoke, one would pull a gun and try to kill him.

Despite the warning, Crook went to Date Creek to investigate the Wickenburg incident and called for a council himself. He did not bring an escort of soldiers, but he had a dozen fully armed packers hovering nearby, ready for action. When all were seated for the council, the Apache leader Ochocama rolled and lit a cigarette. Just then another warrior produced a carbine, but as he fired, Lt. William J. Ross, Crook's aide-de-camp, struck the warrior's arm and deflected the shot.

Bedlam erupted. Other Apaches pulled out weapons, and the packers jumped in with revolvers blazing. Seven warriors were slain and four whites were wounded. Some of the Indians, including Ochocama, fled into the mountains.[599]

Davidson Canyon, in the Empire Mountains (Arizona); view to the north

25 SEPTEMBER 1872
MUCHOS CANYON (Bagdad, Arizona)

After the attempt on Lt. Col. George Crook's life (see previous entry), the Apache-Yumas behind the scheme fled the Date Creek Reservation. With Companies B, C, and K, 5th Cavalry, Capt. Julius W. Mason, taking Al Sieber and his 86 Hualapai scouts, swept the mountains to the northwest for the perpetrators. Sieber figured the Indians would be holed up at the headwaters of the Santa Maria River, and indeed Mason's command found them there.

The 5th Cavalrymen stormed the Indians' camp. Lt. John G. Bourke wrote, "in less than no time everything was in our hands, and the enemy had to record a loss of more than forty."[600] Mason suffered no casualties. The blow demoralized the Apache-Yumas, lessening hostilities in the area.[601]

29 SEPTEMBER 1872
NORTH FORK OF THE RED RIVER (Lefors, Texas)

During the summer of 1872, Col. Ranald S. Mackenzie and Companies A, D, F, I, and L of the 4th Cavalry, one company of the 24th Infantry, and a detachment of 20 Tonkawa scouts under Lt. Peter M. Boehm scoured the Texas Panhandle for Comanche raiders and their hideouts. Along the headwaters of the North Fork of the Red River were several villages of Quahadi Comanches under Parra-o-coom and Kotsoteka Comanches under Mow-way. At 4 P.M. on 29 September, Mackenzie's 231 men surprised one of these villages, a Kotsoteka and Quahadi encampment of 262 lodges under

Site of Mackenzie's fight, North Fork of the Red River (Texas)

Chief Kai-wotche, in charge during Mow-way's absence, about seven miles from the mouth of McClellan's Creek, in present-day Gray County.

Mackenzie sent Company D to capture the large horse herd while the other companies charged the village in columns of four. About 80 warriors made a stand near the riverbank, but by sunset, most had either died or fled, and the remaining women in the camp surrendered. The soldiers burned lodges and destroyed property. The next day, the command camped 18 miles away from the village. The Comanches succeeded in recapturing about 3,000 horses and mules that night. Afterward Mackenzie ordered that, from then on, all captured horses would be shot.

In the fight, the Comanches killed four of Mackenzie's men and wounded four. The soldiers killed at least 32 Comanches, among them chief Kai-wotche and his wife, and captured 124. Eight captives died on the march south. The fight nearly destroyed the Kotsotekas. Mackenzie told the Comanches that to get their women back, they must release all captives to authorities at Fort Sill. Parra-o-coom soon surrendered.[602]

30 SEPTEMBER 1872
CAMP CRITTENDEN (Sonoita, Arizona)

Apache raiders attacked the ranch of a man named Hughs, two miles from Camp Crittenden, killing a Mexican and stealing three horses. Lt. William P. Hall, in command of the post, rode to the ranch with a dozen men of Company F, 5th Cavalry. He found the raiders a mile south, at a strong position in the Canelo Hills. The more than 60 warriors seemed eager to fight. Hall did not engage but sent Sgt. George Stewart and five men to warn nearby ranchers about the Apaches.

The soldiers completed the assignment and were riding back to Camp Crittenden when, four miles from the post, 50 warriors attacked. Stewart and three of his men—Pvts. Andrew Carr, William Nation, and John Walsh—were killed. Of the other two soldiers, a Pvt. Larkin fled to the rear, and the bugler Kershaw charged through the ambuscade. Both safely reached the fort.[603]

25 NOVEMBER 1872
HELL CANYON (Drake, Arizona)

When Lt. Col. George Crook became department commander in Arizona in May 1871, he embarked on a rigorous, five-column offensive to force rebel Apaches onto reservations. On 16 November, Capt. Emil Adams led one column—Company C, 5th Cavalry, and Paiute scouts—out from Camp Hualpai. The troops searched for Apaches in the Chino Valley and into Hell Canyon, in the Red Rocks country. On 25 November, they ran into a band, killing 11 warriors and capturing 3 women and a child. One soldier was killed.[604]

30 NOVEMBER 1872
LOST RIVER (Merrill, Oregon)

After Modoc leader Captain Jack and his band fled the Klamath Reservation in Oregon and refused to return, Capt. James Jackson and 43 men of Company B, 1st Cavalry, left Fort Klamath to force them back. Captain Jack had set up his village on both sides of the Lost River near Tule Lake. Jackson took his men down the west bank of the river, while about 25 armed citizens from Linkville went down the east bank.

Jackson reached Captain Jack and the 17 families on the west bank and demanded their surrender. The soldiers and Modocs parleyed, but tempers boiled over. Jackson and the warrior Scarface Charley both fired their weapons, and a melee erupted. One Modoc, Watchman, was killed; two soldiers were killed or mortally wounded, and six soldiers were wounded.

Arriving on the east bank, the Linkville volunteers attacked Modoc warriors who were crossing the river to help in the fighting. The Modocs, led by Hooker Jim, easily repulsed the citizens, killing two of them and wounding another. One Modoc woman and child were killed.

Captain Jack's people escaped by boat across Tule Lake, while Hooker Jim's band rode around the east side of the lake, killing 14 settlers as they went.[605]

7 DECEMBER 1872
RED ROCKS (Sedona, Arizona)

Another of Lt. Col. George Crook's five columns against hostile Apaches (see Hell Canyon, 25 November), Lt. William F. Rice, 23rd Infantry, with a detachment of Company G, and Lt. Frank Michler, 5th Cavalry, with a detachment of Company K, left Camp Verde on 3 December. They moved northwest, seeking either to defeat Apaches there or drive them east into the Tonto Basin.

On the 7th the column surprised an Apache band heading into the Red Rocks country north of Prescott. They killed 13 warriors, captured 3 women, and burned the Indians' camp. Later that day, Rice's Hualapai scouts ran into another band entrenched on a mountain. The troops lost one man in an unsuccessful attempt to storm the position. With their supplies running out, the column returned to Camp Verde.[606]

11 DECEMBER 1872
BAD ROCK MOUNTAIN (Central Arizona)

Leading a third column in Lt. Col. George Crook's expedition against Apaches (see previous entry), Capt. George M. Randall, 23rd Infantry, took detachments from Companies L and M, 1st Cavalry, a detachment from Company G, 23rd Infantry, and Apache scouts under Corydon E. Cooley west from Camp Apache toward Camp McDowell. As the troops crossed

Tonto Creek, Lt. Thomas Garvey, 1st Cavalry, split north with a squad of 8 soldiers and 20 scouts.

After a difficult overnight march of 30 miles to Bad Rock Mountain in the Mazatzals, on the morning of 11 December, Garvey and his squad struck the band of the Apache chief Delshay. In a two-hour fight, the soldiers and scouts killed 14 warriors, with no casualties of their own. The chief got away, however.[607]

13 DECEMBER 1872
MAZATZAL MOUNTAINS (Central Arizona)

Capt. George M. Randall, 23rd Infantry, continuing his scout to Camp McDowell (see previous entry), was camped north of old Camp Reno on the evening of 13 December. The troops heard what sounded like howling coyotes, but veterans among the men identified the sound as dogs, indicating an Apache camp was near. With a detachment of soldiers and Indian scouts, Lt. Peter S. Bomus, 1st Cavalry, and Lt. William C. Manning, 23rd Infantry, located and crept up on a large rancheria. They killed 11 warriors and captured 6 Apache women and children without loss of their own.[608]

21 DECEMBER 1872
LAND'S RANCH (Tulelake, California)

After the Modocs fled their village on the Lost River (see Lost River, 30 November), they went to the lava beds south of Tule Lake, and the army set up posts on both sides of the lake. Capt. Reuben F. Bernard, Company G, 1st Cavalry, was stationed at Louis Land's ranch, on the southeast side of Tule Lake. A mile from the ranch, Modocs struck an ammunition wagon train, hitting two of the five-man escort in the first volley. Pvt. Sidney Smith was shot and killed, and Pvt. William Donahue was fatally wounded. From Bernard's post, Lt. John G. Kyle, 1st Cavalry, and ten men raced after the Modocs, but with darkness coming on, they soon gave up.[609]

28 DECEMBER 1872
SKULL CAVE (Tortilla Flat, Arizona)

After Apache chief Delshay and his band escaped from Capt. George M. Randall, 23rd Infantry (see Bad Rock Mountain, 11 December), Capt. William H. Brown took Companies G, L, and M, 5th Cavalry, and 30 Apache scouts to follow the band through central Arizona. This force joined 100 Pimas under Capt. James Burns out of Camp McDowell, and the 220 men headed up Salt River Canyon.

In the Four Peaks area, near present-day Tortilla Flat, Arizona, Brown's troops discovered a band of Apaches living in a cave high in the side of a cliff. With a conventional frontal assault impossible, the soldiers and scouts worked their way up the sides of the cliff to spots from which they could fire into the cave. Twice they called on the besieged Indians to surrender, but they received only taunts and curses in reply. The soldiers began to shoot volley after volley into the cave. Hundreds of bullets splintered rocks, ricocheted, and hit the trapped Apaches. Meanwhile, men of Company G worked their way above the cave and dropped boulders down into it.

When Brown's men finally charged the cave, resistance had ceased. Inside, 57 were dead. The soldiers took the remaining 20 women and children, most of them wounded, prisoner. On Brown's side, only one Pima scout was killed. It turned out that the Apaches were not Delshay's people, but Yavapai raiders under Nanni-Chaddi. However, the victory meant that the army could penetrate even the most inaccessible corners of Apacheria, sending a grave warning to fugitive Apaches.[610]

30 DECEMBER 1872
BABY CANYON (Black Canyon City, Arizona)

During Lt. Col. George Crook's campaign (see Hell Canyon, 25 November), even noncommissioned officers led scouts in pursuit of Apaches. Sgt. William L. Day of Company E, 5th Cavalry, led a detachment of his company along the flanks of the Bradshaw Mountains and along the lower Agua Fria River, guided by Lew Ellit and Jack Townsend. In a place called Baby Canyon, which was possibly near the junction of the Agua Fria and Little Squaw Creek, the party surprised eight Apache warriors and killed five. Crossing the river, they killed another warrior, wounded one, and captured nine women and children.[611]

—1873—

16 JANUARY 1873
SUPERSTITION MOUNTAINS (Apache Junction, Arizona)

After Capt. William H. Brown's success in Salt River Canyon (see Skull Cave, 28 December 1872), he continued to pursue the remaining Apaches south of the Salt River. With Companies B, C, G, H, L, and M of the 5th Cavalry, he scoured the Superstition Mountain wilderness. After a difficult night climbing over a mesa, Brown crept up to a small rancheria at sunrise. But according to Lt. John G. Bourke, the occupants were "too smart for us and escaped, leaving three dead in our hands and thirteen captives—women and children." They also captured the old chief of the band, "who, like his people, seemed to be extremely poor."[612]

With this battle, Lt. Col. Crook's campaign in the Superstitions was over.[613]

17 JANUARY 1873
BATTLE OF THE STRONGHOLD (Tulelake, California)

When Captain Jack's Modoc band fled from Lost River, they took shelter in the maze of lava beds on the south shore of Tule Lake (see Lost River,

30 November 1872). Lt. Col. Frank Wheaton gathered 225 men of Companies B, F, and G of the 21st Infantry and Companies B, C, and F of the 1st Cavalry for a showdown. Joining him were about 100 Oregon and California volunteers. As they would face only about 60 Modoc fighting men, they were confident of victory.

Before dawn on 17 January, the troops moved into the lava beds, led by Maj. John Green, 1st Cavalry, on the west and Capt. Reuben F. Bernard, 1st Cavalry, on the east. Shots peppered the darkness as the Modocs fired, popping up and down from their cover in the broken terrain. Soldiers were hit again and again, unable to see their foe. The advance stalled when the men reached an uncrossable chasm. Even after the sun rose and the fog lifted, the soldiers could not see the enemy, yet the Modocs had no trouble finding their targets. The soldiers waited until dark to withdraw.

The volunteers went home and Wheaton's men were demoralized.

The battle cost Wheaton 7 soldiers killed and 19 wounded; 4 volunteers were also killed and 7 were wounded. Not one Modoc was hit. The army settled into a stalemate that would last three months.[614]

19 JANUARY 1873
EAST VERDE RIVER (Central Arizona)

Sgt. William L. Day, 5th Cavalry, continued his hard patrolling throughout the winter (see Baby Canyon, 30 December 1872). Leading a party of Apache scouts along the upper Verde River, they noticed smoke signals in the hills, which the scouts said meant the Indians knew soldiers were in the area. Instead of stopping, however, Day went toward the smoke and picked up a trail that led him up the East Verde River to the bottom of one of the deepest canyons, probably below Polles Mesa. He and his scouts rushed into a rancheria and slew five Apaches. For these and similar actions, Day was awarded the Medal of Honor.[615]

22 JANUARY 1873
TONTO CREEK (Payson, Arizona)

Lt. Frank Michler, with Company K, 5th Cavalry, was en route from Camp Verde to Camp Grant in late January when, on the 22nd, he ran into a sizable rancheria of Tonto Apaches on Tonto Creek. Pvt. George Hooker was killed as he led the first charge into the camp, earning him a posthumous Medal of Honor.

Hooker was the only army casualty; 17 Tontos were slain.[616]

6 FEBRUARY 1873
HELL CANYON (Drake, Arizona)

Capt. Thomas McGregor took a detachment of Company A, 1st Cavalry, out of Fort Whipple to seek out Indians. Marching through deep snows, the soldiers came upon a small Apache camp in Hell Canyon near the Verde

River, north of the fort, and attacked. They killed two Apaches and captured one, then returned cold and hungry to Whipple.[617]

26 FEBRUARY 1873
FORT BASCOM (Tucumcari, New Mexico)

The Cheyenne White Eagle led 17 warriors into the Sangre de Cristo Mountains in New Mexico Territory, looking for Utes. Unsuccessful, they were returning to the reservation when, on the Canadian River, they were attacked by soldiers and civilians. One Cheyenne was killed and one mortally wounded. Three others were also wounded, including White Eagle. Their attackers pressed the Cheyennes so hard that they had to leave their badly injured man behind.[618]

19 MARCH 1873
MAZATZAL MOUNTAINS (Central Arizona)

Following up on his success in January (see Tonto Creek, 22 January), Lt. Frank Michler, with Company K, 5th Cavalry, scouted through the Mazatzal Mountains between the Verde River and Tonto Creek. In a canyon on 19 March, he surprised an Apache band, killing eight and capturing five women.[619]

27 MARCH 1873
TURRET MOUNTAIN (Cordes Junction, Arizona)

Lt. Col. Crook's strategy of pursuing the Apaches year-round was bearing fruit. The harassed bands could find little respite. A column led by Capt. George M. Randall, 23rd Infantry, consisting of men from Company I, a detachment of Company A, 5th Cavalry, and Apache scouts, trailed the hostiles up the Verde River, through Bloody Basin, and west toward Turret Peak.

After some of Randall's mules strayed, the Apaches found them and were alerted to the soldiers' presence. Randall captured an Apache woman and forced her into guiding them to the camp. Both sides knew the other was close, but they continued to play cat-and-mouse among the peaks and canyons. The woman led them into the broken lava flows of the Turret Mountains. Randall's men wrapped their feet and knees in gunny sacks for protection and to muffle the sound.

The soldiers crawled all the way to the top of the mountains to find the Apache camp, and just before dawn on 27 March, they fired a volley into the camp and charged. The Indians were so surprised that some ran right over the precipice.

With no loss of his own, Randall killed 23 Indians and captured 10. The battle broke the will of many Apaches in central Arizona, and they began coming to the forts to surrender.[620]

CANBY MASSACRE (Tulelake, California)

The stalemate in the lava beds of Tule Lake (see Battle of the Stronghold, 17 January) continued until the Modocs agreed to meet with a peace commission. Urged on by tribe members, Jack went along with a plan to assassinate the commissioners under a flag of truce. A friendly Modoc warned the commissioners, but they either discounted it or decided to take a chance.

On 11 April, Good Friday morning, Superintendent Alfred B. Meacham, Commissioner L. S. Dyar, the Rev. Eleasar Thomas, and Brig. Gen. Edward R. S. Canby, commander of the Department of the Columbia, prepared for the council. Frank Riddle and his Modoc wife Tobey were the interpreters. Someone slipped Meacham a Derringer as he mounted up, and the party quietly rode to the council.

There were more Modocs in the tent than was agreed upon, and they were talking and acting aggressively. The negotiations were going nowhere when Schonchin John interrupted Captain Jack and said, "I talk no more."[621]

Captain Jack called out in Modoc, "All ready." He whipped out a revolver, pressed it against Gen. Canby's head and fired. The general staggered back and fell, then Ellen's Man slashed his throat. Commissioner Dyar jumped up and ran, pursued by Hooker Jim, who fired several times but missed. Riddle also broke away. Boston Charley shot Rev. Thomas through the heart. Schonchin John drew his pistol on Meacham, and the superintendent pulled out his Derringer, but it was only half-cocked and did not fire. Schonchin John and Shacknasty Jim blasted away, hitting Meacham several times before he got one shot off, wounding John. Meacham was about to be scalped when Riddle's wife called out that the soldiers were coming. The last of the Modocs turned and fled.

Canby was the highest-ranking officer killed in the Indian wars. The circumstances of his death stunned the nation and assured vengeance. Incredibly, Alfred Meacham survived and remained sympathetic to the Indians, defending the Modocs who were later caught and put on trial for the murders. Some of the guilty Modocs were given amnesty when they helped hunt down Jack. At Fort Klamath on 3 October 1873, Boston Charley, Black Jim, Schonchin John, and Captain Jack were hanged.[622]

LAVA BEDS (Tulelake, California)

Immediately after the Canby Massacre (see previous entry), Col. Alvin C. Gillem of the 1st Cavalry, who had succeeded Lt. Col. Wheaton, ordered an offensive to punish the Modocs, and Jefferson C. Davis, colonel of the 23rd Infantry, replaced Brig. Gen. Canby as department commander. Gillem led Companies B, F, G, H, and K of the 1st Cavalry; Companies E and G of the 12th Infantry; Companies B, C, and I of the 21st Infantry; and Companies A, B, E, G, H, and K of the 4th Artillery in the mission. Most worrisome to the Modocs, 72 Warm Springs Indians from Oregon, who had been friends of Superintendent Meacham, assisted the soldiers.

For three days, Gillem worked his forces slowly into the lava beds, advancing and falling back as soldiers and Indians sniped at each other. The troopers bombarded the Modoc positions with howitzers and mortars. After three days, the Modocs fell back farther south.

The Modocs killed 8 soldiers and volunteers and wounded 17. They left behind the bodies of 3 men and 8 women.[623]

26 APRIL 1873
HARDIN BUTTE/LAVA BEDS (Tulelake, California)

After the first battle at the lava beds (see previous entry), Col. Gillem sent out a reconnaissance force of 59 men—detachments of Companies A and K of the 4th Artillery and Company E of the 12th Infantry, under Capt. Evan Thomas, 4th Artillery—to find the Modocs. Thomas moved his men four miles to a butte at the side of the lava beds, where they halted for lunch. Seeing no Modocs, Thomas called in his skirmishers, but Lt. Arthur Cranston, 4th Artillery, took 12 men forward to "raise some Indians."

Cranston had barely started out when his party was fired upon by Modocs hidden in the rocks on all sides. Every man was hit and most were killed, including Cranston. Hearing the firing, Thomas's soldiers were thrown into confusion. Lt. George M. Harris, 4th Artillery, took a squad up the butte. The Modocs fired down at them. Harris was killed and his men fled. The Indians followed up, killing Thomas and Lt. Albion Howe, 4th Artillery, and Lt. Thomas F. Wright, 12th Infantry. The only officer to survive was Asst. Surgeon B. G. Semig, who was wounded. Donald McKay and 14 Warm Springs scouts came belatedly to the scene, probably preventing a complete annihilation. Scarface Charley called out in English, "All you fellows that ain't dead had better go home. We don't want to kill you all in one day."[624]

In addition to the 5 officers, 18 enlisted men were killed and 17 enlisted men and civilians were wounded. Of the 24 Modocs in the fight, not one of them was hit.[625]

7 MAY 1873
SCORPION POINT (Tulelake, California)

The Modocs, figuring their luck would not last, abandoned their stronghold in the lava beds and moved their camp to higher country, south of Tule Lake. Several days later they returned to the southeast shoreline near Scorpion Point. No one knew exactly where they were until a wagon train carrying supplies to the Scorpion Point camp was jumped by about 20 warriors.

The Modocs wounded 2 soldiers from the 21st Infantrymen and 1 from the1st Cavalry, but not seriously enough to keep them from fleeing with the 17 others in the train while the Indians captured the horses. The Modocs suffered no losses.[626]

10 MAY 1873
SORASS LAKE/DRY LAKE (Tulelake, California)

During the night of 9 May, Modocs under Captain Jack surrounded the lakeside camp of Companies B and G, 1st Cavalry, and Company B, 4th Artillery, under Capt. Henry C. Hasbrouck. At sunrise, the sleeping soldiers were roused by Indian yells. Their first reaction was to run, and several fell to Indian bullets. Hasbrouck and Lt. John G. Kyle rallied them, however, and formed them into skirmish lines to drive the Modocs back. Donald McKay's Warm Springs scouts arrived in time to further frustrate Jack's men.

Ellen's Man was killed, and two other Modocs were wounded. Hasbrouck recaptured the horses that were taken in the 7 May raid on the supply wagons (see previous entry). Two enlisted men were killed, and seven enlisted men and two scouts were wounded. The fight caused an argument among the Modocs, and Hooker Jim and 13 families deserted Captain Jack and headed west.[627]

18 MAY 1873
REMOLINO (Remolino, Coahuila, Mexico)

For years the Kickapoos and Lipan Apaches had been raiding across the Rio Grande from Mexico, but the U.S. forces were hampered in their pursuit by not being able to cross the border. In May 1873 Col. Ranald S. Mackenzie was given an unofficial go-ahead to punish the raiders in their home villages.

Mackenzie led 4th Cavalry Companies A, B, C, E, I, and M and 20 Seminole scouts, about 400 men, out of Fort Clark on 17 May. Carrying five days' rations, the column forded the Rio Grande, near the present-day town of Quemado, at dusk. That night, because the pack mules could no longer keep up, the troopers took all the supplies they could carry and cut the animals loose. By 6 A.M. they had reached their destination on the San Rodrigo River near the Mexican village of Remolino.

There were three Indian villages of about 50 to 60 lodges each. Mackenzie chose a full frontal assault in a succession of companies. Each platoon charged in, fired, wheeled right, and doubled back for another pass. Time after time they repeated the maneuver, sweeping the length of the three camps. Lt. Robert G. Carter, who had seen attacks in the Civil War, affirmed, "I never saw such a magnificent charge as that made by those six troops of the Fourth U.S. Cavalry."[628]

The attack was devastating. The troopers torched the Indians' homes, supplies, and crops. On the return march they trekked straight through Remolino, under the scowls of the Mexican inhabitants. Afterward, some officers learned they had crossed into Mexico without orders and told Mackenzie that had they known, they would not have gone, to which Mackenzie snapped, "Any officer or man who had refused to follow me across the river I would have shot!"[629]

Three soldiers were wounded, Pvt. Peter Carrigan mortally. The cavalry killed 19 Indians, wounded about 12 more, and brought back 42 captives. They also recovered 65 horses with Texan brands.[630]

19 MAY 1873
WILLOW CREEK RIDGE (Dorris, California)

Capt. Henry C. Hasbrouck, with his bloodied companies of 4th Artillery (see previous entry), chased the fragmented bands of Captain Jack's Modocs, moving along the west side of Willow Creek Valley, south of Lower Klamath Lake. Capt. James Jackson, with Company B, 1st Cavalry, went through the valley, and Capt. David Perry, Company F, 1st Cavalry, marched east of the valley along Dome Mountain.

On the west side of Willow Creek Valley, Hasbrouck found an Indian trail. As he started up Willow Creek Ridge he was fired on by Modocs. It was not Jack's band, but Hooker Jim's. Hasbrouck called for Jackson and his mounted men to pursue. They followed Indians eight miles along the ridge, riding and shooting. Jackson claimed to have killed two Modocs, but no bodies were found. The harried Indians tired out one by one, and Jackson's troopers scooped up ten women and children. Three days later, at Fairchild's Ranch, the remainder of Hooker Jim's band surrendered.[631]

16 JUNE 1873
FORKS OF TONTO CREEK (Payson, Arizona)

On a scout out of Camp Apache, on the east fork of the White River, Lt. John B. Babcock, with a detachment of Company C, 5th Cavalry, and Apache Indian auxiliaries, hit the camps of Natotel and Naqui-naquis on upper Tonto Creek in the Diamond Butte country. In what Lt. Col. George Crook called a "brilliant action," Babcock, at the cost of a scout killed and himself wounded, killed 14 Indians and captured 5. The fight resulted in the surrender of most of the Tonto Apaches, but Natotel escaped.[632]

13 JULY 1873
CANADA ALAMOSA (Monticello, New Mexico)

Early in July, a band of Apaches swept down on the Shedd ranch near San Augustin Pass, northeast of Las Cruces, and ran off some horses.

Capt. George W. Chilson, 8th Cavalry, commanding at Fort Selden on the southern end of the Jornada del Muerto, took ten men of Company C and pursued the raiders. Their trail led northwest, across the Rio Grande. Four and a half days later, Chilson found his quarry in a canyon southwest of Canada Alamosa, present-day Monticello, New Mexico.

In the ensuing fight, Cpl. Frank Battling was killed. Three Apaches were killed and a fourth, said to be Chief Victorio's nephew, was wounded. All the stock was recovered. Sgt. James L. Morris, Sgt. Leonidas S. Little, and Pvt. Henry Wills won Medals of Honor.[633]

AUGUST 1873
DEER CREEK (Kingsland, Texas)

When rancher Thomas Phelps and his wife were murdered by a band of Indian raiders near Cypress Creek in Blanco County, local citizens "Capt." Dan W. Roberts and five men scouted the area. They met up with "Capt." James Ingram and three men and combined forces.

Along Deer Creek, north of Round Mountain, the volunteers saw a lone Indian disappearing over a hill, but as they attempted to overtake him, they ran right into an ambush. The civilians were poorly armed; some carried only revolvers. Nevertheless, they tried to flank the Indians, who were firing from a ravine. Dan Roberts's brother George was wounded in the first volley, then Roberts himself took a bullet in the left thigh. The small force carried the two wounded men off the field to a nearby farmhouse, while reinforcements under Capt. Cicero R. Perry rode out. When Perry reached the ambush site, the Indians were gone.

Perry's men reported four Indian graves along the raiders' retreat trail.[634]

4 AUGUST 1873
TONGUE RIVER (Miles City, Montana)

The army acted as escorts for the Northern Pacific Railroad surveyors as they worked their way across the northern plains. The Yellowstone Expedition of 1873, commanded by Col. David S. Stanley, consisted of a formidable force of 1,500 soldiers, including Lt. Col. George Custer and 10 companies of the 7th Cavalry, and 400 civilians.

On 4 August, the advance proceeded under Capt. Myles Moylan of Company B and Lt. Thomas Custer of Company A, with the lieutenant colonel riding along. At 9 A.M., they halted about eight miles above the mouth of the Tongue River, across from Moon Creek. Unsaddling in a grove of cottonwoods, they waited for the command to catch up. Two hours later, after six Indians, probably Lakotas, tried to run off their horses, the troopers saddled up and gave chase. Suddenly the size of the Indian force doubled.

When the soldiers chased them, the Indians ran; when they halted, the Indians halted. Lt. Col. Custer knew it was a decoy game, but he tried to

Lt. Col. George Custer
—Courtesy Little Bighorn
Battlefield National Monument

bring them closer for a talk. When he rode toward them, about 300 Lakotas burst out of the timber by the river. Custer wheeled around and sped back to Moylan, who had dismounted the companies in an open triangle. The troopers fired, but the warriors did not charge through them, trying to burn them out instead. The grass failed to burn, and both sides kept up desultory firing until three in the afternoon. When the Lakotas began drifting away, Custer charged those remaining, driving them across the plain for three miles before calling an end to the chase.

Only one of Custer's men was wounded, and only a few Indians were wounded in turn. Three others, however—the regiment's veterinarian, Dr. John Honsinger; the sutler, Augustus Baliran; and Pvt. John Ball—were caught alone on the plain and killed.[635]

5 AUGUST 1873
PACKSADDLE MOUNTAIN (Kingsland, Texas)

Comanches had been stealing horses and cattle in Llano County for some time when James R. Moss organized a group of eight ranchers to follow their trail. The signs led them to the top of Packsaddle Mountain, where the Indians felt relatively secure. Moss approached undetected.

Killing a guard, the ranchers charged into the camp, trying to cut out the horses. The Comanches made two countercharges but failed to regain the horses. The fight was fast and close, the Texans using Spencers and six-shooters. The Indians retreated into the brush and Moss believed they had gone, but they soon returned. The leader harangued his warriors to go in, but they refused. The chief, alone, took his Winchester and advanced against the Texans. Within a few yards of the ranchers, six bullets pierced the chief and he fell dead. The remaining Comanches fled.

Moss and his men took several hundred pounds of beef from the Indian camp in addition to recovering the stolen horses. It was the last fight between Indians and settlers in Llano County.

Four of the ranchers were wounded during the skirmish, and three Comanches were killed.[636]

11 AUGUST 1873
BIGHORN (Bighorn, Montana)

Col. David S. Stanley's expedition (see Tongue River, 4 August) continued up the Yellowstone River, camping near the mouth of the Bighorn on the night of 10 August. Early the next morning, the camp was greeted by Indian fire from the south shore. The fire became so heavy that Lt. Col. George Custer ordered the horses to be removed from harm's way and pulled back into the timber by the bluffs.

Custer's 450 troopers faced about 500 Lakota warriors. He placed 30 of his best marksmen along the river to counter the Indians' fire. Pvt. John H. Tuttle, Company E, was considered the outfit's best shot. Working his Springfield, he killed three Indians in a row. Finally the Lakotas combined their fire and put a bullet through his head.

The Indians crossed the river downstream and Custer sent Capt. George Yates and Lt. Charles Braden to counter the move. About 200 warriors charged against Braden's line of 120 men. The soldiers drove them off, but Braden caught a bullet in his upper thigh and it broke the bone. More Lakotas crossed upstream, and Lt. Tom Custer and Capt. Myles Moylan met them. Unable to intimidate the soldiers, the warriors ended the action and crossed back to the south bank.

Custer lost 3 enlisted men, with 3 more enlisted men and an officer wounded. The soldiers killed 4 Lakotas and wounded 12.[637]

23 SEPTEMBER 1873
HARDSCRABBLE CREEK (Central Arizona)

On 18 September, Lt. Walter S. Schuyler left Camp Verde with 15 men of Company K, 5th Cavalry, and 23 scouts under Al Sieber to hunt for the Apache chief Delshay, taking 20 days' rations. The men went down the Verde River to Fossil Creek, then upstream, then south over Deadman Mesa to Hardscrabble Creek. There Schuyler split up his command and sent 11 Yuma and Mojave scouts with Corp. Snook, a minor Yavapai chief, toward the East Verde River with orders to find the Apaches then wait until the forces could be united.

Contrary to orders, Snook walked into the rancheria and attacked. The scouts fell upon their traditional enemies with a fury—they killed all 14 Apaches with no loss to themselves. On his way back, Snook found more Apaches on the southern edges of Hardscrabble Mesa. This time he waited for Schuyler, but the Apaches had fled by the time he arrived.[638]

4 DECEMBER 1873
EAST VERDE RIVER (Central Arizona)

During the fall of 1873, in his pursuit of Apaches (see previous entry), Lt. Walter S. Schuyler drove his small command ahead with little rest. Then, on 1 December, he left Camp Verde with 11 men of Company K, 5th Cavalry; 14 Tonto scouts; Al Sieber, Jose de Leon, and his son; two other civilians; and 25 mules with packers. The party went east to Fossil Creek, over Hardscrabble Mesa, and south to the East Verde River.

During a night march through the snow, de Leon saw the fires of a Tonto Apache camp a mile and a half away. Schuyler stopped the command at 10 P.M. The men spent the night without fires or food as more snow fell, and they stomped around in a circle to keep from freezing. At dawn they found two Apache rancherias and Schuyler split up his men to attack both. One of the camps was Chief Natotel's. The soldiers attacked in a blinding snowstorm. "We got within 20 yards of them," wrote Schuyler, "and woke them up firing into the houses."[639]

Because visibility was poor, several Apaches got away, but the soldiers killed 15, taking no prisoners.

Sieber, who was sent to the far camp, could not get there before the gunfire alerted the inhabitants, and they scattered before he could attack. The force joined back up and made a cold, soggy camp on Fossil Creek.[640]

10 DECEMBER 1873
KICKAPOO SPRINGS (Rocksprings, Texas)

In the late fall of 1873, 9 Kiowas and 21 Comanches made a raid into south Texas and Mexico. There were a number of prominent warriors in the group, including Tau-ankia, Lone Wolf's son, and Gui-tain, the 15-year-old son of Red Otter and Lone Wolf's nephew. After killing 14 Mexicans and 2 Americans and capturing 3 Mexicans, the Indians crossed the Rio Grande back into Mexico. But 2 of their prisoners had escaped north of the border and notified United States troops.

Meanwhile, Lt. Charles L. Hudson was on patrol from Fort Clark with 41 men from detachments of Companies A, B, C, and I of the 4th Cavalry. He found a hidden remuda of Indian horses near Kickapoo Springs by the West Fork of the Nueces River and decided to wait for the Indians to return to reclaim their ponies. When he got word of the raid, Hudson moved out to intercept the raiders. After an eight-mile ride he found the Indians' position on a ridge crest.

Plodding up the slope, Hudson held his fire until he gained the top, then, dismounting, he began firing at 75 yards. The warriors took the fire for ten minutes and then broke. Seeing them, Hudson mounted and charged. The fight was a rout. Tau-ankia was left behind, limping badly from the wound he received at Howard's Well (see 20 April 1872). Gui-tain saw his cousin about to be caught and went back to help. Hudson shot down Tau-ankia, and a trooper felled Gui-tan.

Nine Indians were killed and only one trooper was wounded. The soldiers recaptured 50 animals. Lone Wolf, distraught, vowed revenge on all whites.[641]

23 DECEMBER 1873
CAVE CREEK (Cave Creek, Arizona)

The untiring Lt. Walter S. Schuyler kept his small command in the field (see East Verde River, 4 December), giving his men and the Apaches little respite. His guides, knowing he was closing in on their own home villages, suddenly refused to continue, and several of them disappeared. Schuyler had only 11 men of Company K, 5th Cavalry, along with Al Sieber, Jose de Leon, and a few Indian scouts. Near Cave Creek, a small stream coursing southwest out of the New River Mountains north of present Phoenix, Schuyler found an Indian hideout.

As a ruse, Schuyler sent part of his command with the pack mules downstream, as if they were leaving the country and heading toward Camp McDowell. While Schuyler and Sieber watched, the Apaches came out of their holes above Cave Creek and began to draw water. Now Schuyler knew exactly where the Apaches were hiding and collected his men to close in after nightfall.

At sunup, Schuyler assaulted the Apaches. The soldiers killed nine Indians and wounded three. One of the slain was the leader Nanotz. They destroyed the camp along with several tons of mescal. Schuyler returned to Camp McDowell the day after Christmas.[642]

—1874—

10 JANUARY 1874
CANYON CREEK (Central Arizona)

After a short rest and refit at Camp McDowell, Lt. Walter Schuyler, with a detachment of Company K, 5th Cavalry, and Al Sieber, Jose de Leon, his son, and some Apache scouts went out again to continue their search for Apaches (see previous entry). They moved back to the Cave Creek area, then started up the Verde River. They stopped at Canyon Creek, about six miles from the mouth of the East Fork of the Verde, where the scouts noticed two Indians on a far-off ridge, highlighted by the rays of the setting sun. Schuyler waited until about midnight, then started up the mountain in the moonlight.

Reaching the summit at daylight, the men found only tracks. Hurrying along, they saw a small band, still moving away. De Leon and the scouts sped ahead and caught the band near the Verde River. They killed the leader, Natotel, two children, and a woman, and captured a woman and two infants. Only five escaped.

De Leon, who personally slew Natotel, took the chief's double-barreled rifle as a trophy. He would not enjoy it for long—after scouting the Mazatzal Mountains for several more days, both de Leon and his son drowned while crossing the icy and rain-swollen Verde River.[643]

5 FEBRUARY 1874
DOUBLE MOUNTAIN FORK OF THE BRAZOS RIVER
(North-central Texas)

Late in January, Lt. Col. George P. Buell, 11th Infantry, commander at Fort Griffin, got word that Comanches had stolen stock from local ranchers and were heading in the direction of Double Mountain, twin peaks between the Double Mountain Fork and the Salt Fork of the Brazos River. Buell saddled up 55 men from the 10th Cavalry, Company D, under Capt. Phillip L. Lee; Company G, under Lt. Richard H. Pratt; detachments of Companies A, F, and G of the 11th Infantry; and 18 Tonkawa Indian scouts. They headed west for 100 miles.

In the valley of the Double Mountain Fork, the soldiers found the Comanche raiders, and, in a running fight, they killed 10 Indians and captured 65 animals. One trooper was wounded.[644]

8 MARCH 1874
PINAL MOUNTAINS (Globe, Arizona)

Although Gen. George Crook had rounded up most of the Apaches after his 1872–73 campaign, many had escaped the reservations and fell back into their old raiding habits. At Camp Grant, Maj. George M. Randall, 23rd Infantry, took detachments from Companies B, F, H, I, L, and M of the 5th Cavalry, plus Camp Apache White Mountain scouts and guide Archie McIntosh, out after some raiders. Word had it that a large group of renegade Apaches was camped high up in the almost inaccessible Pinal Mountains.

Randall holed up during the day and marched only at night, eventually creeping within 15 miles of the suspected Apache camp. After a great canyon had forced them into a detour of 25 more miles, they finally placed themselves in position surrounding the Apaches' fortified mesa, the camp of chiefs Chunz, Cochinay, and Chan-daisi. The White Mountain scouts attacked at dawn, while the soldiers took the other side.

All three renegade leaders escaped. Not so lucky were 12 slain warriors and 25 captured women and children. Randall did not lose a man and was brevetted a colonel for the action.[645]

25 MARCH 1874
SUPERSTITION MOUNTAINS (Apache Junction, Arizona)

When spring made for milder campaigning weather, Lt. Walter Schuyler was on the trail again (see Canyon Creek, 10 January). With a detachment of Company K, 5th Cavalry, and Al Sieber with 122 Apache-Yuma, Apache-Mojave, and Tonto scouts, he was off from Camp Verde to the Superstition Mountains. The command passed through Camp McDowell on 7 March and spent the next few weeks examining the maze of mountains and canyons in the Superstitions.

On 25 March, somewhere in the jumble of canyons the expedition struck hostile Apaches. With no loss to Schuyler, his men killed 12 Indians and captured 2 more.[646]

2 APRIL 1874
PINAL CREEK (Miami, Arizona)

Continuing the search for renegade Apaches (see Pinal Mountains, 8 March), Lt. Alfred B. Bache and Companies F, L, and M of the 5th Cavalry, with some Apache scouts, left Camp Grant and returned to the Pinal Mountains. Along Pinal Creek, near present-day Miami, Arizona, with the help of a captured woman the men found two rancherias on their northern flank. Planning a dawn attack, Bache sent 24 soldiers and 15 White Mountain scouts under Lt. Ben Reilly and Archie McIntosh up the creek to get on the far side of the camp.

Bache let Reilly have the honor of attacking the larger camp because it was Reilly's first Indian-fighting experience and Bache wanted to give him a chance to distinguish himself. Bache moved in to surround his target and his men shivered in the night waiting for dawn. Reilly's men had to wade through Pinal Creek and reached the attack point with soaked legs. Suddenly a shot was fired; Reilly thought it was Bache and Bache thought it was Reilly. Both forces fired, jumped up, and charged the rancherias.

The premature attack may have allowed more Indians to escape than otherwise might have; nevertheless, the soldiers devastated the Apaches. Reilly's men killed 17, while Bache's accounted for 31. Together they captured 50 women and children. Bache regretted that many noncombatants were killed, but he also regretted that chiefs Chunz, Chan-daisi, and Cochinay were not among the dead.[647]

28 APRIL 1874
ARAVAIPA MOUNTAINS (Southeast Arizona)

Lt. Walter S. Schuyler, 5th Cavalry, with a detachment of Company K of that regiment, guided by Al Sieber and over 100 Indians, continued on their three-month scout (see Superstition Mountains, 25 March). From the Superstitions they went to the Sierra Anchas, then down to the Pinals and into the Aravaipa (Galiuros) Mountains east of old Camp Grant. There, the vanguard, led by Sgt. Rudy Stauffer and the tough cavalrymen of Company K, attacked an Apache rancheria, killing 23 and capturing 12. There were no army casualties.[648]

17–18 MAY 1874
FOUR PEAKS (Roosevelt, Arizona)

Continuing his campaign (see previous entry), Lt. Walter Schuyler drove his Company K, 5th Cavalry, and Indian scouts with little rest. After returning to Camp Verde on 10 May for a four-day layover, the command was off to the Mazatzal Mountains at the junction of Tonto Creek and the Salt River. In the Four Peaks area, they ran into two rancherias on two successive days, killing 38 Apaches and capturing 12. Schuyler returned to Camp Verde on 25 May, after one of the longest and most successful scouts on record.[649]

21 JUNE 1874
BUFFALO CREEK (Buffalo, Oklahoma)

Maj. Charles E. Compton, 6th Cavalry, with a detachment of Company G, 6th Cavalry, and a detachment of Company A, 3rd Infantry, were on the road from Camp Supply to Fort Dodge as a mail escort. Just south of Buffalo Creek they were attacked by about 30 Cheyennes, who wounded one soldier and one civilian. Two Cheyennes were thought to be wounded.[650]

24 JUNE 1874
BEAR CREEK REDOUBT (Ashland, Kansas)

After suffering the 21 June ambush (see previous entry), Maj. Charles E. Compton and his men continued north as escort of the mail to Fort Dodge. They pulled into the redoubt on upper Bear Creek, a new post about 12 miles north of old Bear Creek Station and 33 miles south of Fort Dodge. Cheyennes attacked the party again, but the soldiers were in a more defensible position. The Indians came out badly, having four killed and several wounded.[651]

27 JUNE 1874
ADOBE WALLS (Borger, Texas)

During the early 1870s, buffalo hunters had been increasingly decimating the herds that the nomadic Indians needed for their existence. Encouraged by the Comanche medicine man Isatai (Wolf Ass), who claimed

Adobe Walls (Texas)

he could belch up an endless supply of bullets as well as make the warriors immune to soldier bullets, the angry Indians were ready to strike back. Perhaps 300 warriors, including Cheyennes, Kiowas, and Comanches, selected the post at Adobe Walls as their target. Chiefs included Mow-way, Wild Horse, Lone Wolf, White Horse, and Big Bow, but the leader was the half-white, half-Quahadi Comanche Quanah Parker.

At the fort, about one mile up Adobe Creek from the abandoned Bent's Fort, lived 28 civilian buffalo hunters, some storekeepers, and one woman, the wife of William Olds. For days, word was going around that Indians were in the vicinity attacking buffalo hunters, so those at Adobe Creek kept a watchful eye. As fate would have it, a main ridgepole in James Hanrahan's saloon broke at 2 A.M. and awoke the sleeping men. They pitched in to repair the damage and thus were up when the attack began.

Sleeping outside in a wagon, the two Scheidler brothers were killed in the first charge. The people in Hanrahan's were able to make ready, and their opening fire alerted those sleeping elsewhere. Eleven men defended Hanrahan's; 12 defended Myers and Leonard's store, 300 feet to the north; and Rath and Wright's store, 200 feet south of Hanrahan's, was protected by 6 men and Mrs. Olds.

In the semidarkness the Indians snaked around the buildings as warriors fired into windows and doors. Quanah and others even climbed onto roofs and tried to make holes through which to shoot. Blacksmith Tom

O'Keefe, who had been sleeping near his shop, got up and ran into Rath's store, shouting warning. Quick use of the revolver was the defenders' salvation.

A man who would later become one of the famous names of the West, Bat Masterson, bedded down in the corral, ran to the saloon. Near the corral, a warrior fired through the fence and fatally wounded hunter Billy Tyler. The firepower and marksmanship of the buffalo hunters prevented the warriors from breaking in. The Indians fell back but kept up the siege for two days, though their initial enthusiasm had been severely blunted.

One of the warriors was a black man who carried a bugle, probably a deserter from the U.S. Cavalry. Tired of hearing his bugle blaring, three hunters leveled their rifles and fired at the man as he hid behind a wagon. When he leapt out into the open, reported Masterson, one of the hunters "plunked a big forty-calibre bullet through him, and he bugled no more."[652]

On the third day, 23-year-old guide Billy Dixon made his famous long shot, hitting with his .50-caliber Sharps an Indian on a hill 1,500 yards away. Finally, a wounded Quanah Parker withdrew his warriors, many of them very angry at the false promises of Isatai, who could not even protect his own pony from being killed. Many years later, Quanah said of the buffalo hunters' shooting, "They killed us in sight and out of sight."[653]

In addition to the two Scheidlers and Tyler, William Olds accidentally shot himself in the head while climbing down from a rooftop lookout at Rath's store. Seven Cheyennes and six Comanches were known to be killed, but there certainly may have been more. About 20 were wounded.[654]

After the attack, the occupants of Adobe Walls realized it was not safe to operate a post so deep in hostile territory, and the place was abandoned. By August 1874 the Indians had destroyed the buildings. The Adobe Walls battle also led to the Red River War, which would result in the final subjugation of the local tribes.

3 JULY 1874
HENNESSEY WAGON TRAIN (Hennessey, Oklahoma)

Wagonmaster Patrick Hennessey and three drivers were taking supplies to feed the Kiowas and Comanches at Fort Sill, in spite of having been warned of danger, after Agent James M. Haworth had made repeated pleas for food. About ten miles north of the Cimarron River on Turkey Creek, at present-day Hennessey, Oklahoma, Cheyennes overwhelmed the train.

All four men were killed and mutilated. Hennessey was chained to a wagon wheel, partially buried under his oats and corn, and burned alive.[655]

4 JULY 1874
SNAKE MOUNTAIN (Lysite, Wyoming)

After their Sun Dance in June, the Lakotas, along with the Cheyennes and Arapahos, agreed to make a great raid on the Shoshones of Wind River.

After they crossed the Bighorns, the Indians disagreed as to whether the raid was for war and spoils, or just for horses. The Arapahos broke off and moved their camp into the mountains between the eastern Owl Creek Range and the southern Bighorns.

Shoshone scouts reported the Arapahos' location to authorities at Camp Brown. Capt. Alfred E. Bates was chosen to take his 60 men of Company B, 2nd Cavalry, with 20 Shoshone scouts under Lt. Robert H. Young, 4th Infantry; 167 Shoshones under Chief Washakie; and several civilians to hunt them down. Bates left on the evening of 1 July and headed northeast. The Arapahos, in the meantime, had moved their camp, and it was not until 4 July that Bates found them—112 lodges along a deep ravine and creek branching off the head of Nowood Creek below Snake Mountain (now called Bates Creek and Battle Mountain).

In the early light, Bates saw that he needed to get around to the other side of the valley to surround the camp, but he knew he had little chance of surprise when the Shoshone scouts began singing battle songs. "Their howls were terrific," Bates reported.[656]

The captain ordered the Shoshones to follow him down the ravine and charge through at his rear. Because of the rough ground, he left men behind with the broken-down horses and the packs. He had only 35 men to carry out the charge. The Arapahos, having been alerted, fired from the ravine, which was 15 feet wide and 10 feet deep. Bates drove them out and down the gully.

In less than half an hour, the Arapahos had taken refuge in the cliffs above. Firing from the rocks, the Arapahos killed two soldiers and wounded three in just a few minutes. Lt. Young, wounded, was in danger of being captured when a civilian named Cosgrove pulled him to safety. Meanwhile, Bates had seen nothing of his Shoshones, and he ordered his men to pull back. The Shoshones, however, were in the thick of the fight. Pe-a-quite fought his way into the village and was killed, and another brave died in a hand-to-hand fight in front of a lodge.

When Bates moved out, the Arapahos could not chase after them, having lost too many horses. The command's medical supplies were lost during the battle, and the surgeon had nothing with which to treat the wounded. Washakie lost a sack of scalps when his captured gray horse got away from him and returned to the Arapahos.

Bates lost Pvts. James M. Walker and Peter Engall, and Lt. Young and Pvts. French, Gable, and Pearson were wounded. The Shoshones lost two and three were wounded. Of the Arapahos, 25 were killed and about 20 were wounded, including Chief Black Coal, who was hit in the chest and hand and later got the name Tag-ge-tha-the (Shot-off-Fingers).

Still believing that the Shoshones had failed him, Bates lamented that with more men, he could have completely destroyed the village.[657]

12 JULY 1874
LOST VALLEY (Loving, Texas)

When Indians raided into Jack and Young Counties in the summer of 1874, Maj. John B. Jones took his Frontier Battalion of Rangers to the scene. Jones had a 25-man escort and Capt. G. W. Stevens's Company B with him as he rode across the Salt Creek Prairie. The 36 men came across an Indian trail of what Jones thought were more than 125 horsemen. The trail went by the Salt Creek Prairie, where the Warren Wagon Train was attacked three years earlier (see Salt Creek Prairie/Warren Wagon Train, 18 May 1871), then into Lost Valley, in eastern Young County. There, Kiowas Lone Wolf and Mamanti were waiting for them. They had just unsuccessfully chased four cowboys and were disappointed. Some of the warriors wanted to turn back, but Lone Wolf urged them to stay. Just then they spotted Jones's party, all wearing white hats.

Mamanti put out a few decoys to lure the Texans in, and they took the bait. The Kiowas charged out of the mesquite thickets. While the Indians circled, the Rangers formed up, but they had no cover. Jones charged through the Indians and reached cover in a brushy ravine. Two Rangers, Lee Corn and George Moore, were wounded. Another, Billy Glass, was shot off his horse and called out to the others. His comrades gave a heavy covering fire while three men dashed out to pull him in.

The Rangers settled down for a siege, but they were about a mile from water. Late in the hot afternoon, two of them, Mel Porter and David Bailey, volunteered to make a dash for Cameron Creek. They were filling canteens when 25 Kiowas charged them. Porter dove in the water and swam until he got clear, then crawled out and made his escape. Bailey, however, was lanced off his horse and chopped to pieces.

Satisfied that they had killed at least one of the hated Texans, the Kiowas left the area. Actually they had killed two, because Glass soon died from his wounds. Jones mistakenly thought he had hit six Kiowas, but in fact the Indians had no losses.[658]

22–23 AUGUST 1874
ANADARKO/WICHITA AGENCY (Anadarko, Oklahoma)

After receiving word of possible trouble at the Wichita Agency, Col. John "Black Jack" Davidson, 10th Cavalry, left Fort Sill with Companies E, H, and L on the 37-mile ride north. It was ration day at the agency, and Chief Red Food's 60 lodges of Noconee Comanches were stealing and butchering the beeves of the Wichitas, Caddos, and Delawares. Arriving on 22 August, Davidson ordered Red Food to surrender himself and his band as prisoners.

Kiowa chief Satanta (White Bear)
—Courtesy Denver Public Library,
Western History Department

He sent Lt. Samuel L. Woodward with 40 men to collect the Noconees' bows and arrows. But Red Food refused to give up the weapons.

As mounted soldiers held the reins of Red Food's horse, nearby Kiowas began to taunt the Noconees, saying they would be women if they surrendered. Unable to endure this, Red Food leapt from his horse and waved his blanket, trying to stampede the soldiers' horses. The cavalrymen opened fire on him. Several Kiowas and Comanches fired back, and the fight was on.

In charge of the agency, Capt. Gaines Lawson and his Company I, 25th Infantry, moved in to clear the area. The Indians rushed across the Washita River or took to the hills, but some came back—including the Kiowas Woman's Heart, Satanta, and Big Tree—and returned fire under cover between the agency buildings.

With two of his men hit, Davidson wanted to attack, but because there were so many friendly Indians mixed in he did not want to risk it. Davidson charged a number of warriors firing from the trees along the river, and they disappeared. Later some of the Indians attacked and killed civilians several miles from the agency.

The Indians returned the next morning to find Davidson's men entrenched around the agency. In ensuing crossfire, the Comanche Chee-na-boney was shot in the head. The warriors lit a prairie fire to burn the soldiers out, but the troopers made a backfire to stop the flames. The Indians finally realized they could not take the agency and gave up the assault.

The Indians wounded 4 troopers and killed 4 civilians. Davidson reported 16 Indians killed.[659]

30 AUGUST 1874
MULBERRY CREEK/PALO DURO (Brice, Texas)

In Texas, the Adobe Walls attack (see 27 June) incited the Red River War against the Cheyennes, Kiowas, and Comanches. Five columns of troops converged on the the Staked Plains, in the Texas Panhandle. Col. Nelson A. Miles led one of them, comprising 600 men of Companies C, D, E, and L of the 5th Infantry and Companies A, D, F, G, H, I, L, and M of the 6th Cavalry, plus some civilians and Delaware scouts. Going south from Fort Dodge, the column found a main Indian trail at the Sweetwater River and continued on to the eastern edge of the Staked Plains (Llano Estacado).

At 8 A.M. on 30 August, near Mulberry Creek, Lt. Frank D. Baldwin's scouts entered a canyon and were immediately attacked by about 250 Cheyennes concealed in the bluffs. The frontiersmen and the Delawares under Fall Leaf held their ground until the rest of the cavalry came to reinforce. The troops pressed up the canyon, and as they advanced, the Cheyennes withdrew, but they gathered up Kiowas and Comanches in the process. There may have been 500 or more warriors engaged in the moving battle.

Capt. Adna R. Chaffee called out to the 6th Cavalrymen to keep moving. Even the Gatling guns, under Lt. James W. Pope, got into the action. Every time the Indians tried to make a stand, the artillery and Gatling guns would open up, followed by a charge. The chase proceeded 20 miles, across Mulberry Creek, Battle Creek, Hackberry Creek, and the Prairie Dog Town Fork of the Red River, then up Tule Canyon. The heat and lack of water forced some troopers to open the veins of their arms to moisten their parched mouths with their own blood.

Finally, the Indians climbed out of the canyon and fled onto the Staked Plains, and Miles found it impossible to pursue any farther. He pulled back to wait for provision wagons from Camp Supply.

The soldiers suffered only two men wounded, while about 17 Indians were killed.[660]

9–14 SEPTEMBER 1874
LYMAN WAGON TRAIN FIGHT (Allison, Texas)

Capt. Wyllys Lyman and 104 men of Company I, 5th Infantry, and detachments of the 6th Cavalry, Companies H and I, were taking 36 supply wagons from Camp Supply to Miles's troopers near the Llano Estacado (see previous entry). On 9 September, after crossing the Canadian River,

Col. Nelson A. Miles
—Courtesy Denver Public Library,
Western History Department

the soldiers were rolling south when about 70 Kiowas began to harass them. Sixth Cavalry skirmishers kept the Indians back long enough for the train to advance about 12 miles, to within one mile of the Washita River, near the mouth of Gageby Creek. There, Lyman's men ran smack into about 400 more Kiowas and Comanches under Lone Wolf, Mamanti, Satanta, Big Bow, and Big Tree.

Lyman speedily corralled the wagons and formed the men into lines at the front and rear of the train. The charging Indians broke around them and passed on. A Sgt. De Armond was killed and Lt. Granville Lewis was severely wounded, but the train was still intact.

The warriors contented themselves with long-range firing for the rest of the day, but toward evening, they mounted up and began circling the wagons, putting on an unusually fervent display of horsemanship and bravado. The soldiers threw up dirt breastworks, and sporadic fire continued through the night.

The next day was a repeat of the action. The soldiers were becoming crazed with thirst, tantalizingly close to the water of the Washita River. Toward midnight, scout William Schmalsle volunteered to ride to Camp Supply for help. Some soldiers created a diversion while he sneaked out.

As the days passed, the soldiers became more desperate. Defying orders they broke into the wagon stores, hacking open cans of fruit and drinking the juice. On the 12th, a heavy rain set in, which slaked their thirst but also brought on a cold snap that left them shivering in puddles of mud. The next day it looked like most of the Indians had withdrawn, but the soldiers did not leave their trenches for fear of an ambush. Finally, on the morning of 14 September, a rescue party appeared in the north. Schmalsle had gotten through to Camp Supply.

The Kiowa losses were about 13 killed. One soldier was killed, and one officer and three enlisted men were wounded, a surprisingly low casualty count considering the situation. Lyman received a promotion after the incident, and a number of his men were awarded the Medal of Honor.[661]

12 SEPTEMBER 1874
BUFFALO WALLOW FIGHT (Allison, Texas)

After his fight at Mulberry Creek (see Mulberry Creek/Palo Duro, 30 August), Col. Nelson A. Miles waited ten days for provisions to arrive. Hearing no word, he sent out four soldiers and two civilian scouts under Sgt. Z.T. Woodhall, 6th Cavalry, to determine the supply train's whereabouts. The six left on 10 September, heading north.

Two days later, nearing the south bank of the Washita River around Gageby Creek, the scouts encountered over 100 Kiowas and Comanches, some of whom had been fighting Capt. Wyllys Lyman and his men on the other side of the river (see previous entry). The party was quickly surrounded, and almost at once, four of the six men were hit and wounded. Scout Billy Dixon, who had made a name for himself at the Adobe Walls battle (see 27 June), led his companions to the dubious cover of a nearby buffalo wallow, about six feet square and a foot and a half deep. They kept up a brave front, firing enough to thwart warriors who came too close.

As the scouts lay as flat as possible to avoid Indian bullets, the same cold rain that was also pummeling Lyman's men filled the wallow and almost drowned them. By nightfall, the warriors had backed off, but it would be 36 more hours before help would arrive, in the form of Maj. William R. Price with his column of 8th Cavalrymen from Fort Union in New Mexico.

Scout Amos Chapman, Sgt. Woodhall, and Pvt. John Harrington were wounded, and Pvt. George W. Smith was killed. Chapman thought they had not killed any Indians in the fight, but the army report stated that ten were killed. All six men were awarded the Medal of Honor, but Dixon's and Chapman's were later revoked because they were civilians; Dixon refused to return his.[662]

12 SEPTEMBER 1874
DRY FORK OF THE WASHITA RIVER (Canadian, Texas)

Leading one of the five columns converging on the Texas Panhandle in the Red River War (see Mulberry Creek/Palo Duro, 30 August), Maj.

William R. Price left Fort Bascom on 28 August with Companies C, K, and L, 8th Cavalry, two howitzers, and some Navajo scouts. The column moved down the Canadian River and across to the Salt Fork of the Red. Price met Col. Nelson A. Miles and his column near Mulberry Creek on 7 September, then went north to find his wagon train, which had split from him on the Canadian.

On the 12th, near the Dry Fork of the Washita (also called Gageby Creek), Price ran into the hornet's nest of Comanches and Kiowas who had been fighting Capt. Wyllys Lyman's wagon train (see 9–14 September). With fewer than 200 men, Price decided not to risk an all-out engagement.

After circling Price's men for two hours, the Indians withdrew. Price reported two Indians killed and six wounded, with no army casualties except 14 horses.

Two days later, Price found the survivors of the fight at the buffalo wallow (see previous entry). After having his surgeon examine them, Price moved on, leaving them for Miles to pick up and missing Lyman's besieged train.[663]

17 SEPTEMBER 1874
CAVE CREEK (Cave Creek, Arizona)

After Indians killed a prospector on Humbug Creek, near the lower Agua Fria River, and a herder in the same vicinity, at Marysville Ferry on the Salt River, a call went out to Al Sieber and his scouts at Camp Verde. Sieber and a party of Tonto scouts, accompanied by a detachment of Company K, 5th Cavalry, under Sgt. A. Garner, arrived in the area within a week. The Tontos quickly determined the raiders were Apache-Mojaves, and they were off like bloodhounds.

Four days of trailing brought them to the headwaters of Cave Creek. They came upon the rancheria so suddenly that both sides were surprised, and there was nothing for Garner and company to do but attack. The Apache-Mojaves, about 25 in number, dove into the bush and exchanged fire, bullet for bullet. Some of the Mojaves were seen to fire breech-loading Springfields.

The soldiers and scouts decimated the band, killing 14 and capturing 2. Garner had one man killed and two wounded.[664]

28 SEPTEMBER 1874
PALO DURO CANYON (Canyon, Texas)

Another column converging on the northern Staked Plains during the Red River War (see Mulberry Creek/Palo Duro, 30 August) was Col. Ranald Mackenzie's eight companies of the 4th Cavalry, four companies of the 10th Infantry, one of the 11th Infantry, and a scout detachment of about 30 civilians, Seminoles, Lipans, and Tonkawas. Mackenzie moved the men north, up the edge of the caprock, hindered by cold rains and worsening weather.

Having been harried by soldiers, the Kiowas, Comanches, and Cheyennes had taken refuge in the Palo Duro Canyon, where they hoped to make their winter quarters. With the aid of captured Comanchero Jose Tafoya, whom Mackenzie had strung up until he nearly strangled, the troopers found the Indian camp. On Tafoya's "advice," they moved from the head of Tule Canyon, across the trackless plain, to the yawning edge of Palo Duro's wall. Below them lay over 200 lodges of unsuspecting Kiowas of Lone Wolf and Mamanti, Comanches of Ohamatai and Quanah Parker, and Cheyennes of Iron Shirt.

Mackenzie directed his men to snake their way down the nearly 500-foot canyon wall. Although the soldiers fired shots before they gained the bottom, the Indians took little notice, believing that the troopers could not reach them. When Mackenzie's men finally descended, panic seized the camps and most of the people fled.

The soldiers burned the tipis and captured an immense horse herd, perhaps 2,000 head. Determined not to let the horses be recaptured, Mackenzie had the Indian scouts select the best ones, then ordered the remainder shot, about 1,400 of them. For years, the site was marked by piles of horse bones.

One soldier was killed in the attack and several were wounded. Although Mackenzie's men killed only four Indians, the Palo Duro fight was devastating to the bands. Without horses, lodges, or supplies for the winter, they would either starve or have to go to the reservations. Many chose the latter course.[665]

27 OCTOBER 1874
CAVE CREEK (Cave Creek, Arizona)

After the Cave Creek fight in September (see 17 September), Sgt. A. Garner, Al Sieber, and the Apache scouts returned to Camp Verde. But there were a dozen hostile Indians still unaccounted for, so on 19 October Sgt. Rudolph Stauffer, a detachment of 5th Cavalrymen of K Company, and Al Sieber and his Apache scouts went back to Cave Creek to see if any had returned there. Sure enough, at the head of the creek they found the camp of Big Rump's band. They killed eight warriors and captured five women.[666]

1 NOVEMBER 1874
SUNSET PASS (Winslow, Arizona)

After Tonto Apaches killed a mail carrier near the Little Colorado River on the Mogollon Plateau, Lt. Charles King and Lt. George O. Eaton, 5th Cavalry, took detachments of Companies A and K, with half a dozen Indian scouts, to the scene. They arrived at Sunset Pass, about 20 miles southwest of present-day Winslow, Arizona, early on 1 November.

King, Eaton, and Sgt. Bernard Taylor set out to climb East Sunset Mountain when they ran into an ambush. King was badly wounded in the arm and shoulder. They returned fire and killed one Indian. Eaton tried to get his scouts to go after the ambushers, but they declined. "A more abject set of cowards it has never been my fortune to witness," Eaton growled in his report.[667]

3 NOVEMBER 1874
LAGUNAS QUATRAS (Tahoka, Texas)

After the Palo Duro Canyon fight (see 28 September), Col. Ranald Mackenzie took Companies A, D, F, H, I, K, and L of the 4th Cavalry and 32 Indian scouts south along the eastern edge of the Staked Plains. At Lagunas Quatras (Four Lakes), he attacked a Comanche camp, killed 2 warriors, captured 19 women and children, and took 144 horses.[668]

6 NOVEMBER 1874
MCCLELLAN CREEK (Alanreed, Texas)

Lt. Henry J. Farnsworth and 28 men of Company H, 8th Cavalry, went on a patrol from Maj. William R. Price's command on the Washita River (see Dry Fork of the Washita River, 12 September). On the headwaters of McClellan Creek, south of the present-day town of Pampa, Texas, 100 stirred-up Cheyenne warriors under Grey Beard attacked the party. The Cheyennes were more than a match for the 8th Cavalrymen, pinning them down from 1:30 P.M. until nightfall. Farnsworth pulled his company out under cover of darkness, abandoning his dead on the field, where the bodies were mutilated by the victorious warriors.

Grey Beard's losses were about four men killed and ten wounded; Farnsworth's were two killed and four wounded.[669]

8 NOVEMBER 1874
WAGON CHARGE ON MCCLELLAN CREEK (Jericho, Texas)

Two days after after Grey Beard defeated Lt. Henry J. Farnsworth (see previous entry), his Cheyenne village of about 100 lodges and 200 warriors was hit by more soldiers. Lt. Frank D. Baldwin and Troop D of the 6th Cavalry and Company D of the 5th Infantry, heading to Camp Supply with 23 empty wagons, had permission to attack any hostile Indians they encountered.

Upon spotting Grey Beard's camp on 8 November, Baldwin formed his wagons in a double column, placed the infantry in them, and surrounded them with mounted cavalry. At 8:30 A.M., the bugler sounded the charge and the unorthodox assemblage galloped into the village. Grey Beard's warriors managed to hold the soldiers off for a time while the women and children scattered. Then the warriors fell back, making two stands to give their families more time to escape, as Baldwin chased them about 12 miles across the prairie.

Lt. Baldwin's command had no casualties, but he estimated that the Cheyennes lost about 20 warriors.

When the soldiers returned to destroy the camp, they found two young white girls, age five and seven. They were Adelaide and Julia German, whose parents and brothers had been killed in an attack in western Kansas in September. Their two older sisters, Catherine and Sophia, age 13 and 18, had also been hostages at the camp, but the Cheyennes had taken them during the evacuation. The soldiers were emotionally overcome when they learned of the girls' plight. One teamster remarked, "I have driven my mules over these plains for three months, but I will stay forever or until we get them other girls."[670]

Eventually, after the tribes surrendered, Catherine and Sophia were released. Because the four girls had no other family, Col. Nelson A. Miles became guardian of the youngest three and saw to their upbringing and education.[671]

18 NOVEMBER 1874
BROWNWOOD (Brownwood, Texas)

Lt. B. F. Best, with a 16-man detachment of Company E of the Frontier Battalion, Texas Rangers, was patrolling in Coleman County and found a trail heading east into Brown County. After following it for 20 miles, the Rangers came upon a band of Comanches near Brownwood, Texas. In the fight, the men killed three Indians, wounded one, and confiscated an assortment of weapons. Two Rangers were wounded.[672]

21 NOVEMBER 1874
ROBERTS'S FIGHT (Mason, Texas)

Lt. Dan W. Roberts, with a detachment of Company D of Maj. John B. Jones's Frontier Battalion of Texas Rangers and part of Jones's escort under Lt. L. P. Beavert, came upon an Indian trail in southern Menard County. The tracks headed east through the hill country toward Mason, Texas. Roberts soon found 11 Comanches, and in a running fight, he killed five and wounded and captured a sixth.

By that time, Roberts's horses were exhausted, but a detachment of the better-mounted escort under Lt. Beavert continued the chase. Soon Beavert's horses began to give out one by one, but he and two men rode on and cornered the remaining six Comanches in a cave on the banks of a small creek. They killed one and wounded another before the others could escape.[673]

25–26 NOVEMBER 1874
SNOW LAKE (Snowflake, Arizona)

The failure of Lt. Charles King and Lt. George O. Eaton's probe for renegade Tonto Apaches (see Sunset Pass, 1 November) necessitated another expedition. Leaving 17 November, Eaton led detachments of Companies A and K, 5th Cavalry, with Al Sieber and his Apache scouts, east from Camp Verde along West Clear Creek, then above the Mogollon Rim, trending east and north.

On the 24th Eaton ran into scouts from another expedition under Capt. Robert H. Montgomery, who were covering the territory farther east. Though Eaton was told he did not have to pursue in that direction, he continued anyway. The next day, Eaton found an Indian trail that Montgomery had missed and followed it. Two hours after sunset, a small band of Tontos blundered right into them. In the ensuing skirmish, Eaton's men killed two warriors and captured six women and children, with no loss to themselves.

Sieber questioned the captives about the location of the rest of the band. Early the next morning, he and his scouts went off after them. After chasing them for about 12 miles, Sieber's scouts killed 1 and captured 3 women, then abandoned the pursuit.[674]

1 DECEMBER 1874
CANYON CREEK (Central Arizona)

Capt. Robert H. Montgomery was searching for Apaches on the Mogollon Rim north of Camp Apache with a detachment of Company B, 5th Cavalry, and a party of Indian scouts. He had missed the trail that Lt. George O. Eaton found (see previous entry), but six days after Eaton's fight, Montgomery ran down his own quarry. In the Canyon Creek area, he ran into a group of Tontos, larger than the band Eaton encountered. His men killed 8, wounded 2, and captured 14 with no casualties of their own.[675]

—1875—

6 APRIL 1875
SAND HILLS FIGHT (El Reno, Oklahoma)

In the spring of 1875, many Indians were surrendering to the U.S. Army. The bands of Stone Calf and Grey Beard were told to camp near the Darlington Agency on the North Fork of the Canadian River while the officers at the agency quietly tried to figure out which Indians to hold responsible for bringing on the Red River War. Thirty-three Indians were selected as the worst of the lot, to be sent to Fort Marion, Florida, for incarceration.

Guarding the agency was Lt. Col. Thomas H. Neill, 6th Cavalry, stationed with Company M of the 6th Cavalry, and Companies D and M of the 10th Cavalry. On 6 April the Cheyenne Black Horse was taunted by a Cheyenne woman as an army blacksmith was placing him in leg irons. Black Horse knocked the blacksmith down and ran from the enclosure. As he fled across the compound, he was shot down.

While firing at Black Horse, the soldiers hit other Cheyennes. Some produced weapons and began firing back. Fearing they would all be killed, the bands fled. About 150 Cheyennes from White Horse's Dog Soldier camp across the river soon joined the others. They ran to some sand hills along the North Canadian River, where they had a cache of arms and ammunition.

The cavalrymen, along with a detachment of 5th Infantry, surrounded the sand hills and fought until dark. During the night, the Cheyennes fled. The Indians lost 11 men while the soldiers suffered 19 wounded, one of them mortally.[676]

23 APRIL 1875
SAPPA CREEK (Oberlin, Kansas)

Some of the Indians who fled from the Sand Hills Fight (see previous entry) reached the camp of the Cheyenne Little Bull, 25 miles upriver from the Darlington Agency. The chief had balked at surrendering, and this latest incident sealed his decision. With about 60 people, Little Bull headed north.

Troops had been mobilized in Kansas to cut off the Indians. Lt. Austin Henely and his Company H, 6th Cavalry, entrained in Las Animas, Colorado and sped east to Fort Wallace, where they joined Lt. Christian C. Hewitt and Company K, 19th Infantry. The troops marched northeast, coming upon some buffalo hunters who pointed out an Indian trail to the north, toward the Middle Fork of the Sappa River, in the southeast corner of present-day Rawlins County, Kansas. The soldiers followed it, with the hunters joining them.

At dawn on 23 April, the troopers came upon a sleeping camp and attacked. Instead of fighting back, however, the Indians came out requesting to parley. Henely and his men had already captured the Cheyennes' horses. Through an interpreter, Henely told the Indians to surrender, but they refused, demanding that their horses be returned. Then someone fired. The troops, already surrounding the camp, put in a heavy fire, aided by the long-range shooting of the buffalo hunters. The battle lasted three hours.

Sgt. Theodore Papier and Pvt. Robert Theims were killed. The troopers killed 19 warriors, including Little Bull, Tangle Hair, and White Bear, as well as 8 women and children. However, at least another 33, or more than half the camp, escaped. Henely captured 134 horses and took no prisoners. He was later censured for perpetrating a massacre.[677]

25 APRIL 1875
EAGLE NEST CROSSING (Langtry, Texas)

Lt. John L. Bullis, 24th Infantry, and three Seminole-Negro scouts, Sgt. John Ward and Pvts. Isaac Payne and Pompey Factor, were trailing a raiding party who had about 75 stolen horses. On the west side of the Pecos River, at a place called Eagle Nest, the pursuers discovered about 30 Comanches preparing to herd the stolen stock across the river. Bullis and the scouts dismounted and crept through the brush until they were about 75 yards away, then they opened fire.

In a 45-minute fight, Bullis captured and lost the horses twice. His men killed three Comanches and wounded one, but the firepower of their single-shot Springfields was no match for the Indians' Winchesters, and the four of them made a dash for their horses. The three scouts made it, but Bullis was not with them—he had been cut off from his horse.

Shouting that they must not leave their lieutenant, Ward mounted up and went back for Bullis while Payne and Factor put out as much covering fire as they could. Swinging Bullis onto his horse, Ward caught a bullet in his carbine sling, then another shattered the gun stock. All four of them got away safely, and the three scouts won Medals of Honor.[678]

8 MAY 1875
SPY KNOB (Jermyn, Texas)

In the spring of 1875, seven Comanches left the Fort Sill Reservation and went to Jack County, Texas, to steal horses. They ran off several from near the Loving ranch in Lost Valley. About 20 Texas Rangers from Maj. John B. Jones's Frontier Battalion spotted the Indians from Spy Knob, a hill north of Jermyn, Texas. The Rangers gave chase and killed five of the raiders in a running fight.

Jones reported that the Comanches had been well-armed and fought desperately. He noted that one of them was a woman. Another had reddish hair. The Rangers cut off the heads of the dead and sent them to Washington, where it was confirmed that they were in fact Comanches. The auburn-haired man was identified as Ay-cufty, meaning "Reddish," and the leader was Black Coyote. The woman was the chief's wife. The Fort Sill agent had given them hunting passes and was extremely angered that they had been killed.[679]

1 JULY 1875
EAST VERDE RIVER (Central Arizona)

In the summer of 1875, Capt. George M. Brayton and detachments of Companies A and B, 8th Infantry, with Al Sieber and his Indian scouts, patrolled out of Camp Verde. On 1 July, on the East Verde River, they interrupted a camp of Apaches who were dining on mule meat from stock stolen from area settlements. The soldiers and scouts burst in and killed 25 Indians and captured 9. One enlisted man was wounded.[680]

4 JULY 1875
RED ROCK CANYON (Sedona, Arizona)

Continuing their patrols along the Mogollon Rim, Capt. George M. Brayton and his party (see previous entry) found another Apache camp on Independence Day, at the head of Red Rock Canyon. They killed five Indians and captured six.[681]

CA. 25 AUGUST 1875
BIG LAKE (Big Lake, Texas)

Near present-day Big Lake, Texas, the Texas Ranger Frontier Battalion confronted a band of Lipan Apaches. The Rangers dismounted and advanced on foot, firing as they went. They hit several Indian ponies and wounded one warrior, while the rest fled.

Spying a rider pull an old warrior up onto his horse and ride into a grove of mesquite trees, Ranger James B. Gillett went after them, firing his Sharps carbine. When Gillett killed their pony, the old man hit the ground running, and the rider was pinned under the horse. Gillett saw that the rider was a white youth with red hair. He was Herman Lehmann, who was captured when he was ten years old. Lehmann escaped, and he would live with the Apaches and Comanches until 1878.

One Lipan was killed and three were wounded in the fight. The Rangers had no casualties.[682]

27 OCTOBER 1875
SMOKY HILL STATION (Russell Springs, Kansas)

On 1 October, 30 Arapaho men and 5 women left the Red Cloud Agency and headed south to join the Southern Arapahos in Indian Territory. After moving through Nebraska and halfway through Kansas, near Smoky Hill Station, in present-day Logan County, Kansas, the group stopped while a few of them backtracked to look for stray ponies.

As they were waiting, a detachment of Company H, 5th Cavalry, under Capt. John M. Hamilton, approached their camp. The Arapahos told Hamilton that they had a letter allowing them to travel to the reservation, but one of the men searching for ponies had it. Hamilton left most of his men at the camp while he took an Arapaho youth to find the man with the pass.

Hamilton found the man just outside the camp and demanded he surrender his pistol. The warrior refused and broke away, and Hamilton fired at him. The Arapahos in the camp heard the shots, and general fighting broke out. Two Indians were killed and one soldier was wounded.

The Arapahos turned themselves in at the Cheyenne and Arapaho Agency in early November.[683]

2 NOVEMBER 1875
PECOS RIVER (Langtry, Texas)

Lt. Col. William R. Shafter, 10th Cavalry, was chasing Indians, probably Comanche, on the Staked Plains on what he believed was the main trail near Cedar Lake when he found another trail heading south. Shafter sent Lt. Andrew Geddes, 25th Infantry, with Companies G and L of the 10th Cavalry and Seminole-Negro scouts to follow it. Geddes trailed the Indians across south Texas as they tried to throw him off the scent. The trail traversed the Staked Plains, crossed the Pecos River below the mouth of Independence Creek, and went south. It appeared to Geddes that the Indians were heading for Mexico.

On 2 November, Geddes finally caught up with the Indians in the rough canyonlands near the mouth of the Pecos River. During the chase, most of the Indians had escaped. Geddes and his men killed only one warrior and captured four women and a small boy. After trudging back to Fort Concho, they had made a 650-mile march.[684]

—1876—

17 MARCH 1876
POWDER RIVER/REYNOLDS'S FIGHT (Moorhead, Montana)

A major campaign began in early 1876 when Gen. George Crook led one of three columns searching for nonreservation Lakotas northwest of the Black Hills. At Fort Fetterman, Crook formed up his 900-man command, which consisted of five companies of the 2nd Cavalry, five companies of the 3rd Cavalry, and two companies of the 4th Infantry. Crook placed the units under the command of Col. Joseph J. Reynolds of the 3rd Cavalry. In the bitter cold on 1 March, they marched north.

Traveling down the Tongue River, the column saw tracks heading east. Crook sent Reynolds with six companies, about 370 men, to follow the trail and attack. On the frigid morning of 17 March, Reynolds found a camp of 105 lodges on the Powder River, just downstream of present-day Moorhead, Montana, under the Cheyenne Old Bear and the Oglala He Dog. The village consisted of about 700 people, of whom 200 were warriors.

Capt. James Egan led off the attack by charging his company, pistols blazing, through the center of the camp. Capt. Anson Mills followed in his wake. The Indians scattered, but from the timbered bluffs they began to put up a stiff resistance. Capt. Henry Noyes captured 700 of the Indians' ponies, making it difficult for them to flee. Soon, the warriors were pressing the soldiers back. Reynolds ordered the village destroyed and fell back 20 miles up the Powder.

Reynolds's losses were four killed and six wounded, while the Lakotas and Cheyennes had only two killed and two wounded.

The troopers awoke the next morning to find the warriors in the process of stealing back about 550 of their ponies. Reynolds had assigned no one to guard them. His officers were acrimonious in their denunciation of his command decisions, and back at Fort Fetterman, Crook proffered court-martial charges against Reynolds.[685]

28 APRIL 1876
GRACIE CREEK (Burwell, Nebraska)

Company A, 23rd Infantry, garrisoned the backwater post of Fort Hartsuff, on the north bank of the North Loup River, near present-day Burwell, Nebraska. The post was built to ease the fears of nearby settlers; its soldiers had never seen any action.

Spotting a small band of Lakotas moving away from the reservation, some settlers assumed they were a war party and notified the fort. Lt. Charles H. Heyl and eight enlisted men, with a small party of civilians, pursued the Indians 20 miles northwest to Gracie Creek. With the sun about to set, the Indians entrenched themselves in a blowout on top of a sand hill.

Heyl knew that if he didn't attack, the Indians would disappear during the night. The civilians, however, refused to join him. Leaving some men to block an escape route, Heyl went up against the Lakotas' position with only three soldiers. They charged to the rim of the blowout, and, in simultaneous volleys of gunfire, Sgt. William H. Dougherty was shot dead, one Indian was killed, and a second was wounded. Heyl and the remaining two soldiers retreated.

After dark, the Indians left, and there was nothing for Heyl to do but return Dougherty's body to the fort. Nevertheless, Heyl and two of his men, Cpl. Patrick T. Leonard and Pvt. Jeptha Lytton, received Medals of Honor.[686]

17 JUNE 1876
ROSEBUD CREEK (Decker, Montana)

After the failure at Powder River (see 17 March), Gen. George Crook went out again in search of nonreservation Lakotas and Cheyennes. He left Fort Fetterman on 29 May with ten troops of the 3rd Cavalry, five of the 2nd, two companies of the 4th Infantry, and three of the 9th—about 47 officers and 1,000 enlisted men. Later 176 Crow and 86 Shoshone auxiliaries joined the command.

After traveling down the Tongue River, Crook crossed over to Rosebud Creek. There, on the morning of 17 June, the expedition was attacked by more than 800 Lakota and Cheyenne warriors with an enthusiasm for battle seldom seen. The fight raged for six hours, up and down the broken terrain, on a battlefield that extended several miles along upper Rosebud Creek. Cavalry alternately charged and retired. Indians repeatedly dashed in to shoot, counted coup, and pulled back. On several occasions, the soldiers were saved by the Crow and Shoshone scouts, who did more than their fair share of fighting that day.

After Capt. Anson Mills led a long flank march that threatened their rear, the Lakotas and Cheyennes withdrew. Crook, left in possession of the battlefield, claimed victory, although in fact it was a draw at best. On Crook's side, 9 soldiers were killed and 23 were wounded, and 1 Indian scout was killed and 7 were wounded. The scouts collected 13 scalps. The Lakota leader Crazy Horse later acknowledged that 36 Lakotas and Cheyennes were killed and 63 were wounded.[687]

25 JUNE 1876
LITTLE BIGHORN (Crow Agency, Montana)

The eastern column of the 1876 campaign (see Powder River/Reynolds's Fight, 17 March) left Fort Abraham Lincoln on 17 May, under the command of Gen. Alfred H. Terry. It consisted of all 12 companies of the 7th Cavalry under Lt. Col. George A. Custer, two companies of the 17th Infantry,

Site of Rosebud Creek battle (Montana)

one of the 6th Infantry, a detachment of 20th Infantry with Gatling guns, and 40 Arikara scouts—a total of about 925 officers and enlisted men.

On 22 June, Custer's 7th—including 617 soldiers, 30 scouts, and 20 civilians—marched up Rosebud Creek, following an Indian trail. The trail crossed to the Little Bighorn, where he found a large encampment of Sioux and Cheyennes. About noon on the 25th, believing he had been spotted, Custer decided to lead the regiment down to attack. The village was huge, perhaps 1,200 lodges with 1,500 warriors, but it was nothing the entire 7th Cavalry could not handle.

Custer divided the regiment, sending Capt. Frederick Benteen with Companies D, H, and K toward the river to see if any Indians had fled upstream; sending Maj. Marcus Reno with Companies A, G, and M to cross the Little Bighorn and attack from the south; and taking Companies C, E, F, I, and L along the bluffs east of the river to attempt a flank attack farther downstream.

Reno charged the Hunkpapa Sioux lodges in the south, but he was repulsed and retreated back to the high ground east of the river. Custer, meanwhile, approached from the northeast, aiming for the Cheyenne lodges, then moved downstream to wait for support from Reno and Benteen. The support never came. Custer's scattered companies were picked off in detail. Not a man from his five companies survived.

About 253 soldiers and civilians were killed and 53 were wounded. The Indian loss was about 40 killed and 80 wounded.[688]

Remains at Little Bighorn battlefield (Montana)
—Courtesy Little Bighorn Battlefield National Monument

17 JULY 1876
HAT CREEK/WARBONNET CREEK (Montrose, Nebraska)

The 5th Cavalry had spent late June and early July scouting out of Fort Laramie between the Niobrara and Cheyenne Rivers. On 1 July Col. Wesley Merritt assumed command from Lt. Col. Carr and was expected to meet Gen. George Crook on the Tongue River, but he delayed the march when he learned that a large band of Indians had left the Red Cloud Agency, in northwest Nebraska, intending to join up with the Indians who had just defeated Custer (see previous entry). Merritt marched his seven companies of the 5th Cavalry—346 soldiers plus scouts—to the vicinity of Hat Creek, in extreme northwest Nebraska, near present-day Montrose.

First reports said that 800 Cheyennes had left the Red Cloud Agency, but in reality only Little Wolf's band of less than 100 had done so. Little Wolf had sent a dozen warriors in advance. Near Hat Creek, the advance party spotted Merritt's supply wagons and planned to raid them, not knowing Merritt was waiting for them. While the main body of the regiment hid in the cutbanks of Hat Creek, Companies B, I, and K moved ahead and hid behind a hill. When the Cheyennes went after the wagon train, Lt. Charles King of Company K gave the word to charge.

Some of the scouts, including "Buffalo Bill" Cody, were the first into the fray. Cody shot the Cheyenne Yellow Hair off his horse, then neatly lifted the Indian's scalp, proclaiming it as "the first for Custer."[689]

Yellow Hair was the only Indian killed. The rest fled back to Little Wolf and the entire band returned to the agency. No soldiers were hit.[690]

30 JULY 1876
SARAGOSSA (Saragossa, Coahuila, Mexico)

Even though Col. Ranald S. Mackenzie had successfully attacked the Kickapoos in their Mexican sanctuary in 1873, Kickapoos and Lipan Apaches still raided for horses in Texas, and Lt. Col. William R. Shafter decided to follow the raiders into Mexico. With Companies B, E, and K, 10th Cavalry, detachments of the 24th and 25th Infantry, and 20 Seminole-Negro scouts under Lt. John L. Bullis, the command hit the trail.

About 25 miles upriver from the mouth of the Pecos River, Shafter and his men crossed the Rio Grande into Mexico. They moved south for five days, Shafter wondering if Mexican troops might cut off his retreat back to American soil. He decided to encamp while sending Bullis with the scouts and Lt. George Evans with 20 men of the 10th Cavalry ahead. After a 25-hour march, Bullis and Evans located a Lipan village of 23 lodges about five miles from Saragossa. They attacked at dawn.

The assault crashed through the dwellings and quickly became a hand-to-hand fight, lances against carbines used as clubs. The scouts fought like demons, and in 15 minutes it was over. The Lipans fled, leaving 14 dead warriors behind. Four women and 90 horses were captured. Later reports claimed greatly exaggerated Lipan casualties. Bullis lost three men. Bullis was brevetted to Major.[691]

15 AUGUST 1876
RED ROCKS (Sedona, Arizona)

After prospector Thomas Hammond was killed on upper Tonto Creek in August, the army sent a party out to punish the culprits, thought to be Apaches who had slipped away from the San Carlos Agency. Capt. Charles Porter, 8th Infantry, with a detachment of Company B, 6th Cavalry, and Al Sieber and his Indian scouts, took up the trail. In the Red Rocks country near present-day Sedona, Arizona, they found a band of Apaches. At the cost of one enlisted man wounded, the soldiers and scouts killed seven Apaches and captured seven more. The fight was inconclusive, however, for a number of Apaches escaped and disappeared into the mountains.[692]

9 SEPTEMBER 1876
SLIM BUTTES (Reva, South Dakota)

Ever since Col. Wesley Merritt and his 5th Cavalry joined his column in July, Gen. George Crook had been chasing Indians. After marching down Rosebud Creek and the Tongue and Powder Rivers, cross-country to the

Slim Buttes (South Dakota)

Little Missouri River, and south toward the Black Hills, the expedition was out of supplies and starving. Finally, on 9 September, Lt. Anson Mills and about 130 troopers of the 3rd Cavalry stumbled into Chief American Horse's camp of 37 Lakota lodges, near present-day Reva, South Dakota.

The soldiers drove the surprised Indians into the bluffs south of Gap Creek, but the Lakotas fought back until the rest of Crook's command appeared, around noon. Some Indians trapped in a gulch near the village inflicted several casualties before they surrendered. In the late afternoon, some of Crazy Horse's warriors from a nearby village attacked, but Crook's men drove them off. Crook destroyed the village and continued south on his "starvation march."

Crook's losses were 2 soldiers and 1 guide killed and 15 wounded, including Lt. Adolphus H. Von Luettwitz. About 14 Lakotas were killed, and American Horse was mortally wounded; 23 Indians were captured.[693]

15 SEPTEMBER 1876
FLORIDA MOUNTAINS (Deming, New Mexico)

Capt. Henry Carroll, with a detachment of F Company, 9th Cavalry, scouted the extreme southwestern corner of New Mexico Territory looking for small bands of raiders under Juh and Geronimo. On 15 September, Carroll and 25 hard-riding veterans struck a party of Indians in the Florida Mountains, killing one, wounding three, and capturing 11 ponies. One private was wounded. Carroll returned to Fort Selden after a 9-day, 274-mile march.[694]

18 SEPTEMBER 1876
THE CAVES (Central Arizona)

The Apaches who had gotten away from Capt. Charles Porter and Al Sieber in the Red Rocks fight (see 15 August) were not forgotten. Sieber returned to Camp Verde and readied Company B of Apache scouts. Leaving the fort on 15 September, they quickly found the trail. Three days later they found their quarry, east of Camp Verde in a place called "The Caves." Sieber's scouts killed 5 hostiles and captured 13.[695]

4 OCTOBER 1876
TONTO CREEK (Payson, Arizona)

Within two weeks of bringing in the captives from The Caves fight (see previous entry) to Camp Verde on 22 September, Al Sieber was saddling up with Capt. Charles Porter, 8th Infantry, a detachment of 6th Cavalrymen, and the redoubtable Apache scouts. Looking for the last of the Apaches responsible for killing prospector Tom Hammond (see Red Rocks, 15 August), they followed the Indians' trail across the Mazatzals to Tonto Creek, then up that stream to its source. There they found the Apaches. They killed eight warriors and took two women prisoner.[696]

21 OCTOBER 1876
CEDAR CREEK (Terry, Montana)

With the entire 5th Infantry, 15 officers and 434 enlisted men, Col. Nelson A. Miles tracked Sitting Bull's Hunkpapas through the eastern Yellowstone country. On 20 October, Miles finally ran them down on the headwaters of the East Fork of Cedar Creek, about 20 miles northwest of present-day Terry, Montana. A parley was arranged between Miles and Sitting Bull, with nearly 300 warriors perched on a nearby hill watching the proceedings. The council was long and agitated, and Miles was wary. When the talks broke off, both sides returned to their camps with the understanding that the next day fighting would replace talking.

Miles struck first, bringing his 5th Infantry up to Sitting Bull's camp on the East Fork of Cedar Creek. Another talk was attempted, but Sitting Bull abruptly left the parley. Miles moved his men forward through the valley, Capt. James S. Casey taking his Company A to the bluffs on the left and Lt. Mason Carter taking his Company K to a knoll on the right. Flanks secured, Miles moved the rest of the 5th Infantry toward the Indian camp.

About 900 warriors were there to confront the advance, but their hearts were not in the fight. Miles's skirmishers pushed them back and the howitzers blasted them. The soldiers pushed through and gained the Lakota encampment. The Indians fell back toward Bad Route Creek and eventually fled downstream to the Yellowstone River.

Miles had only two soldiers wounded. He found five Lakota bodies on the field, and perhaps five more were wounded.[697]

25 NOVEMBER 1876
RED FORK OF THE POWDER RIVER (Mayoworth, Wyoming)

In the fall of 1876, the army organized another huge force to round up the last of the recalcitrant bands who had fought Crook and Custer in June (see Rosebud Creek, 17 June, and Little Bighorn, 25 June). The Powder River Expedition consisted of 11 companies of the 2nd, 3rd, 4th, and 5th Cavalry, under Col. Ranald S. Mackenzie; 15 companies of the 4th, 9th, 14th, and 23rd Infantry, plus four companies of the 4th Artillery, under Lt. Col. Richard I. Dodge; and about 400 Bannock, Shoshone, Pawnee, and Lakota allies. Including civilian packers and volunteers, there were almost 2,200 men and 168 wagons.

The command marched to old Fort Reno on the Powder, where Mackenzie split off with the cavalry. On 25 November, scouts guided him to a large Cheyenne camp in a canyon on the Red Fork of the Powder, west of present-day Kaycee, Wyoming. There were 200 lodges under Dull Knife and Little Wolf, with 400 warriors. Mackenzie's 1,100 horsemen burst upon the village, driving the surprised Indians out onto the frozen ridges. A deadly fire ensued. The fight was hand-to-hand at times, the defenders knowing that if they lost their homes and supplies at the onset of winter, they would perish.

When the Cheyennes seemed about to recapture their pony herd, Mackenzie sent Lt. John A. McKinney with Company A, 4th Cavalry, to stop them. Caught in a high-walled ravine and ambushed, McKinney went down with six bullets in him. Capt. John M. Hamilton's company of 5th Cavalrymen helped extricate the company. Finally, the soldiers secured the village, though the Cheyennes continued to pour in harassing fire from the rocks above.

During the fight, the Cheyennes suffered 40 killed and perhaps another 40 wounded. Mackenzie's casualties were 6 men killed and 26 wounded. The soldiers took more than 600 horses and burned all the lodges, leaving the Cheyennes to face the long winter without food and shelter. The night after the battle, the temperature dropped to 30° below zero, and 11 babies froze to death.[698]

18 DECEMBER 1876
ASH CREEK (Brockway, Montana)

Col. Nelson A. Miles sent out battalions of his 5th Infantry to scour the Missouri and Yellowstone Rivers country, searching for the remaining hostile Lakota bands. Lt. Frank Baldwin, with Companies G, H, and I, operated around Fort Peck. In early December, he got word that Sitting Bull's band was south of the Missouri on Redwater Creek. On the 14th, Baldwin crossed the thin ice and trailed them.

The soldiers moved up Ash Creek, a branch of Redwater Creek, southeast of present-day Brockway, Montana. On 18 December, Baldwin found 122 lodges tucked in the creek valley. He placed one company in advance of his wagons, which were drawn up in four columns, and flanked each side of them with the other two companies. He opened the fight by firing several howitzer rounds into the tipis.

When the troops rumbled into the camp, they found that most of the warriors were out hunting. Those remaining put up a feeble resistance, then fled. Baldwin did not pursue. The soldiers captured 60 horses and mules, gathered what supplies they could carry, and destroyed the rest, including the 90 lodges still standing. Only one Indian was killed.[699]

—1877—

8 JANUARY 1877
WOLF MOUNTAIN (Birney, Montana)

Continuing his pursuit of Indians through the winter, Col. Nelson A. Miles (see previous entry) left Cantonment Tongue on 29 December with Companies A, C, D, E, and K of the 5th Infantry and Companies E and F of the 22nd Infantry, heading upstream. On 7 January the soldiers captured eight Cheyennes, and the other Cheyennes, in a camp 20 miles farther upstream at Deer Creek, vowed to rescue them.

Miles, camped on the Tongue near present-day Birney, Montana, expected an attack and threw up breastworks overnight. In the morning, Crazy Horse and about 500 warriors obliged him. Under a fresh layer of snow, both sides maneuvered for advantage, but they did not come to close grips. Miles's artillery bombarded wherever the Indians congregated. After five hours, a new blizzard blew in and the Indians withdrew.

The Cheyenne Big Crow was killed, along with two Lakotas. Three more were wounded, two of them mortally. Miles lost three men and eight were wounded.[700]

9 JANUARY 1877
ANIMAS MOUNTAINS (Animas, New Mexico)

When the army received word that Apaches had stolen horses in the area, Lt. John A. Rucker, 6th Cavalry, was sent out to investigate from Fort Bowie. He left on 4 January with 17 enlisted men and a surgeon from the 6th Cavalry, Companies H and L, and 34 Apaches from Company C, Indian Scouts. Three days later they found a trail across the Animas Valley toward the Leitendorf Hills, an extension of the Pyramid Mountains, south of present Lordsburg, New Mexico.

Rucker moved about 40 miles up the valley to the northern edge of the Animas Mountains, where he found the Chiricahua camp. The troops tried to surround the camp in the dark, and near daylight they were almost in position when Jack Dunn and his scouts opened fire prematurely. The surprise attack drove the Chiricahuas to Rucker's position, about 300 yards north of the camp. The fight lasted two hours. Dunn and his scouts charged twice but were driven back both times, with scout Eshin-e-car severely wounded. When Dunn and Rucker charged simultaneously, they finally prevailed.

Rucker counted ten dead Indians and believed he wounded a large number. A five-year-old boy, identified as a nephew of Geronimo, was captured. The soldiers retrieved equipment that belonged to the Chiricahua Agency. It was believed that this was the first solid punishment the Chiricahuas had suffered from the army.[701]

12–14 JANUARY 1877
EAST VERDE RIVER (Payson, Arizona)

Late in December, several warriors and women fled the San Carlos Reservation, and the agent requested assistance. On 10 January, Capt. George M. Brayton, 8th Infantry, with 9 men of the 6th Cavalry, a medic, Al Sieber and 21 of his scouts, and Mickey Free as interpreter, left Camp Verde and headed southeast. On the first night, as the troops were camped on Fossil

Creek, one of the scouts reported that eight other scouts had cornered the fugitives in a cave below Polles Mesa, six miles from the mouth of the East Verde River.

Brayton took the command to the site. The cave was 15 feet from the top of the cliff and almost 700 feet above the canyon floor. At dawn, the scouts advanced under fire to covering ledges on each side of the cave, about 30 yards from the opening. Sieber spoke to the Indians and learned that the leader was the Tonto Apache Eskeltsetle. Brayton told Eskeltsetle to surrender and return to the reservation, but the old chief declined. With only one pistol and four rifles, Eskeltsetle took on his adversaries.

The siege lasted three days, the scouts on the cliffs enduring frigid weather and nine inches of snowfall, all the while holding their positions and blasting away blindly into the cave mouth. Finally, on 14 January, the trapped Apaches called it quits.

Eskeltsetle and three warriors were killed. The remaining eight Tontos were taken prisoner. Brayton had no casualties.[702]

21 JANUARY 1877
TONTO CREEK (Payson, Arizona)

After the fight at the East Verde River (see previous entry), Capt. George M. Brayton received word that Indians had stolen stock from the Hill ranch in Spring Valley. He took his troops southeast, but snow had covered the raiders' tracks. Guide Al Sieber intuitively chose a likely direction and the command followed toward Tonto Creek, where Sieber picked up the trail again.

On 21 January, about 12 miles south of where the Apache Trail crosses Tonto Creek, Brayton jumped the horse thieves. His men killed seven, captured three, and recovered four horses and mules—the only stock that remained.[703]

24 JANUARY 1877
FLORIDA MOUNTAINS (Deming, New Mexico)

To seek hostile Chiricahuas who had left the reservation and were raiding along the Arizona and New Mexico border, Lt. Henry H. Wright led an undermanned patrol of six troopers from Company C, 9th Cavalry, and three Navajo scouts out from Fort Bayard. Wright found an Indian camp in the Florida Mountains, but, being badly outnumbered, Wright did not attack. Instead he called a parley to try to persuade the Chiricahuas to return to the reservation.

The half-hour council went badly. Wright tried to walk calmly back to the horses and ride away, but warriors blocked his path. The soldiers fired, and with no time to reload, they used their weapons as clubs. Cpl. Clifton Greaves, fighting like a cornered mountain lion, opened a path for the rest to break free.

Amazingly, the troopers suffered only a few minor injuries but killed five Apaches and wounded a few more. Capturing six ponies, they returned to Fort Bayard. Corp. Greaves won the Medal of Honor.[704]

30 JANUARY 1877
NORTH PEAK (Payson, Arizona)

After their two fights earlier in the month, Capt. George M. Brayton, 8th Infantry, a handful of 6th Cavalrymen from Companies B and E, and Al Sieber and his Apache scouts (see East Verde River, 12–14 January, and Tonto Creek, 21 January) rested for three days at Camp McDowell, then went out again on 28 January to look for errant Apaches. They headed up the Verde River and into the Mazatzal Mountains. Only two days later, they struck an Apache band six miles southwest of the 7,888-foot North Peak (Mazatzal Peak). They killed six Indians and captured nine.[705]

18 MARCH 1877
YELLOW HOUSE CANYON (Lubbock, Texas)

In early 1877, a number of Comanches were given permission to leave their Oklahoma reservation to go hunting in Texas. At Charlie Rath's store near Double Mountain, where buffalo hunters bought supplies and swapped stories, word spread that Indians were attacking hunting camps and hunters were disappearing. By March, the hunters figured it was time to do something about it. About 45 men, led by "Captain" Hank Campbell and his "lieutenants" "Limpy Jim" Smith and Joe Freed, headed west.[706]

With an adequate supply of ammunition and whiskey, the buffalo hunters, guided by Jose Tafoya, marched to the edge of the Llano Estacado. Two weeks later, snaking up the North Fork of the Double Mountain Fork of the Brazos River, they found their Indians. Secreted in Yellow House Canyon, in the present-day city of Lubbock, Texas, were Black Horse and a camp of about 300 Comanches.

The hunters divided themselves into three groups, one coming in on each side of the canyon and the third, with the wagons, advancing straight up the canyon. As they charged in, the warriors quickly recovered from their surprise and put up a heavy fire. The three columns got separated, and each made its own desperate fight for over three hours. Scouting farther upstream, Tafoya took a bullet in the shoulder but reported back to Campbell that there was another camp of about 200 Kiowa-Apaches around the bend.

The Indians set a grass fire to smoke out their attackers. The two squads on the plains made their way back into the canyon and joined up with the wagons, then they all pulled back, somewhat faster than they had come in. By 22 March, they were back at Rath's store, facing some harsh comments about their Indian-fighting prowess.

Five buffalo hunters were wounded, including Joe Jackson, who died two months later. Several Comanches were seen to have been hit, but the harried buffalo men did not keep a count.[707]

4 MAY 1877
LAKE QUEMADO (Morton, Texas)

While the buffalo hunters tried to go after the renegade Comanches (see previous entry), the U.S. Cavalry was also on their trail. On 9 April, Capt. Phillip L. Lee and 42 buffalo soldiers of Company G, 10th Cavalry, along with about 70 scouts rode out of Fort Griffin. About 50 miles northwest of the site of the Yellow House fight, west of Silver Lake in present-day Cochran County, Lee came across Black Horse's Comanches.

The Indians were surprised, and Lee chased them about eight miles into the sand hills, then returned to destroy their tipis and supplies. In the fight, Sgt. Charles Butler was mortally wounded. At least four Comanches were killed trying to get away, and several women and children are believed to have been killed, though Lee made no mention of it in his report.[708] He captured six women and 69 horses.

On their return to Fort Griffin, the troopers rode past Rath's store, where Lee told the buffalo hunters that they had killed over 30 Indians at Yellow House Canyon, though few believed it.[709]

7 MAY 1877
LITTLE MUDDY CREEK/LAME DEER FIGHT (Lame Deer, Montana)

On 1 May, Col. Nelson Miles took Companies B and H of his 5th Infantry; Companies E, F, G, and H of the 22nd Infantry; and Companies F, G, H, and K of the 2nd Cavalry, under Capt. Edward Ball, up the Tongue River, searching for the band of Minneconjous under Lame Deer. On the Tongue, the scouts found a trail heading west to Rosebud Creek, and Miles followed with his command of 471 officers and enlisted men.

Spotting the camp of 61 lodges on Muddy Creek, Miles left the infantry behind and hurried in with his cavalry, plus a section of mounted infantry under Lt. Edward W. Casey. They reached the sleeping village at 4:30 A.M. Casey and Lt. Lovell H. Jerome, with Company H, 2nd Cavalry, were the first to thunder through the tipis. When one of the scouts found Lame Deer, Miles asked to parley with him.

Lame Deer approached Miles accompanied by his nephew Iron Star and two others. Miles told Lame Deer to put his rifle down, which he did, but cocked and facing forward. When Miles's scout White Bull tried to take Iron Star's rifle away from him, he shot, and the bullet went through White Bull's coat. Lame Deer grabbed the weapon on the ground and fired it at Miles, the bullet just missing him and killing his orderly, Pvt. Charles Shrenger. Pandemonium erupted.

Several troopers and Indians were hit in the fusillade. Lame Deer was cut down by 17 bullets from L Company, and White Bull scalped him. Companies F and L bore down on the fleeing villagers, with Company G coming up on the flank. It was over in a few moments.

The soldiers killed about 30 Minneconjous and wounded 20. They captured 40, but 200 got away. Four soldiers were killed and 9 were wounded, all from the 2nd Cavalry. Miles captured 450 horses and killed half of them. He also destroyed the village.[710]

17 JUNE 1877
WHITE BIRD CANYON (White Bird, Idaho)

After some young Nez Perce warriors killed settlers on the Camas Prairie in northern Idaho, Capt. David Perry was ordered out from Fort Lapwai with all the horsemen at his disposal—about 100 men of Companies F and H of the 1st Cavalry. Perry left on 15 June and marched to Grangeville, where he learned of more atrocities—drunken warriors had killed about 15 more settlers. Picking up 11 volunteers from nearby Mount Idaho, Perry raced south to try to cut off the Nez Perces before they could escape into the mountains.

White Bird Canyon (Idaho); Chief Joseph's camp was in the trees at right center.

Chief Joseph, camped at the mouth of White Bird Canyon near its junction with the Salmon River, learned that soldiers were coming and hoped he could talk to them. He only had 135 warriors but posted them among the rocks on the cliff sides. Lt. Edward R. Theller, in advance of Perry's column, saw the Indians approaching with a white flag, but the volunteers opened fire and the battle was on.

Though they outnumbered the Indians, Perry's men were exhausted and no match for the warriors. Many of the soldiers were inexperienced, and they could not stand up to the flanking fire. Theller and 18 men, trapped in a ravine, were wiped out. Some fought their way back the 16 miles to Mount Idaho. Stragglers found their way back later.

Perry lost 34 men and 2 were wounded. Only 3 Nez Perces were wounded.[711]

1 JULY 1877
CLEAR CREEK (Kooskia, Idaho)

Capt. Stephen G. Whipple took Companies E and L of the 1st Cavalry, 20 Idaho volunteers, and 2 Gatling guns to the village of the Nez Perce Looking Glass, hoping to capture the chief before he could join up with Chief Joseph. On 1 July Whipple's force came down a hillside opposite the village on Clear Creek, by its junction with the Clearwater River, near present-day Kooskia, Idaho.

Looking Glass, who had maintained neutrality to this point, sent Peopeo Tholekt to tell the soldiers to leave them alone. After treating him roughly, the troopers sent him back with the demand that Looking Glass come to talk himself. The chief refused and sent Peopeo and another Nez Perce back to try to talk again.

While the two Indians talked with Lt. Sevier M. Rains, a volunteer fired from across the river, wounding a Nez Perce named Red Heart. The fight had started, and the soldiers charged across the creek, spraying the 40-family village with gunfire. The Nez Perces fled into the woods.

One Indian was killed, four were wounded, and one woman and her infant were drowned as they tried to cross the swift Clearwater. Whipple destroyed the village. The neutral Looking Glass was now a hostile.[712]

3 JULY 1877
COTTONWOOD CREEK/CRAIG'S MOUNTAIN (Cottonwood, Idaho)

After destroying the Nez Perce Looking Glass's village (see previous entry), Capt. Stephen G. Whipple and his troops rode west across the Camas Prairie to Norton's Ranch on Cottonwood Creek, a post also called Cottonwood House. On 2 July, civilian scouts William Foster and Charles Blewitt spotted Indians, and in the race back to the ranch, Blewitt got lost. The next day, the driver of a stage to Lewiston saw Indians driving a herd of horses and reported the news to Whipple.

Before mounting up his 75 men of Companies E and L, 1st Cavalry, in pursuit, Whipple directed Lt. Sevier M. Rains, Company L, to take 10 men and the scout Foster to reconnoiter and to look for Blewitt. Rains was in a small valley only two miles from the post when he was attacked by Nez Perce warriors hidden at the foot of Craig's Mountain.

Within a few minutes, Rains and the 11 others were killed. Only moments later, Whipple arrived to face the 150 or more warriors who had just overwhelmed the scouting party. Whipple retreated.[713]

4 JULY 1877
COTTONWOOD HOUSE (Cottonwood, Idaho)

After the episode at Cottonwood Creek (see previous entry), Capt. David Perry arrived at Cottonwood House with the remnants of his Company F and took over Whipple's command. The soldiers saw Nez Perces all around the ranch, and the 113 men of the three companies dug in, placing their Gatling guns around the perimeter and prepareing to defend their position. The Indians hovered around all day, engaging in desultory shooting but never coming closer than 500 yards. Two soldiers were wounded.[714]

5 JULY 1877
"BRAVE SEVENTEEN" FIGHT (Cottonwood, Idaho)

When civilian volunteers from Mount Idaho heard that the soldiers at Cottonwood House were in trouble, they went to help. All they could gather up, however, were 17 men. When the "brave seventeen" got within five miles of their destination, they were confronted by a line of Nez Perces. "Captain" D. B. Randall ordered a charge. The volunteers broke through, but the warriors, about 130 of them, quickly closed in and surrounded them. When the horsemen could advance no farther, Randall formed up a defense, only a mile and a half from Cottonwood House.

The firing attracted the attention of Capts. Perry and Whipple at the post, but they did not ride out. Watching the fight, Perry assumed the volunteers were goners. He and his soldiers watched for 25 minutes. Incredibly, during this time, a few of Randall's men broke out and rode up to Perry's men asking for ammunition. Perhaps shame got to them, for finally Whipple and a Lt. Shelton rode out with 42 soldiers and broke the "brave seventeen" free.

Randall and another volunteer were killed, and a third received a mortal wound. Three others were less severely wounded. One Indian was mortally wounded.[715]

11–12 JULY 1877
CLEARWATER RIVER (Stites, Idaho)

After subduing the soldiers at Cottonwood House (see Cottonwood Creek/Craig's Mountain, 3 July ff.), the Nez Perces led their families across the Camas Prairie to the east. They did not have many warriors: Joseph's band combined with Looking Glass's, plus some stragglers, amounted to about 300 fighting men. Pursuing them was Brig. Gen. Oliver Otis Howard, commander of the Department of the Columbia, with Companies B, E, F, H, and L of the 1st Cavalry; A, B, C, D, E, H, and I of the 21st Infantry; four companies of the 4th Artillery acting as infantry; and 50 packers and scouts—almost 500 men.

Howard found the Nez Perce village near the junction of Cottonwood Creek and the Clearwater River, in a valley 1,000 feet below him. He opened the fight by firing his cannons, which did little but alert the Indians that he was there. They filed up the ravines to skirmish with him before he could bring down his entire command. Finally, Howard got his troops down to a gently rolling prairie and deployed in the open in a large circle, with his pack train in the center.

The Nez Perces kept up the fight for seven hours, probing for a weak point, while the artillery kept them at bay. Capt. Evan Miles charged to drive them back in the north, while Capt. Marcus P. Miller did the same in the west. The Nez Perces, however, kept them boxed in. They sniped at each other until dark. Howard's men dug rifle pits during the night.

Clearwater River battle site (Idaho)

The next morning, the firing commenced again. It was another hot day, and the soldiers suffered greatly for lack of water. In an almost unheard-of tactic for Indians, the Nez Perces dug trenches around the soldiers, shooting every time a man looked up. Howard was planning a charge to break out when Capt. James B. Jackson's Company B, 1st Cavalry, came up from the south with 120 pack mules and took on the Indians from the rear. Howard sent out soldiers to meet him and they drove the Indians out of one of the ravines. The rest of the Nez Perces ran back to their village, where they scrambled to gather up what they could and escape across the Clearwater River.

Howard won the field, but it was a costly victory. He lost 17 soldiers and civilians, killed or mortally wounded, and 27 others wounded. The Nez Perces suffered 23 killed, 46 wounded, and 40 captured.[716]

17 JULY 1877
WEIPPE PRAIRIE (Weippe, Idaho)

After the fight at the Clearwater River (see previous entry), Gen. Oliver Otis Howard followed the fleeing Nez Perces, hoping to catch them before they crossed the mountains into Montana. Maj. Edwin C. Mason, 21st Infantry, took detachments of five companies of the 1st Cavalry, Idaho volunteers, under Ed McConville, and some Nez Perce scouts ahead of Howard's main force. The Indians' trail led onto the Weippe Prairie, near the junction of Jim Ford and Grasshopper Creeks, and beyond into a wooded defile.

The scouts who expected an ambush were not disappointed; one was killed and two others were wounded. Finding it impossible to take horsemen through the tangle of undergrowth, Mason dismounted them to trek through the timber, but by the time they got going, the Indians had disappeared.[717]

9–10 AUGUST 1877
BIG HOLE (Wisdom, Montana)

Fleeing Gen. O. O. Howard (see previous entry), the Nez Perces crossed Lolo Pass to Montana and turned south up the Bitterroot Valley. After crossing the mountains to the Big Hole Valley, Looking Glass demanded they stop for a much-needed rest. The delay would be calamitous. Although they had given Howard the slip, Col. John Gibbon from Fort Shaw had taken up the chase. Gibbon had a moderate force, with detachments of Companies B and E of the 2nd Cavalry and detachments of five companies of his 7th Infantry—161 men—later joined by about 45 volunteers.

At dawn on 9 August, Gibbon surprised the 89-tipi village in the valley of the North Fork of the Big Hole River. The soldiers swept through the camp, causing many casualties, and within 20 minutes had secured the area.

Looking Glass and White Bird, however, enraged at the loss of lives and the capture of their property, rallied the warriors. The Nez Perces fired from willow thickets and stream banks with excellent marksmanship.

At this Gibbon fell back across the river to a wooded bluff rising about 30 feet above it. There he dug pits and held on as the Nez Perces surrounded him, picking off his men one by one. The Indians might have overrun the soldiers, but their main interest was to hold them at bay so the women and children could get away. They kept Gibbon pinned in place throughout the next day, with his men needing food, water, and medical attention. Finally, after dark on 10 August, the Nez Perces fired a few parting shots and left.

Gibbon reported 89 Indians dead, but many of them were women and children. The Nez Perces said they lost 50 people and had 30 wounded. On Gibbons's side, 23 enlisted men and civilians were killed or fatally wounded, and 5 officers, including Gibbon, 30 enlisted men, and 4 civilians were wounded.[718]

12 AUGUST 1877
HORSE PRAIRIE (Grant, Montana)

After the Nez Perces abandoned the Big Hole Valley (see previous entry), they went to Horse Prairie, where word of their presence reached the settlers in the area. Most of them fled to Bannack for safety, but some continued going about their work. About 60 warriors went onto the ranch of W. L. Montague and Daniel H. Winters, killing Montague and three others. At the Thomas Hamilton ranch, they killed another man, Andrew Cooper. The raiders stole about 150 horses.[719]

15 AUGUST 1877
BIRCH CREEK (Monteview, Idaho)

On their flight from army pursuers (see Clearwater River, 11–12 July 1877 ff.) the Nez Perces crossed the Continental Divide at Bannock Pass, entered the Lemhi Valley, and continued south. In the Birch Creek Valley, in the southwest corner of present-day Clark County, Idaho, they came across a wagon train. The 8 freight wagons, 3 drivers, 5 other men, and 30 mules were going from Corinne, Utah, to Salmon City, Idaho. Sixty Nez Perces stopped the wagons and forced the freighters to feed them, then made them move upriver two miles to their camp.

At the camp, the freighters may have breathed easier when the Nez Perces asked to buy their goods. Among the cargo was whiskey, however, and after drinking, the Indians' mood became more belligerent. One of the freighters, Albert E. Lyons, edged his way out of the camp and slipped away into the gathering darkness, and the Nez Perces allowed two Chinese passengers to ride on. No one knows what occurred after that. Searchers later found the battered and shot bodies of the men: Albert Green, James

Hayden, Daniel Combs, a man named White, and an unknown man. Combs's dog was patiently keeping watch over the body of his dead master.[720]

20 AUGUST 1877
CAMAS MEADOWS (Kilgore, Idaho)

With Col. John Gibbon's force too hurt from the Big Hole fight (see 9–10 August) to continue their pursuit of Joseph's Nez Perces, Brig. Gen. O. O. Howard came back on the scene. Ahead of his infantry, Companies B, I, and K of the 1st Cavalry, Company L of the 2nd Cavalry, and 53 mounted Montana volunteers under James E. Callaway were only a day behind the Indians. On 19 August they camped at the vacated Indian camp at Camas Meadows, near the junction of East Camas and Spring Creeks.

The next morning, about 200 warriors rode back to the campsite to drive off the cavalry's horses. They had taken 150 mules before daylight, and at dawn Maj. George B. Sanford and three troops went after them. Sanford recaptured some of the mules, but the Indians forced him back. The warriors cut off Capt. Randolph Norwood's Company L for three hours, until Howard came up with his regrouped command, whereupon the Nez Perces renewed their flight to Canada.

Two soldiers were killed or mortally wounded, and ten enlisted men and one civilian were wounded. No Indian casualties were reported.[721]

13 SEPTEMBER 1877
CANYON CREEK (Laurel, Montana)

The army had been pursuing the Nez Perces for weeks (see Clearwater River, 11–12 July 1877 ff.) when Col. Samuel D. Sturgis, 7th Cavalry, finally caught up with the elusive Indians as they were plundering the village of Coulson, Montana, near present-day Billings. Sturgis had about 360 men: Companies F, G, H, I, L, and M of the 7th Cavalry and Company K and detachments of C and I of the 1st Cavalry. He deployed his troops on the plain between the Yellowstone River and the high rimrock walls to the north.

The Nez Perces kept the cavalry at bay by remaining on horseback and firing from long range as their families moved up Canyon Creek, the only escape route from the valley to the high tableland. Then the warriors took position along the rocky defile, where a small number could easily delay a large pursuing force. By the time Sturgis brought up a howitzer to blast the canyon, it was too late. The Nez Perces had escaped.

Sturgis managed to capture a few hundred ponies. Three soldiers were killed and 11 were wounded. The Indians may have had 7 killed and 10 wounded. Sturgis was criticized for his timid handling of the fight.[722]

23 SEPTEMBER 1877
COW ISLAND (North-central Montana)

Cow Island in the Missouri River, in the southeastern corner of present-day Blaine County, Montana, was used as a landing for steamboats to unload their cargo for freighters to pick up, rather than risk the Dauphin Rapids, a troublesome stretch of river 18 miles upstream. Sgt. William Moelchert, 11 soldiers of the 7th Infantry, and 4 civilians were there to guard a government supply delivery when Chief Joseph's Nez Perces, heading toward Canada, reached the Missouri crossing at the island.

The Indians rode near, but Moelchert motioned for them to keep their distance. After some long-distance parleying, the sergeant let a few come in and gave them a side of bacon and half a sack of hardtack. They went away, but a short while later he heard a shot. One of his men, Pvt. Person, had not come into camp with the rest, and Moelchert surmised that the Indians had shot him. He prepared his troopers in the willows by the river, and at dusk, the Indians began to pepper their position with bullets. Through the night, the warriors tried several half-hearted attacks in the pitch dark. In the morning, the Indians took what supplies they wanted and burned the rest. By 10 A.M. they had moved out, up Cow Creek.

No Indians were reported hit. Two civilians and one enlisted man were killed.[723]

Site of Canyon Creek fight (Montana)

25 SEPTEMBER 1877
COW CREEK (Blaine County, Montana)

While the Nez Perces harrassed the soldiers at Cow Island (see previous entry), a train of 15 wagons was moving up the tortuous canyon of Cow Creek. By noon on 24 September, the Indians, following the creek north, had overtaken the train. One of the freighters, O. G. Cooper, estimated there were between 700 and 800 Indians. As they had done before, the Nez Perces threatened no violence at first. They asked to buy or trade for the supplies in the wagons.

As the Indians hovered, the train members bedded down for an uneasy rest. The next morning, it appeared that the Nez Perces were going to let them go, when up the canyon came Maj. Guido Ilges, 7th Infantry, with one enlisted man and about 24 mounted civilian scouts. The mood of the Nez Perces turned violent, and they began shooting. The men in the wagon train scattered; one named Barker was shot in the back before he could escape.

Ilges came in as close as he dared while the Indians fired from the cliffs. After two hours of skirmishing, the soldiers pulled back. About three miles from the creek, Ilges met Lt. Edward E. Hardin and a detachment of Company F, 7th Infantry, with a howitzer. But before Ilges could reengage the Nez Perces, the Indians had burned the wagons and were on their way north again.

Two civilians were killed and one was wounded. Two Nez Perces were wounded.[724]

26 SEPTEMBER 1877
SARAGOSSA (Saragossa, Coahuila, Mexico)

More than a year after Lt. Col. William R. Shafter's expedition into Mexico to punish Lipan and Kickapoo raiders (see Saragossa, 30 July 1876), Gen. Edward O. C. Ord authorized another offensive. Capt. Thomas C. Lebo with detachments of Companies C, 10th Cavalry, and A and F, 8th Cavalry, and Lt. John Bullis, 24th Infantry, with his Seminole-Negro scouts gathered on Pinto Creek near Fort Duncan. They crossed the Rio Grande and made a lightning raid near Saragossa, but most of the Lipans had already scattered. The troopers captured five women and children and destroyed some lodges.[725]

30 SEPTEMBER–5 OCTOBER 1877
BEAR'S PAW/SNAKE CREEK (Chinook, Montana)

After two and a half months of running from U.S. troops, the Nez Perces (see Clearwater River, 11–12 July ff.) appeared likely to reach Canada when they pitched a camp in the ravine of Snake Creek, north of the Bear's Paw Mountains, about 16 miles south of present-day Chinook, Montana, and

Chief Joseph
—Courtesy Denver Public Library,
Western History Department

about 40 miles from the Canadian border. The halt was made at the insistence of Looking Glass, to let the exhausted families rest for a few days. It was enough time to allow a large force under Col. Nelson A. Miles to catch up.

Miles was pursuing Chief Joseph's band with almost 400 men, including mounted Companies B, F, G, I, and K of the 5th Infantry; Companies A, D, and K of the 7th Cavalry; Companies F, G, and H of the 2nd Cavalry; and 30 Lakota and Cheyenne scouts. Among his artillery were a Hotchkiss gun and a howitzer. The 7th Cavalry battalion, under Capt. Owen Hale, led off the charge from the south. The Nez Perces, demonstrating their exceptional marksmanship, cut the charge up. Halted at the bluff's edge south of the camp, Hale dismounted his men. But the Nez Perces' fire was too hot for the troopers to advance. Both Hale and Company K's Lt. Jonathan W. Biddle were killed.

Meanwhile, as the 2nd Cavalry went after the Indians' horse herd, the 5th Infantry came up on the 7th Cavalry's left. But at the Nez Perces' defense, Miles called off the attack. Desultory firing marked the next five days, broken by several peace talks. During a council on 1 October, Miles seized Chief Joseph, but he had to let him go after Lt. Lovell H. Jerome strayed too close and was himself captured by the Nez Perces.

The Indians argued vehemently among themselves as to what course of action to take, but Joseph finally convinced most of them to surrender. They did so on 5 October, Joseph uttering his famous speech: "Hear me, my chiefs! I am tired. My heart is sick and sad. From where the sun now stands I will fight no more forever."[726]

Nevertheless, that night White Bird and nearly 300 warriors, women, and children broke free and eventually made it to Canada. Joseph surrendered 418 others. The battle cost the Nez Perces 17 killed and 40 wounded. Among the dead were Joseph's brother Ollokot and Chief Looking Glass. Miles lost 2 officers and 22 enlisted men, with 4 officers, 38 enlisted men, and 4 civilians wounded.[727]

29–30 NOVEMBER 1877
SIERRA DEL CARMEN (Boquillas del Carmen, Coahuila, Mexico)

Following Capt. Thomas C. Lebo's September raid on the Lipans and Kickapoos in Mexico (see Saragossa, 26 September), Capt. Samuel B. M. Young, 8th Cavalry, led the next expedition across the border. He had Companies A and K, 10th Cavalry; Company C of the 10th, under Lt. William Beck; and Lt. Bullis and his redoubtable scouts. The troops left Fort Clark on 10 November and marched through the rough country between Del Rio and the Big Bend of the Rio Grande.

The expedition lost 11 pack mules over the precipitous cliffs. In the Sierra del Carmen, south of today's Big Bend National Park, the weather was so cold that water froze in their canteens. Nevertheless, the troopers found Alsate's Apaches in a steep canyon near Mount Carmen. Circling soldiers flushed some of the Indians out of their fortified position, and a brief battle ensued. Alsate abandoned his rancheria and climbed into the cliffs above.

Young destroyed the camp and trekked back to Fort Clark with 30 captured horses. One officer, Lt. Frederick E. Phelps, was wounded. Two Indians were killed and three were wounded.[728]

18 DECEMBER 1877
ANIMAS MOUNTAINS (Animas, New Mexico)

Near Stein's Peak, Apache bands under Juh and Nolgee raided a wagon train, killing several men and stealing the livestock, then fled south toward Mexico. At the same time, Lt. John A. Rucker, with detachments of Companies C, G, H, and L, 6th Cavalry, and some Indian scouts, about 80 men, was on his way back from an expedition into Mexico. Passing through the Animas Mountains, in extreme southwest New Mexico, the troops stumbled into the raiders' camp. Rucker attacked, killed 15 warriors, captured 1, and reclaimed 60 animals.[729]

—1878—

5 APRIL 1878
HELL CANYON (Drake, Arizona)

In early spring, Capt. Charles Porter, 8th Infantry, organized a scout consisting of a detachment of Company B, 8th Infantry; Company A, 6th Cavalry; and Al Sieber and his Indian scouts. Their mission was to find and destroy the rancheria of Mojaves and Yumas under Miraha. Porter brought along a captive Mojave who led them upriver from Camp Verde to the camp. It was in a dense thicket of cedar and pinon, near Hell Canyon, about 12 miles west of Bill Williams Mountain.

Porter attacked, killed seven Indians, and captured the camp. One of the dead, badly scarred by smallpox, was believed to be Miraha's brother. Another body bore a pass from the San Carlos agent allowing him to hunt in the Pinal Mountains, far to the south. Five warriors were out hunting at the time of the attack. Porter took one boy, three women, and three infants prisoner. Porter confiscated many goods including blankets, skins, guns, and ammunition, and distributed them to Sieber's scouts.[730]

8 JUNE 1878
SOUTH MOUNTAIN (Silver City, Idaho)

After a band of Bannocks shot and wounded two white men on Camas Prairie, about 90 miles southeast of Boise, Idaho, Chief Buffalo Horn, knowing retribution would come, gathered his followers and left the area. Heading west, with Umatilla and Paiute warriors joining the band along the way, the Indians raided settlements through southwest Idaho, killing about ten whites. When news of the attacks reached Silver City, Idaho, Capt. J. B. Harper organized a volunteer company of 26 men and some friendly Paiute scouts to find the raiders.

The volunteers ran into Chief Buffalo Horn and more than 50 warriors near a small mining camp at South Mountain, about 20 miles southwest of Silver City. The Bannocks were in a good defensive position, but Harper ordered a charge anyway. Although he lost two men and three were wounded, he succeeded in mortally wounding Buffalo Horn and hitting a few other Bannocks. The Indians headed into Oregon with their dying chief, who, two days later, ordered them to leave him in the underbrush to die.[731]

28 JUNE 1878
SILVER RIVER (Riley, Oregon)

After the battle at South Mountain (see previous entry), which killed their chief, the Bannock raiders headed to Steen's Mountain, Oregon. Joining up with some Malheur Paiutes and Cayuses, they chose Chief Egan, a

Paiute, to be their new leader. The band numbered about 700, with 450 warriors. Trying to catch them was Capt. Reuben F. Bernard, with 250 men, including Indian scouts and civilians under Orlando "Rube" Robbins and Companies A, F, G, and L of the 1st Cavalry.

At dawn on 28 June, Bernard caught up with the Indians camped on the Silver River, about 30 miles west of present-day Burns, Oregon. Bernard led off the assault with Robbins and his scouts, who slashed through the village firing six-shooters and yelling like madmen. The Indians, thinking they were being attacked by a much larger force, fled in all directions. Chief Egan and Robbins squared off like two medieval knights, charging each other on horseback. Several bullets went through Robbins's clothes; Egan was hit in the wrist and tumbled off his horse. Robbins then shot him in the chest, but the wound was not fatal and his warriors carried him away.

Many of the Indians who stampeded downriver at Robbins's assault ran into Bernard's cavalry. The others took position on the bluffs surrounding the camp and stiffened their resistance. Bernard was unable to force them off, and when he drew back to consolidate his forces, the fighting sputtered out. The Indians stole away in the night.

The Indians lost five men and two were wounded. Three of Bernard's men were killed and two were wounded.[732]

29 JUNE 1878
NORTH CONCHO RIVER (Big Spring, Texas)

The Comanche Black Horse took 25 warriors from Fort Sill and rode into Texas. Unable to find any buffalo, the Indians stole several colts from a ranch south of Big Spring and ate them. Seven Texas Rangers from Company B, Frontier Battalion, under Capt. Junius "June" Peake, spotted them in a clump of cedar trees near the headwaters of the North Fork of the Concho River.

The Rangers attacked, but they were outnumbered and fell back. They lost two of their pack mules but captured the Indians' mounts. Two Rangers were wounded.

After dark, the Comanches evacuated their position on foot. Though without supplies, blankets, and ammunition, the Rangers followed the Indians' trail at daybreak. The Comanches hid in a nearby buffalo wallow and turned the captured mules out to graze. When the Texans went to reclaim them, the warriors rose up and fired, killing one Ranger, W. G. Anglin, and wounding another man.

The Comanches made it back to Fort Sill, but six of their men had been killed or wounded. The Rangers suffered one killed and three wounded. This was the last Comanche raid into Texas.[733]

2 JULY 1878
NORTH FORK OF THE JOHN DAY RIVER (Dale, Oregon)

After the fight at Silver River (see 28 June), Capt. Reuben F. Bernard and units of the 1st Cavalry pursued the fleeing Bannocks and Paiutes. With Chief Egan's wounding, Oytes became the band's new leader. In a canyon leading up from the North Fork of the John Day River, at the edge of today's Umatilla National Forest, Oytes set up an ambush to slow down Bernard.

The scouts were in the vanguard, and two, Frohman and Campbell, were killed and three others wounded in the first fire. Bernard chased off the warriors, who continued north to the Umatilla Reservation, where they hoped to recruit more followers.[734]

8 JULY 1878
BIRCH CREEK/PILOT ROCK (Pilot Rock, Oregon)

In addition to Capt. Reuben F. Bernard's efforts to stop Chief Oytes's Bannocks and Paiutes (see previous entry), Brig. Gen. Oliver Otis Howard got into the action. With about 480 men, Howard cornered the Indians on Pilot Rock, above Birch Creek, about 20 miles south of present-day Pendleton, Oregon. Bernard was given the honor of leading the attack.

With Companies A, E, F, G, H, K, and L of the 1st Cavalry, Bernard led a frontal advance against the entrenched Indians. The hill was formidable, and Bernard took casualties, but he continued the advance unfalteringly. The Indians retreated to the top, and in a final push, the troops drove them in disorder down the slopes. With exhausted horses, Bernard could pursue no farther.

Surprisingly, only one soldier was killed and four were wounded. The Indians likewise suffered only a few killed and wounded.[735]

13 JULY 1878
UMATILLA AGENCY (Pendleton, Oregon)

Oytes's Bannocks and Paiutes fled south after the Birch Creek fight (see previous entry), but they soon reversed direction and headed for the Umatilla Reservation, just east of present-day Pendleton, Oregon, hoping to entice that tribe into joining them. Capt. Evan Miles, who had a 500-man force of Companies B, D, E, G, H, I, and K of the 21st Infantry; Company K of the 1st Cavalry; and Companies G and D of the 4th Artillery, hurried to the agency, but Oytes's band had already arrived.

Miles waited to see what the Umatillas do. A force of perhaps 1,000 warriors moved out to confront him, but the only ones who attacked were Oytes's warriors, the Umatillas unwilling to commit themselves. Miles easily defended the hesitant, probing attacks against his lines, and after six hours of demonstration, the renegade band pulled away and headed eastward into the mountains.

Miles had only two enlisted men wounded, and the Indians suffered likewise.[736]

20 JULY 1878

NORTH FORK OF THE JOHN DAY RIVER (Northeastern Oregon)

After being rebuffed by the Umatillas, the Bannock and Paiute confederacy (see previous entry) rapidly disintegrated. Near present-day Meachum, Oregon, Umatilla warriors entered Chief Egan's camp under the pretense of joining him, then killed him and took his scalp back to the soldiers to prove their friendship. Oytes hurried south with the discouraged band.

On 20 July, the soldiers again caught up with some of the Indians. Lt. Col. James W. Forsyth, who had taken over for Capt. Reuben F. Bernard, with Companies A, E, F, G, H, and L of the 1st Cavalry, caught up with a rear guard of Oytes's warriors on the headwaters of the North Fork of the John Day River.

In the resulting skirmish, one enlisted man and one civilian were wounded, and one civilian was killed. There were no Indian casualties. The rugged country prevented Forsyth's pursuing Oytes farther.[737]

21 JULY 1878

MIDDLE FORK OF THE CLEARWATER RIVER (Kooskia, Idaho)

Disenchanted Nez Perce warriors who had fled to Canada with White Bird in 1877 after Chief Joseph's surrender (see Bear's Paw/Snake Creek, 30 September–5 October 1877) returned to their homes in Idaho the following summer. On 15 July, they raided in Montana. Lt. Thomas S. Wallace out of Fort Missoula, with 15 mounted men from detachments of Companies D, H, and I of the 3rd Infantry, took up the chase. Wallace caught his quarry on the Middle Fork of the Clearwater River, east of present-day Kooskia, Idaho. Without loss to himself, he killed six Nez Perces, wounded three, and captured 31 horses.[738]

5 AUGUST 1878

DOG CANYON (Alamogordo, New Mexico)

Lt. Col. Nathan A. M. Dudley ordered Capt. Henry Carroll to round up renegade Indians and bring them to the Mescalero Reservation. With Lt. Henry H. Wright, Carroll took 52 men of Companies F and H, 9th Cavalry, and 19 Navajo scouts and headed for the Guadalupe Mountains. Failing to find any Indians, he moved northwest to the Sacramento Mountains.

At the mouth of Dog Canyon, Carroll's men flushed out a small party of Apaches, and in a sharp skirmish they killed three men and captured 22 horses. Up the canyon they found more Indians, who fired at them and rolled rocks down from cliffs nearly 800 feet high. The troopers climbed up the walls in almost intolerable heat, several men suffering heatstroke. They reached the ledge at nightfall, only to find that the Indians had scattered.

In addition to the three warriors killed, the Apaches suffered two wounded and one captured. One corporal from Company H was killed accidentally.[739]

4 SEPTEMBER 1878
CLARK'S FORK (Belfry, Montana)

The Bannocks who fled Oregon after the John Day River fight (see North Fork of the John Day River, 20 July) either returned to their reservation in Idaho or made a dash for Canada. Those in the latter group ran into detachments of the 2nd Cavalry under Lt. William P. Clark. On 29 and 30 August, near Index Peak, Wyoming, Clark drove a small party of Bannocks toward Col. Nelson Miles and detachments of his 5th Infantry. On 4 September, Miles, traveling up Clark's Fork of the Yellowstone, surprised a camp of Bannocks, killing 11 and capturing 31, along with 200 horses and mules. Capt. Andrew S. Bennett of the 5th Infantry was killed, as was the interpreter and one Indian scout. One enlisted man was wounded.[740]

12 SEPTEMBER 1878
SNAKE RIVER (Jackson Hole, Wyoming)

Fugitive Bannock Indians who had escaped from the 4 September fight with Col. Nelson Miles (see previous entry) were caught on a tributary of the Snake River near Jackson Hole, Wyoming. Lt. Hoel S. Bishop with a 30-man detachment of Company G, 5th Cavalry, and some Shoshone scouts struck them, killing one and capturing seven.[741]

13 SEPTEMBER 1878
TURKEY SPRINGS (Camp Houston, Oklahoma)

On 9 September, a band of 92 Northern Cheyenne warriors and 268 women and children under Dull Knife and Little Wolf left their agency at Darlington, trying to return to their home country in the north. After crossing the Cimarron River, they moved to Turkey Springs, where Capt. Joseph Rendlebrock, with Companies G and H, 4th Cavalry, out of Fort Reno, caught them.

Rendlebrock sent an Arapaho named Ghost Man, or Chalk, to parley. Ghost Man told Little Wolf that the Cheyennes would have to surrender, but they would be treated well. Little Wolf said no, they were going home, and asked that the soldiers let them go in peace. Just then, Ghost Man spied several ponies that he believed had been stolen from him. He pulled out his revolver and charged at the Cheyennes, shooting a few of them at close range and receiving bullets in the thighs and bowels in return. With that, the fight was on.

The bugle sounded, and Rendlebrock was about to charge when some Cheyenne warriors attacked from the surrounding bluffs. The soldiers were thrown into confusion. Retreating to a protective draw, Rendlebrock was able to hold his own. While some of the warriors kept up the firing, Little Wolf, who did not want to bring on a major engagement, convinced the others to save their ammunition and continue north. His warriors hemmed in the cavalrymen while the women and children fled. The next morning, Rendlebrock finally broke out of his loose confinement.

Five Cheyennes were wounded, mostly from the surprise fire of Ghost Man. Three of Rendlebrock's men were killed, including Ghost Man, and three were wounded.[742]

27 SEPTEMBER 1878
PUNISHED WOMAN'S FORK (Scott City, Kansas)

After Little Wolf and Dull Knife escaped from Capt. Joseph Rendlebrock (see previous entry), Lt. Col. William H. Lewis, 19th Infantry, with elements of Companies B, F, G, H, and I, 4th Cavalry, and D, F, and G of the 19th Infantry, joined Rendlebrock in the pursuit. Little Wolf halted his band in the cutbanks of Punished Woman's Fork, south of the Smoky Hill River, and planned an ambush. He moved the women and children into a side canyon, and he and Tangle Hair placed the warriors in rifle pits along the bluffs.

On 27 September, about 4 P.M., Lewis followed the Cheyennes' trail right down into the canyon, but an overanxious warrior fired too soon, alerting the soldiers to the trap. Lewis was able to extricate his command and sent some men out to find a way around the canyon, almost trapping a number of Cheyennes in his turn. Little Wolf sent a mounted charge against the soldiers, but by now he had little ammunition left.

On the prairie, Lewis's infantrymen poured out of the wagons. Little Wolf knew the soldiers meant business, but he could not flee and leave the women and children. With the soldiers closing in on three sides of them, led by Lewis on a big bay gelding, Little Wolf called out for his warriors to fire their final bullets. The volleys felled some soldiers, among them Lewis. The troopers retreated. In the night, Little Wolf and Dull Knife gathered their people and crept off to the north. Many of the Indians walked, for they had lost about 80 ponies.

Two warriors were killed and about ten were wounded. The soldiers lost one man and six were wounded. An ambulance sped Lewis to the nearest post, Fort Wallace, but the bullet had struck a femoral artery, and he bled to death that night.[743]

—1879—

9–22 JANUARY 1879
FORT ROBINSON (Crawford, Nebraska)

The Northern Cheyennes under Little Wolf, who had been evading capture since fleeing their Oklahoma agency in September (see previous entries), were eventually rounded up and put in a barracks at Fort Robinson, which garrisoned Companies A, C, E, F, H, and L of the 3rd Cavalry. The Cheyennes resisted all attempts to send them back, so post commander Capt. Henry W. Wessels Jr., after removing most of the women and children from the barracks, cut off their food, water, and heat. A week of this treatment did not break the band's will, and, on the afternoon of 9 January, the 150 warriors decided to break out. One of them, Little Chief, said, "We will all die together."

The Indians had managed to hold onto five guns and hide them under the flooring. After sunset, they burst out of the barracks, shot the guards, and ran for the hills. Unprepared soldiers hurriedly tried to organize a pursuit. It was dark, but the moonlight and heavy snow made the fugitives' tracks easy to see. The soldiers tracked them all night and the next morning, capturing or killing most of them. Some of the Cheyennes managed to hide out for a couple of weeks before being recaptured or killed. Many died of exposure.

The Cheyennes killed 7 soldiers in the escape and wounded 14, including Wessels. In the pursuit, the soldiers killed 64 Cheyennes and recaptured 78. Of the captives, 20 were sent back to the Oklahoma agency, but 58 were allowed to go to the Pine Ridge Reservation, in their home territory. The 8 or 10 others were never heard from again, probably having died in the hills.[744]

17 APRIL 1879
CARELESS CREEK (Ryegate, Montana)

Lt. Samuel H. Loder, 7th Infantry, with 14 mounted men from Company K, 3rd Infantry, and Companies E and D, 7th Infantry, and 6 Indian scouts were looking for Lakotas who had been raiding stock along the Musselshell River. Heading east out of Fort Logan, Loder picked up a trail and caught up with the raiders near Careless Creek, at the head of Musselshell Canyon. The troopers killed eight Lakotas. Loder lost two soldiers and one was wounded.[745]

29 MAY 1879
BLACK RANGE (Southwestern New Mexico)

Learning that Victorio's hostile Apache band was in the vicinity, Capt. Charles D. Beyer and Lt. Henry H. Wright took 31 men of Company C and 15 men of Company I, 9th Cavalry, with two Navajo scouts and guide John R. Foster, out of Fort Bayard. As they headed north they found that in much of the country between the fort and the Gila River, forest fires were raging, and it was with difficulty that they found safe camping grounds.

The Indians kept obliterating their trails by setting more fires. Finally, in the Mimbres Mountains, almost directly atop the Continental Divide, Beyer cornered Victorio's warriors as they were building rock breastworks. He attempted a parley, but the two sides could not agree. Meanwhile, Sgt. Delaware Penn and a few troopers of Company I moved to the Indians' flank.

The talk quickly broke down and firing commenced. At one point, warriors surrounded Wright after killing his horse, and Sgt. Thomas Boyne saved him. After 30 minutes of shooting, Victorio abandoned his position and the Indians retreated down the ridge, leaving behind large quantities of blankets, skins, meat, and mescal.

Two of Victorio's warriors were wounded. Pvt. Frank Dorsey, Company C, was killed, and Pvts. George H. Moore, Company C, and John Scott, Company I, were wounded. Boyne received a Medal of Honor for rescuing Wright.[746]

25 JUNE 1879
TONTO BASIN (Payson, Arizona)

In early June, near Baker Butte, Apaches ambushed two riders on the road from Fort Apache to Camp Verde, killing one. A punitive expedition was put together at Camp Verde, consisting of a detachment of Company B, Indian scouts, under Lt. Frederick Von Schrader, 12th Infantry. After two weeks of tracking, the scouts attacked a rancheria in the Tonto Basin. They killed six warriors and captured one.[747]

17 JULY 1879
MILK RIVER (Saco, Montana)

The Hunkpapas of Sitting Bull, the Minneconjous of Black Eagle, the Sans Arcs of Spotted Eagle, and the Oglalas of Big Road had all fled into Canada, and Col. Nelson A. Miles continued to patrol the border from Fort Peck. In the summer of 1879, Miles had seven companies of the 5th Infantry, seven troops of the 2nd Cavalry, and two companies of the 6th Infantry—about 676 soldiers, plus 143 Indian and white auxiliaries.

The Lakotas were safe in Canada, but lack of game forced them to cross the border on several occasions. On 17 July, as Miles marched his men up the Milk River, his advance units—one company of 5th Infantry, one of the 2nd Cavalry, and some Indian scouts, commanded by Lt. William Philo Clark—ran into more than 300 Indians under Sitting Bull near the mouth of Beaver Creek. Clark was outnumbered, but he harrassed Sitting Bull into retreating.

Clark hounded the Hunkpapas for 12 miles, to a point near the mouth of Frenchman Creek, where the Indians sent the women and children over to the north bank of the Milk, then turned to face their pursuers. Clark was having a tough time in the battle until Miles arrived with the rest of the command. When they appeared, Sitting Bull's warriors sped north across the border with their families.

The Lakotas lost a large amount of property, although only about three were killed and three wounded. Miles took an equal number of casualties.[748]

27 JULY 1879
SALT LAKE (Salt Flat, Texas)

Scouting out of Fort Davis, Capt. Michael L. Courtney, 25th Infantry, with a detachment of H Company of that regiment and a detachment of H Company, 10th Cavalry, attacked Apaches at the salt lakes in present-day Hudspeth County, Texas. They wounded three Indians, two of them mortally, and captured ten ponies. Two of Courtney's men were wounded.[749]

29 JULY 1879
BIG CREEK/VINEGAR HILL (Big Creek, Idaho)

From camps deep in the mountain wilderness of central Idaho, a band of renegade Bannocks and Shoshones known as the Sheepeaters were raiding stock. Several soldier columns were sent to track them down. One of them, under Lt. Henry Catley, left Grangeville, Idaho, with about 50 mounted men of Companies C and K of the 2nd Infantry.

Catley's men were following the raiders' trail single file along a steep slope above Big Creek when suddenly an Indian appeared and called out to his companions. Rifles cracked, knocking two soldiers off their horses. Catley dismounted his men and they fired into the cliffs, but they could not see their assailants.

The troopers backtracked and camped at nightfall. The next morning they continued on but lost their way. On a peak known as Vinegar Hill, Catley's pack train was attacked. The Indians surrounded Catley's men and set fire to the grass, but the soldiers lit a backfire and stopped the flames. Abandoning much of the equipment, Catley quickly retreated. He had been driven out by only 15 warriors. A court-martial later convicted him of misconduct.[750]

4 SEPTEMBER 1879
OJO CALIENTE (Winston, New Mexico)

In a surprise attack at Camp Ojo Caliente, on Alamosa Creek about 18 miles north of present-day Winston, New Mexico, the Mimbres Apache Victorio and 60 warriors swept down on the horse herd of Capt. Ambrose E. Hooker's Company E, 9th Cavalry. The warriors killed five soldiers and three civilians in the raid.[751] They got away with 18 mules and 50 horses, including Hooker's personal mount. It was the beginning round of the "Victorio War."[752]

18 SEPTEMBER 1879
LAS ANIMAS CREEK (Hillsboro, New Mexico)

After Victorio's raid at Ojo Caliente (see previous entry), the Mimbres Apache and his men did not go far. They holed up in the Black Range at

Apache chief Victorio
—Courtesy Denver Public Library,
Western History Department

the head of Las Animas Creek, about 12 miles northwest of present-day Hillsboro, New Mexico. Lt. Col. Nathan A. M. Dudley led a column of Companies B, C, E, and G, 9th Cavalry, and 46 Navajo scouts in pursuit. Dudley, with Capt. Ambrose E. Hooker's E Company and Lt. Byron Dawson's B Company, found perhaps 150 Apaches in a strongly entrenched position and tried to dislodge them. Not far away, Capt. Charles D. Beyer and Lt. William H. Hugo, with the other two companies, heard the gunshots and rushed in to assist. Despite having superior numbers, the soldiers could not overpower the Apaches, and darkness allowed Victorio to slip away.

Dudley lost five troopers, two Indian scouts, and one civilian, with two enlisted men wounded and 32 horses killed.[753]

29–30 SEPTEMBER 1879
CUCHILLO NEGRO CREEK (Chloride, New Mexico)

On 28 September, continuing his raiding, the Mimbres Apache Victorio (see previous entries) attacked a mail party two miles from Camp Ojo Caliente. Maj. Albert P. Morrow, now in command of military operations in New Mexico, quickly followed with detachments of Companies B, C, and G, 9th Cavalry; a detachment of 6th Cavalry; and some Apache scouts—about 190 men.

The next day, Morrow caught up to Victorio on Cuchillo Negro Creek, near present-day Winston, New Mexico. They fought from midafternoon until 10 P.M. Early the next morning, an Apache fired into Morrow's camp, killing a sentinel, and the fighting resumed. Morrow finally drove the Indians from the field, then took his tired men and horses back to Cuchillo Negro Creek for water.

Two soldiers were killed. Morrow's men killed three Mimbres and wounded several others, including Victorio's son, Washington.[754]

29 SEPTEMBER–5 OCTOBER 1879
MILK CREEK (Meeker, Colorado)

At White River Indian agent Nathan C. Meeker's request for help, Maj. Thomas T. Thornburgh, 4th Infantry, left Fort Fred Steele in Wyoming with 153 men of Companies D and F of the 5th Cavalry; Company E, 3rd Cavalry; Company E, 4th Infantry; and 25 civilians. Leaving the infantry on Fortification Creek, Colorado, Thornburgh continued on with about 120 troopers. Sixteen miles northeast of present-day Meeker, Colorado, 300 Ute warriors under Colorow, angry at Meeker and threatened by the soldiers, stopped Thornburgh, and a fight broke out.

Early in the battle, while checking on the wagons, Thornburgh caught a fatal bullet in the head. The command fell upon Capt. J. Scott Payne, 5th Cavalry, who corralled the 25 wagons in an oval, about 200 yards from Milk Creek, and moved the skirmish line to take cover among the wagons. To enlarge the circle, the soldiers shot about 20 wounded mules for barricades, and a six-day siege began.

The Utes were good shots, and they pummeled the corral with a heavy fire. Then they lit a grass fire and very nearly forced the soldiers out of their position. That night, Payne sent couriers for help. At the time, Capt. Francis S. Dodge was moving to the White River Agency from Middle Park with 35 troopers of Company D, 9th Cavalry. When he learned there was a battle going on, he raced 70 miles in 23 hours, riding into Payne's corral on 2 October. Almost immediately, most of Dodge's horses were shot down, but Payne now had fresh men and guns. The persistent Utes did not leave until Col. Wesley Merritt arrived on 5 October with four companies of the 5th Cavalry and five companies of the 4th Infantry.

The Utes lost 37 warriors, but they killed 13 soldiers and civilians and wounded 47 others.[755]

29 SEPTEMBER 1879
WHITE RIVER MASSACRE/MEEKER MASSACRE (Meeker, Colorado)

Nathan C. Meeker, agent of the White River Utes in northwest Colorado, had incited hatred among his charges by demanding that they become farmers and by plowing up the meadows where they grazed their horses. When Meeker called for help from the army to quell the disturbances, the Utes were inflamed. While Colorow's warriors fought the soldiers who came in response (see previous entry), 20 others, led by Douglas, went to the agency and murdered Meeker and eight of his employees. They looted and burned the buildings, then carried off Meeker's wife and daughter, and another woman, Flora Ellen Price, and her two children. The captives were later rescued.[756]

In 1880 Ute leaders traveled to Washington, where they agreed to allow their bands to be relocated to Utah and southwestern Colorado.

13 OCTOBER 1879
LLOYD'S AND SLOCUM'S RANCHES (Nutt, New Mexico)

A score of volunteers from Mesilla, New Mexico, deciding to help the army fight Indians, scouted west into the foothills of the Black Range. Near Lloyd's Ranch, they saw three apparently unattended horses and went after them, riding right into an Apache ambush. Five Mexicans and one American, W. T. Jones, were killed, and the others escaped.

After the incident the Apaches, possibly of Juh's band recently returned from Mexico, saw a wagon train near Slocum's Ranch and attacked. They killed 11 men, throwing the bodies into the flames of the burning wagons, and ran off to the Florida Mountains with a captured woman and child.[757]

27 OCTOBER 1879
GUZMAN MOUNTAINS (Northwestern Chihuahua, Mexico)

Continuing the "Victorio War" (see Ojo Caliente, 4 September ff.), Maj. Albert P. Morrow kept up the search for the Mimbres Victorio. On 4 October, he left Camp Ojo Caliente and marched to Forts Bayard and Cummings with forces that included 113 men in detachments of the 6th and 9th Cavalry (Companies B, G, H, and I), plus 25 San Carlos Reservation scouts.

Three weeks of hard campaigning followed, and he chased Victorio to the Guzman Mountains near Corralitos Creek in northwestern Chihuahua. By this time, sickness, broken-down horses, and exhaustion had reduced his command to 81 men and 18 scouts. Nevertheless, on the evening of 27 October, Morrow pushed his men up the mountainside in the moonlight. The Indians were reduced to throwing rocks down on them. Morrow himself had only three hours' worth of ammunition left. Victorio retreated deeper into Mexico, and Morrow returned to Fort Bayard on 2 November.

One enlisted man was killed and two were wounded. There were no Indian casualties.[758]

—1880—

12 JANUARY 1880
PERCHA CREEK (Hillsboro, New Mexico)

Maj. Albert P. Morrow had chased Victorio's Apaches back into Mexico in late October 1879 (see previous entry), but in early January 1880, the band was back in New Mexico, and Morrow again took up the chase. On the 10th the major received a report that the Mimbres were in the Black Range, and with detachments of Companies B, C, F, G, H, and M of the

Percha Creek (New Mexico)

9th Cavalry, he was on the trail 24 hours behind the band. Morrow caught up with them two days later on upper Percha Creek, west of present Hillsboro, New Mexico, and a sharp fight ensued, lasting from 2 P.M. until dark. Victorio then broke for the San Mateo Mountains, north of Ojo Caliente.

Sgt. D. J. Gross and another enlisted man were killed, and one was wounded. There were no Indian casualties.[759]

17 JANUARY 1880
SAN MATEO MOUNTAINS (Monticello, New Mexico)

After the Percha Creek skirmish (see previous entry), Maj. Albert P. Morrow, with Companies B, C, F, H, and M of the 9th Cavalry, followed Victorio's trail into the San Mateo Mountains. With his 60 warriors, Victorio came within 15 miles of the Ojo Caliente Agency and sent word that he would like to surrender, but not to soldiers. The agent replied that the government in Washington would have to make a treaty.

Meanwhile, Morrow caught up with the wily Mimbreno on 17 January and drove him from his mountain position. After killing Lt. James H. French and wounding two enlisted men, Victorio escaped again, without casualties. Morrow returned to Camp Ojo Caliente for supplies and a rest.[760]

30 JANUARY 1880
CABALLO MOUNTAINS (Caballo, New Mexico)

Fleeing Maj. Albert P. Morrow, Victorio (see previous entries) moved south between the Black Range and the Rio Grande, pursued by Morrow's enlarged command. Victorio's Mimbres band split up for a time, then reunited near the mouth of Las Animas Creek. There, Capt. Louis H. Rucker, with detachments of Companies B and M, 9th Cavalry, struck them, chasing Victorio into the Caballo Mountains. Three of Rucker's men were wounded, and one of Victorio's warriors was killed.[761]

3 FEBRUARY 1880
SAN ANDRES MOUNTAINS (South-central New Mexico)

The hard-riding Maj. Albert P. Morrow directed three commands, including Companies B, C, F, G, H, and M, 9th Cavalry, across the Rio Grande to converge on his target, the Mimbres Apache Victorio (see previous entries). Morrow suspected Victorio's band might join up with the Mescaleros. In the San Andres Mountain, northeast of Aleman's Well, Morrow and his men found Victorio's warriors drawn up in squads of 15 to 20 men on the sides of the canyon. The soldiers drove the Indians from ledge to crevice, only to have them move to new positions in a series of maneuvers that lasted until dark. The next day Victorio broke off the action and disappeared. Morrow, his men exhausted, also pulled out.

Four enlisted men were wounded, and Morrow thought his men had killed some Indians, but he never knew for certain.[762]

9 FEBRUARY 1880
SAN ANDRES MOUNTAINS (South-central New Mexico)

When Maj. Albert P. Morrow left after the 3 February battle (see previous entry), only Capt. Louis H. Rucker's detachment of 9th Cavalrymen were left to poke around the San Andres Mountains to see where Victorio's Mimbres band had gone. Six days after the first encounter, Rucker ran into the Apaches in another fortified position in a narrow canyon. The Indians fired first, hitting several of Rucker's men and horses. Seeing they had the advantage, the Apaches charged the troops, "who gave way, and retreated in pell-mell order."[763] Victorio took the soldiers' bedding and rations. Rucker had about four men wounded.[764]

12 FEBRUARY 1880
PUMPKIN CREEK (Volborg, Montana)

Early in 1880, the Lakotas began warring along the Yellowstone River near Fort Keogh. Hunkpapas fought with Gros Ventres on 3 February, and on the 5th, 40 Lakotas attacked 3 hay cutters on Powder River, wounding two. The workers reported the incident to the fort, and Sgt. T. B.

Glover, 8 men of Company B, 2nd Cavalry, and 11 Indian scouts went after the Lakotas.

A 65-mile chase took the soldiers to Pumpkin Creek, where they cornered six Indians, killing one and wounding two. They captured the last three when a company of 5th Infantry under Capt. Simon Snyder arrived. Glover lost one soldier and one was wounded.[765]

3 APRIL 1880
PECOS FALLS (Grandfalls, Texas)

When Mescalero raiders stole horses from rancher Francis Rooney near the falls of the Pecos River, near present-day Grandfalls, Texas, 10th Cavalry detachments from Companies D and L, under Lt. Calvin Esterly, pursued them. The soldiers found a trail that led north through the sand hills east of the Pecos River, in present-day Ward and Loving Counties. The nearly waterless, three-day pursuit ended when, during a dust storm, Esterly hit the unsuspecting raiders. The soldiers killed one Indian and recovered eight head of stock.[766]

7–8 APRIL 1880
HEMBRILLO CANYON/SAN ANDRES SPRINGS
(South-central New Mexico)

Hiding out in the San Andres Mountains, Mimbres Apache leaders Victorio and Nana joined forces with the Mescaleros, as Maj. Albert P. Morrow had predicted (see San Andres Mountains, 3 February). While the 120 Mescalero and Mimbres warriors were encamped in Hembrillo Canyon, about 40 miles north of present-day Las Cruces, New Mexico, three columns of troops set out to converge on them. Capt. Henry Carroll took Companies A, D, F, and G of the 9th Cavalry, about 100 men, out of Fort Stanton to strike the Indian camp on the south.

On 5 April, Carroll stopped at a mountain spring for water, but it was saturated with gypsum. The next morning, both men and horses were almost too sick to go on, but Carroll pushed them forward. Now they desperately needed the water at Victorio's camp.

About 6 P.M. on 7 April, Carroll and his men staggered into the canyon, heading for the spring. The soldiers' sudden appearance frightened off the Apaches at first, but when they noticed that the troopers were weak, they returned to the cliff sides and poured a hot fire into them, keeping them away from the springs. A few troopers managed to fill their canteens, but it was not enough. Victorio stopped the attack at nightfall, hoping to finish the soldiers off in the morning.

Unbeknownst to the Indians, Capt. Curwin B. McClellan, with Company L of the 6th Cavalry and Indian scouts, about 120 men, were on their way. Delayed because of a broken water pump at Aleman's Well, McClellan's men made a night march to the canyon. They arrived on the morning of

8 April to find Carroll surrounded and under fire. As McClellan's men swarmed in, the Apaches scattered and fled south.

Meanwhile, Col. Edward Hatch and several companies of the 9th Cavalry were also heading to the canyon, going up the same trail that Victorio's and Nana's bands were now on. Before they met the Indians, however, Hatch got a message about Carroll's desperate situation and changed his course, just missing the Apaches. Victorio and Nana split up their bands and all got away.

The Apaches lost three killed and perhaps six wounded. Eight soldiers were wounded, including Carroll, and 25 horses and mules were killed.[767]

9 APRIL 1880
SHAKEHAND SPRINGS (Whites City, New Mexico)

Col. Benjamin Grierson, 10th Cavalry, sent Capt. Thomas C. Lebo and Company K on a scout along the Black River into the Guadalupe Mountains. From there, Lebo was to ride north to the Bluewater River and the settlements on the middle Rio Penasco in New Mexico. The day after they started, the soldiers suddenly came upon an Apache camp at Shakehand Springs, 40 miles south of the Rio Penasco. They killed one chief and captured four women and one child. They also recovered about 25 head of livestock and many provisions from the Mescalero agency. One of the captives was a kidnapped Mexican boy named Coyetano Garcia.[768]

16 APRIL 1880
MESCALERO AGENCY (Mescalero, New Mexico)

On 16 April, Cols. Benjamin Grierson and Edward Hatch assembled about 700 men of the 6th, 9th, and 10th Cavalries at the Mescalero Agency near Tularosa, New Mexico, to oversee the surrender of 309 Apaches. Hatch wanted to disarm them, but agent Samuel A. Russell warned him that if the Indians had known that their weapons would be taken, they would not have come in at all.

About 10 A.M., Army scouts killed two Indians who appeared to be raiding stock. Russell was irate, insisting he had authorized them to drive in some strays. At 2 P.M., Capt. Charles Steelhammer and Company G of the 15th Infantry attempted to disarm the Mescaleros. A fight broke out as the Indians ran. The soldiers killed 14 warriors. Grierson rounded up most of the escapees, but 30 got away, heading south toward the Guadalupe Mountains.[769]

17 APRIL 1880
DOG CANYON (Alamogordo, New Mexico)

The day after the Mescalero Agency fight (see previous entry) the Apache warriors who fled were found in Dog Canyon by Maj. Albert P. Morrow's battalion of Company L, 6th Cavalry, D and L, 9th Cavalry, and Indian scouts. Morrow killed 3 of them and captured 20 horses.[770]

7 MAY 1880
ASH CREEK VALLEY (Fort Thomas, Arizona)

Hiding out somewhere in the mountains, Mimbres Apache leader Victorio (see Hembrillo Canyon/San Andres Springs, 7–8 April) sent his son Washington with about 14 well-armed warriors on a swift strike of the San Carlos Agency. On the way, however, some Indian hunters from the agency spotted Washington's party, and a runner brought word to Capt. Adam Kramer, 6th Cavalry.

Kramer swept up 20 men from Companies D and E, 6th Cavalry, plus 20 scouts, and rushed to the scene. His horsemen outpaced the unmounted scouts, and the soldiers found themselves facing what Kramer thought were more than 40 warriors. Washington's Mimbres fired a volley, forcing Kramer to withdraw. The two sides skirmished until Kramer's scouts arrived, whereupon the Mimbres broke and ran. Lt. Augustus P. Blocksom tried to follow, but the Apaches moved quickly east up Ash Creek Valley and into the Natanes Mountains.

Sgt. Dan Griffin and one Indian scout were killed.[771]

13 MAY 1880
BASS CANYON (Van Horn, Texas)

About 20 Apaches attacked a well-armed westbound train of 20 wagons in Bass Canyon, east of Eagle Springs. Several wagons overturned as the frightened drivers tried to flee. Settlers D. Murphy and his wife and child hid in the brush, while the Indians found several others. The raiders killed Hames Grant, wounded Harry Graham, and mortally wounded Mrs. Graham. When they came upon Murphy and his family, Murphy was hit twice, but he bluffed the Indians away with a disabled rifle.

Meanwhile, driver "Dutch Willie" sped his wagon into the station at Eagle Springs. Capt. Louis Carpenter and Company H, 10th Cavalry, rushed to the scene, but the Indians were gone.[772] About ten people from the train had been killed or wounded.

24 MAY 1880
PALOMAS RIVER (Chloride, New Mexico)

Army regulars had been searching for Victorio's Mimbres band for months (see Guzman Mountains, 27 October 1879 ff.), but it was the civilians and scouts who caused him the most damage. Chief scout Henry K. Parker and about 60 Indians, attached to Hatch's command, looked for Victorio in the mountains west of the Rio Grande. Drawing three days' rations, Parker scouted south along the foothills of the Mimbres Mountains (Black Range), and on 23 May, he found a trail heading upstream on the Palomas River. The scouts found Victorio in a box canyon on the river near Brushy Mountain.

Parker's scouts spent the night stealthily surrounding the camp. Twenty went around the camp, 30 went to the rear, and 10 went with Parker to the side. He left the entrance open, correctly figuring that Victorio would never try to break out the way he had come in. At dawn, the scouts in the rear opened fire, killing several men and women. The Apaches ran in another direction and collided with more scouts, then ran into Parker's group. The trapped Apaches dug in among the rocks, leaving the women and children to face the fire while they entrenched.

Parker's scouts kept up their fire all day. They learned that Victorio had been hit in the leg, and heard the women shout that if their chief died, "they would eat him, so that no white man should see his body!"

At the end of the day, Parker sent a messenger back to Hatch, saying that he had Victorio trapped and needed more ammunition. He then pulled back five miles to wait for assistance, which never came. After two days, Parker took his command back to Camp Ojo Caliente. He had lost not a man, but killed 30 men, women, and children, and captured 74 head of stock.[773]

5 JUNE 1880
COOKE'S CANYON (Deming, New Mexico)

About 25 Apaches fleeing from Parker's attack on the Palomas River (see previous entry) were traveling through Cooke's Range, west of Fort Cummings, on their way to Mexico. Maj. Albert P. Morrow, with four troops of the 9th Cavalry, struck the outnumbered Apaches in Cooke's Canyon. They killed ten and wounded three, and captured much livestock. One of the dead was thought to be Victorio's son, Washington.[774]

30 JULY 1880
TINAJA DE LAS PALMAS (Sierra Blanca, Texas)

Mimbres Apache leader Victorio, leading a combined group of Mimbres, Chiricahua, and Mescalero Apaches, was in Mexico in the summer of 1880. After the Apaches fought with Mexican soldiers under Col. Adolfo J. Valle, Valle sent word to Col. Benjamin H. Grierson, 10th Cavalry, at Fort Davis that Victorio's band was heading north toward the Rio Grande. Grierson already had companies stationed at subposts along the border, such as Viejo Pass, Eagle Springs, and old Fort Quitman, as well as at water holes Victorio was likely to use.

At Fort Quitman on 27 July, Grierson surmised Victorio's location and took a small detachment toward Eagle Springs. In the Quitman Mountains he received word that Victorio was close by. Grierson camped at Tinaja de las Palmas, the only water hole in the area, at the end of Devil's Ridge, about 15 miles southeast of present-day Sierra Blanca, Texas. He had only eight men, including his teenage son Robert, who had accompanied him for a little adventure. That night, Grierson asked a passing stagecoach to take a message to Eagle Springs. At 4 A.M., Lt. Leighton Finley and 13 troopers of Company G rode up, ready to escort Grierson to the post. But the colonel instead placed Finley and his men in position among the rocks and sent another courier for more reinforcements.

At 9 A.M. the Indians came into view, an estimated 60 to 150 warriors. A sharp fight ensued for the next two hours, but Grierson's dogged resistance kept Victorio from the water. At 11 A.M. Capt. Charles D. Viele rode in with men of Companies C and G and stemmed the tide. The Apaches withdrew to a ridge to the south, but Viele drove them out. Then Capt. Nicholas Nolan and Company A rode in from Fort Quitman, and the Apaches fell back to the Rio Grande.

Lt. Samuel R. Colladay was wounded and Pvt. Martin Davis was killed, and three other enlisted men were wounded. The Apaches lost seven killed and an undetermined number wounded.[775]

6 AUGUST 1880
RATTLESNAKE SPRINGS (Van Horn, Texas)

Mimbres leader Victorio was turned back to Mexico at Tinaja de las Palmas (see previous entry), but several days later he was back, heading north to join other Apache bands still in the Guadalupe Mountains of New Mexico. Col. Benjamin H. Grierson believed Victorio and his band would pass Van Horn's Well, so he concentrated his troops there. But the wily Apaches bypassed the well on 4 August.

Grierson figured Victorio would head for Rattlesnake Springs, in the breaks of the Sierra Diablos, about 65 miles north. He sped his men there, covering the distance in 21 hours. The colonel placed Companies C and G, under Capt. Charles D. Viele, in Rattlesnake Canyon. At 2 P.M. on 6 August, Victorio and his band approached. The soldiers held their fire, but Victorio, suspecting a trap, did not come close. When Viele opened up on them, the Apaches fell back to the canyon walls. Seeing the small number of troops, however, Victorio regrouped and counterattacked. The arrival of Capt. Louis H. Carpenter and Companies B and H brought a standoff, and Victorio again went back into the mountains.

At about 4 P.M. Capt. John C. Gilmore and men of the 24th Infantry rode in with supply wagons for Grierson. About eight miles from the springs, Victorio, unable to resist the temptation, attacked the wagons. Soldiers hiding in the wagons threw back the covers and put out a heavy fire, killing one Apache, wounding others, and driving back the rest.

At dusk the Indians made one more attempt to get to the water hole, but the soldiers again repulsed them, this time with Capt. Louis Carpenter pursuing them. The Apaches turned back to Mexico.

Grierson reported three men killed, three seriously wounded, and several minor injuries, with one trooper missing, presumed dead. He believed he had killed or wounded 30 warriors.[776]

1 SEPTEMBER 1880
AGUA CHIQUITA CANYON (Weed, New Mexico)

At Agua Chiquita Canyon, east of the Sacramento Mountains, Sgt. James Robinson and 10 privates of Company G, 9th Cavalry, were driving a herd of army horses and mules when they were attacked by about 25 Apaches, on foot but well-armed. Robinson countercharged into a heavy fire and drove away the Indians. Two privates were killed.[777]

7 SEPTEMBER 1880
FORT CUMMINGS (Deming, New Mexico)

Early in September, Apaches attacked a stagecoach 16 miles west of Fort Cummings, northwest of present-day Deming, New Mexico. The driver and two passengers were killed; one of the victims was Emery S. Madden, the 19-year-old son of Capt. Dan Madden of the 6th Cavalry. Capt. Leopold O. Parker with Company A, 4th Cavalry, was quickly on the Indians' trail, but he exacted no revenge for the killings. When he found the Apaches, the warriors killed one soldier and two Indian scouts, and wounded two other scouts.[778]

Fort Cummings (New Mexico)

28 OCTOBER 1880
OJO CALIENTE (Southwestern Texas)

Renegade Mimbres Apache leader Victorio finally met his destruction at the hands of Mexican soldiers at Tres Castillos in Chihuahua on 14 October 1880. Not knowing his fate, about 35 warriors were about to cross the Rio Grande to join him. On the river below Ojo Caliente, south of the Quitman Mountains, the Apaches spotted 12 soldiers. Under Sgt. Charles Perry, the troopers were on picket duty for Capt. Theodore A. Baldwin's detachments of Companies B, I, and K, 10th Cavalry. The Apaches jumped the soldiers and, firing at point-blank range, killed five.[779] The Indians escaped across the Rio Grande with four horses and two mules.[780]

—1881—

2 JANUARY 1881
POPLAR RIVER (Poplar, Montana)

In late 1880, several Lakota bands were persuaded to surrender at the Poplar River Agency in Montana. As they gathered, however, they became restive and belligerent, and the agent requested more soldiers. Maj. Guido Ilges, 5th Infantry, left Fort Keogh with 180 men—mounted detachments of Companies A, B, C, F, and G, of his regiment—for the 200-mile march to the agency. There he joined up with agency units, adding a detachment of Company F, 7th Cavalry, and Company F, 11th Infantry, to his force.

With 300 men and two howitzers, Ilges moved out to meet the 400 Lakotas camped on the other side of the Missouri River. The Indians fled to some nearby timber, and Ilges attacked, opening up with his howitzers, which quickly convinced the Indians to yield. Eight Indians were killed and 324 gave up, turning over 200 horses and 69 rifles and pistols. About 60 escaped.[781]

29 JANUARY 1881
SIERRA DIABLO (Salt Flat, Texas)

A number of survivors from Victorio's decimated Apache band—12 warriors, 4 women, and 4 children—came back into Texas in January 1881 and attacked a stage in Quitman Canyon, killing the driver, named Morgan, and a passenger named Crenshaw. Capt. George W. Baylor left Ysleta with 15 Texas Rangers and some Pueblo Indian scouts to trail them.

At the Eagle Mountains, the Rangers lost the trail, but about a dozen more Rangers, under Lt. C. L. Nevill from Fort Davis, picked it up. It led north from Eagle Springs to the edge of the Sierra Diablo. On the morning of 29 January, 19 Rangers crept up on the raiders' sleeping camp, and just as the sun rose they opened fire. The Apaches ran, according to Baylor, "like a herd of deer." The fight was over in a short time.

With no losses of their own. the Rangers killed four warriors, two women, and two children. One woman and two children were captured.[782]

3 MAY 1881

SIERRA DEL BURROS (Northern Coahuila, Mexico)

On 14 April, Lipan raiders from Mexico looted ranches at the head of the Frio River in Real County, Texas. They killed a Mrs. McLauren and a boy named Allen Reiss. Lt. John Bullis, 24th Infantry, and 34 Seminole-Negro scouts, with the order to capture or kill the marauders, rode out of Fort Clark and picked up the trail.

With the help of Teresita, a daughter of Lipan chief Costillito captured in 1873, Bullis tracked the raiders west to Devil's River. By this time, however, Teresita realized that the people she was tracking were from her own band, and she deliberately tried to give Bullis false leads. One of the scouts, however, saw the deception and was able to keep the party on the right path.

Six more days of tracking through the Sierra del Burros in Coahuila brought Bullis to the Lipans' camp. Leaving seven men to watch Teresita and the horses, he attacked at daybreak on 3 May. The 27 scouts rushed into the sleeping rancheria and killed 5 Lipans, rescued a kidnapped woman and boy, and reclaimed 21 horses. Lipan leader San-da-ve was mortally wounded. Bullis's scouts took no casualties and crossed safely back into Texas.[783]

25 JULY 1881

SAN ANDRES MOUNTAINS (South-central New Mexico)

From Mexico, Chief Nana, with remnants of Victorio's Mimbres band and 25 Mescalero Apaches, attacked a supply train heading to Fort Stanton in Alamo Canyon on 17 July. The head packer, named Burgess, was wounded. Lt. John F. Guilfoyle, escorting the train, doggedly went after Nana with 20 troopers of Company L, 9th Cavalry, and some Apache scouts. Following the raiders' trail down Dog Canyon, Guilfoyle descended the Sacramento Mountains too late to stop Nana from murdering three Mexicans.

The soldiers pursued west across the blistering White Sands to the San Andres Mountains. On 25 July, while Nana stopped to rest, Guilfoyle caught up with him. The troopers wounded two warriors, while three of their own scouts were hit. They seized 2 horses, 12 mules, and all of Nana's camp supplies, but the old chief got away.[784]

1 AUGUST 1881

RED CANYON (Monticello, New Mexico)

Fleeing from Lt. John F. Guilfoyle, Chief Nana (see previous entry) and his Apache band crossed the Rio Grande and moved northwest to the San Mateo Mountains. Near the river, the Indians killed two miners and a

Mexican, then killed four more Mexicans in the foothills. The band hid in Red Canyon while things cooled off.

The white settlers, meanwhile, were up in arms over the killings. About 36 men organized a party to find the Apaches. By chance they searched the brush-choked Red Canyon, nooning at a freshwater spring on 1 August. Suddenly, Nana's warriors popped out of the bushes, shooting and waving blankets to stampede the horses. It was over in seconds: one white civilian was dead and seven more were wounded. Thirty-eight of their horses were gone. Nana killed one more Mexican on the way out of the canyon and rode on.[785]

3 AUGUST 1881
MONICA SPRINGS (Monticello, New Mexico)

After a day to rest and resupply at Fort Craig, Lt. John F. Guilfoyle and his detachment of L Company, 9th Cavalry, and Indian scouts took up their pursuit of the renegade Apache chief Nana (see previous entries). On 3 August, Guilfoyle caught up with Nana at Monica Springs in the San Mateos Mountains. His men wounded 2 warriors and captured 11 horses, but Nana slipped away again. This time, the worn-out soldiers could not catch up.[786]

12 AUGUST 1881
CARRIZO CANYON (Sabinal, New Mexico)

Capt. Charles Parker, operating out of Fort Wingate with 19 men of Company K, 9th Cavalry, struck a band of Apaches under Nana in Carrizo Canyon, about 25 miles west of Sabinal, New Mexico. Though outnumbered two to one, Parker's men fought the Indians for an hour and a half before the Indians broke off the action. Five troopers were killed and one was captured and later killed. One Apache was killed and three were wounded. For extraordinary courage, Sgt. Thomas Shaw received a Medal of Honor.[787]

16 AUGUST 1881
CUCHILLO NEGRO CREEK (Chloride, New Mexico)

A distraught Mexican rancher told Lt. Gustavus Valois at Camp Ojo Caliente that Indians had killed his wife and three children at Alamosa Creek. Valois sent Lt. George R. Burnett and 15 men of Company I, 9th Cavalry, to confirm the report. Burnett quickly found the raiders' trail, heading down the eastern face of the Black Range. It was that of the renegade Apache chief Nana and his band. Because the raiders were driving livestock, they moved slowly, and Burnett was able to catch them along Cuchillo Negro Creek.

Nana took a strong position in the rocks and Burnett could not dislodge him. Trooper John Rogers rode back to get Valois with more men, but the enlarged company still made no progress against the entrenched

Apaches. When the Apaches cut off four soldiers, Burnett, Sgt. Moses Williams, and Pvt. Augustus Walley braved intense rifle fire to rescue them, for which they all earned Medals of Honor. Nana escaped after nightfall.

Burnett was wounded twice and two enlisted men were slain.[788]

19 AUGUST 1881
GAVILAN CANYON (San Juan, New Mexico)

Col. Edward Hatch, 9th Cavalry, made one last try to stop Nana's Apache band as they moved south toward Mexico (see previous entry). He sent Lt. George W. Smith and a detachment of 46 men from Companies B and H from Fort Cummings to intercept them. Smith only took 20 men on his scout, but 20 cowboys, led by George Daly, joined the soldiers. Nana's trail led into Gavilan Canyon, east of the Mimbres River on the south flank of the Mimbres Mountains.

At the arroyo, Smith slowed down, fearing an ambush, but Daly led his cowboys on. Sure enough, the Indians opened fire. Smith came to the rescue, but both he and Daly were killed, and the cowboys fled the scene. Sgt. Brent Woods of Company B took command and held the ground until the rest of Company H arrived. The two forces now about evenly matched, Nana broke off the action and continued to Mexico.

Three soldiers and three civilians were killed or mortally wounded, and seven more were wounded. Woods received a Medal of Honor.[789]

30 AUGUST 1881
CIBECUE CREEK (Cibecue, Arizona)

After the success of Lt. Col. George Crook's campaigns in the 1870s, the White Mountain Apaches had been relatively quiet for a decade. The medicine man Nochaydelklinne, however, had visions of an Apache resurgence and the white man's disappearance, and he had been stirring up the Indians at the San Carlos Agency. Agent J. C. Tiffany requested assistance. On 29 August, Col. Eugene A. Carr, 6th Cavalry, took 80 soldiers of Companies D and E, 10 civilians, and 23 White Mountain scouts, under Lt. Thomas Cruse, from Fort Apache to investigate.

The command marched about 35 miles northwest to Nochaydelklinne's village on Cibecue Creek and arrived midafternoon on the 30th. The troopers rode up to the prophet's wickiup, announcing that he must come with them or be killed. The old man smiled and said that such a thing would never happen. The watching crowd was tense, but the Apache scouts reassured Nochaydelklinne, and he submitted quietly. The column turned to return to Fort Apache.

A few miles downstream, the troops stopped to set up camp for the night. The Apache scouts were agitated, and an Indian sergeant, Dead Shot, said he would not camp there. Suddenly he gave a war whoop, and the

Apache scouts began blazing away at the soldiers. Dead Shot and Dandy Jim tried to rescue Nochaydelklinne, but a trooper pumped three shots into the old man's head. Incredibly, the medicine man survived the wounds, but later Sgt. John A. Smith finished him off with an ax.

After arranging breastworks out of boxes, cans, and rocks, the soldiers fired back at their attackers, who soon numbered nearly 800. Although they greatly outnumbered the soldiers, the Apaches made no concentrated assault. The firing ended at nightfall. Carr buried his dead—five enlisted men and an officer—inside a tent, then pulled out. Three other enlisted men had been wounded, one mortally. The only Apache casualty was Nochaydelklinne.[790]

31 AUGUST–1 SEPTEMBER 1881
FORT APACHE (Fort Apache, Arizona)

The White Mountain Apaches' anger over Nochaydelklinne's death at Cibecue Creek (see previous entry) was evidenced at Fort Apache and in the surrounding countryside. Warriors killed three freighters in a wagon train and two civilians, a rancher named Fibs and a mail carrier. They also killed three soldiers guarding the ferry at Black River and wounded Lt. Charles G. Gordon, 6th Cavalry. Apache casualties were not reported. The Indians held Fort Apache under siege for about two days. The soldiers finally turned the Apaches back.[791]

2 OCTOBER 1881
CEDAR SPRINGS (Fort Grant, Arizona)

Reports of the affair at Cibecue Creek (see 30 August), many of them exaggerated, inflamed public animosity toward the Apaches, and, fearing they would be punished, the Indians fled their camps. A band of 74 Chiricahuas, including Juh, Geronimo, Naiche, and Chato, headed for Mexico. Department of Arizona commander Col. Orlando B. Willcox, 12th Infantry, led a pursuit himself, with Company G of the 1st Cavalry, A and F of the 6th, a detachment of 8th Infantry, and Indian scouts.

Meanwhile, near Cedar Springs, on the flank of the Pinaleno Mountains, 16 miles northwest of Fort Grant, the renegade Chiricahuas attacked a wagon train. A settler, Mrs. Mowlds, saw from her house the Apaches murder her husband and six other men and loot the train. They were enjoying the plunder when Willcox arrived. The soldiers pitched into the Indians, who withdrew into the rocks and invited the troopers to come after them. The soldiers lost three men killed and three wounded in the attempt.

At dusk, the Apaches charged down a bluff to allow their women, children, and livestock to get away to Mexico. The Indians had no casualties.[792]

4 OCTOBER 1881
DRAGOON MOUNTAINS (Gleeson, Arizona)

After the Gavilan Canyon fight (see 19 August), most of Nana's band went to Mexico's Sierra Madres, but some lingered too long in the States. Capts. Henry Carroll and Charles Parker, with Companies F and K, 9th Cavalry, tracked them to the eastern edge of the Dragoon Mountains. A 15-mile chase ensued.

In the South Pass area, Nana's Apaches joined up with refugees from Gordo's, Bonito's, Naiche's, and Geronimo's bands, who had fought soldiers two days earlier at Cedar Springs and were still being pursued by Companies A and F, 6th Cavalry. The battle lasted from 4:30 P.M. until after dark, when the participants fired at muzzle flashes. A final army charge scattered the Indians, who raced to the Mexican border. Three 9th Cavalry soldiers were wounded, one Apache woman was killed, and four Indians were captured.[793]

—1882—

23 APRIL 1882
HORSESHOE CANYON (San Simon, Arizona)

The Chiricahuas who ran to Mexico after the Dragoon Mountains skirmish (see previous entry) returned in April and persuaded Chief Loco and several hundred other Apaches to flee the White Mountain and San Carlos Agencies. The fugitives hit the Camp Goodwin subagency on the Gila River on 19 April, killing chief of police Albert D. Sterling and Indian policeman Sagotal, then headed south, continuing to raid. By the time they

Gen. George A. Forsyth
—Courtesy Denver Public Library, Western History Department

reached the Peloncillo Mountains on the Arizona–New Mexico border four days later, the band had murdered about 40 whites.

Lt. Col. George A. "Sandy" Forsyth, 4th Cavalry, on patrol in the area, sent Lt. David N. McDonald west toward Stein's Peak with two enlisted men and seven scouts, including Yuma Bill. McDonald found the raiders' trail, heading north into the Peloncillos, and followed it into a canyon so narrow that his scouts would not follow him. Calling the scouts cowards, McDonald continued alone. Shamed, Yuma Bill soon followed with the rest.

The scouts' fears proved justified, for minutes later they were ambushed. Three scouts went down in the first volley. McDonald took a bullet through his hat and another one creased his jaw. Yuma Bill engaged in a gun battle to the death with several Apaches. McDonald forted up with his remaining men, facing Loco's 150 warriors, and sent a courier off to Forsyth.

Later in the day, Forsyth raced up with Companies C, F, G, H, and M of the 4th Cavalry. Forsyth, who had fought his share of Indians, pushed his troops forward, while Loco set fire to the grass to make a smoke screen. His probing attacks forced the Apaches to climb high above the soldiers, firing from points 1,000 or more feet up the cliff sides before melting away. Forsyth called an end to the chase.

One private was killed and a sergeant mortally wounded; Lt. John W. Martin and five enlisted men were wounded. Four scouts were also killed. Two Chiricahuas were killed.[794]

28 APRIL 1882
SIERRA ENMEDIO (Los Huerigos, Chihuahua, Mexico)

Following Loco's Apache band after the Horseshoe Canyon fight (see previous entry), Capts. Tullius C. Tupper and William A. Rafferty and 39 troopers of Companies G and M, 6th Cavalry, with 45 Indian scouts under Lts. Francis J. A. Darr and Albert L. Mills and guides Al Sieber and Pat Keogh, tracked them into Mexico. In the Sierra Enmedio, near the little town of Los Huerigos, about 20 miles south of the border, the soldiers and scouts found the unsuspecting Apaches, apparently secure in their belief that the Americans would not cross the border.

As the scouts moved into attack position around Loco's camp, one warrior and three women, searching for mescal in the predawn, ran into them, so the scouts shot them down, and the battle was on. Tupper's men joined in, firing about 800 rounds in four minutes. Loco's men dove for cover. With the fighting at rock-throwing distance, almost everyone who exposed himself was hit. Lt. John Y. F. "Bo" Blake and his troopers drove off 74 of Loco's horses. Loco called out to the Apache scouts, trying to get them to turn against the troopers, but they only cursed him and fired harder.

By 11:30 A.M., Tupper had only three rounds of ammunition per man left and had to pull out. Moving nine miles north, he halted to rest, where Col. Forsyth joined him with seven more companies of the 6th Cavalry. Forsyth wanted to return immediately to the fight, but Tupper's men were exhausted. When the soldiers returned the next day, the Apaches were gone.

The Indians lost 14 warriors and 7 women, and Loco himself was wounded. Tupper had one man killed, a Pvt. Goodrich, and two wounded.[795]

29 APRIL 1882
FORT WASHAKIE (Fort Washakie, Wyoming)

"Ute Jack," a White River Ute at the Shoshone Agency in Wyoming, was supposedly stirring up trouble. Lt. George H. Morgan took six men of Company K, 3rd Cavalry, to investigate. When Morgan went to arrest Jack, the Ute resisted, wielding a knife, and attempted to escape. The soldiers shot him in the arm, but he ducked into a tipi and grabbed a carbine, then killed a sergeant of the detachment. When Maj. Julius W. Mason, 3rd Cavalry, arrived with more soldiers, Jack was finally captured and killed.[796]

23 JUNE 1882
MESCALERO AGENCY (Mescalero, New Mexico)

In the winter of 1882, the Mescalero Give-Me-a-Horse escaped from confinement at Fort Union and took refuge at the Mescalero Agency near Fort Stanton. After stealing six horses in the Penasco Valley, he was captured by the Indian police, but they released him when he agreed to return the horses.

After this incident, Give-Me-a-Horse took up with some other renegades in Nautzile's camp. Indian agent W. H. H. Llewellyn and some Indian police tried to arrest the renegades. In the resulting battle, Give-Me-a-Horse and two other Indians were killed, and Llewellyn was wounded. He credited the police with saving his life. The rest of the band, about eight warriors, fled the reservation.[797]

17 JULY 1882
BIG DRY WASH/GENERAL SPRING (Long Valley, Arizona)

Still angry about medicine man Nochaydelklinne's death at Cibecue Creek (see 30 August 1881), a White Mountain Apache named Natiotish remained defiant. After raiding in central Arizona's Tonto Basin, he and about 60 warriors stirred up a hornet's nest of soldiers. Holed up above the Mogollon Rim, Natiotish saw a cavalry troop under Capt. Adna R. Chaffee on their way and set a trap for them.

Scout Al Sieber saw the trap and warned Chaffee. On the evening of 16 July, Maj. Andrew W. Evans, 3rd Cavalry, joined Chaffee's men with Companies D, E, and I of the 3rd Cavalry and E, I, and K of the 6th Cavalry, plus two companies of Indian scouts. The next day the troops went in to confront Natiotish, in a narrow canyon about seven miles north of General Spring, in a dry branch of East Clear Creek. Evans let Chaffee run the show while he occupied the Apaches, firing across the canyon rim and hitting the Indians with two companies on each flank.

The soldiers were well-managed and tenacious, and the Apaches could not stand up to them. Twenty warriors died and perhaps another 30 were wounded. Natiotish was killed. This was the last major battle with the Apaches in Arizona.[798]

—1883—

21 MARCH 1883
CANELO HILLS (Canelo, Arizona)

Twenty-six Apache raiders under Chato swept north out of the Sierra Madre in the spring of 1883. The Indians, including Naiche, Mangus, Bonito, Dutchy, Tzoe, Beneactiney, and Kautli, were mainly seeking guns and ammunition, but anyone who crossed their path was marked for death. The slaughter began the first day, as soon as the Apaches crossed the Arizona border. Toward evening, about 12 miles southwest of Fort Huachuca, in the Canelo Hills near Turkey Creek, the band spotted men working at a charcoal camp. Three were felling trees and a fourth was preparing charcoal for the nearby mines.

In a spray of bullets, the Indians killed William Murray, Ged Owens, Joseph Woelfolk, and a man named Armstrong. A fifth worker, P. R. Childs, ducked inside a tent and grabbed his rifle. After calling for him to come out, the Apaches blasted the tent with bullets. Hearing no response, Tzoe and Beneactiney rushed forward. Childs stepped out and shot and killed Beneactiney. Chato led his warriors away to the north.[799]

28 MARCH 1883
MCCOMAS MASSACRE (Lordsburg, New Mexico)

Chato's Apache raiders (see previous entry) looped through southern Arizona, killing and stealing. They entered New Mexico near present-day Virden, and were headed toward the southern end of the Big Burro Mountains when they encountered Judge Hamilton C. McComas, his wife, Juniata, and their six-year-old boy, Charley, coming down the road in a rented buckboard.

About halfway between Silver City and Lordsburg, the family stopped by a lone walnut tree for a picnic lunch. They saw Chato's raiders coming in from the northwest and tried to get to the buckboard, but they were too slow. The judge was shot, but he made it to the wagon and retrieved his Winchester, hoping to hold off the Indians while his wife and son got away. Five or more bullets hit him and killed him instantly.

A mounted Apache caught up with Juniata and smashed her head in with the butt of his rifle, then clubbed her to death. The Indians quarreled over the boy, sitting in shock in the back of the buckboard. Bonito, second in command on the raid, claimed him. The Apaches then rode away for Mexico.

The tragedy caused a great public outburst and led to one of the most famous and lengthy searches in American frontier history, but little Charley McComas was never found.[800]

15 MAY 1883
RIO BAVISPE (Northwestern Chihuahua, Mexico)

In the spring of 1883, Gen. George Crook organized an expedition to go deep into the Sierra Madre of Mexico and find the Apache bands of Geronimo, Nana, Loco, and Bonito. The force consisted of 42 men of Company I, 6th Cavalry; Companies A, B, D, E, F, and G, under Capt. Emmet Crawford, 3rd Cavalry, and Lts. James O. Mackay, 3rd Cavalry, and Charles B. Gatewood, 6th Cavalry; and 193 Chiricahua, White Mountain, Yuma, Mojave, and Tonto scouts. The White Mountain Apache Tzoe, or "Peaches," who had been on a recent raid with Chato, joined the expedition to guide them.

The command went up the Bavispe River, following the river's course into the mountains toward Cumbre. On 15 May, Crawford's Apache scouts, ahead of the cavalry, found Bonito's and Chato's village east of the river, across the Chihuahua border. They killed nine warriors and captured one woman, the daughter of Bonito, and four children, one the granddaughter of Cochise. According to the daughter of Apache chief Chihuahua, a warrior named Speedy grabbed the captive boy Charley McComas (see previous entry) and crushed his head with a rock.

The army's victory deep in territory that the Apaches once considered a refuge convinced many Apaches to surrender over the next several days. Chiefs Nana, Loco, Ka-ya-ten-nae, Geronimo, and Naiche all turned themselves in; only Juh was missing. Crook marched 123 warriors and 251 women and children back to reservations in the United States.[801]

—1885—

22 MAY 1885
DEVIL'S CREEK (Alma, New Mexico)

About 25 Apaches under Chihuahua jumped a party of miners ten miles west of Alma, New Mexico. They killed two and stole some horses. Within 24 hours, Capt. Allen Smith and Lt. James Parker, with Companies A and K, 4th Cavalry, and Lt. Charles B. Gatewood and his Apache scouts were on the scene. They followed the renegades' trail into the Mogollon Mountains.

On Devil's Creek, in a 600-foot canyon about ten miles north of Alma, Smith halted his troopers for a break. While the captain knelt to rinse his bandana in the creek, a bullet punctured the handkerchief but missed his hands. Chihuahua's men, posted in the nearby bluffs, fired more shots. Gatewood and Parker led the Apache scouts up the canyon walls and quickly drove their attackers out. Only 500 yards away was the raiders' now-deserted camp. Chihuahua and his band disappeared into the mountains.

Pvts. Haag and Williams and one scout were wounded, and two horses were killed.[802]

8 JUNE 1885
GUADALUPE CANYON (Northeastern Sonora, Mexico)

Capt. Henry Lawton and Capt. Charles A. P. Hatfield, who operated out of Fort Huachuca with elements of Companies C, D, and G of the 4th Cavalry, were patrolling south of the border near Guadalupe Canyon when Apaches attacked their camp. As the soldiers were having their noon meal, with only 1 sergeant and 7 privates guarding the camp, about 30 warriors of Chihuahua's band swept in. The raiders killed three men, captured livestock, burned equipment, and carried off supplies.[803]

23 JUNE 1885
BAVISPE MOUNTAINS (Oputo, Sonora, Mexico)

In the late spring, Capt. Emmet Crawford, with Henry F. Kendall's Company A, 6th Cavalry, and 92 Apache scouts under Lt. Britton Davis, 3rd Cavalry, went after Apache raiders. The expedition took them into Mexico. At Huachinera the trail turned west toward Oputo. Crawford had Chato, the former renegade Apache chief, now a scout for the army, take the scouts ahead.

On 23 June, Chato stumbled onto a rancheria high in the mountains northeast of Oputo. The Indians fled, and the rough terrain limited Chato's pursuit. Only one hostile was killed, and 15 women and children were captured, including Chihuahua's entire family. One scout was wounded.[804]

7 AUGUST 1885
CASAS GRANDES (Casas Grandes, Chihuahua, Mexico)

Capt. Wirt Davis, 4th Cavalry, with one troop of the 4th Cavalry, 100 Indian scouts of Companies G, H, I, and K under Lt. Matthias W. Day, and guides "Buckskin" Frank Leslie and Charlie Roberts, worked his way through the Sierra Madres in conjunction with Capt. Emmet Crawford (see previous entry). On 28 July, in the Sierra de Joya, Davis's men ran down and killed an Apache woman and a boy.

On 7 August, the command jumped Geronimo's camp near the Rio Janos, west of Casas Grandes. One woman and two boys were killed. Geronimo and Nana escaped. The attack swept away Geronimo's family.

Two of his wives were seized and a third disappeared; five of his children were also taken. Altogether, 15 Apaches were captured.[805]

22 SEPTEMBER 1885
TERES MOUNTAINS (Northeastern Sonora, Mexico)

After decimating Geronimo's Apache camp at Casas Grandes (see previous entry), Capt. Wirt Davis searched for the wily Chiricahua chief, but he had slipped back north of the border. Davis and his Indian scouts found another band of Apaches in the Teres Mountains below the northern loop of the Bavispe River. In the ensuing skirmish, one scout was killed and one was wounded, while the scouts killed one hostile and wounded two. The same day, Geronimo recaptured one of his wives and one of his children from near Fort Apache.[806]

8 NOVEMBER 1885
FLORIDA MOUNTAINS (Deming, New Mexico)

Early in November, two bands of hostile Apaches slipped over the border from Mexico and met in the Florida Mountains, southeast of present-day Deming, New Mexico. There were fewer than 30 warriors, led by Chief Chihuahua's young brother Josanie (Ulzana). The group first killed two Navajo scouts and one White Mountain Apache, then, near the Floridas, they killed two civilians and a scout and wounded one trooper of the 6th Cavalry. Afterward, the bands split up, and Josanie led nine men into Arizona to continue raiding.[807]

19 DECEMBER 1885
LITTLE DRY CREEK (Pleasanton, New Mexico)

After his raiding spree, troops chased the Apache Josanie (see previous entry) across the southwest. Lt. Samuel W. Fountain, with Company C of the 8th Cavalry and Navajo scouts, was tracking Josanie and his band in the Mogollon Mountains near Alma. Fountain was on his way to Fort Bayard for supplies when he was ambushed from a ridge just beyond the road. The troops dismounted, but just as they crossed the road, a Pvt. Wishart, said to be the strongest man in the 8th Cavalry, was killed, as was a Pvt. Gibson; a Cpl. McFarland was wounded.

Fountain looked for his Navajo scouts, who had disappeared. The next volley wounded Asst. Surgeon Thomas J. C. Maddox, then another bullet caught him in the head. Lt. DeRosey C. Cabell was slightly wounded, and the blacksmith, named Collins, took a mortal wound. The Navajo scouts suddenly reappeared and pushed the Apaches off the ridge. The Apaches disappeared in the timber to the west.

Five men were killed and two were wounded. Josanie's men got away unscathed.[808]

—1886—

3 MAY 1886

PINITO MOUNTAINS (Northeastern Sonora, Mexico)

In April 1886, Apache chiefs Geronimo and Naiche led one of their many raids north of the border. In the Santa Cruz Valley, they attacked the Peck ranch, killing Mrs. Peck and one of her children and taking Mr. Peck and another child captive. When Peck went insane, they released him.

Capt. Thomas C. Lebo with Company K, 10th Cavalry, tracked the raiders for 200 miles, finally going 30 miles below the border into the Pinito Mountains. As they rode, the soldiers counted 30 horses the fleeing Apaches had ridden to death. Lebo found the Apaches on a rocky slope and started up. The Indians fired. The first volley killed a Pvt. Hollis and wounded a Cpl. Scott. Lt. Powhatan Clark dragged Scott to safety, an action for which he received a Medal of Honor. After several hours, Geronimo pulled away.

Two Apaches were killed and one was wounded.[809]

Council between Gen. Crook and Geronimo, March 1886;
Geronimo surrendered to Crook but soon ran off.
—Courtesy Denver Public Library, Western History Department

15 MAY 1886
PINITO MOUNTAINS (Northeastern Sonora, Mexico)

After Thomas C. Lebo's fight with Geronimo (see previous entry), Capt. Charles A. P. Hatfield, with Company D, 4th Cavalry, picked up the Apache's trail. He struck a band of hostiles in the little range between the Santa Cruz and San Pedro Rivers and captured their horses and camp equipment. As the soldiers made their way out of the hills, the Apaches ambushed them. The blacksmith and cook were killed, and two sergeants were wounded. The Apaches recovered their ponies, plus some ammunition, with no loss to themselves.[810]

—1887—

5 NOVEMBER 1887
CROW AGENCY (Crow Agency, Montana)

Three years before the Ghost Dance fervor swept the Lakotas on the northern plains, the Crows experienced their own version. The Crow Wraps-Up-His-Tail had a vision of a sword cutting a swath in the trees, which he took to be soldiers falling before him. He inspired followers, who dressed in red flannel and carried swords. Thus he became known as Sword Bearer.

When Sword Bearer's followers went on a horse-stealing raid among the Piegans, the Crow agent Henry E. Williamson took a dim view of the excursion. He sent his police to arrest the raiders, but they were defiant and shot up the agency. Williamson called for help. A deluge of troops from Forts Custer and McKinney responded: Companies A, B, D, E, G, and K, of the 1st Cavalry; Company A of the 7th Cavalry; Company H of the 9th Cavalry; Companies B and E of the 3rd Infantry; Companies C, D, G, and I of the 7th Infantry, with Brig. Gen. Thomas H. Ruger in overall command.

Assured that his medicine was strong, Sword Bearer made a bravery ride in front of the soldiers, but they wounded him and his horse. In the fight that followed, seven Crows were killed, nine more were wounded, and nine were captured. One soldier was killed and two were wounded.

Sword Bearer ran away east of the Little Bighorn, but his father caught up to him and shamed him into returning. Afterward, while taking a drink from the river a few miles north of the agency, the Crow policeman Fire Bear shot him in the back of the head, "for getting all these people into trouble."[811]

—1890—

WOUNDED KNEE CREEK (Wounded Knee, South Dakota)

The Lakota practice of the Ghost Dance ritual on their Dakota reservations had many white soldiers and citizens concerned for their safety. After Indian police killed Sitting Bull on 15 December, trouble was expected. Some of the chief's Hunkpapa band fled to join the Minneconjous (Lakota) under Big Foot, who led his people to Pine Ridge Agency.

On the 28th, units of the 7th Cavalry caught up with Big Foot's band and escorted them to Wounded Knee Creek. That night, Col. James W. Forsyth arrived, and in the morning, Companies A, B, C, D, E, G, I, and K, Light Battery E of the 1st Artillery, and Oglala scouts—about 500 men— surrounded Big Foot's camp of about 350 Indians, including 120 warriors. When the soldiers tried to disarm the Sioux, a medicine man named Yellow Bird called for resistance. A scuffle started, and the Indians fired into the soldiers.

The soldiers had the upper hand in numbers and weapons. Hotchkiss guns raked the village, and soldiers cut down Indians as they fled. After the carnage ended, 128 Lakotas were dead, including Big Foot and Yellow Bird, and 33 were wounded. The battle, however, was not the one-sided affair that is usually portrayed. Forsyth lost 25 men, and 35 were wounded. Only at the Little Bighorn did the 7th Cavalry lose more men.[812]

30 DECEMBER 1890

WHITE CLAY CREEK/DREXEL MISSION (Oglala, South Dakota)

The day after the Wounded Knee incident (see previous entry), several bands of Lakotas—perhaps 4,000 people of which nearly 1,000 were warriors—gathered on White Clay Creek, about 15 miles north of the Pine Ridge Agency. A group of them jumped some supply wagons, killing an enlisted man, and as they retreated back toward the village, they burned a schoolhouse at the Drexel Mission.

Col. James W. Forsyth came to investigate. Although he had nearly 400 7th Cavalry troopers, he marched them into a cul-de-sac among about 50 warriors, who pinned them down for the rest of the day. Finally, Maj. Guy V. Henry rode in with Companies D, F, I, and K of the 9th Cavalry and extricated Forsyth. Two soldiers were killed and seven were wounded.[813]

—Conclusions—

In order to make this compilation of battles, names, places, and numbers more than just a reference book, I tabulated the data and analysed the results to find patterns upon which I could base meaningful conclusions. I drew most of the statistics from the 675 selected battles and skirmishes described in the main part of this book, tallying total casualties (military, civilian, and Indian combined) killed, wounded, and captured as a direct result of a battle. (For example, I counted the 53 Cheyennes captured by force when Custer swept into the village on the Washita in 1868, but not the 418 Nez Perces that gave up after a negotiated surrender to Miles following the 1877 Bear's Paw battle.) I also examined 795 additional fights to supplement the core data.

The numbers of casualties used in this study are inherently biased toward army estimations, since it was the army who kept the records. Although in many cases the exact number of Indian casualties was difficult to determine, there is reason to be confident that the army estimates were reasonably accurate. As Thomas Smith pointed out in his study of Texas battles, the army lived by a strict code of honor, particularly in its official reports, and even if the unit leader tried to inflate numbers, he would face correction and perhaps ostracism by other soldier-witnesses.[814] Given that, I used the army's estimates in nearly every case. Of the 21,586 total casualties tabulated in this survey, military personnel and civilians accounted for 6,596 (31%), while Indian casualties totaled about 14,990 (69%).

Due to the nature of existing records, we have more information regarding military operations than details of the Indian war parties, but even army records are often incomplete. Many reports state the basics, but leave out details from which we might generalize and draw conclusions. Nevertheless, there is enough detailed information to make a workable pool of data in many areas, and I have drawn conclusions wherever I could.

My findings, along with other research I've done, reveal a good deal of evidence to counter several currently held beliefs among historians. First, as I alluded to in the introduction, my evidence debunks those who contend that the American frontier was far less violent than traditionally thought. I will address that issue last. First I'd like to refute the popular notion that during the Civil War, civilians on the western frontier suffered from increased Indian raids because troops were withdrawn from the West to fight in the East.[815] As Robert Utley showed in his book, *Frontiersmen in Blue,* and others have affirmed, the number of soldiers in the West *increased* during the Civil War.[816] Between the Mexican War and the Civil War there were only three mounted regiments to patrol the entire West, the

1st and 2nd Dragoons and the Mounted Rifles. In 1853 the entire army, including cavalry, infantry, and artillery regiments, totaled only 10,417 men of all ranks. Of that number, only about 5,000 effectives were stationed to fight Indians in the West between 1853 and 1863. During the Civil War, however, between 2,500 and 3,500 men were stationed in the central plains; between 4,500 and 5,000 in the northern plains, including Minnesota; between 2,500 and 4,000 in the Southwest; and between 5,000 and 6,000 in the region from the Great Basin to the Pacific coast. Historian Gregory Urwin states that nearly 20,000 men were recruited in western states and territories for home defense. Therefore, there were somewhere between 14,500 to 20,000 men stationed to fight western Indians during the Civil War, three to four times the number of the preceding decade.[817] Thus any increased combat in the West during the Civil War was caused not by a scarcity of troops but by an expansion of them—more fighters mean more fights.

Initially, the army did withdraw troops from the West to battle the Confederates. But did this withdrawal increase fighting in the West? In 1860 there were 42 armed conflicts that resulted in casualties. In 1861, the first year regulars were pulled out of the West, there were 24 conflicts. Rather than increasing, the number of fights declined by almost one-half.

This brings us to another oft-repeated tenet of Indian war history that the data prove wrong—that the volunteers who replaced federal troops during the Civil War killed more Indians than regular soldiers, that they were more "bloodthirsty."[818]

Indian casualties did increase during the Civil War, but does that mean the volunteers were more belligerent? A comparison between the number of Indian battles during the five Civil War years (1861–65) and the number during the five years afterward shows *less* fighting with the state and territorial volunteer forces than with the regular army. In 1862 there were 45 battles with Indians, about the same as in 1860 and an increase from the number in 1861. In 1863 there were 58 battles; in 1864, 64; and in 1865, 72. In 1866, when the regulars were back, fights numbered 63, practically the same as in 1864, the last full year of Civil War. The numbers over the next three years show the contradiction to the conventional wisdom. In 1867, conflicts were at an all-time high, with 139; in 1868 there were 118 battles, and in 1869, the first year of President Grant's "Quaker Peace Policy," there were 101. In 1870 there were 58 battles, the same as in 1863. In total, the volunteers of 1861–65 fought in 257 engagements; the regulars of 1866–70 fought in 479.

According to these figures, it would appear that it was the regular soldiers who were the more violent. Yet I would argue that the increased fighting after the Civil War was due not to differences between regulars and volunteers but to increased white incursions into Indian territory and increased Indian resistance to those incursions, more aggressive military strategies and tactics, and related factors.

Anecdotal evidence is also offered in support of the theory of blood-thirsty volunteers. Among the most commonly cited incidents is the story of John Chivington's Colorado Volunteers at Sand Creek, Colorado, in 1864. While not the bloodiest episode of the Indian wars, Sand Creek has gone down in infamy because of the mutilations and degradations practiced upon the Cheyenne dead by some of the Colorado fighters, and rightly so. While certainly vicious, this incident was part of 270 years of savagery on both sides. Were the Colorado Volunteers worse than the 7th Cavalry regulars at Wounded Knee? Sand Creek resulted in about 130 Indian deaths and 60 soldier casualties; Wounded Knee had about 130 Indian and 70 soldier casualties.

Chivington's attack at Sand Creek brings us to another common asser-tion that is confounded by the numbers. Many histories hold that the Sand Creek massacre so infuriated the Indians that afterward the soldiers and settlers on the surrounding plains suffered a wrath greater than any seen before.[819] Yet a contemporary, settler Elizabeth J. Tallman, wrote, "For a few years after the battle of Sand Creek, the Cheyenne and Arapaho Indians were much quieter."[820] The numbers support her statement. In Colorado in 1864, there were 69 white casualties. In 1865, after the supposedly un-precedented Indian retaliation, there were only 41 white casualties, and in 1866 there were 4. In Kansas for the same three years, white casualties numbered 33, 5, and 0, respectively. In Nebraska the numbers were 88, 39, and 2. In New Mexico, 12, 3, and 1. Rather than causing new heights in bloodshed, it appears that Chivington accomplished his purpose: to drive the warring Indians out of the territory.

Unlike the contentions discussed above, there are claims commonly made in Indian war histories that *are* borne out by the numbers. One is that the power of the Cheyennes was broken after the disastrous defeat of Tall Bull at Summit Springs in July 1869. White casualties in Colorado, Kansas, and Nebraska went down from 56 in 1869 to 21 in 1870. In addition to the decline after Summit Springs and after Sand Creek, the numbers also dropped in Idaho and Utah after the Indian defeat at Bear River in 1863. That year, there had been 70 white casualties; the next year, there were 0. In Washington, before the army's decisive victories at Four Lakes and Spokane Plain in 1858, there had been intermittent battles for a de-cade; afterward, there were no battles, period. The pattern is clear, the conclusion obvious: the way to stop Indian depredations against whites was by defeating them decisively in battle, not by offering them treaties, presents, and promises.

Another common statement in Indian war histories that the data in this survey do support is that Indians attacked only when they had an advantage. In 123 instances, Indians attacked with favorable odds, and 57 of those encounters were ambushes; they attacked only 4 times without a numbers advantage. Conversely, the military attacked 85 times with fewer fighters than their Indian foes, and only 59 times with favorable or even numbers. But if this is so, why did the Indians lose so many fights? Of the 675 battles surveyed, we find that the army, militia, or civilians won 419 (62%) of them. Indians won 201 fights, and there were 55 draws. Greater numbers were apparently no guarantee of success. In the majority of Indian battles, more important than numbers were discipline, tenacity, and tactics.

Contrary to popular myth, the army surprised, ambushed, and forced the Indians to fight at a disadvantage about twice as often as the other way around. Despite the Indians' prowess in mobility, speed, and stealth, they apparently had a fatal flaw in letting their guard down in camp, believing their enemies were far away. The army, militia, civilians, and Rangers hit Indian camps 205 times. Indians ambushed soldiers and settlers about 95 times.

In 216 instances, the military and Indians came upon one another in meeting engagements. In virtually every unexpected encounter, the military's response was to attack, in spite of having little or no time to plan. There were also 206 instances in which the military followed the Indians to their camps or villages and attacked, regardless of the numbers. That was the whole point of the pursuit: find the Indians and attack. No commander, from second lieutenant to general, would expend time and energy to track Indians only to call it off at the crisis point, even with unfavorable odds.

Of the attacks that followed a pursuit (in which the record is complete enough to tally), we find only 60 of them were planned out; 119 were spontaneous. With this in mind, it is easy to see why Lt. Colonel Custer made his attack at the Little Bighorn. He had found the village; it was his duty to attack. Those who say Custer attacked too hastily, without thorough reconnaissance, can see from the data that his actions were well within the norm. Those who condemn him do not understand the basic tactics of the western Indian wars.

Another myth about the Indian wars, this one coming more from movies and novels than from historians, is that most attacks occurred at dawn, or, better still, under the cover of darkness, in order to surprise a sleeping camp. This idea has given rise to another ignorant criticism of Custer, and of others. Why did he attack in the middle of the day? In an ideal situation, it certainly would be best to surprise the enemy at dawn with a superior force and a well-thought-out plan. In reality, that rarely happened. The military attacked whenever it had an opportunity. In accounts that indicated the time of attack, we find opportunity knocked in the daylight hours 221 times. Only 44 times did the army have the luxury of hitting an Indian camp at dawn. The Indians, too, attacked when they had a favorable opportunity, which occurred in the daylight 110 times; they attacked at dawn only 10 times. As for night attacks, the military and the Indians made six nighttime assaults each. Apparently both sides were reluctant to enter the spirit world in the darkness.

Just as both sides preferred to fight in daylight, both Indians and the army, contrary to common conceptions about winter campaigns, found it more convenient to take to the field in summer (see table 1). Indians have always made war in summer, when the grass was up and the ponies were strong. After the Civil War, it has been written, the U.S. military began to adopt the strategy of attacking in winter to strike the Indians when they were least prepared. Generals Sherman, Sheridan, Crook, and Miles, among others, supposedly discovered that the tactic of year-round fighting, employed in the Civil War, could be brought to bear on the Indian. Yet an examination of the data shows that after the Civil War, the army relied *less* on winter campaigns than it did in antebellum years. From 1850 to 1865, there were 181 (43%) winter battles (October through March), and 240 (57%) summer battles (April through September). In a comparable fifteen-year period, from 1866 to 1880, there were 363 winter battles (36%) and 652 summer battles (64%). During the remaining decade, from 1881 to 1890, there is only a 1 percent shift (winter 37%, summer 63%). If the Union generals of the Civil War learned any lessons about how to conduct warfare against the Indians, winter campaigns were not part of the curriculum.

Can we determine from the data what military leader was the most effective Indian fighter? It depends on our criteria. Should we credit the "kills" to the colonel who led the expedition, or to the captains who did the fighting? In either case, George Crook has to rate at or near the top. He led a significant number of detachment and company-sized scouts in California and Oregon as a lieutenant in the 4th Infantry in the 1850s. As a lieutenant colonel of the 23rd Infantry after the Civil War, he directed a number of campaigns against the Shoshone, Paiute, and Pit River bands in the West, much of the time with the 1st Cavalry. He moved to the Department of Arizona in 1871 and directed a three-year campaign against the Apaches, his men engaging in scores of battles. He also fought in the Sioux wars in the late 1870s and was back fighting Apaches in the 1880s. In how many of those confrontations, however, did Crook actually lead units

Table 1: Number of Battles by Month	
May	168
August	165
September	158
June	153
July	148
April	139
October	131
January	116
March	92
December	84
November	83
February	75

into battle? In this study, we find at least 16 casualty-producing engagements with Crook in command on a small-scale tactical level, although he was in overall command of units in more than 100 battles.

Counting only company leaders, Crook would still be in contention, with about 180 casualties. Yet Earl Van Dorn matched that number in only two fights, commanding units of the 2nd Cavalry at Rush Springs and Crooked Creek. On a larger scale, Patrick Connor's Bear River and Tongue River battles caused the Indians more than 430 casualties.

On the fighting level, several individuals stand out as contenders for Indian fighter extraordinaire. Reuben Frank Bernard compiled an amazing record, and in terms of number of engagements he may be the winner. He enlisted in the 1st Dragoons in 1855 and spent the next 26 years fighting. He became a lieutenant colonel of the 9th Cavalry in 1892. In this study, Bernard is mentioned in 14 casualty-producing engagements, although he is reported to have participated in 103 actions.[821]

One of four heroic brothers, Howard Bass Cushing, born in 1838, did not live long enough to fulfill his promise. After serving in the Civil War in the 4th Artillery, he transferred to the 3rd Cavalry, where he had a short, but outstanding career. As a lieutenant in Company F, Cushing led dozens of roving scouts and pursuits in search of marauding Apaches. He was killed in an ambush in Arizona's Whetstone Mountains in 1871. In about two years of Indian fighting, Cushing was in 12 fights.

George Bliss Sanford, born in 1842, served in the 1st Dragoons/1st Cavalry in a number of departments, from California and Arizona to Idaho and Montana, fighting Apaches to Nez Perces. He directly commanded units in at least nine casualty-producing engagements.

Many officers led soldiers in a half dozen or more engagements that resulted in killed or wounded Indians: Henry Carroll of the 3rd and 9th

Cavalry, Rufus Somerby of the 8th Cavalry, Walter Scribner Schuyler of the 5th Cavalry, James Oakes of the 2nd/5th Cavalry, Gerald Russell of the Mounted Rifles/3rd Cavalry, Wirt Davis of the 5th Cavalry, Tulius C. Tupper of the 6th Cavalry, Almond B. Wells of the 8th Cavalry, Jonathan D. Stevenson of the 8th Cavalry, William R. Price of the 8th Cavalry, William McCleave of the 1st California Cavalry and the 8th Cavalry, George M. Randall of the 23rd Infantry, and John Lapham Bullis of the 24th Infantry. There were many more.

If body count is a true indication of success in war, General Alfred Sully could probably be given the title of top Indian killer, an honorific he would have detested since, ironically, Sully would much rather have spent his time studying, drawing, and painting Indians than fighting them.[822] At Whitestone Hill, by conservative estimate, his men killed, wounded, and captured 356 Indians. Some reports indicated 300 warriors were killed. If so, that battle site represents the greatest killing ground of Indians west of the Mississippi. Using the highest estimates claimed by army commanders, perhaps 700 Sioux warriors died in the 1863-65 campaigns of Sully and Henry H. Sibley. The numbers participating in the campaigns, the numbers engaged in the battles, and the numbers of casualties make those Dakota operations the largest Indian wars in the West.[823]

Here I would like to discredit one more misconception, that 1865 was the bloodiest year on record. Again, the numbers belie the orthodoxy. Across the West, casualties declined from 1,715 in 1864 to 789 in 1865. The so-called "bloody year" saw nearly 1,000 fewer casualties than 1864, and 335 fewer than 1866. What was the real "bloody year" on the plains? It was a virtual tie between 1863 and 1864, with 1,712 and 1,715 casualties respectively, mostly the result of Sully and Sibley's large-scale campaigns in the Dakotas.

Just as it is interesting to try to determine the number one military fighter of Indians, so is it intriguing to speculate on who might be considered the top Indian leader in inflicting casualties on the army. It is a difficult assessment, for in many encounters we do not know who led the Indians. Moreover, Indian rules of command differed from army practices—there was not always a single commander, and battle leaders gave few, if any, orders once fighting commenced.

We could nominate Captain Jack, the acknowledged leader of the Modocs, but in the fight where the Modocs thrashed their foes most thoroughly, at Hardin Butte in April 1873, also called the Thomas-Wright Massacre, it was Scarface Charley, not Jack, in command. Chief Joseph of the Nez Perces might be a candidate, because of his famous fight and surrender at the Bear's Paw battle, but in previous battles White Bird or Looking Glass were more in command of the fighters. The Apache Victorio was the leader in at least 16 battles and skirmishes with the military, but the encounters were relatively small in scale, totaling only about 63 casualties. The Paiute Winnemucca inflicted 100 casualties on white forces in a single battle at Pyramid Lake in 1860. More than 300 soldiers were killed or wounded at the Little Bighorn, but who led the Indians? Perhaps we could call Sitting Bull the nominal leader, but he did not directly participate in the fight. Crazy Horse? He had many followers, but was he in charge? Crazy Horse was at the Fetterman fight also, but only as a decoy, not as commander.

The bloodshed on both sides during the Indian wars should help refute those who contend that the American frontier was not particularly violent, and that the "Wild West" image is a fabrication. In support of their position, some historians have noted that the number of casualties of the Indian wars paled in comparison to those of the Second World War. But this comparison is absurd. Would Fort Ridgely or the settlement of New Ulm have held out in 1862 if the Santees had had several hundred tanks? How many Indian villages would have survived heavy artillery and air raids? Who would still be alive if either side had had atomic weapons? A more logical comparison tells a different story: the proportion of casualties to troops during Indian battles in 1876 and 1877 was greater than the average casualty-to-troop ratio during the Civil War.[824]

Furthermore, in assessing the violence of the frontier, we must consider not only warfare between Indians and the army, but also between Indians and civilians. The single military unit that caused the most casualties, the 1st Dragoons/1st Cavalry, killed, wounded, or captured 1,225 Indians; yet, in the battles described in this survey, white civilians and militia surpassed the damage done by the 1st Dragoons/1st Cavalry by more than 600, inflicting 1,834 casualties. And the numbers recorded in this encyclopedia are only the proverbial tip of the iceberg. White civilians took up arms so often we cannot begin to record all the episodes. There were literally thousands of white and Indian deaths reported in state and territorial newspapers that did not make the tally sheets because they were not part of an organized military action.

Whites killed Indians in every state and territory, but perhaps most dramatically along the Pacific coast. In Washington, Oregon, and California, Indian populations declined as if a biblical flood had swept them from the land. The army may have accounted for several hundred fatalities, but thousands more perished from disease, malnutrition, and murder.[825] Next to disease, white civilians with guns were the most dangerous threat to Indian survival.

What about Indian attacks on settlers? Thousands of homesteaders were killed by Indians. Even the trip west was perilous. Some historians, in their quest to downplay the violence of the frontier, would have us believe that the danger along the Overland Trail was minimal. Stewart Udall believes it is a "myth that emigrants in wagon trains faced ever-present threat of attacks" by Indians."[826] Some authors quote from Merrill Mattes's study, which gives an excellent account of the migrations up to 1866, or John Unruh's synthesis, which makes use of Mattes, but goes only up to 1860. In their estimations, about 200,000 people went west on the central route from 1850 to 1860. Unruh figures Indians killed only 316 emigrants in that decade.[827] But he leaves out the attack on the Fancher train, the infamous Mountain Meadows Massacre, in which Mormons and their Indian allies executed 121 emigrants. This brings the number up to 437. It may still look like a small number at first glance—less than 1 percent. But what if "only" 1 out of 100 passenger airplanes flying between New York and San Francisco crashed? It would not seem insignificant.

Granted, in the 1840s there were relatively few conflicts on the trail, but this was because there were relatively few people using it. They were little threat to the Indians. Yet John Faragher's statement in his study of families on the overland trail that "there were no war parties directed at emigrants" during the 1840s and early 1850s is incorrect. Those "nonexistent" war parties killed several hundred travelers! Later, as gold and silver were discovered, particularly in California, Colorado, and Montana, more white people poured in and more conflicts developed. As the casualty numbers in the entries of this book show, there were more than enough confrontations between 1850 and 1860 to belie the assertion that the trail was safe: 62 emigrants were killed at Bloody Point in 1852; 19 died in the 1854 Ward Massacre; 11 were killed in the initial attack on the Utter–Van Ornum trains in 1860; and there were many more emigrant deaths, rapes, and torturings at the hands of Indian attackers. Faragher admits that in the late 1850s and 1860s emigrants "had to be more vigilant." Still, he consoles readers, "most people got through."[828]

I hope I have laid to rest, once and for all, the revisionist theory that the American frontier was not as tough as people think, that it's all just a tall tale passed down from Great-great-grandpa. While we should not romanticize frontier violence, neither should we deny the facts: the West of the late nineteenth century was dangerous, destructive, bloody—in a word, *wild.*

Table A.1: Number of Battles by Year

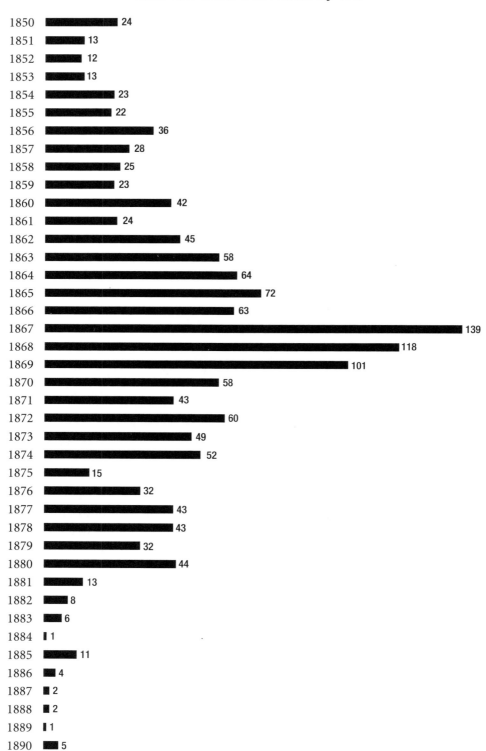

Year	Battles
1850	24
1851	13
1852	12
1853	13
1854	23
1855	22
1856	36
1857	28
1858	25
1859	23
1860	42
1861	24
1862	45
1863	58
1864	64
1865	72
1866	63
1867	139
1868	118
1869	101
1870	58
1871	43
1872	60
1873	49
1874	52
1875	15
1876	32
1877	43
1878	43
1879	32
1880	44
1881	13
1882	8
1883	6
1884	1
1885	11
1886	4
1887	2
1888	2
1889	1
1890	5

—Appendix—
Data and Commentary

By looking at statistics compiled from the survey data, we can answer interesting questions for further study or simply for curiosity's sake. For instance, which battles produced the most casualties killed, wounded, and captured for both sides? Using mostly the data from army records, Connor's fight on Bear River comes out on top, with 451. Second is Custer's battle on the Little Bighorn, at 426. Third, Sully at Whitestone Hill, 414. Fourth, Baker's fight on the Marias, 334. Fifth, Carson at Canyon de Chelly, 262. Sixth, Fetterman's debacle at Fort Phil Kearny, 244. If we leave out the captured, however, the Little Bighorn was the most destructive fight, with Bear River second and Whitestone Hill third.

In which year did the most fighting occur? Table A.1 shows that the greatest number of battles was in 1867, yet, as noted in the Conclusions, 1864 saw the most casualties.

Which Indian tribes had the most fights with the army? Which tribes killed the most soldiers per fight? It is often difficult to determine from the army reports which tribe was engaged in any given battle. At times the report stated only "Indians." Without guessing, and counting only the fights where specific tribes are mentioned, we find the following:

Table A.2: Tribes Ranked by Number of Battles with Army, with Casualties Caused*

TRIBE	NUMBER OF FIGHTS	NUMBER OF CASUALTIES CAUSED	CASUALTIES PER FIGHT
Apache	214	566	2.6
Sioux	98	1,250	12.7
Cheyenne	89	642	7.2
Comanche	72	230	3.1
Kiowa	40	117	2.9
Paiute	33	302	9.2
Navajo	32	33	1.0
Shoshone	31	202	6.5
Rogue	23	196	8.5
Nez Perce	16	281	17.5
Modoc	12	208	17.3
Ute	10	105	10.5
Hualapai	8	22	2.7
Arapaho	6	29	4.8
Kickapoo	5	100	20.0

*Casualties defined as total killed, wounded, and captured

The Apaches, with 213 encounters, were far and away the most pugnacious, but because Apaches never met the army in large numbers in open, pitched battles, engagements with them resulted in relatively few casualties (2.6 per fight). Second place for number of fights belongs to the Sioux (including the Lakota, Dakota, and Nakota), with 98. The largest tribe on the Plains, the Sioux boasted a population of about 40,000 in 1870. Although they fought in only half as many battles as the Apaches, they fought in larger numbers and were more willing to face the army in large battle formations, and they rated number one in number of casualties caused.

A less populous tribe, the Cheyennes, with about 4,000 people in 1875, participated in more than their share of the conflicts, with 89. The Comanches were involved in at least 72 fights, while the Kiowas, another small but aggressive tribe, participated in 40 fights. Both were considered the terrors of the Texas plains, yet we see that they caused relatively few casualties per encounter. Many of the southwestern tribes made their most serious impact raiding stock, murdering civilians, and taking captives, but these numbers do not show up in army battle statistics.

The Paiutes fought 33 times and the Shoshones (counting the Bannocks) 31. The Navajos fought in 32 engagements but caused only about one military casualty per encounter. The Rogue River Indians, a tribe that does not get much attention compared to the Plains Indians, fought in 23 contests, with a substantial casualty ratio of 8.5. The Nez Perces fought only 16 times, virtually all in 1877, and their fighting was superb, causing more than 17 military casualties every time they met. Likewise, the Modocs, with only about 100 warriors at the time they battled the army, probably caused more destruction relative to their numbers than any other tribe—they killed more white men than their own forces numbered. While the Kickapoos had only 5 engagements, they had, by virtue of their punishment of the Texan militia and civilians at Dove Creek in 1865, a tremendous average of 20 casualties per fight. Without Dove Creek the average would be 3.5.

The California Indians always seem to be forgotten. The Yuroks, Hoopas, Pomos, Shastas, Talowas, and others did not live in tribes but in small bands, inhabiting separate sections of river and valley. The bands were often known by the terrain features they lived near, thus there were the Mad Rivers, the Pit Rivers, the Eel Rivers, the Mattole Rivers, and the Goose Lakes, for example. If we combined these small bands, we would get a substantial 32 fights, with 2 military casualties per encounter.

It is interesting to note that Indians also fought with the military against other Indians, particularly from the 1870s on. Native soldiers fought in at least 144 battles and inflicted 340 casualties on other Indians, sometimes without white soldiers to oversee them, occasionally even against people of their own tribes. During the Apache wars, in particular, Apache soldiers helped defeat Apache "hostiles," who were devastated when they saw some of their own people riding with the soldiers and leading them to their most secret hideouts. In the real West, men could be characterized less by white and black hats (or red, brown, and white skin), than by various shades of gray.

There were many U.S. military units that fought in the West between 1850 and 1890, ten of which were cavalry. Unsurprisingly, it was these cavalry regiments that participated in most of the actions. The breakdown is shown in table A.3.

Table A.3: U.S. Cavalry Units in Order, with Number of Indian Battles and Casualties Caused

UNIT	DATE ORGANIZED	NUMBER OF BATTLES	NUMBER OF CASUALTIES	CASUALTIES PER BATTLE
1st Dragoons/1st Cavalry*	03/(18)33	208	1,225	5.9
2nd Dragoons/2nd Cavalry*	05/36	84	731	8.7
Mounted Rifles/3rd Cavalry*	05/46	140	885	6.3
1st Cavalry/4th Cavalry*	03/55	73	405	5.5
2nd Cavalry/5th Cavalry*	05/55	124	955	7.7
3rd Cavalry/6th Cavalry*	05/61	68	365	5.4
7th Cavalry	09/66	40	645	16.1
8th Cavalry	09/66	166	682	4.1
9th Cavalry	09/66	64	229	3.5
10th Cavalry	09/66	63	360	5.7

* Designation changed 08/61

The units organized earliest did not necessarily participate in most of the actions, nor did those organized last participate in the least. The 1st Dragoons/1st Cavalry saw the most action, followed, perhaps surprisingly, by the 8th Cavalry. The famous 4th Cavalry of Ranald Mackenzie is in seventh place, and the renowned 10th Cavalry of Benjamin Grierson is in ninth place. Perhaps most surprising of all, the vaunted 7th Cavalry of George Custer comes in dead last in numbers of engagements, although it is high in casualties per fight because some of its battles were among the most destructive in the Indian wars. Ranked according to total casualties caused, 1st Dragoons/1st Cavalry comes in first, the 2nd Cavalry/5th Cavalry second, and the Mounted Rifles/3rd Cavalry third.

Table A.4 shows all units, federal and state, cavalry and infantry, that effected more than 200 Indian casualties. As we can see, in terms of causing

Indian casualties, the United States Infantry deserves honorable mention. The 6th Infantry killed, wounded, or captured 274 Indians; the 5th, 218; and the 4th, 206. The state volunteer regiments fighting in the West during the Civil War produced significant casualties, especially if we look at the number of casualties per fight. The 2nd California Cavalry caused 601 casualties (in only 22 encounters); the 1st New Mexico caused 297. The 5th California Infantry produced 261 casualties; the 7th Iowa, 224; and the 2nd California Infantry, 221. All together, the California regiments fought in more casualty-producing engagements than any other western state regiment, with about 105 fights.

TABLE A.4: U.S. and State Military Units
Ranked by Number of Indian Casualties Caused

UNIT	NUMBER OF CASUALTIES CAUSED	NUMBER OF BATTLES	CASUALTIES CAUSED PER BATTLE
1st Dragoons/1st Cavalry	1,225	208	5.9
2nd Cavalry/5th Cavalry	955	124	7.7
Mounted Rifles/3rd Cavalry	885	140	6.3
2nd Dragoons/2nd Cavalry	731	84	8.7
8th Cavalry	682	166	4.1
7th Cavalry	645	40	16.1
2nd California Cavalry	601	22	27.3
1st Cavalry/4th Cavalry	405	73	5.5
3rd Cavalry/6th Cavalry	365	68	5.4
10th Cavalry	360	63	5.7
1st New Mexico Cavalry	297	25	11.9
6th Infantry	274	23	11.9
5th California Infantry	261	13	20.1
9th Cavalry	229	64	3.5
7th Iowa Cavalry	224	18	12.4
2nd California Infantry	221	23	9.6
5th Infantry	218	40	5.5
4th Infantry	206	34	6.1

Comparisons of battle statistics by state are inexact; obviously not all had their current state boundaries at the times of the incidents, and it is difficult to pinpoint the exact locations of some encounters. In addition, the army made some pursuits across the Mexican border, going after Apaches and other Indians who had been raiding in the U.S. For this reason, I have included several battles that took place in Mexican states. Table A.5

delineates the recorded fights between Indians and the military from 1850 to 1890 in each western state, using modern boundaries, along with the total casualties of each fight. Table A.6 shows the breakdown by year.

TABLE A.5: States Ranked by Number of Battles, with Total White and Indian Casualties

STATE	NUMBER OF FIGHTS	TOTAL CASUALTIES	CASUALTIES PER FIGHT
Arizona	310	4,340	14.0
Texas	250	2,060	8.2
New Mexico	192	1,629	8.5
Kansas	118	933	7.9
California	88	1,649	18.7
Oregon	87	1,365	15.7
Wyoming	80	1,064	13.3
Montana	60	1,735	28.9
Colorado	49	829	16.9
Nebraska	46	726	15.8
North Dakota	42	1,116	26.6
Idaho	38	1,027	27.0
Oklahoma	30	662	22.1
Nevada	24	482	20.1
Washington	16	542	33.9
Utah	12	219	18.3
Minnesota*	9	610	67.8
South Dakota	6	288	48.0
Iowa	3	55	18.3

* This does not include about 644 white civilians killed in the 1862 uprising.

States bordering Mexico had far more conflicts with Indians than did interior states. Arizona had the most fights, almost as many as the bottom dozen states combined, and as many casualties as the bottom nine states combined, due almost entirely to the warlike nature of the Apaches. Arizona, Texas, and New Mexico combined had 51 percent of the battles and 37 percent of the casualties in the entire country west of the Mississippi. Not only were the Apaches and other southwestern tribes particularly pugnacious, they also felt they could raid somewhat wantonly and afterward find sanctuary against U.S. pursuit in Mexico. While this sometimes worked, at other times American troops crossed the border anyway, occasionally against Mexican sanctions.

For further examination, we can also look at the data according to type of operation. In most cases, military operations fell into one of three general categories: the scout, the pursuit, and the expedition. The lines

TABLE A.6: NUMBER OF BATTLES/NUMBER OF CASUALTIES PER STATE, BY YEAR

Year	AZ	CA	CO	ID	IA	KS	MN	MT	NE	NV	NM	ND	OK	OR	SD	TX	UT	WA	WY
1850	0	3/153	0	0	0	0	0	0	0	0	3/18	0	0	0	0	18/180	0	0	0
1851	1/9	5/163	0	1/8	0	0	0	0	1/1	0	0	0	0	5/87	0	0	0	0	0
1852	1/5	4/203	0	0	0	0	0	0	0	0	2/8	0	0	2/51	0	3/69	0	0	0
1853	0	4/21	2/23	2/26	0	0	0	0	0	0	0	0	0	5/80	0	2/9	1/7	0	1/5
1854	0	2/10	3/76	1/6	0	0	0	0	1/173	0	4/109	0	1/3	2/37	0	8/55	0	4/226	2/38
1855	0	0	0	0	1/50	0	0	0	1/17	0	4/35	0	0	7/170	0	2/17	0	7/100	0
1856	0	0	0	0	0	0	0	0	2/11	1/9	1/5	0	0	12/270	0	15/62	1/121	0	0
1857	2/105	4/42	0	0	0	1/29	0	0	0	0	4/47	0	2/196	0	0	12/72	0	5/216	0
1858	5/36	0	0	1/7	0	1/1	0	0	0	0	8/70	0	1/3	0	0	3/11	0	0	0
1859	4/79	0	0	2/19	0	2/114	0	0	0	0	5/32	0	0	0	0	8/33	1/26	0	0
1860	7/109	2/206	1/21	1/11	0	0	0	0	1/39	6/189	11/91	0	0	1/5	0	10/80	2/8	0	0
1861	1/22	9/209	0	0	0	0	0	0	0	0	9/111	0	1/23	0	0	3/35	0	0	0
1862	2/26	7/152	0	2/27	1/1	0	7/603	0	0	1/24	7/49	3/26	1/10	1/4	0	1/26	2/8	0	3/70
1863	10/211	12/137	1/1	1/451	1/4	0	1/4	0	2/13	2/15	18/194	6/570	1/10	1/4	0	0	0	0	1/11
1864	11/530	9/102	9/223	0	0	6/51	0	0	9/117	4/38	6/111	5/396	0	4/25	0	3/145	0	0	17/235
1865	7/39	0	8/70	1/30	0	12/42	1/3	1/46	7/95	5/187	3/5	5/33	0	3/22	0	1/129	2/2	0	10/296
1866	16/359	2/12	1/17	2/27	0	0	0	3/4	1/13	4/17	2/8	3/9	0	15/172	0	3/20	0	0	18/139
1867	28/216	4/85	6/17	8/138	0	30/204	0	1/45	3/32	1/3	6/29	6/8	3/264	16/300	0	16/88	1/1	0	4/7
1868	30/303	0	9/175	0	0	32/204	0	4/14	3/13	0	7/81	5/15	4/56	7/64	0	5/88	0	0	8/35
1869	39/303	0	3/75	0	0	18/169	0	4/27	3/11	0	16/115	1/4	4/13	0	1/1	8/112	0	0	3/32
1870	17/172	0	1/5	0	0	8/47	0	1/334	5/14	0	3/12	1/5	1/1	0	0	15/103	0	0	0
1871	19/407	0	1/20	0	0	1/8	0	0	1/6	0	3/48	0	0	0	0	14/92	0	0	2/2
1872	36/306	2/7	0	0	0	1/2	0	2/22	1/3	0	3/20	3/17	5/34	1/25	0	8/183	0	0	0
1873	19/262	9/147	0	0	0	0	0	2/30	0	0	7/46	2/17	2/31	0	0	9/51	0	0	3/60
1874	23/451	0	0	0	0	1/7	0	0	0	0	0	1/1	2/13	0	0	19/198	0	0	0
1875	2/45	0	0	10/246	0	3/36	0	1/3	3/5	0	1/9	0	0	0	2/56	6/21	0	0	5/121
1876	6/75	0	0	5/29	0	0	0	10/613	0	0	1/5	0	3/15	0	1/1	2/2	0	0	1/3
1877	5/88	0	0	1/2	0	0	0	8/436	1/163	0	5/69	0	0	0	0	11/34	0	0	1/8
1878	3/34	0	0	0	0	2/21	0	4/52	0	0	2/10	0	0	6/53	0	17/43	0	0	0
1879	1/7	0	3/115	0	0	0	0	9/47	0	0	10/64	0	0	0	0	6/12	0	0	0
1880	1/2	0	0	0	0	0	0	4/16	0	0	26/162	0	0	0	0	13/79	0	0	0
1881	4/37	0	0	0	0	0	0	1/8	0	0	6/37	0	0	0	0	1/11	0	0	0
1882	3/65	0	0	0	0	0	0	1/3	0	0	2/6	0	0	0	0	0	0	0	0
1883	3/9	0	0	0	0	0	0	1/2	0	0	1/3	0	0	0	0	0	0	0	1/2
1884	0	0	1/2	0	0	0	0	0	0	0	0	0	0	0	0	0	0	0	0
1885	0	0	0	0	0	0	0	0	0	0	5/20	0	0	0	0	0	0	0	0
1886	1/8	0	0	0	0	0	0	1/29	0	0	0	0	0	0	0	0	0	0	0
1887	1/1	0	0	0	0	0	0	1/2	0	0	0	0	0	0	0	0	0	0	0
1888	1/2	0	0	0	0	0	0	1/2	0	0	0	0	0	0	0	0	0	0	0
1889	1/9	0	0	0	0	0	0	1/2	0	0	0	0	0	0	0	0	0	0	0

between these categories are somewhat blurred, however, and definitions are inexact. What's more, not all reports indicated the nature of the operation. The scout, or patrol, was the equivalent of a modern search-and-destroy mission. Scouts usually had less than 20 men, led by a lieutenant or a captain. Of the surveyed battles in which the type of operation could be determined, 95 were the result of scouts. The pursuit was usually organized in reaction to an Indian raid. These generally contained from 20 to 40 men, commanded by a lieutenant, a captain, or a major. There were 140 actions of pursuit in the survey. The expedition was a larger operation, similar to a scout in purpose but containing companies from several regiments or nearly a full regiment and taking place over weeks or months, usually led by a field-grade officer. Expeditions account for 108 of the surveyed battles.

From reported battles that specified the number of men in the unit, we find that the army went on scouts or pursuits with fewer than 10 men on 61 occasions; with 11 to 20 men on 69 occasions; with 21 to 30 men, 46 times; and with more than 30 men, or company-strength units, 76 times. Multicompany operations, in which detachments from several companies joined together, occurred 190 times. Likewise, from reports that included such information, we see that lieutenants led operations 141 times; captains commanded 155 times; and majors were in charge only 40 times. Field-grade officers (lieutenant colonel or higher), led units 100 times. Even sergeants and corporals took charge at times, leading patrols, usually of 10 men or less, on 34 occasions.

Using the information above and in the tables, we might construct a model to represent a typical Indian-fighting army operation in the West, keeping in mind that the data is limited, making accuracy uncertain and generalizations tentative.[1] That being said, an "average" western military operation would have taken place in Arizona in 1869. It would have been a detachment of the 8th Cavalry, with fewer than thirty men, commanded by a lieutenant or a captain. Its weapons would have been Civil War issue, Sharps or Spencer carbines and Colt revolvers. The operation would have been a pursuit, going out for two weeks during the late spring or summer and covering about 200 miles. Upon discovery, a band of two dozen or fewer Apaches would be surprised in their rancheria and the soldiers would make an unplanned, daylight attack. The Indians would put up a brief resistance then flee into the mountains, where the troops would give up the chase. The army would have about two casualties, the Indians, six. This basic scenario was acted out time and again by different regiments and different tribes across the West.

---

1 I have based my model on one presented by Thomas T. Smith in his excellent study of military/Indian combat operations in Texas from 1849 to 1881. Smith, *The Old Army in Texas*, 40.

—Notes—

1850

1   Quaife, 136–37; Sabin, 623–24.
2   Smith, T., 136; Adjutant General's Office, 14.
3   Trafzer & Hyer, 24, 57–58.
4   Riddle, 60.
5   Smith, T., 137.
6   Heizer, 244; Davidson, 58–59.
7   Heizer, 245; Davidson, 59–60.
8   Robinson, *Men Who Wear the Star,* 109–10.
9   Groneman, 125–26; Robinson, *Men Who Wear the Star,* 109–10.
10 Smith, T., 137; Adjutant General's Office, 14.
11 Wilbarger, 666–71.
12 Ibid.
13 Ibid.; Smith, T., 138.
14 Adjutant General's Office, 14; Webb, G. W., 10. In the latter, the date is given as 5 July.
15 Adjutant General's Office, 14.
16 Wilbarger, 616–19.
17 Ibid.
18 The men killed were Baker Barton and William Lackey.
19 Wilbarger, 616–19.

1851

20 Trafzer & Hyer, 74, 116.
21 Ibid., 117–18; Harris, 147–48. The men killed were named Little and Sylvester; the injured man was Richard Rillotson.
22 Sometimes I have used quotation marks around the rank titles of volunteer leaders because they were not official titles. How the men got them varied. Often they were self-appointed leaders, or the men under them voted them into leadership. At the same time, they often gave themselves such titles as "Captain," "Colonel," "Major," and the like, or their followers did.
23 Trafzer & Hyer, 119.
24 Thrapp, *Encyclopedia,* 1071; Dunn, J. P., 141–51; Stratton.
25 Some of the men's names were Odeniel, Bogel, Hitchcock, Perely, Lavelle, Clarke, Spencer, O'Donnell, Wilson, and Evans.
26 Trafzer & Hyer, 82–86, 90–93. The *Los Angeles Star* reported: "Persons who have seen the dead bodies describe them as being mangled in a manner shocking to behold."
27 Beckham, 50; Glassley, 53–54.
28 Beckham, 49–50.
29 Glassley, 57; Beckham, 53–58.
30 Glassley, 54; Beckham, 51.
31 Webb, G. W., 11.
32 Beckham, 62.
33 Glassley, 57–58; Beckham, 59–63. The men killed were Patrick Murphy, A. S. Dougherty, John P. Holland, Jeremiah Ryland, and J. P. Pepper.
34 Unruh, 189.

35   Beckham, 67.

36   Glassley, 59–60; Beckham, 65–67. The wounded men were Pvts. French and Williams.

1852

37   Rodenbough, 169–70, 433; Adjutant General's Office, 14. Including a man killed in a later skirmish, the dead were Pvts. Collins, Dayley, Joice, Leland, and Luther.

38   Frazer, 106; Adjutant General's Office, 14. Sweeney, *Mangas Coloradas,* 246–47.

39   Rodenbough, 168–69, 499.

40   Frazer, 35; Adjutant General's Office, 14.

41   Heizer, 249–50.

42   Beckham, 77–78.

43   Glassley, 152; Murray, K. A., 24. Murray believes this attack is a composite of several attacks on emigrants. Casualty estimates range from 33 to 70.

44   Webb, W. P., 144.

45   Glassley, 153; Murray, K. A., 25–27.

46   Groneman, 127; Fehrenbach, *Comanches,* 241.

1853

47   Trafzer & Hyer, 75.

48   Ibid., 120–21.

49   Ibid., 68.

50   Utley, *Frontiersmen,* 113; Hyde, *Red Cloud's Folk,* 70; Unruh, 214.

51   Beckham, 117.

52   Ibid., 118–19; Glassley, 72.

53   Utley, *Frontiersmen,* 177; Adjutant General's Office, 15; Beckham, 119–21; Schwartz, 53.

54   Beckham, 121–22. The volunteers killed were James Mango, Thomas Parnell, and Thomas Frizell.

55   Glassley, 75–76; Beckham, 126–27; Adjutant General's Office, 15.

56   Goetzmann, 286–88; Thrapp, *Encyclopedia,* 598; Trenholm & Carley, 135; Peters, 34. It has been suggested that Mormons had a part in Gunnison's massacre.

1854

57   Crook, 17–20; Heizer, 44–46, 84–86; Beckham, 140–41; Strobridge, 71–72.

58   Glassley, 77–78; Beckham, 134–35.

59   Beckham, 136.

60   Rodenbough, 177.

61   Ibid., 177–78, 433; Utley, *Frontiersmen,* 144; Guild, 199; Adjutant General's Office, 15. Rodenbough calls this battle the "Cagalone." It might be the present-day Canon Largo.

62   Rodenbough, 433; Adjutant General's Office, 15.

63   Sabin, 660–61; Utley, *Frontiersmen,* 144; Oliva, *Fort Union,* 126.

64   Sabin, 660.

65   Rodenbough, 178.

66   Ibid., 180.

67   Ibid., 178–80; Utley, *Frontiersmen,* 145.

68   Smith, T., 139; Wooster, *Recollections,* 82–85.

69 Heizer, 58–62; Beckham, 142–43; Schwartz, 65–66.

70 Sabin, 664–65; Utley, *Frontiersmen,* 146. This campaign cemented the friendship between Carson and Carleton, and Carleton sent Carson a fine "New York" hat for his assistance.

71 Utley, *Frontiersmen,* 146; Rodenbough, 526; Adjutant General's Office, 15. The wounded men were Sgt. Francis Smith and a Pvt. Moore.

72 Smith, T., 139; Webb, G. W., 12.

73 Hyde, *Spotted Tail's Folk,* 56–62.

74 Unruh, 190; Madsen, 58.

75 Unruh, 190; Madsen, 58–59.

76 King, 16.

77 Ibid., 15–16; Smith, T., 139. Smith says Walker was escorting the department commander from El Paso when attacked.

78 Adjutant General's Office, 15. There are at least three Live Oak Creeks between San Antonio and the Rio Grande.

79 Webb, G. W., 12.

80 Hyde, *Spotted Tail's Folk,* 68; Hyde, *Red Cloud's Folk,* 77.

81 Utley, *Frontiersmen,* 146; Sabin, 666.

1855

82 Rodenbough, 200.

83 Ibid., 201.

84 Ibid., 200–02; Utley, *Frontiersmen,* 150–51. The wounded dragoons were Cpl. Katon, bugler William Drown, and Pvt. Pat Rooney. Rooney was taken 95 miles to the nearest settlement, Anton Chico, with an arrow buried more than two inches in his head. He died about 30 January.

85 Utley, *Frontiersmen,* 149–51; Sonnichsen, 83–87; Bennett, 59–62; Adjutant General's Office, 15.

86 Sonnichsen, 88; Adjutant General's Office, 16.

87 Utley, *Frontiersmen,* 147; Sabin, 667–69; Guild, 206.

88 Utley, *Frontiersmen,* 148; Sabin, 669.

89 Utley, *Frontiersmen,* 147–48.

90 Ibid.; Adjutant General's Office, 16.

91 Webb, G. W., 13.

92 Unruh, 215–16; Madsen, 62–63. The Dryer quote is from Unruh, 216.

93 Smith, T., 139–40; Webb, G. W., 13. Smith says the detachment was under Lt. Horace Randal, and eight Indians were killed.

94 Nadeau, 115–23; Hyde, *Spotted Tail's Folk,* 70–73.

95 Utley, *Frontiersmen,* 188; Trafzer & Scheuerman, 63; Glassley, 113–14.

96 Beckham, 152–53; Glassley, 80–81; Schwartz, 85.

97 Beckham, 153–54; Glassley, 81–82. The settler killed on the reservation was William Guin; in subsequent attacks, the Rogues killed Mrs. Jacob Wagner, her daughter Mary, Sarah Pellett, J. K. Jones, his wife, and Isaac Shelton; at George Harris's ranch, in addition to Harris, Frank Reed and David Harris were killed; at the Rogue River, a man named Hamilton was killed in addition to the four teamsters.

98 Beckham, 155; Glassley, 84.

99 Beckham, 157–58; Adjutant General's Office, 16.

100 Adjutant General's Office, 16; Beckham, 157–59; Glassley, 85.

101   Utley, *Frontiersmen,* 190; Adjutant General's Office, 16.
102   Beckham, 161–62.
103   Utley, *Frontiersmen,* 191; Adjutant General's Office, 16.
104   Glassley, 118–23; Trafzer & Scheuerman, 67–69.
105   Beckham, 164; Glassley, 87–88.

1856

106   Beckham, 164; Glassley, 88–89.
107   Beckham, 165.
108   Smith, T., 140; Arnold, 72–73.
109   Beckham, 173–76; Glassley, 93–94.
110   Utley, *Frontiersmen,* 194; Adjutant General's Office, 17.
111   Glassley, 129.
112   Smith, T., 140; Arnold, 74.
113   Trafzer & Scheuerman, 69.
114   *Ibid.,* 69–70.
115   Beckham, 179; Glassley, 95–96.
116   Utley, *Frontiersmen,* 184; Adjutant General's Office, 17; Beckham, 181.
117   Utley, *Frontiersmen,* 154; Thrapp, *Victorio,* 49–50; Sweeney, *Mangas Coloradas,* 325–26.
118   Beckham, 182; Glassley, 99.
119   Schwartz, 119–20. Schwartz says this incident occurred on 25 March.
120   Webb, G. W., 14; Adjutant General's Office, 17. Webb says the fight occurred on 22 March.
121   Beckham, 182; Glassley, 99.
122   Sheridan, 40–45; Utley, *Frontiersmen,* 194–95.
123   Trafzer & Scheuerman, 71, 206; Glassley, 131.
124   Smith, T., 140; Webb, G. W., 15.
125   Beckham, 184; Adjutant General's Office, 17.
126   Utley, *Frontiersmen,* 185–87; Adjutant General's Office, 17; Beckham, 186–87.
127   Beckham, 188; Glassley, 107.
128   Smith, T., 140; Adjutant General's Office, 17.
129   Trafzer & Scheuerman, 73.
130   Utley, *Frontiersmen,* 197–98; Trafzer & Scheuerman, 73.
131   Utley, *Frontiersmen,* 120; Grinnell, *Fighting Cheyennes,* 112–13; Peters, 34.
132   Smith, T., 141; Adjutant General's Office, 17.
133   Smith, T., 141; Adjutant General's Office, 17.
134   Smith, T., 141; Webb, G. W., 16; Arnold, 94–96.

1857

135   Adjutant General's Office, 18.
136   Smith, T., 141; Webb, G. W., 16.
137   Smith, T., 141–42.
138   Clodfelter, 27–33. The first family to die was that of Rowland Gardner. The four women captured near Spirit Lake were Mrs. Luce, Mrs. Nobles, Mrs. Marble, and Mrs. Thatcher.
139   Thrapp, *Victorio,* 53–54; Sweeney, *Mangas Coloradas,* 350.
140   Webb, G. W., 16; Barlow, 155.
141   Wilbarger, 84–86.

142 Utley, *Frontiersmen,* 155–56; Worcester, 65; Sweeney, *Mangas Coloradas,* 353–54.

143 Crook, 34–41; Adjutant General's Office, 18; Strobridge, 145–46.

144 Hamlin, 82.

145 Utley, *Frontiersmen,* 155–57; Worcester, 65; Adjutant General's Office, 18; Hamlin, 82–83.

146 Crook, 44.

147 Ibid., 42–45.

148 Hood, 9.

149 Ibid., 13.

150 Ibid.

151 Smith, T., 142; Hood, 8–13.

152 Crook, 46–47.

153 Grinnell, *Fighting Cheyennes,* 118–22; Hafen & Hafen, *Relations,* 26–29; Chalfant, *Cheyennes,* 182. The Cheyennes reported killed Coyote Ear, Yellow Shirt, Carries the Otter, and Black Bear. The two soldiers killed were Martin Lynch and George Cade. Among the wounded was Lt. James E. B. Stuart, who was shot in the chest.

154 Settle & Settle, *War Drums,* 56–57; Hafen & Hafen, *Relations,* 141–52.

155 Madsen, 78.

156 Dunn, J. P., 253–64; Madsen, 81–82; Brooks, 69–96.

157 Hafen & Hafen, *Relations,* 152–53.

158 Crook, 57.

159 Crook, 55–57; Strobridge, 155–56.

1858

160 Madsen, 86; Trenholm & Carley, 159.

161 Webb, W. P., 154–58.

162 Utley, *Frontiersmen,* 201–03; Trafzer & Scheuerman, 78–82, 207; Adjutant General's Office, 18.

163 Utley, *Frontiersmen,* 203–04; Adjutant General's Office, 19; Crook, 59–64.

164 Utley, *Frontiersmen,* 206.

165 Ibid., 205–07; Adjutant General's Office, 19; Glassley, 147–48.

166 Utley, *Frontiersmen,* 207–10; Adjutant General's Office, 19; Glassley, 148–49.

167 Utley, *Frontiersmen,* 167–68; Adjutant General's Office, 19; McNitt, 341–42.

168 Utley, *Frontiersmen,* 130–32; Nye, *Carbine,* 19–24. The Comanche dead included White Deer, Auti-toy-bitsy, and Tanowine.

169 Utley, *Frontiersmen,* 169; Adjutant General's Office, 19.

1859

170 Utley, *Frontiersmen,* 164–65; Adjutant General's Office, 19.

171 Adjutant General's Office, 19; Utley, *Frontiersmen,* 133.

172 Chalfant, *Without Quarter,* 139.

173 Utley, *Frontiersmen,* 133–35; Chalfant, *Without Quarter,* 80–103, 139; Nye, *Carbine,* 25–26.

174 Ferguson Shepherd, William Shepherd, Bill Diggs, and Clayborne F. Rains were killed. James D. Wright was fatally wounded. Mrs. Wright, her daughter, and I. M. Smith were wounded. Some survivors thought there were white men among the Indians.

175 Madsen, 102–03; Unruh, 195.

176 Madsen, 103–04; Adjutant General's Office, 20. The latter source says this fight occurred on 13 August. Rodenbough, 172, calls it Box Elder Canyon.

177 Madsen, 105–06; Unruh, 195. Unruh claims that some of these "Indians" were white men.

178 Smith, T., 145.

179 Utley, *Frontiersmen,* 159–60; Adjutant General's Office, 20.

1860

180 Trafzer & Hyer, 77.

181 Adjutant General's Office, 20; McNitt, 380–81; Bailey, 39–40.

182 McNitt, 381; Adjutant General's Office, 21. Shepherd's comments appeared in McNitt, 381.

183 Heizer, 255–62; Strobridge, 204, 206. Rains's comments appeared in Strobridge, 206.

184 Utley, *Frontiersmen,* 170; Adjutant General's Office, 21.

185 Settle & Settle, *Saddles,* 145–49; Madsen, 120.

186 Settle & Settle, *Saddles,* 151–52; Madsen, 120; Curran, 188; Paher, 12–14.

187 Settle & Settle, *Saddles,* 152; Paher, 14–15; Madsen, 120–21.

188 Settle & Settle, *Saddles,* 155–56; Madsen, 123–24.

189 Madsen, 124–25; Settle & Settle, *Saddles,* 156–57.

190 The posse included Baylor's brother George, George's two sons, their friend Wat Reynolds, and local men Elias Hale, Minn Wright, John Dawson, and others.

191 Wilbarger, 518–19.

192 Madsen, 115; Adjutant General's Office, 21. The latter source says the fight took place near Harney Lake and occurred on 23 June.

193 Hafen & Hafen, *Relations,* 205–06, 210, 231–33; Mattes, "Patrolling," 586.

194 The settlers killed were Samuel Cousins, John Reed, and Ira Merrill; the two wounded were Solyman Merrill and James Cowan.

195 Madsen, 129–30.

196 Hafen & Hafen, *Relations,* 213, 247–52; King, 31–32.

197 Madsen, 125; Settle & Settle, *Saddles,* 159–60. Madsen dates this incident on 11 August; Settle & Settle indicate it occurred in October.

198 Utley, *Frontiersmen,* 140; Adjutant General's Office, 21; Thrapp, *Encyclopedia,* 1418.

199 In some sources, Utter is listed as Otter. The three other families were those of Joseph Meyers, Daniel Chase, and Alexis Van Ornum (sometimes spelled Van Orman).

200 The three men killed the first day were Lewis Lawson, driver of the lead wagon, and ex-soldiers William Utley and Charles Kishnell. Killed the next day were John Meyers and, later, with the Utters, Judson Cressy.

201 Smith, M. E., 44–46; Unruh, 191–92.

202 Utley, *Frontiersmen,* 170–71; Adjutant General's Office, 22; McNitt, 399–402.

203 Tevis, 213.

204 Thrapp, *Victorio,* 68–71; Tevis, 208–14.

205 Wilbarger, 335–38; Robinson, *Men Who Wear the Star,* 118–20; Exley, 153–59. This battle is sometimes cited as taking place 18 December.

1861

206 Oliva, *Soldiers*, 110.
207 Utley, *Clash of Cultures*, 21–23; Sweeney, *Cochise*, 150–63; Worcester, 75–80. Worcester disputes the "cut the tent" incident.
208 Thrapp, *Conquest*, 19.
209 Ibid.; Sweeney, *Cochise*, 172.
210 *War of the Rebellion*, v. 50/1, 17–18.
211 Ibid., 19.
212 Ibid., 18–19.
213 Ibid., 20.
214 Ibid., 19–20.
215 *Ibid.*
216 Ibid., 21.
217 Ibid.
218 In addition to Thomas and Mills, the party included Joe Roescher, Mat Champion, Robert Aveline, John Wilson, and John Portell.
219 Williams, C. W., 11; Tevis, 229; Sweeney, *Mangas Coloradas*, 414–15.
220 Williams, C. W., 24–28; Frazier, 64–65.
221 *War of the Rebellion*, v. 50/1, 25–26; Adjutant General's Office, 22. In the latter, the date is given as 5 August and the incident is called Goose Lake.
222 Frazier, 65; *War of the Rebellion*, v. 4, 24–25.
223 Frazier, 65; *War of the Rebellion*, v. 4, 25.
224 On 25 September, a few days after this incident, the fort's name was changed to Fort Lyon after Nathaniel Lyon, a recently killed Union brigadier general; Col. Fauntleroy had defected to the Rebels. When the Union army reoccupied the fort in June 1868, they called it Fort Wingate II.
225 Utley, *Frontiersmen*, 238; Frazer, 108; McNitt, 421–27.

1862

226 *War of the Rebellion*, v. 5 Index, 150; Webb, G. W., 24.
227 *War of the Rebellion*, v. 50/1, 70–71.
228 Ibid., 48.
229 Ibid., 46–49.
230 Ibid., 55.
231 Ibid., 56, 72–73.
232 Ibid., 84; Peters, 37. In the latter, this action is called Van Dusen's Creek.
233 *War of the Rebellion*, v. 50/1, 67–68.
234 Ibid., v. 50/1, 59–60, 73–75.
235 Ibid., 74.
236 Ibid., 146.
237 Wellman, *Death in the Desert*, 74–80; Utley, *Clash of Cultures*, 25–27; Cremony, 155–67.
238 *War of the Rebellion*, v. 50/1, 61–62.
239 Webber, *Emigrant Massacre*, 8–10, 33–36; Madsen, 160.
240 *War of the Rebellion*, v. 50/1, 164–65.
241 Anderson & Woolworth, 1, 13–15; Wellman, *Death on the Prairie*, 5–8.
242 Wellman, *Death on the Prairie*, 5.
243 Ibid., 8–10; Schultz, *Over the Earth*, 57–59.
244 Schultz, *Over the Earth*, 97–100, 151–59; Clodfelter, 42.

245 Wellman, *Death on the Prairie*, 10–13; Schultz, *Over the Earth*, 117–20, 145–50.

246 Williams, C. W., 46–48; *War of the Rebellion*, v. 9, 578–79.

247 Schultz, *Over the Earth*, 194.

248 Ibid., 199.

249 Ibid., 188–200; Wellman, *Death on the Prairie*, 17–18; Clodfelter, 54.

250 Schultz, *Over the Earth*, 205–07.

251 Utley, *Frontiersmen*, 266; Clodfelter, 43; Frazer, 109.

252 *War of the Rebellion*, v. 50/1, 171–72.

253 Rogers, 29–31; Madsen, 162. A duplicate attack appears incorrectly in Madsen, 118, as occurring on 12 September 1860.

254 Clodfelter, 53–57.

255 Rogers, 33.

256 Ibid., 32–35; *War of the Rebellion*, v. 50/1, 178–79.

257 Nye, *Carbine*, 29–31.

258 Guild, 225.

259 Sabin, 702–04; Guild, 225–27.

260 *War of the Rebellion*, v. 50/1, 182–83.

261 Madsen, 174.

262 Ibid.; Rogers, 65–66.

1863

263 Faulk, 160.

264 Ibid., 159–60; Thrapp, *Conquest*, 20–23.

265 *War of the Rebellion*, v. 15, 228.

266 *Ibid.* Sitton was cited for gallant behavior in this affair.

267 Rogers, 69–74; Madsen, 180–90.

268 *War of the Rebellion*, v. 22/1, 234.

269 Ibid., v. 50/1, 193–96.

270 Ibid., v. 15, 229–30.

271 Ibid., v. 50/1, 204.

272 Rogers, 91–93; *War of the Rebellion*, v. 50/1, 205–09.

273 *War of the Rebellion*, v. 15, 230.

274 Ibid., v. 50/2, 423.

275 Ibid., 422–23, 431–32.

276 *War of the Rebellion*, v. 50/1, 196.

277 Ibid., v. 50/2, 490; v. 26, 25; v. 5 Index, 151.

278 Rogers, 94; *War of the Rebellion*, v. 50/1, 229.

279 *War of the Rebellion*, v. 26/1, 24; Utley, *Frontiersmen*, 242, 253.

280 Madsen, 208; *War of the Rebellion*, v. 50/1, 230.

281 *War of the Rebellion*, v. 22/1, 378.

282 Clodfelter, 63–64, 72; Anderson & Woolworth, 280–82.

283 *War of the Rebellion*, v. 26/1, 24.

284 Ibid., v. 22/1, 444.

285 Ibid., 444; v. 5 Index, 169; Utley, *Frontiersmen*, 282.

286 *War of the Rebellion*, v. 50/1, 191, 196–98.

287 Ibid., v. 26/1, 24.

288 *Ibid.*

289 Ibid., 25; Peters, 39. Marques cited the exemplary conduct of Cpls. Brigaloa and Gonzales and Pvts. Torres, Romero, Archuleta, Tresquez, and Lopez.

290 *War of the Rebellion,* v. 26/1, 25.

291 Ibid., 25–26.

292 Ibid., 25; v. 5 Index, 150.

293 Clodfelter, 90–99; Robinson, E. B., 100.

294 Clodfelter, 101–04.

295 Ibid., 105–06.

296 Ibid., 113–14.

297 Sabin, 865–68; *War of the Rebellion,* v. 26/1, 26.

298 *War of the Rebellion,* v. 26/1, 27; v. 5 Index, 152. This skirmish is sometimes confused in army compilations with the Paraje fight of 19 July.

299 *War of the Rebellion,* v. 26/1, 27; Peters, 39.

300 Sully, 175.

301 Sully, 168–78; Clodfelter, 122–43.

302 *War of the Rebellion,* v. 26/1, 28.

303 Ibid., v. 50/1, 240.

304 Ibid., v. 26/1, 30; Sabin, 874–76.

305 *War of the Rebellion,* v. 50/1, 240–41.

306 Ibid., v. 22/1, 768–69.

307 Ibid., v. 26/1, 31–32.

308 Clodfelter, 74; *War of the Rebellion,* v. 22/2, 768; v. 34/2, 249.

309 *War of the Rebellion,* v. 26/1, 31; Sonnichsen, 120. Labadie, Fialon, Pvts. Loder and Osier of Company B, 2nd California Cavalry, and Chiefs Ojo Blanco and Cadete were cited for gallantry in the incident.

1864

310 Cremony, 255.

311 *War of the Rebellion,* v. 48/1, 899–900; Sonnichsen, 120, 123; Cremony, 254–57.

312 *War of the Rebellion,* v. 48/1, 900.

313 Sabin, 718–23; Guild, 241–44.

314 Thrapp, *Conquest,* 25–32.

315 Sgt. Thomas Richards and Pvts. Harvey M. McConkey, Thomas Clark, and Lewis W. Mann, of Company D, were the men wounded.

316 *War of the Rebellion,* v. 48/1, 901; v. 34/1, 102.

317 Ibid., v. 34/1, 122–23.

318 Ibid., v. 50/1, 287.

319 Ibid., 257–58.

320 Ibid., 827–30.

321 Ibid., 310–15.

322 Hoig, *Sand Creek,* 36–40; *War of the Rebellion,* v. 34, 883–85. The four soldiers hit were J. G. Brandly, R. E. McBride, A. J. Baird, and John Crosby. Brandly and Baird later died from their wounds.

323 *War of the Rebellion,* v. 34, 219, 881–82.

324 Ibid., v. 50/1, 260.

325 Ibid., 254, 291.

326 Hoig, *Sand Creek,* 44–46; Monahan, 141–44.

327 *War of the Rebellion,* v. 34/1, 909; v. 48/1, 903.

328 Hoig, *Sand Creek,* 51–52; Hyde, *George Bent,* 131–33.

329 *War of the Rebellion,* v. 34/1, 937.

330 The report says the Indians were Shoshones, but they may have been Paiutes under Chief Paunina.

331 *War of the Rebellion,* v. 50/1, 330–31, 345–46. The cavalry casualties were Lt. Watson and Pvts. James Harkinson and Bennett Kennedy of Company B, killed; Cpl. Dougherty and Pvts. Freeman, Henline, Level, and Weeks of Company B, wounded.

332 *War of the Rebellion,* v. 50/1, 284–85.

333 Ibid., 298–99.

334 Utley, *Frontiersmen,* 257–58; *War of the Rebellion,* v. 34, 917–20; v. 50/2, 871.

335 *War of the Rebellion,* v. 50/1, 373.

336 Ibid., 370–73.

337 Becher, 101–02; Williams, S. C., 40–45; *War of the Rebellion,* v. 34/4, 513. New archeological evidence from Dr. J. Jefferson Broome suggests that all four Hungates may have been defending themselves from their house before being overwhelmed.

338 *War of the Rebellion,* v. 26/1, 24.

339 Ibid., v. 50/1, 381.

340 Becher, 93–96.

341 *War of the Rebellion,* v. 48/1, 904.

342 Kelly, 12–35; Farley, 249–50.

343 *War of the Rebellion,* v. 41/1, 81–86.

344 Clodfelter, 167.

345 Ibid., 163–77; Sully, 184–88. The famous scout George Northrup fell in Brackett's charge.

346 *War of the Rebellion,* v. 41/1, 86.

347 Sully, 189.

348 Clodfelter, 178–87; Sully, 189–91.

349 Becher, 270, 451–53. Among the dead were William Bowie and his wife and seven members of the Eubank family. The five captured were Lucinda Eubank and her two children, Laura Roper, and Ambrose Asher.

350 Becher, 253–61; Czaplewski, 14–16; Michno, "Perils of Plum Creek," 36–37.

351 Groneman, 150.

352 *War of the Rebellion,* v. 41/1, 237–39; *Sand Creek Massacre,* 223.

353 Becher, 192–205; *War of the Rebellion,* v. 41/2, 762.

354 *War of the Rebellion,* v. 41/1, 263–64.

355 Ibid., 203–08.

356 Clodfelter, 193–96.

357 Holmes, L. A., 13–15; *War of the Rebellion,* v. 41/1, 246.

358 U.S. House, *Massacre of Cheyenne,* 26.

359 *War of the Rebellion,* v. 41/1, 818; Hoig, *Sand Creek,* 107–09; U.S. House, *Massacre of Cheyenne,* 26.

360 Monahan, 184.

361 *War of the Rebellion,* v. 41/3, 798–99; Monahan, 183–84. White Butte Creek runs west from Summit Springs, also called Buffalo Springs.

362 Michno, "Perils of Plum Creek," 37–38; *War of the Rebellion,* v. 41/1, 839.

363 Taken captive were Milly Durkin's five-year-old daughter, Charlotte "Lottie" Durkin; her two-year-old daughter, Milly Jane; her mother, Elizabeth Ann Carter Fitzpatrick; a boy, Elijah Carter; Mary Johnson, wife of slave Brit Johnson; and her two sons. Contrary to popular writings, Brit Johnson did not rescue his family, nor did Milly Jane grow up to marry a Kiowa chief.

364 Groneman, 151–52; *War of the Rebellion,* v. 41/1, 886; Gallaway, 228–30; Ledbetter, 117–18, 135–36.

365 *War of the Rebellion,* v. 41/1, 934.

366 Brown, *Galvanized Yankees,* 83; *War of the Rebellion,* v. 48/1, 438.

367 Groneman, 153–54; *War of the Rebellion,* v. 41/1, 940–42; Utley, *Frontiersmen,* 298–99; Nye, *Carbine,* 36–37.

368 Czaplewski, 84–85.

369 Hoig, *Sand Creek,* 143–54; Monahan, 187–97; U.S. House, *Massacre of Cheyenne,* 24–25; Williams, S. C., 272–74, 284–88, 309–10. See also Michno, *Battle at Sand Creek* (to be published in 2003). The Colorado State Archives Civil War Casualty Index places the soldier losses even higher, at more than 70 casualties.

370 *War of the Rebellion,* v. 41/1, 937–39.

371 Ibid., 982–83.

372 Ibid., 984–88.

1865

373 *War of the Rebellion,* v. 41/1, 1003–06.

374 Werner, *Heroic Fort Sedgwick,* 19–20; Hyde, *George Bent,* 171–74.

375 Propst, 73–74; *War of the Rebellion,* v. 48/1, 23.

376 Groneman, 155–57; Gallaway, 207–12.

377 Monahan, 212, says that Big Steve survived the battle.

378 Propst, 75–76; Monahan, 212; *War of the Rebellion,* v. 48/1, 41.

379 Three of Godfrey's allies were George Pingrey, Wes Mullin, and Si Perkins.

380 Propst, 77–79.

381 Ibid.

382 *War of the Rebellion,* v. 48/1, 57–58. Killed was Pvt. Fields, Company F, 2nd Colorado. Wounded were Pvt. Donihue of the same company and Pvt. Robert F. Cole of Company A, 1st Colorado.

383 Ware, 367.

384 Hyde, *George Bent,* 181–83; Ware, 363–67.

385 Hyde, *George Bent,* 187–90; Spring, 61–63.

386 Pvt. John A. Harris, Company D, 7th Iowa, and Pvt. William H. Hartshorn, Company C, 11th Ohio, were the men killed.

387 Spring, 64–66; Hyde, *George Bent,* 191–93; McDermott, 82–84.

388 *War of the Rebellion,* v. 50/1, 400–01.

389 The guides were T. W. Murch and W. H. Wilson.

390 *War of the Rebellion,* v. 50/1, 403–04.

391 The men killed were Pvts. John Odum and William Hughes.

392 Brown, *Galvanized Yankees,* 89; *War of the Rebellion,* v. 48/1, 208–09.

393 *War of the Rebellion,* v. 48/2, 1254; v. 5 Index, 148. Paul, 218. This skirmish is erroneously listed as occuring in 1864 in Peters, 41.

394 Brown, *Galvanized Yankees,* 23–25.

395 Vaughn, *Platte Bridge,* 14–15; Connelley, 197; *War of the Rebellion,* v. 48/1, 273.

396 Paher, 42.

397 Ibid.

398 *War of the Rebellion,* v. 48/1, 306.

399 The men killed were Pvt. William T. Bonwell, Company F, 11th Kansas, and Pvt. Tilman Stahlnecker, Company G, 11th Ohio Cavalry.

400 *War of the Rebellion*, v. 48/1, 306; Vaughn, *Platte Bridge*, 15; Connelley, 197–98; Unrau, *Talking Wire*, 253–54. Unrau incorrectly places this action at Deer Creek Station.

401 *War of the Rebellion*, v. 48/1, 295–96.

402 Ibid., 313–14.

403 Ibid.

404 Ibid., 320–21.

405 In addition to Capt. Fouts, Pvts. Edward McMahon and Richard Groger, Company D, 7th Iowa, and Pvt. Philip Alder, Company B, were killed; Pvts. Samuel Kersey and Lewis Tuttle, Company B, and Pvts. James H. May and John W. Trout, Company D, were wounded.

406 *War of the Rebellion*, v. 48/1, 322–23: Hyde, *Red Cloud's Folk*, 120–22; Bettelyoun & Waggoner, 87–89.

407 Nadeau, 186.

408 *War of the Rebellion*, v. 48/1, 326–28; Nadeau, 185–86.

409 *War of the Rebellion*, v. 50/1, 420–21.

410 Ibid.

411 Ibid., 424.

412 Spring, 85.

413 The men killed with Collins were Pvts. George McDonald, Sebastian Nehring, George Camp, and Moses Brown.

414 Spring, 82–89; Vaughn, *Platte Bridge*, 55–70, 75–76, 101; Powell, 342.

415 Vaughn, *Platte Bridge*, 34; Spring, 90.

416 Pvts. Edwin Summers and James Ballau were killed; Cpl. James Schrader, Pvt. Bryam Swain, and Pvt. Henry C. Smith survived.

417 The Cheyennes killed were Young Wolf, Young Bear, Old Bull Hair, Stray Horse, Spit, and Left Hand. High Backed Wolf had been killed the day before.

418 Vaughn, *Platte Bridge*, 22–34; Spring, 90–92; Powell, 342.

419 Clodfelter, 211–12.

420 Rogers, 180.

421 Ibid., 179–80.

422 Hafen & Hafen, *Powder River*, 222, 227, 238, 245–58; Rosenburg, 69–82; Powell, 377–78.

423 Grinnell, *Two Great Scouts*, 90–93; Rogers, 180–81; Hyde, *George Bent*, 227.

424 Hafen & Hafen, *Powder River*, 131.

425 Varley, 238–46; Hafen & Hafen, *Powder River*, 25, 47, 130–35.

426 Hafen & Hafen, *Powder River*, 100.

427 Varley, 246–52; Utley, *Frontiersmen*, 328–30; Hyde, *George Bent*, 233–40; Springer, 44–51.

1866

428 Thrapp, *Conquest*, 33–35; Farish, v. 4, 103.

429 Thrapp, *Conquest*, 34–35; Farish, v. 4, 117–18.

430 Williams, C. W., 61–62.

431 Doyle, 430.

432 Johnson, D. M., 207–08; Doyle, 431.

433 Johnson, D. M., 208–09; Doyle, 432.

434 Wilbarger, 493–97.

435 Rodenbough, 373–74; Adjutant General's Office, 25; Dinges, 41–42.

436 Dinges, 42.
437 Brown, *Fort Phil Kearny,* 160–65.
438 Ibid., 174.
439 Ibid., 173–82; Hyde, *Red Cloud's Folk,* 148–49; Powell, 456–61.
440 Crook, 143–44.

1867

441 Thrapp, *Conquest,* 37–38.
442 Crook, 148–49.
443 Ibid., 151–52.
444 Williams, C. W., 69; Smith, T., 147–48; Adjutant General's Office, 26.
445 Thrapp, *Conquest,* 57–58.
446 Burkey, 6; Lee & Raynesford, 95–98. The three victims were Robert Anderson, John Reynolds, and Frank Carter.
447 Powell, 474–75; Adjutant General's Office, 26.
448 Thrapp, *Conquest,* 41; Adjutant General's Office, 27.
449 Lee & Raynesford, 108–09; Chandler, 7.
450 Chandler, 6.
451 Thrapp, *Conquest,* 58.
452 Crook, 153; Adjutant General's Office, 27.
453 Lee & Raynesford, 110; Chandler, 7.
454 Powell, 477; Burkey, 35.
455 Frost, *Court-Martial,* 53–58; Kennedy, 118–20.
456 Utley, *Custer's Cavalry,* 68.
457 Thomas & Heinz, 26–30; Utley, *Custer's Cavalry,* 68–78.
458 Frost, *Court-Martial,* 60–64; Chandler, 4.
459 Powell, 486–87; Frost, *Court-Martial,* 251–54; Johnson & Allan, 32–38.
460 Crook, 151–52; Adjutant General's Office, 28.
461 Thrapp, *Conquest,* 58.
462 Moore, 14–16; Adjutant General's Office, 28.
463 Wilbarger, 472–77.
464 Knight, 36–43; Adjutant General's Office, 29.
465 Johnson & Allan, 277.
466 Johnson, D. M., 276–80; Hagan, 116–25; Adjutant General's Office, 29.
467 Burkey, 35; Lee & Raynesford, 116; Burton, 178.
468 Keenan, 19–20.
469 Keenan, 9–22; Hyde, *Red Cloud's Folk,* 159.
470 Michno, "Perils of Plum Creek," 38, 76.
471 Ibid.
472 Ibid., 76.
473 Ibid.; Adjutant General's Office, 29.
474 Leckie, *Buffalo Soldiers,* 24.
475 Powell, 492–96; Leckie, *Buffalo Soldiers,* 23–24; Adjutant General's Office, 29; Burkey, 36–37.
476 Knight, 46–47; Adjutant General's Office, 29.
477 Leckie, *Buffalo Soldiers,* 25.
478 Knight, 55.
479 Crook, 154.
480 Ibid., 153–55; Knight, 48–56; Adjutant General's Office, 30.

481 Leckie, *Buffalo Soldiers,* 84–85; Adjutant General's Office, 30; Williams, C. W., 88.

482 Thrapp, *Conquest,* 46; Adjutant General's Office, 30. In the latter, the fight is listed as occurring at Trout Creek.

483 Thrapp, *Conquest,* 41–43; Adjutant General's Office, 30–31. This fight is also reported as having taken place on 3 November.

484 Billington, 8.

485 Burton, 152–53.

1868

486 Thrapp, *Conquest,* 48–51; Adjutant General's Office, 31.

487 Carter, W. H., 138–39. The wounded men were Pvts. John F. Butler and Charles Hoffman of Company I, and Pvt. James Regan of Company F.

488 Peters, 7.

489 Crook, 156–57.

490 Ibid.; Adjutant General's Office, 32.

491 Thrapp, *Conquest,* 43–45; Adjutant General's Office, 32.

492 Peters, 7; Adjutant General's Office, 32.

493 The men's names were Williams, Schultz, and McCarthy.

494 Michno, "Perils of Plum Creek," 76.

495 Moore, 30; Adjutant General's Office, 33.

496 The privates were Merrill, Theely, and two named Murphy.

497 Thrapp, *Conquest,* 56–57; Adjutant General's Office, 33.

498 Thrapp, *Conquest,* 59–60; Adjutant General's Office, 33.

499 Williams, C. W., 99.

500 The women's names were Bacon, Foster, and Shaw.

501 Mills, 150–52.

502 Ibid.

503 Ibid., 150–52; Burkey, 39–40; Adjutant General's Office, 34.

504 Peters, 8; Chandler, 25.

505 Billington, 16; Adjutant General's Office, 35.

506 Peters, 10; Webb, G. W., 40.

507 Peters, 10–11; Webb, G. W., 40; Chandler, 28, 426. Chandler reports the fight took place on 9 September.

508 Chandler, 10–11, 26–27; Utley, *Custer's Cavalry,* 186–90; Carriker, *Fort Supply,* 10–12.

509 Williams, C. W., 102–03; Adjutant General's Office, 36; Leckie, *Buffalo Soldiers,* 87.

510 Leckie, *Buffalo Soldiers,* 33.

511 Ibid.

512 Dixon, *Hero of Beecher Island,* 75–88.

513 Ibid.

514 Ibid.

515 Ibid.; Utley, *Frontier Regulars,* 152–53.

516 Price, 131–32.

517 King, 81–87.

518 Ibid.

519 Ibid.; Leckie, *Buffalo Soldiers,* 37–38; Brady, 124–34.

520 King, 86

521 Ibid.; Keim, 78–80; Price, 132.

522 Leckie, *Buffalo Soldiers,* 43.

523 Hoig, *Washita,* 141; Michno, *Mystery of E Troop,* 12.

524 Hoig, *Washita,* 127–42; Michno, *Mystery of E Troop,* 10–12.

525 Nye, *Carbine,* 78–82.

1869

526 There are several Mulberry Creeks in Kansas. Two of the most likely sites are the one southeast of Fort Dodge and the one west of Salina.

527 Leckie, *Buffalo Soldiers,* 44; Burton, 180–81.

528 Stuart, 85–87; Peters, 19. The latter source says this action took place on the Musselshell River.

529 Randall, 48; Webb, G. W., 45.

530 Billington, 17; Webb, G. W., 45–46; Peters, 19.

531 Billington, 17; Webb, G. W., 45–46; Peters, 19.

532 Williams, C. W., 112; Adjutant General's Office, 40.

533 Cody, 245–48.

534 King, 96–97; Cody, 245–48; U.S. War Department, Eugene Carr Papers, Box 3.

535 King, 97–98; Cody, 248–49; U.S. War Department, Eugene Carr Papers, Box 3.

536 Burkey, 75–76; Bernhardt, 41–42; White, "Indian Raids," 377. Alexander McKeever and John Lynch were killed; foreman George Sealy and Adolph Roenigk, Charles Sylvester, and Louis Taylor were wounded.

537 Williams, C. W., 115; Webb, G. W., 47; Robinson, *Bad Hand,* 50.

538 White, "Indian Raids," 382–83; Webb, G. W., 47.

539 King, 109.

540 Ibid., 102–09; Powell, 727; U.S. War Department, Eugene Carr Papers, Box 3.

541 King, 110; Price, 136; U.S. War Department, Eugene Carr Papers, Box 3; Grinnell, *Two Great Scouts,* 191–92; Powell, 727.

542 King, 111.

543 Grinnell, *Two Great Scouts,* 191–92; King, 110–16; Powell, 728–33; U.S. War Department, Eugene Carr Papers, Box 3.

544 Wilbarger, 466–68.

545 Rodenbough, 392; Peters, 24.

546 Leckie, *Buffalo Soldiers,* 88–89; Adjutant General's Office, 42; Robinson, *Bad Hand,* 50–51. Robinson reports that the scout consisted only of 61 men of Companies F and M.

547 U.S. War Department, Thomas Duncan Papers, Box 3.

548 The murdered passengers included John F. Stone, owner of the Apache Pass Mine.

549 Sweeney, *Cochise,* 270–72; Adjutant General's Office, 43.

550 Sweeney, *Cochise,* 273.

551 Ibid., 273–75; Adjutant General's Office, 43. In the latter the fight is dated 20 October.

552 Leckie, *Buffalo Soldiers,* 89–91; Webb, G. W., 50; Williams, C. W., 119.

553 Peters, 25; Adjutant General's Office, 43; Randall, 49.

554 Williams, C. W., 120; Adjutant General's Office, 43.

555 Peters, 25; Webb, G. W., 51. The former places the action on 2 December.

556 Peters, 25; Adjutant General's Office, 43; Randall, 49–50; Smith, T., 150.

1870

557   Williams, C. W., 122; Adjutant General's Office, 44; Leckie, *Buffalo Soldiers*, 90.

558   Welch, 31.

559   Ibid., 30–33; Peters, 26.

560   Rodenbough, 392; Peters, 27; Frazer, 185; Trenholm, *Arapahoes*, 236.

561   Paul, 219–20; Webb, G. W., 53. All five troopers, Sgt. Leonard and Pvts. Hubbard, Heath Canfield, George W. Thompson, and Michael Himmelsbach, received Medals of Honor for gallantry, more than for any other episode in Nebraska's Indian wars.

562   Kenner, 161.

563   Leckie, *Buffalo Soldiers*, 93, 95; Kenner, 161.

564   Thrapp, *Conquest*, 64–66.

565   Carriker, *Fort Supply*, 49–50; Webb, G. W., 53–54.

566   Burkey, 93; Thrapp, *Encyclopedia*, 395; Chandler, 426.

567   Thrapp, *Conquest*, 66–67; Bourke, 30–33; Randall, 51–52; Adjutant General's Office, 45. In the last source, the battle is listed as Apache Mountains.

568   Price, 142–43; King, 283.

569   Carriker, *Fort Supply*, 51–52; Leckie, *Buffalo Soldiers*, 53.

570   Carriker, *Fort Supply*, 52–53; Peters, 28.

571   Nye, *Carbine*, 113; Carter, W. H., 141–46; Smith, T., 151–52. Eighteen Medals of Honor were awarded for gallantry in this battle.

572   Thrapp, *Conquest*, 70; Webb, G. W., 55; Randall, 52–53.

573   Nye, *Carbine*, 119; Carter, W. H., 149; Adjutant General's Office, 47. The last source reports that the fight took place near the Little Wichita River.

574   Thrapp, *Conquest*, 70; Randall, 57; Adjutant General's Office, 47. The last source says this action took place in the Pinal Mountains.

1871

575   Johnson's body was disemboweled, with his little pet dog stuffed into his gut. The men were scalped, but the Kiowas threw the scalps away because the hair was too short to be of value. An alternative explanation for the Kiowas not keeping the scalps, perhaps, is that Johnson and friends sold their lives too dearly for the Indians to celebrate.

576   Wilbarger, 581–82; Ledbetter, 199, 204; Nye, *Carbine*, 123. Nye believes there were four black settlers in this fight.

577   Robinson, *Men Who Wear the Star*, 163–64.

578   Randall, 60; Webb, G. W., 57. This engagement probably took place in the Pinal Mountains, branches of which, between the Pinal and the Superstition Mountains, were once called the Apache Mountains. This fight may be the same as the Bloody Tanks fight.

579   Wilbarger, 549–51. In addition to Graves, the 12 ranchers included Jason McLean, George and John Lemley, Shap Carter, and Tom Crow. Crow, Carter, and John Lemley died.

580   Thrapp, *Conquest*, 89.

581   Thrapp, *Conquest*, 80–92.

582   Ibid., 72–76; Adjutant General's Office, 48; Randall, 62–70.

583   Among those involved were Chiefs Satanta, Satank, Eagle Heart, and Big Tree.

584 Fehrenbach, *Comanches,* 505–06; Robinson, *Satanta,* 116–22; Capps, 35, 38–54. The teamsters killed were Nate Long, Jim Elliott, Sam Elliott, M. J. Baxter, Jesse Bowman, John Mullins, and James Williams.

585 Nye, *Carbine,* 132; Adjutant General's Office, 48.

586 Thrapp, *Conquest,* 100; Adjutant General's Office, 49.

587 Nye, *Carbine,* 150, 154; Leckie & Leckie, *Unlikely Warriors,* 198; Adjutant General's Office, 49. Nye names the dead soldier as Foster Larkin, wagoner.

588 Groneman, 166–67; Nye, *Carbine,* 151; Fehrenbach, *Comanches,* 511, 513; Carter, R. G., 174–78, 198–99.

589 Bourke, 166–67; Thrapp, *Conquest,* 105. The six men killed included two members of a survey party returning to California, Lt. George M. Wheeler, the survey leader, and Frederick W. Loring, a young scientist and writer from Massachusetts.

1872

590 Leckie, *Buffalo Soldiers,* 101–02; Williams, C. W., 154–57.

591 Paul, 220; Adjutant General's Office, 50. Due to Meinhold's glowing report, Col. Joseph J. Reynolds, commander of the 3rd Cavalry, recommended Medals of Honor for Cody, Foley, Sgt. Leroy Vokes, and Pvt. William H. Strayer.

592 Nye, *Carbine,* 153; Adjutant General's Office, 51.

593 Thrapp, *Conquest,* 114; Adjutant General's Office, 51.

594 Carriker, *Fort Supply,* 67; Peters, 32.

595 Thrapp, *Conquest,* 115; Adjutant General's Office, 51.

596 Williams, C. W., 160; Adjutant General's Office, 51.

597 Brown, *Plainsmen,* 199–200; Peters, 33.

598 Thrapp, *Conquest,* 115–16; Adjutant General's Office, 52. The latter source additionally shows two civilians killed in this fight. The Banta quote is from Thrapp, *Conquest,* 116.

599 Bourke, 169–70; Crook, 174; Thrapp, *Al Sieber,* 97–100.

600 Bourke, 171.

601 Crook, 174; Thrapp, *Al Sieber,* 100–103; Bourke, 170–71.

602 Groneman, 168–69; Nye, *Carbine,* 161–63; Fehrenbach, *Comanches,* 518–19; Carter, R. G., 377–81.

603 Thrapp, *Conquest,* 116–17; Adjutant General's Office, 52.

604 Thrapp, *Conquest,* 121; Adjutant General's Office, 52.

605 Utley, *Frontier Regulars,* 206–07; Glassley, 165–67; Murray, K. A., 86–90.

606 Thrapp, *Conquest,* 122–23; Adjutant General's Office, 53.

607 Thrapp, *Conquest,* 124; Adjutant General's Office, 53.

608 Thrapp, *Conquest,* 124; Adjutant General's Office, 53.

609 Murray, K. A., 107–08; Webb, G. W., 63.

610 Thrapp, *Conquest,* 124–30.

611 Ibid., 132; Adjutant General's Office, 53.

1873

612 Bourke, 205.

613 Ibid., 205; Adjutant General's Office, 53; Thrapp, *Conquest,* 131–32.

614 Utley, *Frontier Regulars,* 207–08; Glassley, 170–71.

615 Thrapp, *Conquest,* 132–33; Adjutant General's Office, 53.

616 Thrapp, *Conquest,* 133; Adjutant General's Office, 53.

617 Thrapp, *Conquest,* 133; Adjutant General's Office, 53.

618 Powell, 828; Carriker, *Fort Supply,* 75–76; Berthrong, 375. This may be the fight labled "Angostura" in Adjutant General's Office, 53, and the soldiers engaged were 8th Cavalrymen.

619 Thrapp, *Conquest,* 135; Adjutant General's Office, 53.

620 Thrapp, *Conquest,* 135–37; Crook, 177–78.

621 Glassley, 185.

622 Utley, *Frontier Regulars,* 210–12; Glassley, 184–87, 206.

623 Utley, *Frontier Regulars,* 210; Glassley, 191–94.

624 Glassley, 196.

625 Utley, *Frontier Regulars,* 211; Glassley, 195–96.

626 Glassley, 197; Murray, K. A., 244; Peters, 46. The latter incorrectly dates the fight on 2 May.

627 Glassley, 198; Utley, *Frontier Regulars,* 211; Murray, K. A., 247–49.

628 Robinson, *Bad Hand,* 139.

629 Robinson, *Bad Hand,* 143.

630 Ibid.

631 Utley, *Frontier Regulars,* 211; Murray, K. A., 257–58.

632 Crook, 182; Adjutant General's Office, 55; Thrapp, *Al Sieber,* 119.

633 Thrapp, *Victorio,* 160; Adjutant General's Office, 55.

634 Groneman, 170–71.

635 Frost, *Custer's 7th,* 66–68.

636 Groneman, 171–72; Wilbarger, 639–42.

637 Frost, *Custer's 7th,* 83–85; Peters, 36.

638 Thrapp, *Al Sieber,* 125–26; Adjutant General's Office, 55. The latter source also lists five captured.

639 Thrapp, *Al Sieber,* 130.

640 Ibid., 128–30; Adjutant General's Office, 56.

641 Nye, *Carbine,* 182–83; Adjutant General's Office, 56.

642 Thrapp, *Al Sieber,* 132–33; Adjutant General's Office, 56.

1874

643 Thrapp, *Al Sieber,* 135–36; Adjutant General's Office, 56.

644 Leckie, *Buffalo Soldiers,* 80; Webb, G. W., 68.

645 Thrapp, *Conquest,* 157–58; Adjutant General's Office, 56.

646 Thrapp, *Al Sieber,* 138–42; Adjutant General's Office, 57.

647 Thrapp, *Conquest,* 158–59; Adjutant General's Office, 57.

648 Thrapp, *Conquest,* 159; Thrapp, *Al Sieber,* 143–44; Adjutant General's Office, 57.

649 Thrapp, *Conquest,* 159; Thrapp, *Al Sieber,* 144–45; Adjutant General's Office, 57.

650 Carriker, *Fort Supply,* 89; Haley, 96; Webb, G. W., 70. Haley lists the escort as 2nd Infantry.

651 Haley, 96; Carriker, *Fort Supply,* 89; Webb, G. W., 70. The last source claims 6 Indians killed and 11 wounded.

652 Baker & Harrison, 68–69.

653 Ibid., 66.

654 Groneman,174–75; Nye, *Carbine,* 190–91; Baker & Harrison, 50–55, 66, 68–69.

655 Haley, 97–98.

656 Trenholm & Carley, 239–43; Rodenbough, 396–99; Adjutant General's Office, 57.

657 Trenholm & Carley, 239–43; Rodenbough, 396–99; Adjutant General's Office, 57.

658 Wilbarger, 574–75; Robinson, *Men Who Wear the Star,* 173–77.

659 Davidson, 187–89; Nye, *Carbine,* 206–10; Adjutant General's Office, 58.

660 Groneman, 178–79; Miles, 166–70; Adjutant General's Office, 58.

661 Groneman, 180–81; Miles, 172–73; Nye, *Carbine,* 215–19; Adjutant General's Office, 58.

662 Groneman, 181–82; Miles, 173–74; Nye, *Carbine,* 219; Dixon, O., 199–214. The only unwounded soldier was Pvt. Peter Rath, Company A, 6th Cavalry.

663 Nye, *Carbine,* 218–19; Leckie, *Buffalo Soldiers,* 125; Webb, G. W., 71.

664 Thrapp, *Al Sieber,* 149–50; Adjutant General's Office, 58.

665 Robinson, *Bad Hand,* 164–78; Fehrenbach, *Comanches,* 541–42.

666 Thrapp, *Al Sieber,* 150; Adjutant General's Office, 59. The latter source says this action took place on 29 October.

667 Thrapp, *Al Sieber,* 151; Adjutant General's Office, 59.

668 Smith, T., 159; Adjutant General's Office, 59.

669 Groneman, 185; Adjutant General's Office, 59.

670 Miles, 175.

671 Groneman, 186–87; Miles, 174–75; Nye, *Carbine,* 226–27; Utley, *Frontier Regulars,* 233; Feldman-Jauken, 191.

672 Wilbarger, 575; Webb, W. P., 316.

673 Webb, W. P., 316–17; Wilbarger, 575.

674 Thrapp, *Al Sieber,* 152–54; Adjutant General's Office, 59. The site of this fight is not pinpointed in the sources, but it could very well have been near present-day Snowflake, Arizona; "Snow Lake" may have been a mistranscription.

675 Thrapp, *Al Sieber,* 155; Adjutant General's Office, 59.

1875

676 Berthrong, 401–02; Adjutant General's Office, 59.

677 Monnett, *Cheyenne Hole,* 66–77.

678 Williams, C. W., 186; Burton, 96–97.

679 Nye, *Carbine,* 235–36; Webb, W. P., 317.

680 Thrapp, *Al Sieber,* 180; Adjutant General's Office, 60.

681 Thrapp, *Al Sieber,* 180; Adjutant General's Office, 60.

682 Williams, C. W., 182–84; Gillett, 40–45. Lehmann and Gillett met and exchanged experiences at a pioneer reunion 50 years later.

683 Carriker, *Fort Supply,* 109–10; Peters, 48.

684 Williams, C. W., 189–90; Leckie, *Buffalo Soldiers,* 147.

1876

685 Gray, 53–56; Utley, *Frontier Regulars,* 255–58.

686 Paul, 221–22; Adjutant General's Office, 61.

687 Gray, 121–23; Utley, *Frontier Regulars,* 261–62.

688 Michno, *Mystery of E Troop,* 16–18; Utley, *Frontier Regulars,* 259, 265–68.

689 Hedren, 68.

690 Ibid., 48–68.

691 Burton, 99; Williams, C. W., 201; Leckie, *Buffalo Soldiers,* 150–51.

692 Thrapp, *Al Sieber,* 183–84; Adjutant General's Office, 62.

693 Utley, *Frontier Regulars,* 278–79; Greene, *Slim Buttes,* 59–88.

694 Leckie, *Buffalo Soldiers,* 177; Billington, 48–49; Adjutant General's Office, 62. Leckie places this fight on 15 April.

695 Thrapp, *Al Sieber,* 184; Adjutant General's Office, 62.

696 Thrapp, *Al Sieber,* 184; Adjutant General's Office, 62.

697 Greene, *Yellowstone Command,* 90–104.

698 Utley, *Frontier Regulars,* 283–84; Robinson, *Bad Hand,* 215–22.

699 Greene, *Yellowstone Command,* 139–43.

1877

700 Greene, *Yellowstone Command,* 163–76; Utley, *Frontier Regulars,* 285.

701 Thrapp, *Victorio,* 183–85; Adjutant General's Office, 63. This fight is sometimes listed as Leitendorf Hills.

702 Thrapp, *Al Sieber,* 185–87.

703 Ibid., 187–88.

704 Leckie, *Buffalo Soldiers,* 178; Billington, 50–51.

705 Thrapp, *Al Sieber,* 188.

706 Among the men were Johnny Cook, Sol Rees, Jim Harvey, Hi Bickerdyke, Smoky Hill Thompson, Louis Keyes, and Rath's agent, George West.

707 Groneman, 188; Sandoz, *Buffalo Hunters,* 272–80.

708 Sandoz, *Buffalo Hunters,* states that Black Horse was killed in this fight. Rister, *Fort Griffin,* states that Butler killed Black Horse before being wounded himself. Leckie, *Buffalo Soldiers,* indicates the wounded soldier was named Baker, from Company C.

709 Sandoz, *Buffalo Hunters,* 281–82, 291; Leckie, *Buffalo Soldiers,* 156; Adjutant General's Office, 63; Rister, *Fort Griffin,* 187–89.

710 Greene, *Yellowstone Command,* 202–13; Utley, *Frontier Regulars,* 288–89.

711 Utley, *Frontier Regulars,* 309–10; Brown, *Flight of the Nez Perce,* 130–41.

712 Brown, *Flight of the Nez Perce,* 167–68.

713 Ibid., 173–75.

714 Ibid., 176–77.

715 Ibid., 177–80.

716 Utley, *Frontier Regulars,* 313–14; Brown, *Flight of the Nez Perce,* 188–97; Adjutant General's Office, 64.

717 Brown, *Flight of the Nez Perce,* 203–04.

718 Utley, *Frontier Regulars,* 315–16; Brown, *Flight of the Nez Perce,* 246–64. Capt. William Logan and Lt. James H. Bradley were killed, and Lt. William L. English received a mortal wound.

719 Brown, *Flight of the Nez Perce,* 275–77. The other three men killed were Thomas Flynn, James Smith, and James Farnsworth.

720 Ibid., 281–85.

721 Ibid., 290–97; Utley, *Frontier Regulars,* 317–18.

722 Brown, *Flight of the Nez Perce,* 359–63; Utley, *Frontier Regulars,* 320.

723 Brown, *Flight of the Nez Perce,* 371–73; Adjutant General's Office, 65.

724 Brown, *Flight of the Nez Perce,* 374–76; Adjutant General's Office, 65.

725 Leckie, *Buffalo Soldiers,* 154; Adjutant General's Office, 65.

726 Utley, *Frontier Regulars,* 323.

727 Ibid., 320–23; Chandler, 74–76.

728 Leckie, *Buffalo Soldiers,* 154–55; Williams, C. W., 214–15; Adjutant General's Office, 66; Smith, T., 162. Most sources label the range the Carmel Mountains.

729 Peters, 75; Adjutant General's Office, 66; Thrapp, *Conquest,* 178–79.

1878

730 Thrapp, *Al Sieber,* 201–02; Adjutant General's Office, 67. The latter source labels this fight Mogollon Mountains.

731 Glassley, 229–30.

732 Ibid., 231–32; Utley, *Frontier Regulars,* 334–35; Adjutant General's Office, 67.

733 Nye, *Carbine,* 238–39; Leckie, *Buffalo Soldiers,* 167–68.

734 Glassley, 233–34.

735 Utley, *Frontier Regulars,* 335–36; Adjutant General's Office, 67.

736 Glassley, 234–35; Utley, *Frontier Regulars,* 336.

737 Utley, *Frontier Regulars,* 336–37; Adjutant General's Office, 67.

738 Peters, 78.

739 Leckie, *Buffalo Soldiers,* 191; Billington, 56–57.

740 Peters, 78.

741 Ibid.; Adjutant General's Office, 68.

742 Carriker, *Fort Supply,* 123–25; Powell, 1162–63; Grinnell, *Fighting Cheyennes,* 404–05; Sandoz, *Cheyenne Autumn,* 38–40. The fight is also said to have occurred on Little Medicine Lodge River.

743 Powell, 1167–70; Sandoz, *Cheyenne Autumn,* 75–82.

1879

744 Grinnell, *Fighting Cheyennes,* 417–27.

745 Peters, 85; Adjutant General's Office, 69.

746 Billington, 87–89; Adjutant General's Office, 69.

747 Thrapp, *Al Sieber,* 207; Adjutant General's Office, 69.

748 Peters, 87.

749 Williams, C. W., 229; Peters, 86.

750 Utley, *Frontier Regulars,* 339–40; Glassley, 243–44.

751 The soldiers killed were Sgt. S. Chapman and Pvts. Graddon, Hoke, Murphy, and Percival.

752 Billington, 89.

753 Ibid., 90–91. Lt. Matthias W. Day and Sgt. John Denny received Medals of Honor for this action.

754 Ibid., 91–92.

755 Peters, 88–91; Burton, 218–20; Sprague, 205–26.

756 Wellman, *Death on the Prairie,* 255–57; Sprague, 233–38.

757 Thrapp, *Conquest,* 186; Adjutant General's Office, 71.

758 Billington, 92–93; Adjutant General's Office, 71.

1880

759 Thrapp, *Victorio,* 261; Adjutant General's Office, 71; Peters, 93. The latter two sources incorrectly call this fight Rio Puerco.

760 Thrapp, *Victorio,* 261–62.

761 Ibid., 262.

762 Ibid., 262–63; Adjutant General's Office, 71.

763 Thrapp, *Victorio,* 263.

764 Ibid.; Thrapp, *Conquest,* 192–93.

765 Brown, *Plainsmen of the Yellowstone,* 324; Peters, 93.

766 Williams, C. W., 235; Leckie, *Buffalo Soldiers,* 217. Other sources indicate that the troop with Company L was either Company B or F.

767 Thrapp, *Conquest,* 194–96; Leckie, *Buffalo Soldiers,* 215–16.

768 Williams, C. W., 235–36; Leckie, *Buffalo Soldiers,* 217. Leckie says the boy's last name was Segura.

769 Thrapp, *Victorio,* 271–73; Leckie, *Buffalo Soldiers,* 219.

770 Leckie, *Buffalo Soldiers,* 220; Adjutant General's Office, 72.

771 Thrapp, *Al Sieber,* 216–17; Adjutant General's Office, 73.

772 Leckie, *Buffalo Soldiers,* 223; Williams, C. W., 239–40.

773 Thrapp, *Victorio,* 277–80.

774 Ibid., 281; Thrapp, *Conquest,* 202–03.

775 Thrapp, *Victorio,* 286–87; Leckie, *Buffalo Soldiers,* 224–25; Utley, *Fort Davis,* 42–43. This fight has been known variously as Rocky Ridge, Quitman Canyon, and Eagle Pass.

776 Thrapp, *Victorio,* 288–89; Leckie, *Buffalo Soldiers,* 226–27.

777 Billington, 97–98.

778 Thrapp, *Conquest,* 207; Adjutant General's Office, 73.

779 Leckie, *Buffalo Soldiers,* 230; Peters, 97; Adjutant General's Office, 73. Some sources indicate this fight took place on 29 October.

780 The men killed were Cpl. William Backus and Pvts. Jeremiah Griffin, James Stanley, Carter Burns, and George Mills.

1881

781 Peters, 98.

782 Utley, *Fort Davis,* 45; Webb, W. P., 403–06; Robinson, *Men Who Wear the Star,* 244.

783 Burton, 100–01; Adjutant General's Office, 74.

784 Thrapp, *Conquest,* 212–13; Billington, 103–05.

785 Thrapp, *Conquest,* 213–14; Adjutant General's Office, 75.

786 Thrapp, *Conquest,* 214; Billington, 105.

787 Billington, 105; Burton, 161.

788 Billington, 106; Thrapp, *Conquest,* 214.

789 Billington, 106–07; Thrapp, *Conquest,* 215; Adjutant General's Office , 75. The latter two sources incorrectly label the canyon "Guerillo."

790 Wellman, *Death in the Desert,* 218–21; Thrapp, *Conquest,* 221–26.

791 Wellman, *Death in the Desert,* 221; Thrapp, *Conquest,* 226–27.

792 Thrapp, *Conquest,* 232–34; Ludwig & Stute, 7–8.

793 Leckie, *Buffalo Soldiers,* 233–34; Ludwig & Stute, 12.

1882

794 Thrapp, *Conquest,* 235–45; Utley, *Frontier Regulars,* 385; Adjutant General's Office, 76.

795 Thrapp, *Conquest,* 245–48; Thrapp, *Al Sieber,* 228–35; Kraft, *Gatewood,* 9; Adjutant General's Office, 76. The last source says this fight took place in the Hatchet Mountains near the Mexican line.

796 Peters, 101–02.

797 Ibid., 102; Sonnichsen, 234–35.

798 Thrapp, *Conquest,* 254–56; Utley, *Frontier Regulars,* 386; Adjutant General's Office, 76.

1883

799 Simmons, *Lordsburg Road,* 86–91.

800 Ibid., 109–11.

801 Thrapp, *Conquest,* 277, 286–87, 291; Kraft, *Gatewood,* 27–35; Betzinez, 118, 120.

1885

802 Thrapp, *Conquest,* 318–19; Kraft, *Gatewood,* 91–92.

803 Thrapp, *Conquest,* 324–25; Webb, G. W., 94.

804 Thrapp, *Conquest,* 328–29; Kraft, *Gatewood,* 97.

805 Thrapp, *Conquest,* 330–31; Kraft, *Gatewood,* 103–04.

806 Thrapp, *Conquest,* 332; Webb, G. W., 94.

807 Thrapp, *Conquest,* 334–35; Webb, G. W., 94. In Adjutant General's Office, 77, this fight is dated 7 November.

808 Thrapp, *Conquest,* 337; Carroll, 87–89; Adjutant General's Office, 77.

1886

809 Leckie, *Buffalo Soldiers,* 243–44; Adjutant General's Office, 78.

810 Thrapp, *Conquest,* 351; Adjutant General's Office, 78.

1887

811 Brown, *Plainsmen of the Yellowstone,* 441–42; Adjutant General's Office, 78.

1890

812 Utley, *Frontier Regulars,* 415–17; Adjutant General's Office, 79.

813 Utley, *Last Days,* 233–41; Adjutant General's Office, 79.

Conclusions

814 Smith, T., 14.

815 Examples are in Schultz, *Freezing Moon,* 50–51; Osborn, 200; Oliva, *Soldiers,* 139–140; Nadeau, 145; Worcester, 80; Hebard & Brininstool, 71, 139; Bender, 170; Springer, 1.

816 Utley, *Frontiersmen,* 216–17.

817 Urwin, 92–93, 134; Sawicki, 42, 44; Utley, *Frontiersmen,* 216.

818 Josephy, 36, indicates volunteers were more than eager to kill Indians "on any excuse."

819 Osborn, 217–18. Osborn liberally quotes from numerous sources and repeats the consensus that Sand Creek was the primary cause of subsequent Indian fighting.

820 Tallman, 146.

821 Thrapp, *Encyclopedia,* 101–02; Russell, 97. The majority of Bernard's fights were against Rebels, not Indians.

822 Sully, 201–09.

823 Clodfelter, 217–20.

824 McDermott, *Indian Wars,* 28.

825 Trafzer & Hyer, xiii.

826 Udall, "'Wild' Old West," 67.

827 Mattes, *Platte River Road,* 23; Unruh, 185.

828 Faragher, 31–32.

—Bibliography—

Books

Afton, Jean, David F. Halaas, and Andrew E. Masich, with Richard N. Ellis. *Cheyenne Dog Soldiers: A Ledgerbook History of Coups and Combat.* Denver: University Press of Colorado and Colorado Historical Society, 1997.

Anderson, Gary Clayton, and Alan R. Woolworth, eds. *Through Dakota Eyes: Narrative Accounts of the Minnesota Indian War of 1862.* St. Paul: Minnesota Historical Society Press, 1988.

Arnold, James R. *Jeff Davis's Own: Cavalry, Comanches, and the Battle for the Texas Frontier.* New York: John Wiley & Sons, 2000.

Athearn, Robert G. *William Tecumseh Sherman and the Settlement of the West.* Norman: University of Oklahoma Press, 1995.

Bailey, Lynn R. *Bosque Redondo: The Navajo Internment at Fort Sumner New Mexico, 1863–1868.* Tucson: Westernlore Press, 1998.

Bain, David Haward. *Empire Express: Building the First Transcontinental Railroad.* New York: Viking Penguin, 1999.

Baker, T. Lindsay, and Billy R. Harrison. *Adobe Walls: The History and Archaeology of the 1874 Trading Post.* College Station: Texas A & M University Press, 1986.

Barlow, J. W. *Outline Descriptions of the Posts in the Military Division of the Missouri.* Chicago, 1876. Reprint, Belleview, Nebr.: Old Army Press, 1969.

Becher, Ronald. *Massacre along the Medicine Road: A Social History of the Indian War of 1864 in Nebraska Territory.* Caldwell, Idaho: Caxton Press, 1999.

Beckham, Stephen Dow. *Requiem for a People: The Rogue Indians and the Frontiersmen.* Corvallis: Oregon State University Press, 1996.

Bender, Averam B. *The March of Empire: Frontier Defense in the Southwest 1848–1860.* New York: Greenwood Press, 1968.

Bennett, James A. *Forts and Forays: A Dragoon in New Mexico, 1850–1856,* Ed. Clinton E. Brooks and Frank D. Reeve. Albuquerque: University of New Mexico Press, 1996.

Bernhardt, C. *Indian Raids in Lincoln County, Kansas, 1864 and 1869.* Lincoln, Kans.: Lincoln Sentinel Print, 1910.

Berthrong, Donald J. *The Southern Cheyennes.* Norman: University of Oklahoma Press, 1963.

Bettelyoun, Susan Bordeaux, and Josephine Waggoner. *With My Own Eyes: A Lakota Woman Tells Her People's History.* Lincoln: University of Nebraska Press, 1999.

Betzinez, Jason, with Wilbur Sturtevant Nye. *I Fought with Geronimo.* Lincoln: University of Nebraska Press, 1987.

Billington, Monroe Lee. *New Mexico's Buffalo Soldiers, 1866–1900.* Niwot: University Press of Colorado, 1991.

Bourke, John G. *On the Border with Crook.* Lincoln: University of Nebraska Press, 1971.

Brady, Cyrus Townsend. *Indian Fights and Fighters.* Lincoln: University of Nebraska Press, 1971.

Brooks, Juanita. *The Mountain Meadows Massacre*. Norman: University of Oklahoma Press, 1991.

Brown, Dee. *Fort Phil Kearny: An American Saga*. Lincoln: University of Nebraska Press, 1971.

———. *The Galvanized Yankees*. Lincoln: University of Nebraska Press, 1986.

Brown, Mark H. *The Flight of the Nez Perce*. Lincoln: University of Nebraska Press, 1967.

———. *The Plainsmen of the Yellowstone: A History of the Yellowstone Basin*. Lincoln: University of Nebraska Press, 1969.

Burkey, Blaine. *Custer, Come at Once!* Hays, Kans.: Thomas More Prep, 1976.

Burton, Art T. *Black, Buckskin, and Blue: African-American Scouts and Soldiers on the Western Frontier*. Austin: Eakin Press, 1999.

Capps, Benjamin. *The Warren Wagon Train Raid*. Dallas: Southern Methodist University Press, 1974.

Carriker, Robert C. *Father Peter John de Smet: Jesuit in the West*. Norman: University of Oklahoma Press, 1995.

———. *Fort Supply: Indian Territory*. Norman: University of Oklahoma Press, 1970.

Carroll, John M., ed. *The Papers of the Order of Indian Wars*. Ft. Collins, Colo.: Old Army Press, 1975.

Carter, R. G. *On the Border with Mackenzie; or, Winning West Texas from the Comanches*. Mattituck, N.Y.: J. M. Carroll & Co., n.d.

Carter, W. H. *From Yorktown to Santiago with the Sixth Cavalry*. Baltimore: Lord Baltimore Press, 1900. Reprint, Austin: State House Press, 1989.

Cashin, Herschel V. *Under Fire with the Tenth U.S. Cavalry*. Niwot: University Press of Colorado, 1993.

Castel, Albert. *Civil War Kansas: Reaping the Whirlwind*. Lawrence: University Press of Kansas, 1997.

Chalfant, William Y. *Cheyennes and Horse Soldiers*. Norman: University of Oklahoma Press, 1989.

———. *Without Quarter: The Wichita Expedition and the Fight on Crooked Creek*. Norman: University of Oklahoma Press, 1991.

Chandler, Melbourne C. *Of Garryowen in Glory: A History of the Seventh U.S. Cavalry Regiment*. Annandale, Virg.: Turnpike Press, 1960.

Clodfelter, Michael. *The Dakota War: The United States Army versus the Sioux, 1862–1865*. Jefferson, N.C.: McFarland & Co., 1998.

Cody, William F. *The Life of Hon. William F. Cody, Known as Buffalo Bill, the Famous Hunter, Scout, and Guide: An Autobiography*. Lincoln: University of Nebraska Press, 1978.

Coffman, Edward M. *The Old Army: A Portrait of the American Army in Peacetime, 1784–1898*. New York: Oxford University Press, 1986.

Connelley, William E. *The Life of Preston B. Plumb, 1837–1891*. Chicago: Browne & Howell, 1913.

Coward, John M. *The Newspaper Indian: Native American Identity in the Press, 1820–90*. Urbana: University of Illinois Press, 1999.

Craig, Reginald S. *The Fighting Parson: The Biography of Colonel John M. Chivington.* Tucson: Westernlore Press, 1959.

Crawford, Samuel J. *Kansas in the Sixties.* Ottawa: Kansas Heritage Press, 1994.

Cremony, John C. *Life among the Apaches.* San Francisco: A. Roman & Co., 1868. Reprint, Norman: University of Oklahoma Press, 1983.

Crook, George. *General George Crook: His Autobiography.* Norman: University of Oklahoma Press, 1986.

Curran, Harold. *Fearful Crossing: The Central Overland Trail through Nevada.* Las Vegas: Nevada Publications, 1987.

Custer, Elizabeth B. *Tenting on the Plains; or, General Custer in Kansas and Texas.* Norman: University of Oklahoma Press, 1994.

Custer, George Armstrong. *My Life on the Plains.* Norman: University of Oklahoma Press, 1988.

Czaplewski, Russ. *Captive of the Cheyenne: The Story of Nancy Jane Morton and the Plum Creek Massacre.* Lexington, Nebr.: Dawson County Historical Society, 1993.

Danziger, Edmund Jefferson, Jr. *Indians and Bureaucrats: Administering Reservation Policy during the Civil War.* Urbana: University of Illinois Press, 1974.

Dary, David. *The Santa Fe Trail: Its History, Legends, and Lore.* New York: Alfred A. Knopf, 2000.

Davidson, Homer K. *Black Jack Davidson, a Cavalry Commander on the Western Frontier: The Life of John W. Davidson.* Glendale, Calif.: Arthur H. Clark, 1973.

Derounian-Stodola, Kathryn Zabelle, and James Arthur Levernier. *The Indian Captivity Narrative, 1550–1900.* New York: Twayne Publishers, 1993.

Dick, Everett. *Conquering the Great American Desert: Nebraska.* Lincoln: Nebraska State Historical Society, 1975.

Dickson, Arthur Jerome, ed. *Covered Wagon Days: A Journey across the Plains in the Sixties, and Pioneer Days in the Northwest; from the Private Journals of Albert Jerome Dickson.* Lincoln: University of Nebraska Press, 1989.

Dippie, Brian W. *Custer's Last Stand: The Anatomy of an American Myth.* Lincoln: University of Nebraska Press, 1976.

———. *The Vanishing American: White Attitudes and U.S. Indian Policy.* Lawrence: University Press of Kansas, 1982.

———, ed. *Nomad: George A. Custer in Turf, Field and Farm.* Austin: University of Texas Press, 1980.

Dixon, David. "Custer and the Sweetwater Hostages." In *Custer and His Times, Book 3,* edited by Gregory J. W. Urwin and Roberta E. Fagan. El Paso: Little Big Horn Associates; and Conway: University of Central Arkansas Press, 1987.

———. *Hero of Beecher Island: The Life and Military Career of George A. Forsyth.* Lincoln: University of Nebraska Press, 1997.

Dixon, Olive K. *Life of "Billy" Dixon, Plainsman, Scout and Pioneer.* Austin: State House Press, 1987.

Doyle, Susan Badger, ed. *Journeys to the Land of Gold: Emigrant Diaries from the Bozeman Trail, 1863–1866.* Helena: Montana Historical Society Press, 2000.

Drago, Harry Sinclair. *The Great Range Wars: Violence on the Grasslands.* Lincoln: University of Nebraska Press, 1985.

Drimmer, Frederick, ed. *Captured by the Indians: Fifteen Firsthand Accounts, 1750–1870.* New York: Dover Publications, 1985.

Dunlay, Thomas W. *Wolves for the Blue Soldiers: Indian Scouts and Auxiliaries with the United States Army, 1860–90.* Lincoln: University of Nebraska Press, 1982.

Dunn, J. P., Jr. *Massacres of the Mountains: A History of the Indian Wars of the Far West 1815–1875.* New York: Archer House, 1886.

Dunn, William R. *"I Stand by Sand Creek": A Defense of Colonel John M. Chivington and the Third Colorado Cavalry.* Fort Collins, Colo.: Old Army Press, 1985.

———. *War Drum Echoes: A Narrative History of the Indian Wars in Colorado.* Colorado Springs, Colo.: privately published, 1979.

Ellis, Richard N. *General Pope and U.S. Indian Policy.* Albuquerque: University of New Mexico Press, 1970.

Exley, Jo Ella Powell. *Frontier Blood: The Saga of the Parker Family.* College Station: Texas A & M University Press, 2001.

Faragher, John Mack. *Women and Men on the Overland Trail.* New Haven: Yale University Press, 1979.

Farish, Thomas Edwin. *History of Arizona.* 8 vols. San Francisco: Filmer Brothers Electrotype Company, 1915–18.

Faulk, Odie B. *Crimson Desert: Indian Wars of the American Southwest.* New York: Oxford University Press, 1974.

Fehrenbach, T. R. *Comanches: The Destruction of a People.* New York: De Capo Press, 1994.

———. *Lone Star: A History of Texas and the Texans.* New York: Collier Books, 1980.

Feldman-Jauken, Arlene. *The Moccasin Speaks: Living as Captives of the Dog Soldier Warriors.* Lincoln, Nebr.: Dageforde Publishing, 1998.

Forsyth, George A. *Thrilling Days in Army Life.* Lincoln: University of Nebraska Press, 1994.

Franzwa, Gregory M. *Maps of the Oregon Trail.* St. Louis: Patrice Press, 1990.

———. *The Oregon Trail Revisited.* Tucson: Patrice Press, 1997.

Frazer, Robert W. *Forts of the West: Military Forts and Presidios and Posts Commonly Called Forts West of the Mississippi River to 1898.* Norman: University of Oklahoma Press, 1965.

Frazier, Donald S. *Blood and Treasure: Confederate Empire in the Southwest.* College Station: Texas A & M University Press, 1995.

Frederick, J. V. *Ben Holladay, the Stagecoach King: A Chapter in the Development of Transcontinental Transportation.* Glendale, Calif.: Arthur H. Clark, 1940. Reprint, Lincoln: University of Nebraska Press, 1989.

Frost, Lawrence A. *The Court-Martial of General George Armstrong Custer.* Norman: University of Oklahoma Press, 1968.

———. *Custer's 7th Cav and the Campaign of 1873.* El Segundo, Calif.: Upton & Sons, 1986.

Gallaway, B. P., ed. *Texas, the Dark Corner of the Confederacy.* Lincoln: University of Nebraska Press, 1994.

Gard, Wayne. *The Chisholm Trail.* Norman: University of Oklahoma Press, 1954.

Gillett, James B. *Six Years with the Texas Rangers, 1875 to 1881.* Lincoln: University of Nebraska Press, 1976.

Glassley, Ray Hoard. *Indian Wars of the Pacific Northwest.* Portland, Ore.: Binfords & Mort, 1972.

Goetzmann, William H. *Exploration and Empire: The Explorer and the Scientist in the Winning of the American West.* New York: W. W. Norton, 1966.

Goodrich, Thomas. *Scalp Dance: Indian Warfare on the High Plains, 1865–1879.* Mechanicsburg, Penn.: Stackpole Books, 1997.

———. *War to the Knife: Bleeding Kansas, 1854–1861.* Mechanicsburg, Penn.: Stackpole Books, 1998.

Gray, John S. *Centennial Campaign.* Fort Collins, Colo.: Old Army Press, 1976.

Greene, Jerome A. *Slim Buttes, 1876: An Episode of the Great Sioux War.* Norman: University of Oklahoma Press, 1982.

———. *Yellowstone Command: Colonel Nelson A. Miles and the Great Sioux War 1876–1877.* Lincoln: University of Nebraska Press, 1991.

Grinnell, George B. *The Cheyenne Indians.* Lincoln: University of Nebraska Press, 1972.

———. *The Fighting Cheyennes.* Norman: University of Oklahoma Press, 1966.

———. *Two Great Scouts and Their Pawnee Battalion: The Experiences of Frank J. North and Luther H. North.* Lincoln: University of Nebraska Press, 1973.

Groneman, Bill. *Battlefields of Texas.* Plano: Republic of Texas Press, 1998.

Guild, Thelma S., and Harvey L. Carter. *Kit Carson: A Pattern for Heroes.* Lincoln: University of Nebraska Press, 1988.

Hafen, Leroy R. *Broken Hand: The Life of Thomas Fitzpatrick, Mountain Man, Guide and Indian Agent.* Norman: University of Oklahoma Press, 1981.

———, and Ann W. Hafen. *Handcarts to Zion: The Story of a Unique Western Migration, 1856–1860.* Lincoln: University of Nebraska Press, 1992.

———. *Powder River Campaigns and Sawyers Expedition of 1865.* Glendale, Calif.: Arthur H. Clark, 1961.

———. *Relations with the Indians of the Plains, 1857–1861.* Glendale, Calif.: Arthur H. Clark, 1959.

Hafen, LeRoy R., and Francis Marion Young. *Fort Laramie and the Pageant of the West, 1834–1890.* Lincoln: University of Nebraska Press, 1984.

Hagan, Barry J. *"Exactly in the Right Place": A History of Fort C. F. Smith, Montana Territory, 1866–1868.* El Segundo, Calif.: Upton & Sons, 1999.

Haley, James L. *The Buffalo War: The History of the Red River Indian Uprising of 1874.* Norman: University of Oklahoma Press, 1985.

Hamlin, Percy Gatling, ed. *The Making of a Soldier: Letters of General R. S. Ewell.* Richmond, Virg.: Whittet & Shepperson, 1935.

Harris, Benjamin Butler. *The Gila Trail: The Texas Argonauts and the California Gold Rush.* Norman: University of Oklahoma Press, 1960.

Hebard, Grace Raymond, and E. A. Brininstool. *The Bozeman Trail.* Lincoln: University of Nebraska Press, 1990.

Hedren, Paul L. *First Scalp for Custer.* Lincoln: University of Nebraska Press, 1987.

Heitman, Francis B. *Historical Register and Dictionary of the United States Army.* Washington: GPO, 1903.

Heizer, Robert F., ed. *The Destruction of California Indians.* Lincoln: University of Nebraska Press, 1974.

Hoig, Stan. *The Battle of the Washita: The Sheridan-Custer Campaign of 1867–69.* Lincoln: University of Nebraska Press, 1979.

———. *The Peace Chiefs of the Cheyennes.* Norman: University of Oklahoma Press, 1980.

———. *The Sand Creek Massacre.* Norman: University of Oklahoma Press, 1961.

———. *Tribal Wars of the Southern Plains.* Norman: University of Oklahoma Press, 1993.

Holmes, Kenneth L., ed. *Covered Wagon Women: Diaries and Letters from the Western Trails.* 2 vols. Lincoln: University of Nebraska Press, 1999.

Holmes, Louis A. *Fort McPherson, Nebraska, Fort Cottonwood, N.T.: Guardian of the Tracks and Trails.* Lincoln: University of Nebraska Press, 1963.

Hood, John B. *Advance and Retreat: Personal Experiences in the United States and Confederate Armies.* New Orleans: G. T. Beauregard, 1880. Reprint, Cambridge, Mass.: Da Capo Press, 1993.

Howbert, Irving. *Indians of the Pike's Peak Region.* New York: Knickerbocker Press, 1914.

Hutton, Paul Andrew. *Phil Sheridan and His Army.* Lincoln: University of Nebraska Press, 1985.

Hyde, George E. *Life of George Bent, Written from His Letters.* Norman: University of Oklahoma Press, 1968.

———. *The Pawnee Indians.* Norman: University of Oklahoma Press, 1988.

———. *Red Cloud's Folk: A History of the Oglala Sioux Indians.* Norman: University of Oklahoma Press, 1937.

———. *A Sioux Chronicle.* Norman: University of Oklahoma Press, 1956.

———. *Spotted Tail's Folk: A History of the Brule Sioux.* Norman: University of Oklahoma Press, 1974.

Jackson, W. Turrentine. *Wagon Roads West: A Study of Federal Road Surveys and Construction in the Trans-Mississippi West, 1846–1869.* New Haven: Yale University Press, 1965.

Johnson, Dorothy M. *The Bloody Bozeman: The Perilous Trail to Montana's Gold.* Missoula, Mont.: Mountain Press, 1983.

Johnson, Randy, and Nancy P. Allan. *A Dispatch to Custer: The Tragedy of Lieutenant Kidder.* Missoula, Mont.: Mountain Press, 1999.

Jordan, David M. *Winfield Scott Hancock: A Soldier's Life.* Bloomington: Indiana University Press, 1996.

Josephy, Alvin M., Jr. *The Civil War in the American West.* New York: Alfred A. Knopf, 1991.

Keenan, Jerry. *The Wagon Box Fight.* Boulder, Colo.: Lightning Tree Press, 1992.

Keim, De B. Randolph. *Sheridan's Troopers on the Borders: A Winter Campaign on the Plains.* Lincoln: University of Nebraska Press, 1985.

Kelly, Fanny. *My Captivity among the Sioux Indians.* New York: Carol Publishing Group, 1993.

Kennedy, W.J.D. *On the Plains with Custer and Hancock: The Journal of Isaac Coates, Army Surgeon.* Boulder, Colo.: Johnson Books, 1997.

Kenner, Charles L. *Buffalo Soldiers and Officers of the Ninth Cavalry, 1867–1898: Black and White Together.* Norman: University of Oklahoma Press, 1999.

King, James T. *War Eagle: A Life of General Eugene A. Carr.* Lincoln: University of Nebraska Press, 1963.

Knight, Oliver. *Following the Indian Wars: The Story of the Newspaper Correspondents among the Indian Campaigners.* Norman: University of Oklahoma Press, 1960.

Kraft, Louis. *Gatewood and Geronimo.* Albuquerque: University of New Mexico Press, 2000.

Larson, Robert W. *Red Cloud: Warrior-Statesman of the Lakota Sioux.* Norman: University of Oklahoma Press, 1997.

Lavender, David. *Bent's Fort.* Lincoln: University of Nebraska Press, 1972.

———. *Westward Vision: The Story of the Oregon Trail.* Lincoln: University of Nebraska Press, 1985.

Leckie, Shirley A. *Elizabeth Bacon Custer and the Making of a Myth.* Norman: University of Oklahoma Press, 1993.

Leckie, William H. *The Buffalo Soldiers: A Narrative of the Negro Cavalry in the West.* Norman: University of Oklahoma Press, 1967.

———, and Shirley A. Leckie. *Unlikely Warriors: General Benjamin Grierson and His Family.* Norman: University of Oklahoma Press, 1984.

Ledbetter, Barbara A. Neal. *Fort Belknap: Frontier Saga.* NL Ranch Headquarters, Tex.: Lavender Books, 1982.

Lee, Wayne C., and Howard C. Raynesford. *Trails of the Smoky Hill: From Coronado to the Cow Towns.* Caldwell, Idaho: Caxton Printers, 1980.

Liddic, Bruce R., and Paul Harbaugh, eds. *Camp on Custer: Transcribing the Custer Myth.* Spokane, Wash.: Arthur H. Clark, 1995.

Limerick, Patricia Nelson. *The Legacy of Conquest: The Unbroken Past of the American West.* New York: W. W. Norton, 1987.

———. *Something in the Soil: Legacies and Reckonings in the New West.* New York: W. W. Norton, 2000.

———, Clyde A. Milner II, and Charles Rankin, eds. *Trails: Toward a New Western History.* Lawrence: University Press of Kansas, 1991.

Lowe, Percival G. *Five Years a Dragoon ('49 to '54) and Other Adventures on the Great Plains.* Norman: University of Oklahoma Press, 1991.

Ludwig, Larry L., and James L. Stute. *The Battle at K-Y Butte: Apache Outbreak, 1881, Arizona Territory.* Tucson: Westernlore Press, 1993.

Madsen, Brigham D. *The Shoshoni Frontier and the Bear River Massacre.* Salt Lake City: University of Utah Press, 1985.

Mattes, Merrill J. *The Great Platte River Road*. Lincoln: Nebraska State Historical Society, 1969.

———. *Indians, Infants and Infantry: Andrew and Elizabeth Burt on the Frontier*. Lincoln: University of Nebraska Press, 1988.

Mayhall, Mildred P. *The Kiowas*. Norman: University of Oklahoma Press, 1962.

McDermott, John D. *Frontier Crossroads: The History of Fort Caspar and the Upper Platte Crossing*. Casper, Wyom.: City of Casper, 1997.

———. *A Guide to the Indian Wars of the West*. Lincoln: University of Nebraska Press, 1998.

McNitt, Frank. *Navajo Wars: Military Campaigns, Slave Raids and Reprisals*. Albuquerque: University of New Mexico Press, 1972.

Meyers, Frank. *Soldiering in Dakota, Among the Indians, in 1863–5*. Pierre: State Historical Society of South Dakota, 1936.

Michno, Gregory F. *Battle at Sand Creek*. El Segundo, Calif.: Upton & Sons, 2003 (forthcoming).

———. *The Mystery of E Troop: Custer's Gray Horse Company at the Little Bighorn*. Missoula, Mont.: Mountain Press, 1994.

Miles, Nelson A. *Personal Recollections and Observations of General Nelson A. Miles*. Lincoln: University of Nebraska Press, 1992.

Mills, Charles K. *Harvest of Barren Regrets: The Army Career of Frederick William Benteen, 1834–1898*. Glendale, Calif.: Arthur H. Clark, 1985.

Monahan, Doris. *Destination Denver City: The South Platte Trail*. Athens: Ohio University Press, 1985.

Monnett, John H. *The Battle of Beecher Island and the Indian War of 1867–1869*. Niwot: University Press of Colorado, 1992.

———. *Massacre at Cheyenne Hole*. Niwot: University Press of Colorado, 1999.

Moore, William Haas. *Chiefs, Agents and Soldiers: Conflict on the Navajo Frontier, 1868–1882*. Albuquerque: University of New Mexico Press, 1994.

Murray, Keith A. *The Modocs and Their War*. Norman: University of Oklahoma Press, 1959.

Murray, Robert A. *The Army on the Powder River*. Bellevue, Nebr.: Old Army Press, 1969.

———. *Military Posts in the Powder River Country of Wyoming, 1865–1894*. Buffalo, Wyom.: The Office, 1968.

Nadeau, Remi. *Fort Laramie and the Sioux*. Lincoln: University of Nebraska Press, 1967.

Namias, June. *White Captives: Gender and Ethnicity on the American Frontier*. Chapel Hill: University of North Carolina Press, 1993.

Nash, Gerald D. *Creating the West: Historical Interpretations 1890–1990*. Albuquerque: University of New Mexico Press, 1991.

Neider, Charles, ed. *The Great West: A Treasury of Firsthand Accounts*. New York: Da Capo Press, 1997.

Nichols, David A. *Lincoln and the Indians: Civil War Policy and Politics*. Urbana: University of Illinois Press, 2000.

Nye, Wilbur Sturtevant. *Carbine and Lance: The Story of Old Fort Sill.* Norman: University of Oklahoma Press, 1969.

———. *Plains Indian Raiders: The Final Phases of Warfare from the Arkansas to the Red River.* Norman: University of Oklahoma Press, 1968.

Oliva, Leo E. *Fort Union and the Frontier Army in the Southwest.* Santa Fe: National Park Service, 1993.

———. *Soldiers on the Santa Fe Trail.* Norman: University of Oklahoma Press, 1967.

Osborne, William M. *The Wild Frontier.* New York: Random House, 2000.

Ostrander, Alson B. *An Army Boy of the Sixties.* New York: World Book, 1936.

Paher, Stanley W., ed. *Fort Churchill: Nevada Military Outpost of the 1860s.* Las Vegas: Nevada Publications, 1981.

Paul, R. Eli, ed. *The Nebraska Indian Wars Reader, 1865–1877.* Lincoln: University of Nebraska Press, 1998.

Perkins, J. R. *Trails, Rails and War: The Life of General G. M. Dodge.* New York: Arno Press, 1981.

Peters, Joseph P. *Indian Battles and Skirmishes on the American Frontier, 1790–1898.* Ann Arbor, Mich.: University Microfilms, 1966.

Powell, Peter John. *People of the Sacred Mountain: A History of the Northern Cheyenne Chiefs and Warrior Societies, 1830–1879.* 2 vols. San Francisco: Harper & Row, 1981.

Price, George F. *Across the Continent with the Fifth Cavalry.* New York: Antiquarian Press, 1959.

Propst, Nell Brown. *The South Platte Trail: The Story of Colorado's Forgotten People.* Boulder, Colo.: Pruett Publishing, 1989.

Prucha, Francis Paul, ed. *Documents of United States Indian Policy.* Lincoln: University of Nebraska Press, 1990.

Quaife, Milo Milton, ed. *Kit Carson's Autobiography.* Lincoln: University of Nebraska Press, 1961.

Randall, Kenneth A. *Only the Echoes: The Life and Times of Howard Bass Cushing.* Las Cruces, N.M.: Yucca Tree Press, 1995.

Rickey, Don, Jr. *Forty Miles a Day on Beans and Hay.* Norman: University of Oklahoma Press, 1963.

Riddle, Kenyon. *Records and Maps of the Old Santa Fe Trail.* Stuart, Fla.: Southeastern Printing, 1963.

Riley, Glenda. *The Female Frontier: A Comparative View of Women on the Prairie and Plains.* Lawrence: University Press of Kansas, 1988.

———. *Women and Indians on the Frontier 1825–1915.* Albuquerque: University of New Mexico Press, 1984.

Rister, Carl Coke. *Border Captives: The Traffic in Prisoners by Southern Plains Indians, 1835–1875.* Norman: University of Oklahoma Press, 1940.

———. *Fort Griffin on the Texas Frontier.* Norman: University of Oklahoma Press, 1956.

Robinson, Charles M., III. *Bad Hand: A Biography of General Ranald S. Mackenzie.* Austin: State House Press, 1993.

Robinson, Charles M., III. *The Men Who Wear the Star: The Story of the Texas Rangers.* New York: Random House, 2000.

———. *Satanta: The Life and Death of a War Chief.* Austin: State House Press, 1997.

Robinson, Elwyn B. *History of North Dakota.* Lincoln: University of Nebraska Press, 1966.

Rodenbough, Theophilus R. *From Everglade to Canyon with the Second United States Cavalry.* New York: D. Van Nostrand, 1875. Reprint, Norman: University of Oklahoma Press, 2000.

Roenigk, Adolph. *A Pioneer History of Kansas.* Lincoln, Kans.: privately published, 1933.

Rogers, Fred B. *Soldiers of the Overland: Being Some Account of the Services of General Patrick Edward Connor and His Volunteers in the Old West.* San Francisco: Grabhorn Press, 1938.

Root, Frank A., and William Elsey Connelley. *The Overland Stage to California.* Topeka, Kans.: privately published, 1901.

Royster, Charles. *The Destructive War: W. T. Sherman, Stonewall Jackson, and the Americans.* New York: Random House, 1993.

Sabin, Edwin L. *Kit Carson Days, 1809–1868: Adventures in the Path of Empire.* Lincoln: University of Nebraska Press, 1995.

The Sand Creek Massacre: A Documentary History. New York: Sol Lewis, 1973.

Sandoz, Mari. *The Buffalo Hunters: The Story of the Hide Men.* Lincoln: University of Nebraska Press, 1978.

———. *Cheyenne Autumn.* New York: Hastings House, 1953.

Sanford, Mollie D. *Mollie: The Journal of Mollie Dorsey Sanford in Nebraska and Colorado Territories, 1857–1866.* Lincoln: University of Nebraska Press, 1976.

Sawicki, James A. *Cavalry Regiments of the U.S. Army.* Dumfries, Virg.: Wyvern Publications, 1985.

Schlissel, Lillian. *Women's Diaries of the Westward Journey.* New York: Schocken Books, 1982.

Schubert, Frank N. *Outpost of the Sioux Wars: A History of Fort Robinson.* Lincoln: University of Nebraska Press, 1993.

Schultz, Duane. *Month of the Freezing Moon: The Sand Creek Massacre, November 1864.* New York: St. Martin's Press, 1990.

———. *Over the Earth I Come: The Great Sioux Uprising of 1862.* New York: St. Martin's Press, 1992.

Schwartz, E. A. *The Rogue River Indian War and Its Aftermath, 1850–1980.* Norman: University of Oklahoma Press, 1997.

Scott, Bob. *Blood at Sand Creek: The Massacre Revisited.* Caldwell, Idaho: Caxton Printers, 1994.

Scott, Douglas D., P. Willey, and Melissa Connor. *They Died with Custer: Soldiers' Bones from the Battle of the Little Bighorn.* Norman: University of Oklahoma Press, 1998.

Secoy, Frank Raymond. *Changing Military Patterns of the Great Plains Indians.* Lincoln: University of Nebraska Press, 1992.

Settle, Raymond W., and Mary Lund Settle. *Saddles and Spurs: The Pony Express Saga.* Lincoln: University of Nebraska Press, 1972.

———. *War Drums and Wagon Wheels: The Story of Russell, Majors and Waddell.* Lincoln: University of Nebraska Press, 1966.

Sheridan, Philip H. *The Personal Memoirs of P. H. Sheridan.* New York: Da Capo Press, 1992.

Simmons, Marc. *Following the Santa Fe Trail: A Guide for Modern Travelers.* Santa Fe: Ancient City Press, 1984.

———. *Massacre on the Lordsburg Road.* College Station: Texas A & M University Press, 1997.

Slotkin, Richard. *Fatal Environment: The Myth of the Frontier in the Age of Industrialization, 1800–1890.* New York: Harper Collins, 1994.

———. *Gunfighter Nation: The Myth of the Frontier in Twentieth-Century America.* New York: Harper Collins, 1992.

Smedley, William. *Across the Plains: An 1862 Journey from Omaha to Oregon.* Boulder, Colo.: Johnson Books, 1994.

Smith, Sherry L. *The View from Officer's Row: Army Perceptions of Western Indians.* Tucson: University of Arizona Press, 1990.

Smith, Thomas T. *The Old Army in Texas: A Research Guide to the U.S. Army in Nineteenth-Century Texas.* Austin: Texas State Historical Association, 2000.

Sonnichsen, C. L. *The Mescalero Apaches.* Norman: University of Oklahoma Press, 1958.

Sprague, Marshall. *Massacre: The Tragedy at White River.* Lincoln: University of Nebraska Press, 1957.

Spring, Agnes Wright. *Caspar Collins: The Life and Exploits of an Indian Fighter of the Sixties.* New York: AMS Press, 1967.

Springer, Charles H. *Soldiering in Sioux Country: 1865.* San Diego: Frontier Heritage Press, 1971.

Stallard, Patricia Y. *Glittering Misery: Dependents of the Indian Fighting Army.* Norman: University of Oklahoma Press, 1992.

Stanley, Henry M. *My Early Travels and Adventures in America and Asia.* London: Sampson Low, Marston & Co., 1895.

Steckmesser, Kent Ladd. *The Western Hero in History and Legend.* Norman: University of Oklahoma Press, 1997.

Stratton, R. B. *Captivity of the Oatman Girls.* Lincoln: University of Nebraska Press, 1983.

Strobridge, William F. *Regulars in the Redwoods: The U.S. Army in Northern California, 1852–1861.* Spokane, Wash.: Arthur H. Clark, 1994.

Stuart, Granville. *Pioneering in Montana: The Making of a State, 1864–1887.* Lincoln: University of Nebraska Press, 1977.

Sully, Langdon. *No Tears for the General: The Life of Alfred Sully, 1821–1879.* Palo Alto, Calif.: American West Publishing, 1974.

Sweeney, Edwin R. *Cochise: Chiricahua Apache Chief.* Norman: University of Oklahoma Press, 1991.

Sweeney, Edwin R. *Mangas Coloradas: Chief of the Chiricahua Apaches.* Norman: University of Oklahoma Press, 1998.

Tatum, Lawrie. *Our Red Brothers and the Peace Policy of President Ulysses S. Grant.* Lincoln: University of Nebraska Press, 1970.

Taylor, Quintard. *In Search of the Racial Frontier: African Americans in the American West, 1528–1990.* New York: W. W. Norton, 1998.

Tevis, James H. *Arizona in the Fifties.* Albuquerque: University of New Mexico Press, 1954.

Thomas, Gary M. *The Custer Scout of 1867.* Kansas City, Mo.: Westport Publishing, 1987.

Thrapp, Dan L. *Al Sieber, Chief of Scouts.* Norman: University of Oklahoma Press, 1964.

———. *The Conquest of Apacheria.* Norman: University of Oklahoma Press, 1967.

———. *Encyclopedia of Frontier Biography in Three Volumes.* Lincoln: University of Nebraska Press, 1991.

———. *Victorio and the Mimbres Apaches.* Norman: University of Oklahoma Press, 1974.

Trafzer, Clifford E., and Richard D. Scheuerman. *Renegade Tribe: The Palouse Indians and the Invasion of the Inland Pacific Northwest.* Pullman: Washington State University Press, 1986.

Trafzer, Clifford E., and Joel R. Hyer, eds. *Exterminate Them: Written Accounts of the Murder, Rape, and Slavery of Native Americans during the California Gold Rush, 1848–1868.* East Lansing: Michigan State University Press, 1999.

Trenholm, Virginia Cole. *The Arapahoes, Our People.* Norman: University of Oklahoma Press, 1970.

———, and Maurine Carley. *The Shoshonis: Sentinels of the Rockies.* Norman: University of Oklahoma Press, 1964.

Unrau, William E., ed. *Tending the Talking Wire: A Buck Soldier's View of Indian Country, 1863–1866.* Salt Lake City: University of Utah Press, 1990.

Unruh, John D., Jr. *The Plains Across: The Overland Emigrants and the Trans-Mississippi West, 1840–60.* Urbana: University of Illinois Press, 1993.

Urwin, Gregory J. W. *The United States Cavalry: An Illustrated History.* London: Blandford Press, 1983.

Utley, Robert M. *Cavalier in Buckskin: George Armstrong Custer and the American Military Frontier.* Norman: University of Oklahoma Press, 1988.

———. *A Clash of Cultures: Fort Bowie and the Chiricahua Apaches.* Washington: National Park Service, 1977.

———. *Fort Davis National Historic Site, Texas.* Washington: National Park Service, 1965.

———. *Frontier Regulars: The U.S. Army and the Indian 1866–1891.* New York: Macmillan Publishing, 1973.

———. *Frontiersmen in Blue: The United States Army and the Indian, 1848–1865.* New York: Macmillan Publishing, 1967.

———. *The Lance and the Shield: The Life and Times of Sitting Bull.* New York: Henry Holt, 1993.

Utley, Robert M. *The Last Days of the Sioux Nation*. New Haven: Yale University Press, 1963.

———, ed. *Life in Custer's Cavalry: Diaries and Letters of Albert and Jennie Barnitz, 1867–1868*. Lincoln: University of Nebraska Press, 1987.

Varley, James F. *Brigham and the Brigadier: General Patrick Connor and His California Volunteers in Utah and along the Overland Trail*. Tucson: Westernlore Press, 1989.

Vaughn, J. W. *The Battle of Platte Bridge*. Norman: University of Oklahoma Press, 1963.

———. *Indian Fights: New Facts on Seven Encounters*. Norman: University of Oklahoma Press, 1966.

Vestal, Stanley. *The Old Santa Fe Trail*. Lincoln: University of Nebraska Press, 1996.

———. *Warpath: The True Story of the Fighting Sioux Told in a Biography of Chief White Bull*. Lincoln: University of Nebraska Press, 1984.

Walker, Henry Pickering. *The Wagonmasters: High Plains Freighting from the Earliest Days of the Santa Fe Trail to 1880*. Norman: University of Oklahoma Press, 1966.

Walton, George. *Sentinal of the Plains: Fort Leavenworth and the American West*. Englewood Cliffs, N.J.: Prentice-Hall, 1973.

Ware, Eugene F. *The Indian War of 1864*. Lincoln: University of Nebraska Press, 1994.

Webb, George W. *Chronological List of Engagements between the Regular Army of the United States and Various Tribes of Hostile Indians*. St. Joseph, Mo.: Wing Print & Publishing, 1939.

Webb, Walter Prescott. *The Texas Rangers: A Century of Frontier Defense*. Austin: University of Texas Press, 1965.

Webber, Bert. *Oregon Trail Emigrant Massacre of 1862 and Port-Neuf Muzzle-Loaders Rendezvous, Massacre Rocks, Idaho*. Medford, Ore.: Webb Research Group Publishers, 1987.

———, ed. *The Oregon and California Trail Diary of Jane Gould in 1862*. Medford, Ore.: Webb Research Group Publishers, 1987.

Welch, James. *Killing Custer*. New York: W. W. Norton, 1994.

Wellman, Paul I. *Death in the Desert: The Fifty Years' War for the Great Southwest*. Lincoln: University of Nebraska Press, 1987.

———. *Death on the Prairie: The Thirty Years' Struggle for the Western Plains*. Lincoln: University of Nebraska Press, 1987.

Werner, Fred H. *The Beecher Island Battle, September 17, 1868*. Greeley, Colo.: Werner Publications, 1989.

———. *Heroic Fort Sedgwick and Julesburg: A Study in Courage*. Greeley Colo.: Werner Publications, 1987.

———. *The Sand Creek Fight*. Greeley, Colo.: Werner Publications, 1993.

———. *The Summit Springs Battle, July 11, 1869*. Greeley, Colo.: Werner Publications, 1991.

West, Elliot. *The Contested Plains: Indians, Goldseekers, and the Rush to Colorado*. Lawrence: University Press of Kansas, 1998.

———. *The Way to the West: Essays on the Central Plains*. Albuquerque: University of New Mexico Press, 1995.

Wheeler, Homer W. *Buffalo Days*. Lincoln: University of Nebraska Press, 1990.

White, Lonnie J. *Hostiles and Horse Soldiers: Indian Battles and Campaigns in the West*. Boulder, Colo.: Pruett Publishing, 1972.

White, Richard. *"It's Your Misfortune and None of My Own": A New History of the American West*. Norman: University of Oklahoma Press, 1991.

Wilbarger, J. W. *Indian Depredations in Texas*. Austin: Hutchings Printings House, 1889.

Williams, Clayton W. *Texas' Last Frontier: Fort Stockton and the Trans-Pecos, 1861–1895*. College Station: Texas A & M University Press, 1982.

Williams, Scott C., ed. *Colorado History through the News: The Indian Wars of 1864 through the Sand Creek Massacre*. Aurora, Colo.: Pick of Ware Publishing, 1997.

Wilson, D. Ray. *Fort Kearny on the Platte*. Dundee, Ill.: Crossroads Communications, 1980.

Wooster, Robert. *The Military and United States Indian Policy, 1865–1903*. Lincoln: University of Nebraska Press, 1995.

———, ed. *Recollections of Western Texas by Two of the U.S. Mounted Rifles, 1852–55*. Lubbock: Texas Tech University Press, 1995.

Worcester, Donald E. *The Apaches: Eagles of the Southwest*. Norman: University of Oklahoma Press, 1979.

Worster, Donald. *Under Western Skies: Nature and History in the American West*. New York: Oxford University Press, 1992.

Young, Harry. *Hard Knocks: A Life Story of the Vanishing West*. Portland, Ore.: Wells & Co., 1915.

Magazines and Journals

Barry, Louise. "The Ranch at Cimarron Crossing." *Kansas Historical Quarterly* 39, no. 3 (Fall 1973).

———. "The Ranch at Great Bend." *Kansas Historical Quarterly* 39, no. 1 (Spring 1973).

———. "With the First U.S. Cavalry in Indian Country, 1859–1861." *Kansas Historical Quarterly* 24, no. 3 (Fall 1958) and no. 4 (Winter 1958).

Beck, Paul N. "Firm but Fair: The Minnesota Volunteers and the Coming of the Dakota War of 1862." *Journal of the Indian Wars* 1, no. 3 (2000).

Cooper, Marilyn. "The Kidder Massacre Site on the High Plains of Kansas." *Research Review* 13, no. 1 (Winter 1999).

Dinges, Bruce J. "The Irrepressible Captain Armes: Politics and Justice in the Indian-Fighting Army." *Journal of the West* 32, no. 2 (April 1993).

Duncan, Charles, and Jay Smith. "The Captives." *Research Review* 7, no. 2 (June 1993).

Farley, Alan W. "An Indian Captivity and Its Legal Aftermath." *Kansas Historical Quarterly* 21, no. 4 (Winter 1954).

Farrell, Ellen. "The Most Terrible Stories: The 1862 Dakota Conflict in White Imagination." *Journal of the Indian Wars* 1 no. 3 (2000).

Goodwin, Carol G. "The Letters of Private Milton Spencer, 1862–1865: A Soldier's View of Military Life on the Northern Plains." *North Dakota History* 37, no. 4 (Fall 1970).

Hughes, Michael A. "Nations Asunder: Western American Indians during the American Civil War, 1861–1865. *Journal of the Indian Wars* 1, no. 3 (2000).

Hull, Myra E., ed. "Soldiering on the High Plains: The Diary of Lewis Byram Hull, 1864–1866." *Kansas Historical Quarterly* 7, no. 1 (February 1938).

Hutcheson, Grove. "The Ninth Cavalry." *By Valor & Arms: The Journal of American Military History* 1, no. 3 (Spring 1975).

Janda, Lance. "Shutting the Gates of Mercy: The American Origins of Total War, 1860–1880." *Journal of Military History* 59, no.1 (January 1995).

Jones, Douglas C. "Medicine Lodge Revisited." *Kansas Historical Quarterly* 35, no. 2 (Summer 1969).

Justus, Judith P. "The Saga of Clara H. Blinn at the Battle of the Washita." *Research Review* 14, no. 1 (Winter 2000).

Kraft, Louis. "Edward W. Wynkoop: A Forgotten Hero." *Research Review* 1, no. 1 (June 1987).

Lindley, William R. "Ned Wynkoop and Black Kettle." *Research Review* 9, no. 2 (June 1995).

Marrs, James David, Sr. "Grant's 'Quaker' Policy and the Bishop of Niobrara." *South Dakota Historical Collections* 38 (1976).

Mattes, Merrill J. "Patrolling the Santa Fe Trail: Reminiscences of John S. Kirwan." *Kansas Historical Quarterly* 21, no. 8 (Winter 1955).

McCall, Kimberly S. "'Vindictive Earnestness' in Practice: The Campaigns of Ranald S. Mackenzie as a Model of Post–Civil War Indian Policy." *Journal of the West* 34, no. 3 (July 1995).

McDermott, John D. "'We Had a Terribly Hard Time Letting Them Go': The Battles of Mud Springs and Rush Creek." *Nebraska History* 77, no. 2 (Summer 1996).

Michno, Gregory F. "The Perils of Plum Creek." *Wild West* 13, no. 6 (April 2001).

Millbrook, Minnie Dubbs. "Custer's First Scout in the West." *Kansas Historical Quarterly* 39, no. 1 (Spring 1973).

———. "The West Breaks in General Custer." *Kansas Historical Quarterly* 36, no. 2 (Summer 1970).

Miller, Nyle H., and Robert W. Richmond. "Sheridan: A Fabled End-of-Track Town on the Union Pacific Railroad, 1868–1869." *Kansas Historical Quarterly* 34, no. 4 (Winter 1968).

Monnett, John H. "A Scout's Perceptions of Indians at the Battle of Beecher Island." *Montana: The Magazine of Western History* 43, no. 4 (Fall 1993).

Murray, Robert A. "Wagons on the Plains." *By Valor & Arms: The Journal of American Military History* 2, no. 4 (Summer 1976).

———. "Water Walking War Wagons: Steamboats in the Western Indian Campaigns." *By Valor & Arms: The Journal of American Military History* 3, no. 1 (Fall 1976).

Niderost, Eric. "Failed Peace on the Plains: The Treaty of Medicine Lodge." *Research Review* 13, no. 1 (Winter 1999).

Pfaller, Louis. "Sully's Expedition of 1864." *North Dakota History* 31, no. 1 (January 1964).

Reid, John Phillip. "Punishing the Elephant: Malfeasance and Organized Criminality on the Overland Trail." *Montana: The Magazine of Western History* 47, no. 1 (Spring 1997).

Rickey, Don. "An Indian Wars Combat Record." *By Valor & Arms: The Journal of American Military History* 2, no. 1 (Fall 1975).

Ridge, Martin. "Reflections on the Pony Express." *Montana: The Magazine of Western History* 46, no. 3 (Fall 1996).

Roberts, Gary L. "Condition of the Tribes, 1865. The McCook Report: A Military View." *Montana: The Magazine of Western History* 24, no. 1 (January 1974).

Robinson, W. Stitt, ed. "The Kiowa and Comanche Campaign of 1860 as Recorded in the Personal Diary of Lt. J.E.B. Stuart." *Kansas Historical Quarterly* 23, no. 4 (Winter 1957).

Rowen, Richard D., ed. "The Second Nebraska's Campaign against the Sioux." *Nebraska History* 44, no. 1 (March 1963).

Russell, Don. "One Hundred and Three Fights and Scrimages: The Story of General Reuben F. Bernard." *The Cavalry Journal* 45, no. 2 (March-April 1936).

Rzeczkowski, Frank. "The Crow Indians and the Bozeman Trail." *Montana: The Magazine of Western History* 49, no. 4 (Winter 1999).

Sampson, Joanna. "Sand Creek Massacre: A Dilemma at the University of Colorado." *Journal of the West* 34, no. 4 (October 1995).

Sawyers, James A. "Niobrara–Virginia City Wagon Road." *South Dakota Historical Review* 2, no. 1 (October 1936).

Schlesinger, Arthur, Jr. "What Should We Teach Our Children about History?" *American Heritage* 43, no. 1 (February-March 1992).

Smith, Jay. "The Indian Fighting Army." *Research Review* 3, no. 1 (June 1989).

Smith, Maurice E. "The Oregon Trail's Utter Tragedy." *Wild West* 12, no. 6 (April 2000).

Snell, Joseph W., and Robert W. Richmond. "When the Union and Kansas Pacific Built through Kansas." *Kansas Historical Quarterly* 32, no. 2 (Summer 1966) and no. 3 (Fall 1966).

Stanley, Henry M. "A British Journalist Reports the Medicine Lodge Peace Councils of 1867." *Kansas Historical Quarterly* 33, no. 3 (Fall 1967).

Tallman, Elizabeth J. "Pioneer Experiences in Colorado." *Colorado Magazine* 13, no. 4 (July 1936).

Tate, Michael L. "Comanche Captives: People between Two Worlds." *The Chronicles of Oklahoma* 72, no. 3 (Fall 1994).

Taylor, Morris F. "Kicking Bird: A Chief of the Kiowas." *Kansas Historical Quarterly* 38, no. 3 (Fall 1972).

Thomas, Gary, and Ralph Heinz. "Quite a Desperate Little Fight." *Research Review* 5, no. 1 (January 1991).

Udall, Stewart L. "The 'Wild' Old West: A Different View." *Montana: The Magazine of Western History* 49, no. 4. (Winter 1999).

———, Robert R. Dykstra, Michael L. Belleisles, Paula Mitchell Marks, and Gregory H. Nobles. "How the West Got Wild: American Media and Frontier Violence, a Roundtable." *Western Historical Quarterly* 31, no. 3 (Fall 2000).

Unrau, William E. "The Story of Fort Larned." *Kansas Historical Quarterly* 23, no. 3 (Fall 1957).

Voight, Barton R. "The Death of Lyman S. Kidder." *South Dakota History* 6, no. 1 (Winter 1975).

Welty, Raymond L. "The Policing of the Frontier by the Army, 1860–1870." *Kansas Historical Quarterly* 7, no. 3 (August 1938).

———. "Supplying the Frontier Military Posts." *Kansas Historical Quarterly* 7, no. 2 (May 1938).

Wetzel, Charles W. "Monument Station, Gove County." *Kansas Historical Quarterly* 26, no. 3 (Fall 1960).

White, Lonnie J. "Indian Raids on the Kansas Frontier, 1869." *Kansas Historical Quarterly* 38, no. 4 (Winter 1972).

———. "White Women Captives of the Southern Plains Indians, 1866–1875." *Journal of the West* 8, no. 3 (July 1969).

Government Publications

U.S. Army, Adjutant General's Office. *Chronological List of Actions &c., with the Indians from January 15, 1837 to January, 1891.* Washington: GPO, 1891.

U.S. Bureau of Indian Affairs. *Report of the Commissioner of Indian Affairs for the Year 1861.* Washington: GPO, 1861.

U.S. Bureau of Indian Affairs. *Report of the Commissioner of Indian Affairs for the Year 1865.* Washington: GPO, 1865.

U.S. Bureau of Indian Affairs. *Report of the Commissioner of Indian Affairs for the Year 1866.* Washington: GPO, 1866.

U.S. House. *Difficulties with Indian Tribes.* 41st Congr., 2nd sess. Ex. Doc. 240.

U.S. House. *Letters of Maj. Gen. W. S. Hancock, 22 May 1867.* 41st Congr., Ex. Doc. 240, 1867.

U.S. House. *Southern Column Kiowa-Comanche Expedition.* Report by Capt. S. D. Sturgis. 36th Congr., Ex. Doc. 1079, 1860–61.

U.S. House. Joint Committee on the Conduct of the War. *Massacre of Cheyenne Indians.* 38th Congr., 2nd sess., 1865.

U.S. Senate. *How We Built the Union Pacific Railway.* Report by Grenville M. Dodge. 61st Congr., 2nd sess., 1910.

The War of the Rebellion: A Compilation of the Official Records of the Union and Confederate Armies. Washington: GPO, 1880–1901.

Unpublished Sources

Little Bighorn Battlefield National Monument, Crow Agency, Mont.: Camp Collection, folder 10, no. 11729 (N. Cole report); Hammer Collection, folder 7, no. 18117 (A. C. Leighton letter).

Rosenberg, Robert G. "Historical Investigations of the Sawyers Wagon Road Expeditions of 1865 and 1866 and Related Rifle Pit Sites, Campbell County, Wyoming." Prepared for AMAX Coal Co., February 1987. Private Collection.

U.S. War Department, Records of U.S. Army Commands, Record Group 98: General Duncan's Journal, 22 November 1869; Marches and Scouts, Report of Lt. Col. Luther P. Bradley, 1868; Republican River Expedition, Report of Maj. E. A. Carr, 25 July 1869; Republican River Expedition, Report of Lt. Col. Thomas Duncan, 7 October 1869; Republican River Expedition, Report of Col. W. H. Emory, 22 November 1969. National Archives, Washington, D.C.

—Acknowledgments—

I would like to thank several people for helping me with this project: Carl Katafiasz at the Monroe County, Michigan, Library for locating documents regarding George Custer's and Eugene Carr's fights in Kansas; Anita Donofrio for providing very helpful source material; Dr. Jeff Broome for showing where he located battle artifacts at sites such as Kidder's fight and Summit Springs; Robert and Betty Lu Rosenberg for sharing their research concerning the Bone Pile Creek Fight and Sawyer's Expedition; and my wife, Susan, for allowing me to spend most of our money on books and resources and accompanying me on so many trips to research these battle sites. I will soon attempt to repay her in a like manner as she researches her own historical projects.

—Index of Battles by Place—

This index lists modern-day locations. Battle names and original place names are listed in the general index.

—Index of Indian Tribes—

—General Index—

—About the Author—

Gregory F. Michno is the author of *Lakota Noon: The Indian Narrative of Custer's Defeat* and *The Mystery of E Troop: Custer's Gray Horse Company at the Little Bighorn*, both published by Mountain Press, as well as *USS Pampanito: Killer-Angel*, and *Death on the Hellships*. He has also written numerous articles in *Montana: The Magazine of Western History*, *Journal of the West*, *Wild West*, and other western history publications. A member of the Western History Association, Order of the Indian Wars, Little Big Horn associates, and several other organizations, Michno holds a master's degree in history from the University of Northern Colorado. He lives in Longmont, Colorado.

We encourage you to patronize your local bookstore. Most stores will order any title that they do not stock. You may also order directly from Mountain Press using the order form provided below or by calling our toll-free number and using your credit card. We will gladly send you a catalog upon request.

Some history titles of interest:

_____	The Arikara War: The First Plains Indian War, 1823	$18.00/paper	$30.00/cloth
_____	Bleed, Blister, and Purge: A History of Medicine on the American Frontier	$15.00/paper	
_____	The Bloody Bozeman: The Perilous Trail to Montana's Gold	$16.00/paper	
_____	Chief Joseph and the Nez Perces: A Photographic History	$15.00/paper	
_____	Children of the Fur Trade	$15.00/paper	
_____	Crazy Horse: A Photographic Biography	$20.00/paper	
_____	Discovering Lewis & Clark from the Air	$24.00/paper	$40.00/cloth
_____	Encyclopedia of Indian Wars: Western Battles and Skirmishes, 1850 to 1890		$28.00/cloth
_____	The Journals of Patrick Gass: Member of the Lewis and Clark Expedition	$20.00/paper	$36.00/cloth
_____	Lakota Noon: The Indian Narrative of Custer's Defeat	$18.00/paper	$36.00/cloth
_____	Lewis & Clark: A Photographic Journey	$18.00/paper	
_____	The Mystery of E Troop: Custer's Gray Horse Company at the Little Bighorn	$18.00/paper	
_____	The Oregon Trail: A Photographic Journey	$18.00/paper	
_____	The Piikani Blackfeet: A Culture Under Siege	$18.00/paper	$30.00/cloth
_____	The Pony Express: A Photographic History	$22.00/paper	
_____	Sacagawea's Son: The Life of Jean Baptiste Charbonneau _(for readers 10 and up)_	$10.00/paper	
_____	The Saga of the Pony Express	$17.00/paper	$29.00/cloth
_____	Stories of Young Pioneers: In Their Own Words _(for readers 10 and up)_	$14.00/paper	
_____	William Henry Jackson: Framing the Frontier	$22.00/paper	$36.00/cloth

Please include $3.00 for 1-4 books or $5.00 for 5 or more books for shipping and handling.

Send the books marked above. I enclose $

Name_____

Address_____

City/State/Zip_____

☐ Payment enclosed (check or money order in U.S. funds)

Bill my: ☐ VISA ☐ MasterCard ☐ American Express ☐ Discover

Card No._____ Exp. Date:_____

Signature_____

MOUNTAIN PRESS PUBLISHING COMPANY
P.O. Box 2399 • Missoula, MT 59806 • fax: 406-728-1635
Order Toll Free 1-800-234-5308 • Have your credit card ready
e-mail: info@mtnpress.com • website: www.mountain-press.com